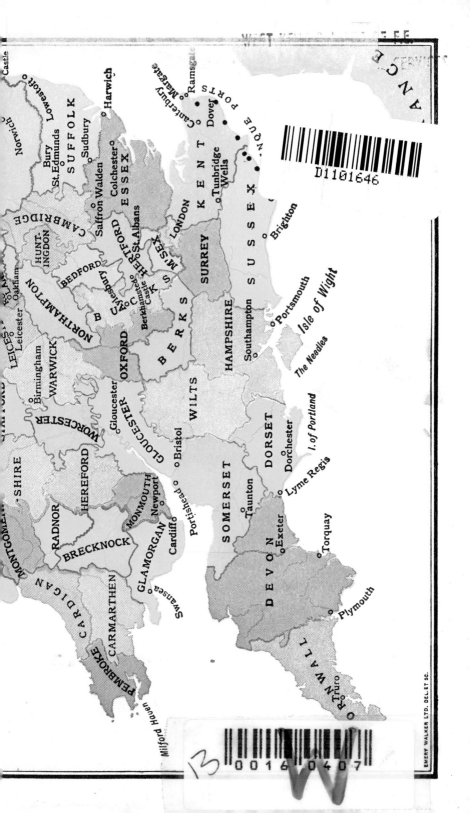

ENGLISH SOCIAL HISTORY

A Survey of Six Centuries
Chaucer to Queen Victoria

BY

G. M. TREVELYAN, O.M.

LONGMAN

LONGMAN GROUP LIMITED
London

Associated companies, branches and
representatives throughout the world

FIRST PUBLISHED IN USA AND CANADA

FIRST EDITION IN GREAT BRITAIN 1944
Second edition 1946
Third edition (reset) 1946
New impression 1972

ISBN 0 582 11342 3

PRINTED IN GREAT BRITAIN BY
WILLIAM CLOWES AND SONS LIMITED
LONDON, COLCHESTER AND BECCLES

To the memory
of
EILEEN POWER
economic and social
historian

Works by
George Macaulay Trevelyan, O.M.

HISTORY OF ENGLAND

BRITISH HISTORY IN THE NINETEENTH CENTURY AND AFTER

ENGLAND IN THE AGE OF WYCLIFFE

ENGLAND UNDER QUEEN ANNE:

* BLENHEIM

** RAMILLIES AND THE UNION WITH SCOTLAND

*** THE PEACE AND THE PROTESTANT SUCCESSION

GARIBALDI AND THE THOUSAND

GARIBALDI AND THE MAKING OF ITALY

GARIBALDI'S DEFENCE OF THE ROMAN REPUBLIC

GREY OF FALLODON

AN AUTOBIOGRAPHY AND OTHER ESSAYS

CARLYLE: AN ANTHOLOGY

CLIO, A MUSE AND OTHER ESSAYS

LORD GREY OF THE REFORM BILL

ILLUSTRATED ENGLISH SOCIAL HISTORY VOLS., 1, 2, 3 AND 4

A LAYMAN'S LOVE OF LETTERS

SELECTED POETICAL WORKS OF GEORGE MEDEDITH

CONTENTS

v

MAPS AND DIAGRAMS

PUBLISHERS' NOTE

An American edition of this work was published in 1942, but owing to paper shortage over here in war time, it was only possible to publish it in Great Britain in 1944.

INTRODUCTION

ALTHOUGH I have attempted to bring this book up to date in the light of the most recent publications (1941), it was nearly all written before the war. I then had in view a social history of England from the Roman times to our own, but I left to the last the part that I would find most difficult, the centuries preceding the Fourteenth. The war has rendered it impossible for me to complete the work, but it has occurred to me that the chapters which I have already finished constitute a consecutive story of six centuries, from the Fourteenth to the Nineteenth, and as such some readers may give it welcome.

Social history might be defined negatively as the history of a people with the politics left out. It is perhaps difficult to leave out the politics from the history of any people, particularly the English people. But as so many history books have consisted of political annals with little reference to their social environment, a reversal of that method may have its uses to redress the balance. During my own lifetime a third very flourishing sort of history has come into existence, the economic, which greatly assists the serious study of social history. For the social scene grows out of economic conditions, to much the same extent that political events in their turn grow out of social conditions. Without social history, economic history is barren and political history is unintelligible.

But social history does not merely provide the required link between economic and political history. It has also its own positive value and peculiar concern. Its scope may be defined as the daily life of the inhabitants of the land in past ages : this includes the human as well as the economic relation of different classes to one another, the character of family and household life, the conditions of labour and of leisure, the attitude of man to nature, the culture of each age as it arose out of these general conditions of life, and took ever-changing forms in religion, literature and music, architecture, learning and thought.

How far can we know the real life of men in each successive age of the past ? Historians and antiquarians have amassed by patient scholarship a great sum of information, and have edited innumerable records, letters and journals, enough to provide reading for whole lifetimes ; yet even this mass of knowledge is small indeed compared to the sum total of social history, which could only be mastered if we knew the biographies of all the millions of men, women and children who have lived in England. The generalizations which are the stock-in-trade of the social historian, must necessarily be based on a small number of particular instances, which are assumed to be typical, but which cannot be the whole of the complicated truth.

And small as is the mass of accumulated knowledge in proportion to the vastness of the theme, how pitifully small is the selection from that mass which I have been able to set down in this volume of 200,000 words dealing with six whole centuries of the variegated and wonderful life of England. Yet even a millionth part of a loaf may be better than no bread. It may at least whet the appetite. If it makes a few people more eager to study the literature and records of the past, this book will have served its turn.

Disinterested intellectual curiosity is the life-blood of real civilization. Social history provides one of its best forms. At bottom, I think, the appeal of history is imaginative. Our imagination craves to behold our ancestors as they really were, going about their daily business and daily pleasure. Carlyle called the antiquarian or historical researcher ' Dryasdust.' Dryasdust at bottom is a poet. He may find difficulty in expressing to his neighbour the poetry he finds for himself in the muniment room. But the main impulse of his life is the desire to feel the reality of life in the past, to be familiar with ' the chronicle of wasted time ' for the sake of ' ladies dead and lovely knights.'

Scott began life as Dryasdust—as an antiquarian— because that way he could find most poetry, most romance. Carlyle, like every great historian, was his own Dryasdust. Indeed he is really the greatest defender of Dryasdust in the whole field of literature. He declared, with a striking exaggeration, that the smallest real fact about the past of man which Dryasdust could unearth was more poetical than all Shelley and more romantic than all Scott.

Consider all that lies in that one word *Past* ! What a pathetic, sacred, in every sense *poetic*, meaning is implied in it ; a meaning growing ever the clearer the farther we recede in time—the more of that same Past we have to look through ! History after all is the true poetry. And Reality, if rightly interpreted, is grander than Fiction.

It is the detailed study of history that makes us feel that the past was as real as the present. The world supposes that we historians are absorbed in the dusty records of the dead ; that we can see nothing save—

> The lost-to-light ghosts, grey-mailed,
> As you see the grey river mist
> Hold shapes on the yonder bank.

But to us, as we read, they take form, colour, gesture, passion, thought. It is only by study that we can see our forerunners, remote and recent, in their habits as they lived, intent each on the business of a long-vanished day, riding out to do homage or to poll a vote ; to seize a neighbour's manor-house and carry off his ward, or to leave cards on ladies in crinolines.

And there is the ' fair field full of folk.' Generation after generation, there is the ploughman behind the oxen, or the horses, or the machine, and his wife busy all day in the cottage, waiting for him with her daily accumulated budget of evening news.

Each one, gentle and simple, in his commonest goings and comings, was ruled by a complicated and ever-shifting fabric of custom and law, society and politics, events at home and abroad, some of them little known by him and less understood. Our effort is not only to get what few glimpses we can of his intimate personality, but to reconstruct the whole fabric of each passing age, and see how it affected him ; to get to know more in some respects than the dweller in the past himself knew about the conditions that enveloped and controlled his life.

There is nothing that more divides civilized from semi-savage man than to be conscious of our forefathers as they really were, and bit by bit to reconstruct the mosaic of the long-forgotten past.　To weigh the stars, or to make ships sail in the air or below the sea, is not a more astonishing and ennobling performance on the part of the human race in these latter days, than to know the course of events that had been long forgotten, and the true nature of men and women who were here before us.

Truth is the criterion of historical study ; but its impelling motive is poetic.　Its poetry consists in its being true.　There we find the synthesis of the scientific and literary views of history.

Since, however rashly and inadequately, some attempt is to be made in this volume to imagine the life of our ancestors in such partial light as modern research can afford, in what form can the story best be told ?　It cannot, like the web of political history, be held together by the framework of well known names of Kings, Parliaments and wars.　These indeed have their influence on social development which has often to be noted.　The Puritan Revolution and the Restoration were social as well as political events.　But, on the whole, social change moves like an underground river, obeying its own laws or those of economic change, rather than following the direction of political happenings that move on the surface of life.　Politics are the outcome rather than the cause of social change.　A new King, a new Prime Minister, a new Parliament often marks a new epoch in politics, but seldom in the life of the people.

How then is the tale to be told ?　Into what periods shall social history be divided up ?　As we look back on it, we see a continuous stream of life, with gradual change perpetually taking place, but with few catastrophes.　The Black Death is perhaps one, and the Industrial Revolution another.　But the Industrial Revolution is spread over too many generations to be rightly regarded either as a catastrophe or as an event.　It is not, like the Black Death, a fortuitous obstruction fallen across the river of life and temporarily diverting it ; it is the river of life itself in the lower part of its course.

In political history one King at a time reigns ; one Parliament at a time sits.　But in social history we find in every period several different kinds of social and economic organization going on simultaneously in the same country, the same shire, the same town. Thus, in the realm of agriculture, we find the open-field strip cultivation of the Anglo-Saxons still extant in the Eighteenth Century, side by side with ancient enclosed fields of the far older Celtic pattern, and modern enclosures scientifically cultivated by methods approved by Arthur Young. And so it is with the varieties of industrial and commercial organization— the domestic, the craft, the capitalist systems are found side by side down the centuries. In everything the old overlaps the new—in religion, in thought, in family custom. There is never any clear cut ; there is no single moment when all Englishmen adopt new ways of life and thought.

These things being so, it has seemed to me best to tell the story as life is presented on the stage, that is to say by a series of scenes divided by intervals of time. There will be a good deal in common between one scene and the next, between the age of Chaucer and the age of Caxton, the age of Dr. Johnson and the age of Cobbett—but there will also be a good deal that is different.

To obtain a true picture of any period, both the old and the new elements must be borne in mind. Sometimes, in forming a mental picture of a period in the past, people seize hold of the new features and forget the overlap of the old. For example, students of history are often so much obsessed by the notorious political event of the Peterloo massacre that they imagine the Lancashire factory hand as the typical wage-earner of the year 1819 ; but he was not ; he was only a local type, the newest type, the type of the future. The trouble was that the rest of old-fashioned society of the Regency period had not yet adjusted itself to the change heralded by his advent. They were annoyed with him, they could not place him, because he was not then, as he is now, the normal.

So then the method of this book is to present a series of successive scenes of English life, and the first of these scenes presented is the lifetime of Chaucer—(1340–1400). I have already confessed that the reason why the book begins at that point is personal and accidental. But in fact it is a good starting-point. For in Chaucer's time the English people first clearly appear as a racial and cultural unit. The

component races and languages have been melted into one.
The upper class is no longer French, nor the peasant class
Anglo-Saxon: all are English.   England has ceased to be
mainly a recipient of influences from without.   Henceforward she gives forth her own.   In the age of Chaucer,
Wycliffe, Wat Tyler and the English bowmen, she is
beginning to create her own island forms in literature,
religion, economic society and war.   The forces moulding
England are no longer foreign but native.   She no longer
owes her progress to great foreign churchmen and administrators, to Norman ideas of the feudal manor, to
Angevin lawyer Kings, to cavalry armed and trained on
French models, to the friars coming over from Latin lands.
Henceforward England creates her own types and her own
customs.

When, in the Hundred Years' War (1337–1453) the
' Goddams ' (as Joan of Arc called them) set out to conquer
France, they went there as foreign invaders, and their
successes were due to the fact that England was already
organized as a nation and conscious of her nationhood,
while France as yet was not.   And when that attempted
conquest at length failed, England was left as a strange
island anchored off the Continent, no longer a mere offshoot
or extension of the European world.

It is true that there was nothing sudden in this growth of
our distinctive nationhood.   The process neither began
nor ended in the lifetime of Chaucer.   But during those
years the principle is more active and more observable than
in the three previous centuries, when the Christian and
feudal civilization of Europe, including England, was not
national but cosmopolitan.   In the England of Chaucer's
time we have a nation.

ENGLISH SOCIAL HISTORY

CHAPTER I

CHAUCER'S ENGLAND [1340–1400]

I

Field, Village and Manor-house.

In Chaucer's England we see for the first time the modern mingling with the mediaeval, and England herself beginning to emerge as a distinct nation, no longer a mere oversea extension of Franco-Latin Europe. The poet's own works register the greatest modern fact of all, the birth and general acceptance of our language, the Saxon and French words happily blended at last into ' English tongue ' which ' all understanden,' and which is therefore coming into use as the vehicle of school teaching and of legal proceedings. There were indeed various provincial dialects of English, besides the totally distinct Welsh and Cornish. And some classes of society had a second language : the more learned of the clergy had Latin, and the courtiers and well-born had French, no longer indeed their childhood's tongue but a foreign speech to be learnt

' after the school of Stratford-atte-Bowe.' [1]

Chaucer, who spent long hours of his busy day in Court circles, had the culture of mediaeval France at his fingers' ends : when therefore he set the pattern of modern English poetry for centuries to come, he set it in forms and metres

---

[1] ' Some can French and no Latin
    That have used courts and dwelled therein :
    And some can of Latin a party
    That can French full febelly :
    And some understandeth English
    That neither can Latin nor French :
    But lerid and lewid [learned and ignorant], old and young
    All understanden English tongue.'
So, in Chaucer's day, wrote William Nassyngton.

1

derived from France and Italy, in both of which countries
he had travelled several times on business of State.   None
the less he struck a new English note.   It was he who, in
the *Canterbury Tales*, gave the first full expression of ' the
English sense of humour,' one quarter cynical and three
quarters kindly, that we do not look for in Dante, Petrarch
or the *Roman de la Rose*, and do not find even in Boccaccio
or Froissart.

Other characteristics of the new-born nation were expressed in Langland's religious allegory, *Piers the Plowman*.
Though he too was a learned poet and a Londoner most
of his life, he was by origin a Malvern man, and used the
form still common in the West country, the alliterative
blank verse derived from Anglo-Saxon poetry.   That native
English form was soon to be generally displaced by
Chaucer's rhymings, but the spirit of *Piers the Plowman*
lived on in the religious earnestness of our fathers, their
continual indignation at the wrong-doing of others and their
occasional sorrow for their own.   English Puritanism is
much older than the Reformation, and the two ' dreamers,'
Piers the Plowman and Bunyan the tinker, are more alike
in imagination and in feeling than any other two writers
divided by three centuries.

While Langland and Gower, without straying into heresy,
bewailed the corruptions of mediaeval society and religion,
looking back to the ideals of the past rather than forward to
a different future, Wycliffe hammered out red-hot a programme of change, most of which was long afterwards put
into force by English Anti-clericalism and English Protestantism.   An open Bible in the new common tongue of
England was part of this programme.   Meanwhile John
Ball asked in mediaeval terms the most modern question
of all :

> When Adam delved and Evé span
> Who was then a gentleman ?

For in the economic sphere also the mediaeval was beginning to yield to the modern, and England was beginning to
develop social classes peculiar to herself.   The break-up of
the feudal manor and the commutation of field-serfdom were
proceeding apace.   The demand advanced by the rebellious
peasants that all Englishmen should be freemen has a

familiar sound to-day, but it was then a novelty and it cut
at the base of the existing social fabric. Those workmen
who already enjoyed this boon of freedom, were constantly
on strike for higher pay in approved modern English
fashion. Moreover, the employers against whom these
strikes were directed were not so much the old feudal lords
as new middle classes of leasehold farmers, manufacturers
and merchants. The cloth trade, destined to make the
wealth and remould the society of England, was already in
the reign of Edward III fast encroaching on the mediaeval
marketing of our raw wool oversea. And the State was
already making intermittent attempts to unite the interests
of the mutually jealous mediaeval towns in a common
policy of protection and control for the trade of the nation.

In pursuit of this policy, sea-power must be maintained
in home waters, and Edward III's new gold coinage represents him standing armed and crowned in a ship.
Chaucer's merchant

> ‘Wold the see were kept for anything
> Betwix Middleburgh and Orewell’

(viz. between Holland and Suffolk). National self-consciousness is beginning to dissolve the local loyalties and
the rigid class divisions which had characterized the cosmopolitan society of the feudal age. And so, in the
Hundred Years' War to plunder France, the King and
nobles find themselves supported by a new force, a democratic Jingoism of the modern type, taking the place of
feudal polity and warfare. At Crecy and Agincourt, that
‘ stout yeoman,’ the archer, is in the forefront of his country's
battle, fighting shoulder to shoulder with the dismounted
knights and nobles of England and shooting down, in heaps
of men and horses, the antiquated chivalry of France.

The institution of Justices of the Peace, local gentry
appointed by the Crown to govern the neighbourhood in
the King's name, was a move away from inherited feudal
jurisdictions. But it was also a reversal of the movement
towards bureaucratic royal centralization : it recognized
and used local connections and influence for the King's
purposes, a compromise significant of the future development of English society as distinct from that of other lands.

All these movements—economic, social, ecclesiastical, national—are reflected in the proceedings of Parliament, a characteristically mediaeval institution in origin, but already on the way to be modernized. It is not merely a council of great nobles, churchmen, judges and civil servants, brought together to advise or harass the King. The Commons are already acquiring a limited importance of their own. In high politics it may be that the members of the Lower House are only pawns in the game of rival parties at Court, but on their own account they voice the economic policy of the new middle classes in town and village, often selfish enough ; they express the nation's anger at the misconduct of the war by land and sea, and the perpetual demand for better order and stronger justice at home, not to be had till Tudor times.

Thus the age of Chaucer speaks to us with many voices not unintelligible to the modern ear. Indeed we may be tempted to think that we ' understanden ' more than in fact we do. For these ancestors of ours, in one half of their thoughts and acts, were still guided by a complex of intellectual, ethical and social assumptions of which only mediaeval scholars can to-day comprehend the true purport.

The most important of the changes proceeding during the lifetime of Chaucer (1340–1400) was the break-up of the feudal manor. Farm leases and money wages were increasingly taking the place of cultivation of the lord's demesne by servile labour, so beginning the gradual transformation of the English village from a community of semi-bondsmen to an individualist society in which all were at least legally free, and in which the cash nexus had replaced customary rights. This great change broke the mould of the static feudal world and liberated mobile forces of capital, labour and personal enterprise, which in the course of time made a richer and more varied life in town and village, and opened out new possibilities to trade and manufacture as well as to agriculture.

In order to understand the meaning of this change, it is necessary to give a brief account of the older system that was gradually displaced.

The most characteristic, though by no means the only,

method of cultivation in mediaeval England was the ' open field.' [1] It was established throughout the Midlands from the Isle of Wight to the Yorkshire Wolds. It implied a village community, working huge unenclosed fields on a principle of strip allotments. Each farmer had a certain number of arable strips, of half an acre or one acre each. His long, narrow strips did not lie next to one another in a compact farm, which would have involved the expense of hedging ; they were scattered over the ' open field ' between those of his neighbours.

The outline of many of these ' strips,' ploughed by the farmers of Saxon, mediaeval and Tudor-Stuart times can still clearly be seen. The ' ridge and furrow ' of pasture-fields that once were arable is one of the commonest features of the English landscape to-day. The long, raised round-backed ' ridges ' or ' lands,' were divided from one another by drains or ' furrows,' made by the turn of the plough in order to carry off the water. [2]   Often, though not always, the curved ' ridge ' or ' land,' thus clearly visible to-day, represents a ' strip ' that was held and worked long ago by a peasant farmer, who also held and worked many other strips in other parts of the ' open field.' The strips were not, in most cases, divided from one another by grass balks, but only by the open drain made by the plough.

The strips or ' lands ' were not severally enclosed. The whole vast ' open field ' was surrounded, when necessary, not by permanent hedges but by movable hurdles. There might be two, three or more of these great arable ' fields ' belonging to the village and subdivided among the farmers ; one of the fields lay fallow while the others were under crop.

The meadowlands for hay were cultivated on a similar principle. Both meadowland and arable, after hay and corn had been cut, were thrown open for common pasture, the grazing rights being ascribed to each man by stints

---

[1] See *The Open Fields*, by C. S. Orwin (1938), for the best account of the system.

[2] The first sentences of Dorothy Wordsworth's *Journal*, written after a night of rain, illustrate the nature and appearance of this system of surface drainage, once almost universal in English ploughlands.

' Alfoxden, Jan. 20, 1798. The green paths down the hillsides are channels for streams. *The young wheat is streaked by silver lines of water running between the ridges.*'

and regulations settled by the village community as a whole, to do justice to each of its members.

This system of cultivation, originated by the first Anglo-Saxon settlers, lasted down to the time of the modern enclosures. It was economically sound as long as the object of each farmer was to raise food for his family rather than for the market. It combined the advantages of individual labour and public control ; it saved the expense of fencing ; it gave each farmer a fair share in the better and worse land ; it bound the villagers together as a community, and gave to the humblest his own land and his voice in the agricultural policy to be followed for the year by the whole village.

On this democracy of peasant cultivators was heavily superimposed the feudal power and legal rights of the lord of the manor. The peasant cultivators, in relation to each other were a self-governing community, but in relation to the lord of the manor they were serfs. They had not the legal right to leave their holdings : they were *ascripti glebae,* ' bound to the soil.' They must grind their corn at the lord's mill. They could not give their children in marriage without his consent. Above all they owed him field service on certain days of the year, when they must labour not on their own land but on his, under the orders of his bailiff. In some villages many of the strips in the great field belonged to the lord ; but he also had in most cases a compact demesne land of his own.

This system of servile tenure with the fixed ' work-days ' of service on the lord's demesne held good all over England, not only in the regions of open-field strip cultivation, but in the south-east, the west and the north, lands of old enclosure where other systems of cultivation were practised. The Norman lawyers had made the feudal law of the manor more or less uniform for all England. In Norman and early Plantagenet times the typical rural village was a society, constituted by the lord of the manor or his agents on the one side and by his peasant serfs upon the other. The freemen were few and far between, fewer than they had been in Anglo-Saxon times, particularly in the Danelaw.

But, for a true picture of mediaeval agriculture in England, we must never forget sheep farming and the shepherd's life. Our island produced the best wool in Europe, and had for centuries supplied the Flemish and Italian looms with material with which they could not dispense for luxury production, and which they could get nowhere else. The woolsack, the symbolic seat of England's Chancellor, was the true wealth of the King and of his subjects, rich and poor, cleric and lay, supplying them with coin over and above the food they wrung from the soil and themselves consumed. Not only the distinctively pastoral regions, the great Yorkshire dales and the Cotswold hills and Sussex downs and the green oozy islands of the fens, but ordinary arable farms had sheep in abundance. Not only the great sheep-farming barons, Bishops and Abbots—with their flocks counted by thousands and tens of thousands, tended by professional shepherds—but the peasants of ordinary manors themselves dealt in wool, and often together owned more sheep than were fed on the lord's demesne. Indeed the proportion of English sheep reared by the peasants was increasing in the reign of Edward III as against the number reared by lay and ecclesiastical landlords. (Eileen Power, *Mediaeval English Wool Trade*, 1941, Chap. II.)

The lifetime of Chaucer roughly corresponds with the years when the disruption of the old manorial system was in most rapid and painful progress. But the change was not complete till long after his death, and it had begun long before his birth. As early as the Twelfth Century the lords of a number of manors had adopted a custom of commuting, for money rents, the forced services due on their demesne lands. The serfs did not thereby become freemen in the eye of the law, they were still subject to other servile dues, and even their liability to work for certain days on their lord's land might be revived if he chose to renew his claim. Meanwhile it stood commuted from year to year. For experience had taught the bailiff that the demesne was better cultivated by hired men working all the year round, than by the grudging service of farmers called off from labour on their own strips, only on such 'workdays' as the custom of the manor assigned to the lord. In some cases the villeins themselves actually preferred the old system of personal service.

The commutation of field services had thus made some headway before the Twelfth Century closed. But in the following Century the process was very frequently reversed. 'Workdays,' for which money payments had been substituted in the age of Becket, were being again demanded in the age of Simon de Montfort, and in some cases new burdens were imposed. A general tightening up and defining of the lords' claims characterized the Thirteenth Century, particularly on certain great ecclesiastical estates where commutation had formerly been creeping in.

One cause of this 'feudal reaction' was the rapid increase of population and the consequent land-hunger of the Thirteenth Century. As the families of the villeins multiplied, the number of strips in the open field assigned to a single farmer grew less. The pressure of population on the means of subsistence, and the competition for land to farm, enabled the lord's bailiff to drive harder bargains with the villeins, and to re-enforce or enforce more strictly the demand for fieldwork on the home farm as the condition for tenure of other lands.

When therefore the Fourteenth Century began, the lords of the manors were in a strong position. But then the tide turned once more. The increase of population had slowed down in the reign of Edward II and it was again becoming usual to commute field services for money rents, when the disaster of the Black Death (1348–1349) came to speed the change.

When a third or possibly a half of the inhabitants of the Kingdom died of plague in less than two years, what was the effect on the social and economic position in the average English village? Obviously the survivors among the peasantry had the whip-hand of the lord and his bailiff. Instead of the recent hunger for land there was a shortage of men to till it. The value of farms fell and the price of labour went up at a bound. The lord of the manor could no longer cultivate his demesne land with the reduced number of serfs, while many of the strip-holdings in the open fields were thrown back on his hands, because the families that farmed them had died of plague.

But the lord's difficulty was the peasant's opportunity. The number of strips in the open field held by a single farmer were increased by the amalgamation of derelict holdings ; and the villein cultivators of these larger units became in effect middle-class yeomen employing hired labour. Naturally they rebelled all the more against their own servile status and against the demands of the bailiff that they should still perform their ' workdays ' in person on the lord's demesne. Meanwhile free labourers who had no land were able, in the general scarcity of hands, to demand much higher wages than before, whether from the bailiff of the demesne or from the farmers of the open field.

Some lords still relied on the compulsory labour of the serfs to cultivate the home farm, but the decreased numbers and the increasing recalcitrance of the villagers from whom such services were due clogged the wheels of the old system. Often, when the bailiff pressed a villein to perform his field-work, he ' fled ' to better himself on the other side of the forest, where every town and every village were so short of labour after the Black Death that high wages were given to immigrants, and no questions asked as to whence they came. A serf, ' bound to the soil ' of a manor by law, might detach himself in physical reality, unless indeed he was encumbered by a wife and children whose migration was more difficult. Such ' flights ' of single villeins, usually the young and energetic men, left on the lord's hands the holding in the open field that the fugitive had deserted, and often there was no one willing to take it except for a low money rent.

More and more, therefore, as Chaucer was growing to manhood, the lords abandoned the attempt to cultivate their demesne lands by the old method, and consented to commute field services for cash. Since there was more coin per head of the reduced population, it was easier for the serf to save or borrow enough shillings to buy his freedom and to pay money rent for his farm. And many of the peasants kept sheep, by the sale of whose wool they obtained coin to buy their freedom.

With the money received in lieu of field service, the lords could offer wages to free labourers. But they could seldom offer enough, because the price of labour was now so high. Many landlords therefore ceased to cultivate the demesne themselves, and let it on lease to a new class of yeoman

farmer.   These farmers often took over the lord's cattle on
a stock-and-land lease.   Sometimes they paid money rents,
but often it was agreed that they should pay in kind, supplying the household of the manor with its food and drink.
The lord's ' family ' had always been fed from the produce
of the home farm and, now that it was let, the old kindly
connection was continued with mutual convenience.   On
some manors in pastoral districts where the peasants grew
rich by selling wool, the bondage tenants took a lease of
the whole of the lord's demesne and divided it among
themselves.

In a number of different ways, therefore, new classes of
substantial yeomen came into existence.   Some of them
farmed the lord's demesne, others the new lands lately
enclosed from the waste, others took over strips in the old
open field.   Some dealt in corn, others in sheep and wool,
others in a mixed husbandry.   The increase in their
numbers and prosperity set the tone of the new England
for centuries to come.   The *motif* of the English yeoman
—his independence, his hearty good nature, his skill in
archery—fills the ballads from the time of the Hundred
Years' War to the Stuart era.[1]

The wide gap between lord and villein that had characterized the society of the feudal manor is being filled up.
Indeed the villein serf is in process of extinction.   He is
becoming a yeoman farmer, or else a landless labourer.
And between these two classes enmity is now set.   The
peasantry are divided among themselves as employers and
employed, and an early phase of their strife is seen in the
famous ' Statutes of Labourers.'

These Parliamentary laws to keep down wages were
passed at the petition of the Commons, at the instance of
the smaller gentry and tenant farmers—' husbands and
land-tenants ' as the Statutes called them.   The policy was
dictated by the new agricultural middle class rather than
by the old-fashioned feudal magnates, though the great

---

[1] The word ' yeoman ' meant any sort of countryman of the middling classes,
usually a farmer, but sometimes a servant or an armed retainer (like the Knight's
and the Canon's yeomen in the *Canterbury Tales*).   In the earlier ballads Robin
Hood is not a disguised earl but a ' yeman.'   The idea that a yeoman must be a
freeholder owning his own land is very late indeed.

landlords supported the demand of their tenants, because high wages indirectly endangered the payment of rents. But the direct quarrel lay between two classes of peasants, the small farmer and the landless labourer whom he hired : their fathers might have worked their strips of land side by side in the village field and laboured together as serfs on the lord's demesne, but the sons' interests were opposed.

These Parliamentary laws in restraint of wages mark the gradual change from a society based on local customs of personal service to a money-economy that is nation wide. Each mediaeval manor had been governed by its own custom, which had now in many cases broken down, and here we have an early attempt of Parliament to substitute national control. The avowed purpose of the Statutes of Labourers is to prevent the rise of wages, and to a lesser degree of prices also. Special Justices are appointed to enforce the Parliamentary rates, and to punish those who demand more.

So the battle of the landless labourers against the farmers backed by the Parliamentary Justices went on, from the time of the Black Death to the Rising of 1381 and after. Strikes, riots and the formation of local unions were met by prosecution and imprisonment. But on the whole the victory lay with the wage-earner, because of the shortage of labour caused by the great pestilence and by its continual local recurrence. Prices indeed rose, but wages rose faster still. During this period the landless labourer stood in the fortunate position described by Piers Plowman (B.VI, 308–319).

> Labourers that have no land to live on but their hands
> Deigned not dine a-day on worts a night old.
> May no penny-ale pay, nor no piece of bacon,
> But if it be fresh flesh or fish fried or baked
> And chaude or plus chaude [hot and hot] for chill of their maw
> And but if he be highly hired else will he grieve
> And that he was workman wrought wail the time
> [And bewail the time when he was born a working man.]
> And then curseth he the King and all his council after
> Such laws to loke [enforce] labourers to grieve.

So let us leave the landless labourer, eating, occasionally at least, his dinner of hot meat, or growling seditiously over his cold bacon and stale cabbage, and turn back to the small peasant cultivator, the farmer of the open-field strips.   How was it going with his fight for freedom—while Chaucer was reaching plump and prosperous middle age at the court of the boy King Richard ?

On some manors the change in the relation between landlord and tenant had taken place without a struggle, in accordance with the clearly perceived interest of both parties to replace villein services by money rents.   But even on manors where field service had thus been commuted, the lords often continued to claim other servile dues : such were the *merchet*, the fine paid for marriage ; the *heriot*, the seizure of the family's best beast on the death of a tenant ; the compulsory use of the lord's mill for grinding the family corn at a monopoly price—and many more such galling instances of servitude.   The half-freed farmers would be content with nothing less than complete emancipation, and the status of freemen before the law with all the rights of the *liber homo* of Magna Carta.   Moreover, on many estates the attempt was still being made to enforce the field work of the villein on the demesne lands, rendering strife yet more acute.

The battle for freedom, differing in its precise character from manor to manor and from farm to farm, led to sporadic acts of violence that prepared the way for the rising of 1381. The preamble of a Statute passed by the Parliament of 1377 is significant.   The lords of manors, ' as well men of Holy Church as other,' complain that the villeins on their estates

' affirm them to be quit and utterly discharged of all manner of serfage, due as well of their body as of their tenures, and will not suffer any distress or other justice to be made upon them ; but do menace the ministers of their lords of life and member, and, which more is, gather themselves in great routs and agree by such confederacy that every one shall aid other to resist their lords with strong hand.'

(*Stats. of Realm*, II, p. 2.)

If such had for years been the state of the countryside, we can better understand the astonishing events of 1381. In the villages within a hundred miles of London, and in many regions yet more distant to west and north, unions

of labourers to resist the Parliamentary laws fixing wages,
and unions of villein farmers to resist the custom of the
manor, had taught whole communities to defy the governing class by passive and active resistance. Nor was social
discontent confined to the village. In the market towns
overshadowed by great abbeys, like St. Albans and
Bury St. Edmunds, not only the serfs but the burghers
were at constant strife with the monks who refused the
municipal liberties which successive Kings had readily
sold to towns fortunate enough to have grown up on royal
land.

The English rebels were not, like the *Jacquerie* of
France, starving men driven to violence by despair. In
wealth and independence their position was improving fast,
but not fast enough to satisfy their new aspirations. And
many of them had the self-respect and discipline of soldiers,
having been armed and drilled in the militia. Not a few
of the famous English long-bowmen were found in the
rebel ranks. And in the forests lurked formidable allies of
the movement, Robin Hood bands of outlaws, peasants
whom upper-class justice had driven to the greenwood,
professional poachers, broken men, criminals and discharged soldiers of the French war.

These various formidable elements of social revolt had
been inflamed by a propaganda of Christian Democracy,
demanding in God's name freedom and justice for the poor.
Such was the preaching of John Ball and of many itinerant
priests and friars. And the parish priest, being usually of
much the same class as the villein farmer, often sympathized
with his desire for freedom. The idealism of the movement was Christian, in most cases not unorthodox, though
some of Wycliffe's Lollard preachers were involved. But
whether orthodox or heretic, the rebels had lost all respect
for the privileges of the wealthy Churchmen, ' the Caesarean
clergy ' allied to the upper class in resistance to the demands
of the poor. The rich monasteries, prelates or laymen who
took the tithe of the parish and starved the parson, were
hateful alike to the priest and his parishioners.

In the south-eastern half of England, the chief area of
the revolt, the monasteries were specially unpopular, and
suffered much from the violence of the rebels. The Prior

of Bury St. Edmunds was murdered by his own serfs. In London, Wat Tyler's men beheaded the Archbishop of Canterbury on Tower Hill, because as Chancellor of the realm he represented the unpopular government. In revenge, the fighting Bishop of Norwich led in person the army that suppressed the rising in East Anglia. Thus the equalitarian and the conservative elements, always present together in the Christian Church, were for a while at open war with one another.

The Rising originated from an unpopular poll-tax. Its oppressive and corrupt administration caused local revolts in Essex and Kent, which became the signal for a national rebellion in no less than twenty-eight counties. The word was sent round by the popular leaders that ' John Ball hath rungen your bell.' Headed sometimes by the parish priest, sometimes by old archers, in a few cases by sympathetic gentry, the half-armed villagers and townsfolk rose. They invaded the manor-houses and abbeys, extorted the rights they claimed, and burnt obnoxious charters and manor rolls. Some murders were committed, and the gentry fled from their homes to hide in the thickets of the woods, whence the outlaws had just emerged.

Then took place the most remarkable incident of our long social history—the capture of London. Many of the village bands had been advised to march on the capital, where the popular leaders had allies. The London mob and a party among the aldermen opened the gates to the rustic armies. The panic of the governing class was such that the impregnable royal fortress of the Tower was surrendered to the rebels, much as the Bastille was surrendered in 1789. Unpopular characters were murdered, including the mild Archbishop Sudbury, whose head was placed over London Bridge. Lawyers were specially obnoxious. And a massacre of foreign artisans was perpetrated by their trade rivals.[1]

---

[1] The only reference in the *Canterbury Tales* to the events of 1381 occurs in the *Nun's Priest's Tale* when the farm hands are chasing the fox:

> ' Certés Jack Straw and his meinie
> Ne maden never shoutes half so shrille
> When that they wolden any Fleming kille
> As thilke day was made upon the fox.'

The cause of law and order had been lost by the poltroonery of the government ; it was revindicated, partly by courage and partly by fraud. The boy King Richard II, whom the rebels had everywhere declared to be on their side, met their London army at Mile End and granted commutation of all servile dues for a rent of four pence an acre, and a free pardon for all the rebels. Thirty clerks were set to work drawing up charters of liberation and of pardon for the men of each village and manor, as well as more generally for every shire. After this great concession, which satisfied the majority of the rebels, it became possible to deal sternly with the more recalcitrant. Wat Tyler was slain at Smithfield in the presence of the mob he led. After that bold stroke by Mayor Walworth, the upper class recovered its courage, called out its men-at-arms, put down the rising in London and in the provinces, and punished it with cruel severity. The charters of liberation, which had served their turn, were repealed by Parliament as having been extorted under duress.

The rebellion had been a great incident, and its history throws a flood of light on the English folk of that day. Historians cannot decide whether it helped or retarded the movement for the abolition of serfdom, which continued at much the same pace after 1381 as before. But the spirit that had prompted the rising was one of the chief reasons why serfdom died out in England, as it did not die out on the continent of Europe.

Personal freedom became universal at an early date in our country, and this probably is one reason for the ideological attachment of Englishmen to the very name of ' freedom.' But many of the serfs won this freedom at the price of divorce from the soil ; and the ever increasing wealth of the country was accompanied by greater inequalities of income. The feudal manor under its lord had been a community of serfs, all poor, but nearly all with rights of their own in the lands to which they were bound ; the land was tied to them as well as they to the land. The modern village under the squire was a society of wealthy farmers, village craftsmen, and a proletariat of free but landless labourers constantly drifting off to the towns. The change from the one form of society to the other was long-drawn-out through centuries, from the Twelfth to the Nineteenth.

Typical of the new England of Chaucer's day was the yeoman farmer, Clement Paston, whose descendants became great landowners and politicians in East Anglia in the following Century. Of him it was told that—

'He was a good plain husband[man], and lived upon his land that he had in Paston, and kept thereon a plough all times in the year, and sometimes in barleysell two ploughs. The said Clement yede [went] at one plough both winter and summer, and he rode to mill on the bare horseback with his corn under him, and brought home meal again under him ; and also drove his cart with divers corns to Wynterton to sell, as a good husband[man] ought to do. Also, he had in Paston a five score or a six score acres of land at the most [about four times a normal villein holding], and much thereof bond-land to Gemyngham Hall, with a little poor water-mill running by the river there. Other livelode nor manors had he none, nor in none other place.'

Himself free, he married 'a bondwoman.' He saved enough money to send their son to school and thence to the law, and so founded the fortunes of the famous Norfolk family that in two generations acquired many Manors in many 'other places'—and left to posterity the *Paston Letters*.

The story of the Rising of 1381 reminds us how ill policed was the England of that day and how weak the arm of the law. Murder, rape, beating and robbery by violence were everyday incidents. Lord, miller and peasant must each guard his own family, property and life. The King's peace had never been very strong, but it had probably been stronger in the reign of Edward I and possibly even under Henry II. The Hundred Years' War enriched individuals with plunder and ransoms from France, and swelled the luxury of court and castle, but was a curse to the country as a whole. It increased disorder and violence, by raising the fighting nobility and their retainers above the control of the Crown.

The King was powerless to act against the great nobles, because his military resources were the resources commanded by the nobles themselves. His army consisted, not of his own Life Guards and regiments of the Line, but of numerous small bodies of archers and men-at-arms enlisted and paid by earls and barons, knights and professional soldiers of fortune, who hired out their services to the government for a greater or less time. Such troops might do well for the French war, and might rally round the throne on an occasion like the Peasants' Rising, when all the upper classes were threatened by a common danger. But they could scarcely be used to suppress themselves, or to arrest the employers whose badges they wore on their coats, and whose pay jingled in their pockets. Once indeed, in 1378, the Commons insisted that a special commission should be sent into the country to restore order. But the new body was necessarily composed of great lords and their retainers, who were soon found to be even more intolerable than the law-breakers whom they were sent to suppress. The Commons next year asked that they might be recalled, as the King's subjects were being brought into ' serfage to the said Seigneurs and commissioners and their retinues.'

A very similar story is told in *Piers Plowman*, where ' Peace ' comes to Parliament with a petition against ' Wrong,' who, in his capacity of King's officer, has broken into the farm, ravished the women, carried off the horses, taken the wheat from the granary, and left in payment a tally on the King's exchequer. ' Peace ' complains that he has been unable to get the law of him, for ' he maintaineth his men to murder mine own.' Such were the King's officers as known in the country districts. They were really ambitious lords using the King's name to acquire wealth for themselves. These evils were partly the result of the bankruptcy of the government. The King could not change the military system, because he could not hire men to take the place of the nobles' retainers. He had to accept the aid of the lords for the French wars very much on their own terms.

Yet the peasant profited as much as he lost by the absence of police. The villein farmer striving for freedom, the free workman in constant revolt against the Statute of Labourers, were neither of them in such real subjection to their ' betters ' as the agricultural labourer in the well-policed countryside of the Nineteenth Century, when the poor had been deprived of bow and club, and had not yet been armed with the vote. In the Fourteenth Century, when every man was expected to ' take his own part ' with stick or fist, with arrow or knife, a union of sturdy villagers was less easily overawed.

The military system by which England fought the Hundred Years' War, strengthened the power not of the King himself but of more than one class of his subjects. While the armies that invaded France were raised by the King contracting with lords and gentry for the service of their retainers, home defence was provided for by a militia compulsorily raised among the common people. And this conscript militia was so well armed and trained that the Scots often rued their temerity in invading the land while the King and nobles were away in France. The good yeoman archer ' whose limbs were made in England ' was not a retrospective fancy of Shakespeare, but an unpleasant reality for French and Scots, and a formidable considera-tion for bailiffs and Justices trying to enforce servile dues or statutory rates of wages in the name of Law, which no one, high or low, regarded with any great respect.[1]

In most of the counties of England the King's writ ran, though it was often evaded or defied. Murderers and thieves, when not in the service of some great lord, were often obliged to fly to the greenwood, or to take sanctuary and then forswear the realm. Sometimes they were actually arrested and brought into court. Even then they often slipped through the meshes of law by pleading their ' clergy ' or by some other lawyer's trick. But, at worst, a great many thieves and a few murderers were hanged by the King's justice every year. The engine of law worked

---

[1] The secret of that greater efficacy of which English archers had the monopoly in Europe lay in the fact that

' the Englishman did not keep his left hand steady, and draw his bow with his right ; but the keeping his right at rest upon the nerve, he pressed the whole weight of his body into the horns of his bow. Hence probably arose the phrase " bending a bow," and the French of " drawing " one.' (W. Gilpin in *Remarks on Forest Scenery*, 1791.)

This is what Hugh Latimer meant when he described how he was early taught ' not to draw with strength of arms as divers other nations do, but with the strength of the body.' It was an art not easily learned.

in the greater part of England, though cumbrously, corruptly and at random.

But in the counties bordering on Scotland the King's
writ can scarcely be said to have run at all.   War seldom
ceased, and cattle-raiding never.   On those roadless fells,
society consisted of mounted clans of farmer-warriors, at
feud among themselves and at war with the Scots.   No
man looked to the King's officers to protect or avenge him.
In the land of the Border Ballads all men were warriors and
most women were heroines.

To Chaucer it was an unknown, distant, barbarous land
—much further off than France—'far in the North, I
cannot tellen where.'   There the Percies and other border
chiefs were building magnificent castles to resist the siege
of the King of Scotland's armies—Alnwick, Warkworth,
Dunstanburgh, Chipchase, Belsay and many more.   The
lesser gentry had their square ' peel towers,' smaller copies
of the castles of the great ; there were no manor-houses, a
product of relative peace.   The peasants lived in wooden
shanties that the raiders burnt as a matter of course, while
the inhabitants and their cattle hid in the woods or sheltered
in the peels.

This state of things outlasted the Tudors who gave
such firm peace to the rest of England.   Only after the
union of the Crowns on the head of James Stuart had made
an end of Border War (1603) did peaceful manor-houses
begin to rise beside the castles and peel towers of the North.

One result of this long continuance of warlike habits,
amid a sparse population, was that a greater familiarity
between high and low prevailed in those wild regions and
lasted into modern times.   The moorland shepherd and the
' hind,' as the Northern farm hand was called, never became
as subject to ' squire and farmer ' as the pauper labourer of
the South in days to come.   There was always a breath of
freedom blowing off the moors.

While the North was still armed and fortified for war,
and while the Marcher lords still relied on their castles to
hold down the Welsh, in the more civilized parts of England
it was no longer usual for lords and gentlemen to build
fortress-homes meant to withstand the siege of a regular

army.   While the Black Prince was ravaging France, **war** was no longer a normal incident in the English country-side.   But local violence was always to be feared, whether from the retainers of a bad neighbour, the rebellious peasants of the village, or outlaws from the greenwood.

Modified precautions were therefore taken in the domestic architecture of the day.   The manor-houses that rose throughout the southern and midland counties were seldom more than two storeys high and they were not completely castellated ;   but they presented narrow shot-hole windows on the sides that overlooked the moat, across which entry was made by the drawbridge.   The inner and safer aspect that looked on to an enclosed courtyard had larger windows and more domesticated architecture. The courtyard was surrounded by suites of rooms ;   the demands of luxurious living had recently added more accommodation to the high hall, parlour and kitchen which had met the needs of a simpler age.   Holes in the roof no longer sufficed to conduct the smoke of the hearth away from throats and eyes ;   noble fireplaces were now built in the dwelling rooms and great chimneys in the thickness of the walls.   But the farm and the cottage were still without chimneys.   Near the manor-house lay the formal garden or lady's pleasaunce, the traditional place for flirta-tion according to the poetry of the ' laws of love.'

In hilly country a moat filled with water was less usual and the rise of ground took its place in the scheme of defence.   Haddon Hall in Derbyshire is a perfect example of a half-fortified English manor-house, built round two courtyards and adapted by constant enlargements to the use of many succeeding generations.

In the West, fine houses were sometimes built of wood and plaster instead of stone, with a lessening regard for con-siderations of defence.   Brick was very rare in England from the time of the departure of the Romans until the Fifteenth Century, when it came into general use in East Anglian and other regions where local stone was scarce, and where the timber of the forests was beginning to run short.

In Chaucer's day, life was already somewhat safer and **a** good deal more comfortable than in the warlike era when the most wealthy families had been crowded into the darkness of grim, square Norman keeps. In the Thirteenth Century, Kenilworth Keep had resisted the force of the Kingdom for six months, but the cannon of the Hundred Years' War would soon have breached its antique strength. Nor was it any longer regarded as tolerable quarters for a great man's court. John of Gaunt therefore built at its foot a palace with a banqueting hall, into which light flooded through wide windows of delicate tracery. But he took care to protect his new home, at each end, with a tower suitable to carry cannon.

While the square keeps of the Norman warriors were being deserted as no longer habitable, some of the finer Plantagenet castles were being enlarged and adapted to the uses of a new age. Not a few of them continued as royal or private palaces down to the time when Milton's *Comus* was acted in Ludlow Castle. Finally Cromwell's men stormed and dismantled a large proportion of the castles which had till then served as homes of the great.

The farms and cottages of the poor were built of logs or planks, or of uprights and beams supporting rubble and clay. The floors were usually bare earth, and the roof of thatch. But since these humble homes have disappeared, we know very little about them. Something has already been said about their inhabitants, during this period of social change and strife. But nothing is more difficult to assess than the real degree of the peasants' poverty or well-being, which differed greatly not only from place to place but from year to year. Many of them by feeding sheep acquired considerable wealth by the sale of the wool ; the great English wool mart was supplied largely by the peasants. Their bread and ale depended on the uncertain harvest of the common field, and in bad seasons there was local shortage or famine. But meat, cheese and vegetables made up an equally important part of their diet. Many peasants kept poultry and ate the eggs. Most had a plot of land with their cottage, where peas, beans or more primitive ' worts ' were grown, and where sometimes a cow or pig was kept. The farmers of the open field, whether serf or free, had each his oxen on the village stubble and pasture ; the poor beasts, half the size of modern cattle,

B

were lean with scant fare and tough with years of tugging at the plough ; but some were slaughtered every Martinmas to be salted for the winter's food, or were killed fresh for Christmas feasting.

Bacon was a more common dish on the cottage table ; but the number of pigs in the village herd depended on the extent and character of the ' waste.' On some manors the heaths and woods had shrunk to small proportions before the encroachments of ' assart ' farms enclosed for agriculture. In others, particularly in West and North, the waste was essential to the life of many families. Lonely squatters, with or without leave, built their huts and fed their beasts on some outlying bit of land. And every lawful villager required timber from the trees on the waste, to build his cottage, to warm his hearth and cook his food, to make his carts, ploughs, farm tools and household furniture. The rights of the customary tenants differed from manor to manor, but often they had the privilege of cutting wood for building and carpentry, and of taking sticks for fuel by ' hook and crook,' that is, by pulling branches from standing trees. The waste, too, meant pig-pannage and extra pasture for cattle and sheep, the latter often the most valuable item in a peasant's budget by the sale of the wool. In these respects the comfort and wealth of the villager diminished as the cornfields encroached on wild nature. There was gain with loss and loss with store.

But there is other meat besides beef and mutton, poultry and bacon. The waste and the woodland swarmed with game. In the King's forests, an ever diminishing area, and in the warrens and enclosures of lords and gentry, which were always on the increase, the deer and lesser game were guarded by severe laws, and still more effectively by keepers who administered club law of their own without bothering the King's courts. Poaching was not only the livelihood of outlaws, but the passion of men of all classes—gentry, clerks of Holy Church, besides farmers and workmen seeking a pheasant or hare for the pot.[1]

---

[1] The proverbial efficiency of ' the poacher turned gamekeeper ' is as old as Chaucer :

> ' A thief of venison, that hath forlaft
> His likerousness and all his olde craft.
> Can kepe a forest best of any man.' (*Doctor's Tale.*)

In 1389 the Commons complained in Parliament that 'artificers and labourers, and servants and grooms keep greyhounds and other dogs, and on the holy days, when good Christian people be at Church, hearing divine service, they go hunting in parks, warrens and coneyries of lords and others, to the very great destruction of the same.' Evil indeed is the heart of man ! Henceforth let no layman with less than forty shillings a year in land, and no priest or clerk with less than ten pounds income a year, be so bold as to keep sporting nets or dogs. So the Statute decreed ; how far it was observed may well be doubted. (*Stats. of Realm*, II, p. 65.) There were, moreover, great regions of moor, fen and woodland where game was not strictly preserved and could be taken with little or no risk of challenge.

Rabbits, then called ' coneys,' were a plague in many parts of mediaeval England, and were snared and dug out by all classes, except in private warrens. To take and eat small birds like thrushes and larks was then as usual in our island as it still is on the Continent ; they were limed and netted in great numbers both by the peasants and by the sporting gentry. But most of all did it rejoice the farmer's heart to slay secretly for his own pot one of the legion of privileged birds from the dovecot of the manor-house whose function in life was to grow plump on the peasants' corn till they were fit for the lord's table.[1] Then there were trout in the streams and meres, and great pike in the ' stews ' (ponds) of manor-house and abbey. Of Chaucer's Franklin we read—

> ' It snowed in his house of meat and drinke
> Of alle dainties that men coulde thinke.
> After the sundry seasons of the year,
> So changed he his meat and his supper.
> Full many a fat partridge had he in mewe [cage]
> And many a bream and many a luce in stewe ' [pike in fishpond].

The gentry spent much of their lives hunting the deer with horse and hound, or flying hawks at pheasant, partridge

[1] In the Fifteenth Century, the Fellows of King's College, Cambridge, ate or sold from two to three thousand doves a year from the great dovecot of their Grantchester estate.

and heron, or lying out at night to net the fox and the badger. Such field sports, and tilting in tournaments before the gallery of ladies, were the lighter sides of their life ; the more serious were war abroad, and at home law-suits, national politics and local administration.[1] The improvement of agricultural methods did not interest them as much as their descendants. The historian of English farming has said : ' Feudal barons are rarely represented as fumbling in the recesses of their armour for samples of corn.' (Ernle, p. 31.) But the break-up of the feudal manor and the new opportunities it afforded of producing for the market, opened the way to agricultural improvement and thereby encouraged the landlord class to take a greater interest in farming methods. Indeed, Lord Berkeley, though very exceptional, was a great improver of his land, a Fourteenth Century Coke of Norfolk.

By self-flattering fallacy, some of our city-bred folk to-day suppose that their ancestors, because they were accustomed to country sights and sounds on workdays as well as week-ends, cared nothing for the loveliness around them. No doubt many of them raised their eyes to nature's beauty as little as the Philistines of to-day. But the poetry of the age of Chaucer and Langland shows that they were by no means all so indifferent.

Here, in an alliterative poem of the mid-Fourteenth Century, is a poacher's account of dawn in the woods, as he waits for the deer :

> In the monethe of Maye when mirthes bene fele,
> And the sesone of somere when softe bene the wedres,
> Als I went to the wodde my werdes to dreghe,
> In-to the schawes my-selfe a schotte me to gete
> At ane hert or ane hynde, happen as it myghte :
> And as Dryghtyn the day droue from the heuen,
> Als I habade one a banke be a bryme syde,
> There the gryse was grene growen with floures—
> The primrose, the pervynke, and the piliole the riche—
> The dewe appon dayses donkede full faire,

---

[1] The ' knights of the shire ' (county members in the House of Commons) were busy in local administration. Miss Wood-Legh has ascertained that of 1636 persons who were knights of the shire in the fifty odd Parliaments of Edward III, 125 served as escheators, 371 as collectors at ' tenths and fifteenths ' (taxes), 381 as sheriffs and 641 as Justices of the Peace. Chaucer's Franklin is an example. (*Review of English Studies*, April 1928.)

Burgons and blossoms and braunches full swete,
And the mery mystes full myldely gane falle :
The cukkowe, the cowschote, kene were they bothen,
And the throstills full throly threpen in the bankes,
And iche foule in that frythe faynere than other
That the derke was done and the daye lightenede :
Hertys and hyndes one hillys thay gouen,
The foxe and the filmarte thay flede to the erthe,
The hare hurkles by hawes, and harde thedir dryves,
And ferkes faste to hir fourme and fatills hir to sitt.

At last the hart appears, with tall antlers. The poet-poacher watches him, cross-bow in hand :

And he statayde and stelkett and starede full brode,
Bot at the laste he loutted doun and laugt till his mete
And I hallede to the hokes and the herte smote,
And happened that I hitt hym be-hynde the lefte sholdire.

* * *

Dede as a dorenayle doun was he fallen.[1]

The poet then hides the body lest the game-keepers should find it.

In men's dress, as well as in so much else, the beginning of the change from mediaeval to modern might be ascribed to the age of Chaucer. He himself, like Dante, is known to us clad in the dignified long gown and plain hood—the distinctively mediaeval dress that the Franciscan brother-

---

[1] *The Parlement of the Three Ages.* Ed. Gollancz, 1915. The following is the translation of these lines given in H. S. Bennett's *Life on the English Manor,* p. 271 :

'In May, when there are many things to enjoy, and in the summer season when airs are soft, I went to the wood to take my luck, and in among the shaws to get a shot at hart or hind, as it should happen. And, as the Lord drove the day through the heavens, I stayed on a bank beside a brook where the grass was green and starred with flowers—primroses, periwinkles and the rich penny-royal. The dew dappled the daisies most beautifully, and also the buds, blossoms and branches, while around me the soft mists began to fall. Both the cuckoo and pigeon were singing loudly, and the throstles in the banksides eagerly poured out their songs, and every bird in the wood seemed more delighted than his neighbour that darkness was done and the daylight returned. Harts and hinds betake themselves to the hills ; the fox and polecat seek their earths ; the hare squats by the hedges, hurries and hastens thither to her forme and prepares to lurk there.

'The hart paused, went on cautiously, staring here and there, but at last he bent down and began on his feed. Then I hauled to the hook [i.e. the trigger of the cross-bow] and smote the hart. It so happened that I hit him behind the left shoulder . . . he had fallen down, dead as a door nail.'

hood still preserves in our midst in its simplest form. But Chaucer's fashionable contemporaries, especially the younger sort, abandoned the decent gown for a short coat or jacket and displayed the symmetry of their legs in tight-fitting ' hosen.' The new mode resembled in fundamental form the ' coat and trousers ' of the modern male biped, but by no means in our drab detail and monotony of dullness. In Richard II's court, coats and ' hosen ' blazed with colour. One leg might be draped in red, the other in blue. Men ' wore their estates on their backs,' and flashed in jewels and costly stuffs no less than their wives. Following the fashion of an extravagant court, gilded youth was every-where ' expressed in fancy.' Sleeves ' slod upon the earth ' ; shoes with long toe-points chained to the waist prevented the wearer from kneeling to say his prayers.

The long gown did not, however, go out of use among the more sober part of mankind till Tudor times. And sometimes the gown itself became an extravagance ; men of high rank wore rich gowns trailing behind them on the ground as if they were women. Both men and women of fashion wore enormous head-dresses of fantastic shape, like horns, turbans or towers.

With much absurd and ephemeral luxury came in much solid comfort and new habits of life, that have survived. Now for the first time in our country, gentlemen's families retired from the great hall where they used to feed in patri-archal community with their household, and ate their more fashionable meals in private. The tribute and plunder of France that had been poured into England during the early and more successful part of the Hundred Years' War, revo-lutionized the primitive economy of the English feudal household, just as, among the ancient Romans, the tribute and plunder of the Mediterranean overturned the austere simplicity of Camillus and Cato. French nobles, taken in war, waited sometimes for years till their ransoms could be wrung from their peasants, and meanwhile they lived as honoured guests in the country houses of their English captors ; they hunted with the men, made love to the ladies, and taught English provincial simplicity that every gentleman must have this fashion in his clothes or that dish on his table.

Under such tutors luxury increased, and with it commerce grew and refinement spread by the very means which the moralists denounced. The merchants of the town rejoiced to supply the noblemen's courts with every new fashion and requirement, in dress, furniture or food. By their own magnificence and outlay the feudal lords were helping the rise of the mercantile classes who were one day to take their place. Most of our town manufactures and overseas commerce, and almost all European trade with the East were conducted to supply the luxuries of castle and manor-house, and not, as in modern times, the needs of the mass of the population. English towns and English trade would have made little headway in those days if they had catered only for the farm and the cottage, which produced their own food, while almost all their clothing, furniture and farm implements were home-made either by the peasant family itself or by the craftsmen of the village.

CHAPTER II

CHAUCER'S ENGLAND (*continued*)

II

Town and Church

IN the Fourteenth Century the English town was still a rural and agricultural community, as well as a centre of industry and commerce. It had its stone wall or earth mound to protect it, distinguishing it from an open village. But outside lay the 'town field' unenclosed by hedges, where each citizen-farmer cultivated his own strips of cornland ; and each grazed his cattle or sheep on the common pasture of the town, which usually lay along the riverside as at Oxford and Cambridge.[1] In 1388 it was laid down by Parliamentary Statute that in harvest time journeymen and apprentices should be called on to lay aside their crafts and should be compelled ' to cut gather and bring in the corn '; Mayors, bailiffs and constables of towns were to see this done. (*Stats. of Realm*, II, 56.) In Norwich, the second city of the Kingdom, the weavers, till long after this period, were conscripted every year to fetch home the harvest. Even London was no exception to the rule of a half rustic life. There was none of the rigid division between rural and urban which has prevailed since the Industrial Revolution. No Englishman then was ignorant of all country things, as the great majority of Englishmen are to-day.

The town was more insanitary than the village and was often visited by plague. But it was not, as in later centuries, crowded thick with slums. Its houses still stood pleasantly amid gardens, orchards, paddocks and farm-yards. For the number of inhabitants was still very small—two or three thousand for a town of fair size.

The life of the burgher combined the advantages of town

---

[1] Cambridge was protected not by walls but by water, the river on the west, the King's ditch on the east.

and countryside. The all-pervading atmosphere of natural beauty unconsciously affected the language and thoughts of all. Chaucer was a Londoner, but, in describing a beautiful and sprightly young woman, he employs four metaphors, one taken from the Tower mint, the other three from familiar, vulgar sights, sounds and smells of the rustic farm :

> ‘ Full brighter was the shining of her hewe
> Than in the Tower the noble yforged newe.
> But of her song, it was as loud and yerne [brisk]
> As any swallow sitting on a berne.   [barn]
> Thereto she could skip and make game
> As any kid or calf following his dame.
> Her mouth was sweet as brachet or the meeth [honeyed
>   ale or mead]
> Or hoard of apples laid in hay or heeth.’

How simple, strong yet exquisite it is—a lost quality, because the influences of daily life that made it are lost, or at least are overmastered by others more ugly and mechanical. It was equally characteristic of the age of Chaucer that the young woman so beautifully described was no better than she should have been !   (*The Miller's Tale.*)

But these little towns, half rural though they were, had burgher pride of the most exclusive kind.   Their constant preoccupation was to keep and extend the privileges of self-government and the monopoly of local trade, which they had bought from King or Lord, Abbot or Bishop.   To defend the merchants of their own town in their dangerous journeys, and to gather in their debts owing in other towns, municipal action was quasi-diplomatic ; Norwich talked to Southampton like England to France.   Commercial treaties between towns were common.   As to London, its power of self-government, which included jurisdiction over wide territories up and down the river, might have been the envy of many German ‘ free cities.’   Woe to the King's officer, or to one of John of Gaunt's ‘ meinie,’ who infringed the right of a London citizen or challenged the jurisdiction of the Mayor.

Yet, great as was the power of London and considerable as were the ‘ liberties ’ of other towns, they were loyal members of a State, whose Parliament legislated, partly

by their advice, on their economic concerns in so far as
they were national ; and in the Fourteenth Century trade
was becoming more and more national without ceasing to
be municipal.   The history of all English towns was
swallowed up in the history of England which they helped
to make ; while in Germany, not then a nation, the history
of Nuremberg and of the Hanse Towns form separate
chapters in the annals of Europe.

But even in England and even during the Hundred
Years' War, national sentiment and loyalty to the Kingdom
at large made no such daily and urgent claims as did the
civic patriotism that a man felt for his own town.   The first
duty of the burgher was to play his part in the city militia,
to defend the walls and if possible the fields of the town
against French or Scottish raiders, bands of outlaws, or the
retainers of great men at feud with the privileges of the
borough.   The principle of ' conscription ' raised no
difficulty in the mind of the mediaeval Englishman.   How
indeed could he expect other people to defend him and his
fellows from dangers constantly at his door ?   For purposes
of war and police, and for town-works of all sorts like
digging a town ditch or drain, repairing the town bridge,
helping in the harvest of the town fields, very occasionally
cleaning or mending the street in front of his own house, a
man might be called on for personal service by the civic
authorities.   Such work in the common cause was not
regarded as ' servile,' like work on the lord's demesne.   No
one then thought that ' liberty ' consisted in avoiding
military or other obligations on the performance of which
the cherished ' liberties ' of his town and of his fellow
burghers ultimately depended.   Self-help and self-government were for long centuries taught to the English in the
school of town life, and to a less degree in the shire-court
and in the manor-court of the village.   There were no
rights without duties.

Political strife ran strong and fierce in the streets of every
town of England, not the strife of national parties, but the
politics of the craft and of the town which touched the
burgher in his daily life.   The struggle for power was
constantly being waged in disputes of the crafts with
the corporation ; of the big merchants with the small

manufacturing masters ; of the masters with their men ; of the whole body of citizens with outsiders trying to settle and trade in the town ; of all the inhabitants of the borough with the King's Sheriff, the lord's or bishop's bailiff, or the monks of the Abbey the worst enemies of all. In a hundred ever-changing forms such disputes went on for centuries, with different fortunes in a hundred different towns, from great London, itself a State within the State, to the smallest would-be borough that was struggling to rise above the position of a feudal village ruled by the lord's bailiff and manor-court. In all these civic battles, external and internal, each party used every appropriate weapon of legal proceedings, open riot and economic pressure.

In London, ' sea ' coal, so called because it was brought by ship from Tyneside, was being more and more used in place of wood and charcoal, causing ' clergy and nobility resorting to the city of London ' to complain of danger of contagion from ' the stench of burning sea-coal.'[1] For fear of fire, thatch was gradually giving way to red tiles on London roofs. The walls of the houses were still of mud and timber, though the number of fine stone mansions built by great lords or wealthy citizens was on the increase, like John of Gaunt's Savoy on the way between London and Westminster. But the chief architectural glory of the capital was its hundred churches. The streets were ill paved and had no side walks ; the crown of the causeway sloped down on both sides to the ' kennels,' into which the filth ran ; weaker passengers, shoved down off the centre of the road, ' went to the wall ' and splashed through the mud. Too little checked by municipal authority, householders and tradesmen threw their garbage, litter and offal into the street from doors and windows, without regard to amenity or sanitation.

Two miles from London lay Westminster, clustering round its Abbey, and its Hall which Rufus had built and which Richard II was adorning with rafters of oak. Westminster had become the recognized centre of royal administration, law and Parliament, although it had no

---

[1] There was a prejudice against coal as domestic fuel until the shortage of wood brought it increasingly into use. In the country at large it was, till Tudor times, chiefly used by smiths and lime burners.

commerce and no municipal privileges of its own, and was only a village at great London's gate. There was no royal foothold inside the English capital corresponding to the Louvre in Paris. When the King came up to town, he lived sometimes at Westminster on one side of London, sometimes in the Tower on the other. But the City that lay between was not his ground, and Richard II was no more able than Charles I to dictate to its militia, its magistrates and its mob. The mediaeval balance and harmony of powers, from which modern English liberty has sprung, is clearly illustrated in the relation of the Plantagenet Kings to their capital.

The richest citizens of London were now on a par with the great territorial nobles, not only because they had at their command the City militia and a large proportion of the shipping of England, but because they lent money to government. In 1290 Edward I had expelled the Jews from England, so putting an end to the older method of raising royal loans. This expulsion of the Jews is one cause why anti-semitism is to-day less strong in England than in many countries of Europe : our forefathers were compelled by the action of Edward I to undertake their own financial and intellectual life unaided by Jewry, so that when in Cromwell's time the Jews were allowed to return, the English had learnt to stand alone, and could meet without jealousy that gifted race on equal terms.[1]

And so, in the absence of the Jews, Edward III borrowed money for his wars from Florentine bankers, who also supplied the needs of his barons. In the Second Day of Boccaccio's *Decameron* we read how three Florentines ' coming to London, took a little house, and lived as frugally as possible, letting out money on interest.' When they had made enough money they returned to Florence, but ' keeping on their banking trade in England, they sent a

---

[1] The expulsion of the Jews had been preceded by a decline in their wealth and power of lending ; otherwise they would not have been expelled. English and foreign Christians had already been taking their place as moneylenders to the King and to his subjects. Industry and agriculture were changing and expanding all through the later middle ages and required the borrowing of capital by King, lord of manor, farmer, villein and trader. The laws against usury prohibited interest instead of limiting it ; the result was that very high interest, often 50 per cent., was asked and given, as the transaction was illegal. (*Lipson*, I, pp. 616-620.)

nephew thither, named Alessandro, to manage their business. . . . He let out money to the barons upon their castles and other estates, which turned to good account.'

But the King also borrowed from his own subjects, the ' great City men ' as we may already call them, and from the wealthy merchants of other towns, like Sir William de la Pole of Hull, the first English business man to become the founder of a great noble house. The relation of the Crown to these new creditors was very different from its previous relation to the Jews, who had been mere sponges in the King's hand to suck up his subjects' wealth, helpless clients whom he alone protected from popular malice and massacre. But the English merchants who lent money to government for the Hundred Years' War could give or withhold their aid as they chose, and they took advantage of the need the King had of them to bargain for commercial or other advantages for themselves or their families, for their city, their craft or their trade.

It was in these circumstances that the network of Edward III's financial, home and foreign policy was elaborated. The Hundred Years' War was not merely an adventure for military plunder and dynastic ambition ; it was also an attempt to keep open the market for our wool and cloth trade in Flanders and in France. The alliance with Van Artevelde and the Flemish burghers against France, was at once diplomatic and commercial.

English national policy was continually changing under the pressure of the King's necessities, and of rival interests among his own subjects and among his allies oversea. Experiments in Protection and Free Trade, neither yet an established doctrine, were made in bewildering alternation. The ' mercantilist ' era of a fixed Protectionist policy had not yet come, but the country was already groping towards it. Navigation laws to exclude foreign vessels from trading in English ports were passed as early as the reign of Richard II, but could not be enforced, because our merchant shipping was not large enough, until Stuart times, to cope alone with the ever increasing volume of our trade. English merchants did much of their overseas trade in foreign bottoms.

But the English marine was at last beginning to be

formidable. Edward III used it to clear the Channel of foreign pirates, and succeeded for a number of years. Tne fleet that defeated the French at Sluys (1340) was not a royal navy : it was composed of the merchant ships of many different towns, temporarily conscripted to fight under a royal Admiral. Cannon had as yet no place in warfare at sea. Still, as at Salamis, ships rammed and grappled each other, and the fight was conducted with swords, spears and arrows, like a battle on land.

The ' Staple,' where English goods for export had to be collected, taxed and sold, was necessary for levying the customs duties on which the King's finances depended, and it was thought also to be of service in protecting English merchants against the fraud and violence of international commerce in that age. But ' the Company of the Staple ' obtained a partial monopoly in export that was not at all agreeable to many wool growers and to many rival merchants. Numerous and divergent interests, agricultural, industrial and mercantile, held conflicting views about the Staple, and particularly about its proper location. At one time it was fixed in certain English towns, then in Flanders, finally in Calais, which English arms won and held as the port of entry into France. ' When the wool reached Calais, it was the common practice for the foreign buyer to pay a certain sum in cash and give bills for the rest. The discounting of bills by *assigning* or transferring them was also usual, so that the trade custom of circulating bills from one creditor to another is at least five hundred years old.' (*Lipson*, I, 549, ed. 1937.)

Most of the English goods exported through the Staple at Calais consisted of raw wool ; but woollen cloth was constantly gaining ground, till in Tudor times the export of cloth killed the export of raw wool. But in Chaucer's day and for long after, the men who lent most money to the King were the Staplers who exported wool to feed the foreign looms ; and the customs levied at the Staple on exported wool were the great source of royal revenue.[1]

---

[1] Both wool and cloth were collected, taxed and sold at the Staple. But the ' Staple Company,' the ' Staplers ' *par excellence*, dealt in wool, not in cloth, and their gradual decline was due to the increase of the export of cloth by the Merchant Adventurers. In the early Fourteenth Century wool exports were 30,000 sacks a year and cloth exports about 5000 cloths. In the middle of the Sixteenth Century

These London–Calais merchants, with whom the King
had to bargain for loans and levies as if with a fourth estate
of the realm, had extensive business and personal connections with wool-growing districts like the Cotswolds,
where they and their rivals the clothiers bought estates and
founded many of the great county families of Western
England. In 1401 was laid to rest in Chipping Campden
the body of William Grevel ' late citizen of London and
flower of the wool merchants of England,' and his stone
house is still an ornament of the most beautiful village
street now left in the island : for Chipping Campden was
not an ordinary Gloucestershire village but a collecting
centre for England's greatest trade.

It is, in fact, to the age of Chaucer that Professor Postan
points as the ' great breeding season of English capitalism ;
in the early phases of the Hundred Years' War, the time
when the exigencies of Royal finance, new experiments in
taxation, speculative ventures with wool, the collapse of
Italian finance and the beginning of the new cloth industry,
all combined to bring into existence a new race of war
financiers and commercial speculators, army purveyors and
wool monopolists.' (*Ec. Hist. Review*, May 1939, p. 165.)

If the capitalist as financier and public creditor was
found chiefly in the wool trade, the beginnings of the
capitalist as organizer of industry were found during the
same period in the cloth manufacture.

While raw wool was still the chief article of export,
domestic needs were supplied for the most part by cloth
made in England. In the times of Ancient Britons,
Romans and Saxons and ever since, the spare moments of
the housewife, her maids and daughters had been devoted
to spinning—the supposed occupation of our mother Eve.
And equally from the earliest times the more difficult art
of weaving had been practised by men specially trained as
websters, sitting all day each at the loom in his own cottage,
to provide the coarse clothes of the local peasantry. In
the Twelfth and Thirteenth Centuries a better class of

---

the wool exports were 4000 sacks and the cloth exports well over 100,000 cloths.
See E. E. Rich, *The Ordinance Book of the Merchants of the Staple*, 1937.
    On the early history of the Staple, see Eileen Power, *Mediaeval English Wool
Trade*, 1941.

manufacture was conducted by Weavers' Gilds in many towns, including London, Lincoln, Oxford and Nottingham. In Henry III's reign, Stamford cloth was well known in Venice, while Yorkshire, both east and west, was already famous for its woollens.

In the Thirteenth and early Fourteenth Centuries the production of standardized cloth for the market began to deteriorate in English towns, where the number of weavers seriously declined. The fact was that the manufacture had begun to move into the country districts, particularly to those of the West where running water was obtainable to work fulling-mills. One of the many processes necessary in cloth-making, that which was conducted by the fuller, had in all previous ages been done by human labour with hand, foot or club ; but it was now beginning to be done by water-power. Already therefore when the Fourteenth Century opened, the Cotswold and Pennine valleys and the Lake District had begun to compete seriously with Eastern England in the manufacture of cloth. And the country was already vying with the town as the seat of the industry. It was an early case of technical invention having important social results. (*Ec. Hist. Rev.*, 1941, Miss Carus Wilson's article, ' An industrial Revolution of the 13th Century.')

Government action in the reigns of Edward II and III further stimulated our greatest industry. The importation of cloth from abroad was prohibited. Skilled artificers with trade secrets were invited over, particularly into London and East Anglia, and were protected by the Government against native jealousy ; special privileges were at the same time extended to English clothiers. During the lifetime of Chaucer the production of broadcloth in England was trebled, and the export of broadcloth was increased ninefold. The enormous advantage that England had over other countries as a feeder of sheep and a producer of the best wool gave her the opportunity gradually to win the command of the world's cloth market, as she had long commanded the European market for raw wool.

The growth of the cloth trade was destined to go on for generations to come, creating new classes in town and country, adding to the luxury of the manor-house and relieving the poverty of the cottage, altering the methods and increasing the rewards of agriculture, supplying our ships with their cargoes, spreading our commerce first over all Europe and then over all the world, dictating the policy of our statesmen and providing the programmes of our parties, causing alliances, treaties and wars. The cloth trade held its place as incomparably the most important English industry, till the far distant day when coal was wedded to iron. For centuries it occupied men's daily thoughts in town and village, second only to agriculture ; our literature and common speech acquired many phrases and metaphors borrowed from the manufacture of cloth— 'thread of discourse,' 'spin a yarn,' 'unravel a mystery,' 'web of life,' 'fine-drawn,' 'homespun,' 'tease'—while all unmarried women were put down as 'spinsters.'

Already in the Fourteenth Century it was evident that the rapid expansion of the cloth trade required a new economic organization. The manufacture of raw wool into the best cloth called not for one craft alone but for many— carding, spinning, weaving, fulling, dyeing, cloth-finishing. Therefore a large expansion of the cloth industry for the market at home and abroad could not be organized by the Craft Gilds which had done so much to improve weaving in former centuries. The *entrepreneur*, with a more than local outlook and with money at his command, was required to collect the raw material, the half-manufactured and the finished article, and pass them on from craftsman to craftsman and from place to place, from village to town, from town to port, and finally to bring a standardized article to the best market. For all this capital was needed.

Capitalism as the organizer of industry is first clearly visible in the cloth trade. Already in the lifetime of Chaucer, the capitalist clothier could be found, employing many different people in many different places. He was a social type more modern than mediaeval, and quite different from the master craftsman labouring at the bench with his apprentices and journeymen.[1] The ultimate future lay with the capitalist employer, in the far distant days of the

[1] Until the coming of elaborate machinery in the Eighteenth Century, capitalism did not mean factories. Except for the water-worked fulling-mills, the capitalist employed the various workmen in their own homes, and they owned their own tools and plant. This is the 'domestic' system of industry. The capitalist had indeed to provide warehouses to store the goods.

Industrial Revolution. But the cloth manufacture had brought him into existence four hundred years before he swallowed industry whole. Shipping, the coal trade and the building trade were also conducted in part on a capitalist basis at this early date.

But, for centuries to come, most industries were still conducted by the old-fashioned master craftsman, with a few apprentices and journeymen sleeping and working under his roof, subject to the general supervision of the Craft Gild. Here too trouble was brewing between the master craftsmen and the journeymen whom they employed, corresponding to the trouble between the farmers and the free labourers. The journeyman in the shop felt the same movement of aspiration and unrest as the labourer in the field. He too struck for higher wages when the Black Death made labour scarce, and the Statute of Labourers was in part directed against his claims.

But there was more in it than a struggle for wages. The unrest in the towns had deeper causes. Owing to the expansion of trade and the increase of its rewards, the harmony of the mediaeval Craft Gild was being disturbed by social and economic cleavage between master and man, which had not been felt in the simpler day of small things.

In the earlier stages of the Craft Gild, masters, apprentices and journeymen were more or less of one class. They were all ' small men ' together, brother labourers in the shop, sharing the same meals. Though poor by any modern standard, they were a proud fraternity, the skilled men of the trade. Their Gild represented their common interest and, subject to the general control of the Municipality, it managed the affairs of the craft within the town, fixing prices, wages and conditions of work to the general satisfaction of masters and men. The apprentices at the expiry of their indentures, became either masters or journeymen, and most journeymen sooner or later became small masters. The master-craftsman worked with his men. He often beat his apprentices and sometimes beat his journeyman, for blows were common currency in those days. But there was no marked division of social standard and way of life. Outside the Gilds, indeed, there had always been a pool of unskilled labour in the town, ill paid

and uncared for. But in the Gilds themselves there had
been much harmony and content.

In the age of Chaucer these things were changing. The
expansion of industry and trade were bringing variety of
function and an increasing difference of monetary reward.
The master was becoming less the brother craftsman and
more the *entrepreneur*, engaged in organizing the business
and selling the goods. Some apprentices became masters,
especially if they ' married their master's daughter.' But
most apprentices could only look to become journeymen,
and few journeymen could any longer look to become
masters. In proportion to the increasing numbers engaged
in the trade, the number of masters was less than of old.
The harmony of the Craft Gild had depended on the
identity of interest of its members, and on a certain sense
of social equality among them. But this was growing less
every year. The distinction between ' employer and employed ' was becoming more marked. There was also an
increasing difference between the rich trading master and
the poor manufacturing master, who worked with a couple
of journeymen to make the goods that the great man sold.

And so we find in the towns of the Fourteenth Century
not only occasional strikes for higher wages inside the Gild,
but in some cases the formation of permanent ' Yeomen
Gilds,' to champion the interest of the employees and perform the fighting functions of a modern Trade Union. In
some trades and in some towns these Yeomen Gilds also
included small master-craftsmen. For they too were opposed to the richer masters, who were ceasing to be craftsmen at all and were concerned only in selling the goods.
The trader and the manual worker were in some trades
beginning to be separated, and the trader was assuming
control of the industry, by his command of the Craft Gild or
the Livery Company. The manual worker, whether journeyman or small master, was losing much of his economic independence and was acquiring an inferior status. The government of the towns was in the hands of the big merchants.
But the modern trade union spirit was already active.[1]

---

[1] The gangs of workmen who built the glorious Cathedrals and lovely churches
and manor-houses of the later middle age were organized not as a gild but on a
capitalist basis. Trade unionism was therefore strong among the ' free masons '

These economic and social changes, begun in the Four-teenth Century, were going on all through the succeeding epoch. But there was no uniformity, and generalization is necessarily inaccurate. The history of each craft and of each town differs from every other. But such was the general direction of growth in industry and commerce during the Hundred Years' War and the Wars of the Roses.

Great changes, therefore, were taking place in Chaucer's day in the structure of society. Servitude was disappearing from the manor and new classes were arising to take charge of farming and of trade. Modern institutions were being grafted on to the mediaeval, in both village and town. But in the other great department of human affairs—the religious and ecclesiastical, which then covered half of human life and its relationships—institutional change was prevented by the rigid conservatism of the Church authorities, although here too thought and opinion were moving fast.

Change indeed was long overdue. The ' corruption ' of the clergy was being denounced not merely by Lollard heretics but by the orthodox and the worldly, by Langland, Gower and Chaucer no less than by Wycliffe. ' Corrupt ' the Church certainly was, but that was not the whole of the matter : she had been ' corrupt ' yet perfectly safe for centuries past, and was no more ' corrupt ' in the time of Chaucer than was royal justice or the conduct of the lords and their retainers. Most institutions in the Middle Ages were ' corrupt ' by modern standards. But whereas the laity were moving with the times, the Church was standing still. Entrenched behind her immutable privileges and her inalienable and ever increasing wealth, her leaders took no steps to pacify the clamour of moral disapprobation and

—a very different folk from modern ' free masons.' Wycliffe thus describes their trade union policy which seems to have been already highly developed :

' Also men of sutel craft, as fre masons and othere, . . . conspiren togidere that no man of here [their] craft schal take lesse on a day than thei setten [agree] . . . and that noon of hem schal make sade trewe work to lette othere mennus wynnyng at the craft [viz. that none of them shall do steady true work which might hinder the earnings of other men of his craft] and that non of hem schal do ought but only hewe stone, though he migght profit his maister twenty pound bi o daies werk by leggyng on a wal [laying stones on a wall] without harm or penyng [paining] to himself.' (Wycliffe, *Select Eng. Works*, III, p. 333, and *Stats. of Realm*, III, p. 227.)

the growls of envious greed that rose on every side against
her and her possessions. The laity were not only more
critical but were far better educated and therefore more
formidable than in the days of Anselm and Becket, when the
clergy had enjoyed a fairly close monopoly of trained intelligence. The Church, however, refused to do anything
to satisfy the general discontent, and during the Fifteenth
Century the storm subsided. But the respite was not
lasting, and the refusal of all reform under the Plantagenets
led under the Tudors to revolution.

Many of the clergy themselves were critics of the Church
as outspoken as the laity. The scholars of Oxford and not
a few of the priests serving parishes whose tithes went to
rich monks and foreign prelates, were reformers and even
rebels. Moreover the accused parties themselves denounced one another with the intemperance of language
habitual in mediaeval controversy. The friars attacked the
Bishops and secular clergy, who repaid their abuse with
interest. In Chaucer's *Tales* it is the friar and the summoner who expose each other's tricks, to make mirth for
the company of laymen. From every quarter, within and
without the Church, the air resounded with attacks on the
various orders of clergy.

Yet nothing was done. The Church, unlike the manor
and the gild, could not be transformed by the natural
working of economic change or by the mere pressure of
opinion. Definite measures of administrative and legislative reform were required, and there was no machinery to
effect them, except such as rested in the hands of the Pope
and the Bishops. But the Pope, who in former ages had
done so much, now did less than nothing to improve the
condition of the Church in England. He used his powers
to foster abuses that brought wealth to the Roman Court—
simony, non-residence, plurality, the sale of indulgences, all
of which offended the roused conscience of a censorious age.

Yet even without the support of the Pope, the English
Bishops might have done at least something. And the
Bishops in the age of Chaucer were, with scarcely an
exception, able, hard-working, highly respectable men.
Why then did they not at least attempt to make some
reform in the Church ?

The main reason was their preoccupation with secular interests. Though paid out of the revenues of the Church, the Bishops gave their lives to the service of the State. In spite of Parliamentary laws, the best places in the Church were disposed of by collusive agreement between Pope and King. The Pope thrust foreign favourites into many rich benefices, but as part of the bargain he usually left the appointment of Bishops in royal hands. So the King paid his Ministers and civil servants not out of the public taxes but out of the episcopal revenues. Among the twenty-five persons who were Bishops in England and Wales between 1376 and 1386, thirteen held high secular office under the Crown, and several others played an important part in politics. Sometimes they were sent abroad as ambassadors to foreign powers. Others had risen by secular services rendered to the King's sons : the Bishop of Bath and Wells had been Chancellor of Gascony for the Black Prince, the Bishop of Salisbury had been Chancellor of Lancaster for John of Gaunt. The Chancellor of the Realm was usually a Bishop like the Primate Sudbury, and William of Wykeham.

In the days of the Norman Kings, the close connection between the bench of Bishops and the royal ministry had supplied a barbarous land with able and learned bureaucrats, who derived from their episcopal authority a prestige which enabled them to cope as the King's servants with an ignorant and brutal baronage. But the need for a system once so valuable to the country was growing less with every generation. The laity, of whom Chaucer was one, were many of them now qualified to be the King's civil servants. The monopolization of secretarial work by the clergy, and of the principal offices of State by the Bishops, was beginning to arouse a reasonable jealousy. There were now ready to hand intelligent and highly trained lawyers, like Knyvet, and gentlemen, like Richard Scrope, well capable of conducting the highest business of the State. It was men of this type who, under the Tudor monarchs, replaced both prelates and nobles as the instruments of royal government. Already under the later Plantagenets the first signs of such a change were visible. Owing to a petition of the House of Commons of 1371 against the employment of clergy in

the royal service, laymen for some years alternated with
clerics as Chancellors and Treasurers of the Realm.

Occupied as they were by the cares of secular office, the
Bishops paid little attention to the deplorable state of their
dioceses.   If Rectories were empty or filled with scandalous
persons or underpaid substitutes, it had always been so. If
the Pope pushed the sale of indulgences and sham relics,
the Bishops could only regard it as a legitimate piece of
business ; without thinking more of the matter, they
supplied the Pardoners with episcopal letters commending
their wares to the public.

One branch of their duties, the proper control of the
Spiritual Courts, the Bishops neglected with unfortunate
results.   As regards the business of wills and marriages,
then conducted by the Church, the ecclesiastical tribunals
were no more corrupt or inefficient than the lay Judges and
lawyers of that time.   But the more specifically religious
function of the Bishop's Court, which he usually left to
the Archdeacon, was causing grave scandal in Chaucer's
day, as his *Friar's Tale* illustrates.   Punishment for sins
not cognizable by the lay Courts, particularly sexual incontinence, was then undertaken by the Church.   But in
fact the habit of commuting penance for money payment
had become general.   And from that official practice the
step was short to blackmail of sinners in their own homes
by the officers of the Bishop's Court, particularly the
' summoners,' who had a most evil reputation :

> ' Art thou than a bailiff ? '   ' Yea,' quod he
> He dorste not for veray filth and shame
> Say that he was a Sompnour, for the name. (*Friar's Tale*.)

But the Bishops, though they neglected many of their
duties, were so far interested in ecclesiastical affairs as to
fight for Church privileges and endowments against all
comers, and hunt down heretics, when heresy, now for the
first time, seriously raised its head in England with
Wycliffe's denial of transubstantiation in the sacrifice of the
Mass (1380).

Many parishes, no doubt, were faithfully and sufficiently
served by men like Chaucer's ' poor parson,' the only type
of Churchman for whom the poet seems to have felt affection

and respect. But a large proportion of the livings in lay gift were presented to people not in priests' orders at all, or to mere laymen. And far too often the church belonged to a monastery or to a wealthy absentee pluralist, and was served by some underpaid and ignorant 'mass-priest,' who scarcely understood the Latin words he mumbled, any better than his audience. Other parsons, who might have done their duty well, wandered off from their charges to London, Oxford, or some great man's house, in search of a more free and exciting life and additional stipends. The parish priest was seldom the Rector, very often not even the Vicar, but a chaplain or clerk miserably paid to do the duty neglected by the incumbent.

It followed that teaching and preaching often amounted to very little in an English village, so far as the resident priest was concerned, though Mass was regularly performed. But this deficiency was to a large extent supplied by the preaching friar on his regular beat, by the travelling Pardoner with his wallet ' bretful of pardons come from Rome all hot,' by Wycliffe's heretical missionaries, by John Ball's agitators of Christian Democracy. Whether we regard these interlopers as sowing tares in the wheat, or as enriching the Lord's harvest, they played a great part in the religious and intellectual life of the nation. They carried the latest thoughts, teaching and news of the time to remote farms and hamlets, whose inhabitants never moved from the neighbourhood and could read no written word. These religious roundsmen, on foot and on horse-back, were always on the move along the winding muddy roads and green lanes of England ; and to their peripatetic fellowship must be added the more secularly minded minstrels, tumblers, jugglers, beggars and charlatans of every kind, and pilgrims pious and worldly alike. All these wayfarers acted the part of ' microbes,' as their historian Jusserand [1] has said, infecting the stationary part of the population with the ideas of a new age and of a larger world. They too were preparing the change from mediaeval to modern.

But the parish priest reigned within the walls of his Church and there he said the Mass, attended on Sundays

[1] *English Wayfaring Life in the Middle Ages (XIVth Century).* J. J. Jusserand.

by the greater part of the village.   It was the heart of mediaeval religion.

The peasant as he stood or knelt on the floor of the Church each Sunday, could not follow the Latin words, but good thoughts found a way into his heart as he watched what he revered and heard the familiar yet still mysterious sounds. Around him blazed on the walls frescoes of scenes from the scriptures and the lives of saints ; and over the rood-loft was the Last Judgment depicted in lively colours, paradise opening to receive the just, and on the other side flaming hell with devil executioners tormenting naked souls.   Fear of hell was a most potent force, pitilessly exploited by all preachers and confessors, both to enrich the Church and to call sinners to repentance.   The ortho-dox consigned the heretics and the heretics consigned the Bishops to eternal flames, and all parties agreed there would scarce be room in hell ' of friars there is such throng ! '

The peasant knew some of the sayings of Christ, and incidents from his life and from those of the Saints, besides many Bible stories such as Adam and Eve, Noah's flood, Solomon's wives and wisdom, Jezebel's fate, Jephthah and his daughter ' the which he loved passing well.'   All these and much more with many strange embellishments, he learnt from ' pious chansons' and from the friars' sensa-tional and entertaining sermons.   He never saw the Bible in English, and if he had he could not have read it.   There was nothing in his own home analogous to family prayers and Bible reading.   But religion and the language of religion surrounded his life.   The crucifix was often before his eyes, and the story of the crucifixion in his mind.

Confession was a compulsory duty, normally made to the parish priest, but very frequently to the intruding friar, who gave absolution more easily, often it may well be more intelligently, and often (so all said) more corruptly for money, for a good meal, or for other favours.

But there is a great deal more to be said about the friars than that.   Like Rob Roy they were ' ower bad for blessing, and ower gude for banning.'   The black friars of St. Dominic and yet more the grey friars of the gentle St. Francis had been the true evangelical force in England in the Thirteenth Century, and in the Fourteenth they still shouldered most of the missionary work of the Church. They were still the great preachers and had created a demand for preaching. The illiterate folk of an age awakening to intelligence, demanded more and yet more of the spoken word, and could seldom get enough of it from the parish priest.

And so the friars still set the pace in the age of Chaucer. It was in imitation as well as in rivalry that the Wycliffites laid such stress on preaching to the people. If Protestants in times to come attached more importance to the pulpit than to the altar, they were only carrying further a movement begun by the friars.

If the orthodox secular clergy denounced the friars for filling their sermons with idle and unedifying stories to attract the vulgar, it was partly because those sermons attacked the sloth of Bishops, monks and clergy and the corruption of the Archdeacon and his summoner. In the first part of Wycliffe's career the friars were his allies against the ' possessionate clergy,' and it was only when he propounded his heresy on transubstantiation that the mendicant orders became his most effective enemies. In theory the friars, unlike the monks, lived by begging alms, had no property of their own and preached the doctrine of evangelical poverty so dear to St. Francis. In practice they had now amassed wealth and treasure which they stored in their magnificent convents. Wycliffe liked their theory and condemned their practice.

If we seek the origins of some of the distinctive traits of English Puritanism, of its asceticism, its war on sin, its sabbatarian rigour, its fear of hell, its attacks on the Bishops and wealthy clergy, its crude denunciation of opponents, its vigorous and soul-stirring sermons, its tendency to unctuous sentiment, its lapses into hypocrisy, its equalitarian appeal to the poor and lowly, they are all to be found in the mediaeval Church, and particularly in the work of the friars. But not of the friars alone ; clerk Langland was Bunyan's forerunner, and Wycliffe would have found his ideal of priesthood realized by Latimer and Wesley. Those scholars who have most recently and most fully studied the sermons and other pious literature in prose and verse of the Fourteenth Century, are most averse to ' the appropriation of mediaeval religion by any modern party or the repudiation of it by any other party. For the mediaeval Church is the mother of us all.' [1] As Chaucer himself said :

'Ther n'is no newé guise that it n'as old.'

On the other hand there were elements in later English Protestantism which were not mediaeval at all. Family worship and the religious dedication of family life and of business life are later Protestant accretions. They had no place in mediaeval ideals or practice. For mediaeval ideals derived from more purely ascetic and anti-mundane sources in primitive Christianity, to which practice indeed seldom conformed but which held the field in theory.

While the enemies of the friars complained that they did too much and intruded too busily where they had no rightful place, the monks of this age were accused of doing too little. The fire of religious enthusiasm and the light of learning burnt low within the walls of monasteries that once had supplied England with noble leadership. The King no longer sent for some saintly abbot, to implore him to take pity on the land and exchange the government of his House for the government of a great diocese. The cloister of Canterbury no longer rivalled the University of Paris in scholarship and philosophy : the higher thought and education of the country was now concentrated at Oxford, and there the chief intellectual influences were the friars and the secular clergy. Nor did the monks any longer, as in the days of the Barons' War, play a patriotic and formidable part in politics. Chronicles were still compiled in monasteries, but they merely carried on the literary tradition of a former age, while the worldling Froissart was setting up a new standard of history. In the Thirteenth Century, Matthew Paris of St. Albans cloister had been a truly great historian, but the monastic chroniclers of Chaucer's day, even the best of them like Walsingham, had no power to grasp the relative importance of events, or to appreciate the significance of what was going on in the world outside

[1] *The People's Faith in the time of Wyclif*, B. Manning, pp. 186–188 and *passim*. *Preaching in Mediaeval England*, G. R. Owst, pp. xii, 91–95 and *passim*. (Cambridge Press.)

the abbey close. The monk had little thought except for the interests of his House. His whole life was passed within its precincts, except when he was sent out to gather in the rents of distant estates, or to accompany the abbot on a hunting expedition or an occasional visit to London. At home he spent his time with brethren whose interests and experience were as limited as his own. It is then, not wonderful that the monks offered so stubborn a resistance to the claims of the townsfolk and peasantry, to whom the local privileges of the Abbey had, under changed conditions, become galling and vexatious. In every way the world was moving on, but the monastic life was standing still. Only in Yorkshire and the North the monasteries were popular, and continued to be so up to the time of the Dissolution.

The monks in Chaucer's England were worldly and well-to-do, living lives of sauntering comfort in the monastery, or roaming the land dressed like laymen, to hunt game or look after their estates. They were not numerous—probably rather more than the 5000 at which they were estimated at the time of their Dissolution in the reign of Henry VIII. But, having themselves abandoned the manual labour practised by their predecessors, they maintained armies of servants to carry on the daily routine of their great establishments, which often covered many acres of ground, as at Bury St. Edmunds and Abingdon. The monks performed in person their obligations of prayers and masses for the living and the dead, their patrons and their founders. They gave daily alms in money and broken meats to the poor, and showed a lavish hospitality to travellers, many of whom were wealthy and exacting guests. The rich fed at the table of the Abbot or Prior, while humbler wayfarers were accommodated in the guest house of the Monastery. Founders' kin, influential nobles and gentry, claimed rights as guests, officers and agents of the monasteries, consuming much of their wealth ; and at the same time the monks, especially the abbots, spent plenty upon themselves. (Snape, *English Monastic Finances*, Cambridge Press, 1926 ; Savine, *English Monasteries on the eve of the Dissolution*, Oxford Studies, ed. Vinogradoff, 1909.)

The monasteries had by this time accumulated vast endowments in land, tithes, appropriated churches, treasures, and clerical patronage—enough to cause them to be bitterly envied as idle drones, living at the expense of the impoverished Kingdom. The Commons declared that a third of the wealth of England was in the hands of the Church, most of it belonging to the regular clergy. And yet the monks were constantly in financial straits, sometimes through their magnificent architectural zeal for enlarging and beautifying the abbey and its church, sometimes through sheer mismanagement. The abbot who, like Carlyle's Samson, had good business ability among his other qualities, seems to have been rare in later times, though some of the Cathedral Priories, like Canterbury, continued to manage their finances and administer their far scattered manorial estates well. The Black Death hit the monastic landlord as hard as the lay. The Italian and English moneylenders, who had succeeded the Jews, charged just as high interest, and the monks were reckoned an easy prey. The monasteries often speculated in a form of life annuity known as a 'corrody,' whereby the abbey borrowed money in return for an undertaking to keep the creditor for the rest of his life—and often he lived disastrously long.

In earlier times the demesne lands of monastic manors, administered by the Abbey's own officials direct, had often been admirable examples of estate management and agricultural improvement, not only in the sheepruns of Yorkshire dales but in mixed arable and pasture regions of the South. But in the Fourteenth and Fifteenth Centuries the demesne lands of the Abbeys were increasingly let out on long leases to laymen, who either farmed them or sublet them to others. In this and other ways the lay control and enjoyment of monastic wealth began long before the final Dissolution.

There were occasional scandals in monasteries, and the orthodox Gower was as certain as Wycliffe that the monks were unchaste. But if allowance is made for the low standard of all classes in that age and for the peculiar difficulties of the celibate clergy, there is no reason to think that the monasteries were wonderfully bad in that respect. Certainly the ascetic impulse of former ages had died away, and the monks were no longer famous for strict adhesion to their rule. The ordinary monk lived luxuriously by

the standards of that age, dressed smartly and was fond of
good food. The former restrictions on his meat diet had
been relaxed. He was fond of field sports—but so were
other men. It was not the sinfulness but the uselessness
of the monk on which the world commented most. The
worst that Langland could say of him was that when outside
the cloister he appeared as—

' A rider, a roamer by streets
A leader of lovedays [manor-court sittings] and a land buyer
A pricker on a palfrey from manor to manor,
An heap of hounds at his arse as he a lord were.[1]

And the poet looks forward to a day which indeed came in
the fullness of time—

' Then shall the abbot of Abingdon and all his issue for ever
Have a knock of a King and incurable the wound.'

Already it was to the kingly power that Church reformers,
baffled by Pope and Bishops, were beginning to turn their
hopes. Parliament was already demanding a large disendowment of the Church, which had swallowed so much
land from countless generations of benefactors and gave
not an acre back. But the time had not yet quite come
when the general conscience considered that lay power
could dispose of the sacred endowments of the Church.
The omnicompetence of the King in Parliament was not
yet an established constitutional doctrine. The parallel
authorities of Church and State, of Convocation and Parliament still represented the actual balance of society.

In one great branch of service to mankind the Church in
the age of Chaucer was neither decadent nor even stagnant.
The continuous but ever moving tradition of ecclesiastical
architecture still proceeded on its majestic way, filling
England with towering forests of masonry of which the
beauty and grandeur have never been rivalled either by the

---

[1] Langland's criticism of the monk's life was not, like much modern criticism
including Wycliffe's, due to want of appreciation of the retired, contemplative
life of self-abnegation, but to Langland's perception that the monks had ceased
to realize that ideal. ' The Middle Ages had no doubt that the Contemplative
Mary had chosen her part better than the Active Martha.' But the monks had
ceased to be Maries without becoming Marthas.

For the understanding of *Piers the Plowman* I would recommend the reader
to the illuminating essays on the subject in Professor R. W. Chambers' *Man's
Unconquerable Mind* (1939).

Ancients or the Moderns. With a brief pause in building caused by the Black Death, the march of English architecture in Cathedral, Abbey and Parish Church went forwards through the *Decorated* and the *Flamboyant*, to the *Perpendicular*, the chief new feature being the elaboration of tracery, and the size of the great windows each with its framework of stone shafts. Archdeacons, on their visitations would condemn a little old Norman church, perfect in its own way, as 'too small and too dark.' In the newer churches the light no longer crept but flooded in, through the stained glass, of which the secret is to-day even more completely lost than the magic of the architecture. No doubt the mediaeval Church became too wealthy, no doubt her rival chiefs and corporations suffered from the sins of pride and luxury and narrow *esprit de corps* ; but if the Church had been as St. Francis or as Wycliffe wished, a poor, devoted evangelist, those cathedrals and minsters would never have been built in such supreme magnificence, to stand, century after century, silently praising God, giving to one generation of men after another the purest and highest delight of worship that can be kindled through the eye.

The section of the mediaeval Church that was under least discipline and had only too little ' corporate sense,' was the army of unbeneficed priests, deacons and clerks in holy orders who were scattered about the country, in every variety of employment, often under no control beyond that of their lay employers. In most cases they fulfilled functions performed in the modern world by laymen. They were the ' clerks ' (in both senses of the word) who wrote papers and kept accounts for men of affairs, whether merchants, landowners or officials. Others fulfilled sacred functions, as private chaplains in castle or manor-house, or as ' chantry priests,' paid by laymen to say masses for the souls of departed relations. Many drifted about from one job to another, forming lazy and criminal habits that made them in the end ' unemployable ' for any good purpose.

The ' clerks ' in business houses and legal or State offices were performing functions necessary for society, and were neither better nor worse men than their neighbours. But in view of the fact that they were under such slight ecclesiastical

discipline it was perhaps unfortunate that they were
' clergy ' at all.　Except those in minor orders, clerks were
expected not to marry,[1] and many of them would have
been better with a wife and a settled home.　In the literature of the time the ' clerk ' is often the hero of an amorous
intrigue.　Moreover, when they committed crimes of theft
or murder they could plead benefit of clergy and so escape
from the severe justice of the King to the lighter penances
of the Spiritual Court.　No wonder that ' criminous clerks '
often earned an ill name for themselves and for the Church
to which they were so loosely attached.

There was already considerable provision for the education of clerks in reading, writing and Latin.　Three or
four hundred grammar schools, most of them indeed very
small establishments, were scattered through the length of
England.　They were usually under the control of Monasteries or Cathedrals, Hospitals, Gilds, or Chantries ; the
masters whom these authorities appointed were secular
clergy.　Clever boys of humble origin rose through such
schools to be clerks and priests, for the Church was still
the career of ambition most easily open to the poor.　But
no attempt was made to teach reading and writing to the
mass of the people until the Eighteenth Century brought
the Charity Schools.

In 1382 William of Wykeham, desiring better education
for the secular clergy, founded at Winchester a grammar
school on a scale of unexampled magnificence, which
became the model for later foundations of equal splendour,
like Eton.　A certain proportion of the scholars were to
be ' sons of noble and powerful (*valentium*) persons,' a
provision which the historian of our mediaeval schools
has called the ' germ of the public school system.' (*Winchester College*, A. F. Leach, p. 96.)

The two ancient Universities of England already existed ;
but scarcely yet as rivals, for Cambridge only rose to national
importance in the Fifteenth and Sixteenth Centuries.

---

[1] In fact a number of clergymen, including parsons of parishes, were married.
Such marriages were irregular and voidable, but not void until challenged.　Others
lived in concubinage of a more or less permanent kind.　Many English clergy
had always resented the rule of clerical celibacy gradually forced on the island
after the Norman Conquest.　The struggle against it continued till the Reformation gave victory to the rebels.

In Chaucer's day, Oxford was the intellectual centre of
England, and Wycliffe's influence was the chief fact in
Oxford, until he and his followers were driven out or
silenced by the interference of Bishops and King with the
independent life of the University (1382). If Oxford had
been united, the invasion of her liberties would have been
more difficult. But there had long been two academic
parties, the secular and the regular clergy ; the former took
Wycliffe's side, while the latter turned against him.

The ' regulars ' were the monks and friars who had
several great convents of their orders attached to the University. In the previous century the friars had been the
leaders of academic thought, with their Grossetete, Roger
Bacon and Duns Scotus, and they were still a great power
in Oxford.

The ' seculars,' who regarded themselves as the
University proper, consisted of secular clergy, priests like
Wycliffe, or deacons and clerks in lower orders. These
men were academicians first and churchmen second. They
were as jealous for the ' liberties ' of their University as a
burgher for those of his town. They were always on guard
against Papal and episcopal interference, royal mandates,
and the claims and privileges of the town. Their rights
were defended against all aggression by the hosts of turbulent undergraduates herding in the squalid lodging-houses
of Oxford, who, when occasion called, poured forth to
threaten the life of the Bishop's messenger, to hoot the
King's officials, or to bludgeon and stab the mob that
maintained the Mayor against the Chancellor.

Town and gown used daggers, swords and even bows and
arrows in their pitched battles in High Street. In 1355
the townsmen made a regular massacre of clerks and
students : the survivors fled in terror from Oxford, and
the University closed down until the King intervened to
protect and avenge the scholars. At Cambridge, in the
riots of 1381, the town destroyed the University charters
and records.

The mediaeval student, before the development of the
College system had done its work, was riotous, lawless and
licentious. He was miserably poor ; he often learnt very
little for want of books and tutoring, and left without taking

c

a degree. Yet many were enthusiastically eager for learning or at least for controversy. Some were only fourteen years old, but most were of an age rather more nearly resembling that of modern undergraduates. Many were still laymen, but nearly all intended to become clerks if not also priests. There can be little doubt that the habits contracted at Oxford and Cambridge account for the violent and scandalous character of so many of the clergy in later life. The authorities of the Universities, imitating the folly of authorities in Church and State elsewhere, forebade athletic exercises among the youth in their jurisdiction, but made no great effort to keep them out of the tavern and the brothel ; some of them roamed the countryside in robber bands.

But England found a remedy for these evils. The College system, though it had originated in Paris, became in the end the unique characteristic of the two English Universities. In the late Thirteenth Century several Colleges had been founded at Oxford, and Peterhouse at Cambridge. But College life was still the exception, and in the early part of Wycliffe's career it may be doubted whether more than a hundred of the three thousand Oxonians were under any such discipline—except the monks and friars in their convents. But before Wycliffe died, William of Wykeham had already founded his magnificent New College, with its quadrangular buildings and its ' hundred clerks.' With such a pattern to copy, the English College system grew apace with ever new foundations during the next two centuries.

The demand for Colleges and the readiness of founders to supply the need were stimulated by religious controversy. The orthodox desired to place the boys, who were to be the clergy of the next generation, in the safe keeping of such institutions and Masters as would preserve them from the Wycliffe heresy, which raged in the lodging-houses and inns where the students lived crowded together, discussing all things in heaven and earth with the freedom of irresponsible and ardent youth. And, apart from all questions of divinity, parents and practical men saw the advantage of academic homes to shelter the young from material and moral dangers possibly as bad as the intellectual errors of Wycliffe.   The College system struck root in England and flourished as nowhere else.   The business management of the College revenues at this period seems to have been more often efficient than the management of monastic finance.

And so, in the Fifteenth Century, while the forcible suppression of debate on religious and ecclesiastical questions crippled for a hundred years the intellectual vigour of the English Universities, the rapid growth of the College system brought about an improvement in morals and discipline, and a civilizing of academic life, for which later generations of Englishmen stand deeply in debt to the Oxford and Cambridge of the late mediaeval period.

One very important branch of learning had found for itself a home that was neither Oxford nor Cambridge.   The lay lawyers who were building up the common law administered in the King's Courts, had formed for themselves the Inns of Court between London and Westminster, where legal education, other than that of the ecclesiastical courts, was carried on.   Maitland has thus described them (*Collected Papers*, II, 482) : ' They were associations of lawyers which had about them a good deal of the club, something of the College, something of the trade-union. They acquired the *inns* or *hospices*—that is, the town houses —which had belonged to great noblemen : for example, the Earl of Lincoln's inn.   The house and church of the Knights of the Temple came into their hands. . . . The serjeants and apprentices who composed the inns of court enjoyed an exclusive right of pleading in court.'   These common lawyers were, as a class, the first learned laymen, and as such were of great importance to the growth of the nation.

BOOKS FOR FURTHER READING FOR CHAPTERS I AND II

H. S. Bennett, *Life on the English Manor*, 1150–1400 ; Eileen Power, *Mediaeval English Wool Trade* ; Trevelyan, *England in the Age of Wycliffe* ; E. Lipson, *Economic History of England*, Vol. I ; *Social England* (edited by Traill) Vol. II ; Prof. Postan, *The Chronology of Labour Services*, in *R.H.S.* 1937 ; G. R. Owst, *Preaching in Mediaeval England* ; B. L. Manning, *The People's Faith in the Age of Wycliffe* ; Coulton, *Chaucer and his England* ; Chaucer's *Canterbury Tales* and Langland's *Piers the Plowman*, ed. Skeat.   *Mediaeval England*, edited by H. W. C. Davis, 1924 ; Rashdall, *The Universities of Europe in the Middle Ages* ; Leach, *The Schools of Mediaeval England*, and review of it by A. G. Little in *E.H.R.*, 1915, pp. 525–529.   For the Church a hundred years before, see **Church Life in England in the Thirteenth Century**, J. R. Moorman, 1945.

CHAPTER III

England in the Age of Caxton

Henry VI, 1422. Edward IV, 1461. Edward V, 1483. Richard III, 1483
Henry VII, 1485.

It is difficult for us to-day to imagine how slow was the
pace of change before the era of inventions. After the
social and intellectual unrest of the English Fourteenth
Century, it might have been expected that something big
and dramatic would soon occur. Yet the Fifteenth Century
proved markedly conservative in most aspects of life and
thought.

If Chaucer in the ghost had haunted England during
the lifetime of Caxton (1422–1491), he would have found
little to astonish him, except perhaps that nothing had come
of all the talk against the Church. As he rode along the
familiarly bad highways, still dangerously beset by robbers,
and crossed the deep fords and ill-mended bridges, he
would see the peasants with their oxen cultivating the same
strips in the big open fields, and only if he attended the
manor-court would he learn that very few of them were any
longer serfs. The wayfarers who accosted him would still
be the types he knew so well—pilgrims as many and as
jolly as those with whom he had ridden to Canterbury ;
friars, summoners and pardoners still at their old games
with simple folk ; merchants guarding their pack-horse
trains ; gentry and churchmen with hawk and hound ;
lords' retainers with bow and spear bound on the same
dubious errands as when John of Gaunt's men held the
countryside in awe. From their talk of Red and White
Roses and battles fought on English soil, he might surmise
that disorder was even worse than it had been in his own
day, but the nature and cause of misrule was the same, the
terrorising of honest folk by the retainers of great men, and
the corruption and intimidation of the law courts and of
the Privy Council itself. It would not take Chaucer long
to discover from wayside chat that a battle at Agincourt

had revived in the minds of his countrymen ideas first implanted there by Crecy when he himself was a boy, to the effect that one Englishman could beat three foreigners and that it was England's proper business and pastime to rule and rob France. And therefore England's own social ills remained incurable as ever. For her success in France had proved no more durable after Agincourt than after Crecy ; again driven back over the Channel, the privately enlisted armies had again disturbed peace at home as the retainers of great men.

Most of the towns, our ghostly visitor might notice, had not grown since his day and some had even shrunk. But London and Bristol flourished and thrust out new suburbs. In town and country there were some splendid new churches, guildhalls and chantries, and equally splendid enlargements of old churches. They were all built in an intricate and ornate style of masonry which would seem to Chaucer a ' newe guise,' as also would the brick buildings now to be seen in the Eastern counties—manor-houses, gatehouses, Cambridge colleges like Queens', and noblemen's palaces like Tattershall, towering up in red brick— and the King's College at Eton.[1]

In the port towns, bearded mariners, much the same as a certain ' Shipman ' whom Chaucer had described long ago, told rough tales of trade and tempest in the Channel and the Biscay Bay ; of the luck of English pirates who preyed on the merchandise of Spanish galleys, Genoese carracks and Breton and Flemish ballingers, and of adventures with foreign pirates who tried to retaliate ! And amid all this old, familiar chat about the home seas, might be noted a strange rumour of something new : that certain foreign shipmen were hoping to reach the Indies by sea, round Africa or across the Ocean westward, and that some folk in Bristol were inclined to give ear.

In the gentleman's manor-house, the nobleman's castle and the King's Court, the poet's ghost would find the

[1] There had been no bricks made or used in England after the thin tile bricks of the Roman period, until in the Fourteenth Century bricks began to come in from Flanders (the very name *bricks* is of French or Walloon origin). In the Fifteenth Century brick was widely used in parts of the Eastern Counties where there was little or no stone except clunch and where timber was now running short. Already the bricks were manufactured in England of local clay.

culture he loved still alive in a faded kind of way. It was
good that they should still be reading his poems, but his
successors did not seem to do much except imitate with
indifferent success. The imagination of youth still seemed
prisoner to the formal allegories of mediaeval love-longing
and its conventional discipline, and still delighted in the
war of the Greek knights against Troy—as interminable as
the English war against France. But the stories of King
Arthur's Table were being newly rendered from the
' Frenssche book ' into Malory's immortal English prose.

And if Chaucer's spirit could have peeped over the
shoulders of Edward IV at the machine which Master
Caxton had brought from Flanders, as it stamped off in
quick succession copies of the *Canterbury Tales* to look
almost like real manuscripts, the flattered poet would have
smiled at so pleasant a toy. He would hardly have foreseen in it a battering-ram to bring abbeys and castles
crashing to the ground, a tool that would ere long refashion
the religion and commonwealth of England.

After the second expulsion of the English armies from
France came the Wars of the Roses at home (1455–1485).
How far did they affect the social life of England ? The
answer depends on what we mean by ' the Wars of the
Roses.' Very little, if we mean only those brief occasional
campaigns conducted by 2000 to 10,000 men a side, which
ended in battles like St. Albans, Towton, Barnet and
Bosworth Field.[1] The verdict of such a battle, even if
fought far away in Yorkshire or in the Midlands, was
usually accepted without more ado by London and by the
whole realm, as deciding which group of noblemen was for
the time being to govern England. It was not possible
for the Houses of York and Lancaster to wage civil war
after the manner afterwards employed by Charles I and the
Long Parliament, when numerous and enthusiastic armies
were maintained by systematic plunder and by national
taxation, to make regular campaigns, to besiege walled
cities by the score and castles and manor-houses by the

---

[1] These battles were still fought with the same infantry tactics as Crecy and
Agincourt, by archers shooting arrows, and knights and men-at-arms dismounted
to fight by the archers' side. But cannon were now occasionally used in the
field with effect.

hundred. The Lords of the Roses had no such hold over their countrymen : since they could make no appeal to any principle or to any popular sentiment on behalf of rival pretensions to the Crown, neither side could venture to antagonize opinion by heavy war taxation, by the interruption of trade or the devastation of the countryside, according to the recent and evil example of our armies in France. In this sense it is true that the ' Wars of the Roses ' were, militarily speaking, only a skin eruption on the surface of English life.

But if by ' the Wars of the Roses ' we mean a period of social disorder which gave rise at intervals to spurts of real warfare, it is clear that the whole social fabric was affected by the general state of misrule. So deep and so widespread was the damage done by ' overgreat subjects ' and ' lack of governance,' that in the succeeding century the Tudor monarchy was popular because it was strong and could ' bridle stout noblemen and gentlemen.'

In what did this social disorder consist ? It was a rural phenomenon, not much affecting the towns. But the population of England was nine-tenths rural, and the social disorder was mainly a struggle of landowners among one another for land.

Most men's conduct is determined by the prevailing fashion of the society in which each lives. Just as in the Eighteenth Century the squire was little thought of who did not drain and enclose land, rebuild farm houses, plant trees, enlarge his hall and adorn his grounds—so in the Fifteenth Century, a country gentleman was likely to imitate his most highly esteemed neighbours, when he observed them devote their time and energy, partly indeed to holding their manor-courts and exacting their rents, but still more to increasing their family estates and fortunes by marriage treaties, and frequently by the armed occupation of a neighbour's estate on some trumped-up claim of law. And those who were themselves the victims of such injustice, could only defend their rightful heritage by a similar combination of legal proceedings and brute force. An English county such as the Pastons' Norfolk was not unlike Europe, with its great and small powers, its alliances sealed by child-marriage, its balance of power, its territorial claims and counterclaims always simmering and occasionally leading to some act of violence or legal chicane. The connection between this state of society and the official Wars of the Roses is illustrated by the siege of Caister Castle in 1469 by an army of 3000 men in the pay of the Duke of Norfolk, acting in a purely private quarrel over the right of possession.

The technique of estate-jumping included assault and battery, or downright murder, often committed in a public place and in the eye of day to produce the greater effect. For not only the rival claimant but the jurors in court must be made to go in fear of their lives. Justice was not to be had from juries on the mere merits of a case. The livery of a powerful lord or knight gave immunity for the cutting of purses and even of throats.

Under these conditions, any aspirant to importance in the county, any ambitious man covetous of his neighbour's lands, or any quiet man who wished to remain safe in possession of his own, had need to secure the patronage of some magnate of the realm to be ' good lord ' to him, to overawe the judge and jury when his case came on, and to speak the word for him at the Privy Council that should invoke or prevent interference by the Crown in the course of local justice. Redress was not to be had, unaided by fear or favour, whether in the law courts or at the Council Board.[1]

In the following century the Tudors freed the Privy Council and the courts of law from the dictation of the nobility, put down retainers and enforced order in the land. But even they could not change human nature, either in themselves or their subjects, and in the palmy days of Elizabeth, Shakespeare put into the mouths of Justice Shallow and his serving-man Davy, the principle on which justice was conducted in the Fifteenth Century, and to a less degree in the later and better times in which Shakespeare himself lived :

DAVY : I beseech you, sir, to countenance William Visor of Woncot against Clement Perks of the Hill.

SHALLOW : There is many complaints, Davy, against that Visor ; that Visor is an arrant knave on my knowledge.

---

[1] E.g., in 1451 the Sheriff of Norfolk told John Paston that it was useless to think of suing Robert Hungerford, Lord Moleyns, because the Sheriff had received ' writing from the King that he make such a panel (as) to acquit the Lord Molynes.

DAVY : I grant your worship that he is a knave, sir : but yet, god forbid, sir, but a knave should have some countenance at his friend's request. An honest man, sir, is able to speak for himself when a knave is not. I have served your worship truly, sir, this eight years ; and if I cannot once or twice in a quarter bear out a knave against an honest man I have but very little credit with your worship. . .

SHALLOW : Go to : I say he shall have no wrong.

In the Fifteenth Century perpetual law-suits about title to land, often dragging on for years without settlement, were a serious matter for the farmer of the land in question, especially when both claimants for a manor sent in armed men and extorted the rents by force. The expense of retainers and actions at law, and the agricultural depression of the period, made landlords niggardly about repairs and exorbitant about rents. For the country gentleman looked to his rent-roll to keep him in ready money. In those days, unless he were a breeder of sheep, he had seldom any other source of income in cash other than his money rents, though food and clothing for his household might come off his home farm, or from rents paid in kind.[1]

The relation of the landlord to the tenant—whether of open-field strips or of an enclosed farm—was assimilating itself year by year to modern practice. Feudalism proper and serfdom were dying out. But the quasi-feudal position of the landlord still survived in his powerful chairmanship of the manor-court or court-leet, exercised by himself in person or by his steward. There the affairs of lord of the manor and his copyhold tenants were decided and registered, as well as the internal relations of the community of farmers of the open field and sharers of the common pasture and waste. It might not always be possible in practice for the

[1] The regular 'investments' by which the upper and middle classes live to-day did not then exist for ordinary people. But great lords and prelates often had other forms of acquiring wealth besides agriculture. Politics, though a very dangerous, were a very lucrative profession. Moreover, statesmen in close touch with the great merchants were let in to good things in trade. Cardinal Beaufort was supposed to deal in wool and certainly worked silver mines in Cornwall and Devon. Henry VI paid Adam Moleyns, Privy Seal and Bishop of Chichester, £1000 to cancel a patent that had authorized him to ship wool where he pleased. (Ramsay, *York and Lancaster*, II, p. 79.) This Moleyns was a characteristic figure of that epoch ; Clerk of the Council and a politician useful to the great men, he was rewarded for his services to the State with the Bishopric of Chichester and licence to impark 12,000 acres and to fortify twelve manor-houses.

tenants to override the will of the lord or his steward, but the tenants were judges in the court, and the procedure of an open court guided by the traditional custom of the manor was a real check on landlord tyranny, as well as an exercise in self-government for all, in which ' the poorest he ' might take his part.

Disputes between landlord and tenant as to the obligation to do repairs, and as to the amount and regularity of rent payments, characterized this period of transition from the old feudal ways to a new leasehold money-system, of which the rules had not yet been regularized by tradition. Landed proprietors, as their correspondence shows, were kept busy over these controversies, and their agents, lay and clerical, had no easy task with a recalcitrant peasantry. James Gloys, the Pastons' chaplain and factotum, who acted as tutor to their sons, and as confidential secretary and land-agent, distrained and threatened to distrain cattle and ploughs. But he too was human : one tenant he declared he could never touch—' I could never do it, unless I would have distrained him in his mother's house, and this I durst not for her cursing.'

The functions of land-agent were often performed by a gentleman's private chaplain, or even by the parish priest who ' visited ' his flock in this secular capacity. Such mundane employment by the patron of the living must often have involved the parson in questionable proceedings.[1] The use of the beneficed clergy by the laity for their own secular purposes, deriving from a past age when only the clergy could read and write, still prevailed from top to bottom of society. For did not the saintly King Henry VI pay his civil servants with Bishoprics and other Church preferment ? How else indeed could he pay them, in a land whose people would not endure taxation ?

Sometimes the parish priest spent most of his time as a farmer, cultivating his own glebe farm (normally forty to sixty acres of the open field) like the peasant born that he

---

[1] The relation of the parson, Sir Oliver Oates, to his master, Sir Daniel Brackley, in Stevenson's *Black Arrow* is, like most other social facts in the book, taken from a close study of the Paston Letters, in spite of the fact that R. L. S. does not seem to have known the difference between a friar and a monk. Another illuminating and more learned study of Fifteenth Century thought and social practice is to be found in Mr. Evan John's *Crippled Splendour* (1938).

was, and even hiring other lands. Parson Trulliber, the agricultural enthusiast in Fielding's *Joseph Andrews*, was a survival from mediaeval custom.

Very occasionally the open field was enclosed and divided up into consolidated farms by agreement among the peasant cultivators themselves. And always there was a free land-market among the customary tenants. The thrifty peasant of Fifteenth Century England, like the peasant of Nineteenth Century France, often saved up money to enlarge his little holding by purchase of his neighbours' strips.

Taken as a whole, the Fifteenth Century was a good time for the peasant and labourer and a bad time for the landlord. Owing to the continual recurrence of plague, the shortage of the population had not yet been made up since the Black Death, and the decay of serfdom enabled the labourer to take full advantage of this fact by putting a high price on his free service. Not only did the landlord find it very expensive to work his demesne land by hiring labour, but he found it equally difficult to let farms, whether on the demesne or in the open field of the village. The land-hunger of the Thirteenth Century, so favourable to the landlord, had been replaced by a glut in land and a hunger for men to cultivate it, and this state of things lasted throughout most of the Fourteenth and Fifteenth Centuries, until the beginning of the Tudor period.

England during the Wars of the Roses was poorer than she had been owing to the unsuccessful French war, followed by civil strife at home, and owing also to the fall in population. The recurrence of plague was most frequent in the towns and ports, where the flea-bearing rats multiplied most ; that is to say, the part of the community where wealth was chiefly made was the part most often disorganized and reduced by epidemics. For these reasons the total national income was less than in Chaucer's day ; but it was more evenly distributed. The general economic situation was favourable to the peasant and the poor.[1]

[1] Similarly, to-day the national income is less than it recently was, but is more evenly distributed. See Professor Postan's important article on *The Fifteenth Century* in the *Ec. Hist. Review*, May 1939 :

' Of the 450 odd manors for which the Fifteenth-Century accounts have been studied, over four hundred show a contraction of land in the hands of tenants and a corresponding fall in the rents. The effect of a falling population and depressed

This period of rural society is best known to us from the letters of the Paston family and other smaller collections, like the Stonor and Cely Papers.   The Fifteenth Century was the first in which the upper classes of both sexes, and their agents, lay as well as clerical, customarily wrote letters —in 'English tongue' it is to be observed.   The times might be out of joint, but education had clearly made great strides since the time when Kings and Barons had set their seals and inked their crosses to documents they had not the skill to read.

In the age of Caxton, letters were not written for pastime or gossip, but had some practical purpose in view, usually of law, business or local politics.   But they tell us by the way something of domestic customs.   The picture of family life, love and marriage, that emerges from these Fifteenth Century letters is well worth consideration ; and some of the aspects so revealed which modern readers will find strange, were, we have reason to think, equally or yet more characteristic of earlier ages which have left no such intimate records.

The extreme and formal deference that children were made to show to their parents, the hardness of home and school discipline, the constant 'belashing' of boys and girls and of servants will perhaps cause no surprise.   But to some readers, vaguely accustomed to think of the Middle Ages as a period of chivalry and love, with knights ever on their knees to ladies, it may come as a shock to realize that, in the knightly and gentle class, the choice of partners for marriage had normally nothing whatever to do with love ; often the bride and bridegroom were small children when they were pledged for life, and even if adults, they were sold by their parents to the highest bidder.   The Pastons and other county families regarded the marriages of their children as counters in the game of family aggrandizement, useful to buy money and estates, or to secure the support of powerful patrons.   If the victim destined for the altar

---

prices on the condition of the peasants is easily imagined.   It meant a greater supply of land and lower rents.   The improvement in the position of the landholder was accompanied by an improvement in the position of the hired labourer.   The real sufferers from the agricultural depression were therefore the landlords.'

See also the article by Mr. John Saltmarsh entitled ' Plague and economic decline in England in the later Middle Ages ' in the *Cambridge Historical Journal* for 1941.

resisted, rebellion was crushed—at least in the case of a daughter or a female ward—with physical brutality almost incredible. Elizabeth Paston, when she hesitated to marry a battered and ugly widower of fifty, was for nearly three months on end ' beaten once in the week or twice, sometimes twice in one day, and her head broken in two or three places.' Such were the methods of her mother Agnes, a highly religious, respectable and successful controller of the large Paston household. Many parents seem to have cared very little who married their children, provided they themselves got the money ; John Wyndham, one of the Pastons' neighbours, proposed to sell to a London merchant the right to dispose of his young son in marriage.

These old-established mediaeval customs, still vigorous in the Fifteenth Century, may at first seem inconsistent with the tone of mediaeval literature ; for three centuries past, poetry had been the analysis of love-longing, the service and devotion of the knight to his lady, sung in strains of rapture and in forms of mystic allegory. Such indeed was literature as known to the Pastons and their neighbours. But this poetry of love, from its most heavenly flight in Dante's chaste worship of another man's wife, to the more usual idealization of courtly adultery, had seldom anything to do with marriage.

To the educated mediaeval man and woman, marriage was one relation of life, love another. Love might indeed chance to grow out of marriage, as doubtless it often did. If it did not, the wife tried to assert her rights by her tongue, sometimes with success. But the ' lordship ' was held to be vested in the husband, and when he asserted it by fist and stick, he was seldom blamed by public opinion. In this unequal struggle, the woman also laboured under the handicap of constantly bearing children—most of whom soon died and had to be replaced. Such marriage was not an ideal state of things, but for centuries it served to people England, a difficult task in those days of plague and medical ignorance.

A nobler view of what marriage might and should mean had not yet been envisaged by general opinion. Even the Church had scarcely been helpful, for her ascetic ideal was unsuited to average human nature. The Fathers had regarded women with suspicion as potential snares of Satan.

The Church had indeed endeavoured to protect them by her authority from lawless lust and violence, and her support of the marriage tie had at least made it more difficult for a man to discard his wife—though divorce was sometimes obtained for money. But ecclesiastical authority, which insisted that priests must be celibate, regarded marriage as a lower state. In this imperfect world the laity must be permitted to marry, but the relation of man and wife was not held to touch a high spiritual plane. It was not therefore wonderful that the clergy sanctioned by their ceremonials the customs of child betrothal and child marriage, thereby accepting the materialistic view of the laity, that the rational choice of the parties most concerned was not necessary, and that the marriage of a boy and girl might be a proper subject for barter between other persons.[1]

Since, therefore, love was not the normal basis of marriage, the Troubadours of Languedoc at the end of the Eleventh Century, and the French and English poets who succeeded them in chanting the service of a pagan ' God of Love,' regarded the passion of love as being under no obligation to respect so irrelevant a thing as the marriage bond. It has been shrewdly said that ' any idealization of sexual love in a society where marriage is purely utilitarian, must begin by being an idealization of adultery.' But it need not so end.[2]

The great gift of the mediaeval poets to the Western world was this new conception of the love of man and woman as a spiritual thing—the best of all spiritual things, raising men and women above their normal selves in all gentleness and virtue.

> The God of love, a benedicite !
> How mighty and how great a lord is he !
> For he can make of low hertes high,
> And of high low, and like for to die,
> And hard hertes he can maken free.

* * *

[1] The degree to which the Church tried to limit and in fact allowed child marriage is discussed in Coulton's *Chaucer and his England*, pp. 204-208, ed. 1921.

[2] It was said that a Court of Love had pronounced that married persons could not be in love with one another. I would refer the reader to a very remarkable and scholarly book on the whole subject—*The Allegory of Love*, a study in mediaeval tradition, by C. S. Lewis of Magdalen, Oxford, 1936.

And thereof cometh all goodnesse,
All honour and all gentilnesse,
Worship, ease and all hertes lust,
Parfit joy and ful assured trust,
Jolitee, pleasaunce and freshnesse,
Lowlihead, largesse and curtesye,
Semlihead and true companie,
Drede of shame for to doon amis ;
For he that trewly love's servaunt is
Were lother be shamed than to die.

(*The Cuckoo and the Nightingale*
by Sir Thomas Clanvowe, temp. H.IV.,
formerly attributed to Chaucer.)

Here was a new and constant source of inspiration to the life of mankind, based on the facts of nature. It was an idea unknown to the Ancients,[1] and unknown to the early Church. Could this thrice precious concept of the mediaeval poets be allied, by a further revolution, to the state of Marriage ? Could the lovers themselves become husband and wife ? Could the bond of young love be prolonged till age and death ? This change has actually taken place in England in the gradual evolution of the idea and practice of marriage. It was not an inevitable change. In France, for instance, the arranged marriage is still normal, though of course the civilized French parent pays far greater consideration to the wishes and mutual compatibility of the young people than did Mistress Agnes Paston. And such marriages are often very happy. But in England the arranged marriage has given place to the love match ; the parents have yielded to the children the choice of their own destiny. The battle of Gretna Green has been won.

This victory of freedom and love has behind it a long roll of unknown warriors and martyrs. No doubt there were many cases of lovers marrying, all through the Middle Ages. Men did not always obey their fathers, and fathers were sometimes human, and often died young. Chaucer's *Franklin's Tale* is a beautiful story of a marriage made and maintained by love. And in the Fifteenth Century things

---

[1] There is a very shrewd analysis of marriage and love in the Graeco-Roman world in John Buchan's *Augustus*, p. 244.

were slowly moving. The poet-King, James I of Scotland, made his love his Queen, and wrote *The Kingis quair* in her honour.

Even in the society of the prosaic Pastons we have epistolary record of at least two love marriages. In the first case, that of Margery Brews and John Paston in 1477, the girl won over her soft-hearted mother to the romantic view. Here, in the original spelling, is Margery's love letter to John while the matter was still being negotiated, not very hopefully, on the usual purely financial ground.

Right reverent and wurschypfull, and my ryght welebeloved Voluntyne (Valentine)
. . . My lady my moder hath labored the mat(t)er to my ffadur full delygently, but she can no mor gete (viz. she can get no more dowry provided with me) than ye knowe of, for the wheche God knowythe I am full sory. But yf that ye loffe (love) me, as I tryste verely that ye do, ye will not leffe (leave) me therefor.

Her next letter on the same situation, though not very grammatical, is as moving as anything in English prose (I give it in modernized spelling).

Wherefore, if ye could be content with that good (viz. that amount of dowry) and my poor person, I would be the merriest maiden on ground. And if ye think not yourself so satisfied, or that ye might have much more good as I have understood by you before ; good, true and loving Valentine, that ye take no such labour upon you as to come (any) more for that matter but let it pass and never more be spoken of, as I may be your true lover and bedewoman during my life (viz. pray for you the rest of my life).

This was too much for John. He was more his own master than many young men, for his father was dead, and he put the matter through in spite of the doubts of his mother and relations.

The other Paston love story had a longer and rougher course but reached an equally happy haven. Margery Paston had the courage secretly to plight herself to Richard Calle, the bailiff of the Paston estates. Such betrothals were regarded as binding and the Church could not refuse to maintain them, but they were sometimes broken by the consent of the parties. For years the girl stood out against the fury and bullying of her family, till at last, wearied out by her obstinacy and still desiring to retain the indispensable services of their too aspiring bailiff, the Pastons allowed the lovers to complete their marriage.

Already in the popular ballad literature of the later Fifteenth Century the *motif* of the love marriage was more and more making itself heard, as in the *Nut Brown Maid*, ancestress of the *Bailiff's Daughter of Islington* and a hundred other romantically married heroines of ballad. When we reach the age of Shakespeare, literature and the drama treat mutual love as the proper, though by no means the invariable, basis of marriage. The struggle of children against parents for matrimonial freedom has got hold of the sympathetic popular imagination, and the commonest interest on the Elizabethan stage is the devotion of lovers aiming at marriage, and the adventures of runaway couples like Master Fenton and Anne Page. Clearly the love marriage was more frequent by the end of the Tudor period, but child marriages were still all too common : in this matter the reformed Church was at first as much in fault as the mediaeval. In 1582, Bishop Chaderton married off his only daughter Joan, aged nine, to a boy of eleven : the result was bad. On another occasion John Rigmarden, aged three, was carried in the arms of a clergyman who coaxed him to repeat the words of matrimony to a bride of five. Before the end he struggled to get down, saying he would learn no more that day ; but the parson said, 'You must speak a little more and then go play you.' (*E.E.T.S.*, 1897, *Child Marriages*, etc., p. xxii.)

And so the slow and long contested evolution towards the English love match goes on throughout our social history, until in the age of Jane Austen and the Victorians free choice in love is accepted as the basis of marriage, even in the best society, and any more mercenary arrangement is regarded as exceptional and suspect. The lawless and pagan ' God of Love,' whose altar the mediaeval poets had erected, has been baptized, and has settled down as a married man in the England of Alfred Tennyson and Mr. and Mrs. Robert Browning.

Among the poor, it is probable that marriage choice had always been less clogged by mercenary motives. We have but slight evidence on the subject, but we may presume that among the peasantry in the Middle Ages, as in all ages, Dick and Nan walked together in the wood and afterwards to church for reason of love-liking, added to the belief that Nan would make a good mother and housewife, and that Dick was a good workman, or ' had a pig put up in a stye ' besides some strips in the open field. Marriage to legalise the consequences of incontinence was exceedingly common, especially in the lower ranks of society where maidens could not be so carefully guarded at all hours. But girls of the class of the Pastons were under their mother's strict watch and ward, so that the licentious amours of the gentry had usually to be conducted either with the daughters of the poor or the wives of the rich.

When once a lady was married, she entered on a sphere of activity, influence and even authority. The Paston letters tell the tale of several generations of matrons by no means slaves to their husbands, but rather their counsellors and trusted lieutenants. They seem utterly devoted to their lords' interests, to which their numerous children must be sacrificed. They are better wives and housekeepers than mothers. Their letters show them taking part in the legal and business interests of the family, as well as in the purely domestic sphere where they ruled supreme.

To organize the feeding and clothing of the inhabitants of one or more manor-houses was in itself a task for a life, requiring the same sort of administrative ability as ladies in our day so often devote to public work or professional employment. The household requirements could not in those days be met by hasty ' shopping.' Everything that could not be supplied by the estate must be ordered in the requisite quantities months beforehand—wines of France, sugar grown in the Mediterranean, spices, pepper, oranges, dates and the better kinds of cloth. It was the lady's business to make these provident calculations of coming needs and to see that orders were placed with solid merchants of the County capital or more often in London, for even Norwich failed to supply such overseas goods as would now be found in the shops of any small market town. As to home produce, the preparation, curing and storing of the meal, meat and game off the estate and the fish from the ponds, besides the command of the dairy, the brew-house and of the kitchen with its fire of logs roaring up the great chimney, were all under the supervision of the lady chatelaine. Much of the clothing, too, of the inmates of the manor-house was spun and woven, cut out and made up in the house or the neighbourhood under the lady's orders. Her daughters did not go to town to buy their dresses, though one might hope to have the stuff for one's best dress fetched from London. The young men, as brightly and fancifully clothed as their sisters, having more liberty to travel, could more often deal with a city tailor.

Thus we can imagine the innumerable and constant activities of a wealthy matron, and *mutatis mutandis* the housewife's round of work in all ranks of life.

The walls of manor-house rooms in this period were hung with cloth : the hall and better chambers with the rich ' Cloth of Arras,' tapestries to-day of Museum value, representing hunting scenes or religious or allegorical subjects ; the commoner rooms with woven hangings either of one bright colour or of variegated stripes. Framed pictures had as yet no place in the English mansion, but the walls themselves were often painted. To judge by what is left of the mural painting in Eton College Chapel, done by an English artist, William Baker, between 1479 and 1488, there must have been much fine painting on walls in the England of the Wars of the Roses—almost all perished long ago.

Chimneys in the wall were more and more replacing the open hearth in the middle of the room, whence the smoke had escaped as best it could through open windows. The Pastons were making this great improvement in their manor-houses as early as the reign of Henry VI, but the change was gradual, for as late as the reign of Elizabeth, William Harrison remembered and regretted the old system :

Now have we manie chimnies, and yet our tenderlings complaine of rheumes, catarhs and poses. Then had we none but reredoses [braziers in the centre of the hall], and our heads did never ache. For as the smoke of those daies was supposed to be a sufficient hardning of the timber of the houses, so it was reputed to be a far better medicine to keep the good man and his family. (Book II, chap. XXII.)

Harrison would have sympathized with the most conservative remark ever made by Doctor Johnson, who in
1754 said to Thomas Warton about the old 'Gothic'
Halls : 'In these halls the fire-place was anciently always
in the middle of the room, till the Whigs removed it on
one side.' But this terrible innovation had been going
gradually forward for three or four hundred years before
there was a Whig in the world !

In the somewhat hard conception of family life that
prevailed in manor-house and castle, there was little welcome
extended to a superfluity of maiden aunts or elderly
spinsters. If a girl were not married off, she must if
possible be placed in a nunnery. To be well rid of her,
money was piously paid and there was the girl respectably
settled for life. It was rarely possible to become a nun
without a dowry. In this way the English nunneries were
recruited and in part financed, at least in the Fourteenth
and Fifteenth centuries. Whatever they may have been in
theory, or in the distant past, they were not in this era
refuges for the poor, or houses for women with a special
call to the religious life. The records of the frequent
episcopal visitations show that there was a good deal of
female human nature in the nunneries, and that discipline
was relaxed, though scandal was only occasional. The nun,
and particularly the lady abbess or prioress, seldom forgot
that she was a lady born and bred. Like Chaucer's Madam
Eglentyne, she was a model of fashion and deportment
rather than of devotion.

The rules for dress and conduct drawn up long ago by
founders with ascetic ideas were very generally neglected :
'for more than six weary centuries the bishops waged a
holy war against fashion in the cloister and in vain.' The
episcopal visitor was often deafened by a flood of shrill
female eloquence, the prioress complaining of the nuns, and
all the dozen nuns together accusing the prioress, till the
good man fled before the storm, having effected little by
his visitation. In vain the bishops attempted to dislodge
the regiments of 'hunting dogs and other hounds'—and
sometimes the monkeys [1]—with which, contrary to rule,

[1] We know how the nuns' monkeys reached this island. The author of the
Libel of English Policy (1436) complained that

the poor ladies solaced their long leisure. ' At one nunnery in the Lincoln diocese, when the bishop came and deposited a copy of the Bull in the house and ordered the nuns to obey it, they ran after him to the gate and threw the Bull at his head, screaming that they never would observe it.'

The nunneries, though numerous, were very small. Of the one hundred and eleven Houses in England only four had over thirty inmates. The total number of nuns in the country was between 1500 and 2000. But of course each nunnery had also servants attached and one or more priests.

In the Fifteenth Century these establishments were going downhill financially and otherwise. Before Henry VIII took the matter so drastically in hand, eight nunneries had been suppressed in the course of forty years at the instigation of orthodox Bishops. For example, Bishop Alcock of Ely in 1496 founded Jesus College, Cambridge, in place of St. Radegund's nunnery, of which he procured the dissolution on the ground of ' the negligence and improvidence and dissolute disposition and incontinence of the religious women of the same house, by reason of the vicinity of Cambridge University.' The successors of those two Cambridge scholars who visited the Trumpington Mill in Chaucer's day, had apparently been paying too much attention to the nuns of St. Radegund. At the very end there were only two nuns left, one an absentee and the other an ' infant.' So at least said the Bishop, anxious to clear the ground for a more useful institution.

St. Radegund's was an exceptionally bad case, but it remains true that the nunneries of England were less useful and admirable houses of religion in the later Middle Ages than they are to-day.[1]

' The grete galees of Venees and Florence
Be well ladene wythe thynges of complacence,
All spicerye and other grocers ware,
With swete wynes, all manere of chaffare,
Apes and japes and marmusettes taylede,
Nifles, trifles that litell have availed,'
in return for which they take away our good cloth.

[1] The authoritative works which I have quoted on the subject are Eileen Power's *Mediaeval English Nunneries* and her chapter on ' Madame Eglentyne ' in *Mediaeval People*.

Between the time of Wycliffe's criticism on the great endowments of the church, and the onslaught of Henry VIII,
gifts of land and money were still commonly made, but
they now went less often to houses of monks, nuns and
friars than to chantries and schools.   In these latter days,
wealthy gentry and burghers in their gifts and bequests
seemed to be thinking more of themselves and of their
fellow laymen, and less of Holy Church.   The endowment
of a school was in the Fifteenth Century as useful for the
education of laymen as of priests.   And the foundation of
a chantry was largely a self-regarding act : in a chantry,
one or more priests were paid to say Mass for the soul of
the founder.   And whatever one's expectations about the
next world, it was clearly a way of endowing a living monument to one's own memory here below.   A chantry often
took the architectural form of a delicately wrought side-
chapel in a church, with the founder's tomb large therein ;
sometimes it was a separate building, a small church or
chapel, carrying down to posterity the founder's name.
' There's hope a great man's memory may outlive his life
half a year : but by'r lady he must build churches, then, or
else shall he suffer not thinking on. . . .'

The Fifteenth Century, for all its troubles, was a great
time for increased educational facilities and endowments.
There had been many schools in Chaucer's England, but
there were many more on the eve of the Reformation.   The
Fifteenth Century Bishops, often worldly-wise men of a
good type, loved to endow schools.   Municipal gilds and
individual burghers and merchants, increasing in wealth
and in family connections with the landed gentry, took
pride in founding schools which would give to other boys
of their town or shire the chance to rise, either to be future
priests and bishops, or equally well to be future Mayors,
merchants, royal ministers and clerks, judges and lawyers,
gentry capable of managing their estates and ruling their
county for the King.[1]

England, in fact, acquired a fine system of secondary

---

[1] Between 1390 and 1415 Papal and Episcopal registers frequently mention
'Literate laymen '—a phenomenon then coming into notice.   As the Fifteenth
Century goes on the expression drops out of use, because the class it describes has
become too common for remark, and the grammar schools educated an ever increasing proportion of laymen.   M. Deansely, *The Lollard Bible*, 1920, p. 209.

education. Many of these schools were endowed to teach
'the poor' gratis ; but the poor who benefited by them
were not the labouring class but the relatively poor, the
lower middle class, the sons or protégés of small gentry,
yeomen and burghers who rose through these schools to
take part in the government of the land. Thus were
prepared the social and intellectual changes of the next
century, by the training up of a new middle class of scholarly
laymen and scholarly priests, for both had their part in
the great movements that shortly took place. Grammar
schools were not, as used to be thought, the result of the
English Reformation : they were its cause.

Before the Greek and Ciceronian Renaissance reached
our island at the end of the Fifteenth Century, secondary
education, from aristocratic Winchester and Eton downwards, was based on the teaching of Latin—Vergil, Ovid,
and some Christian authors. The Mediaeval Church had
long ago acquired a liberal reverence for the ancient writers
in spite of their pagan errors, and out of that liberality grew
much that was finest in European civilization. Boys in
the grammar schools wrote Latin verse and prose composi-
tions, and stood up in class to translate the Latin authors
into English, already the universal medium of instruction ;
only in some schools French was used alternatively, not
because it was any longer spoken by the boys at home, but
on the contrary ' lest the French tongue be wholly lost.'
But out of school hours no language must be talked except
Latin ! For some centuries to come this amazing rule
was sanctioned by the usual brutalities of flogging. Sometimes a ' lupus ' or spy was paid to sneak among the boys
and report if any of them used an English word in their
play. How fully, one wonders, did this harsh prohibition
actually take effect ? Was Latin less ' a dead language '
and more a real medium of speech to the Grammar School
boy of the Fifteenth Century than to the Public School boy
of the Nineteenth ? There are many reasons to suppose
that it was. Familiarity with Latin such as the Grammar
Schools set out to supply, was indeed essential in those
days to any professional career. It was not merely the
priest who needed it ; it was required also by the diplomat,
the lawyer, the civil servant, the physician, the merchant's

accountant, the town clerk, in many of the documents connected with their daily work.

The sons of the nobility and gentry were educated in various ways, differing according to the rank or the personal views of their parents. Some stayed in the manor-house and were taught letters by the chaplain, field sports by the forester, and the use of arms by an old retainer or a neighbour knight. More usually they were sent away from home, an English practice that seemed heartless to foreigners, but was perhaps more good than bad in its results. Some sat in the Grammar Schools, conning Latin, cheek by jowl with the ablest sons of burghers and yeomen. Others went to smaller private schools, even then sometimes kept by a married master. (*Stonor Letters*, I, p. 21.) Others again were boarded in monasteries under the special care of the abbot.[1] At some time between the ages of fourteen and eighteen they might go on to Oxford or Cambridge, while others completed their education as ' henchmen ' or squires at the King's Court, or in the Court-like households of great noblemen. There the acquirements most valued were not Latin, but skill in riding, jousting at tournaments, field sports, dancing, harping, piping and singing—and doubtless all the forms of love-making. Moralists denounced these establishments as the ruin of the youth trained in them. No doubt some were better than others, but the noblemen as a class and their retinues were going downhill at the latter end of the Fifteenth Century, and the men from the manor-house, the counting-house, the Grammar School and the University, were coming up. To them the new age was destined to belong. Many of the gentlemen's sons who did best in after life were those who had been apprenticed to craftsmen and merchants, a custom which increasingly differentiated English from French society, merging the gentles with the burghers.

William of Wykeham's Winchester, and Eton College founded by Henry VI in 1440, were gradually approxi-

---

[1] Shortly before the Dissolution, the Abbot of Reading writes to Lord Lisle : ' I have set your young gentleman with William Edwards, my under-steward, that he may be well seen to by a woman for his dressing, for he is too young to shift for himself. He is the most forwardly child in learning that I have known.' G. Baskerville, *English Monks and the Suppression of the Monasteries*, p. 37.

mating to the character of ' Public Schools ' in the English
sense of the word—schools where the sons of the gentry
were educated. Winchester from the first had a con-
tingent of this class, and from the first was a national, not
merely local, grammar school ; it drew boys from all over
the South, the Midlands, and even from Cheshire and
Lancashire. Many of the scholars stayed till the age of
eighteen. Eton was in great financial difficulties during
the Wars of the Roses. But this, says Mr. Leach,

' perhaps hastened rather than retarded the development of the school
into a great public school for the upper classes and the aristocracy,
who while paying nothing for their education, paid large sums for
boarding in the houses of the fellows, and in the town of Eton, whence
they came to be called Oppidans.' (Leach, *Schools of Med. England*,
p. 259.)

And so in 1477 young William Paston was sent from the
Norfolk manor-house to Eton, to learn Latin translation
and composition in verse and prose, and to consort with
other young gentlemen, though his parents were lamentably
slow at paying his boarding expenses which fell nine
months in arrear. His tutor on one occasion lent him
twenty shillings, which we should multiply many times to
get the modern equivalent.

In a previous generation, the first John Paston had gone
to the neighbouring University of Cambridge, to learn law
at Trinity Hall, prior to going on to the Inner Temple.
In that litigious era, a squire had need to know law to
preserve his property, as his worldly-wise mother, Agnes,
wrote to him :

' I advise you to think once of the day [every day] of your father's
counsel to learn the law, for he said many times that whosoever
should dwell at Paston should need to conne [know how to] defend
himself.'

John's son, Walter Paston, was sent to the more distant
Oxford under charge of the family chaplain and man-of-all-
works, James Gloys. His mother Margaret was anxious
lest the clerks of the University should persuade him to
take Holy Orders : ' I would love him better to be a good
secular man than a lewit (unworthy) priest.'

While Walter Paston was at Oxford in 1474, he must

have seen the walls of Magdalen, the College founded by Bishop Waynflete two decades back, at length beginning to rise after a long delay caused by the Wars of the Roses. Wykeham's New College, already a hundred years old, had a fair rival in the architecture of Magdalen, where the quadrangle received the novel form of a roofed cloister adorned with stone figures. At Cambridge also the building of Henry VI's King's College was retarded by the troubles of his reign : even the chapel had to wait till the Tudor age for completion, with the happy result that it obtained the modern splendour of its fan-vaulted roof. (Willis and Clark, I, p. 494.) But Queens' College on the riverside, founded by Margaret of Anjou, rose in the lifetime of her meek husband, giving, with his own Eton, proof of what fine things could now be done with brick.

Throughout the Fifteenth Century, Cambridge was gaining ground as a serious rival to Oxford. Though Church and State had in 1382 successfully purged the older university of Wycliffism, it was still suspect of heresy in the minds of pious parents choosing a University. Partly for this reason, the number of Oxford students fell, and the number of Cambridge students rose during the next hundred years, and royal patronage was turned to the foundation of Colleges on the banks of the hitherto neglected Cam. By the end of the Century a high proportion of Bishops were Cambridge men. But though the younger University was rising fast in numbers, wealth and importance as a place of education, neither Cambridge nor Oxford added much to scholarship or thought until the coming of the New Learning in the first years of the Tudor Kings. Speculation and scholarship had to be orthodox, and orthodoxy was no longer mentally creative, as in the days of the great mediaeval schoolmen.

But during this conservative age the College system took firm root, and thereby an end was put in England to the uncared for and undisciplined life of the mediaeval student. It is the tendency of all movements to go too far in the first blush of success, and undergraduate discipline became in some respects too strict in the Fifteenth and Sixteenth Centuries. At least this must have been so if all the

College and University rules of Yorkist and Tudor times were actually carried out, for in that case the undergraduates were treated like schoolboys. One of the sanctions was flogging, previously unknown in Universities. This is the more remarkable as the age of undergraduates was tending to rise : when Erasmus was at Oxford and Cambridge there were more students of seventeen and fewer of fourteen than in the days of Wycliffe. But it is always difficult to know how far and how often rules were enforced, and presumably matters adjusted themselves to circumstances and cases. At any rate the time had gone by for ever when there was no such thing as academic discipline. Already by the end of the Fifteenth Century the framework of Collegiate Oxford and Cambridge had been created once for all.

With the increase in the numbers of readers taught in the schools and Universities of England, what were the books they read ? Works of piety and religion were much in demand, but the Bible was little known. Its possession in English without licence was regarded by the Church authorities as presumptive evidence of heresy. Lollardry, now without learning or leadership, was confined to the poor. It was proscribed and driven underground ; it was not dead, but ready to sprout up again as soon as times changed. A score of heretics were burned alive in the Fifteenth Century ; many more recanted to evade the stake ; many escaped notice or at least arrest.

Apart from books of piety, Latin classics taught at school, and heavy tomes of learning for real scholars, the commonest types of reading among gentry and burghers were chronicles of England and of France in verse and in prose, endless romances in prose and in ' rhyme doggrel ' about Troy, King Arthur, and a hundred other traditional tales.[1] The constant reproduction of copies of Chaucer, Langland and

---

[1] Roger Ascham, Queen Elizabeth's schoolmaster, wrote retrospectively : ' In our forefathers' time, when papistry, like a standing pool, covered and overflowed England, few books were read in our tongue saving certain books of chivalry, as they said for pastime and pleasure. . . . As one, for example, *La morte d'Arthure*, the whole pleasure of which book standeth in two special points, in open manslaughter and bold bawdry. . . . Yet I know when God's Bible was banished the Court, and *La Morte d'Arthure* received into the Princes Chamber.'

Mandeville's Travels (how the crocodile weeps as it eats men) proved the abiding popularity of those old authors. Political satires in English verse were much circulated in manuscript ; so was the *Libel of English Policy* written in 1436 to urge that the first duty of government was to keep the home seas with an adequate royal fleet, alike for reasons of military defence and commercial policy.

> ' Kepe thou the see abought in speciall
> Which of England is the rounde wall,
> As though England were lykened to a cité
> And the wall environ were the see.'

Besides private libraries, public libraries were being formed, such as Duke Humphrey's at Oxford, the University Library at Cambridge, Whittington's at Grey Friars in London, and another at Guildhall. Of lighter literature there was little except ballads, and they were more often recited or chanted than written and read. The eternal human appetite for stories was for the most part satisfied by word of mouth. To kill the long hours, men and women still practised the social art of story-telling, besides music on all sorts of instruments, and singing of songs.

Such was the state of society and letters when Caxton set up his printing press in England.

William Caxton (1422–1491) was a product of the new middle class and its improved education. He was an early and a noble example of a well-known modern type that has done so much for the world, the individualistic Englishman following out his own ' hobbies ' with business capacity and trained zeal. As a successful merchant of the London Mercers' Company, he made enough money during his thirty years' residence in the Low Countries to be able to devote his later years to the literary pursuits he loved. He began by translating French books into English. While so engaged, he fell in with the new mystery of printing with movable types, and studied it at Bruges and Cologne. In 1474–1475 he produced abroad two of his own translations (one of them a mediaeval romance and the other *The Game and Playe of Chesse*), the first books to be printed in our language.

Then in 1477 he brought over his press to England, set it up at Westminster, under the shadow of the Abbey, and there, during the remaining fourteen years of his life, under royal and noble patronage, he poured out nearly a hundred books, many of them in folio, and most in the English tongue. Among them were Chaucer, Gower, Lydgate, Malory's *Morte Arthur* and translations of Cicero and of Aesop's Fables. His industry was prodigious. Besides his constant and arduous labours at the press he translated as many as twenty books. He had indeed a missionary zeal for the dissemination of good and useful books among his countrymen 'in our English language.' His diligence and success as translator, printer and publisher did much to lay the foundations of literary English, and to prepare the way for the great triumphs of our language in the following century.

His own use of the machine which he established as part of our island life was at once ideal and practical, but it was not controversial. Yet the press would henceforth be the weapon of every political or religious controversy ; the *tempo* of the spread of ideas and of knowledge would be immensely accelerated. But in the year Caxton died that consequence had scarcely yet been realised.

On the other hand, Caxton was well aware of the importance of his work in fixing the form of the English language for educated people, and he therefore gave much thought and asked much advice as to the dialect into which he had best translate the books he printed. He describes these difficulties, in his Prologue to the *Eneydos*,[1] his translation from a French paraphrase of Vergil's Aeneid :

After dyuerse werkes made translated and achieued, hauing noo werke in hande, I, sittyng in my studye where as laye many dyuerse paunflettis and bookys, happened that to my hande came a lytyl booke in frenshe, whiche late was translated oute of latyn by some noble clerke of fraunce, whiche booke is named *Eneydos* made in latyn by that noble poete and grete clerke Vyrgyle.

And whan I had aduysed me in this sayd boke, I delybered and concluded to translate it in-to englysshe, And forthwyth toke a penne and ynke, and wrote a leefe or tweyne whyche I ouersawe agayn to corecte it. And whan I sawe the fayr and straunge termes therin,

[1] E.E.T.S., 1890, pp. 1-4.

I doubted that it sholde not please some gentylmen whiche late
blamed me, sayeng that in my translacyons I had ouer curyous termes
whiche coude not be vnderstande of comyn peple and desired me to
vse olde and homely termes in my translacyons.   And fayn wolde I
satysfye euery man ; and so to doo, toke an olde boke and redde
therin and certaynly the englysshe was so rude and brood that I coude
not wele understand it. . . . And certaynly our langage now vsed
varyeth ferre from that whiche was vsed and spoken when I was
borne. . . . And that comyn englysshe that is spoken in one shyre
varyeth from another.   In so moche that in my dayes happened that
certayn marchauntes were in a shippe in Tamyse, for to haue sayled
ouer the see into Selande, and for lacke of wynde thei taryed atte
Forlond [North Foreland in Kent], and wente to lande for to re-
freshe them ; And one of theym named Sheffelde, a mercer, cam
in-to an hows and axed for mete ; and specyally he axyed after
eggys ; and the goode wyf answerde, that she coude speke no frenshe.
And the marchaunt was angry, for he also coude speke no frenshe,
but wolde haue hadde ' egges ' and she vunderstode hym not.   And
theene at laste another sayd that he wolde haue ' eyren ' then the
good wyf sayd that she vnderstod hym wel.   Loo, what sholde a
man in thyse dayes now wryte, ' egges ' or ' eyren ' ?

Certainly it is harde to playse euery man by cause of dyuersite
and chaunge of langage.   And som honest and grete clerkes haue ben
wyth me, and desired me to wryte the moste curyous termes that I
coude fynde.   And thus between playn, rude and curyous, I stande
abasshed, but in my judgemente the comyn termes that be dayli vsed,
ben lyghter to be vnderstonde than the olde and auncyent englysshe.
And for as moche as this present Booke is not for a rude vplondyssh
man to laboure therein ne rede it, but onely for a clerke and a noble
gentylman that feleth and vnderstondeth in faytes of armes, in loue,
and in noble chyualrye, therefor in a meane bytwene bothe I haue reduced and translated this sayd booke in to our englysshe, not ouer
rude ne curyous, but in suche termes as shall be vnderstanden, by
goddys grace, accordynge to my copye.

We thus see that Caxton had a choice to make.   He had
no dictionaries to cramp or to guide him.   As he sat in his
book-littered study considering the matter, he had not, as
we have and as even Shakespeare had, an English language
' given ' whose limits he might extend but whose framework he must accept.   The number of dialects were almost
as numerous as the counties of England, and moreover
they were perpetually changing.   The Northerner, the
West countryman, even the housewife of Kent with her

'eyren,' could not easily understand either the London merchant or one another. The victory of the speech of London and the Court may perhaps have been ultimately inevitable, but it was rendered certain and rapid first by Chaucer and his Fifteenth Century imitators, who drove the west-midland dialect of *Piers Plowman* out of the field among the educated classes ; then, by the products of Caxton's press ; and last and most of all by the English Bible and Prayer Book, which in Tudor times, thanks to the printing press, reached everyone who could read and many who could only listen. Thus, in the course of the Fifteenth and Sixteenth Centuries, the educated English obtained a common dialect, corresponding to 'literary English ' ; and, as education spread, this dialect became the language of all the land.

Throughout the troubled reigns of the Lancastrian and Yorkist Kings, London remained peaceful and her wealth constantly increased : the pomp and parade of her magistrates on solemn occasions grew ever more imposing in the streets and on the river ; her civic, ecclesiastical and domestic architecture grew more rich and beautiful, till no wonder at the end of the century the Scottish poet Dunbar exclaimed, ' London, thou art the flower of cities all.' [1]

The government of London during this period was conducted, not by the democracy of manufacturing crafts but by members of the great merchant Companies. The Mercers, Grocers, Drapers, and to a lesser extent the Fishmongers and the Goldsmiths, supplied nearly all the Mayors and Aldermen of Fifteenth Century London. The members of these great Companies, whatever their names might portend, were not in fact confined to the business of mercers, drapers and so forth : their chief profits came from the export overseas of all kinds of goods, principally of corn, wool and cloth. They had their houses and their

---

[1] In the reign of Henry VII an Italian traveller wrote : ' in one single street, named *Strada*, leading to St. Paul's, there are fifty-two goldsmiths' shops, so rich and full of silver vessels, great and small, that in all the shops in Milan, Rome, Venice and Florence put together, I do not think there would be found so many of the magnificence that are to be seen in London.' (*Italian relation of England.* Camden Soc., 1847, p. 42.) *Strada* is probably not the Strand, but Cheapside ; see Miss J. Davis' article in *History*, April 1932.

agents, like William Caxton, established in Bruges and other great trading cities of Europe. They owned good plenty of English ships, not only in London but in other ports, and traded also in hired foreign bottoms. But the merchants of Italy and of the North German Hanse still brought their own goods in their own ships to London. The wharves, crowded with vessels of many nations, stretched down the river from the Bridge, battlemented with tall houses and decorated with ever fresh supplies of traitors' heads, to the royal palace and armoury at the Tower.

The merchant aristocracy that ruled the capital, wisely resisted the temptation to take an active part in the struggle of the rival families for the Crown (it was only in Stuart times that London was in a position to make and unmake Kings). But they compelled the armies of the Red and White Roses to respect London's liberties and commerce, and each successive government whether of Henry VI, Edward IV, Richard III or Henry VII, regarded the friendship of her merchants as indispensable to the solvency of the national exchequer. Edward IV courted their friendship in personal and domestic visits to the City, almost beneath the dignity of a King. The Staplers continued to lend money to government. The wool off the royal estates, and off the land of political magnates like Lord Hastings and the Earl of Essex, was sold abroad through the good offices of London merchants. Gentry like the Stonors, owning West Country sheep runs, were proud to be styled Merchants of the Staple. The 'landed and monied interests' were often indistinguishable, even at this early date. Wealth acquired in trade already flowed into and fertilized the land. The younger sons of the gentry, apprenticed to London masters, rose to be City magnates.

Not only London but the other towns enjoyed peace during the Wars of the Roses by the practice of virtual neutrality, and by paying small sums for presents to the King and other political personages, national and local, as also to the Judges for their favour in court. Thus in the accounts of the Borough of Cambridge in 1484–1485 we read such items as :

For a present given to the Lord the King, namely, in fishes £6.5.0.
In a present given to the Chief Justice of the Lord King, namely
in wine, spice, fish and bread 5s.
In a present given to the Bishop (sic) of York 8s. 8d.
For a present given to the Duke of Norfolk 6s. 8d.
To William Copley for having his friendship 6s. 8d.
In wine to the Duke of Norfolk 2s. 8d.

(Cooper's *Annals of Cambridge*, I, pp. 230–231.)

Cambridge town also paid its burgesses of Parliament
12d. a day each during the session, total 33s., though one
of the two members 'released his part.' The new Mayor
had 20s. each year to buy his magnificent robes, and much
money was paid for ' minstrels,' and for their ' vestments.'
These sums of course represented something very much
larger in terms of modern money : a country parson who
had £10 a year from all sources was considered to have a
tolerable income.

From the middle of the Fourteenth Century onwards,
the manufacture and export of cloth were growing at the
expense of the export of raw wool. In other words the
Merchant Adventurers were gaining ground at the expense
of the Staplers. The cloth trade enriched inland towns
like Colchester, where it was collected, and the ports whence
it was shipped, especially London. But the actual manufacture of the cloth was carried out chiefly in rural areas,
and many country villages acquired a richer and more
varied life that was partly industrial. The skilled manufacture of cloth for the open market had, ever since the
Thirteenth Century, been leaving the towns and migrating
to the country. The day was still far distant when the
mechanical inventions of the Eighteenth and subsequent
Centuries would reverse the movement and herd English
workmen back into the cities. Except London, most
English towns in the Fifteenth Century were stationary or
declining in wealth and population.[1]

---

[1] See Professor Postan (*Ec. Hist. Rev.*, May 1939, pp. 164–165) : according
to him the great increase in the cloth trade had been made in the second half of
the Fourteenth Century, and was resumed in Tudor times in the last twenty years
of the Fifteenth. During most of the Fifteenth Century the total production of
cloth remained nearly stationary—it was expanding in the villages and towns
of East Anglia, Yorkshire and the West, but decreasing in the older clothing

D

The migration of the cloth trade to the country was bound to be unpopular with the clothing gilds in the towns, who attempted to prevent the competition of rival manufacture by prohibiting the merchants of their towns from dealing with country cloth makers. But these restricting efforts were spasmodic and vain. For in this question the town merchants had the opposite interest to the town craftsmen, and were more influential in the control of municipal policy. The great merchants therefore continued on an ever increasing scale to operate the cloth trade in both town and country on a capitalist system. They supplied the raw material to the village craftsman who owned his own loom. They then took back the woven cloth, passed it on to other workers for the finishing processes, and finally put it on the market.

' All over Essex there lay villages famous for cloth making, Coggeshall and Braintree, Bocking and Halstead, Shalford and Dedham, and above all Colchester, the great centre and mart of the trade. The villages throve on the industry and there was hardly a cottage which did not hum with the spinning wheel, and hardly a street where you might not have counted weavers' workshops, kitchens where the rough loom stood by the wall to occupy the good man's working hours. Hardly a week but the clatter of the pack-horse would be heard in the straggling streets, bringing in new stores of wool to be worked, and taking away pieces of cloth to the clothiers of Colchester and the surrounding villages. Throughout the Fifteenth Century Coggeshall was an important centre second only to the great towns of Norwich, Colchester and Sudbury, and to this day its two inns are called the " Woolpack " and the " Fleece." ' (Eileen Power, *Mediaeval People*, p. 149.)

In Coggeshall lived the famous cloth merchant, Thomas Paycocke, and there he built his fine house with carved timbers, now belonging to the National Trust. Such mansions in the village street and brasses in the parish church mark the rise of a new rural class, as wealthy as the neighbouring gentry with whom they were not long in forming marriage alliances, and whose privileged circle they entered by the purchase of landed estates.

---

towns. But the Staplers' export of raw wool was declining still more rapidly, and 'even at the topmost Fifteenth Century level, the cloth exports were not large enough to account for the whole decline of the wool trade.'

And it was the same in the West ; after two more centuries had passed, Defoe observed that ' many of the great families who now pass for gentry in the Western counties have been originally raised from and built up by this truly noble manufacture ' of cloth.   In the Fifteenth Century, Cotswold wool was considered the best in England and therefore in Europe.   It was the basis of the prosperity of that lovely region, of which the record still stands in magnificent stone farm-houses, and old fulling-mills beside the streams of the valleys.

The character of an English merchant of this period is made very real to us by the life and letters of Thomas Betson (Eileen Power, *Mediaeval People*, Chap. V).   He was a wool merchant of the Staple, often resident at Calais on his business, but well acquainted with the West country manor-houses of gentlemen like the Stonors ; for he bought the wool of their sheep-runs to sell at Calais.   These business connections were cemented by matrimonial alliance. Betson married Katherine Ryche, a relation and ward of the Stonors.   He did not in fact marry her till she was fifteen and the marriage proved a happy one, but they had been betrothed some years before, and we have a letter of Thomas to his Katherine, then aged twelve or thirteen ; he writes in 1476 from his business house in Calais to Katherine at Stonor in Oxfordshire.   If one must be engaged to a girl of twelve this is certainly a good way to write to her. He bids little Katherine :

' Be a good eater of your meat alway, that ye may wax and grow fast to be a woman . . . and to greet well my horse and pray him to give you four of his years to help you withal.   And I will at my coming home give him four of my years and four horse-loaves to make amends.   Tell him that I prayed him so. . . . And All-mighty Jesu make you a good woman and send you alway many good years and long to live in health and virtue to his pleasure.   Written at Calais the first of June, when every man was gone to his dinner, and the clock smote noon and all our household cried after me and bad me come down.   " Come down to dinner at once ! "   And what answer I gave to them ye know of old.'

More than four and a half centuries have slipped by since that old clock ' smote noon ' at Calais, but Thomas

Betson as he rises from his writing-desk and folds the letter
with a smile on his face is an Englishman we can all understand and like.[1]

The hours of labour in field and workshop were very
long by the standards of to-day.   But men rested on Sundays and on an indefinite number of the greater Saints' days.
Custom enforced this good rule, and the Church Courts
did useful service in exacting penance or fine for work
on Sundays and Holy Days.   Much besides work went on
in old England, which in all ages has been both ' merry
England ' and miserable England, though the forms of
misery and merriment have changed from age to age.
The joyful background of country life was hunting and
hawking, snaring and fishing, conducted with all the pomp
of ' venery ' by the inhabitants of castle and manor-house,
monastery and parsonage—and more quietly by the unprivileged poacher from farm and cottage.   Much money
was spent on ' stage-plays, enterludes, maye games, wakes,
ravells,' and much money changed hands in ' wagers at
shootinge, wrestlinge, runninge, and throwing the stone or
barre.'

It was during this period that playing-cards came in, very
much in the form in which we have them to-day : the dress
of our court cards is still based on late Fifteenth Century
costume.   Cards served, like chess, to while away the tedious
winter evenings of the manor-house and supplied the
gambler with an alternative to dice.

Shooting at the butts was encouraged by Proclamation
and Statute at the expense of rival forms of amusement, such
as ' handball, football or hockey,' in order to preserve
England's military monopoly of archery with the long-bow.
It remained a monopoly, because it was an art not easily
acquired.   Hugh Latimer described how his yeoman father
in Henry VII's reign :

[1] *Stonor Letters, Camd. Soc.* II, pp. 6–8 (spelling modernized). The English
merchants of the Staple, like Betson, were the principal buyers of wool in the
Western shires, but they had to compete with Italian merchants who rode about
the Cotswolds on a like errand.   The Staplers shipped to Calais the English wool
that supplied the Low Countries and Northern Europe, but they did little business
in the Mediterranean.   The Italian merchants had royal licence to ship English
wool direct by the Straits of Gibraltar to the Italian looms.

'taught me how to draw, how to lay my body in my bow. .... I had my bows bought me according to my age and strength ; as I increase in them, so my bows were made bigger and bigger. For men shall never shoot well unless they be brought up to it.' (See note, p. 18.)

At the archery competitions, leaders dressed in the parts of ' Robin Hood ' and ' Little John,' led the village procession to the butts.

In towns and wealthier villages, many gilds—not merely the craft gilds—helped to organize pageantry and merriment. On every possible occasion, national or local, men rejoiced in solemn processions, of which the Lord Mayor's Show and the King's opening of Parliament are to-day among the few survivors. In those times, before it was easy to invest one's savings, much money was spent on splendour. Rich men wore the most magnificent and expensive clothes, and showed their wealth in plate upon their sideboards. The gilds, from which priests were generally excluded, represented the growing intelligence and initiative of the laity. But they were permeated, as was most of life and thought, by religious ideas. The line between religion and daily life was not so strictly drawn as in modern times. Men combining in a gild for a benevolent, a useful, or even a convivial purpose liked to give a religious tinge to their proceedings and to invoke a saint's blessing on their association. Even if they were anticlerical, they were not irreligious.

Besides the maintenance of a chantry, a school, an almshouse or a bridge, one of the chief activities of Gilds was the staging of Miracle Plays ' in a scaffold hye.' Such plays were very popular in the Fifteenth Century, and taught versions of the Bible stories, and many legends beside, in an age when the Bible as a book was known to few.

' The actors announced themselves as I am Abraham or I am Herod. They dressed in contemporary clothes, and contemporary clothes were symbolical of status. God Almighty was bearded and wore a tiara, a white cope and gloves. Wicked kings wore a turban and swore by Mahound. High priests were vested as bishops and sat " in convocation." Doctors of the law wore round caps and furred gowns. Peasants and soldiers wore the dress of the day, and Mary Magdalene before her conversion was tricked out in overmuch finery.

Angels went up to heaven and came down by real ladders, and the gloomy portal called Hell's-mouth was contrived to open and shut. Black, blue and red devils came out to claim the damned, while a clanging of unseen pots and pans signified the discord that prevailed within.' [1]

Such was the drama a hundred years and more before Shakespeare.

So too the Christmas Carols represented the homely religious feeling of the laity on the eve of the Reformation.

> The shepherd upon a hill he sat ;
> He had on him his tabard and his hat,
> His tarbox, his pipe and his flagat [flageolet],
> His name was called jolly, jolly Wat,
>   For he was a good herd's boy
>   With hoy
> For in his pipe he made so much joy.
>
> Now must he go where Christ was born :
> Jesus I offer thee here my pipe
> My skirt, my tarbox and my scrip ;
> Home to my fellows now will I skip,
> And also look unto my sheep,
>   For he was a good herd's boy
>   With hoy
> For in his pipe he made so much joy.

More directly under the patronage of the clergy were the 'Church ales,' forerunners of the religious tea and philanthropic bazaar. Men and women sold and drank ale in the church itself or the churchyard, to raise funds for the fabric or for some other good purpose. Church ales were very common in the Fifteenth Century though they had been frowned upon by the more ascetic churchmen of earlier times. The nave of the church was the 'village hall' for most communal purposes.

The ceremony of the Boy Bishop, very strange to modern ideas, was patronized equally by the high-and-dry orthodox clergy and by the reforming Dean Colet. On the day of St. Nicholas, patron saint of boys, or on Holy Innocents' Day, a boy was dressed up as a Bishop in schools and cathedrals,

---

[1] Canon Maynard Smith's *Pre-Reformation England* (1938), p. 146 ; it is a book much to be recommended.

went in procession and preached a sermon, to which not only his schoolmates but the Church dignitaries were expected to listen with reverence. Sometimes regular endowments were left to meet the expense and pageantry of this pretty scene, in which the Dean knelt for the child's blessing.

BOOKS FOR FURTHER READING

H. S. Bennett, *The Pastons and their England ;* C. L. Kingsford, *Prejudice and Promise in 15th Century England ;* Eileen Power, *Mediaeval People ;* Professor Postan, article on the Fifteenth Century in *Ec. Hist. Rev.,* May 1939 ; *Cambridge Hist. Journal,* 1941, J. Saltmarsh's *Plague and Economic Decline ;* Alice Stopford Green, *Town Life in the 15th Century ;* E. Lipson, *Ec. Hist.* Vol. I ; H. Maynard Smith, *Pre-Reformation England ;* Rashdall's *Universities of Europe in the Middle Ages* (ed. Powicke and Emden) Vol. III ; *Libel of English Policy* (1436), ed. Sir George Warner, 1926 ; *Paston Letters, 1422-1589,* ed. James Gairdner.

CHAPTER IV

Tudor England.—Introduction

'The End of the Middle Ages'?

Henry VII, 1485. Henry VIII, 1509. Dissolution of Monasteries, 1536–1539. Edward VI, 1547. Mary, 1553. Elizabeth, 1558–1603.

DATES and periods are necessary to the study and discussion of history, for all historical phenomena are conditioned by time and are produced by the sequence of events. Dates, therefore, apply a necessary test to any historical statement, and are apt to be found inconveniently cumbering the path and tripping up the heels of glib generalization rushing forward with head in air. There is no appeal from the verdict of a date.

But, unlike dates, ' periods ' are not facts. They are retrospective conceptions that we form about past events, useful to focus discussion, but very often leading historical thought astray. Thus, while it is certainly useful to speak of ' The Middle Ages ' and of the ' Victorian Age,' those two abstract ideas have deluded many scholars and millions of newspaper readers into supposing that during certain centuries called ' The Middle Ages,' and again during certain decades called ' Age of Victoria,' everyone thought and acted more or less in the same way—till at last Victoria died or the ' Middle Ages came to an end.' But in fact there was no such sameness. Individual character, variety and an urge to change were marked features of the English over whom Victoria presided ; and the end of her reign was very different from the beginning. So, too, mediaeval society can only be studied fruitfully if we conceive it not as a static order but as a continuous evolution, without any definable date for its beginning or end.

The habit of thinking about the past as divided into watertight ' periods ' is most dangerous of all in economic and social history. For ' periods ' have usually been assorted, as their names imply, for purely political reasons—

'the age of the Tudors,' 'the age of Louis XIV' and so forth. But economic and social life takes little heed of the deaths of Kings or the accession of new dynasties : absorbed in its own daily task it flows on, like an underground river, only occasionally making eruption into the upper daylight of politics, though it may all the time be their unacknowledged and unconscious arbiter.

And it is all the more difficult to think about economic and social history in ' periods,' because there is always an overlap of the old and the new continuing side by side in the same country for generations and even for centuries. Different systems of production—craft and domestic and capitalist—all went on in England both in late mediaeval and in modern times. So, too, in the agricultural world, open fields and enclosures, Anglo-Saxon and modern methods were found together, from the Middle Ages to the Nineteenth Century. And in the social sphere, the feudal and the democratic spirit have had a marvellous aptitude for co-existence in our tolerant island.

If, then, we are asked to name a date, or even a period, when ' the Middle Ages came to an end,' what can we safely say ? Certainly not ' 1485,' the year when Tudor rule began, though it has been found by teachers and examiners a convenient point at which to wind up the Middle Ages in England. But in the real year 1485, when our simple ancestors ' gaped and rubbed the elbow at the news ' that Henry Tudor and his Welshmen had overthrown Richard III at Bosworth, they had no thought that a new era was beginning. They supposed merely that the Lancastrians had again got the better, for the time, of the Yorkists, in the endless and tiresome wars of the Roses. It is true that the events of the next twenty years showed that in fact the Wars of the Roses had, almost but not quite, ended on Bosworth Field. But the end of the Wars of the Roses is by no means the same thing as the end of the Middle Ages—in whatever way the Middle Ages are defined.

The victory of Henry the Welshman made no change distantly comparable in importance to the victory of William the Norman at Hastings. For half a century after 1485, until Henry's son took the Papal power and the monastic wealth into his own hands, English society continued very much as I have described it in the last chapter. The agricultural changes still continued at a slightly accelerated pace. The Church went on just as before, though exposed to re-newed unpopularity and denunciation, very similar to the anti-clerical outcry in the days of Langland, Chaucer and Wycliffe ; but there was no evident certainty that such strictures would have any more practical outcome this time than so often of old. Henry VII and young Henry VIII were both zealous in their orthodoxy ; they were dutiful in the roasting of heretics ; they frequently employed Bishops as their counsellors of State, after the mediaeval custom, culminating in the grand finale of Cardinal Wolsey, who displayed on a colossal scale the pride and power of the mediaeval Church. Himself the instrument of Papal power, he greatly increased its control over the *Ecclesia Anglicana.* He treated the lay nobles and gentlemen like dirt beneath his feet, thereby helping to prepare the anti-clerical revolution that accompanied his fall. He kept a household of nearly a thousand persons, and marched in state with silver pillars and pole-axes borne before him. Besides many other sources of wealth, he drew the revenues and neglected the duties of Archbishop of York, Bishop of Durham and Abbot of St. Albans ; the biographer of Wolsey and of Henry VIII estimates that the Cardinal was almost as rich a man as the King (Pollard's *Wolsey,* pp. 320–321). He obtained for his natural son four arch-deaconries, a deanery, five prebends and two rectories, and only failed in his endeavour to have him succeed in the fabulously rich see of Durham. In proportion to Wolsey's pride, luxury and greed was his munificence in founding schools and Colleges of splendour then unparalleled. Here was a prince indeed, of the cosmopolitan hierarchy of Europe before which men had bowed for centuries, but should never again bow in England. Yet he served the King as Chancellor with far more devotion than he served the religious interests of the Church. In all this, Wolsey is one of the greatest and the most characteristic of ' medi-aeval ' figures in our history, and his power was at its fullness more than forty years after Bosworth Field.

Another aspect of that half century of calm before the

storm, was the Renaissance of classical scholarship and biblical exegesis under Grocyn and Linacre, Colet and More, the English friends of Érasmus. Their work, more than all Wolsey's pride, was preparing the future, but it was not much altering the present. None of those friends thought that their new knowledge of the classics and of the Greek Testament would destroy the 'Mediaeval' Church, which they hoped to liberalize and to reform. More radical was the intention of William Tyndale, as in penury and danger he translated the Bible into words of power and beauty that unborn millions were to have daily on their lips, and to interpret in a hundred different ways disruptive of the past.

In the secular sphere, Henry VII restored order to the countryside, and put down retainers. That was an important social change, but it was not 'the end of the Middle Ages'; rather it was the belated fulfilment of a hope of mediaeval Englishmen. One mediaeval institution indeed, Parliament, was in grave danger under Henry VII and under Wolsey of perishing through disuse; but in England, unlike France and Spain, the mediaeval Parliament was destined to be revived and strengthened by Henry VIII for modern purposes. So, too, another great mediaeval institution, the English Common Law, survived the Tudor period to become the basis of modern English life and liberty.

In the early Sixteenth Century, English trade, though again on the increase after a period of relative stagnation, still ran in its old mediaeval channels along the coasts of northern Europe, with a new thrust into the Mediterranean, for vent of cloth. In spite of Cabot's voyage from Bristol to Newfoundland in the reign of Henry VII, the wider outlook across the Atlantic did not greatly affect Englishmen before Elizabeth was on the throne. Until the reign of her sister Mary, the English were still a French-hating, not a Spaniard-hating, people, for the quarrel about the Inquisition and about the possession of the New World had not yet arisen.

It is indeed useless to look for any date, or even for any period, when the Middle Ages 'ended' in England. All that one can say is that, in the Thirteenth Century, English thought and society were mediaeval, and in the Nineteenth Century they were not. Yet even now we retain the mediaeval institutions of the Monarchy, the Peerage, the Commons in Parliament assembled, the English Common Law, the Courts of Justice interpreting the rule of law, the hierarchy of the established Church, the parish system, the Universities, the Public Schools and Grammar Schools. And unless we become a Totalitarian State and forget all our Englishry, there will always be something mediaeval in our ways of thinking, especially in our idea that people and corporations have rights and liberties which the State ought in some degree to respect, in spite of the legal omnicompetence of Parliament. Conservatism and Liberalism, in the broadest sense, are both mediaeval in origin, and so are trade unions. The men who established our civic liberties in the Seventeenth Century, appealed to mediaeval precedents against the ' modernizing ' monarchy of the Stuarts. The pattern of history is indeed a tangled web. No simple diagram will explain its infinite complication.

As to the economic side of things in town and country, Mr. Tawney, the social historian of the Sixteenth Century, regards the Tudor epoch as a ' watershed ' whence things moved downward with ever increasing momentum towards the big estates and farms of the Eighteenth and Nineteenth Centuries, and the industrial capitalism of modern times. This may well be true. But it is a question whether ' the end of the Middle Ages ' might not as well be sought in the consummation of economic and social change in the reign of George III, as in the Tudor beginnings. Nor in fact did these things begin first under the Tudors : as noted in former chapters of this book, ' capitalism ' was established in some important trades long before. So too the emancipation of serfs and the consequent break-up of the mediaeval manor system had actually been accomplished before ever Bosworth Field was fought.

Where then shall we place the end of mediaeval society and economics—in the Fourteenth, the Sixteenth or the Eighteenth Centuries ? Perhaps it matters little : what does matter is that we should understand what really happened. It is probable that ere long a new perspective of periods in the past will replace the old. Owing to the mechanization of life, man has changed more in the last hundred years than in the previous thousand. It is not unlikely therefore that the real beginning of ' modern times '—if ' modern times ' are to include our own—will be allocated to the growth of the Industrial Revolution rather than to the Renaissance and Reformation. And even in the realm of thought and religion, the impact of Science and Darwin may come to seem as memorable as the impact of Erasmus and Luther.

It is of course the Renaissance and the Reformation of which people are chiefly thinking when they ascribe the end of the Middle Ages to the Sixteenth Century.[1] In the spheres of thought and religion, of clerical power and privilege, we may indeed say that the mediaeval scheme of things was abolished in Tudor England. Yet even this is not true without qualification about the land that Elizabeth ruled. The Protestantizing and secularizing of England was not complete till after the Puritan Rebellion and the Whig-Tory Revolution—or rather it has never yet been made complete. The Church of England, both in its organization, its privileges, its ceremonies and its thought has always remained in part ' mediaeval.'

The Elizabethan system, the grand finale of Tudor triumph, was as much a triumph of the Renaissance as of the Reformation. The two became one, and partly for that reason Shakespeare's England had a charm and a lightness of heart, a free aspiring of mind and spirit not to be found elsewhere in the harsh Jesuit-Calvinist Europe of that day. And at the same auspicious moment England's old song of the sea became a new ocean song. The Elizabethan adventurers—Drake, Frobisher, Hawkins, Raleigh and the rest—were sailing the wide world, discovering ' islands far away,' opening to their countrymen at home new realms of hope and fancy—committing indeed crimes in Ireland and in the slave-trade but without knowing that they were crimes or what the dreadful consequences were to be in the deep of time. The music of the Elizabethan madrigal and

---

[1] Another alleged reason is the ' rise of National Monarchies.' But England, unlike France and Spain, had already been a ' national Monarchy ' in the days of Crecy and Agincourt. No doubt Henry VIII's assumption of religious power carried nationalism one step further.

the lyric poetry to which it was wedded, expressed the reasonable joy in life of a people freed from mediaeval and not yet oppressed by Puritan complexes and fears ; rejoicing in nature and the countryside in whose lap they had the felicity to live ; moving forward to a healthy agricultural and mercantile prosperity, and not yet overwhelmed by the weight of industrial materialism.

All this found its perfect expression before it passed away —in Shakespeare's plays. In them we see the immense step forward that had been taken in the realm of thought and feeling, away from the ancient limits. The play of *Hamlet*, that at least is modern. Also in the English Church Service in every parish, and in the wide study of the English Bible in the homes of rich and poor, we can say the English mind and imagination had in those respects already ceased to be mediaeval. But society, politics and economics still very much more closely resembled those of the Fourteenth than of the Twentieth Century ; the author of *Richard II* and *Henry IV* found it easy to understand and portray that not very distant world.

If all aspects of life are taken into consideration, we may perhaps agree with the Historian of the reign of Henry VIII, that ' of all the schisms which rend the woven garment of historical understanding, the worst is that which fixes a deep gulf between mediaeval and modern history.' (A. F. Pollard, *Wolsey*, p. 8.)

But before this brief golden age corresponding to the lifetime of Shakespeare (1564–1616), Tudor England had known a long period of *malaise*. She did not, indeed, suffer from ' wars of religion ' such as devastated France, because here Monarchy was stronger and religious fanaticism less strong. But the Tudor Reformation was not carried through without attendant misery and violence. And the disturbances caused by the quick changes of ecclesiastical policy under Henry VIII, Edward VI and Mary coincided with a grave economic crisis in trade and agriculture, due chiefly to a rise in prices. That rise we must ascribe partly to world causes and partly to Henry's wanton debasing of the coinage. Of these things, among much else, it will be my business to deal in the chapters that follow.

CHAPTER V

ENGLAND DURING THE ANTI-CLERICAL REVOLUTION

THE advent of the first English antiquary, John Leland, may, if we wish, be taken for a sign that the Middle Ages were indeed passing away and becoming matter for retrospect. For nearly ten years (1534–1543) Leland travelled through the length and breadth of Henry VIII's kingdom, diligently seeking out and observing things new and old.[1] He noted much that was flourishing, but he had also a loving and learned eye for the past, to discern

> ' by Time's fell hand defaced
> The rich-proud cost of outworn buried age.'

Many ' lofty towers ' he saw ' downrazed,' especially three kinds of ruin—dilapidated castles, crumbling walls of towns, and the housebreakers beginning their work upon the roofs of the Abbeys.

Many castles, indeed, Leland saw that had been adapted to the domestic uses of a later age, and had long years of splendour still before them. But many others (like royal Berkhamstead where the Black Prince kept court) had after the Wars of the Roses been abandoned by the frugal policy of Henry VII ; while private owners often condemned their ancestral fortresses as fit neither to withstand cannon planted on a neighbouring eminence, nor to house nobles and gentlemen with modern comfort. Leland, therefore, reports on many a feudal stronghold that ' tendith to ruin,' some stripped of their roofs, their walls a quarry for the village or the new manor-house, the slighted remains sheltering poor husbandmen and their cattle.

In the Middle Ages, the glory and safety of every town had been its encircling walls, but military, political and economic reasons had combined to bring about their decay. The thin stone curtain, such as can still be seen in the grounds of New College, Oxford, could no longer avail to

---

[1] *The Itinerary of John Leland.* Edited by Lucy Toulmin Smith, 1906–1910.

protect a town against the cannon of Tudor times. A hundred years later, in the wars of Charles and Cromwell, places like London, Oxford and Bristol were defended by earthworks thrown up on newer principles of military engineering, well outside the too narrow circuit of the mediaeval walls.   Indeed such prosperous cities had already in Leland's day outgrown their antique suits of stone armour, and had thrust out suburbs and ' ribbon development ' along the roads of approach.   Other less fortunate towns, shrunk and impoverished by economic change, had no money to waste on keeping up walls which the Tudor peace rendered no longer needful.   More generally, the decadence of the walls was a symptom of the decline of that intense civic patriotism which had inspired mediaeval townsfolk.   National control and individual initiative were taking the place of the corporate spirit of town and gild, not only in matters of government and of military defence, but in trade and industry, as witness the cloth manufacture continuing to move ever more rapidly into the rural parts to escape municipal and gild regulation.

But the third kind of ruin that Leland saw was the most recent.   The crash of monastic masonry resounding through the land was not the work of the ' unimaginable touch of time '—not at least in the physical sense—but the sudden impact of a King's command, a demolition order to resolve at one stroke a social problem that had been maturing for two centuries past.

During the decade in which Leland was travelling and making his notes, Henry VIII, through the instrumentality of Parliament, effected the anti-clerical revolution which more than any other single event may be held to mark the end of mediaeval society in England.   The claim of national independence for a Church repudiating the Pope's authority, rendered possible the subjection of the clergy to the laity, and the division of the vast estates and social influence of the Monasteries among laymen.   Taken together, these proceedings constitute a social revolution. It was accompanied by just that amount of religious change which Henry VIII, a child of the new learning, approved— the diffusion of the English Bible among all classes, the destruction of the cruder forms of idolatry and relic-mongering, the substitution at Oxford and Cambridge of Renaissance scholarship for scholastic philosophy and Canon Law—measures which constituted in Henry's eyes an orthodox and Catholic reform. Having done all this, he continued to abhor and persecute Protestants, and if he had not done so he might have lost his throne in the then state of opinion. None the less, he had created a new social and ecclesiastical order of things which, as the changing years went by, could only be maintained on a more definitely Protestant basis.

The Reformation in England was at once a political, a religious and a social event. All three of its aspects were closely interwoven but, so far as division is possible, this volume is concerned only with its social causes and effects. Anti-clericalism is a social phenomenon, compatible with many different forms of belief about religion. And anti-clericalism was the keynote of the movement of opinion, equally felt among the learned and the vulgar, which rendered possible the breach with the Papacy and the Dissolution of the Monasteries, at a time when English Protestants were still a persecuted minority.

Henry VIII had himself been educated in the scholarly anti-clericalism of Erasmus and his Oxford friends—men sincerely religious and in the main orthodox, but inflamed with indignation at the tricks by which the baser sort of clergy conjured money from the ignorant and superstitious. They were specially hostile to the monks and friars, as protagonists of obscurantism, upholders of scholastic philosophy and opponents of that direct study of the Greek Testament to which Erasmus and Colet appealed as a criterion of religious truth.

Some, indeed, of the writings of Erasmus conveyed the most uncompromising spirit of anti-clericalism. In the *Praise of Folly* he denounces the monks for

'observing with punctilious scrupulosity a lot of silly ceremonies and paltry traditional rules,'

for which Christ cares nothing, yet managing therewith to lead a life of luxury,

'gorging the carcase to the point of bursting.'

The ' contemptible friars ' and their preaching come off no better :

'Their whole demeanour in preaching is such that you might swear they had taken lessons from a set of itinerant mountebanks, though indeed the mountebanks are out and out their superiors,'

and so forth for pages together.

If the most learned and polished man in Europe, who deprecated Luther's robust and headlong proceedings, could write thus in Latin about monks and friars, it be imagined what was the tone of popular anti-clerical writers, appealing to the common English in their own tongue. The printing press busily circulated such attacks, making direct appeal to the greed of the laity in view of the vast landed wealth of a Church that had for a while lost its only defences against spoliation—moral influence and religious awe.

For example, a few years before the Dissolution of the Monasteries, Henry VIII read without apparent disapproval, and Londoners read with loudly expressed delight, the pamphlet of Simon Fish entitled *The Supplication of the Beggars.*   Its form was an address to the King :

In the times of your noble predecessors past, craftily crept into this your realm an other sort, (not of impotent but) of strong, puisant and counterfeit, holy and idle beggars and vagabonds . . . the Bishops, Abbots, Priors, Deacons, Archdeacons, Suffragans, Priests, Monks, Canons, Friars, Pardoners and Sommoners.   And who is able to number this idle, ruinous sort, which (setting all labour aside) have begged so importunately that they have gotten into their hands more than the third part of all your Realm ?   The goodliest lordships, manors, lands and territories, are theirs.   Besides this they have the tenth part of all corn, meadow, pasture, grass, wool, colts, calves, lambs, pigs, geese and chickens. . . . Yea, and they look so narrowly upon their profits, that the poor wives must be countable to them of every tenth egg, or else she [sic] getteth not her rights at Easter, shall be taken as a heretic. . . . How much money get the Sommoners by extortion in a year, by citing the people to the Commissaries Court, and afterwards releasing their appearance for money ? . . . Who is she that will set her hands to work to get 3d. a day, and may have at least 20d. a day to sleep an hour with a friar, a monk or a priest ?

The conclusion reached by the pamphleteer is that the clergy, especially the monks and friars, should be deprived of their wealth for the benefit of the King and Kingdom, and made to work like other men ; let them also be allowed to marry and so be induced to leave other people's wives alone.

Such crude appeals to lay cupidity, and such veritable coarse anger at real abuses uncorrected down the centuries, had been generally prevalent in London under Wolsey's regime, and at his fall such talk became equally fashionable at Court. In those days, whenever the capital and the Court were agreed on a policy, the battle was already half won. And judging by the readiness with which the Reformation Parliament followed Henry's lead, similar feelings must have been widely spread in the country at large, though least in the Northern Counties, where feudal and religious loyalty to the Church and the Monasteries still prevailed.

In the face of this storm of opinion, now directed to practical issues by the King, what would be the attitude of the clergy, thus threatened and arraigned ? Their submission or their resistance would be an event of the utmost importance to the whole future development of English society. If the clerical body—Bishops, priests, monks and friars—had stood together for the high privileges and liberties of the Mediaeval Church, and had arrayed themselves under the Papal banner, they would scarcely have been overcome ; certainly not without a struggle that would have rent England to pieces. But in fact the clergy were not only scared by the union against them of the King and so many of his subjects ; they were themselves genuinely divided in opinion. A large number of clergymen were in close and daily contact with laymen and understood their way of thinking. The English priesthood had not got the spiritual isolation or the discipline of a caste, like the Roman Catholic clergy of to-day.

The Bishops, for example, were first and foremost royal nominees and civil servants. And in like manner parish priests and chaplains, as has been noted in an earlier chapter, often acted as business agents and trusted confidants of lords, squires and other lay patrons. Even the monks were wont to have their estates managed for them largely by laymen and to submit in many things to the wishes of patrons and founders' kin, who were not infrequently lodged in the Abbey precincts.

It was not therefore natural to the clergy to draw together to defend themselves against lay attack. The hostility with which Bishops and parish priests regarded monks and friars was centuries old and was in no degree abated. So too was the feeling against the Papal authority which had so long mercilessly bled and exploited the Church in England. And of recent years Wolsey, as the Pope's *legatus a latere*, had infuriated the English clergy by over-riding episcopal authority and clerical freedom. ' Better the King than the Pope ' was a general feeling among them at the time of his fall. There was no third choice before Convocation. Wolsey, says his biographer, ' always rode furiously ; he rode Papal jurisdiction in England to its death.' [1]

Moreover, the reforming doctrines, whether of Erasmus or of Luther, had many secret sympathizers and open missionaries among the clergy ; otherwise there would never have been a reformation in England, but only a brutal struggle of anti-clerical hatred with clerical privilege, such as seemed to be foreshadowed in propaganda like Fish's *Supplication of the Beggars*, such as in later times has actually taken place in countries that rejected the Reformation.

Many different currents of thought were moving in the English clerical mind. Just as the Oxford reformers responded to Erasmus in the reign of Henry VII, so in the reign of his son the Cambridge reformers, including Cranmer and Latimer, Tyndale and Coverdale responded to the impulse of Luther from oversea. And without being definitely Lutherans, many of the clergy sincerely desired to reform their own profession and were by no means in

---

[1] Professor Pollard adds (*Wolsey*, pp. 369-370) :

' The essential difference between Wolsey and Henry VIII was that the Cardinal was the protagonist of the *Sacerdotium* and the King of the *regnum ;* and that, rather than any question of theology, distinguished the Roman from the Anglican Church. The one was a priest-ridden, the other a king-ridden body. . . Wolsey had reduced the Church to a despotism whose liberties consisted in its jurisdiction over the laity and not in its government of itself. By Henry's conquest and annexation the *Ecclesia Anglicana* was saved from sinking into a church of Wolsey's conception, purely papal and autocratic and incompatible with the spirit of self-determination which was informing and transforming the nation as a whole. And into the sphere of church government was thereby injected the discords and debates which are the representative signs of popular interest and intellectual life.'

love with all its privileges. Many even of the expropriated monks and dissolved friars became Protestant clergymen under Edward VI, and there is no reason to suppose that they were hypocrites.

English opinion, lay and clerical, was a shifting kaleidoscope. It was not yet divided between two fixed and clearly divided parties, one of reform the other of reaction. And in the confusion the King's eclectic will prevailed. His anti-Papal, anti-monastic policy, in the year that it was challenged by the northern rebellion known as the Pilgrimage of Grace (1536), was saved by the support of conservative noblemen like Norfolk and Shrewsbury, and Bishops like Gardiner and Bonner, all of whom desired to burn Lutherans as much as Henry himself.[1] On the other hand, two chief lights of academic renaissance and reform, More and Fisher, the dear friends of Erasmus, suffered death rather than agree to the repudiation of Papal authority and the subjection of the Church to the State.

The dissolution of the orders of monks and friars was a natural outcome of the attitude towards religion, life and society that Erasmus and his English friends had done so much to propagate. The men of the new learning in classical and Biblical study, now dominant at Court as well as in the Universities, had been taught to regard the monks and friars as the obscurantist enemies of the new movement. And the ascetic ideal, which had founded the monasteries in ages long ago, was no longer either admired by the world or practised by the monks. Why, then, should the monasteries any longer be maintained at vast expense ?

That question was asked by the man in the street, particularly in London. And it was pressed by certain interested parties. The weakest of these were reforming clergymen, like Latimer, who hoped that the monastic wealth would go to endow education and religion ; they were the more deceived. Then there were the lay neighbours and patrons of the monasteries, who looked to succeed to their estates on

---

[1] ' It is indeed worthy of comment that of the leading figures concerned in the Dissolution (of the monasteries) in Cornwall, not one was a Protestant ; Sir Thomas Arundell, no more than Sir John Tregonwell, neither Prideaux nor Prior Mundy. The sympathies of each were unmistakably Catholic.' Rowse's *Tudor Cornwall*, p. 222.

easy terms of purchase, and who were seldom disappointed. Next, the King himself, whose profligate finance and foolish wars in France had emptied his treasury, sought to refill it by confiscation. And lastly, the House of Commons was only too glad to evade the unpopularity of voting taxation of their constituents, by passing the Bills for the disendowment of the monasteries.

An obstinate refusal to pay taxes was a characteristic of the English at this period. A new tax of any weight, even though voted by Parliament, was liable to produce a rebellion in some part of the country, and the Tudors had no standing army. Henry, therefore, in the last part of his reign sought relief for his financial embarrassments from two sources, first the monastic wealth, and, after that, the debasement of the coinage. Both these expedients had, as we shall see, important social consequences.

For a short while the sale of the monastic lands replenished the King's treasury. If Henry had not been bankrupt, he might never have dissolved the monasteries at all ; or he might have kept all their lands and tithes for the Crown, and so perhaps enabled his successors to establish absolute monarchy in England ; or again, he might have given more of their wealth to education and charity, as at first he intended to do, had not his financial needs been so pressing. Even as it was, he founded Trinity as a College on a larger scale than any other at Cambridge. He was probably inspired to that good deed by the example of Cardinal College (Christ Church) which Wolsey had recently founded at Oxford, also out of the spoils of monasteries ; for the diversion of monastic lands and tithes was not an invention either of Henry or of the Reformation. But considering the enormously greater opportunities of the King, he did very little for the endowment of institutions beneficial to the public. Some indeed of the monks' money he spent on fortifying the harbours of the Kingdom and the arsenals of the Royal Navy.

Henry did not, as it is sometimes stated, distribute any large proportion of the monastic lands and tithes gratis among his courtiers. He sold much the greater part of them.[1]

---

[1] See Appendix II, pp. 497–499 of H. A. L. Fisher's Vol. V of the *Political History of England*—table of Disposition of Monastic Lands.

He was driven by his financial necessities to sell, though he would have preferred to keep more for the Crown. The potential value of the estates, enjoyed in times to come by the lay purchasers or their heirs, was very great compared to the market prices they had actually paid to the necessitous King or to the merchant speculators who bought them up from Henry to re-sell to the local squirearchy. Therefore the ultimate beneficiary of the Dissolution was not religion, not education, not the poor, not even in the end the Crown, but a class of fortunate gentry, of whom more will be said when we come to consider the changes going on in social and agricultural life.

A good deal of monastic, chantry and other ecclesiastical land and tithe remained in the hands of the Crown for several generations. But financial necessity induced Elizabeth, James and Charles I gradually to part with it all to private purchasers.

The coal-fields, particularly in Durham and Northumberland, had been, to a predominant extent, ecclesiastical property. But owing to the action of Henry VIII this source of future wealth, which from Stuart times onwards was to be developed on an immense scale, passed into the hands of private gentlemen, whose descendants founded many powerful and some noble families out of coal. Yet even from the remnant left to the Church, the Ecclesiastical Commission a few years ago was drawing nearly £400,000 a year—a seventh part of all coal royalties. (Nef, *Rise of the British Coal Industry*, I, pp. 134–135.)

Besides the gentry, another class that benefited by the Dissolution of the Monasteries were the citizens of towns like St. Albans and Bury St. Edmunds, now released from the stranglehold of monastic lordship, against which they had been in fierce rebellion for centuries past. On the other hand, the destruction of great monastic establishments and the suppression of popular centres of pilgrimage reduced the wealth and importance of some towns and some rural districts, which were not in a position to make good the loss as independent centres of industry and trade. The destruction of many monastic libraries with their irreplaceable MSS. was a cruel injury to learning and literature.

The monks suffered personally much less than used to be supposed until recent research has revealed the facts.[1] They were given adequate pensions, which were really paid. Many of them found employment, particularly as beneficed clergymen and some even as Bishops. Under the successive Catholic and Protestant regimes of Henry, Edward, Mary and Elizabeth, the Church was served by former monks and friars, who appear to have been as well able as the rest of the clerical body to adapt their views to the frequent changes of the times. A few of the Heads and inmates of the dissolved houses resisted the new order of things and were ruthlessly executed by the tyrant King. But the great bulk of the monks and friars accepted changes which to many of them were not unwelcome as opening to them personally a freer life and greater opportunity in the world. They did little to build up a party against Henry's innovations, except in the North where social conditions still resembled those of feudal ages gone by.

With the monks disappeared also the preaching friars, so long the auxiliaries and rivals of the parish clergy. The familiar grey and black-gowned figures of Franciscan and Dominican were no longer seen upon the roads of England, tapping at the cottage door, or perorating to an audience of rustics. Their functions were in part taken over by ' hot gospellers ' and itinerant Protestant preachers, working sometimes for, sometimes against the authorities of the Church. The life of Bernard Gilpin, ' the Apostle of the North,' in his religious peregrinations of the Border Counties under Mary and Elizabeth, recalls the earlier days of the friars, and looks forward to Wesley.

In all, about 5000 monks, 1600 friars and 2000 nuns were pensioned off and sent out into the world. The disappearance of the Nunneries made the least social difference. Their wealth and estates were not comparable to those of the monks, nor their popular activities to those of the friars. The nuns of this period were ladies of good family whom their relations had provided for in the life of religion, as they could not be suitably married.

---

[1] See G. Baskerville, *The English Monks and the Suppression of the Monasteries*, 1938. See also Rowse's *Tudor Cornwall*, 1941, Chaps. VIII–IX.

The convents were not an important factor in English social life.[1]

But the social consequences of the Dissolution of the Monasteries require more consideration. How far did their tenants, their servants and the poor suffer by the change ?

As regards estate management, there is less than no reason to suppose that either the secular or regular clergy were easier landlords than laymen before the Dissolution. The Domesday of Enclosures of 1517 shows that evictions were as common on ecclesiastical as on lay estates and that ' while the average rental value of lands in the hand of owners are considerably lower in the case of ecclesiastics than of lay owners, the rents of lands let by ecclesiastics are higher.' (R.H.S. *Domesday of Enclosures*, Leadam, pp. 48, 65.) The Abbeys were accused by Sir Thomas More of turning tillage into pasture and by popular rhymers of extortionate renting as well as of enclosing :

> How have the abbeys their payment ?
> A new way they do invent
> Letting a dozen farms under one,
> Which one or two rich franklins
> Occupying a dozen men's livings
> Take all in their own hands alone.
>
>   *   *   *
>
> Where a farm for twenty pounds was set,
> Under thirty they wold not it let.
>
> (Date 1527-1528 ; Tawney and Power, *Tudor Ec. Docs.*, III, pp. 20-21.)

In fact the monks had to a large extent handed over the control of their estates to laymen. The Abbey lands were often managed, and the farms taken on lease and sublet, by noblemen, gentlemen and ' franklins,' who ran them very much as other estates were run, enclosing land where it was profitable to enclose, turning copyholders into tenants at will, and raising rents if prices rose or the value of the farms increased. When, at the Dissolution, the monastic property passed into lay ownership, the existing lay management

---

[1] For the nuns in the Fifteenth Century see Eileen Power's *Mediaeval English Nunneries*. Something has been said of them on pp. 72-73 of this book.

continued as before in much the same spirit towards the
tenants.   But as, owing to Henry VIII's debasement of the
coinage, the reign of his son was a period of soaring prices,
all landlords new and old, if they would not be ruined, had
to raise their rents whenever leases and copies fell in.   The
' new men ' were therefore denounced, sometimes rightly
but very often unfairly, for doing what the monks would
have had to do in like price-conditions, and for continuing
an estate policy for which Abbots had, in former times, been
abused with equally good or bad reason.   As years went
by, the past was seen through a golden haze, and a tradition
grew up that the monks had been particularly easy landlords—a tradition that modern research has not confirmed.[1]

Apart from the tenants of the monastic lands, who cannot
be positively said to have either gained or lost by the Dissolution, there was also a great army of servants, more
numerous than the monks themselves, who were employed
in the domestic service of the Abbeys.   It had been the
custom to denounce them as ' idle abbeylubbers, apt to do
nothing but only to eat and drink ' (Starkey's *England*,
temp. H. VIII, E.E.T.S., p. 131).   They were probably
no better and no worse than the great households of serving-
men that noblemen and gentlemen loved to keep up, after
Henry VII had disarmed their military retainers.   ' Serving-
men ' were not admired, even in Shakespeare's day.   These
monastic dependants were many of them taken over by the
new proprietors, especially by such as converted the abbey
buildings into a manor-house.   But no doubt a certain
proportion lost their places and swelled the ranks of the
' sturdy beggars,' which the monks themselves had no need
to do, owing to their pensions.

Many of the abbey ' servants ' had been young gentlemen
of the squire class attached to the monastery, ' wearing its
livery, administering its estates, presiding over its manorial
courts, acting as stewards, bailiffs, gentlemen farmers.'
Besides these gentlemen servants, paid officers of the monks,
there were wealthy guests and corrodians living in the abbey

---

[1] For what I say about the monasteries in this chapter, see Baskerville, *English
Monks and the Suppression of the Monasteries* ; Savine, *English Monasteries on the
Eve of the Dissolution* (*Oxford Studies*, edited by Vinogradoff, 1909) ; Snape,
English Monastic Finances, 1926.

at its charges. And there were noblemen and gentlemen who, as patrons or Founders' kin, exerted great influence over the administration of the House. The lay upper class had got its fingers deep in the monastic pie long before the Dissolution. In some aspects, the secularization of the monastic lands was a gradual process, and the Dissolution only a last step.[1]

But there were always the poor at the gate. They duly received broken meats and a dole of money. The custom represented an ancient tradition and doctrine of Christian duty which was of priceless value. But in practice, according to the historian of our Poor Law, the monastic charity being 'unorganized and indiscriminate,' did 'nearly as much to increase beggars as to relieve them.' (Leonard, *Poor Law*, p. 18.) Presumably the cessation of the dole at the Abbey Gate did something in the first instance to increase the number of beggars elsewhere, but there is no evidence that the problem which mendicancy presented was seriously worse after the Dissolution than it had been before. It was certainly less bad at the end of the reign of Elizabeth.

How far, when the new order of things was well established, did the heirs of those who had purchased the abbey lands carry on the work of charity ? Did the lord and lady of the manor in Elizabethan times give more or less of their income to the poor than the monks before them ? It is impossible to say ; probably some gave more and others less.[2] Early in the Stuart era the care of the village was a duty recognized by many a squire's wife, sometimes even by a Peeress, like Letice, Lady Falkland, who used to visit the

---

[1] Baskerville, Chap. II and *passim* ; Savine, *English Monasteries*, etc., pp. 244–267.

[2] In 1539, while the Dissolution of the Monasteries was still proceeding, Robert Pye wrote to Thomas Cromwell on the state of opinion in the country about the King's ecclesiastical changes :

' I asked what relief they had since the suppression of religious houses and was told they were never in so good case, were it not for the unreasonable number of hounds and greyhounds which the gentlemen keep and compel their tenants to keep, and many tenants keep them for their own pleasures. These dogs eat up the broken meats and bread which should relieve the poor. [Exactly the same complaint had been made against the monks !] They say they must keep dogs, or the foxes would kill their lambs. There are men enough if they might be suffered with traynes [traps] who would not leave a fox in the country. Howbeit they have always been resisted by gentlemen for killing their game.' (*Cal. L. and P., H.* VIII, Vol. XIV (2) p. 354.)

sick, dose them and read to them.   The ' Lady Bountiful '
of the manor-house and her lord often did as much for the
poor as had been done by the later monasteries.

How far the poor positively lost by the dissolution of the
monasteries remains obscure, but it is plain as noonday that a
great chance was missed of endowing the poor, as well as
education and learning.   This was realized by many at the
time, especially by the reforming clergy, like Latimer and
Crowley.   About 1550 Crowley wrote :

> As I walked alone, and mused on things
> That have in my time been done by great Kings,
> I bethought me of the Abbeys that sometimes I saw,
> Which are now suppressed all by a Law.
> O Lord (thought I then) what occasion was here
> To provide for learning and make poverty cheer !
> The lands and the jewels that hereby were had
> Would have found godly preachers which might well had led
> The people aright that now go astray,
> And have fed the poor that famish every day.

Instead of that, a further impetus had been given to a tendency already strong enough, the rise to dominance of the
class of landowning gentry, whose power replaced that of
the great nobles and ecclesiastics of the feudal ages and
whose word was to be law in the English countryside for
centuries to come.

The bands of ' sturdy beggars ' who alarmed society in
the early Tudor reigns were recruited from many sources—
the ordinary unemployed, the unemployable, soldiers discharged after French wars and the Wars of the Roses,
retainers disbanded at Henry VII's command, serving men
set adrift by impecunious lords and gentry, Robin Hood
bands driven from their woodland lairs by deforestation and
by the better enforcement of the King's peace, ploughmen
put out of work by enclosures for pastures, and tramps who
prudently pretended to belong to that much commiserated
class.   All through the Tudor reigns, the ' beggars coming
to town ' preyed on the fears of dwellers in lonely farms
and hamlets, and exercised the minds of magistrates,
Privy Councillors and Parliaments.   Gradually a proper
system of Poor Relief, based upon compulsory rates, and

discriminating between the various classes of the indigent, was evolved in England, first of all the countries of Europe. It was soon found that the whipping of 'sturdy beggars' was by itself no solution. The double duty of providing work for the unemployed, and charity for the impotent was gradually recognized by Tudor England as incumbent not merely on the Church and the charitable, but on society as a whole. In the reign of Henry VIII some great towns, like London and Ipswich, organized the administrative relief of their poor. At the end of Elizabeth's reign and under the early Stuart kings, it had become a duty prescribed by national legislation, enforced upon the local magistrates by a vigilant Privy Council, and paid for by compulsory Poor Rates.[1]

After the monasteries, the chantries! Henry VIII was already preparing an attack upon them when death took him where Kings can steal no more. On the accession of Edward VI (1547) Protestant doctrine triumphed, and prayers for the dead were pronounced 'superstitious.' As that was the specific purpose of chantries, their spoliation had now the cover of religious zeal. The 'ramp,' as our generation would call it, of greedy statesmen and their parasites at Court, and of rural gentry living near to chantry lands, became more shameless under the boy King than under his formidable old father; Henry had at least protected the interests of the Crown, so far as his financial incompetence permitted.

The chantries were not purely ecclesiastical establishments. Many of them were the property of lay gilds, and their endowments went to pay not only for prayers on behalf of the dead, but for the maintenance of bridges, harbours

---

[1] About the year 1550 Robert Crowley thus writes in his *Epigrams :*
I heard two beggars that under an hedge sate,
Who did with long talk their matters debate.
They had both sore legs most loathsome to see,
All raw from the foot well most to the knee.
'My leg,' quoth the one, 'I thank God is fair.'
'So is mine,' quoth the other, 'in a cold air,
For then it looketh raw and as red as any blood,
I would not have it healed for any world's good.
No man would pity me but for my sore leg,
Wherefore if I were whole I might in vain beg.
I should be constrained to labour and sweat,
And perhaps sometime with scourges be beat.'

and schools. When therefore their 'superstitious' uses were to be suppressed, the secular purposes for which the endowments were also used ought clearly to have been separated off and protected. In some cases this was done : the burgesses of Lynn secured the funds of their Holy Trinity Gild to maintain their piers and seawalls. But many public services suffered in the scramble, especially in the case of the poorer and less influential gilds. School endowments lost heavily.

For three hundred years after his death, Edward VI enjoyed an undeserved reputation as a very good boy who had founded schools. But in fact the ' Edward VI Grammar Schools ' were simply those old establishments which his counsellors refrained from destroying and to which his name was sycophantically appended. Most of the chantry and gild schools affected by the legislation of this period suffered, some more, some less. Lands of great potential value were taken from them, and they were compensated with fixed stipends in a rapidly depreciating currency.[1]

Another great chance had been missed. If all, or even half, the endowments of masses for the dead had been devoted to schools, and if at the same time those schools had been left with their old landed property, England would soon have had the best secondary education in the world, and the whole history of England and of the world might have been changed for the better. Latimer denounced the waste of opportunity—and appealed for a new form of endowment more suited to the religious needs of the time :

' Here I will make a supplication that ye would bestow so much to the finding of scholars of good wits, of poor men's sons, to exercise the office of salvation, in relieving scholars, as ye were wont to bestow in pilgrimage matters, in trentals, in masses, in pardons, in purgatory matters.'

Such appeals had little effect on the policy of the councillors and courtiers who were greedily exploiting the

---

[1] Christ's Hospital, indeed, was really founded by Edward VI on the site of Grey Friars Monastery, originally as a foundling hospital, though it soon became the famous ' blue-coat school.' Some monastic hospitals had been destroyed by Henry VIII, but ' Barts,' St. Thomas's and Bedlam were saved and refounded under lay control. The disendowment of hospitals was more injurious to the poor than the disendowment of monasteries. The hospitals had been founded to help the poor and had been placed where they were most needed.

minority of Edward VI. But they were not without influence on individuals. The Tudor English were not all of a piece. Members of the rising class of gentry and individual lawyers, merchants and yeomen did much by private beneficence to retrieve the educational position. In Elizabeth's reign, Camden notices newly founded schools at Uppingham, Oakham and other towns ; the yeoman, John Lyon, founded a free grammar school for boys at Harrow, where Greek was to be taught in the upper forms. In the first year of King James, a grammar school was founded in the remote but flourishing dale of Dent in Yorkshire, by subscription among its ' statesman ' free-holders, and thence for centuries to come the University of Cambridge and the parsonages of the North drew many valuable recruits, down to the days of Professor Adam Sedgwick. The grammar school at Hawkshead, where the poet Wordsworth was educated, had been founded in the reign of Elizabeth by Archbishop Sandys.

A typical ' new man ' of the Tudor age was Nicholas Bacon, father of Francis, and son of the sheepreeve to the Abbey of Bury St. Edmunds. Nicholas Bacon rose by law and politics to be owner of many of the farms on which his father had served the monks as one of their bailiffs. He founded a free grammar school on those lands, with scholarships thence to Cambridge, and gave other endowments to his old College of Corpus Christi. At Cambridge he had first met his lifelong friends Matthew Parker and William Cecil, the future leaders of Church and State under Elizabeth. The younger and hitherto lesser University was coming rapidly to the front, and her sons played the leading part in the great changes of the period.

At the same time the educational methods and ideals of the men of the new learning, eager to study the classics and the Bible in the original tongues, gave an increased value to school and University teaching. The influence of John Cheke and Roger Ascham, the ' Grecians ' of St. John's, Cambridge, had a profound and lasting effect. Shakespeare got a classical education of the new type at Stratford Grammar school, and he got it free of charge, which was fortunate, as his father was at the time gravely embarrassed. Our humble and hearty thanks are therefore due to the mediaeval founders of Stratford School and to the educational reformers of the English Renaissance.

If under Henry VIII and Edward VI the Catholic families had refused to purchase confiscated Church property, it is probable that their children and grandchildren would less often have become Protestants. In the days of Elizabeth, when a vigorous Catholic reaction threatened England from overseas, the new owners of abbey and chantry lands found their own interest had become involved in that of the Reformation.[1]

Throughout Tudor times, as for centuries before, ' enclosure ' of land with permanent hedges was going on in various forms : the enclosure of waste and forest for agricultural purposes ; the enclosure of open field strips into a smaller number of hedged fields to promote better individual tillage ; the enclosure of village commons ; and the enclosure of arable land for pasture. All of these forms of enclosure increased wealth, and only some of them defrauded the poor or reduced the population. Some were carried out with the active collaboration of the peasants themselves. Others, especially the enclosure of commons, were deeply resented, and provoked riot and rebellion.

In the reign of Henry VII a cry arose against the throwing together of small peasant holdings into pasture farms, as being injurious to population and leading to the ' pulling down of towns ' (viz. villages). In 1489 and 1515 Acts were passed to restrain this practice, apparently without result. After that, the proclamations, commissions and statutes of Henry VIII's middle and later years indicate a growing alarm at the increase of pasture at the expense of arable, and the consequent reduction of the village population. But enclosure does not appear to have been conducted on any large scale except in certain midland shires where Royal Commissioners were sent to report. And even in the midlands, enclosure, whether for arable or pasture, must in fact have been very limited, for in these same counties, in the Eighteenth Century, we find that the open

---

[1] On the treatment of chantries and schools under Edward VI see Pollard, Longmans' *Political History of England*, Vol. VI, 1547-1603, pp. 15-20 ; and Leach, *English Schools at the Reformation*.

fields and commons of the mediaeval manors are, with few exceptions, still unhedged and waiting to be enclosed by Hanoverian Acts of Parliament. (Gonner, *Common Land and Enclosure*.)

The amount of noise made over economic and social change is determined, not by the extent and importance of the changes that actually occur, but by the reaction of contemporary opinion to the problem. For example, we hear much of rural depopulation in Tudor times, because it was then regarded as a grave evil. Enclosures for pasture were therefore denounced by More and Latimer and a hundred other writers and preachers, Catholic and Protestant alike. ' Where forty person had their livings, now one man and his shepherd hath all '—such was the outcry. There were some such cases, and there would have been more but for the agitation and the consequent action by government to restrain such enclosure. But the ' rural depopulation ' in Tudor times was only sporadic and local, and was more than made up elsewhere. When, however, ' rural depopulation ' really set in on a national scale about 1880, as a result of the import of American foodstuffs, the later Victorians looked on with indifference at this tremendous social disaster, as a natural and therefore acceptable outcome of Free Trade, and did nothing to check it at all. Only in our own day, the fear of island starvation in time of war has attracted some general interest to a problem of rural depopulation twenty times more serious than that which four centuries ago occupied the thoughts of our ancestors as much perhaps as the Reformation itself.

Social and economic grievances caused Kett's rising in Norfolk (1549), when the rebellious peasantry, encamped on Mousehold Heath, slaughtered 20,000 sheep as a protest against the landlords who kept an unconscionable number of their own sheep upon the common lands. But enclosure of arable for pasture was not the grievance in Norfolk, where, a generation later, Camden recorded that the county was ' almost all champion,' to wit unenclosed, though he also notes its ' great flocks of sheep.'

Agrarian trouble had not been to any large extent aggravated by the Dissolution of the Monasteries. But it was aggravated as we shall presently see, by Henry's next

E

financial expedient, the debasement of the coinage. The
bottom of the trouble lay deeper, in the growing pains of
historic change. Society was passing from a system of wide
distribution of land among the peasants at easy rents which
had prevailed during the shortage of labour of the Fourteenth and Fifteenth Centuries, to a gradual abolition of
peasant holdings and their consolidation into larger, highly
rented farms. This implied a further reduction of mere
' subsistence agriculture,' and a greater production for the
market. It may or may not have been a change from
a better form of life to a worse, but it was certainly a
change from a poorer to a richer countryside. And
some such change was necessary in order to feed the increasing number of inhabitants of the island ; to
multiply the nation's wealth ; and to allow the rise of
the general standard of living, which modern conditions
ultimately brought about at the expense of the old order
of life.

Sixteenth-Century England was ahead of Germany and
France in having got rid of the servile status of the peasant,
of which little was left in the reign of Henry VII and practically nothing in the reign of Elizabeth. But the agrarian
changes of the epoch were beginning another evolution less
to the peasants' advantage, which in the course of the Seventeenth and Eighteenth Centuries gradually got rid of the
peasant himself, converting him either into farmer or
yeoman, or into the landless labourer on the large leasehold farm, or into the town workman divorced from the
land. Agrarian discontent in Tudor times was the protest
against an early stage of this long process. The circumstances under which it began require further examination
here.

Long ago, in the Thirteenth Century, there had been
' land-hunger '—too many men and not enough land in
cultivation—greatly to the advantage of the landlords.
But, as has already been noticed, during the next two
centuries, largely owing to the Black Death, there had been
a glut of land and a hunger for men to till it—to the advantage of the peasant, who had effected his emancipation
from serfdom under these favouring conditions. And now
in the Sixteenth Century there was land-hunger again.

The slow advance of the birth-rate against the death-rate had at last made good the ravages of the Black Death— though its local recurrence still periodically took toll of London and other towns. Only the rich had medical attendance of any value, and even their children died off at a rate that would appal modern parents, but was then taken as a matter of course. But in spite of the ' dance of death,' a favourite subject for the artists at that time, the population was slowly on the rise, probably reaching four millions for all England. So there was again under the Tudors a surfeit of labour in proportion to the land available. And as yet there was no colonial and little industrial development to absorb the superfluous men. Hence the ' sturdy beggars ' ; hence increased deforestation and taking in of waste land for agriculture, which had been held up in the Fifteenth Century ; hence also the economic opportunity of the landlord to do what he liked with land so much in demand, and to exact higher rents so far as the character of his tenants' leases allowed him.

While the land-hunger enabled the landlord to effect changes in rent and in agricultural method, the rise in prices compelled him to do so or be ruined. Between 1500 and 1560 the prices that the landlord had to pay for the things he bought for himself and his household, had much more than doubled ; food had nearly trebled. Unless then the landlords were to accept ruin they must raise rents when leases fell in, and they must turn land to its most profitable use—even in some cases to pasture instead of arable.[1]

But this excuse was scarcely considered at all by popular anger and religious sentiment. Catholic and Protestant alike still applied mediaeval ethical judgments to economic actions. For example, in spite of the long established

[1] There were three stages of the price-rise under the Tudors : (1) 1510–1540. Owing to production of silver in Germany, and the dispersal of Henry VII's hoarded treasure by Henry VIII, prices of food stuffs go up 30 per cent. Other prices rise less. (2) 1541–1561. Owing to Henry VIII's debasement of the coin (and a little later to American silver mines beginning to take effect) prices of all kinds rush up about 100 per cent. more. (3) 1561–1582. Owing to Mary's better finance and Elizabeth's re-coinage, prices are stabilized, and rise more slowly. Then in early Stuart times American silver mines again raise prices to peak 1643–1652 ; after that prices fall.

practice of business men, law and opinion still attempted to forbid as usury all interest on money lent.   So far did legislation lag behind reality that as late as 1552 an Act of Parliament prohibited all taking of interest as ' a vice most odious and detestable.'   At length, in 1571, this Act was repealed and interest not exceeding ten per cent. ceased to be criminal.

It is not then surprising that preachers, pamphleteers and poets denounced enclosures as immoral and higher rents as extortionate.   Some of them were so, no doubt; but on the whole the landlords were acting under financial compulsion.   ' Economic necessity ' became indeed the tyrant's plea for much oppression, and was too glibly used in later centuries when the ' dismal science ' of Political Economy bore iron rule over the minds of men.   But much of the Tudor writing on these questions suffered from the opposite fault and was not economic enough. It blamed the wickedness of individuals alone, instead of looking for root causes and remedies.

But there were exceptions.   A remarkable dialogue, written at the height of the social trouble under Edward VI, entitled *A Discourse of the Common Weal*, managed to elucidate the real truth with fairness to all parties, perceiving the unavoidable effect that the price-rise must have on rent, as well as its main cause in Henry's debasement of the coinage.   And early in Elizabeth's reign Thomas Tusser grew lyrical as well as economic in praise of the much abused enclosures :

> More plenty of mutton and beef,
> Corn, butter and cheese of the best,
> More wealth anywhere (to be brief)
> More people, more handsome and prest,
> Where find ye (go search any coast)
> Than there, where enclosures are most ?

But, more usually, indiscriminate abuse was poured on all enclosure, which might better have been reserved for the cases of real injustice, when lords of the manor ' enclosed from the poor their due commons.'   Equally indiscriminate was the attack on the gentry as ' cormorants and greedy gulls ' because they ' raise our rents.'   Yet owing to the price-rise, peasants and farmers were selling their produce at two or three times the old money, while their landlords were paying proportionately more for all they bought.[1] How then could rents fail to rise? But the mind of the community, still essentially mediaeval in outlook, thought the right basis of social economics was not competition but immemorial custom, even when the fall in the value of money and the soaring of prices was rendering old custom every day more impossible and unfair.

A chief cause of social *malaise* was the casual and irregular incidence of the price-rise on various classes of men. One part of the peasantry, who were lucky enough to have long-term leases or copyhold tenures of the kind that was by law not breakable, reaped the full advantage from the soaring prices of their products because their rents could not be raised. Since therefore the landlords could not raise rents all round in moderation, they recouped themselves by extorting high rents and heavy fines for renewal of leases from the other less fortunate part of the peasantry and farmers, whose leases were renewable annually or fell in upon death or after a period of years. The result was that one group of peasants was coining money without paying an extra penny of rent, while another group, not socially distinguishable except by the date of their leases or the legal forms of their tenure, were being oppressed all the more to make up for the immunity enjoyed by the others. Meanwhile the yeoman freeholder who paid no rent or a purely nominal one to the lord of the manor, was selling his corn and cattle for three times the price that his grandfather had been able to ask.

Thus, while some men flourished exceedingly, others, including many lords and squires, were in real distress during the reigns of Edward VI and Mary, largely as a result of their royal father's unscrupulous juggle with the coinage. For the same reason the landless labourer suffered from the

---

[1] This point, though noted in the *Discourse of the Common Weal*, is shirked in most of the literature of the time. But the poet Gascoigne, early in Elizabeth's reign says of the peasants in his *Piers Ploughman* :

> Nor that they can cry out on landlords loud
> And say they rack their rents an ace too high,
> When they themselves do sell their landlords' lamb
> For greater price than ewe was wont be worth.

time-lag of wages behind prices.[1] But the landless labourer was then a much smaller proportion of the working class than he is to-day, and as he was to some extent paid in kind, his loss from the fall of the value of money was often not very great. On the other hand, the craftsman, manufacturer and merchant gained by the rise of prices as much as the peasant whose rent could not be raised. More generally, the rise of prices, which brought poverty to some and wealth to others, had the effect of stimulating trade, production and enterprise both in the towns and on the land. It was a factor in the development of the new England of adventure and competition, replacing the old England of custom and settled rights.

Before the end of the Century equilibrium had been reached for a time. In the last years of Edward VI a real financial reform had been begun which Mary continued and Elizabeth carried to fruition. As early as the second year of her reign (1560–1561) the great Queen was able to restore the purity of the currency. Prices were for awhile stabilized. Gradually, as more and more leases fell in, rents were adjusted all round, and in the age of Shakespeare there was agrarian peace and a high general level of prosperity and content, except in times of bad harvest.

By the time that this new balance had been adjusted, important changes had been brought about under the pressure of the bad times. The number of farmers in the modern sense of the word, men with a considerable acreage held on terminable leases, was greater than before, and the typical peasant holder of the middle ages was rather less common. But there were still many small peasants, and the bulk of the best arable land in the Midlands was still cultivated in open-field strips, either in large or small holdings.

The continuous effort of successive Tudor Governments, by legislation, Commissions and the judicial action of the Star Chamber and Court of Requests, had done something to check the abuses of enclosure and to protect the old-

---

[1] Between 1501 and 1560 food prices had gone up as from 100 to 290, while wages in the building trade had gone up only from 100 to 169. Agricultural wages cannot be given.

fashioned peasant against his landlord. But it had not stopped the gradual process of inevitable change.

As a result of these conditions, the class denominated 'yeomen' was more numerous, more wealthy and more important than in any former age. The term 'yeoman' covered at least three different classes, all now prosperous : the freeholder cultivating his own land ; the capitalist farmer, who might be a tenant-at-will ; and the peasant who was lucky enough to enjoy a secure tenure at an unalterable rent. All these three types of yeoman might be cultivating either land enclosed by hedges, or scattered strips in the open field. The wealth of many of them was derived wholly or in part from the fleeces of their sheep. The praise of the yeoman as the best type of Englishman, holding society together, neither cringing to the high nor despising his poorer neighbour, hearty, hospitable, fearless, supplies a constant motif of literature under Tudors and Stuarts. And it corresponded to a social fact.

The yeomen were held to be the real strength and defence of the nation. Of old they had won Agincourt and but yesterday Flodden, and were still the nation's shield and buckler. ' If the yeomanry of England were not, in time of war we should be in shrewd case. For in them standeth the chief defence of England.' (Starkey's *England, Temp. H. VIII*, E.E.T.S., p. 79.) Other nations, Englishmen boasted, had no such middle class, but only an oppressed peasantry and the nobles and men-at-arms who robbed them.

A strong feeling already existed among the English against professional soldiers, largely derived from memories of what had been endured by quiet folk at the hands of the lords' retainers. The Tudor Kings had put all that down, and had no standing army of their own : hence their popularity. The English were conscious and proud of their liberty, not yet defined as the liberty of governing their King through Parliament, or of printing what they liked against the authorities of Church and State, but simply freedom to live their own lives undisturbed either by feudal or royal oppression. In the *Discourse of the Common Weal* in Edward VI's reign, the Husbandman and Merchant

discuss whether there should be a standing force in England
to repress tumults :

HUSBANDMAN : God forbid that we have any such tyrants amongst
us ; for, as they say, such will in the country of France take poor
men's hens, chickens, pigs and other provision and pay nothing
for it ; except it be an evil turn, as to ravish his wife and daughter
for it.

MERCHANT : Marie, I think that would be rather occasion of com-
motions to be stirred, than to be quenched, for the stomachs of
Englishmen would never bear it.

The English yeomen would not stand that kind of thing !

The new age was bringing into increasing prominence
not only the yeoman, but the squire. He survived the
difficulties of his family budget during the price-crisis, and
emerged under Elizabeth as the principal figure in the life
of the countryside. The wealth and power of the country
gentlemen had been increased, partly by their easy purchases
of monastic land, partly by the recent changes in the agricultural economy of their estates, which the land-hunger
had enabled them, and the price-rise had forced them, to
accomplish. And many of them had other interests beside
land, in the cloth trade and commerce oversea.

Apart from the absolute increase in their wealth, they
had acquired a new relative importance by the disappearance
of their former superiors, the feudal nobles, and the abbots
and priors. The gentry who now governed the counties
for the Crown as Justices of the Peace had no longer cause
to dread interference in their duties by ' overgreat subjects '
and their retainers. The old nobility who had disturbed
and terrorized Plantagenet England had lost their lands
and their power in the confiscations of the Wars of the
Roses ; and the policy of the early Tudor Kings continued
to depress their order, as in the Attainder of the lordly
Buckingham. The last nobles of the old type maintained
their feudal power along the Scottish border, where men
said ' there was no King but Percy.' They too were broken
by Elizabeth after the rebellion of the northern Earls in
1570. In other parts of England, such semi-sovereign
nobles had disappeared long before.

The families whom the Tudors raised up in their stead,

the Russells, Cavendishes, Seymours, Bacons, Dudleys, Cecils and Herberts rose to influence, not because they were feudal magnates, but because they were useful servants of the Crown. Their social affinities were with the rising class of gentry, whence they derived their origin, and to whom they still essentially belonged even when they were raised to be Peers of the Realm.

Not only political but economic causes were depressing the old nobility. They suffered from the fall in the value of money even more than the gentry, because they paid too little personal attention to the management of their far-flung properties, and were less quick than the smaller land-lords to evict tenants, terminate leases, impose fines and raise rents. In the Tudor period taken as a whole, the gentry rose while the nobles declined.

A distinguishing feature of the English gentry, which astonished foreign visitors as early as the reign of Henry VII, was their habit of turning their younger sons out of the manor-house to seek their fortunes elsewhere, usually as apprentices to thriving merchants and craftsmen in the towns. Foreigners ascribed the custom to English want of family affection. But it was also, perhaps, a wise instinct of ' what was best for the boy,' as well as a shrewd calculation of what was best for the family fortunes. The habit of leaving all the land and most of the money to the eldest son built up the great estates, which by steady accumulation down the years, became by Hanoverian times so marked a feature of English rural economy.

The younger son of the Tudor gentleman was not per-mitted to hang idle about the manor-house, a drain on the family income like the impoverished nobles of the Conti-nent who were too proud to work. He was away making money in trade or in law. He often ended life a richer and more powerful man than his elder brother left in the old home. Such men bought land and founded county families of their own, for they had been bred in the countryside and to the countryside they loved to return.

Foreigners were astonished at the love of the English gentry for rural life. ' Every gentleman,' they remarked, ' flieth into the country. Few inhabit cities and towns ; few have any regard of them.' (Starkey's *England, Temp.*

H. VIII, E.E.T.S., p. 93.) Though London might already be the greatest city in Europe, England was still in its essential life and feeling a rural community, whereas in France and Italy the Roman had deeply implanted the civilization of the city, that drew to itself all that was most vital in the life of the surrounding province. The English squire did not share the feelings of the ' Italian gentlemen of quality ' described by Robert Browning, pining unwillingly in his country home—

> Had I but plenty of money, money enough and to spare
> The house for me, no doubt, were a house in the city square.

The place for the squire, whether he were rich or poor, was at home in his manor-house, and he knew and rejoiced in the fact.

Owing to the habit among the gentry of apprenticing their younger sons to trade, our country avoided the sharp division between a rigid caste of nobles and an unprivileged bourgeoisie, which brought the French *ancien régime* to its catastrophe in 1789. Unlike the French, the English gentry did not call themselves ' nobles '—except the select few who sat in the House of Lords. The manor-house, its hospitality open to neighbours and friends of many different classes, was not ashamed to acknowledge a son in trade, besides another at the Inns of Court and a third perhaps in the family living. The ' landed ' and ' moneyed ' men might talk as if they were rivals, but in fact they were allied by blood and by interest. Recruits from the landed class were constantly entering town life, while money and men from the towns were constantly flowing back to fertilize the countryside.

Throughout Tudor, Stuart and early Hanoverian times, successful lawyers formed a large proportion of the ' new ' men who introduced themselves into the county circle by purchase of land and by building of manor-houses. The number of English county families who were founded by lawyers is even greater than those derived from the cloth trade. The process had begun in the Middle Ages : the fortunes of the Norfolk Pastons had been founded by one of Henry VI's judges. And the road opened yet wider before the men of law in the exciting, litigious and rapacious times of Henry VIII and his children, when lawyers of an adventurous turn had unusual opportunities to serve the government, and receive a very full reward, especially when, as in the case of the Bacons and Cecils, law was blended with courtiership and politics. Many of the lovely Tudor homes, small and great, that still adorn the English landscape, were paid for by money made in the Courts of Law.

There was much in common between the squire, the lawyer, the merchant and the yeoman. They were all men of the new age, not hankering after feudal ideals now passing away. And they tended to become Protestant, alike from interest and conviction. They evolved a kind of religion of the home, essentially ' middle class ' and quite unmediaeval.

The tendency of Protestant doctrine was to exalt the married state, and to dedicate the business life, in reaction against the mediaeval doctrine that the true life of ' religion ' was celibacy and monastic separation from the world. The permission to marry, conceded to the clergy under Edward VI and Elizabeth, was one symptom of this change of thought. The religious home was the Protestant ideal, with family prayer and private Bible reading in addition to the services and sacraments of the Church. These ideas and practices were by no means confined to the dissident Puritans : in late Tudor and in Stuart times they were the practice of Anglican families who loved and fought for the Prayer Book. The religion of the home and of the Bible became a social custom common to all English Protestants. It was found most often, perhaps, in the households of squires, yeomen and tradesmen, but it was widely extended among the cottages of the poor.

The new type of English religion idealized work, dedicating business and farming to God. As George Herbert quaintly and nobly wrote :

> ' Who sweeps a room as for Thy laws
> Makes that and the action fine.'

It was a good religion for a nation of shopkeepers and farmers.

The seed-time of these practices and ideas, which in the following century became so general, was the reign of

Edward VI and his elder sister, while Cranmer was producing the Prayer Book to stand beside the Bible, and
Queen Mary was providing English Protestantism with a
martyrology.   The anti-clerical revolution of Henry VIII,
with its unedifying scramble for Church property, had
lacked a moral basis, but the martyrs recorded in Foxe's
book provided one for the new national religion beginning
to emerge out of chaos.   When Elizabeth came to the
throne, the Bible and Prayer Book formed the intellectual
and spiritual foundation of a new social order.

The institutions of a country are always reflected in its
military system.   During the Hundred Years' War there
had been two military systems.   Home defence, against
domestic rebellion and Scottish invasion, was conducted
chiefly by local militia levied on a conscript basis.   The
more difficult war in France, which required a more professional soldiery, was conducted by war-bands following
fighting nobles and gentlemen who enlisted and paid them ;
the King indented with their employers to furnish him with
so many of these professionals for so much money.   This
dual system continued under Henry VII and Henry VIII,
with this difference, that the destruction of the military
power and landed wealth of the old nobility by the confiscations of the Wars of the Roses had taken the value out
of the indenture system.   Indeed, the system of indenting
with private individuals to supply an army for foreign war
was incompatible with the Tudor domestic policy of suppressing the retainers and military establishments of great
subjects.   But as the Kings could not afford to keep up a
standing army of their own, the troops hastily levied for
occasional foreign service were undisciplined, mutinous and
often useless, as the history of the Tudor war on the Continent was to show again and again.   The steady, devoted
bands who had followed the great lords to Crecy and Agincourt, no longer existed.   And as yet there was no royal
army.
English archery was still so good that firearms had not
yet displaced it.   Flodden was won by the archers.   Bow
and bill for the infantry, the lance for the cavalry was still
the rule.   The artillery, of which the King had a monopoly

in his Realm, was becoming an important arm, not only for sieges but for battles against rebels or Scots, as at Loose-Coat Field and Pinkie Cleugh. Under these conditions, the democratic conscript militia sufficed to make the King safe at home, so long as his policy was not too unpopular. But he was powerless to make conquests in Europe.

While the royal army did not exist, the royal navy was growing strong. Sole reliance could no longer be placed on conscripted merchant ships to hold the narrow seas in time of war. Henry VIII has been called ' the father of the English navy,' though Henry VII might perhaps dispute the title. The navy was placed under a separate government department and organised as a standing force in the King's pay. Henry VIII spent much of the royal and monastic wealth on this project. He not only built royal ships, but established dockyards at Woolwich and Deptford, where the Thames estuary made a surprise raid difficult, developed Portsmouth as a naval base, and fortified many harbours such as Falmouth Roads.

The formation of a professional navy for war purposes only, was the more important because naval tactics were, after 2000 years, entering on a new era. The placing of cannon in the broadside of a vessel transformed naval war from a mere grappling of ship with ship (the method used from the days of the ancient Egyptians and Greeks till late mediaeval times), into the manœuvring of floating batteries, which first showed their strength against the Armada. By proficiency in that new game England was to attain her sea-power and Empire, and Henry VIII's naval policy first put her in a way to win it.

In spite of much economic trouble, the standard of life was slowly going up in the early and middle Tudor period. When the more marked advance under Elizabeth had diffused a general sense of prosperity, William Harrison, the parson, recorded in 1577 the improvement in household conditions that had taken place since his father's day, ' not among the nobility and gentry only but likewise of the lowest sort in most places of our south country.'

' Our fathers [he writes] yea and we ourselves have lien full oft upon straw pallets, covered only with a sheet, under coverlets made of dagswain or hop harlots (I use their own terms) and a good round log under their heads instead of a bolster.   If it were so that our fathers or the good man of the house had a mattress or flockbed and thereto a sack of chaff to rest his head upon, he thought himself to be as well lodged as the lord of the town [village], that peradventure lay seldom in a bed of down or whole feathers.   Pillows were thought meet only for women in childbed.   As for servants, if they had any sheet above them, it was well, for seldom had they any under their bodies, to keep them from the pricking straws that ran oft through the canvas of the pallet and razed their hardened hides.'

Straw on the floor and straw in the bedding bred fleas, and some fleas carried plague.

Harrison also notes that chimneys have become general even in cottages, whereas ' in the village where I remain,' old men recalled that in ' their young days ' under the two Kings Harry, ' there were not above two or three chimneys if so many, in uplandish towns [villages], the religious houses and manor places of their lords always excepted, but each one made his fire against a reredoss in the hall where he dined and dressed his meat.'   The increasing use of coal instead of wood for the domestic hearth made it more disagreeable not to have chimneys, and the increasing use of bricks made it easier to build them, even if the walls of the house were of some other material.

Common houses and cottages were still of timber, or of ' half-timber ' with clay and rubble between the wooden uprights and cross-beams.   Better houses, especially in stone districts, were of stone.   But brick was gradually coming in, first of all in regions where stone was not to be had on the spot, and where timber was running short owing to the process of deforestation—chiefly, that is to say, in the eastern Counties.

Harrison also records a change during his own lifetime ' of treen [wooden] platters into pewter, and of wooden spoons into silver or tin.'   The age of forks was not yet come ; where knife and spoon would not avail, even Queen Elizabeth picked up the chicken bone deftly in her long fingers.   Until her reign ' a man should hardly find four pieces of pewter in a farmer's house.'   Of china there was as yet no question at all.

So primitive, in the early Tudor period, had been

household conditions. Such or worse they had been in all previous ages. But things were now on the way to the marked improvement noted by the Elizabethan parson. We must never forget, in picturing the past and specially the remoter past, the want of comforts and luxuries which we take for granted. Yet they have only been made general by slow processes of change, some of which, like the new farming, we call in question as having been in some respects unjust to the poor.

In the reign of Henry VIII, the long predominance of Gothic architecture may be said to have come to an end, after bursting out into the final magnificent flourishes of Wolsey's hall at Christ Church, Oxford, and the fan-vaulted roof of the chapel of King's College, Cambridge, completed by his royal master. Then the new age came in. Italian workmen ornamented the new quadrangle of Hampton Court with terracotta busts of Roman Emperors, entirely Renaissance in feeling and in design.

The Tudor period was not one of church building. Rather the lead and stones of Abbey churches were requisitioned for the ' gentleman's seats ' that took their place, or for the yeomen's farms of the new age. In the manorhouses, now everywhere being built or enlarged, spacious rooms, well-lighted galleries, wide lattice windows and oriels, instead of narrow loopholes, proclaimed the Tudor peace and comfort. The commonest form of large manorhouse was now an enclosed court, entered through a turretted gateway of gigantic proportions, frequently of brick. A generation later, under Elizabeth, when the need for fortifying a house had even more completely disappeared from men's minds, it became usual to build an open courtyard with three sides only, or to adopt the E-shaped form.

Every manor-house of any pretensions had a deer-park dotted with clumps of fine trees at various stages of growth, the whole enclosed by a high wooden pale. Sometimes two parks, one for fallow deer and one for red, diminished the arable land of the demesne, and sometimes, it is to be feared, the common lands of the village. On hunting mornings, the chime of hounds ' matched in mouth like bells ' chased the deer round and round the enclosure, while the gentlemen and ladies of the manor and their guests followed easily on horseback—and Lady Jane Grey stayed indoors and read Plato ! But there were also plenty of deer at large beyond the park pales, to be hunted more nobly ' at force ' across the countryside. Great herds of red deer roamed over the Pennines, the Cheviots and the northern moors. In the South, fallow deer ran wild in the forests, woods and fens, often issuing forth to attack the crops. One use of the enclosure was to provide fences against these visits made while the village slept.

Hunting did not usually mean fox-hunting : farmers for the most part were free to kill the red thief as best they could.[1] Gentlemen hunted the deer ; and everyone, on foot and horseback, hunted the hare—' poor Wat, far off upon a hill ! ' Horsemen and greyhounds pursued the swift-footed young bustards over the downs. The poaching of deer was a great feature of life ; the scholars of Oxford openly hunted Radley Park, till the owner was fain to throw down the pales in despair. As to fowling, though the hawk, the bow and the cross-bow were still the most usual methods, the ' fowling-piece ' was sometimes employed. (*Merry Wives*, iv. 2, 58.) But snaring, liming and trapping all sorts of birds and beasts were still conducted not only for use but for sport.

The English were already notorious in Europe for their devotion to horses and dogs, of which they bred and kept many varieties in great numbers. But the horse was still a cumbrous animal. The slim racer and hunter of eastern blood had not yet come in, and a gentleman's mount was still bred to carry a knight in his armour at full trot, rather than a huntsman at full gallop. The farm-horse was gradually beginning to share with the ox the labours of the plough.

It was still the age of the tournament, ridden before the eyes of sympathetic ladies and critical populace,

> The gravelled ground, with sleeves tied on the helm.
> On foaming horse, with swords and friendly hearts,

---

[1] Yet in some districts in Elizabeth's reign foxes and badgers were ' preserved by gentlemen to hunt and have pastime withal ' when they would otherwise have been ' rooted out,' Harrison says (Book III, ch. IV).

as Surrey, Henry VIII's courtier poet describes it. He
sings also of other play at that Court :

The dances short, long tales of great delight ;
With words and looks that tigers could but rue,
When each of us did plead the other's right.
The palme-play [courtyard tennis] where, despoiled for the game
With dazed eyes oft we by gleams of love
Have missed the ball, and got sight of our dame,
To bait her eyes that kept the leads above.

That gay Court owed its character to the young, athletic
Henry, one of the best archers in his own kingdom, not yet
grown an obese and angry tyrant, but himself the glass of
fashion and the mould of form. Leaving policy to his still
trusted Wolsey, he spent in delights and pageants and
masques the treasure which his careful father had laid up for
the nation's need. Not to have been at Court was indeed,
in Touchstone's words, to be damned. There the gentlemen of England learnt not only the intrigues of love and
politics, but music and poetry, and a taste for scholarship
and the arts, seeds which they took back to their rural homes
to plant there. The culture, art and scholarship of the
Italian Courts of the Renaissance had great influence on
the courtiers and nobles of England, from the time of the
Wars of the Roses until the reign of Elizabeth. The
mediaeval distinction between the learned clerk and the
barbarous fighting baron was coming to an end, blending
in the ideal of the all-accomplished 'gentleman.' The
' Courtier's, soldier's, scholar's, eye, tongue, sword,' the
Elizabethan ideal afterwards realized in Sir Philip Sidney,
had been rehearsed two generations before by Sir Thomas
Wyatt (1503–1542), a kind and faithful public servant in
a hard-hearted and faithless Court. He was just as happy
in the privacy of his country estate :

This maketh me at home to hunt and hawk
And in foul weather at my book to sit.
In frost and snow then with my bow to stalk
No man doth mark where I so ride or go ;
In lusty lees my liberty I take. . .
Here I am in Kent and Christendome
Among the muses where I read and rhyme.

The ' cultivated country gentlemen ' already existed, often like Wyatt, half a courtier. (See E. K. Chambers' and E. M. Tillyard's books on *Sir Thomas Wyatt*.)

At Court, Holbein and his studio were turning out apace portraits of Henry and of his chief nobles. Thence the fashion spread to the country houses, and family portraits took their place beside the tapestry that adorned the walls. Some of them were fine pictures by the Court painters, but most were creations of local talent—white-faced knights and ladies looking stiffly out at posterity from the painted boards. It was the beginning of a fashion that led up to Gainsborough and Reynolds.

The music in the Chapel Royal was perhaps the best in Europe. And it was the fashion at that Court, from the King downwards, to compose musical tunes, and verses to go with them. The Tudor age was the great age of English music and lyrical poetry, two sisters at a birth, and the impulse may in part be traced to the Court of the young Henry VIII. But the whole country was filled with men and women singing songs, composing the music and writing the verses. It was a form taken in England by the free, joyful spirit of the Renaissance ; but here it was a rustic spirit, mingled with the song of birds in the greenwood, and leading up to the full chorus of Shakespeare's England.

When the Tudor age began, Venice still held the East in fee. The precious goods of the Indies, still borne on camels' backs, continued as for ages past to reach the Levant overland. Thence Venetian ships carried the spices to England, returning with cargoes of wool to feed the looms on the Adriatic. The Venetian trader was therefore a well-known figure in our island. In 1497 one of them reported home the discovery of Newfoundland made by his country-man John Cabot, five years after Columbus' greater exploit.

The Venetian, our countryman, who went with a ship from Bristol in quest of new islands, is returned, and says that 700 leagues hence he discovered land, the territory of the Grand Cham. He coasted for 300 leagues and landed ; saw no human beings, but found some felled trees, wherefore he supposed there were inhabitants. He is now at Bristol with his wife. Vast honour is paid him ; he dresses in silk, and these English run after him like mad people ; . . . This discoverer of these places planted on his new found land a large cross, with a flag of England and another of St. Mark's by reason his being a Venetian, so that our banner has floated very far afield.

But it was significant of the future that the flag of St. Mark had not gone thus ' far afield ' in a Venetian ship.

After this discovery, prophetic of an end of things for Venice and a beginning of things for England, nothing much came of it for two generations, except indeed cod-fishing by English, French and Portuguese fishermen off the New Foundland coast.[1]   Throughout the early and middle Tudor period our commerce was conducted as before with the coast of Europe from the Baltic round to Spain and Portugal, most of all with the Netherlands, and above all with Antwerp, the centre of European business and finance. Even more rapidly than in the Fifteenth Century, the export of manufactured cloth by the Merchant Adventurers gained on the export of raw wool by the Staplers, and the volume of London's foreign trade continued to increase.   In the reigns of Henry VII and VIII English ships began to trade in the Mediterranean as far as Crete.   In 1486 an English Consul was established at Pisa, where there were English merchants exploiting Florentine rivalry against the Venetian monopoly.   But our goods still reached Italy chiefly in Italian ships.

Meanwhile the Portuguese were rounding the Cape of Good Hope and opening the oceanic route to the Eastern trade, a fatal blow to Venice.   More slowly the English followed them along the West Coast of Africa, in defiance of their claim to monopolise the Dark Continent.   As early as 1528 William Hawkins, father of a great line of seamen, traded in friendly fashion with the negroes of the Guinea coast for ivory.   It was his more famous son John who in Elizabeth's reign made the negroes themselves an article of export, and thereby almost destroyed the legitimate trade

---

[1] The increase of deep sea fishing was a feature of early Tudor times, and helped to build up the maritime population and strength of the country, soon to be turned to such great account.   The herring had recently moved from the Baltic into the North Sea, and our herring fishery had sprung to importance as a result.   ' These herrings,' wrote Camden, ' which in the times of our grandfathers swarmed only about Norway, now in our times by the bounty of Providence swim in great shoals round our coasts every year.'

with the natives, who learnt to regard the white man as their deadly enemy. In the reigns of Edward VI and Mary the West African trade in its proper form was still being developed, besides voyages to the Canaries, to Archangel and ventures as far as Moscow ; but except the cod-fishing off Newfoundland, nothing was done beyond the Atlantic by Englishmen before the reign of Elizabeth.

Although the ' vent of cloth ' was still conducted mainly on the old lines and in the old European markets, it was constantly on the increase, supplied by the even growing cloth manufacture in the towns and still more in the villages of England. After a stationary period in the Fifteenth Century, the cloth trade was again increasing by leaps and bounds. ' Enclosure for pasture ' was a result. Even before such enclosures were much complained of, foreigners had marvelled at the incredible number of sheep in England.

The manufacture of wool into finished cloth involved a number of processes, not all carried on by the same folk or in the same place. The capitalist *entrepreneur* passed on the raw material, the half-manufactured and the finished cloth from place to place, employing various classes of workmen or buying from various classes of masters in the process. William Forrest, in Edward VI's reign, grows prosaically lyrical over the ubiquitous cloth trade that employed so many kinds of skill.

> No town in England, village or borough
> But thus with clothing to be occupied.
> Though not in each place clothing clean thorough,
> But as the town is, their part so applied.
> Here spinners, here weavers, there clothes to be dyed,
> With fullers and shearers as be thought best,
> As the Clothier may have his cloth drest.

In another stanza he urges the now popular policy of encouraging the cloth trade at the expense of the declining export of raw wool :

> The wool the Staplers do gather and pack
> Out of the Royalme to countries foreign,
> Be it revoked and stayed aback,
> That our clothiers the same may retain,

> All kind of work folks here to ordain,
> Upon the same to exercise their feat
> By tucking, carding, spinning and to beat.

Most of the weaving was done on the domestic system ; the loom, owned and plied by the goodman of the house, was set up in garret or kitchen. But the fulling-mills on the western streams must needs be more like factories, and some weaving was already done on what may be called the factory system. The clothier, John Winchcomb, was so rich and so princely that after his death in 1520 he became a legendary hero of ballad as ' Jack of Newbury,' a rival in fame to Dick Whittington himself. Tradition said that he led a hundred of his prentices to Flodden Field and feasted King Harry at his house. The Elizabethan Ballad proceeds to describe his factory of cloth:

> Within one room, being large and long
> There stood two hundred looms full strong.
> Two hundred men, the truth is so,
> Wrought in these rooms all in a row.
> By every one a pretty boy
> Sate making quilts with mickle joy.
> And in another place hard by
> A hundred women merrily
> Were carding hard with joyful cheer
> Who singing sat with voices clear.

Possibly the cheerfulness, certainly the numbers, of the hands in the factory, are exaggerated by the retrospective ardour of the poet (E. Power, *Mediaeval People*, p. 158). Jack of Newbury of course founded a county family. His son supported the King against the Pilgrimage of Grace, acquired Abbey land, and sat in Parliament.

The volume of internal trade was far greater than the external. England still imported only luxuries for the rich. Her people were fed, clothed, housed and warmed by home products.

The rivers were a great means of transport especially for the heaviest goods, like the railways to-day. Even inland towns like York, Gloucester, Norwich, Oxford, Cambridge, were to a large extent ports on rivers.

But the roads were used, then as now, for all local distribution and for much traffic in bulk. The badness of the roads, though execrable by our standards, was not absolute. In dry weather they were used by waggons, and in all weathers by pack-horse trains.   As far as possible the roads followed by commerce kept to chalk and other hard soils, of which much of England is composed.   Where they had to cross marshy or clay belts, the traffic was helped by causeways ; some of these were built by the merchants who needed them, in the absence of any effectual road authority. Leland notes the causeway between Wendover and Ayles-bury, ' else the way, in wet time, as in low stiff clay, were tedious to pass.'

Even for long distance traffic of heavy goods the supremacy of water over road was not complete.   South-ampton, for example, flourished as a port serving London. Certain classes of goods were regularly unshipped at Southampton and sent by road to the capital, to save the vessels from the necessity of rounding Kent.

Books for Further Reading

Darby's *Historical Geography of England* (1936), Chap. IX ; Miss Toulmin Smith's edition of *Leland's England* ; Lord Ernle, *English Farming*, chap. III ; Tawney, *Agrarian problem in the Sixteenth Century* ; and *Religion and the Rise of Capitalism* ; *Social England*, ed. Traill, vols. II and III ; Baskerville, *English Monks and the Suppression of the Monasteries* ; Lipson, *Ec. Hist. England*, II.   In working on this Chapter, I have been much indebted to the advice and notes of Mr. John Saltmarsh of King's College, Cambridge.

CHAPTER VI

SHAKESPEARE'S ENGLAND [1564-1616]

I

The Towns. The Countryside. Classes and modes of life. Wales. The Northern counties. Elizabethan homes. Inns. Social relationships. Militia. Law. J.P.s. Poor Law.

(Queen Elizabeth, 1558-1603. The Armada, 1588.)

AFTER the economic and religious unrest of the middle Tudor period, followed the golden age of England. Golden ages are not all of gold, and they never last long. But Shakespeare chanced upon the best time and country in which to live, in order to exercise with least distraction and most encouragement the highest faculties of man. The forest, the field and the city were there in perfection, and all three are needed to perfect the poet. His countrymen, not yet cramped to the service of machines, were craftsmen and creators at will. Their minds, set free from mediaeval trammels, were not yet caught by Puritan or other modern fanaticisms. The Elizabethan English were in love with life, not with some theoretic shadow of life. Large classes, freed as never before from poverty, felt the upspring of the spirit and expressed it in wit, music and song. The English language had touched its moment of fullest beauty and power. Peace and order at last prevailed in the land, even during the sea-war with Spain. Politics, so long a fear and oppression, and soon in other forms to be a fear and oppression again, were for a few decades simplified into service paid to a woman, who was to her subjects the symbol of their unity, prosperity and freedom.

The Renaissance, that had known its springtime long ago in its native Italy, where biting frosts now nipped it, came late to its glorious summer in this northern isle. In the days of Erasmus, the Renaissance in England had been confined to scholars and to the King's Court. In Shakespeare's day it had in some sort reached the people. The Bible and the world of classical antiquity were no longer left to the learned few. By the agency of the grammar schools, classicism filtered through from the study into the theatre and the street, from the folio to the popular ballad which familiarized the commonest auditories with *The Tyranny of Judge Appius* and *The Miserable state of King Midas* and the other great tales of Greece and Rome. The old Hebrew and the Graeco-Roman ways of life, raised from the grave of the remote past by the magic of scholarship, were opened to the general understanding of Englishmen, who treated them not as dead archaeological matter, but as new spheres of imagination and spiritual power, to be freely converted to modern use. While Shakespeare transformed Plutarch's *Lives* into his own *Julius Caesar* and *Antony*, others took the Bible and fashioned out of it a new way of life and thought for religious England.

And during these same fruitful years of Elizabeth, the narrow seas, amid whose tempests English mariners had for centuries been trained, expanded into the oceans of the world, where romance and wealth were to be won by adventurous youth, trading and fighting along newly discovered shores. Young, light-hearted England, cured at last of the Plantagenet itch to conquer France, became conscious of herself as an island with an ocean destiny, glad, after that Armada storm, to feel the safety and freedom that the guarded seas could give, while the burden of distant Empire was not yet laid upon her shoulders.

There is, of course, another side to all this, as there is to every picture of human well-being and well-doing. The cruel habits of centuries past were not easily or quickly to be shed. The overseas activity of the Elizabethans paid no regard to the rights of the negroes whom they transported into slavery, or the Irish whom they robbed and slaughtered: some even of the noblest English, like John Hawkins on the Gold Coast and Edmund Spenser in Ireland, failed to see what dragons' teeth they were helping to sow. At home, the woman hunted by her neighbours as a witch, the Jesuit missionary mounting the scaffold to be cut to pieces alive, the Unitarian burning at the stake, the Puritan dissenter hanged or ' laden with irons in dangerous and loathsome gaols,' had little joy of the great era. But in Elizabeth's England such victims were not numerous, as elsewhere in Europe. We escaped the pit of calamity into which other nations were being thrust—the Spanish Inquisition and the vast scale of martyrdom and massacre that turned the Netherlands and France into a shambles in the name of religion. Looking across the channel and seeing these things, the English rejoiced that they were islanders and that wise Elizabeth was their Queen.

As the tour of Henry VIII's England was made and recorded by the antiquary Leland, so the tour of Elizabeth's happier kingdom was made and recorded by the greatest of all our antiquaries, William Camden, in his *Britannia*. And just before him William Harrison, the parson, and just after him Fynes Moryson, the traveller, left us pictures of the English life of their day, which it is a pleasure to collate with the more vivid glimpses in Shakespeare.

It is probable that the population of England and Wales at the end of the Queen's reign had passed four millions, about a tenth of its present size. More than four-fifths lived in the rural parts ; but of these a fair proportion were engaged in industry, supplying nearly all the manufactures required by the village, or, like the clothiers, miners and quarrymen, working for a more general market. The bulk of the population cultivated the land or tended sheep.

Of the minority who inhabited towns, many were engaged, at least for part of their time, in agriculture. A provincial town of average size contained 5000 inhabitants. The towns were not overcrowded, and had many pleasant gardens, orchards and farmsteads mingled with the rows of shops. Some smaller towns and ports were in process of decay. The recession of the sea, the silting up of rivers (which gradually put Chester on the Dee out of action as a port), the increase in the size of ships demanding larger harbours, the continued migration of the cloth and other manufactures in rural villages and hamlets, were all causes of the decline of some of the older centres of industry or commerce.

Yet the town population was on the increase in the island taken as a whole. York, the capital of the North ; Norwich, a great centre of the cloth trade, welcoming skilled refugees from Alva's Netherlands ; Bristol with mercantile and inland trade of its own wholly independent of London—

these three were in a class by themselves, with perhaps 20,000 inhabitants each. And the new oceanic conditions of trade favoured other port towns in the West, like Bideford.

But, above all, London, absorbing more and more of the home and foreign commerce of the country at the expense of many smaller towns, was already a portent for size in England and even in Europe. When Mary Tudor died it may have had nearly 100,000 inhabitants ; when Elizabeth died it may already have touched 200,000. It was spreading most rapidly in the ' liberties ' outside its old walls ; in the heart of the City there were small open spaces, and houses with gardens, courtyards and stables. In spite of the recurrent visits of the Plague (the old Black Death) and the novel visitation of the ' sweating sickness,' Tudor London was relatively healthy and deaths were fewer than births. It was not yet as congested as it became in the early Eighteenth Century, when its still vaster population was more closely packed in slums, further removed from access to the country, and more unhealthy, although the Plague had by that time disappeared, to give place to smallpox and typhus.

The London of Queen Elizabeth, by its size, wealth and power, was the most formidable unit in the Kingdom. Socially, intellectually and politically it exercised an influence that went far to secure the success of the Protestant revolution in the Sixteenth Century and of the Parliamentary revolution in the Seventeenth. The area of the City was now the fortress of a purely civic and mercantile community, unchallenged within its own borders by any rival influence. The great monasteries and convents of mediaeval London had disappeared ; the laity were supreme, and refashioned their religion in the City churches and in their own homes after the Protestant and individual patterns of their preference. Neither monarchy nor aristocracy had any strongholds within the City boundaries. The royal power lay outside in Whitehall and Westminster on one flank, and in the Tower upon the other. Even the great nobles were leaving their mediaeval quarters in the City and migrating to mansions in the Strand or in the neighbourhood of Court and Parliament at Westminster. The power and privilege of the Mayor and citizens, with their formidable militia, formed a State within the State—a society that was purely bourgeois, inside the larger England that was still monarchical and aristocratic. And the leaven of London worked throughout the land. The feeding of Tudor London governed the agricultural policy of the home counties, and the same influence was felt in varying degrees further afield. Food was wanted in the capital, in vast quantity for the population, and of the best quality for the richest tables of the kingdom. Kent with its enclosed fields, already called ' the garden of England,' was specifically London's fruit-garden, rich with ' apples beyond measure and also with cherries.' The barley of East Anglia, coming through brewing towns like Royston, quenched the daily thirst of the Londoner ; while Kent and Essex were learning to train hops to flavour his beer. For the rest, the wheat and rye that made London's bread, were grown all over the south-eastern counties.

Thus the great market of the capital helped to change agricultural methods, by inducing districts best fitted for one particular crop to specialize on that. Near London, Norden the topographer noticed ' another sort of husband-man, or yeoman rather, who wade in the weeds of gentle-men, . . . who having great feedings for cattle,' sell their fat stock at Smithfield, ' where also they store themselves with lean. There are also those that live by carriage for other men, and to that end they keep carts and carriages, carry milk, meal and other things to London, whereby they live very gainfully.' In regions so fortunately situated, the pressure to enclose the land was strong.

Besides London, there were other markets for agricultural produce. Few towns, if any, could grow all the food they required in the ' town fields ' without need to purchase outside. And even in the country, if one rural district had a bad season, it could buy the surplus of other districts through middlemen, unless the harvest had been poor all over England, when, perhaps once in a decade, there might be considerable importation from abroad. In normal years some English corn was exported. Huntingdonshire, Cambridgeshire and other regions of the Ouse valley, sent great quantities of wheat through Lynn and the Wash to

Scotland, Norway and the cities of the Netherlands. Much food came to Bristol and the Western towns from the granary of central England, the open fields of south-eastern Warwickshire, the ' Feldon ' lying between the Avon and Edgehill. But the other half of Warwickshire lying north-west of Avon, as Leland and Camden both noted, was deep woodland, thinly studded with pastoral settlements ; it was the Forest of Arden. Thus the winding Avon, spanned by Stratford's famous bridge of ' fourteen arches of stone,' divided the lonely forest from the populous cornlands. One born and bred in the town upon its banks saw, in his boyhood's rambles, what was best in wild nature on one side of the river, and what was most characteristic of man upon the other.

Until the Eighteenth Century with its highly capitalized farming, it was not possible to ripen enough wheat to feed the whole population. Oats, wheat, rye and barley were all grown, some more, some less, according to the soil and climate. Oats prevailed in the North ; wheat and rye in most parts of England, except the south-west where rye was little grown. Everywhere barley abounded, and much of it went into beer. The West, with its apple orchards, drank cider ; and the pears of Worcestershire gave perry, which Camden condemned as ' a counterfeit wine, both cold and flatulent.' In all parts of England the village grew a variety of crops for its own use, and its bread was often a mixture of different kinds of grain. Fynes Moryson, who knew the chief countries of Europe well, wrote, shortly after Queen Elizabeth's death—

' The English husbandmen eat barley and rye brown bread, and prefer it to white bread as abiding longer in the stomach, and not so soon digested with their labour ; but citizens and gentlemen eat most pure white bread, England yielding all kinds of corn in plenty.[1]

' The English have abundance of white meats, of all kinds of flesh, fowl and fish and of all things good for food. In the seasons of the year the English eat fallow deer plentifully, as bucks in summer and

---

[1] Harrison, writing a generation earlier (circa 1577) says the same thing :

' The bread throughout our land is made of such grain as the soil yieldeth, nevertheless the gentility commonly provide themselves sufficiently of wheat for their own tables, whilst their household and poor neighbours in some shires are forced to content themselves with rye or barley, yea and in time of dearth many with bread made out of beans, peason or oats and some acorns among.'

does in winter, which they bake in pasties, and this venison pasty is a dainty, rarely found in any other kingdom.   England, yea perhaps one County thereof, hath more fallow deer than all Europe that I have seen.   No kingdom in the world hath so many dove-houses. Likewise brawn is a proper meat to the English, not known to others. English cooks, in comparison with other nations, are most commended for roasted meats.'

This experienced traveller goes on to praise our beef and mutton as the best in Europe, and our bacon as better than any except that of Westphalia.

'The English inhabitants [he continues] eat almost no flesh com-moner than hens, and for geese they eat them in two seasons, when they are fatted upon the stubble after harvest and when they are green about Whitsuntide.   And howsoever hares are thought to nourish melancholy, yet they are eaten as venison both roast and boiled.   They have also great plenty of conies [rabbits] the flesh whereof is fat, tender and more delicate than any I have eaten in other parts.   The German conies [our traveller declares] are more like roasted cats than the English conies.'

Meat and bread were the chief foods.   Vegetables were little eaten with meat ; cabbages helped to make the pottage.   Potatoes were just beginning to come in to some garden plots, but were not yet grown as a crop in the fields.

Puddings and stewed fruit did not yet play so great a part in the Englishman's table as in later centuries, though sugar was already obtained in moderate quantities from Mediter-ranean lands.   The time of dinner, the chief meal, was at eleven or twelve, and supper some five hours later.

Since the English village, whether in the western lands of old enclosure or in the ' champion ' regions of the open field, still grew its own food, ' subsistence agriculture ' was the basis of English life.   But, as we have seen, the self-supply-ing village also grew wool and food-stuffs for some special market at home or abroad.   ' Industrial crops ' were also coming much into use : flax grew well in some parts of Lincolnshire ; woad, madder and the great fields of saffron in Essex (whence ' Saffron Walden ' already had taken its name) supplied the dyers of cloth, who had previously depended on foreign imports.

Such specialization for the market demanded enclosure and private methods of farming.   The new lands won from forest, marsh and waste, were now always enclosed with hedges and farmed on the individualist system. The area of open field and common pasture did not increase as the total area under cultivation increased. The bleak open fields, though not much reduced in acreage, were relatively a smaller part of the farmlands of the Kingdom than they had formerly been.

It was the low-lying clay districts that produced the surplus corn for the home and foreign market. The sheep, that supplied the wool and cloth trades, fed on the thin up-land pastures which alternate with the clay valleys in the geographic structure of the island. The chalk downs and the wolds—the Chilterns, the Dorset Heights, the Isle of Wight, the Cotswolds, the Lincoln and Norfolk ridges, and many moorlands of the North, had always produced the best wool. On such hillsides, foreign and native travellers in Tudor England marvelled at the number and size of the flocks, unparalleled elsewhere in Europe. The sheep on the less fertile lands were often half starved, but their fleeces were the most valuable in the world, owing to some quality latent in the soil.

The increased demand for sheep and cattle in Tudor times caused, as we have seen, some highly unpopular en-closures of arable clay-land for pasture. The valley sheep were fatter, but their wool proved less good than that of their leaner brethren of the uplands. Yet the new lowland pastures were not unprofitable : though their fleeces were less fine, the demand for coarser wools was also on the increase, and larger supplies of mutton and beef were con-sumed by a prosperous and hospitable generation, whose carnivorous habits amazed foreign visitors accustomed to a more farinaceous diet. The Midlands therefore continued in Elizabeth's reign to add sheep and cattle to corn. Rugby ' abounded in butchers.' The cattle fairs of Leicestershire and Northamptonshire were famous. The great quantities of cattle in the island helped all leather industries : the southern English walked on leather, and disdained the ' wooden shoes ' that foreigners were fain to wear. Clogs, however, were very generally worn in the thrifty North, and Scots lads and lasses went barefoot.

The breeding of horses had to keep pace with an ever-increasing demand. The horse was very gradually replacing the ox at cart and plough ; [1] and the general prosperity of the country demanded more riding-horses, as in good years we demand more motor-cars. In many parts of Yorkshire and on the grass moors of the turbulent Border country, the breeding of horses and cattle was more important than the sheep-farming which prevailed there in later and more settled times. It was not sheep but cattle that the Mosstroopers drove off in their midnight raids.

Though sheep and cattle were now reared in such abundance in England, they were, by our modern standards, small and thin until the era of the Eighteenth Century improvements. For as yet there were only very inadequate means of feeding them during the winter months.

> ' From Christmas to May
> Weak cattle decay '

sang Thomas Tusser, the poet of Elizabethan agriculture. And the open-field system, still prevalent in half the country, afforded neither sufficient shelter nor sufficient grazing for beasts.

One region of England was still a world by itself, the great fen that stretched from Lincoln to Cambridge, from King's Lynn to Peterborough. Already in the later years of Elizabeth there were projects debated in Parliament, to drain Fenland as the Dutch had drained Holland, and so reclaim its watery, reedy solitudes to rich cornfields and pasture. But the great design was not carried out till an age when more capital was to be had for such ventures—in Stuart times for the south half of the fen, and in Hanoverian times for the north. Meanwhile the fenmen continued to dwell round its shores and on its innumerable oozy islands —living an amphibious life, and varying their traditional occupations with the changing seasons of the year.

' The upper and north part of Cambridgeshire [Camden writes] is all over divided into river isles, which all summer long afford a most delightful green prospect, but in winter time are almost all laid under water, farther every way than a man can see, and in some sort re-

---

[1] The process was very gradual, from Tudor to Hanoverian times ; persons now living have seen oxen ploughing in Victoria's England.

sembling the sea itself. The inhabitants of this and the rest of the fenny country (which reaches 68 miles from the borders of Suffolk to Wainfleet in Lincolnshire) are a sort of people (much like the place) of brutish, uncivilized tempers, envious of all others, whom they call *Upland men ;* and usually walking aloft upon a sort of stilts they all keep to the business of grazing, fishing and fowling. All this country in the winter time, and sometimes for the greatest part of the year, is laid under water by the rivers Ouse, Grant (Cam), Nen, Welland, Glene and Witham, for want of sufficient passages. But when they once keep to their proper channels, it so strangely abounds with rich grass and rank hay (by them called *Lid*) that when they've mown enough for their own use, in November they burn up the rest to make it come again the thicker. About which time a man may see all the moorish country round about of a light fire, to his great wonder. Besides it affords great quantity of turf and sedge for firing, reeds for thatching. Elders also and other watershrubs, especially willows, either growing wild, or else set on the banks of rivers to prevent their overflowing ; which being frequently cut down come again with a numerous offspring. 'Tis of these that baskets are made.' (Camden's *Britannia*, p. 408, Gibson's edition.)

The taking of wild fowl for the market was conducted by the fenmen on an immense scale. The wild geese and duck were captured hundreds at a time, being driven or lured into long cages of netting called ' decoys.' Rents were paid largely in fixed quantities of eels, counted by the thousand. It may perhaps be doubted whether the Fenmen had such ' brutish uncivilized tempers ' as the ' upland men ' told Camden. In any case it is a mistake to suppose, as many writers have done, that because their life was amphibious, because they herded their cattle and sheep on stilts, and because they went about in boats, fishing, fowling and reed cutting, that therefore they were any more ' lawless ' than the farmer who carted his corn on dry land. Recent research (H. C. Darby, *The Mediaeval Fenland*, 1940) has shown that throughout the Middle Ages, from the time of Domesday Book and beyond, the laws and customs of the Manorial system held good throughout Fenland ; that rents and services were regularly paid to the great Abbeys and to their successors after the Dissolution ; that the most complicated laws, rules and divisions of proprietary and fishing rights were observed among the fenmen ; that the most elaborate system of embankment and 'sewerage' was maintained by constant labour and skill, without which the great waterways would have become unnavigable, and Lincoln, Lynn, Boston, Wisbech, Cambridge, St. Ives, Peterborough and the lesser towns of the region would have lost most of their trade and communications. 'Almost every stream and bank in Fenland,' writes Dr. Darby, ' had, in one way or another, someone who was held responsible for it.' In short, the Fenland, before its reclamation by the great drainage operations of Stuart and Hanoverian times, was indeed an amphibious region, but with a highly specialized economic system of its own.

In the midst of these scenes of wild nature, Ely Cathedral had for centuries floated like an ark upon the waters, its two towers and two long shining roofs far seen on distant horizons. In its shadow lay the Palace where the Bishop held his court. He still exercised remnants of the authority which his mediaeval predecessors had enjoyed in the so-called ' County Palatine ' of Ely Isle. But in fact the Reformation had reduced the independent power of the Clergy. The State now held the Church in check, sometimes with an arrogant disregard of spiritual interests. Queen Elizabeth compelled Bishop Cox to surrender Ely Place in Holborn, London, and its famous fruit-gardens to her favourite, Sir Christopher Hatton. And when Cox died she kept the see vacant for eighteen years for the benefit of the Crown. Yet whenever a Bishop of Ely was allowed to exist, he was the chief ruler of Fenland—till first Oliver Cromwell and then the draining Dukes of Bedford acquired in the region an influence more than episcopal.

Besides Fenland, two other regions, the Principality of Wales and the Northern Border, differed from the social and economic structure of the rest of Elizabethan England. But they were approximating to the general pattern, and of the two, Wales had recently moved furthest along the road leading to modern life.

Throughout the Middle Ages, Wales had been the seat of military and social conflict between the wild Welsh, nursing their ancient tribal ways in the high places of the hills, and the ' Marcher Lords,' champions of English feudalism

F

in their castles along the valleys.   During the Wars of the
Roses, the Marcher Lords had turned eastwards to play
leading parts in the dynastic strife of England, with the
happy result that their independent power was extinguished.
By the end of the Fifteenth Century their principal castles
and estates had passed into the King's hands.

Here then was an opportunity for the amalgamation of
Wales with England under the Crown, provided only that
the operation were effected without wronging and exacer-
bating the national feeling and traditions of the Welsh, as
the sentiment of the Irish was so disastrously alienated by
Tudor policy.   Fortunately in Wales the circumstances
were more propitious.   No religious difference arose to
divide the old inhabitants from the English, and there was
no movement to ' colonize ' the Principality by robbing the
natives of their land.   By good chance, Bosworth Field
placed a Welsh dynasty on the throne of England, thereby
making loyalty to the Tudors a point of national pride with
all the inhabitants of Wales.

Under these happy auspices Henry VIII effected the
legal, parliamentary and administrative union of the two
countries.   The English county system, the rule of the
Justices of the Peace, and the body of English law were
extended all over the Principality, and the leading Welsh
gentry were flattered by representing their counties in the
Parliament at Westminster.   The Council of Wales, a court
of monarchical power analogous to the Star Chamber and
the Council of the North, usefully enforced order during the
long period of transition from old to new.   Feudalism in
the valleys had been extinguished with the Marcher Lords,
and tribalism in the hills now also disappeared, without any
violent conflict such as marked its end in the Scottish Highlands two centuries later.   In Elizabeth's reign Wales was
in process of settling down as a part of England.   Already
the structure of government, and to a large extent the form
of society had been adapted to the English model.   But
Wales retained her native language, poetry and music.
Her soul was still her own.

The Welsh gentry, an amalgam of former tribal chiefs,
former Marcher Lords, and ' new men ' of the type so well
known in that era, were well content with the Tudor rule,

which gave their class the same advantages in Wales as in England. Some of them were already accumulating great estates under the recently introduced English land-laws, and these properties swelled to vast size in years to come. But in Elizabeth's reign and for some time afterwards there was also a numerous class of Welsh gentry of smaller wealth and pretension. Major General Berry reported to Oliver Cromwell from his command in Wales—'You can sooner find fifty gentlemen of £100 a year than five of £500.' Most of them, like the corresponding class of small squires in England, flourished in Tudor and early Stuart times, but disappeared in the course of the Eighteenth Century, leaving Wales a land of great estates.

But the essential part of the Welsh people was to be sought not among the landowners but among the small tenant farmers. Large farms of the commercial type did not grow up in Wales to the same extent as in England. Nor, on the other hand, were the farms divided and sub-divided to excess as among the unfortunate peasantry of Ireland. The sound basis of modern Welsh society was laid in tenant farms of the peasant and family type, small, but not too small to maintain the cultivators in hardy self-respect. Their relation to the landlords, who undertook improvements and repairs, resembled the system of agricultural England, rather than the less happy relationship of the impoverished tenant to the exploiting landlord in Ireland or the Scottish Highlands.

The Dissolution of the Monasteries had been carried through in Wales in the same way and with the same social consequences as in England. There had been no revolt against it, like the northern Pilgrimage of Grace. The Welsh upper class found their advantage in the Reformation, and the peasantry accepted it with indifference born of ignorance. If they did not understand the Prayer Book and Bible in the foreign tongue of England, neither had they understood the Latin Mass. As yet religion passed them by. Early in Elizabeth's reign the Welsh peasantry were in a state of intellectual torpor and educational neglect, compatible indeed with all that is good in country life and old tradition, but certain ere long to be disturbed by some outside influence. What would it be? The Jesuit missionaries, who might have broken the virgin soil, left Wales alone.   At length, in the last decades of Elizabeth's reign the Established Church began to do its duty, and brought out a Welsh translation of Bible and Prayer Book. The foundations were thereby laid for popular Welsh Protestantism, and for the great educational and religious movements of the Eighteenth Century.

Under the Tudor Kings the life of England north of the Trent bore a character of its own.   The constant troubles of the Scottish border, the poverty of the whole region except the clothing valleys and the mining districts, the greater strength of old feudal loyalties and pretensions, and the greater popularity of the monasteries and the old religion differentiated it from the rest of England in the reign of Henry VIII, and to a less extent under Elizabeth.

In the early years of Henry, the Border was still ruled by its fighting families, particularly the Percies and Nevilles, of whom the Earls of Northumberland and Westmorland were the heads.   Among the armed farmers of these pastoral shires, a fierce spirit of personal independence was combined with loyalty to the hereditary chiefs who led them to war, not only against occasional Scottish invasion and frequent cattle raiding, but sometimes against the Tudor government itself.   The Pilgrimage of Grace (1536) was made in defence of monasteries, and also in defence of the quasi-feudal power of the noble families of the Border against the intruding force of the new Monarchy.   Henry seized the opportunity of the suppression of that rising to crush feudalism, and to extend the royal power, governing Yorkshire and the Border Counties through Wardens of the Marches dependent on the Crown's commission instead of their own hereditary influence.   Much of Henry's work was never undone, particularly in Yorkshire.   But Northumberland and Cumberland were seldom really at rest. The policy of Henry VIII and Edward VI was foolishly hostile to Scotland, and the occasional wars and perpetual illwill between the two nations prolonged the disturbed state of the border shires.   Under Mary the Roman Catholic influence was revived, and with it the power of the Percy family which Henry VIII had broken.

And so, when Elizabeth came to the throne, the battle between the old and the new religion, between the power of the Crown and the power of feudalism was not yet fully decided in the far North. Such was the state of things in the more civilized parts of the Border, the seaward plains of Northumberland on the East, and of Cumberland on the West. Between them lay the Middle Marches, the moors and hills of the Cheviot district, where a yet more lawless and primitive state of society survived in the regions of Redesdale and North Tyne. Those robber valleys, cut off by trackless wastes of grass ' bent,' heather and wet moss-hag from the more civilized lands round about, were inhabited by clans who paid little heed to the King's writ or even to the feudal power of the Percies, Nevilles and Dacres. Indeed, the only allegiance of the warriors of these wild regions was loyalty towards their own clans. Family feeling served, more than anything else, to protect culprits and defy the law. Stolen property could not be followed up and recovered in the thieving valleys, because each raider was protected by the revengeful jealousy of a warlike tribe. Small families came for protection under the rule of the Charltons who answered for North Tyne. The Halls, Reeds, Hedleys, Fletchers of Redesdale, the Charltons, Dodds, Robsons and Milbournes of North Tynedale, were the real political units within a society that knew no other organization. The Crown when it raised taxes, secured the tribute through the agency of the clan chiefs.

The royal commissioners, reporting in 1542 and 1550 on the state of the Border (Hodgson's *Northumberland*, ii, pp. 171–248), estimated that there were 1500 armed and able-bodied men in these two lawless valleys. The meagre soil could not yield food enough for their families, so, like the Scottish Highlanders, they eked out their living by raids on the cattle of their richer neighbours in the seaward plains to east and west. They were in close league with the robbers of Scottish Liddesdale, where a similar state of society existed. The Mosstroopers of either nation, when close pressed by the ' fray ' of the men they had robbed, could slip over the Border and be safe till the danger had passed. But usually no English officer dared ' follow the fray ' even into North Tyne or Rede, still less into Liddes-dale. The robber strongholds, built of oak trunks, covered with turf to prevent the application of fire, were hid in unapproachable wildernesses, among treacherous mosses, through which no stranger knew the paths. Henry VIII's commissioners did not venture to suggest to their royal master the expense of conquering and occupying North Tyne and Rede, but only a better system of watch and ward against the raiders, and a stronger force of lances in Har-bottle and Chipchase Castles on the edge of the lawless region, to bridle the constant invasion of the Lowlands.

Such was the society, much the same on both sides of the Border, which produced the popular poetry of the Border Ballads, transmitted by word of mouth from one generation to another. Many of the stanzas took the shape we know in the days of Elizabeth and Mary Queen of Scots. These ballads, almost always tragic, describe such incidents of life and death as were of daily occurrence in those regions. Utterly different from the songs and poetry of Shakespeare's more gentle England, are these rough outpourings of the sombre North. A pair of lovers in South English song or ballad run a fair chance of ' living happily ever afterwards.' But to assume the part of lover in a Border Ballad is a desperate undertaking. No father, mother, brother or rival will have pity before it is too late. Like the Homeric Greeks, the Borderers were cruel and barbarous men, slaying each other like beasts of the forest, but high in pride and honour and rough faithfulness ; and they were also (what men no longer are) untaught natural poets, able to express in words of power the inexorable fate of man and woman, and pity for the cruelties they nevertheless con-stantly inflicted on one another.

In Elizabeth's reign political relations with Scotland were greatly and permanently bettered, because the government of the two countries had now a common interest in defending the Reformation against its enemies at home and abroad. Border warfare between Scottish and English armies came to an end, and cattle raiding as between the two nations was at least diminished. But the English robbers of Redesdale and North Tyne continued to raid the farms of their more civilized fellow-countrymen. In the middle of Elizabeth's

reign, Camden was unable to pay an antiquarian visit to
Housesteads on the Roman Wall 'for fear of the Mosstroopers,' who occupied that region in force.   And the
Grahams of Netherby, a clan situated on the Esk near where
it flows into Solway, were perpetually harrying the lands of
their Cumbrian neighbours.   The levy of blackmail and
the abduction of men and women from their homes to be
held to ransom, were common incidents of life till the end
of the Queen's reign.

But although mosstrooping continued, the feudal power
of the Percies, Dacres and Nevilles was wholly destroyed
after the suppression of their rebellion in 1570.   After that
crisis, Northumberland and Cumberland were governed
by noblemen loyal to government.

Early in the reign, Mass was still said in parish churches
within thirty miles of the Border, under the protection of
Catholic nobles and gentry.   But Protestantism made
progress among the people with the help of missionaries
like Bernard Gilpin, 'the Apostle of the North.'   The
Bishops of Carlisle were zealous in the work of gradually
enforcing uniformity, as the Queen's government grew
stronger.   But the warrior farmers of the 'riding' districts
were not men to be coerced or easily led, either in religion or
anything else.   Change came slowly up that way.

Until the end of Elizabeth's reign many farmers of Cumberland and Northumberland held their land by rendering
military service when called upon by the Wardens of the
Marches.   These light horsemen of the North, whether in
the service of the government or of freebooting clans, wore
leather coats and steel caps, were armed with a lance and
bow or pistol, and rode surefooted nags of a local breed that
knew their way through the mosses.

After the Union of the Crowns of England and Scotland
on the head of James I (1603) co-operation became possible
between the authorities on the two sides of the Border who
were able at last to suppress the Mosstroopers and carry the
King's peace into the heart of the thieving valleys. 'Belted
Will Howard' of Naworth, though a Catholic recusant,
loyally served King James as his Warden of the Western
March.   He hunted down the Grahams and the other
mosstrooping clans, following them into their lairs with

sleuth-hounds. North Tyne and Redesdale were gradually brought under the law. In the early years of the Seventeenth Century the gentlemen of Northumberland first ventured to build manor-houses instead of peel-towers and castles, as homes in which it was safe to live.

It is strange that the barbarous old-world life of the Border, as it still was in Queen Elizabeth's day, lay in close juxtaposition to the most forward-looking of industries, the coal-mining of the lower Tyne and East Durham. The winning of surface coal dated from before the Roman occupation ; but now the pits were getting deeper and the work of the miner was beginning to approximate to that of his present-day successor. Newcastle, the centre of the great business of shipping the ' sea-coal ' of London, was unique as a meeting-point of the feudal world of the Percies, the tribal world of the mosstrooper, and the coal trade not fundamentally different from that of to-day. (For the Border under the Tudors, see *Victoria County History*, Cumberland, Rev. J. Hodgson's *Hist. of Northumberland*, and Dr. Rachel Reid's *North Parts under the Tudors* in *Tudor Studies*, ed. Seton Watson, 1924.)

Everywhere, south of the still vexed Border with its grim stone castles and peel-towers, the England of Elizabeth was becoming *par excellence* the land of manor-houses, bewilderingly different from one another in size, material and style of architecture, but all testifying to the peace and economic prosperity of the age, its delight in display, in beauty and in the glory of man's life on earth. Wealth and power, and with them the lead in architecture had passed from the Princes of the Church to the gentry. The great era of ecclesiastical building, after lasting for so many centuries, had at length come to an end. The new religion was the religion of the Book, the sermon and the psalm, rather than of the sacred edifice : there were already fine churches enough to satisfy the religious requirements of Protestant England.

Elizabethan architecture contained strong elements both of the Gothic and the classical, in other words, the old English and the new Italian. In the early part of the reign the more irregular and picturesque Gothic was most used, especially in converting old fortified manor-houses into more peaceful and splendid homes, such as Penshurst and Haddon Hall.   But side by side with them, and increasingly as the reign went on, came in the more regular planning of new private palaces in an Italianate or classical style, like Longleat, Audley End, Leicester's buildings at Kenilworth, and Montacute in its glory of dull gold—just a country gentleman's house in a remote district of Somerset, built in the local stone, yet certainly one of the most beautiful and magnificent homes in the world.

In country houses of the new style like Audley End, and in public buildings like Gresham's Royal Exchange, intricate Renaissance ornament adorned the stone-work of the fabric and the woodwork of the interior.   A fine and pure example is the Gate of Honour at Caius College, Cambridge (1575), and a later instance is found hard by in the roof and screen inside the hall of Trinity (1604–1605).   The design and ornamentation of Elizabethan mansions were often carried out by Germans brought over for the purpose.   As their taste and tradition were none of the best, it was fortunate that there were also many competent native builders and architects.

Besides the lordlier rural palaces, there were innumerable smaller manor-houses arising in every variety of style and material, some of stone, some of black-and-white half timber like Moreton Old Hall in Cheshire, and some of red brick in regions where neither stone nor timber were plentiful.[1] Though the windows were not yet plate glass but lattice, they occupied a much larger area of the wall space than in former times, and let floods of light into the pleasant chambers and long Elizabethan galleries.   Plain clear glass was now used in the lattices, which in early Tudor times had often been filled up with ' wicker or fine rifts of oak in chequerwise,' as Harrison tells us, ' but now only clearest glass is esteemed.'

[1] Harrison (1577) writes,
' The ancient manors and houses of our gentlemen are yet, and for the most part, of strong timber, in framing whereof our carpenters have been and are worthily preferred before those of like science among all other nations. Howbeit such as be lately builded are commonly either of brick or of hard stone, or both, their rooms large and comely, and houses of office further distant from their lodgings.'

F 2

Formerly the best glass had come from abroad, but early in Elizabeth's reign the industry in England was improved by foreign workmen from Normandy and Lorraine. Works in the Weald, Hampshire, Staffordshire and London supplied not only window glass but bottles and drinking-glasses, in imitation of the fashionable Venetian ware from Murano that only the wealthy could afford.

In rooms of the better kind the stucco work on the white-washed ceiling was often ' most expressed in fancy,' and its mouldings were sometimes picked out in colours or in gold. The walls were warmed and adorned with ' tapestry, arras work or painted cloth, wherein either diverse histories, or herbs, beasts or knots and such like are stained ' ; or else they are panelled with ' oak of our own, or wainscot brought hither out of the east countries,' that is, the Baltic lands. (Harrison.)

A less expensive way of decorating the walls, recommended by Falstaff to the Hostess, was to paint pictures on them :

HOSTESS : I must be fain to pawn both my plate and the tapestry of my dining-chambers.
FALSTAFF : Glasses, glasses, is the only drinking. And for thy walls,—a pretty slight drollery, or the story of the Prodigal, or the German hunting in the water-work, is worth a thousand of these bed-hangings and these fly-bitten tapestries.

Framed pictures, except family portraits, were few even in gentlemen's houses. But the more princely mansions had pictures in the Venetian style. Thus the lord's servants say to the bewildered Christopher Sly

' Dost thou love pictures ? We will fetch thee straight
Adonis painted by a running brook
And Cytheraea all in sedges hid.'

The homes of common folk in town and village had changed less than the manor-houses of the rich. They were still the old-fashioned gabled and thatched cottages of timber—with clay, loam, rubble and wattle-work filling up the spaces between the uprights and crossbeams.

' Certes this rude kind of building [wrote Harrison] made the Span-iards in Queen Mary's days to wonder, but chiefly when they saw what large diet was used in many of these so homely cottages. In so much that one of no small reputation amongst them said after this manner—"These English (quoth he) have their houses made of sticks and dirt, but they fare commonly so well as the King." '

The greatness of the Elizabethan English in poetry, music and the drama was not equalled by their school of painting, though many competent portraits of the Queen and her courtiers were produced, on canvas. Nicholas Hilliard, son of a citizen of Exeter, founded the school of English miniature. There was much demand for this delicate and beautiful art, not only among courtiers ostentatiously vying with one another for the Queen's ' picture in little ' at ' forty, fifty or a hundred ducats apiece,' but among all who desired mementoes of their family or friends. Miniature painting went on at a high level in England until the era of Cosway at the end of George III's reign, and indeed it was only killed by photography, as so many other arts have been killed by science.

The expense and fantasticalness of men's dress was a constant theme of satire. ' Fashions from proud Italy ' and France were always being imitated, and the tailor played a great part in the life of the Elizabethan gentleman. Jewels, gold chains and costly trinkets of all sorts were worn by men as much as by women. Both sexes wore round the neck ruffs of various sizes and shapes. Such fashions were confined to the well-to-do—but all classes wore beards. ' Twas merry in hall when beards wagged all.'

Gentlemen had the privilege of wearing swords as part of their full dress in civil life. The laws of the duel, endorsed by the code of honour, were beginning to replace the more savage ' killing affray,' the murder of an enemy by a man's retainers and serving-men. The fashions of fencing, whether in sport or earnest, were of foreign origin, when men of fashion quarrelled in print, by the book, ' on the seventh cause,' and fought with rapier and dagger, to cries of ' ah, the immortal *passado ! the punto reverso ! The hai !* '

With the continuous growth of commerce, land-development and general prosperity, the roads were more busy than ever with the passage of riders and pedestrians of all classes on business and pleasure. The mediaeval custom of Pilgrimage had helped to give people a taste for travel and sightseeing, which survived the religious custom of visiting shrines. The medicinal spa was taking the place of the holy well. Already, as Camden tells us, Buxton in distant Derbyshire was a fashionable resort for ' great numbers of nobility and gentry,' who came to drink its waters, and were housed in fine lodgings erected by the Earl of Shrewsbury to develop the place. Bath was not yet in full fashion, for although its waters were famous its accommodation was squalid.

The inns of Elizabethan England had a character of their own for individual attention accorded to travellers. Fynes Moryson, who had sampled the wayside hospitality of half Europe, wrote in the light of his experience :

' The world affords not such inns as England hath, either for food and cheap entertainment after the guests' own pleasure, or for humble attendance on passengers, yea even in very poor villages. For as soon as a passenger comes to an inn, the servants run to him, and one takes his horse, and walks him till he be cold, then rubs him and gives him meat [food], yet I must say that they are not much to be trusted in this last point, without the eye of the Master or his servant to oversee them. Another servant gives the passenger his private chamber, and kindles his fire ; the third pulls off his boots and makes them clean. Then the host or hostess visit him ; and if he will eat with the host, or at a common table with others, his meal will cost him sixpense, or in some places but four pence ; yet this course is less honourable and not used by gentlemen. But if he will eat in his chamber, he commands what meat he will, yea the kitchen is open to him to command the meat to be dressed as he best likes. And when he sits down at table, the host or hostess will accompany him, or if they have many guests will at least visit him, taking it for courtesy to be bid sit down. While he eats, if he have company especially, he shall be offered music, which he may freely take or refuse. And if he be solitary, the musicians will give him good day with music in the morning. . . A man cannot more freely command in his own house than he may do in his inn. And at parting, if he give some few pence to the chamberlain and ostler, they wish him a happy journey.'

Unfortunately, behind all this hearty welcome, something sinister might be concealed. Shakespeare has given us the seamy side of inns as he knew them, in words muttered before dawn in the inn-yard at Rochester (1 H. IV, II, i),

' while Charles' wain is over the new chimney, and yet our horse not packed ' : the honest carriers, one learns, have not had such clean quarters, nor enjoyed so undisturbed a night as Fynes Moryson's gentleman. And they know the chamberlain for a rogue, who lives by betraying travellers to bolder thieves than himself.

Shakespeare is fully borne out by the account of the inns of that date given by William Harrison. He praises indeed the food, the wine, the beer, the scrupulously clean linen at bed and board, the tapestry on the walls, the key of his room given to every guest, and the freedom he enjoys as contrasted to the more tyrannous treatment of travellers on the Continent. But, alas, the willing servants and the jolly host himself are often in league with highwaymen. The obsequious attendance on the guest may cover a wish to learn what route he will take next day and whether he is in charge of money. Before the days of cheques, large sums of gold and silver were carried along the roads in the ordinary way of business. The servants of the inn officiously handle every article of the traveller's baggage, to judge by its weight in hand if it contain coin. Then they pass on the result of their researches to confederates outside. The inn keeps its good name, for no robbery is done within its walls ; the thieves spring out from a thicket some miles off upon the road.

This system, Harrison concludes, works ' to the utter undoing of many an honest yeoman as he journeyeth on his way.' Even so did the chamberlain of the Rochester inn betray to Falstaff's gang the ' franklin in the wild of Kent,' who ' brought three hundred marks with him in gold.'

But the inn was not the resort of wayfarers alone. It frequently happened that the inhabitants of the manor-house and their guests, after dining at home, would adjourn to the neighbouring hostelry, and spend long hours there in a privy chamber round the glasses and tankards ; for in the difficult matter of foreign wine the squire was often more ready to trust mine host's cellar than his own. This custom continued among the smaller gentry for several generations after the death of Elizabeth. And in all ages the ale bench has been the social centre of the middling and lower classes of town, village and hamlet.

The study of the history and literature of Elizabethan England gives an impression of a greater harmony and a freer intercourse of classes than in earlier or in later times. It is not a period of peasants' revolts, of levelling doctrines, of anti-Jacobin fears, or of exclusiveness and snobbery in the upper class such as Jane Austen depicts in a later age. Class divisions in Shakespeare's day were taken as a matter of course, without jealousy in those below, or itching anxiety on the part of the ' upper and middling classes ' to teach ' the grand law of subordination ' to the ' inferior orders,' which is so painfully evident, in the Eighteenth and early Nineteenth Centuries, for example, in Charity School education. The typical unit of Elizabethan education was the Grammar School, where the cleverest boys of all classes were brought up together : the typical units of Eighteenth and Nineteenth Century education were the Charity School, the village school and the ' great Public School,' where the classes were educated in rigorous segregation. Elizabethans took the social world as they took everything else, naturally, and consorted together without self-consciousness or suspicion.

Class divisions, recognised without fuss on either side, were not rigid and were not even strictly hereditary. Individuals and families moved out of one class into another by acquisition or loss of property, or by simple change of occupation. There is no such impassable barrier as used to divide the Lord of the manor from his peasantry in mediaeval England, or such as continued till 1789 to mark off the French *noblesse* as an hereditary caste separate from everyone else. In Tudor England such rigid lines were rendered impossible by the number and variety of men in intermediate classes and occupations, who were closely connected, in the business and amusement of daily life, with those above and those below them in social status. English society was based not on equality but on freedom— freedom of opportunity and freedom of personal intercourse. Such was the England known and approved by Shakespeare : men and women of every class and occupation were equally interesting to him, but he defended ' degree ' as the necessary basis of human welfare.

The Peers of the Realm were a small section of the gentry

enjoying great personal prestige and some invidious legal
privileges, though not that of exemption from taxation.
They were expected to keep up great households and to
extend munificent patronage to clients, which their estates
could often ill support. The nobility had lost the independent military and political power which their order had
exercised up till the Wars of the Roses. And the Tudors
kept them few in number by abstaining from lavish creations. The acreage owned by members of the House of
Lords was much smaller in Elizabethan than in Plantagenet
or in Hanoverian times ; the recent price revolution had
hit them even harder than other landlords, and the process
by which Peers like the Dukes of Bedford afterwards bought
up the estates of small gentry and freeholders had not yet
got under way. For all these reasons the House of Lords,
especially after the mitred abbots had disappeared, was a
less important body in Tudor times than it had been in the
past and was to be again in the future. The old aristocracy
had been pruned away, and the new aristocracy had not yet
fully grown up to take its place.

But, if Elizabeth's reign was not a great age for the
peerage, it was a great age for the gentry. Their numbers,
wealth and importance had been increased by the decay of
the old nobility that had stood between them and the
Crown ; by the distribution of the monastic estates ; and
by vitality of commerce and land-improvement in the new
era. The squire in Tudor and Stuart times led by no
means so isolated and bucolic a life as some historians have
imagined. He was part of the general movement of an
active society. Yeomen, merchants and lawyers who had
made their fortunes, were perpetually recruiting the ranks
of the landed gentry ; while the younger sons of the manor-
house were apprenticed into industry and trade. In these
ways old families were kept in personal touch with the
modern world, and the country was kept in touch with the
town. No doubt there was more rural isolation in the West
and North, the future Cavalier districts, than in the counties
more closely associated with the trade of London ; but the
difference, though real, was only relative.

The sensible custom of apprenticing the younger sons of
squires to trade became less common in Hanoverian times,

partly because of the diminution (almost the disappearance)
of the class of small squire. The contemptuous attitude
affected by some gentlefolk in the Eighteenth and Nineteenth Centuries towards 'soiling the hands with trade,'
was particularly absurd, because nearly all such families had
risen wholly or in part by trade, and many were in fact
still engaged in it though the smart ladies of the family may
not have known much about it. But in Elizabeth's time
there was much less of this snobbish nonsense. The
London apprentices, as we read in Stow, were 'often
children of gentlemen and persons of good quality,' who
served their masters obediently, hoping to rise to a share in
the business, but in their leisure time 'affected to go in
costly apparel and wear weapons and frequent schools of
dancing, fencing and music.'

'The Elizabethan and Jacobean monuments to be found in parish
churches record the origin of many a squire's wealth in his prosperity
as " Citizen and Mercer," " Citizen and Haberdasher " of London
or some other town, in a way for which it would be hard to find
parallels on the mural tablets of a later date.' (W. J. Ashley, *Economic Organization of England*, p. 131.)

While the landed gentry were thus closely intermingling
with the commercial classes, the status of 'gentleman' was
not supposed to be confined to landed proprietors. Harrison
tells us how liberally and how loosely the matter was
regarded in the days of Shakespeare's boyhood :

'Whosoever studieth the laws of the realm, whoso abideth in the University giving his mind to his book, or professeth physic and the
liberal sciences, or beside his service in the room of a captain in the
wars, or good counsel given at home whereby his commonwealth is
benefitted, can live without manual labour, and thereto is able and
will bear the port, charge and countenance of a gentleman, he shall
be called 'master,' which is the title that men give to esquires and
gentlemen, and be reputed a gentleman ever after. Which is so
much the less to be disallowed of, for that the Prince doth lose nothing
by it, the gentleman being so much subject to taxes and public payments as is the yeoman or husbandman, which he likewise doth bear
the gladlier for the saving of his reputation.'

He is expected to tip largely, not to look too closely at a
bill, and to remember that it is the privilege of a gentleman
to get the worst of a bargain. On these terms his easy-

going, obsequious countrymen will touch their caps to him
and call him ' Master '—though behind his back they will
say they remember his father, honest man, riding to market
astride his sacks of corn.   In that way everyone is pleased.
As Professor Tawney has said, the gentry ' held a position
determined, not by legal distinctions, but by common
estimation.   Mere caste had few admirers—fewer probably
among the gentry militant of the early Seventeenth Century
than among the gentry triumphant of the early Eighteenth.
Common sense endorsed the remark that *gentility is nothing
but ancient riches*, adding under its breath that they need not
be very ancient.'   (*Ec. Hist. Rev.* 1941, pp. 2–4.)
    Harrison then passes on from the gentry to the citizens
and merchants, and remarks on the expansion of the area of
their trade :

' And whereas in times past their chief trade was into Spain, Portingall,
France, Danske, Norwaie, Scotland and Iceland only, now in these
days, as men not contented with these journeys, they have sought
out the east and west Indies, and made voyages not only into the
Canaries and New Spain, but likewise into Cathaia, Moscovia, Tar-
taria and regions thereabout, from whence (as they say) they bring
home great commodities.'

The increasing importance of the merchant class is told in
their monuments in parish churches with effigies worthy of
noblemen, and bas-reliefs below of their sons and daughters
in ruffs kneeling all in a row, and inscriptions commemor-
ating the foundations of hospitals, alms-houses and schools.
Society is getting so mixed, that even a theatre manager, if
he has made his money and settled down as a leading citizen
in his native town, shall, when he dies, have his bust within
the chancel.
    After the merchants Harrison places the yeomen.   Some
of them are ' forty-shilling freeholders,' farming their own
land and enjoying the Parliamentary franchise.

' But for the most part the yeomen are farmers to gentlemen ; and
with grazing, frequenting of markets and keeping of servants (not
idle servants such as gentlemen do, but such as get their own and
part of their master's living) so come to great wealth, in so much that
many of them are able and do buy the lands of unthrifty gentlemen,
and often setting their sons to the schools and to the Universities and

to the Inns of Court ; or otherwise leaving them sufficient lands whereupon they may live without labour, do make them by those means to become gentlemen.'

To-day the countryside, in almost every region of England, is full not only of Elizabethan mansions, but of more modest houses built in the Tudor or early Stuart type of architecture, now occupied by tenant farmers, which once were manor-houses of small gentry or seats of freehold yeomen on much the same economic level. Such houses remind us that from Elizabethan times down to the Restoration of 1660 the number of small gentry and yeomen freeholders was on the increase, while the great estates of the old feudal nobility were diminishing. It was a great age for the rural middle class.

After the merchants and yeomen came the ' fourth and last sort of people,' the wage-earning class of town and country.

' As for slaves and bondmen we have none,' Harrison says in a proud parenthesis, and boasts that by the privilege of our island every man who sets foot upon it becomes as free as his master. This principle, that to touch the soil of England in itself confers freedom, was two centuries later extended for the benefit even of negroes, by Lord Mansfield's celebrated judgment in the case of the runaway slave Somersett.

But the wage-earning class, though now free from all taint of servile position, ' have neither voice nor authority in the Commonwealth,' says Harrison ; ' yet they are not altogether neglected, for in cities and corporate towns, for default of yeomen, they are fain to make up their inquests of such meaner people. And in villages they are commonly made churchwardens, sidesmen, ale-conners, constables, and many times enjoy the name of headboroughs.' This principle of democratic self-government had subsisted even among the serf-farmers of mediaeval times. It was strong in the Court Leet, or Manor Court where petty justice was done : even so mean a member of village society as Christopher Sly could threaten to ' present ' the hostess of the tavern ' at the Leet because she brought stone jugs and no sealed quarts.' And in the Leet Court, too, the agricultural policy to be pursued on the open field and the common pasture was discussed and decided by all. The English villager had not only rights but functions in the society of which he was member. Many were always very poor, and some were victims of oppression, but there was a spirit of independence running through all classes under the old system of land-tenure, before the Eighteenth Century enclosures broke up the village community.

Another sign of the self-respect and self-reliance of the English commonfolk was training for military service. It was only during the long period of peace and safety after Waterloo, that men began to regard it as part of English liberty not to be trained for defence. In all previous ages the opposite and more rational idea had prevailed. In the later Middle Ages the national skill in archery and the obligation to serve in the militia of town and country had fostered the spirit of popular independence which Froissart, Fortescue and other writers had noticed as peculiarly English. And so it still was under Elizabeth, though the long-bow was yielding to the caliver or hand-gun.

' Certes [writes Harrison] there is almost no village so poor in England (be it never so small) that it hath not sufficient furniture in a readiness to set forth three or four soldiers, as one archer, one gunner, one pike, and a billman at the least. The said armour and munition is kept in one several place appointed by the consent of the whole parish, where it is always ready to be had and worn within an hour's warning.'

A newly established County officer, the Lord Lieutenant, took the place in 1557 of the Sheriff as commander and organizer of the Militia of each Shire. He and his sub-ordinates held frequent reviews of men, armour and muni-tions. The parsimony of Elizabeth's finance threw as much of the expense as possible on local and volunteer resources, but the system worked. The Rising of the Northern Earls was suppressed without a battle because 20,000 militiamen, ready armed and trained, took the field on the first alarm to defend the Queen and the Protestant religion. Twice as many were assembled when the Armada was off our shores, and more were mustering daily when that danger passed away before the wind. England had no regular army, but she was not defenceless. Each locality had to supply so many men trained and armed for the militia ; each man of property had to find one or more men. Partly by volunteering, partly by compulsion the national duty was fulfilled.

For expeditions oversea such a system was gravely at fault ; indeed the only English troops who won any credit upon the continent between the Hundred Years' War and the time of Cromwell were the long-service regiments of Englishmen in Dutch or other foreign pay.

It was as well that the veterans of Spain did not effect a landing. For the English militia no longer had the superiority over other nations that the long-bow had once given. All through the Queen's reign the caliver or harquebus man was displacing the archer, in proportion as the gun, once so much inferior to the long-bow in an expert hand, increased in range, in rapidity of fire, and in force to penetrate plate-armour. At the beginning of the reign, most even of the well-appointed London militia were still bowmen, but the best companies already consisted of ' shot ' and heavily armoured pikemen. After another generation had passed, not one of London's 6000 trained militiamen bore the bow during the alarm of the Armada, and it was the same in many Southern counties. A decade later, Shakespeare wrote a scene in which Falstaff is pressing Cotswold yokels by the authority of the Justices of the Peace ; he is not seeking archers but only ' shot ' ; ' put me a caliver into Wart's hand, Bardolph.' In 1595 the Privy Council decreed that bows should never again be issued as weapons of war ; and so a great chapter in English history came to its end.

In sport the substitution of firearms for bows followed more slowly. As late as 1621 the Archbishop of Canterbury had the misfortune to aim at a buck and kill a gamekeeper with his cross-bow. But by that time many sportsmen used the ' long gun ' especially in the stalking of wild fowl, though ' to shoot flying ' was still regarded as something of a feat.

The good order preserved in Elizabeth's kingdom, in spite of religious differences and foreign dangers, was due to the power of the Crown exerted through the Privy Council, the real governing body of Tudor England, and the Prerogative Courts which represented the Council's judicial power. Those Courts—The Star Chamber, the Councils of Wales and of the North, the Chancery Court, the ecclesiastical Court of High Commission—were (all except Chancery) afterwards abolished in the Parliamentary Revolution of Stuart times, because they were the rivals of the Common Law Courts, and because they were a danger to individual liberty with their inquisitorial procedure and their avowed bias in favour of the Crown. Yet in the Tudor age it was precisely these Prerogative Courts that saved the liberties of Englishmen by enforcing respect for law, and saved the English Common Law by enabling and compelling men to administer it without fear or favour. The Privy Council and the Prerogative Courts stopped the terrorization of Judges and Juries by local mobs and local magnates ; this restoration of the free working of the Jury system in ordinary cases was a service to society that far outweighed the Privy Council's occasional interference in cases of a political complexion. In this way the Common Law and its tribunals were saved by the very jurisdiction that was their rival. Moreover, the Prerogative Courts introduced many new principles of law suited to modern times, which were eventually absorbed into the law of the land.

In foreign countries the old feudal law was not so good a system as the Common Law of mediaeval England, and could not be adapted to the uses of modern society. And so the feudal law of Europe and with it the mediaeval liberties of Europe were swept away in this epoch, by the ' reception ' of Roman law, which was a law of despotism. But in England the mediaeval law, fundamentally a law of liberty and private rights, was preserved, modernized, supplemented, enlarged, and above all enforced by the Council and Courts of the ' Tudor despotism,' so that both the old system of law and the old Parliament survived into a new age with a renewed vigour.

So, too, in the sphere of administration, the Tudor Privy Council blended the old with the new, local liberty with national authority. The will of the central power was imposed on the localities, not as in France by sending down bureaucrats and King's Intendents to govern the provinces in place of the local gentry, but by using the more influential local gentry themselves as the Queen's Justices of Peace. They were Elizabeth's maids of all work. They had not only to carry out her political and ecclesiastical policy, but to administer petty justice, and to execute all the ordinary functions of local government, including the new Poor Law, the Statute of Artificers and the regulation of wages and prices. These matters were neither left to adjust themselves on a principle of *laissez-faire*, nor abandoned to the whims of local authorities. They were regulated on nation-wide principles by Parliamentary Statutes, which it was the business of the J.P.s to enforce in every shire. If they were slack in performing these arduous duties, the vigilant eye of the Privy Council was upon them, and its long arm was soon extended. The J.P.s were not yet a law unto themselves, as they became in Hanoverian times. Squirarchical power and local interests were under the wholesome supervision of a central authority thinking for the whole nation.

Nothing is more characteristic of this aspect of the Elizabethan and early Stuart regime than the manner of providing for the poor and unemployed. Times were on the average better in that period (1559–1640) than during the earlier Tudor reigns, but there were recurrent periods of distress. Though complaints were less loud of agricultural troubles and depopulating enclosures, the growth of industries in the country districts was accompanied by periodic unemployment, especially under the domestic system then prevalent in most trades. Under the factory system, which was still in its infancy, a capitalist employer is often able and anxious to keep his works going as long as possible even in bad times, and to accumulate stock, which he hopes to get rid of when times improve. But the domestic worker was less able to carry on, if the demand for his goods grew slack. Whenever under Elizabeth there were bad times, as when a quarrel with the Spanish Governors of the Netherlands closed Antwerp to English goods, our cloth workers perforce left their looms idle as soon as the merchants ceased to buy their cloths or provide them with raw material. Periodic unemployment was a feature of the cloth trade, even during this period, which, taken as a whole, saw it greatly increase.

To meet such exigencies the Poor Law took shape in a long series of experiments and enactments. They were enforced locally by the J.P.s under the strict surveillance of the Privy Council ; the Council had a real regard for the interests of the poor, with which the interests of public order were so closely involved. There were to be no more bands of ' sturdy beggars ' such as had terrorized honest folk in the days of Henry VIII. A compulsory poor-rate was now levied with increasing regularity. From this fund, not only was poor relief given, but the Overseers of the Poor in every parish were compelled to buy material to provide work for the unemployed—' a convenient stock of flax, hemp, wool, thread, iron and other stuff to set the poor to work.' (Statute of 1601.)

So, too, in time of dearth, as during the series of bad harvests 1594–1597, the Privy Council, acting as always through the instrumentality of the J.P.s, controlled the price of grain, and saw that it was imported from abroad and distributed where famine was worst. No doubt both the Poor Law and the supply of food in time of dearth were imperfect, and more so in some districts than in others, but a compulsory national system existed both in theory and in fact ; the provision for the poor was better than anything there had been in an older England, and better than anything there was to be for many generations to come in France and other European countries. (E. M. Leonard, *English Poor Relief* ; W. J. Ashley, *Economic Organization of England*.)

The judicial, political, economic and administrative powers of the Justices of the Peace were so various and, taken together, so important that the J.P.s became the most influential class of men in England. They were often chosen for Parliament, where they could speak as experienced critics of laws and policies which they themselves administered. They were the Queen's servants, but they were not in her pay, or in her dependence. They were country gentlemen, living on their own estates and off their own rents. In the last resort what they valued most was the good opinion of their neighbours, the gentry and common folk of the shire. Whenever, therefore, as sometimes happened in Stuart times, the class of country gentlemen strongly opposed the King's political and religious policy, on such occasions the Crown had no instrument with which to govern the countryside. So it proved, for example, in 1688 ; but it was not so in 1588. Some of the gentry, especially in North and West, disliked Elizabeth's Reformation policy, but an increasingly large majority of their class favoured the new religion, and J.P.s of that persuasion could be used by government to restrain and occasionally to arrest their more recalcitrant neighbours. Such coercion if it had been exerted by paid officials sent down from London, would have been more resented by the opinion of the County—and would have been more expensive to the Queen's exchequer.

CHAPTER VII

II

Religion and Universities. The social policy of the Elizabethan State. Industry
and Seafaring. Shakespeare.

(Queen Elizabeth, 1558-1603. The Armada, 1588.)

IN seafaring and discovery, in music, drama, poetry, and in
many aspects of social life, we can speak with assurance of
the golden age of Shakespeare's England, an age of harmony
and creative power.   But the religious life of the time seems
on the face of it more obscure, less attractive and certainly
less harmonious.   Except ' the judicious Hooker,' there is
no name of the first order that springs to the mind as connected with Elizabethan religion.   Yet, if we consider the
fate that in those years befell Spain, France, Geneva, Italy
and the Netherlands on account of religion, we may see
reason to be thankful that in England ecclesiastical feuds
were so kept in check by the policy of the Queen and the
good sense of the majority of her subjects, lay and clerical,
that religious fanaticism never got loose to destroy or
pervert the activities of Elizabethan man.   Nor is that
negative merit the only one to be attributed to religious
life in the age of Shakespeare.   He himself, and Edmund
Spenser, were children of their time and breathed its religious
atmosphere, just as the poets of other ages, Langland,
Milton, Wordsworth and Browning were each the outcome
and highest expression of a religious philosophy characteristic of their respective epochs.   There were among
Shakespeare's contemporaries many violent Puritans and
Romanists and many narrow Anglicans, but there was also
something more characteristically Elizabethan, an attitude
to religion that is not primarily Catholic or Protestant,
Puritan or Anglican, but which evades dogma and lives
broadly in the spirit.   It is common to Shakespeare and
to the Queen herself.

The first year of Elizabeth saw a crisis in the social life of every parish. Cranmer's bequest to posterity, the English Prayer Book, was again ordered to be read in place of the Latin Mass. But this change of religion was not accompanied by a corresponding change in the person of the parish priest. Out of some 8000 beneficed clergy not more than 200 were deprived. The parson obeyed the law as a matter of course, and his neighbours, themselves equally obedient, thought none the worse of him for that. If he was a middle-aged man he was well accustomed to altering his religious practice at the behest of the powers that be. In some cases he was an ex-monk or friar who had known a good many ' varieties of religious experience.' In the year when Queen Mary was succeeded by her sister, the average parson was seldom a convinced Protestant ; but he had no respect for the authority of the Pope ; the idea of consulting his own ' private judgment ' was alien to his thought ; and if he sincerely wished to obey ' the Church,' where was he to hear her voice ?   It issued, he had been taught to believe, from the mouth of the Prince, and in 1559 it came to him from no other quarter. To accept religious services and doctrines because they were ordained by Crown, Parliament and Privy Council, seemed to clergy and people not only expedient but positively right.

Such was the Erastian attitude to religion that carried Englishmen through that dangerous century of change. It is repugnant to our modern ideas of denominational and personal freedom, but it was at that time a doctrine sincerely held by the majority of conscientious men. Bishop Jewel, the best exponent of the ideas of the early Elizabethan settlement, declared

' This is our doctrine, that every soul, of what calling soever he be, —be he monk, be he preacher, be he prophet, be he apostle,—ought to be subject to King and magistrates.'

The sphere of King and magistrates covered religion. All were agreed that there could be only one religion in the State, and all except Romanists and very rigorous Puritans were agreed that the State must decide what that religion should be.

This doctrine, equally opposed to mediaeval and modern

conceptions, suited Elizabeth's England. It was the political corollary of the social revolt of the laity against the clergy in the time of the Queen's father. The Tudor English were not irreligious, but they were anti-clerical, and therefore they were Erastian. This attitude of mind affected the clergy themselves, who had not been brought up in seminaries as a priestly caste, but were themselves an integral part of English society.

The clergy as a whole were therefore obedient and supine in the first years of Elizabeth. But there was an active and proselytizing minority among them of zealous Protestants, who had escaped the Smithfield fires by the accident of Queen Mary's death, or had returned from exile abroad full of Calvinist zeal imbibed at the Genevan fountain-head. Such men were not Erastian at heart. They would have disobeyed a Popish Prince, but they knew that Elizabeth alone stood between England and a Papal restoration, so they accepted her Church compromise, intending to reform it as time and occasion should permit. As against Rome and Spain they were the strongest defence of the new settlement, but from another point of view they were its most dangerous enemies.

The majority of the parish priests of 1559, who were prepared to take their religion ready-made from a Parliamentary Statute, were lacking in any definite tradition that could give enthusiasm and authority to their ministrations. But the extreme Protestants had a living faith that made them for some decades the most influential section of the clergy, at a time when the average parson was deficient both in learning and in zeal.

Since the anti-clerical revolution of King Henry's day, priests were no longer envied or hated, but they were often despised and ill-used. Elizabeth herself continued to filch Church lands and property, and sometimes to keep Bishoprics vacant in order that the Crown should enjoy the rents of the manors. Her Archbishops constantly sought the advice of her Secretary, William Cecil, on purely religious matters, while complaining to him unceasingly of the petty oppressions of powerful laymen. ' The Church was treated very much as an arm of the Civil Service, a dignified but pleasantly helpless prey of an impecunious sovereign and a rapacious court.' In the smaller sphere of parish politics, the squire was equally dominant over the parson. The young author of *Love's Labour's Lost* had seen much of the half kindly, half contemptuous attitude of the laity towards the parish priest, ' a foolish, mild man, an honest man look you and soon dashed. A marvellous good neighbour, faith, and a very good bowler.'

All this betokened that the ground-swell caused by the great anti-clerical earthquake of Henry's reign was subsiding only by degrees. Nevertheless it was subsiding. By the end of the Queen's reign the Anglican clergy were already in a better position, more respected by their neighbours, more sure of themselves and of their message. When the Stuart Kings took the Church by the hand in an honourable partnership, the laity were soon complaining once more ' of the pride of the clergy.' Laud encouraged the parson to look the squire in the face.

It was an important change in social life that the clergy under Elizabeth were again, and this time finally, authorised to take unto themselves wives. Many parsons, who had been ready to accept the restoration of Roman Catholicism in 1553, had been deprived of their livings under Mary, for no reason except that they had been legally married by the laws of Edward VI. Under Elizabeth their connubial liberty was restored. It has been shrewdly suggested that ' as the distribution of monastic property created among certain classes a vested interest in the future of the Reformation, so the removal of restrictions on the marriage of the clergy created what we may call a family interest in its progress among sections of the clergy not sufficiently enlightened to grasp the higher issues, an interest which was not without importance in guaranteeing its ultimate success.' (Miss Hilda Grieve's study of the personal fortunes of the clergy in Essex deprived under Mary. *R.H.S.* 1940.)

Freedom to marry must have been a real comfort to many honest men ; and a fine race of children were reared in the parsonages of England, for generations to come, filling all the professions and services with good men and true, and most of all the Church herself. But, in the first instance, clerical marriage involved certain difficulties : priests' wives were looked at askance by Elizabeth and many of her subjects, still under the prejudice of old use and wont. Time was needed before the parson's wife acquired the honourable and important position in parish society that she afterwards filled.

The need to support a wife and children made the parson's poverty yet more acute. Because they were poor, it was not usual for the parish clergy to marry gentlemen's daughters. Clarendon himself, devoted as he was to the Anglican Church, noted as a sign of the social and moral chaos produced by the Great Rebellion, that the daughters of noble and illustrious families bestowed themselves upon divines ' or other low and unequal matches.' The great rise in the economic and social status of the clergy took place only during the Hanoverian epoch. In Jane Austen's novels the squires and parsons form one social group, but that was not the case in Tudor or Stuart times.

Clerical poverty helped to prolong simony and pluralities. Those practices did not cease with the disappearance of Papal jurisdiction, though the holding of English benefices by foreigners living in France and Italy had come to an end for ever.

In the middle of the reign, during the foreign and domestic crisis that culminated in the Armada and the execution of Mary Queen of Scots, English society in town and country was gravely disturbed by the religious differences of neighbours ; the Jesuit mission was hard at work in the houses of the unfortunate gentry of the old religion, distraught between the claims of the two rival loyalties. Fear brooded over the land. Men waited, expecting every day to hear of Spanish invasion, Roman Catholic rebellion, the assassination of the Queen. The Jesuits flitted about in disguise, hiding in ' priest holes ' in the thickness of manor-house walls, pursued by Justices of the Peace, occasionally caught and executed.

Meanwhile the Puritans, not yet ' dissenters ' but parish clergymen and Justices of the Peace on whom the State depended for its existence in this crisis, were working hard to overturn and remodel the Church establishment from within. They denounced the Bishops as ' limbs of anti-Christ.' They held lectures and prayer-meetings forbidden by the authorities. Every merchant of London, Elizabeth

complained, ' must have his schoolmaster and nightly conventicles, expounding scriptures and catechizing their
servants and maids, insomuch that I have heard how some of
their maids have not sticked to control learned preachers,
and say that " Such a man taught otherwise in our house." '
In many counties the Puritan clergy held conferences of
ministers which were dangerously like Presbyterian Synods,
and were intended, with the help of Parliament, soon to
wrest authority from the Bishops.

Already the Puritans showed that gift for electioneering
and Parliamentary lobbying and agitation which in the next
century remodelled the English constitution. In 1584
they flooded Parliament with petitions from clergy, town
corporations, Justices of the Peace and the leading gentry
of whole counties. The House of Commons and even the
Privy Council were half converted. But Elizabeth stood
her ground. It was well that she was firm, for a Puritan
Revolution in the Church, effected at that time, would almost
certainly have resulted in a religious civil war of Catholic
and Protestant from which Spain would not improbably
have emerged as victor. In 1640 England was sufficiently
strong and sufficiently Protestant to indulge safely in a
course of ecclesiastical revolution and counter-revolution
which would have been fatal to her half a century before.

Queen Elizabeth and her stiff Archbishop Whitgift
weathered the storm, and the Anglican vessel slipped safely
on between the clashing rocks of Romanism and Puritanism.
By the end of the reign there had been a certain reaction.
The Puritans had for a time been reduced to some show of
obedience within the Church. Those who were outside
the Church, like the ' Brownists,' were few and despised.
There had been hard hitting : some of the more extreme
Puritans had been hanged and many more imprisoned.
And yet the bulk of the Puritan clergy, gentry and merchants
were loyal to the Queen. The wonderful woman still
' reigned with their loves.' But a person even more far-
seeing and intelligent than Elizabeth —' if ever such wight
were '—might have wondered how much longer the State
would be able to impose ' one religion ' on this divided
and obstinate race of Englishmen, where even maid-
servants ' sticked not to control learned preachers ' ! The

abomination of Toleration might yet be the ultimate issue, and England become famous for the ' hundred religions,' which so much amused Voltaire on his visit to our island. But Elizabeth still hoped that all her subjects would accept ' one religion,' that of the middle way, wherein, as Hooker was so eloquently and learnedly explaining, human reason and common sense were to have their place beside scripture and beside Church authority. Certainly there was more chance that such a religion would be acceptable to the English than the scripture-pedantry of the Puritan who must find a text to justify every act of daily life, or the crushing Church authority preached by the Jesuit. Yet the idea of enforcing ' one religion ' of any kind on all England was utterly vain, and meant another hundred years of strife and hatred, imprisonments and confiscations, with blood tragically shed on the battlefield and the scaffold. And out of all that misery it was destined that there should be plucked the flower of our civil liberties and our Parliamentary constitution. Truly the ways of man's history are strange and the fate of nations is inscrutable.

As we still use the Prayer Book, it is not very hard to reconstruct in our minds an Elizabethan service. But we must imagine a wooden table in the body of the Church, instead of an altar railed off in the east end. There was no intoning, either of prayers or psalms. The prayers were said and the psalms were sung. Congregational singing was a great part of the appeal of Protestant worship. But instead of the modern hymns now sung in Church, the psalms appointed for the day were sung in the rhymed, metrical version of Sternhold and Hopkins. That old psalter, so dear to many generations of Englishmen, is now utterly forgotten ; only the ' Old Hundredth ' psalm is still familiar as a modern hymn :

> All people that on earth do dwell,
> Sing to the Lord with cheerful voice ;
> Him serve with fear, His praise forth tell,
> Come ye before Him, and rejoice.

The Elizabethan psalters, containing these rhymed versions of the psalms, often supplied the music of the tunes in four parts, ' Cantus,' ' Altus,' ' Tenor ' and ' Bassus,' so that ' the unskilful with small practice may attain to sing that part which is fittest for their voice.' The music of viols and wind instruments might or might not accompany the psalm-singing of the congregation.[1]

The sermon was the parson's great opportunity, particularly if he were a Puritan. It might be endured or even welcomed for an hour, or haply for two. But the less learned or self-confident of the clergy, especially those of the older generation, confined themselves to occasional reading of the Homilies provided by the Church. Both sermon and homily, besides making for edification, helped to form religious and therefore political beliefs.

Weekly attendance at church was a duty enforced by the State. There was a statutory fine on absentees, but it was probably not very regularly exacted, except from a known ' Popish recusant.' We may be sure that in that highly individualistic society not everyone consented to be ' knolled to church ' every Sunday of the year.

A Catholic gentleman of Cornwall, John Trevelyan, who used to attend church to avoid the fine, endured the reading of the lesson and the singing of the ' Geneva jig ' which was his name for Sternhold and Hopkins' psalms, but always went out before the sermon, calling aloud to the parson in the pulpit ' when thou hast said what thou hast to say, come and dine with me.' He used to frighten Protestant old ladies of his acquaintance by telling them ' they should expect worse days than they suffered in Queen Mary's time, and that faggotts should be dear ' ! He was a merry old gentleman of whom many stories were told. (*Trevelyan Papers. Camden Soc.*, P. II [1863, pp. 113–118] and Pt. III [1872, p. xxii.]

In the course of Elizabeth's long reign, the younger generation, brought up on Bible and Prayer Book, and sharing

---

[1] In Hanoverian times, before organs and harmoniums were common in parish churches, the metrical versions of the psalms was still sung to the accompaniment of various instruments played in the gallery : Hardy in the *Return of the Native*, Chap. V, recalls such homely music :

' One Sunday, I can well mind, a bass-viol day that time and Yeobright had brought his own. Twas the Hundred-and thirty-third [psalm] and [to the tune of] "Lydia " ; and when they'd come to *Ran down his beard and o'er his robes its costly moisture shed*, neighbour Yeobright, who had just warmed to his work, drove his bow into them strings that glorious grand that he e'en a'most sawed the bass-viol in two pieces. Every winder in church rattled as if 'twere a thunderstorm.'

the struggle for national existence against Spain, Pope and Jesuits, became for the most part fervent Protestants. Bible reading and family prayer were becoming customs of the English. So early as the first decade of the reign, Roger Ascham wrote in his *Schoolmaster* ' Blessed be Christ, in our city of London, commonly the commandments of God be more diligently taught, and the service of God more reverently used, and that daily in many private men's houses, than they be in Italy once a week in their common churches.' No doubt such family worship was then more general among the London citizens than in the country as a whole, but the custom spread fast and far.

In the year when the Queen succeeded her sister Mary, Puritanism was mainly a foreign doctrine imported from Geneva and the Rhineland ; when she died, it was rootedly and characteristically English and had added to itself some peculiarities unknown to continental Calvinism, such as rigid Sabbatarianism, ' the English Sunday ' already at war with the idea of ' Merry England.' Anglicanism also had taken root and shape in the Queen's reign. In 1559 Anglicanism had been hardly so much a religion as an ecclesiastical compromise, decreed by a shrewd, learned and moderate young woman, with the consent of Lords and Commons. But at the end of her reign it had become a real religion ; its services were dear to many, after more than forty years of use in the ancient churches of the land ; and its philosophy and spirit were being nobly set forth in Hooker's *Ecclesiastical Polity*. George Herbert (1593–1633) is the poet of an Anglican religion that is something better than a convenience of State.

The improvement in the quality of the clergy and in the learning of clergy and laity alike, which marked the end of Elizabeth's reign, was largely due to the grammar schools and Universities. The mass of the people were either quite illiterate, or half taught to read by village dames. But the clever boys of the most various ranks of society received a good Latin education together, sharing the benches and the floggings of the grammar school. Classes were not segregated, as in the schools of later generations.

The Universities, like most other institutions, had gone

G

through a bad time during the religious and economic troubles of 1530–1560. Their numbers and wealth had fallen, with the disappearance of the convents of monks and friars which had composed an important part of mediaeval Oxford and Cambridge. At the same time an Act of Parliament sent back to their parishes the crowds of middle-aged clergymen, who still, as for centuries past, were wont to desert their cures and live in idleness at the University in no too reputable manner. The mediaeval character of the two English seats of learning disappeared during these distressful years of change and impoverishment.

It was a new and more secular Oxford and Cambridge that revived under Elizabeth and flourished exceedingly up to the outbreak of the Civil War. A larger proportion of the undergraduates now looked forward to careers as laymen. The number of great Elizabethans who had been at Oxford or Cambridge is significant of a new attitude to learning in the governing class. A gentleman, especially if he aspired to serve the State, would now finish his education at one of the ' learned Universities,' whence he usually came away with a familiar knowledge of the Latin language and of classical mythology, a smattering of Greek, and a varying measure of mathematical and philosophical acquirements. Sidney and Raleigh, Camden and Hakluyt were at Oxford ; the Cecils, the Bacons and Walsingham were at Cambridge, not to mention Spenser and Marlowe. Master Silence, J.P., is at the cost of keeping his son, Will, at Oxford, for some years before he goes on to the Inns of Court ; after that double training in the humanities and in law, the young man will be fit to succeed his father as a Gloucestershire landowner and Justice of the Peace. (2 H. IV, III, ii.)

One reason for this growing connection between the Universities and the governing class, was the improvement in the conditions of academic life. The College system, rapidly replacing the hostelries and lodging-houses of mediaeval times, afforded some guarantee to careful parents. At Oxford and Cambridge, alone of the Universities of Europe, the Colleges were at this time taking over discipline, which the University had grossly neglected, and the function of teaching, which it had fulfilled very indifferently as regards the majority of students. There was as yet no such officer as the College Tutor, but the student or his parents contracted privately with one of the Fellows of the College to act both as teacher and guardian. Each of these private tutors had half a dozen such pupils whom he lectured and coached. Sometimes they slept in his rooms. It was a relationship analogous to that of master and apprentice.

On the whole this system of private tutoring worked well. But there was a tendency for the tutor to neglect those of his pupils who could not pay high fees, and to be too indulgent with those who could. His richer pupils loved to wear ' excessive ruffs, apparel of velvet and silk, swords and rapiers,' contrary to academic rules, and to engage in forbidden pastimes, such as cards and dice in the parlours of inns, fencing, cockfighting and bear-baiting. In 1587 William Cecil, Lord Burleigh, whose paternal eye was turned into every corner of the kingdom over whose welfare he watched, was credibly informed that through

' the great stipends of tutors, not only the poorer sort are not able to maintain their children at the University, but the richer be so corrupt with liberty and remissness that the tutor is afraid to displease his pupil through the desire of great gain.'

Dons, like everyone else in those days, were ' respecters of persons.' Early in Elizabeth's reign, parson Harrison complained that

' gentlemen or rich men's sons often bring the Universities into much slander. For, standing upon their reputation and liberty, they ruffle and roist it out, exceeding in apparel, and riotous company which draweth them from their books unto another trade. And for excuse, when they are charged with breach of all good order, think it sufficient to say they are gentlemen, which greeveth many not a little.'

One may well guess that, without some eye-winking on the part of the authorities, smart young men accustomed to the outdoor life of the manor-house or the gay life of the Court, would never have endured the rigid College rules of that day, which seem indeed more suitable to schoolboys than undergraduates.[1] In 1571 the Vice-chancellor forbade

---

[1] In Elizabeth's time undergraduates usually came up at sixteen ; many were two or three years younger, but it was becoming increasingly recognized that such boys were too young for the studies of the place.

even the innocent diversion of swimming in any stream or pool in Cambridgeshire to all members of the University. Probably the objection was to the danger of the exercise, like that of climbing the roof of the chapel in our own more adventurous age. Organized games and athletics did not exist, and sports were either discouraged or forbidden. But since youth must be served somehow, no wonder there was much breaking of rules. But there were rules to break : there had been none to speak of in the mediaeval University.

In an age of patronage, nepotism was inevitable, and Fellowships were freely given to the sons or clients of wealthy and powerful men, or of lawyers who would intrigue and work for the College. The Colleges were growing rich, while the University remained poor. During Elizabeth's reign the Great Court of her father's foundation of Trinity at Cambridge grew up as the rival of Tom Quad at Christ Church.

A generation later, in the reign of James I, when Simon d'Ewes studied at St. John's, Cambridge, the chief undergraduate diversions were walking, swimming (in spite of the prohibition !), bell-pulling, running, pitching the bar, and football, which was little better than an excuse for a free fight in the backs between two Colleges.

Most of the students slept four or more in a room. The poorer were usually destined for the Church, the richer for the world. The Dons who taught them were still compelled to take holy orders, and even to refrain from marriage which was now legalized for other clergymen. To that extent Oxford and Cambridge remained clerical and even quasi-monastic, until the Gladstonian legislation of the late Nineteenth Century. Daily attendance at College Chapel was enforced on all.

A number of the undergraduates, including Kit Marlowe at Corpus, Cambridge, and Philip Sidney at Christ Church, Oxford, were interested in poetry and the drama, which played so great a part in the life of those days. Plays and interludes, some in Latin, were often acted by the students. One elaborate ' rag,' played off on the town by the gown in 1597, was recorded by Fuller in his history of Cambridge University :

' The young scholars, conceiving themselves somewhat wronged by
the townsmen, betook them for revenge to their wits. . . They composed a merry but abusive comedy (which they called *Club Law*) in
English, as calculated for the capacities of such whom they intended
spectators thereof.   Clare Hall was the place wherein it was acted, and
the Mayor with his brethren and their wives were invited to behold
it, or rather themselves abused therein.   A convenient place was
assigned to the townsfolk riveted in with scholars on all sides where
they might see and be seen.   Here they did behold themselves in their
own clothes (which the scholars had borrowed) so lively personated,
their habits, gestures, language, lieger-jests and expressions, that it was
hard to decide which was the true townsman, whether he that sat by
or he that acted on the stage.   Sit still they could not for chafing,
go out they could not, for crowding, but impatiently patient were fain
to attend till dismissed at the end of the comedy.'

The Corporation, like all Englishmen in Tudor times
who felt themselves aggrieved, appealed for remedy to the
Privy Council.   Her Majesty's sage advisers gave indeed
' some slight and private check to the principal actors' but,
when the town became importunate for their further punishment, put an end to the matter by merrily proposing to
come down in state to Cambridge to see the play acted again
and judge it on the spot !

This curious incident illustrates not only the traditional
hostility but the personal intimacy that then existed between
town and gown.   Elizabethan Cambridge was a small
community in which all the leading characters were likely
to be known to one another and to the double public of
townsmen and undergraduates.   In 1586 there were 6500
inhabitants of Cambridge, of whom 1500 belonged to the
University.

A large proportion of the tradesmen cultivated a few acres
each in the town field beyond the Cam, and there were besides many small farmers (' husbands ') in the borough :
the shops and farm buildings on the street were timber-
framed, of ' mud and stud,' hiding labyrinthine alleys and
courtyards, of which relics still survive behind the modern
street-fronts of brick.   Such was the town in which Hobson
the carrier inherited in 1568 a cart and eight horses from
his father, and from that slender beginning built up a
transport service of riding and wheeled traffic which became famous throughout all East Anglia, enriched our

language with the expression ' Hobson's choice,' and the town of Cambridge with Hobson's Conduit, and finally was immortalized by two short poems of indifferent merit by young Mr. Milton of Christ's.

Cambridge was scarcely more famous for its University than for its Fair, held for three weeks in September on the stubble of the town fields, between the Newmarket road and the river.   There North and South England exchanged goods, brought by land and water.   Streets of booths were erected, where the North bought its hops and sold its wool and cloth.   Traders from the Netherlands and the Baltic and great merchants of London did big business there in cloth, wool, salt-fish and corn.   In days before the commercial traveller, fairs of this kind were essential to trade, and Stourbridge was the greatest in England : goods of every kind, wholesale and retail, were sold ; housewives, thrifty and gay, came from far to furnish their houses or replenish their cupboards and to see ' the fun of the fair.' And there too were many of the farmers and half the bailiffs of East Anglia.   The strange thing to our modern notions is that the jurisdiction over this vast annual hive of commerce lay with the University.   Stourbridge Fair could not be begun till the Vice-chancellor had come in full academic pomp and proclaimed it open.

The first necessary condition of the recovery and growth of national prosperity under Elizabeth, was an honest coinage.   Her father, as recorded above, had left behind him untold trouble by debasing the currency in the last years of his reign, and so causing under Edward VI and Mary a leap in prices with which neither wages nor fixed rents could keep pace.   After the ' settling of religion ' in 1559, Elizabeth's next great action was an equally bold grasp of the financial nettle.   In September 1560 she called in by proclamation the existing currency of debased coins, to be paid for in new money at a rate somewhat below their nominal value.   The skill and success with which this dangerous operation was carried through, bore witness that the new Queen and her Privy Council well understood the economic aspects of government, wherein many otherwise great rulers have gone fatally astray.   From that moment

forward, prices steadied themselves. They continued to
rise gradually throughout the reign, and more rapidly under
James and Charles I, because of the increasing effect of
new gold and silver from the mines of Spanish America.
But wages were now better able to keep pace, and rents were
gradually adjusting themselves as leases fell in. The
steady, but no longer catastrophic, rise in prices helped
trade and industry to prosper, to start new types of
manufacture and to find new markets. (See pp. 119–122
above.)

A great expansion of mining of all sorts—lead, copper,
tin, iron and coal—marked the reign of Elizabeth. German
miners opened out copper and other diggings in various
parts of the remote Lake District. The Mendip hills
yielded more and more lead for export by the merchants of
Bristol. The innumerable small tin-mines of Cornwall and
Devon flourished. Salt pans multiplied. Our iron was
recognized as the best in the world. In 1601 an enthusiast
told the House of Commons that iron ' appeareth to be a
particular blessing of God given only to England, for the
defence thereof, for albeit most countries have their iron,
yet none of them all have iron of that toughness and validity
to make such ordnance of.' And the navy demanded not
only cannon but gunpowder, of which the ingredients
were still collected at home, till the East India Company
in Stuart times brought them back in greater quantities
from the East.

These industrial activities were a drain on the timber of
the island, increasingly felt. Iron, lead and the new manufacture of glass, all burnt vast quantities of wood or charcoal.
' As the woods about here decay,' said a native of Worcester
late in Elizabeth's reign, ' so the glass houses remove and
follow the woods with small charge.' Salt-works, Camden
noticed, had recently consumed Feckenham Forest in
Worcestershire. Even the forests of the Weald, in Sussex,
Surrey and Kent, which had supplied the iron furnaces with
charcoal for thousands of years, were running short at last,
owing to the drain on the timber made by the increased demand for iron, and by Kent's new agricultural industry
which required poles for the hops to climb and charcoal
for the oast-houses to burn.

Household warmth and cooking still depended normally on wood fuel. The yearly increase of shipping, and men's now clear perception that the future of England lay on the sea, made it needful but difficult to maintain growing timber within reach of the docks. Already it was noted that in the lands near the sea, even as far away as Pembrokeshire, ' the woods are consumed and the ground converted to corn and pasture.' No doubt there were trees enough in the island to supply all its furnaces, hearths and shipyards a while longer, if all the timber in the realm could have been used. But it could not. The horse-transport of that day and the soft state of the roads made it economically and even physically impossible to move great masses of timber for any distance, except by water. In many upland districts, therefore, particularly in the West, the ' youthful poet ' of *Il Penseroso* could still find untouched primaeval woodlands

> ' Of pine or monumental oak,
>   Where the rude axe with heaved stroke
>   Was never heard the Nymphs to daunt
>   Or fright them from their hallowed haunt,'

while in other districts the disappearance of wood fuel gave the cottager a cold hearth and a bread-and-cheese diet, and sorely restricted the output of the manufacturer. Indeed, works had often to be moved to some place where timber could still be found. Ironworks were destined soon to invade and consume the Forest of Arden.

Under these conditions of increasing wood shortage, coal came more and more into use under Elizabeth, both for household purposes and for manufacture. But the difficulty of carriage limited the supply of coal to regions near the pits or near to navigable water. ' Sea-coal ' as it was called from its method of transport, was in general use in London and the Thames valley, and among other coastwise and riverside populations, as along Trent, Severn and Humber. Chimneys and hearths originally constructed for wood fuel had to be remade, and until this was done the ' sulphurous ' fumes were a constant nuisance. The great increase of chimneys in Elizabeth's reign was largely due to the increased use of coal. The manufacture of cast-iron fire-backs for coal fires became an important part of the work of the Sussex forges. An attempt to smelt iron with coal was made at this period, but proved premature. Many other trades already used coal where it could be got cheap. In 1578 it was said that brewers, dyers, hat-makers and others ' have long since altered their furnaces and fiery places, and turned the same to the use and burning of sea-coal.'

Not only London but the Netherlands and other foreign parts were supplied from Tyneside and Durham. Much of the coal went abroad in foreign bottoms, but the still greater trade to London was carried on by fleets of ' colliers ' from Tyne. The inadequacy of roads compelled everyone to send heavy goods of all sorts by sea or river as far as possible, and even at the end of the Queen's reign the coastwise trade of England was more than four times as great as the growing export trade.

The two chief nurseries of English seamen were the ' colliers ' plying between the Northern ports and London, and the fishermen of Cornwall and Devon, many of whom ventured to the foggy shores of Newfoundland for cod. No less important was the growth in Tudor times of the herring-fleets of the East Coast. Camden noted the size of Yarmouth, the outport of Norwich, now outstripping its rival Lynn, ' for it seems incredible what a great and throng fair is here at Michaelmas, and what quantities of herring and other fish are vended.'

The fishermen were favourites of government, because they so often helped to man the mercantile and royal navies. Laws were passed ordering the observance of ' fish days ' : none of the Queen's subjects were to eat meat during Lent, or on Fridays—sometimes Wednesdays were added. It was expressly stated that the object was not religious but political—to maintain our seafaring population, to revive decayed coast towns, and to prevent the too great consumption of beef and mutton which resulted in the conversion of arable into pasture. These fish laws were enforced by actual penalties. In 1563 we read of a London woman being pilloried for having flesh in her tavern during Lent. In 1571 we find the Privy Council busy with returns from Justices of the Peace as to enforcement of this law in various counties. Since people had been accustomed for centuries

G 2

to observe, more or less, the fasts of the Church, it was relatively easy to prolong the fish-eating habit into a new age for purposes of State. The 'fish days' may not have been always observed in upland districts where it was difficult to get fresh fish from the sea, but no doubt salt fish was sent far inland ; even in Northants and Bucks the Justices of 1571 were busy enforcing the law. It helped to prolong the use of the stews and fishponds which had been so common in the mediaeval countryside, and of which the dry beds are still to be observed near many an old manor-house.

In this and every other way, Secretary Cecil strove to maintain the seafaring population and shipping of the country. He exempted seamen from military service on land ; and he enforced Navigation Laws against foreign ships, particularly in the coasting trade. The English marine could not yet carry the whole of English exports, but the Navigation Laws were aiming in that direction.

In the reign of Elizabeth, under the vigorous leadership of Cecil and the Privy Council backed by Parliament, the industrial, commercial and social system of the country was brought under national instead of municipal control.

In the Middle Ages each locality, through its town council or craft gilds, had decided questions of wages and prices ; the relations of master, apprentice and journeyman ; the right to trade in a place ; and the conditions under which trade should there be carried on. In the Fourteenth Century national control had begun to impinge upon municipal control, when Edward III's foreign policy in France and the Netherlands had affected the whole course of English trade, and when the Statute of Labourers had vainly attempted to fix a maximum wage for the whole country.

Under Elizabeth the national control of wages and prices by the Justices of the Peace was more wisely carried on, without attempting to impose everywhere a fixed maximum wage. At the same time, municipal control of conditions of trade and industry was replaced by State control. The reasons for this great change were various : the decay of many towns and the spread of industry into the country districts where there was no municipal authority ; the decline of the craft gilds, which had received their *coup de grâce* in the confiscatory legislation of Edward VI against gild property ; the growth of the power of the Crown, working through Privy Council and Parliament ; and the joyous sense of nationhood which inspired the Elizabethan English. A man no longer felt his first loyalty owing to his town, his gild, or his ' good lord,' but to his Queen and country.

Under these circumstances the Elizabethan State undertook the control not only of wages and prices, but of apprenticeship, of the right to set up trade and the conditions under which it must be carried on. In these matters the substitution of national policies for the narrower interests of individual towns and gilds gave freer play to the initiative of individuals and to the operations of the capitalist employer and merchant.

The Elizabethan State was more liberal than most towns and gilds in encouraging the settlement of the foreign immigrant : he was usually a Protestant refugee, and he often brought new skill and new processes of manufacture into the land of refuge. Economic nationalism, as interpreted by the Tudors, gave greater liberty to the individual, freeing him from the local jealousies that usually inspired municipal policy.

But this economic liberty was not unconditional *laissez-faire*. The State that gave the individual Englishman or Huguenot the right to manufacture and to trade, laid down rules that he had to obey in the interests of the public. And the craftsman whom he employed was placed under the discipline of a national system of apprenticeship.

The Statute of Artificers (1563) enacted that every craftsman in town or country had for seven years to learn his craft under a master who was responsible for him. The object was quite as much social and educational as it was economic. ' Until a man grow into 23 years,' it was said, ' he for the most part, though not always is wild, without judgment and not of sufficient experience to govern himself.' After the age of 24, having served his apprenticeship, he was at liberty to marry, and either to set up a business of his own, or to become a journeyman for hire.

The good or bad working of apprenticeship varied greatly with the character of the master. There must have been many hard cases, with some of which the Justices of the Peace, who were responsible for the granting of the indentures, were able to interfere, as in the case recorded in the third chapter of *Oliver Twist*. But, on the whole, the relation of master and apprentice—at once domestic, educational and economic—served the purposes of society well. For centuries apprenticeship was the school of Englishmen. It was the very practical answer made by our ancestors to the ever-present problems of technical education and the difficult ' after-school age.' Apprenticeship continued until, in the Nineteenth Century, the Industrial Revolution destroyed it, and substituted, in the first instance, a *laissez-faire* chaos by no means to the advantage of the uncared-for youth of the land. The situation so created has scarcely yet been made good.

But, after all, the greatest social change in Elizabeth's England was the expansion of overseas enterprise. In her reign our merchants found new and more distant markets, some of them on the other side of the globe, in place of that commerce with the Netherlands and France which had from time immemorial furnished the principal vent of English goods. Corresponding to the change of markets was the change of mental outlook. In Court and City, in Parliament and manor-house, in workshop and field-furrow, talk ran upon the ocean and the new lands beyond it, on Drake and Frobisher and Raleigh, on the romance and profit of the explorer's and privateer's life, on sea-power as England's wealth and safety, on the prospect of colonization as a means of personal betterment and national strength. What was the loss of Calais beside all this ? Let the dead past bury its dead.

Englishmen looked forward to new things. The most influential writer in the age of Shakespeare, if it were not Foxe the Martyrologist, was Hakluyt, author of *The Principall Navigations, Voiages and Discoveries of the English Nation.* That book was published in the year after the Armada, and ten years later it was enlarged and brought up to date in three magnificent volumes. Hakluyt, in narrating the deeds of our explorers and seamen, directed across the ocean the thoughts of adventurous youth, of scholars, statesmen and merchants and of all who had money to invest. Even up-country squires and farmers began to dream of boundless expanses of virgin soil, waiting since the dawn of time to be broken by the English plough.

In the lifetime of Elizabeth no colony was successfully planted, though Sir Humphrey Gilbert tried in Newfoundland and Raleigh in Virginia. But the expediency of occupying the temperate regions of North America became a familiar doctrine of State. As early as 1584 Hakluyt had won the Queen's favour and patronage by urging it in his *Discourse of Western Planting*. Meanwhile the actual achievement of the reign in Atlantic sea-power and exploration made ready the path for the folk-wandering of the English people that began in the next generation.

The character of the war with Spain, and the limited and peculiar use to which our victory was turned in the years after the Armada, proved fundamental to the future development of English-speaking lands, and impressed a special character on England herself. The triumph of Elizabeth's subjects over the Spaniards was not a military conquest organized by an Alexander, a Pizarro or a Napoleon. Elizabeth had little in common with those heroes, or with her famous predecessor Henry V : though the tale of Agincourt berattled the common stages and made Englishmen proudly conscious of their past greatness, no one desired to renew such conquests on the continent, or even to find a new field for them in Spanish America. The victory over the Spaniards was merely the establishment of a naval superiority of our ships over theirs, through the co-operation of individual initiative with a thrifty and cautious policy of State. Drake's idea of glory was not Caesar's. He wanted no inch of Spanish soil in the old world or the new. His objects were booty, trade, freedom to sail the seas and to worship God aright, and ultimately to colonize empty lands where the Red Indian nomad would be the only person aggrieved. If Elizabeth's subjects had been less averse to taxation and more in love with the glories of war, the energy that afterwards peopled North America might have been misdirected to the conquest and development of the tropical colonies of Spain.   But our sea-victory was not thus abused.

If indeed our triumph over Spain had been won by great armies carried by the fleet, as the Spaniards had intended their victory of the Armada to be achieved ; if Spanish colonies had been subjected by force to English rule, then the United States, Canada and Australia that we know to-day might never have come into existence.   And in all probability the character of such a military effort would have diverted English society and politics in a martial and monarchical direction.[1]

The Elizabethan sea-war had the opposite influence ; it promoted a tendency towards freedom.   The possession of a royal navy does not enable the monarch to hold down his subjects, as a royal army may do.   In England there was no royal army, and in the Civil War of Charles I, the royal navy actually took the side of Parliament !   The other element of the new English sea-power was private enterprise—the action of Drake, Hawkins and their like in American waters, and the merchant companies formed in London to push trade into distant parts of the world : these activities fostered the spirit of self-reliance and self-government.

These novel elements in English society—the new City companies and the fighting seamen—exercised a great influence over the country as a whole.   Drake and his rivals and companions became the national heroes.   They and the capitalist merchants who backed them were strong Protestants, the more so as their enemies were the Spaniards, and a common result of capture was death by torture in the hands of the Inquisition.   Their allies were the French Huguenots from Rochelle and the Dutch Sea-beggars, with many a tale to tell of the tender mercies of Alva and Guise. This rough sea-fellowship, which saved the world from Philip and the *auto-da-fé*, was inspired by a fighting religion of Protestantism which reacted powerfully on English landsmen.   The seamen who beat Spain were rough

---

[1] It is true that in 1759 French Canada was conquered and annexed, but by that time the free character of the British polity at home and overseas had been fixed.   In Elizabethan and Stuart times our political and social constitution was still flexible and might have moved either towards or away from freedom.

customers, no respecters of persons in Church or State, but faithful to their proved captains, of whom the greatest was the Queen. They took their lives in their hands, and few of them survived many years the chances of battle, shipwreck and sea accident, and the terrible epidemics that raged in the ill-provisioned ships of the period, where food was rotten and the rules of hygiene were unknown.

During the Tudor reigns England changed her national weapon. She laid aside the long-bow and acquired the broadside. The long-bow, that had rendered her soldiers superior to all others in Europe, had lured her into a hundred years of military adventure in France. The broadside— the rows of cannon protruding between the timbers— showed her a better way, along the paths of the ocean to new lands. By the broadside, sea warfare was completely changed. It ceased to be a game of soldiers seeking to grapple their ship to the enemy and fight deck to deck as if on land ; it became, instead, a game of sailors, manœuvring their ship so as to fire her cannon with most effect. The ship ceased to be a platform for a storming party and became a moving battery of guns.

This change in the character of warfare at sea was better understood and more quickly exploited by the English than by their enemies. The Spaniards had Mediterranean traditions connected with the oared galley and the grappling of ship to ship. As late as 1571 they fought the great battle against the Turks at Lepanto, by sea tactics the same as those by which the Greeks had defeated the Persians at Salamis. These ancient and honourable traditions hampered Spanish seamanship, even after Philip improvised an ocean-going navy to conquer England in the Atlantic and the Channel. His Armada was, in its real spirit, an army embarked ; the soldiers outnumbered and bullied the sailors, regarding them as mechanic drudges, whose privilege it was to bring the gallant soldado to grips with his enemies.

But in the English fleet—commanded by Howard, Frobisher, Hawkins, Drake—the Admiral and his Captains were seamen and they were in full command of everyone on board. The soldiers were few and knew their place at sea. Drake, on his voyage round the world (1577–1580) had established the rule that even the gentleman volunteer must haul at the ropes with the mariner.   The discipline and equality of the crew at sea was accepted by the Englishman, while the Spaniard could not lay aside his military and aristocratic pride even to save the ship.   It was a social difference between the countries, translated into terms of war.[1]

In the twenty years before the coming of the Armada, ocean sailing and the tactics of the broadside had been perfected by English seamen, who learnt their trade in various capacities—in service in the royal ships, as merchants, as explorers, and as privateers.   These parts could be easily combined or interchanged.   The fighting merchantship, accustomed to defend herself and to force her trade in all the waters of the world, took a large share in the battle against the Armada.   But without the Queen's own professional warships the victory could not have been won.

Henry VIII had founded the royal navy.   Under Edward VI and Mary it had been permitted to decay. Under Elizabeth it was revived.   Yet during the first twenty years of her reign improvement in the royal dockyards was slow.   Elizabeth inherited a bankrupt State, and she dared not lay heavy taxes on her impatient and obstinate subjects.   Her proverbial parsimony, though sometimes applied in the wrong place, was as a general rule necessary to the bare survival of her government.   Moreover, what money she was able to squeeze out for the navy was much of it grossly ill spent.   Cecil and the vigilant Privy Council lacked not the will but the technical knowledge to detect and reform the traditional corruption of the shipyards. Then, in a fortunate hour (1578), Elizabeth put John Hawkins in charge of the building and upkeep of her ships. During the decade before the coming of open war, which the Queen had so long and so wisely postponed, Hawkins did as great a work in the dockyards as Drake on the Pacific and Atlantic coasts.

The Queen's money was at last honestly spent for full

---

[1] Hawkins and a long race of successors carried negro slaves, crimped on the coast of Africa, to the Spanish Colonies of America.   But the English seamen as among themselves had the spirit of freedom.   They always regarded with horror the use of galley slaves by French and Spaniards.   That was not the English idea of the way in which a ship should be manned.

value received. But Hawkins did more than stop corruption. This great public servant, who in his trading and privateering days between Africa and Spanish America had had experience second only to Drake's, well understood what kind of ships he ought to build for the new kind of warfare. His critics, clinging to the ideas of an older school, clamoured for vessels with a high superstructure, impregnable to assault but difficult to manœuvre, affording houseroom for crowds of soldiers who would consume the stores. Hawkins would have no more of such castles. In spite of protest, he built the Queen's ships low, long in proportion to their beam, easy to handle and heavily gunned. Such a ship was the *Revenge*, destined many years later to justify her designers when she fought the Spanish navy for a day and a night.

The English merchants, in seeking out more distant markets, were encouraged by the new potentialities of seamanship, and inspired by the adventurous spirit of the age ; but they were also compelled along the new course by the closing of old markets nearer home. The loss of Calais, where the wool Staple had functioned for so many generations past, occurred a few months before Elizabeth ascended the throne. It was a blow to English wool-exporters from which they never fully recovered, as the general trend of things was against them and in favour of their rivals, the manufacturers and merchants of cloth.

After the loss of Calais there still remained the yet more ancient trade centres of Bruges and Antwerp in the Netherlands, as marts of English wool and cloth. But in the next few years that opening also was closed. The quarrel of the young Elizabeth and her Privy Council with Granvelle, then governing the Netherlands for Philip of Spain, arose from a diversity of political, religious and economic motives. English piracy in the channel ; English friendship with the Protestants in the cities where they traded, encouraged by the magistrates and people of Antwerp ; Spanish intolerance of heretical foreigners, all played their part in the breach. But no less important was the economic clash of the two mercantilist policies of Granvelle and Elizabeth. Each side believed that the other was at its mercy. Granvelle was sure that if the English were forbidden to sell their cloth in the Netherlands they would not be able to sell it anywhere else, and must perforce be content to bring their raw wool to be wrought on the looms of the Netherlands. The English were sure that the Netherlands could not flourish without English trade.

The quarrel came to a head in the first decade of Elizabeth's reign, twenty years before actual war broke out between England and Spain. Excluded from the Netherlands, the English cloth merchants moved in 1567 to Hamburg as their port of entry into Europe, only to be driven thence ten years later by the mercantilist jealousy of the Hanse Towns.[1]

These changes of market caused much distress and periodic unemployment in the cloth manufacture at home, but gradually new markets were found further afield. New trading Companies were formed in London which successfully pushed trade into Russia, Prussia, the Baltic, Turkey and the Levant. Persia was first reached by way of the Russian river system, and finally India by way of the Cape of Good Hope. In 1600 the old Queen granted a charter to the East India Company, destined to an economic and political future surpassing all the tales of romance. These new world-wide adventures rescued the trade of England from the otherwise inevitable consequences of the loss of her old markets on the coast opposite to her own shores. The change-over was rendered possible by the adventurous spirit of the capitalists of the City of London, by the quality of the new school of sailors and sea-captains, and by the enterprise of English explorers by land as well as sea.

Already in 1589, Hakluyt in dedicating to Walsingham the first edition of his *Voyages*, had proudly written :

'Which of the Kings of this land before her Majesty, had their banners ever seen in the Caspian sea ? Which of them hath ever dealt with the Emperor of Persia as her Majesty hath done, and obtained for her merchants large and loving privileges ? Who ever saw, before this regiment, an English Ligier in the stately porch of the Grand Signor at Constantinople ? Who ever found English Consuls and Agents at Tripoli in Syria, at Aleppo, at Babylon, at Bakara, and, which is

---

[1] E. E. Rich, *The Ordinance Book of the Merchants of the Staple* (1937), chap. IV, tells the story of the loss of the Netherlands market and its consequences.

more, who ever heard of Englishmen at Goa before now ? What
English ship did heretofore ever anchor in the mighty river of Plate ?
Pass and repass the unpassable (in former opinion) strait of Magellan,
range along the coast of Chili, Peru and all the backside of Nova
Hispania, further than any Christian ever passed, traverse the mighty
breadth of the South Sea, land upon the Luzones, in despite of the
enemy, enter into alliance, amity and traffic with the Princes of
Maluccas, and the isle of Java, double the famous Cape of Bona
Speranza, arrive at the isle of St. Helena, and last of all return home
richly laden with the commodities of China, as the subjects of this
now flourishing monarch have done ? '

By the end of Elizabeth's reign not only was English
commerce and finance thus reviving and expanding on a
modern basis, but her ancient rivals were in rapid decline.
The withdrawal of English trade might not by itself have
proved fatal to the prosperity of the Spanish Netherlands,
but there followed the appalling religious persecutions and
wars of Alva's rule. The complex of these events put an
end to the supremacy which Antwerp had long held in the
trade and finance of Europe. Amsterdam and the other
towns of the rebel Dutch republic rose instead. Ere long
the Dutch seamen were to be chief rivals of the English in
all the waters of the world ; but to the subjects of Elizabeth
the Dutch mariners were more important as allies in war
than as rivals in trade.

Meanwhile the merchant cities of Italy were being ruined
by the increasing difficulties of the overland trade-routes to
the East, and by the rivalry of the Cape route, which they
left to the Portuguese, Dutch and English. Italian traders
abandoned the big field of world competition. Venetian
merchants ceased to visit England in quest of Cotswold
wool. In 1587 the last of the argosies sent by Venice to
Southampton was wrecked off the Needles ; with her sank
the mediaeval system of trade and all that it had meant to Italy
and to England. Southampton, which had been the Italian
depot, declined, and London was further enriched, as the
trade with the Mediterranean and the Far East now entered
the Thames in English ships.

In the following century, tobacco played a great part in
English colonial and commercial expansion and in the trade
of Bristol. There were as yet no English colonies, but

already in 1597 the new American weed was being smuggled into the creeks of Cornwall on a large scale, by French, Flemish and Cornish ships, in open and armed defiance of the custom-house officers. The habit of taking tobacco in long clay pipes was very general by the time the Queen died.

The expansion of overseas enterprise was closely connected with the growth of merchant capitalism, inimical to the old municipal and gild system.

'The guild system [writes Mr. Fay] was not favourable to capital accumulation. In their technique and the ordering of their life the merchants and craftsmen of the Middle Ages surpassed perhaps the centuries which followed. But the guild outlook was municipal and its structure inelastic, and therefore it gave way to a system which lent itself to expansion and change. This we call merchant capitalism, with its complement domestic industry. The merchant capitalist was a middleman who broke down ancient barriers. He defied corporate towns by giving out work to the country, and evaded the monopolies of privileged companies by interloping. . . He committed excesses, but he was the life-blood of economic growth.' [1]

This movement of merchant capitalism athwart the old municipal and gild system had been apparent in the wool trade as early as the age of Chaucer. In Elizabeth's reign it took another great step forward in the rise of oversea trading Companies of a new type. They were of two kinds. First the 'regulated company,' in which each member traded on his own capital, subject to the common rules of the Corporation : such were the Merchant Adventurers, who had a great past as well as a great future as exporters of cloth ; the Eastland or Baltic, the Russia, and the Levant Companies. The other class was joint-stock—the East India Company ; the African ; and two generations later the Hudson's Bay. In this second class, trade was conducted by the corporation as a whole, and the profits and losses were divided among the shareholders.

To each of these companies, whether regulated or joint-stock, a geographical sphere of operations was assigned by royal charter, and no 'interloper' from England might trade therein. Such monopoly was both just and necessary,

---

[1] C. R. Fay, *Great Britain from Adam Smith to the Present Day*, p. 107.

because of the expenses in the way of forts, establishments and armaments which the Companies had to maintain ; for the royal navy could offer them no protection in distant waters. These Elizabethan companies were in many respects similar in their privileges and functions to the ' Chartered Company ' that helped to develop and disturb the interior of Africa late in Victoria's reign. That was, perhaps, an age too late for such political and military powers to be wisely entrusted to a private group of the Queen's subjects—as Jameson's raid showed. But under Elizabeth there was no other way of promoting distant trade, and if the Company mismanaged its policy in distant lands, its members suffered but the English State was not involved in the consequences.

These great London companies, only very slightly dependent on the State, worked under conditions which fostered the spirit of private enterprise, self-government and self-reliance. Supreme as was the ultimate importance of these corporations in the history of India and North America, their influence at home was also very great on the development of the English character and on social and political change, as the history of Stuart and Hanoverian times was to show. A generation after the death of Elizabeth, the traveller Peter Mundy noted as one of the ' seven things wherein England may be said to excel, traffic and discoveries, viz. so many incorporated companies of merchants for foreign trade, who employ their study and means for the increase thereof, by adventuring their goods and sundry fleets and ships into most parts of the known world.' [1] Mediaeval England had been ' traded with ' by Italians, French and Germans ; Elizabethan England herself traded with remote shores. Commercially we had ceased to be the anvil ; we had become the hammer.

To remote posterity the memorable fact about Elizabethan England will be that it produced the plays of Shakespeare. It is not merely that the greatest of mankind happened to be born in that age. His work would never

---

[1] Mundy's Travels (Hakluyt Soc. 1924) IV, pp. 47–48. An account of the origin (chiefly Elizabethan) of these companies will be found in vol. II of Lipson's *Economic History of England*.

have been produced in any other period than those late Elizabethan and early Jacobean times in which it was his luck to live. He could not have written as he did, if the men and women among whom his days were passed had been other than they were, in habits of thought, life and speech, or if the London theatres in the years just after the Armada had not reached a certain stage of development, ready to his shaping hand.

It was no accident that Shakespeare's plays were more poetry than prose, for the audience he addressed, as indeed the common English in town and country alike, were accustomed to poetry as the vehicle of story-telling, entertainment, history and news of contemporary incidents and sensations. Not newspapers and novels but ballads and songs were hawked about by Autolycus and his comrades to satisfy the common appetite in the city street and on the village green. Ballads were multiplied and sold, many thousand of them, each with a story from the Bible, or classical myths and histories, mediaeval legend or happenings of the day, whether the Armada, the Gunpowder Plot or the latest murder or runaway match. And lyrics and lovesongs, of which the words survive as masterpieces of literature in our modern anthologies, were sung as the common music and sentiment of the people.

Under these conditions, in the twenty years before Shakespeare's first plays were acted, a new drama had suddenly grown up, with a new school of playwrights of whom Marlowe was the chief, and companies of highly-trained actors, taking their profession with a high seriousness. To the mediaeval clown and barn-stormer out-heroding Herod had been added men of subtler art, of whom Burbage ere long became the most notable ; these men carried the art of interpretative acting to its height, and with them were boy apprentices, strictly trained from childhood to take the women's parts with dignity, gaiety and skill.

In the middle years of Elizabeth a way to wealth and honour had been opened to the actor and the playwright. The travelling companies had the patronage of literary noblemen, whose castles and manors they visited as welcome guests, acting in hall or gallery, like the players who had such princely entertainment at Elsinore. But even better

' both for reputation and profit ' were the theatres built in the meadows on the Southwark bank of Thames, to play before the motley and critical audience of the capital ; while citizens with their wives, and apprentices with their sweethearts, walked over London Bridge to see the play, men of rank and fashion came over by boat from Whitehall, and sharp young lawyers from the Inns of Court.

The performances were given in the day-time ; there was neither curtain nor footlights. The front of the stage was in the open air. The most privileged of the audience sat on ' stools ' almost among the actors. The ' groundlings ' stood below, gaping up at the spectacle, exposed to rain and sun. The covered galleries, that enclosed the ' wooden O ' of the theatre, were also full of folk. Here then were gathered together several classes of society, differing from one another, more or less, in tastes and education. It was Shakespeare's business to please them all.

When he first knew this exacting audience, they were eager for plot and pageant, noise and knock-about, gross clowning and bouts of courtly and learned wit, and music of the best, for the English had then the finest songs and music in Europe ; and they were eager too, as the ordinary modern audience is not, for the rhetoric of poetry as a vehicle for play and passion. All these things Marlowe and his fellow labourers had supplied, creating in a few years the new drama that Shakespeare found ready to his hand. He accepted the tradition, and in twenty more years expanded it into something far greater than the most consummate of public entertainments.

His poetry was of a yet higher strain than Marlowe's ' mighty line,' and he invented a prose dialogue as subtle, as powerful, and sometimes as lovely and harmonious as his verse. He made both forms the vehicles not only of beauty, terror, wit and high philosophy, but of a thing new in the drama, the presentation of individual characters, in place of the types and personified passions that had hitherto held the stage. Even the plot, even the action, became subordinate to the character, as in *Hamlet*, and yet the play pleased. So real were his men and women that we are for ever discussing them as if they had a life of their own off the scene. Indeed, for two hundred years past his plays have lived even more in the study than on the stage.   Yet plays they are, even when acted in the theatre of the mind ; and only the stage can give them full force, though too often it mars them.   It is to the Elizabethan theatre that we owe Shakespeare and all that he created.   For that let praise be given to the theatre —and to the Elizabethans.

The social historian of to-day cannot really describe the people of the past ; the most he can do is to point out some of the conditions under which they lived.   But if he cannot show what our ancestors were like, Shakespeare can.   In his pages we can study the men and women of those times. More, for instance, can be found out in his plays about the real relations of the two sexes, the position and character of Elizabethan women, than could possibly be expressed in a social history.

As our study of the English scene emerges from mediaeval into modern times, we obtain in increasing profusion that aid of which Chaucer gave us a foretaste, the literature and fiction that described men and women of the writer's own time, their habits of thought, speech and conduct—contemporary impressions which have by the passage of years become historical documents of priceless value.   At the same time, intimate diaries and memoirs become common in the Seventeenth Century, like those of Evelyn, Pepys and, later, Boswell's *Johnson*.   These, and the English drama, and the novels of Fielding, Jane Austen, Trollope and a hundred others help social history in just that region where legal and economic documents stop short.

All who crave to know what their ancestors were like, will find an inexhaustible fount of joy and instruction in literature, to which time has added an historical interest not dreamt of by the authors.   These are the ' books, the arts, the academes' of the social study of the past, and the greatest of them all is Shakespeare.

Books for Further Reading

Besides those mentioned in the text above, Darby *Historical Geography of England* (1936) Chap. X ; Miss Taylor's *Camden's England ;* James Williamson, *The Age of Drake* (1938) and J. Corbett's *Drake and the Tudor Navy ;* W. Cunningham, *Growth of English Industry and Commerce : Modern Times*, Part I ; Lipson *Ec. Hist. of England*, Vol. II, III, *Age of Mercantilism* (1934) ; Granville-Barker, *Prefaces to Shakespeare and Henry V to Hamlet* (British Academy Lecture, 1925) ; *Social England*, Vol. II (ed. H. D. Traill) ; Blomfield, *Short History of Renaissance Architecture in England ;* J. U. Nef, *The Rise of the British Coal Industry.* For Elizabethan ballads see the first Essay in Sir Charles Firth's posthumously published *Essays* (Oxford 1938) ; Rowse, *Tudor Cornwall*, 1941 ; Mildred Campell (Professor in Vassar College), *The English Yeoman under Elizabeth and the Early Stuarts* (Yale Press 1942).

CHAPTER VIII

THE ENGLAND OF CHARLES AND CROMWELL

The beginning of Colonial expansion. East India Company. Fen Draining.
Social conditions and consequences of the Great Rebellion. Household Life.

(James I, 1603–1625. Charles I, 1625–1649. Long Parliament meets,
1640. Outbreak of Civil War, 1642. Oliver Cromwell, Protector, 1653–
1658.)

In the realm of social and economic history, the period of
the Stuart Kingship in England up to the outbreak of the
Great Rebellion may be regarded as an uneventful prolongation of the Elizabethan era, under conditions of peace and
safety instead of domestic danger and foreign war. Agriculture, industry and commerce all continued very much in
the manner described in the two preceding chapters. A
rural society, in which land-ownership, opportunity and
modest wealth were widely distributed, gave ample scope
and importance to the country gentlemen of large and of
small estates, and to the freehold and leasehold yeomen.
But there were hard times for many, partly owing to the
rise of prices. Industry and commerce moved forward on
the lines laid down in Tudor times. The companies
founded in the reign of Elizabeth for trading to distant
parts of the world grew in wealth and influence, and with
them grew London, outstripping other cities more completely than before in population, wealth, and all the attri-
butes of power. In the country at large, the apprentice
system, the poor law, the regulation of wages and prices,
the economic and administrative functions of the Justices
of the Peace under the control and stimulus of the Privy
Council, were all much the same on the day when the Long
Parliament met as on the day when Queen Elizabeth died.
No industrial, agricultural or social change of importance
took place in England during the forty years when the
Parliamentary and Puritan Revolution was germina-
ting beneath the soil of an apparently stable and settled
society.

The slow pace of change in the economic and social life of England in the first forty years of the new century was but little accelerated by the union of the English and Scottish Monarchies in the person of Elizabeth's successor. The peoples, Parliaments, laws, Churches and commercial systems of the two Kingdoms remained for another century as separate and as different as before. Nor did any exchange of population result from the union of the Crowns. Scotland was too poor to attract, too jealous to welcome immigrants from England. When James Sixth of Scotland and First of England moved from Holyrood to Whitehall in 1603, he was accompanied or followed by a crowd of courtiers and needy adventurers, the first trickle of the great stream of Scots who have since come across the Border to seek their fortunes. But it was long before that stream swelled to proportions of national significance. Several generations were to pass before Scottish farmers, mechanics, gardeners, administrators, physicians and philosophers came swarming south, bringing with them skill, industry and knowledge sufficient to affect the life and increase the prosperity of England. Throughout the Seventeenth Century it was not to Scotland but to Holland that Englishmen looked for new ideas in religion, politics, agriculture, land-draining, gardening, commerce, navigation, philosophy science and art.

Nor, under the Stuart Kings, did English thought and practice greatly affect the Scots, whose pride took quick alarm at influences emanating from their too powerful neighbour. Scottish religion had clothed herself in a strongly woven garment of native fabric, and was equally inimical to Anglicanism with its Prayer Book and to English Puritanism with its unorthodox sects. So, too, the peculiar spirit of Scottish society, feudal in the personal loyalty of the vassal to his lord, but equalitarian in the human intercourse between classes, was utterly unintelligible to the English mind until Sir Walter Scott's novels retrospectively afforded the key.

In overseas trade the merchants of the two countries were still rivals, the purse-proud English everywhere bearing the upper hand, and shutting out the Scots from foreign and colonial markets to the best of their power. At home the two peoples glowered at each other across the pacified border. Three hundred years of periodic warfare might be brought to an end by the union of the Crowns, but the long tradition of mutual injury and revenge, from Falkirk and Bannockburn to Flodden and Pinkie Cleugh, had left animosities that took long to abate. In the civil and religious troubles of Stuart times, English and Scottish parties, Churches and soldiers often acted together for Parliament or for King, but the more they saw of one another the less they agreed, for the men of the two nations still moved on different planes of thought and feeling.

Slight and gradual as were the changes in England herself during the first forty years of the Seventeenth Century, little as the dynastic union with Scotland affected the social life of the time, these quiet years witnessed the greatest change of all, the beginning of the permanent expansion of the English race overseas. The successful founding of Colonies in Virginia, New England and West Indian Islands like Barbados, and the establishment of the first trading stations on the coast of Hindoostan, were the greatest events of the reign of James I and the early years of King Charles.

The English race began once more to move outside its island borders, this time in the right direction. The attempt made during the Hundred Years' War to reduce France to an English province had been the first instinctive gesture of an awakening national consciousness and a new-felt power to expand. After it had failed, the English had for a century and a half been confined to England, strengthening themselves there in wealth, intelligence and naval power ; now they began once more to expand, by very different methods and under very different leadership from those of the day when

> ' Our King went forth to Normandy
> With grace and might of chivalry.'

This time the ' good yeomen whose limbs were made in England ' went forth again, but not with chivalry and not under the King, not with the long-bow to sack and conquer an ancient civilization, but with axe and plough to found a new civilization in the wilderness.

For this enterprise the first requisite was peace. So long as the war with Spain continued, England's limited stock of wealth and energy would run into fighting at sea, in Ireland and in the Netherlands. Under war conditions, the Elizabethan attempt to found Virginia had failed. In the first year of the new reign, James I had the merit of making peace, on good terms which successful war had won. In many respects his subsequent foreign policy was feeble and inept : he let down the strength of the navy and cut off Raleigh's head to please Spain. But at any rate his pacifism gave peace to England, and his subjects made use of that breathing space to sow the seed of the British Empire and of the United States. The restoration of an effective navy by Charles I and its maintenance by subsequent rulers enabled the movement to go forward in safety. Government maintained the conditions under which colonization was possible, but private enterprise supplied the initiative, the money and the men.

London Companies like the Virginia Company and the Massachusetts Bay Company financed and organized the emigration, which could never have taken place without such backing. The object of the noblemen, gentry and merchants who found the money, was partly to earn a good percentage on their immediate investments, but even more to create beyond the Atlantic a permanent market for English goods, in exchange for the products of the new world, such as the tobacco that Virginia soon produced in great quantities. Both patriotic and religious motives inspired many of those who supplied the funds, the ships and the equipment for the enterprise. Between 1630 and 1643 £200,000 was spent in conveying 20,000 men, women and children to New England in 200 ships : in the same period 40,000 more emigrants were conveyed to Virginia and other colonies.[1]

The very efficient ' promoters ' of the movement included some of the noblest born and many of the wealthiest of the King's subjects : but the colonists themselves were of the middling and lower orders of town and village. In their minds, also, the motives of colonization were in part self-regarding and economic and in part ideal and religious.

[1] Godfrey Davies, *Early Stuarts* (Oxford Hist. Eng.) p. 337.

The religious motive had little or no weight with the majority of the settlers ; but it inspired the leaders in New England, like the Pilgrim Fathers (1620), and after them John Winthrop and his colleagues. Their zeal imposed on the Northern group of colonies a Puritan character which was destined to affect powerfully the social development of the future United States.

Those who crossed the Atlantic for religious reasons desired, in the words of Andrew Marvell, to escape from ' prelate's rage.' Under James, Charles and Laud, only one religion was tolerated in England and it was not the Puritan. Some of these religious refugees to New England desired to set up in the wilderness a Kingdom of God on the Geneva model, to be enforced upon all who chose to become citizens of the theocratic republic—for such in effect was early Massachusetts. But another type of Puritan exile, like Roger Williams the founder of Rhode Island, and the various groups of settlers in New Hampshire and Connecticut, not only wished to enjoy religious freedom themselves but were ready to extend it to others. Williams had been driven from Massachusetts because he maintained that the civil power had no authority over the consciences of men. Thus the difference between the two Puritan ideals, the coercive and the liberal, which soon afterwards split the ranks of the victorious Roundheads in the old country, had come to a head in New England as early as 1635. An easy-going attitude towards varieties of religion prevailed in Anglican Virginia, and in Maryland founded by the Roman Catholic Lord Baltimore.

The settlers in Virginia, the West Indian Islands and to a large extent even in New England, had not emigrated for religious motives at all. The ordinary colonist had been drawn oversea by the Englishman's characteristic desire to ' better himself,' which in those days meant to obtain land. Free land, not free religion was the promise held out in the pamphlets issued by the companies promoting the emigration. It was a period of land-hunger in England. Many younger sons of peasants and yeomen could obtain no land at home, and former copyholders often found themselves pushed out of their old secure franchise into the position of lease-holders or tenants at will. Rents were rising and tenants were competing hotly for farms. Unemployed craftsmen, too, could be sure that in the new settlements their skill would be in great demand. Many gentlemen adventurers were attracted not only by the prospect of land, but by the lure of the unknown and the marvellous, and by stories of fabulous riches to be won in America, which in fact only their remote descendants were to realize in ways undreamt. Early New England was not a land of great fortunes or of great contrasts in wealth.

All these classes of emigrants went freely, at the instigation of private enterprise and persuasion. The government only sent out convicts, and later on prisoners of the Civil Wars. These unfortunates, and other youths kidnapped by private enterprise to be sold into servitude in Barbados and Virginia, worked out their freedom if they lived long enough, and often founded prosperous families. For it was soon tacitly agreed that only negroes from Africa ought to be kept in perpetual bondage. The slave-trade, which Hawkins had begun with the Spanish colonies, now supplied Virginia and the English West Indian Islands.

During the Civil Wars of Charles and Cromwell the flow of voluntary emigration diminished. Virginia and Maryland were passively loyal to the King ; and even the New England colonies, though sympathizing with the Puritan cause, remained neutral. For already the instinct of ' isolation ' from the affairs of Europe was strong in America. Three thousand miles was a very long way, a voyage of several months of misery, during which death took its toll in the ill-found ships. And so, after the first few years, the social history of America ceased for ever to be a part of the social history of England. The new society began to work out its own characteristics, under pioneer conditions of life very different from those that prevailed in the ' garden of England ' in the days of Shakespeare and Milton. None the less the Colonies were an offshoot of English Seventeenth Century life, and derived thence ideas and impulses that were to carry them far along new paths of destiny.

England at that period and for two hundred years to come was peculiarly fitted to provide colonists of the right sort. That is why the English language is spoken in North America and Australasia to-day. Until the later Nineteenth

Century agricultural life and tradition flourished in England. The ordinary Englishman was not yet a townee, wholly divorced from nature ; he was not yet a clerk or a specialized workman of one trade only, unable to adapt himself to pioneering conditions, unwilling to abandon the advantages of a high standard of living at home for a life of hardship and incessant toil in an unknown land. The Englishman of Stuart and Hanoverian times was more adaptable than his descendants and had stronger incentives to emigrate. No standard of life and no pension for old age were secured to him at home beyond what he could win by his own efforts. The poor law would keep him from starving, but no more. Moreover, the inhabitant of the Seventeenth Century English town still knew something of agriculture, and the inhabitant of the English village still knew something of craftsmanship. The townsmen tilled their ' town fields.' The village contained not only men to farm its land but men to build its cottages and barns, weave and cut its clothes, make its furniture, farm implements and harness. The cottage wives could bake, milk, cook, help in the harvest, spin, mend or make clothes, as well as rear families of children. A shipload of emigrants drawn from a number of such self-sufficing villages were capable of creating and maintaining a new village in the wilderness, even where there was no shopping town behind it to supply its needs.[1]

The makers of the early American settlements must have been men and women of most admirable versatility, endurance and courage. The greater part of the first colonists—more than three-quarters it is calculated—died prematurely, succumbing to the miseries of the voyage, or to disease, famine, exposure and Indian war. It was only a residue who survived the first years, to people and extend the woodland townships. In many respects it was the story of the Anglo-Saxon settlement of Britain over again—the struggle with virgin forest and marsh, the warfare with the old inhabitants. But the Anglo-Saxon invaders had been barbarians accustomed to savage life ; the American settlers

---

[1] In some of the New England townships the first settlers established for a time the system of open village fields and common pasture to which they had been accustomed in England. Gilbert Slater, *English peasantry and the enclosures,* Chap. XVI.

were men of civilized intelligence, some of them highly educated. In Massachusetts one of their first acts was to found a University—a Cambridge in the new land. For civilized people to endure the hardships incident to primitive life requires fine qualities, which the England of that day was able richly to supply.

The newly founded colonies, whether on the mainland or on the islands, whether under the control of London Companies or more directly under the Crown, at once assumed a large degree of independence. They elected assemblies for the whole colony, and made each township a self-governing unit. In New England the Church congregation strengthened the tie and dominated the policy of the township. The instinct to extrude the authority of the homeland, whether exercised by King or by Company, was present in the earliest settlements, especially in Massachusetts, though it only assumed continental proportions under George Washington.

The instinct of the first English settlers to manage their own affairs cannot be attributed solely to the great distance from Europe. Spanish, French and Dutch colonies in America and South Africa were no less remote, yet they long remained undemocratic in government and amenable to the authority of the homeland. The self-dependent attitude of the English settlements was partly due to the circumstances of their origin : they had not been founded by an act of State but by private initiative. And many of the colonists had come out with rebellious hearts, seeking to escape from the ecclesiastical government of England. The King of France, on the other hand, would allow no Huguenots in Canada.

Moreover, there were habits of self-government in old English society that were easily transplanted oversea. Thus the squirarchical tradition at home, the local government of the English shire by Justices of the Peace who were the local landowners, gave rise ere long in Virginia to the rule of an outdoor equestrian aristocracy of planters, whose life differed from that of English country gentlemen chiefly in the possession of negro slaves. This aristocratic system grew up naturally with the tobacco plantations that soon became the staple of that Colony's wealth.

H

In New England a Puritan democracy of farmers and tradesmen arose, which also had its roots in habits brought from the old country.   In the early Seventeenth Century, the English shire and village still retained elements of communal self-government, beneath the higher control of the squires and Justices of the Peace.   The freeholders had their part in the proceedings of the County Court.   The Court Leet of the Manor was still attended by the peasantry who were, nominally and to some extent actually, the judges of the business there transacted.   And in every English village there were various humble offices—such as constable, overseer of the poor, headborough, ale-conner, road-repairer, churchwarden, sidesman and innumerable other small public posts—which the common people filled, either by election or rotation.   These habits of local self-government at home helped the creation of the New England Township and Court House.

The emigrants also carried with them the jury system and the English common law, a law of liberty.   Last but not least, the right of Parliament, as representing the people, to vote or refuse taxes was a doctrine widely diffused in the England of James and Charles I, especially among the opposition leaders, like Sir Edwyn Sandys, who did so much for the plantation of Virginia, and among the Puritan gentry and yeomen of East Anglia who took so leading a part in the settlement of New England.   To such men the immediate establishment of colonial Assemblies seemed a matter of course.

The spirit of independence was further stimulated by the Bible-religion which the Colonists brought with them from home.   Even in Massachusetts where the ministers and the godly at first tyrannized over the plain man, there was no sanction for the spiritual and social power they assumed, beyond the temporary acquiescence of their fellow-citizens. The New England ministers could not, like Laud's Anglican clergy, claim authority drawn from the King.   Still less could they, like the Catholic priests who directed life in French Canada, exercise a spiritual rule of dateless antiquity derived from Rome.   The only foundation for Church power in New England or in Virginia was popular opinion.   And so the religion of English-speaking America soon became congregational rather than ecclesiastical, and served further to enhance the democratic spirit of trans-atlantic society.

In this way the American colonies were founded, by private enterprise—financial, commercial, agricultural, and politico-religious. The first application of State policy and military power to promote imperial development was Cromwell's conquest of Jamaica from Spain (1655), followed by Charles II's acquisition from the Dutch of the regions that became New York, New Jersey and Pennsylvania (1667). By that time it was beyond the power of State action to alter the self-dependent character of English colonial society. But the increasing need for the protection of colonial trade by the Royal fleet in the Atlantic, in the face of foreign enemies, rendered possible a policy of State inter-ference with the course of that trade, exercised through the Navigation Laws. From the time of Cromwell onwards these laws were partially at least enforced. They aimed, not without a large measure of success, at enlarging the proportion of English commerce carried in English ships, and in keeping the trade of English colonies mainly for England.[1]

Meanwhile, on the other side of the globe, the ships of another London trading company were beginning another chapter of England's destiny. The East India Company founded by Elizabeth's charter of 1600, held thereby the monopoly among her subjects of trading with the 'East Indies,' the power of legislation and justice among its own servants oversea, and by implication the power of making peace and war beyond the Cape of Good Hope. For generations to come no ship of the Royal Navy rounded the Cape. The Crown made no pretence of being able to take action in the Far East to protect the nation's trade in those parts, as it protected the Atlantic trade with the American colonies. The Company had therefore to defend its fac-tories with sepoys in its own pay ; and at sea the great 'East Indiamen' built, equipped and manned at once for

---

[1] A high authority on the original Settlements is Charles M. Andrews, *The Colonial Period of American History*, Vol. I, *The Settlements*. (Yale Univ. Press, 1933.)

commerce and for war, replied with their broadsides to attacks made by Portuguese and Dutch rivals and by the pirates of all nations. But the Company was wisely careful to avoid quarrels with Indian Princes, and had no territorial or political ambition.

The first great Anglo-Indian statesman, Sir Thomas Roe, James I's Ambassador and the Company's agent at the Court of the Mogul Emperor, laid down the policy which guided the action of his countrymen in the East for more than a century to come.

'A war and traffic are incompatible. Let this be received as a rule that if you will profit, seek it at sea, and in quiet trade ; for without controversy it is an error to affect garrisons and land-wars in India.'

So long as the Mogul Empire maintained its authority, as it did during the Stuart era, the Company was able to follow Roe's prudent advice. Only when the great Peninsula relapsed into anarchy, the English merchants, in the days of Clive, were unwillingly drawn into war and conquest to save their trade from Indian and French aggression.

Under the early Stuarts the Company established small trading stations at Madras, at Surat north of Bombay,[1] and by 1640 in Bengal. The power and privileges they exercised within the walls of the towns and ' factories ' assigned them were held by treaty with the native princes. Their enemies were the Portuguese, who soon ceased to be formidable, and the growing power of the Dutch, who drove them by force out of the coveted trade of the Spice Islands farther east (1623), compelling them to develop instead their position on the mainland of the Peninsula. From their factories in Madras and Bombay the English learnt to trade with Canton ; ignorance of conditions in the Farther East prevented the London merchants from doing direct trade with China to any purpose, but the Company's servants in India had local knowledge enough to conduct it themselves, and to tap the great resources of Chinese commerce. The London Company also sent ships direct to the Persian Gulf (first in 1628) to the annoyance of the Levant Company,

---

[1] Later on, Charles II's Portuguese marriage brought Bombay itself as part of the Queen's dowry.

which endeavoured to trade with the Shah's dominions by the overland route.

The East India trade, implying voyages a year long of ten thousand miles without breaking bulk, did more even than the American trade to develop the art of navigation and the character of ship-building. Already in the reign of James I the East India Company built ' goodly ships of such burthen as never were formerly used in merchandise.' While the ships of the Levant Company ranged from 100 to 350 tons for the Mediterranean traffic, the first voyage to India was made in a vessel of 600 tons, and the sixth voyage (1610) in a vessel of 1100 tons.[1]

The long Indian voyages would not have been possible as a means of regular trade if the crews had been much exposed to the ravages of scurvy. But from the very first (1600) the East India Company supplied its crews with ' lemon water ' and oranges. The Royal Navy of Stuart and Hanoverian times was not protected in this manner, and the King's sailors suffered terribly, until Captain Cook, almost as great a sea-doctor as a discoverer of new continents, introduced marked improvement in naval drinks and diet.

In Stuart times the East India Company owned some thirty great vessels for the voyage round the Cape, besides numerous smaller craft that never left the Eastern seas. A considerable proportion were wrecked, or taken by pirates or by Dutch. But those great ships that survived were so strongly built of the best English oak as to be able to face the high seas for thirty or even for sixty years. Already in James I's reign ' the Company laid out at one time £300,000 in building shipping, which was more than King James had then in the navy.' The Indian trade thus ' filled the nation with great ships and expert mariners.'

Here was a private navy, heavily armed, added to the strength of England. Knowledge of the most difficult parts of navigation, and the habit of distant maritime enterprise became widely spread among the English. London, as the headquarters of the East India Company, drew to

[1] Grenville's *Revenge*, one of the large ships of the Elizabethan navy, was 500 tons. The *Mayflower* was only 180 tons ; she had previously been engaged in the wine trade between English and Mediterranean ports.

itself England's trade with the Orient. Bristol shared in the tobacco and slave trades across the Atlantic, and Liverpool soon followed suit ; but the general effect of the American and Indian trades, and the increase in the size of merchant ships, was to enhance yet further the supremacy of London at the expense of many lesser ports that had sufficed for the small ships and short voyages of earlier times.

The Indian trade increased not only the shipping, but the wealth of England. It proved indeed impossible to sell more than a limited quantity of English cloth in the warm climate of the Far East, and the enemies of the Company always made that a ground of accusation. But Queen Elizabeth had very wisely permitted the Company to export a certain quantity of coin of the realm, on condition that as much gold and silver was returned after each voyage. By 1621, £100,000, exported in bullion, brought back oriental wares worth five times as much, of which only a quarter was consumed at home. The rest was resold abroad at great profit and so, to meet the bullionist criticism, ' the treasure of the realm was increased.'

Before the Civil War, the chief articles conveyed to the Thames in the Company's great ships were saltpetre (for warlike Europe's gunpowder), raw silk, and above all spices, particularly pepper. The scarcity of fresh meat in winter before the era of roots and artificial grasses was a chief reason why our ancestors craved for spices ; they were used both to preserve meat, and to season it highly when it had little else to recommend it. After the Restoration, tea and coffee came in, and silks manufactured in the East for the European market, and porcelain of China. By the time of Queen Anne, the East Indian trade had materially altered the drink, the habits of social intercourse, the dress and the artistic taste of the well-to-do classes among her subjects.

These long-distance trading companies, with their great losses and greater profits, became an important part of social and political life under the Stuarts. Their wealth and influence were generally thrown against the Crown in the Civil War, partly for religious reasons and because London was prevalently Roundhead, and partly because the merchants were discontented with the treatment they had received from James and Charles I. Monopolies for the production and sale in England of many articles in common use, had been granted to courtiers and intriguing patentees. This policy, enlarged by Charles I as a means of raising non-Parliamentary revenue by his Prerogative, was frowned on by the common lawyers and Parliament men, and was for very good reasons unpopular with the consumer who found the price of the articles raised, and with the merchant community who saw trade restricted and disturbed.

But the merchants of the East India House felt even more aggrieved because the King, while granting such unneeded monopolies in the home market, infringed their own much needed monopoly of trade in the Far East, though the whole cost of political and military action on that side of the globe fell on the Company and not on the Crown. Charles I had set up a second company for Indian trade—the Courteen Association—which by its rivalry and its mismanagement had nearly ruined all English trade in the Far East, at the time the Long Parliament met. The policy of Pym and Parliament, to suppress Monopolies in England and maintain them for the companies trading oversea, was much better liked in the City. One of the most important results of the victory of the Parliamentary armies in the Civil War was the virtual abolition of monopolies inside the country. Henceforward, though foreign and Indian trade was subject to regulation, industry in England was free, as compared to European countries where mediaeval restrictions still hampered its growth. This was one reason why England in the Eighteenth Century led the world in the race of the Industrial Revolution.

The early Stuart Kings had done nothing effective either in Europe or in Asia to restrain the Dutch from destroying the Company's ships and factories in the East. The ' massacre of Amboyna ' (1623) when the Dutch drove the English traders from the Spice Islands, was a memory that sank deep. More than thirty years later Cromwell exacted compensation for this old injury, by war and diplomacy in Europe. The Protector indeed did much to ' protect ' English trade and interests all over the world. But the expense of his military and naval establishment was a burden that before he died was getting too heavy for commerce, and the Restoration, bringing disarmament and lower taxes, came as an economic relief. Cromwell's posthumous reputation as the great ' Imperialist ' was in no sense undeserved. By his conquest of Jamaica he set an example to all future governments, which Elizabeth had never set, of taking the opportunities afforded by war to seize distant colonies from other European powers.

The rivalry of the Courteen Association followed by the troubles of the Civil Wars in England, had almost destroyed the East India Company and put an end to the English connection with India. But during the Protectorate the old Company, with Cromwell's help, re-established its shaken prosperity and assumed its permanent financial form as a single joint-stock enterprise. Hitherto, money had been raised for each separate voyage (usually indeed on the joint-stock principle). The earliest voyages had often realized 20 or 30 per cent., sometimes 5 per cent., sometimes a dead loss due to battle or wreck. But in 1657 a permanent fund, the ' New General Stock ' was instituted for all future purposes. For thirty years after the Restoration the profit on the original stock averaged first 20 and later 40 per cent. per annum. The market price of £100 stock touched £500 in 1685. There was no need to increase the amount of the original stock, since the Company was in so strong a position that it could borrow short loans at very low interest, sometimes 3 per cent., and reap enormous profits with these temporary borrowings.

The great wealth derived from Eastern trade therefore remained in a few hands, chiefly of very rich men. Under the last Stuart Kings, Sir Josiah Child could set aside great sums of money to bribe the Court before 1688, and Parliament afterwards, in the interest of the Company's monopoly. The general public, having to pay very high prices for the stock if they were allowed to buy it at all, grew every year more indignant that no one except a few fortunate shareholders in a close concern was permitted to trade beyond the Cape. ' Interlopers ' from Bristol and elsewhere sent out ships to carry on a ' free trade.' But the Company's monopoly, however unpopular, was legal, and its agents enforced the law with a high hand, in regions a year's sail

distant from Westminster, where strange, unreported incidents took place by sea and land between English rivals in
high rage with one another.

The struggle between Josiah Child and the Interlopers in
the reigns of Charles and James II and William, was only a
repetition on a larger scale of the struggle between the Company and its rivals under James and Charles I and Cromwell.
All through the Stuart era, there was eager and angry competition, economic and political, for a share in the profits of
the Indian trade, all the more because there was no easy,
common way of finding investment for money, though
savings were rapidly accumulating. There was no regular
stock market where a man could make his choice among a
number of reasonably hopeful ventures offering shares for
sale. The usual way of investing money was to purchase
land or mortgages on land. But the amount of land was
limited, and it was, moreover, an article which owners were,
for reasons other than economic, exceedingly unwilling to
sell ; the social and the sporting value of landed estate made
it hard to buy. And so the question what to do with one's
money, other than keep it in a strong-box at home, puzzled
many people, from the nobleman to the thrifty yeoman and
artisan.

Four-fifths of the population was tilling the land, but a
gradually increasing proportion were engaged in trade or industry, more often in the country than in the town. It was
a day of small businesses, rapidly increasing in number. A
yeoman or craftsman who had saved a little money could not
in those days use it to buy Consols or railway or brewery
shares. He might spend some of it in a marriage portion
to provide his daughter with a husband as an establishment
for life. For the rest he would very likely invest his savings
in a new venture of his own, employing a few apprentices and
journeymen to set up an industry or a shop, or perhaps
buying horses, carts and pack-saddles to serve the neighbourhood as a carrier.

The number of such small employers and tradesmen
was on the increase, and they, like the East India Company,
often wanted to borrow money for their business. So,
too, did landowners—not only the squire in distress due to

H 2

extravagance, but the squire prudently eager to drain, clear
and improve his land, and increase the agricultural acreage
at the expense of wood and waste. How did these various
classes of 'adventurers' borrow money for their enterprises ?
How were they put in touch with persons wishing to lend
and to invest ?

Society had at last, very gradually, in the course of the
Tudor reigns, abandoned the mediaeval doctrine that it was
wrong to lend money on interest. Lending money on
reasonable terms had now been made legal by Act of Parliament, and therefore interest was less exorbitant. Thinkers
who led opinion under the early Stuarts, clearly saw the use
of a money market. ' 'Tis a vain thing,' Selden told his
friends, ' to say money begets not money, for that no doubt
it does.' And the very practical mercantile philosopher,
Thomas Mun, wrote : ' How many merchants and shopkeepers have begun with little or nothing of their own, and
yet are grown very rich by trading with other men's money.'

As yet indeed there were no banks in England. But
there were persons who performed some of the functions of
modern bankers, receiving deposits and lending out money
on interest. Brokers and scriveners, in the way of their
ordinary business, had special opportunities to oblige clients
by arranging such operations, or by bringing borrower and
lender together.

During the Commonwealth and after the Restoration the
holding and lending of money passed more and more into
the hands of the goldsmiths of London. The merchants of
the City had been accustomed to keep their spare cash in the
Tower Mint, but after Charles I had seized it there, they
preferred to trust the goldsmiths. At the outbreak of civil
strife, when the wealthy of both sides melted their plate into
' pikes and musketeers,' the goldsmiths' ordinary occupation
of selling gold and silver vessels was suspended during the
years of war, and they were glad instead to become ' the
merchants' cash-keepers, to receive and pay for nothing, few
observing or conjecturing the profit they had for their pains.'
So great indeed was the profit, that the goldsmiths soon
found it worth while to encourage deposits by paying interest
—under Charles II they gave six per cent. ! For they employed the deposits to great advantage in lending to others.

The principal goldsmiths thus engaged were those in Lombard Street.[1]

The goldsmiths' business as ' proto-bankers ' was by no means confined to dealings with city merchants. Many landowners had their rents paid into the goldsmiths' hands ; while others, all the country over, came to Lombard Street for loans. The value of these new conveniences can be illustrated by examining the actual method by which a certain noble family managed its extensive affairs in the reign of Charles I.

In 1641, the year of Strafford's execution, died Francis Russell, Fourth Earl of Bedford.[2] There was no bank in which his money could be kept ; there were no cheques by which his heir could pay it out. There was, however, a ' great trunk ' in Bedford House in the Strand, where his current cash lay guarded by the family servants. The young Earl William, the first time he opened the trunk as its owner, found therein £1557.14.1. Out of this he paid all the expenses of his father's funeral and other bills, in money of the realm. But the trunk was speedily replenished : in the next twelve months, immediately preceding the outbreak of the Civil War, the cash poured into it amounted to £8500, a sum worth many times as much in terms of present-day money. It represented rents, and ' fines ' for the renewal of leases, while a thousand pounds were accounted for by sales of wood, malt, tallow, sheepskins, hay and other produce of the Russell home farms.

The Earl's principal Steward lived in Bedford House, kept the key of the all-important trunk, and was, in fact, the family treasurer or receiver-general, permanently residing in London. Everything paid to the Earl, or almost everything, came up to the Steward and was by him placed in the trunk and taken out again as required. In 1641 the largest

---

[1] The origin, or one of the origins, of cheques, took the form of notes sent to goldsmiths or others asking them to pay out so much money to such and such a person from the money the writer of the note had lodged with its recipient. The first printed cheques were issued by the Bank of England early in the Eighteenth Century.

[2] For what follows see the excellent book of Miss Scott Thomson, *Life of a noble household 1641-1700* (1937), a remarkable contribution to social history in many of its aspects.

single item came from the great estates in Devon and
Cornwall, which sent up £2500 that year. For these
western estates—and for them alone—a modern and convenient method had already been adopted of transferring
the money to London. The estates in East Anglia and
other parts sent up hard money guarded from highwaymen
by the Earl's mounted servants. But at Exeter there sat a
' Steward of the West.' His office was an old Russell
mansion in the western capital, to which the Bailiffs of the
various manors in Devon and Cornwall came with hard cash
and accounted for the audit at Lady Day and Michaelmas.
The Steward of the West, with the moneys thus received
by him at Exeter, arranged for a bill of exchange to be
drawn upon one of the London goldsmiths, the celebrated
Thomas Viner of Lombard Street. When Viner had
received the bill, he gave notice to the Steward at Bedford
House, who went with bags and porters to fetch away an
equivalent sum of coined money from ' Lumber-Street ' and
deposit it in the trunk.[1]

But the Earls of Bedford, though certainly ' spacious in
the possession of dirt,' were by no means mere passive receivers of rent. Francis, the Earl who died in 1641, and
his son William the first Duke, who died in 1700, nearly
covered the century between them as owners of the Russell
property, and as such did a greater work for England than
they achieved by their cautious political patronage of ' the
good old Cause ' in its more moderate aspect. The labour
of their lives was given to the improvement of their great
and widely scattered properties in London, Bedfordshire,
the South-west and in the Fen District. Their very genuine
but unobtrusive Puritan religion strengthened and in no
wise disturbed their fulfilment of the duties of an English
country gentleman upon the national scale.

To these two men, more than to any others, was due the
successful initiation of the drainage of Fenland. One of
their ancestors while serving Queen Elizabeth in the Low
Countries, had observed with wonder how Holland had

---

[1] The importance of the operations of some of these ' goldsmiths ' may be
judged from the fact that this Thomas Viner supplied large quantities of bullion
and plate both to Cromwell and to the East India Company, and contracted for
coining it into money. In 1656 he and Alderman Blackwell bought Spanish
prize plate to the value of £60,000.

been built up out of the waters, and brought back with him a Dutch engineer to look at the Russell estate in the Fens, formerly the land and water of the Thorney monks. The project thus engendered in the family mind was given reality forty years later by Earl Francis. In 1630 he promoted the formation of a company of 'adventurers' to drain a large region of South Fenland round Ely Isle. The Earl 'adventured' by far the greatest sum—ultimately at least £100,000. The 'adventurers' were each allotted portions of the land to be drained, answering to the amount of their several investments.

On the advice of Vermuyden, another Dutch engineer, it was decided that it would not suffice to deepen the old winding river-courses ; a straight canal, seventy feet wide and twenty-one miles long, was cut from Earith to Denver Sluice. This became known as the Old Bedford River, when twenty years later the New Bedford River was cut in a parallel line to help it at its work. The waters, constantly piling up from the distant catchment area of the Ouse, at last ran freely away down these new channels, instead of spreading over the Fenland as they had done from time immemorial. Arable and pasture were rapidly substituted on the reclaimed lands for fishing, fowling, and reed-growing. The change was resented by the fenmen, whose ancestors had for countless generations lived an amphibious life with a fixed economy of its own. (See pp. 147–149 above.) Now, at one blow, their occupation was gone. Whether they received proper compensation for this loss of livelihood we have not the evidence to decide. At any rate they waged a war of midnight raids to cut the dykes as fast as they were built, seriously impeding progress.

During the Civil War the work of drainage was at a standstill, or rather went back, for the destruction of the dykes by their enemies went on apace in the disordered time. But under the Commonwealth, partly through the labour of Scottish and Dutch prisoners of war, the first great stage was completed. Under the Protector, who favoured the enterprise,[1] crops were already growing and cattle feeding

---

[1] In 1638 ' Mr. Cromwell,' then of local celebrity only, had opposed the injustice of the drainage award in the interest of the Commoners, but he was not opposed to the scheme of reclamation, and in 1649 advocated an Act for its completion.

over scores of thousands of acres, of late the reedy home of
bittern and wild duck.   The Earl reaped the reward of his
own and his father's ' adventure.'   Before 1660 he had
paid off the mortgages on all the Russell estates, many of
them incurred to drain the fenland which had now made
good the investment.

At the Restoration, the draining of the fens, so far as it had
yet gone, seemed to be an engineering and an economic success. But before the end of the Century new and grave difficulties had arisen, due to the opposition not of man but of
nature.   At first the rapid outfall of the new canals had
scoured and kept open the estuaries of Ouse and Nene, but
as time went on these exits to the sea began to silt up.
Moreover, the level of the lands drained by the new system
began unexpectedly to fall ; the black peaty earth shrank
as soon as it was dry, as a sponge shrinks when water is
squeezed out of it.   The consequence was that the Bedford
River and the other canals stood up above the surrounding
country, like the similar ' rivers ' that drain Holland.
Means had therefore to be devised to pump the water up
out of the low fields into the high ditches and thence into
the still higher canals that were to take it to the sea.
Throughout the Eighteenth Century this was the problem,
partly solved by the erection of hundreds of windmills to
raise the water ; they formed a picturesque feature in the
flat landscape, but they were not wholly effective.   The
solution came—so far as it has ever come—in the early
Nineteenth Century, when steam-driven pumps were
employed instead of windmills.

Even during the Eighteenth Century, when the drainage
difficulty was at its worst, the success of the work of reclamation done in Southern Fenland in the valleys of the Ouse and
Nene, was so manifest that similar undertakings were carried
out in the Northern Fens, watered by the Welland and the
Witham, round Spalding, Boston and Tattershall.   Wherever draining took place, the shrinking and attrition of the
peat brought the underlying layer of rich clay nearer the
surface.   In the Eighteenth and Nineteenth Centuries the
clay was increasingly dug up to manure the land, or became
the land itself by the total disappearance of the peat.   To-day
the Fenland is one of the best arable soils in England.

Thus, in spite of natural difficulties which are not yet entirely overcome, a great work was accomplished, and a new, rich province, eighty miles long, and ten to thirty miles broad, was added to the farmland of the Kingdom. It had not, like the older fields of England, been won from the waste by the gradual encroachment of innumerable peasants and landowners, diligently working through centuries to increase bit by bit each his own estate. The victory over nature in Fenland was due to the accumulation of capital and its application to an enterprise conceived beforehand on a large scale by men who were ready to risk great sums of money and wait twenty years or more for a return. The draining of the fens is an old-world story, but it is an early example of the working of modern economic methods, and as such worthy of special remark in a social history of England. (H. C. Darby, *Historical Geography of England*, Chap. XII, and his book on *The Draining of the Fens*, 1940 ; Gladys Scott Thomson, *Life of a noble household*.)

Before we return to the early Stuart period, let us follow a little further the economic history of the House of Russell, after the great venture of the fen-draining had turned out so well under the Commonwealth. The family fortunes had been laid long ago in trade with Gascony from Weymouth quay in the days of Chaucer. Three hundred years later, in the days of William III, the Russells went back into overseas trade by a marriage alliance with the governing family of the East India Company. The first Duke of Bedford, who had inherited the Earldom and the family trunk from his father in 1641 and had seen the fens successfully drained, was living at the close of the century in honoured and prosperous old age, but melancholy from the loss of that loved son William who, with less political moderation than his father and grandfather, had given his life for ' the good old cause ' by the scaffold and axe in 1683. A dozen years later the old Duke married his grandson and heir to Elizabeth, grand-daughter of Josiah Child and daughter of John Howland of Streatham, the rulers of the East India Company. The bridegroom was 14, the bride 13 years old. It was a marriage of great splendour, with many coaches attendant. Bishop Burnet performed the ceremony. But after the banquet arose a hue and cry. ' The bride and bridegroom were missing. They had slipped away after dinner to play together, and in their play the costly point lace trimming of the young lady's dress had been torn to pieces. She was found hiding in a barn, while her new lord and master was strolling back with seeming innocence to the wedding company.'

And so, by this child marriage, which in the course of years proved happy enough, the Russells got in on the ground floor of the East India Company. They did not come empty handed. As they had formerly put their money into fen drainage, so now they put it into building new docks at Rotherhithe and great vessels for the Cape voyage, which they presented in noble style to the Court of Directors. One ship was called the *Tavistock*. Another called the *Streatham*, built by the old Duke in the year of his death in 1700, survived so many voyages that it carried Clive back to India in 1755.

If the ' great families ' had an overlarge share in governing England in the Eighteenth Century, they had done something to earn it. By wise activity in other spheres besides politics and administration they played a great part in the development of the country by land and by sea, they had the interests of trade as much in their minds as the interests of land, and in their veins flowed the blood of merchants and lawyers no less than of soldiers and country gentlemen. The French *noblesse*, with greater privileges, including exemption from taxes, was a close caste with few functions and limited outlook.

But let us return to the generation that followed the death of Queen Elizabeth. The gradual but constant rise of prices, largely due to the flow of silver from the Spanish-American mines into Europe, made it impossible for James and Charles I to ' live on their own revenues,' and their Parliaments were unwilling to make good the deficiency except on religious and political conditions which the Stuart Kings were unwilling to accept. And the same rise of prices, though always injurious to people with fixed incomes and often to wage-earners, tended to enrich the more enterprising of the landowners and yeomen and above all the merchants—precisely the classes who were becoming most opposed to the monarchy on religious and political grounds. These economic causes contributed to bring about the Civil War and to decide its issue.

The financial embarrassments of the Crown had an unfortunate effect on the economic policy of the State. We have already seen how the royal power to control trade, by the grant of ' monopolies ' in the manufacture and sale of certain classes of goods, was used not for the public interest but to raise revenue for a distressed monarch, endeavouring to make his Prerogative financially self-supporting. Those expedients were harmful to trade and politically injurious to the popularity of the royal cause.

But in one aspect of economic and social policy—the Poor Law—the continuance and enlargement of the system laid down under Queen Elizabeth was a credit to the Crown, and to the system of Privy Council government with which the names of Strafford and Laud are associated. The historian of the English Poor Law has written [1] that the survival of an effective system of poor relief in England alone of the greater nations of Europe—

was mainly caused by the coexistence in England of a Privy Council active in matters concerning the poor and of a powerful body of county and municipal officers who were willing to obey the Privy Council. Even in the reign of Elizabeth the Privy Council sometimes interfered in enforcing measures of relief, but only as a temporary expedient for relieving the distress caused by years of scarcity. But from 1629 to 1640 they acted continuously in that direction, and by means of the Book of Orders succeeded, as far as children and the impotent poor were concerned, in securing the due execution of the law. The Council also succeeded in inducing the Justices of the Peace to provide work for the able-bodied poor in many of the districts in the eastern counties and in some places in almost every county. This provision of work was provided either in Houses of Correction or in the Parishes. . . The substance of the orders does not appear to have excited opposition. Men of both parties sent in their reports to the Privy Council, and more energetic measures to execute the poor law were taken in the Puritan counties of the east than in any other part of England.

[1] Miss E M. Leonard, *Early History of English Poor Relief*, 1900, pp. 293-294. See also pp. 113, 171 above.

We shall have occasion in later chapters to consider the serious faults of poor law administration in the Eighteenth Century. Some of them resulted from the decline of the control exercised by the Privy Council over local magistrates and parishes, a decay of much-needed central authority which was the heavy price paid for Parliamentary government and constitutional freedom. But the Poor Law had taken such firm root in the days of Royal Prerogative that it survived as custom of the country in Parliamentary times.

The worst horrors of failure, of unemployment and of unprovided old age were not suffered by the poor in England to the same extent as in the continental countries of the *ancien régime*. The regiments of beggars, such as continued to swarm in the streets of Italy, and of France under Louis XIV, were no longer known over here. The scandal and danger of such congregations had alarmed the Tudor and early Stuart governments ; the Poor Law was meant to prevent them, and did prevent them by the only practical method, the relief of distress and the provision of work.[1] That is one reason why there was never anything like the French Revolution in our country, and why through all our political, religious and social feuds from the Seventeenth to the Nineteenth Centuries the quiet and orderly habits of the people, even in times of distress, continued upon the whole as a national characteristic.

There was no effective system of police until that begun by Sir Robert Peel in 1830. It was a disgraceful condition of things, and had many evil consequences. But the wonder is that society held together at all without the protection of a strong civic force trained to control mob violence and to detect theft and crime. That we dispensed so long with a proper police force is a testimony of the average honesty of our ancestors and to the value of the old Poor Law, in spite of all its defects.

The personal liberty of the poor was not a thing of which much account was taken. The philanthropic action of the State was curtailed by no such consideration. The Poor Law system involved sending the idler (the ' unemployable ')

---

[1] In 1631 the Mayor and Recorder of King's Lynn reported that they had ' bought materials to set the able-bodied poor on work, not suffering to our knowledge any poor to straggle and beg up and down the streets of this Burgh.'

to the House of Correction and clapping the drunkard in the stocks. Some, though by no means all, of the Puritans' interference with the lives of their fellow-citizens, that became so intolerable under the Commonwealth, was common form to all religious sects and all shades of political opinion.

The clear modern distinction between offences punishable by the State on the one hand, and ' sins ' not cognizable by a court of law upon the other, was not yet so rigid in men's minds as it afterwards became. Mediaeval ideas still survived and the Church Courts still existed to punish ' sin,' though with diminished powers. In Scotland indeed the Presbyterian Church exacted penance for sexual offences more rigidly than the Roman Church had been able to do. In Laud's England the Church Courts attempted something of the same kind, but much more cautiously and even so with disastrous results. The ' libertines ' joined the Puritans in the outcry against the Bishops' Courts, though for very different reasons. The ' libertine ' objected to standing publicly in a white sheet for adultery or fornication. The Puritan, on the other hand, thought even more strongly than the Bishop that ' sin ' should be punished, but he thought that he and not the Bishop should punish it. The outcome was that the Englishman threw off the yoke first of Bishop and then of Puritan, and the attempt to punish ' sin ' judicially lapsed after the Restoration and was never seriously renewed south of the Border.

Under English Puritan rule, it was not the Church Courts but the ordinary lay Courts of the land that were charged with the suppression of sin. In 1650 an Act had been passed punishing adultery with death, and the savage penalty was actually inflicted in two or three cases. After that even Puritan juries refused to convict and the attempt broke down. But during this period, public opinion supported the laws to suppress duelling, which had more success, until the Restoration restored the liberty of the bravo. The employment of soldiers to enter private houses in London to see that the Sabbath was not being profaned, and that the Parliament fasts were being observed —carrying off meat found in the kitchens—aroused the fiercest anger. So, too, in many places did the cutting down of Maypoles and the forbidding of sports on Sunday afternoon. Yet the ban on ' Sabbath ' games substantially survived the Restoration. In spite of the Anglican and liberal reaction of 1660, the Puritans left their sad mark on the ' English Sunday ' in permanence.

The horrible mania for persecuting witches, common to Catholic and Protestant lands during the period of the religious wars, was less bad in England than in some countries, but touched its highest point in the first half of the Seventeenth Century. It was caused by a sincere belief in the reality of witchcraft held by all classes, including the most educated, and it only receded as the governing class in the later Seventeenth and early Eighteenth Century gradually reached a point of scepticism on the subject that induced them to stop the witch-hunt, in spite of the continued credulity of the mass of the population. The two worst periods in England were during the first half of the reign of the credulous James I, and during the rule of the Long Parliament (1645–1647) when 200 witches were executed in the eastern counties, chiefly as a result of the crusade of Matthew Hopkins the witch-finder. The government of Charles I and of the Regicide Republic and Protectorate were both honourably marked by a cessation of this foolish atrocity.

In England before the Restoration it would have been difficult to find more than a handful of men who openly avowed a disbelief in the miraculous sanctions of the Christian faith, in one or other of its forms. But there were many Englishmen in whom a dislike of the pretensions of the pious, whether Anglican priests, or Puritan ' saints,' was stronger than positive enthusiasm for any religious doctrine. In this limited, English sense of the word, ' anti-clericalism ' has again and again been the decisive make-weight in the balance between religious parties in England. Anti-clericalism had been the chief motive force in the destruction of the mediaeval Church under Henry VIII. In his daughter's long reign it had nerved the national resolution against the Spain of the Inquisition, while at home it had no quarrel with the modest and unprovocative clergy of Elizabeth's tame Church. But when, under Charles I's patronage, Bishops and clergy raised their heads again in social and political life, and even occupied offices of State once more as in the Middle Ages, the jealous laity took alarm.   The anti-clerical feeling of great nobles, angry at the presence of clergymen in the Council Chamber and the Royal Closet, and of the London mob howling against Bishops in Palace Yard (1640–1641), joined itself in a blind alliance with Puritanism, then at the apex of its influence, and enabled the Long Parliament to break the Laudian Church.

After the triumph of the Parliamentary armies came the ' rule of the saints,' with their canting piety used as a shibboleth to obtain the favour of the dominant party ;   their interference with the lives of ordinary people ;   their closing of the theatres and suppressing of customary sports.   Anti-clerical feeling, thus provoked, reacted so violently as to become one of the chief causes of the Restoration of 1660. A generation later it was one of the chief causes of the anti-Romanist Revolution of 1688.   For many generations to come, hatred of Puritanism took its place beside hatred of Romanism in the instincts and traditions of the chapel-burning mobs, as well as of the great majority of the upper class.

The Cromwellian revolution was not social and economic in its causes and motives ;   it was the result of political and religious thought and aspiration among men who had no desire to recast society or redistribute wealth.   No doubt the choice of sides that men made in politics and religion was to some extent and in some cases determined by pre-dispositions due to social and economic circumstance ;   but of this the men themselves were only half conscious.   There were more lords and gentlemen on the side of the King, more yeomen and townsfolk on the side of Parliament. Above all, London was on the side of Parliament.   Yet every class in town and country was itself divided.

The stage of economic and social development which had been reached in the England of 1640 was not the cause, but it was a necessary condition, of the political and religious movements that burst forth into sudden blaze.   The astonishing attempt of Pym, Hampden and the other Parliamentary leaders to wrest power from the Monarchy in good earnest, and to govern the State through an elected debating assembly of several hundred members, and the degree of success which that bold innovation actually attained in politics and war, pre-supposed not only an old Parliamentary tradition but the existence of a powerful bourgeoisie, gentry and yeomanry, long liberated from ecclesiastical and feudal control, and long accustomed to share with the monarchy in the work of government.   So too the rapid rise to national importance, and for a while to national predominance, of innumerable sects such as Baptists and Congregationalists could not have occurred except in a society where there was much personal and economic independence in the yeomen and artisan classes, and in a country where for nearly a century past the individual study of the Bible had been a great part of religion, and the chief stimulant of popular imagination and intellect.   If there had been newspapers, magazines and novels to compete with the Bible in manor-house, farm and cottage, there would have been no Puritan revolution—and John Bunyan would never have written *Pilgrim's Progress.*

Indeed, the Puritan Revolution was itself, in its basic impulse, a ' Pilgrim's Progress.'   ' I dreamed [wrote Bunyan], and behold I saw a Man clothed with rags, standing in a certain place, with his face from his own house, a Book in his hand, and a great burden upon his back.   I looked, and saw him open the book and read therein ; and as he read, he wept and trembled ; and not being able longer to contain, he broke out with a lamentable cry, saying " *What shall I do ?* " '

That lonely figure, with the Bible and the burden of sin, is not only John Bunyan himself.   It is the representative Puritan of the English Puritan epoch.   When Bunyan was a young man in the years that followed Naseby, Puritanism had come to its moment of greatest force and vigour, in war, in politics, in literature, and in social and individual life. But the inner pulse of the machine that drove all that tremendous energy tearing its way athwart the national life

> ' To cast the Kingdoms old
> Into another mould,'

the prime motive force of it all was just this lonely figure of the first paragraph in *Pilgrim's Progress*—the poor man seeking salvation with tears, with no guide save the Bible in his hand. That man, multiplied, congregated, regimented, was a force of tremendous potency, to make and to destroy. It was the force by which Oliver Cromwell and George Fox and John Wesley wrought their wonders, being men of a like experience themselves.

But it would be a mistake to suppose that this earnestness of personal and family religion was confined to the Puritans and the Roundheads. The Memoirs of the Verney family and many other records of the time show us Cavalier households as religious as the Puritan, though not so wearisomely obtrusive with scripture phrases for every common act of life. Many of the small gentry and yeomen, particularly in the northern and western half of England, felt, like humble and patient Alice Thornton, that the Church of England was that ' excellent, pure and glorious church then established, which for soundness in faith and doctrine, none could parallel since the Apostles' time.' As her biographer has said :

Her account of the religious life of the family must dispel any illusion that to be Church of England, as opposed to the Nonconformists, meant that religion was to be taken any more lightly. The whole family was called to prayers by a little bell at six in the morning, at two in the afternoon and again at nine at night. (Wallace Notestein, *English Folk*, p. 186.)

Many families in all ranks of life who fought and suffered for the Church and the Prayer Book, by those sufferings learnt a love of the Church of England which had not been so consistently felt and expressed before the Civil War as it was after the Restoration. And that love for the Church as Laud had refashioned it continued, until the Nineteenth Century, to be combined with a family and personal piety and a study of the Bible that was common to all English Protestants who took their religion seriously.

But there are other things in *Pilgrim's Progress* besides the most perfect representation of evangelical religion. The way of the Pilgrims, and of the reader withal, is cheered by the songs, the rural scenery, the tender and humorous human dialogues. It is the England of Izaak Walton's *Angler*. It is still in great measure the England of Shakespeare, though it is the scene of a soul's conflict that afflicted the contemporaries of Shakespeare less often than those of

Bunyan. But the human background has little changed. We should feel no incongruity if Autolycus displayed his wares to the Pilgrims on the footpath way, or if Falstaff sent Bardolph to bid them step aside and join him in the tavern.

The country through which the Pilgrims travel and the ways along which they have to pass, are the countryside, the roads and the lanes of the English East Midlands with which Bunyan in his youth was familiar. The sloughs, the robbers, and the other accidents and dangers of the road were real facts of English Seventeenth Century travel. We must indeed except the dragons and giants ; but even those Bunyan got from no more alien source than *Sir Bevis of Southampton* and other old English ballads, legends and broadsides that used then to circulate among the common people, instead of the flood of precise newspaper information that has killed the imaginative faculty in modern times.

In those days men were much left alone with nature, with themselves, with God. As Blake has said :

> Great things are done when men and mountains meet.
> These are not done by jostling in the street.

The principle, thus poetically expressed, of the effect of quiet contact with nature upon human achievement and quality, is true not only of the mountains that nursed Wordsworth's genius, but also of the far-stretched horizons of the fenland and of Cambridgeshire, over which the rising and setting sun and the glories of cloudland were often watched by solitary men—Squire Cromwell for instance, and the yeomen farmers who became his Ironsides. In the wide spaces of the East Anglian countryside each of these men had felt himself to be alone with God, before ever they joined to form a regiment. And that same principle is true of the meadows, the lanes and the woodland fens of Bedfordshire, the nurse of Bunyan and all the strivings and visions of his youth.

Fortunately most of the common people who kept the sheep in Shakespeare's countryside, or wandered by Izaak Walton's streams, fishing-rod in hand, were untroubled by Bunyan's and Cromwell's visions of heaven and hell ; but, saint and sinner, happy fisherman and self-torturing fanatic, all were subject to the wholesome influences of that time and landscape. Their language was the crisp pure English from which the translators of the Bible drew their style, now irrecoverable. As to the songs of the common people, they are well described in a dialogue by Izaak Walton.

PISCATOR : I pray, do us a courtesy that shall stand you and your daughter in nothing, and yet we will think ourselves something in your debt. It is but to sing a song that was sung by your daughter when I last passed over this meadow, about eight or nine days since.

MILK-WOMAN : What song was it, I pray ? Was it ' Come shepherds, deck your herds ? ' or ' As at noon Dulcina rested ? ' or ' Phillida flouts me ? ' or ' Chevy Chace ? ' or ' Johnny Armstrong ? ' or ' Troy Town ? '

PISCATOR : No, it is none of those ; it is a song that your daughter sung the first part, and you sung the answer to it.

MILK-WOMAN : Come, Maudlin, sing the first part to the gentleman with a merry heart ; and I'll sing the second when you have done.

So the song is sung : it is ' Come, live with me and be my love.' When it is finished, *Venator* says :

Trust me, master, it is a choice song, and sweetly sung by honest Maudlin. I now see it was not without cause that our good Queen Elizabeth did so often wish herself a milkmaid all the month of May.

Such were simple country-folk under the Puritan Commonwealth, most of them little disturbed by its interfering rigours and stern aspirations.

Here is a letter of June 1653 by that charming girl Dorothy Osborne, reporting to her lover what she saw and heard one morning near the ' open field ' of a village :

You ask me how I pass my time here. . . The heat of the day is spent in reading or working, and about six or seven o'clock I walk out into a common that lies hard by the house where a great many young wenches keep sheep and cows and sit in the shade singing of ballads. I talk to them and find they want nothing to make them the happiest people in the world, but the knowledge that they are so. Most commonly when we are in the midst of our discourse, one looks about her and spies her cows going into the corn, and then away they all run as if they had wings at their heels.

Not all the year round could maids ' sit in the shade singing of ballads,' and Queen Elizabeth only desired to be a milkmaid in the month of May ! There was much hardship, poverty and cold in those pleasant villages and farms ; but the simplicity and beauty of the life with nature was an historical reality, not merely a poet's dream.

The great generation of men who between them produced the high English tragedy of Roundhead and Cavalier, were not brought up on the Bible and on the influences of the country life alone—though such a limitation would almost be true of Bunyan. The age of Milton, Marvell and Herrick was an age of poetry and learning often in close alliance. Not only were simple and beautiful songs being written and set to music and sung by all classes, but in cultivated households more elaborate and scholarly poems circulated in manuscript before they found their way into print or passed into oblivion. When the music of Lawes was married to the immortal verse of Milton's *Comus* for the private theatricals of Lord Bridgewater's family (1634), English domestic culture touched perhaps the highest mark to which it ever attained. And the learning of the time, classical as well as Christian, was very widely spread.

Political and religious controversy was conducted in books and pamphlets forbiddingly learned to the modern eye, yet in spite of their heavy display of erudition, they caught the eager audience to which they made appeal. Even the famous pamphlet in favour of tyrannicide, entitled *Killing no Murder*, written by a Republican and reissued by the Cavaliers with the very practical object of inducing someone to assassinate Cromwell, is made up of learned citations of classical as well as Biblical authorities. Even under Puritan rule, what the Greeks and Romans had said about tyrannicide counted with ordinary readers as much as the views of Hebrew Judges and prophets.

There were in fact a great many students among the upper and middle classes both of town and country. Every reader had in some sort to be a student, for, apart from poetry and the stage, there was hardly any literature that was not serious. Fiction scarcely existed except in ballads for the common folk, and in the heavy ' tomes ' of French romances like *Grand Cyrus*, which seem to us as dull as sermons, but in those days pleased cultivated young ladies like Dorothy Osborne.

Professor Notestein has in our day unearthed the diaries

of a Yorkshire yeoman named Adam Eyre, who at one time served in the Parliament's army, but by 1647 had come home to his farm in the Dales. No doubt he read and thought more than the majority of his class, but the range and character of his reading throws light on the intellectual habits of the time and shows why yeomen were quite capable of choosing a side for themselves, in politics and religion, often different from that of the neighbouring gentry.

Adam had a carpenter in to furnish his study with shelves and his friends (yeomen like himself) were always borrowing from those shelves. Rarely did he return from a visit to one of the larger towns without bringing home a book ; sometimes he had a whole package sent to him, and he went through them with care. ' This day I rested at home, and spent most of the day reading,' such is a typical entry. He began to make a table of a book called *The State of Europe.* He read *A Discourse of the Council of Basel,* ' wherein as in all the actions of men is little save corruption,' a comment that gives us an inkling of Adam's philosophy of history. He read Lilly's queer books of prophecy, and Walter Raleigh's *History of the World,* a best seller of the century ; he dipped into Erasmus' *Praise of Folly* and James Howell's *Dendrologia* (a political allegory of events from 1603-40). He owned Dalton's Country Justice, a practical manual concerning the duties of Justices of the Peace and other local officials. A larger part of his reading was in religious books, pleas for presbytery, arguments for independency or congregationalism, volumes of sermons by this or that famous preacher. The number of religious books he covered is astonishing. ' This day I rested at home all day and had various thoughts by reason of the variety of men's opinions I find in reading.' Surely it was the beginning of wisdom to reflect upon the variety of opinions. Adam was not a deeply spiritual man ; he read these books because religion was in the air. It filled the newsletters and pamphlets [1] of the day, as strikes and sports items crowd our dailies. Religion was involved with village squabbles in the West Riding as with factions at Westminster. (W. Notestein, *English Folk*, pp. 250–251.)

Such was the reading of this Cromwellian yeoman. In the manor-houses of the gentry a larger proportion of poetry and of classical learning circulated, or settled down on the

---

[1] There was a spate of printed pamphlets between 1640 and 1660, but few printed newspapers. News was conveyed by news-letters written in London, and sent down in manuscript to subscribers in the country who circulated them among their neighbours. This continued to be the chief way of spreading news till after the end of the century.

library shelves, besides the sermons and pamphlets. No doubt most yeomen, most squires, and most merchants read very little, but many of them read a great deal. The Civil War was a war of ideas, and the ideas had been spread in print and in manuscript, as well as by the voice of the preacher and the talk of men.

The Civil Wars of Charles and Cromwell were not, like the Wars of the Roses, a struggle for power between two groups of aristocratic families, watched with disgusted indifference by the majority of the population, particularly by the townsfolk. In 1642 town and country alike rushed to arms. Yet it was not a war of town against country, though to some extent it became a struggle for London and its appendages against the rural North and West. Least of all was it a war between rich and poor. It was a war of ideas in Church and State.

Men chose their sides largely from disinterested motives and under no compulsion. They made their choice on account of their own religious and political opinions, and most of them were in such an economic and social position as to be able to exercise that choice with freedom. In the rural districts, feudal dependence was mainly a thing of the past, and the great consolidated estates were mainly a thing of the future. It was the golden age of the small squire and the yeoman, who prided themselves on their political independence, whereas the tenant farmers on the large estates a hundred and two hundred years later were proud to follow their landlords to the poll, in the interest of Whig or Tory. But in 1642 many yeomen drew sword against the neighbouring squires.

In the towns also it was an age of independence and individualism. Corporate life had decayed ; a man's municipal loyalty to his town was already less important than his national loyalty to a party or a sect which he chose for himself. Personal opinions were strongly held in a society composed chiefly of small masters and their apprentices, so the inhabitants of the towns took free and intelligent interest in the land's debate.

But on the outbreak of the Civil War it was easier for the majority to seize power and muzzle the minority in a town, than in a large country district. Thus the Roundheads were able to suppress the Cavaliers at once in London, the seaports and the manufacturing cities. But in many shires of England a local civil war dragged on spasmodically for several years together, distinct from the campaigns of the main armies, though they too sometimes became involved in these regional struggles.

Where the local wars were conducted under the command of gentlemen who had known each other as neighbours and often as friends, though now differing in politics, there was little bitterness and much personal courtesy, especially in the first year or two. But some local wars had a fiercer character, where two sharply contrasted systems of society were at each other's throats. For example, in Lancashire the squires were many of them Roman Catholics, representing the old half-feudal world of the Pilgrimage of Grace ; a deep gulf of misunderstanding and hatred was fixed between them and their Puritan neighbours in the towns that had recently sprung up with new industries of woollens, fustian, cotton and linen.

But in the great majority of the counties of England the Royalists were Anglicans, decisively Protestant ; many of them had been opposed to Laud. Such a one was grand old Sir Edmund Verney, the King's standard-bearer, who died for his master at Edgehill but declared, ' I have no reverence for Bishops for whom this quarrel subsists.'

To speak in general terms, Royalism was strongest where the economic and social changes of the previous hundred years had been least felt. The King and the Church were best loved in rural regions and market towns furthest from the capital, and least connected with overseas commerce. Parliamentary and Puritan sympathy was strongest where recent economic change had gone furthest, as in London under the influence of the great Elizabethan trading companies ; in the seaports (including the King's own ships and dockyards) : and in the newer type of manufacturing town or district like Taunton, Birmingham and the clothing Dales on both sides of the Pennines. The squires who had most business connection with London, or with trade and industry anywhere, tended most to the Roundhead side in politics and religion. The London area, including Kent,

Surrey and Essex, was at once seized for Parliament, and the Royalist minority there was never able to raise its head. The same happened in the counties of East Anglia, organized in the 'Eastern Association' and held in the firm grip of Colonel Oliver Cromwell—the region whence in the previous generation the majority of the Puritan emigrants to New England had been drawn, and where the first Ironsides were now enlisted among the Bible-reading yeomen.

Cromwell himself was a man of good family, related to several of the most important people in the House of Commons. He was a gentleman farmer, owning a small estate near Huntingdon which he worked himself until, in 1631, he sold his land to buy leases of rich river pastures near St. Ives. This sale of his patrimony shows that he regarded land as a means of making a livelihood, rather than as an hereditary possession and a matter of social and family pride. He preferred to be a hard-working farmer and business man, mixing on equal terms with common folk, whose champion he became, in various local quarrels, rather than to be a mere squire. This point of view is characteristic of the kind of business agriculturist who was likely to be a Puritan and a Roundhead, while the old-fashioned, west country squires, who took a more feudal attitude to life and society, were the typical Cavaliers. Even the great landed magnates of the Puritan party, like the Earls of Bedford and Manchester, were deeply interested in increasing their fortunes and estates by modern capitalistic methods. The Puritan, high or low, was taught by his religion to idealize business, enterprise and hard work. The Cavalier was usually of a more easy-going and enjoying nature.

The Civil War was not therefore a social war, but a struggle in which parties divided on political and religious issues, along a line of cleavage that answered, roughly and with many personal exceptions, to certain divisions of social type. In the events that followed the War, during the Roundhead Commonwealth (1649–1660), the class cleavage became more marked. The gentry as a whole became more and more alienated from the Roundhead cause and its leaders. Meanwhile democratic ideas of the equality of men irrespective of their rank and wealth affected the political happenings of the period. But these 'levelling' ideas were more political than social. The theorists in the ranks of the New Model Army advocated manhood suffrage for Parliament, but not a socialist redistribution of property. Only the small sect of ' Diggers,' under Winstanley, claimed that the land of England belonged to the people of England and had been stolen by the squires. They were quickly suppressed by the army chiefs. When the Diggers warned the Regicide Government that the political revolution would not stand its ground unless it was based on a social revolution, they spoke the truth, as the Restoration shortly afterwards showed.

Even the idea of political democracy was almost confined to the Radicals of the triumphant army. There was no movement in that direction among the mass of the people, and if a general election had been held on a wide franchise it would have resulted in a Cavalier Restoration.

But although there was no breaking up of estates into smaller units of land on a democratic basis, a certain amount of land passed for a short time from Cavalier to Roundhead ownership. This consisted chiefly of the Church and Crown lands sold to meet the needs of the Revolutionary government, as the monastic lands had been sold a century before. The purchasers were for the most part men of the advanced Republican party. But all these lands went back to Church and King at the Restoration, so that no ' new aristocracy ' was founded out of them. And indeed the soldiers and merchants who held them for a decade on this insecure tenure had made little attempt to set up as country gentlemen in their new estates, which they had bought chiefly as commercial speculations.

Otherwise the amount of land that changed hands was remarkably small. The Cavalier squire had the government of the county taken out of his hands, and had to pay heavy fines for ' malignancy.' But severe as these fines were, they were paid by cutting of woods, borrowing, economy and various arrangements with family and friends.[1] For the

---

[1] One of Charles I's wealthiest and most loyal supporters, the last Earl of Southampton (owner of Bloomsbury property that went to the Russells by the marriage of his daughter Rachel) was fined £6466 for the part he had taken in the Civil War, a sum reckoned to be a tenth of all his landed property. He paid it, retired to his country estates for awhile, and emerged as a very wealthy nobleman

squires were ready to make great sacrifices to avoid parting
with their lands.　Recent detailed research into ownership
land-holding in several Midland counties in the Seventeenth
Century, shows how little private land changed hands under
the Commonwealth.　Indeed, small estates were more freely
sold after the Restoration, from economic causes which
then became prevalent ; but it is indeed possible that the
Parliamentary fines may have permanently embarrassed
some small estates and helped to compel their sale in a later
generation.

In any case it does not appear to be true that, as has sometimes been conjectured, the ' Whigs ' of Charles II's reign
were a new type of landowner who had risen in the county
during the Commonwealth period.　The older squirearchy
suffered much indignity and distress and was put to many
mean shifts, but it was not uprooted.　When in the autumn
of 1654 the Cavalier diarist, John Evelyn, made a sporting
tour among his friends' country houses in the Midlands,
from the ' pleasant shire of Nottingham, full of gentry,' to
Cambridge and Audley End, he noted many ' noble seats '
and says nothing of the ruin or absence of their proprietors,
or of any changes of ownership.

The nobility were even more in eclipse than the squirearchy, for hardly any of the House of Peers followed the
fortunes of the Roundhead party in the regicide period.
Under the rule of Saints and Soldiers, Lords ceased to count
for much in England.　Dorothy Osborne, ever sensible and
ever gay, remarked on the folly of her cousin in choosing a
wife because she was an Earl's daughter, ' which methought
was the prettiest fancy and had the least sense in it, considering that it made no addition to her person, and how
little it is esteemed in this age, if it be anything in a better.'
The ' better age ' of the Restoration brought back, sure
enough, a respect for Earls and a more general desire to
marry their daughters.

On the other hand, many important results of the victory
of the Parliamentary armies survived the Restoration.　One
of these was the increased power of London and of the

---

at the Restoration.　This is very far from rooting out a class, or forcing property
to change hands by fines.　*The Russells in Bloomsbury*, Miss Scott Thomson,
Chap. II.

merchant community in high politics.   Another was the
triumph of the English Common Law over its rivals.

In Tudor times, to strengthen the Royal Prerogative and
meet the real needs of that age, there had been a great increase in the number and the power of independent Courts
each administering its own legal system with little regard to
the procedure and principles of the Common Law.   But the
Parliaments that opposed James and Charles I, instructed
by Edward Coke, the greatest of English lawyers, endeavoured to uphold the supremacy of the Common Law, and in
1641 were able to enforce it by legislation ; the Star
Chamber, the Ecclesiastical Court of High Commission and
the jurisdiction of the Councils of Wales and of the North
were then abolished.   The Admiralty Court had already
been compelled to accept the control of the Common Law
in the development of the important commercial law of
England.

Thus the English judicial system escaped the fate of being
broken into fragments.   The only dualism left was the independence of the Court of Chancery ; but even that ceased
to be a weapon of Royal Prerogative, and became a complementary system of Judge-made law, ingeniously dovetailed
into the principles enforced in the ordinary Courts.

The victory of the Common Law involved the abolition of
torture in England long before other countries, and paved
the way for a fairer treatment of political enemies of government when brought to trial.   Above all, the victory of the
Common Law over the Prerogative Courts preserved the
mediaeval conception of the supremacy of law, as a thing
that could not be brushed aside for the convenience of
government, and could only be altered in full Parliament,
not by the King alone.   This great principle, that law is
above the executive, was indeed violated during the revolutionary period of the Commonwealth and Protectorate.
But it re-emerged at the Restoration, and was confirmed at
the Revolution of 1688, which was effected against James II
precisely to establish the principle that law was above the
King.   That mediaeval idea of the supremacy of law as
something separate from and independent of the will of
the Executive, disappeared in continental countries.   But
in England it became the palladium of our liberties and

I

had a profound effect on English society and habits of thought.

Under the Commonwealth and Protectorate, constitutional law was trodden underfoot in the exigencies of Revolution, but even during that period the common law and the lawyers were very strong, strong enough unfortunately to prevent the fulfilment of a loud popular demand for law reform, a crying social need which Cromwell vainly endeavoured to supply.   The lawyers were too many for him. Even he was not wholly a dictator : the soldiers on one side, the lawyers on the other, at once supported him and held him in check.   When at the Restoration the army was disbanded, the lawyers were left victorious.

It may well be imagined that there was scant building of manor-houses between 1640 and 1660.   But the peaceful generation that preceded the Civil War had been, on the whole, a prosperous period for the gentry, great and small, who had continued the work of the Elizabethan age in filling the English countryside with more and yet more lovely and commodious dwellings.

Certain changes were taking place in the structure of the houses newly built.   The lofty, raftered hall, the essential feature of the country house from Saxon to Elizabethan times, went out of fashion.   ' Dining-rooms ' and ' drawing-rooms ' were now built of one storey's height, as the various purposes of the old ' hall ' were divided up among a number of different chambers of ordinary size.   The courtyard in the centre of the older type of manor-house, where so much of the life of the establishment used to go on, also shrank or disappeared in the plans of the Jacobean mansion ; the yard was placed no longer in the middle of the house but behind it.

Cornices and pilasters decorated the exterior in classical style.   Inside, the staircase and its landings were broad, and the baluster elaborately carved.   On the walls, Jacobean panelling more and more displaced tapestry, hangings and wall paintings, for common use, though much fine tapestry was still manufactured and highly valued.   Framed pictures and marble sculpture were becoming common, after the example set by the art-loving Charles I and his great subject the Earl of Arundel. Rubens, Van Dyck and the homelier Dutch painters did much work for English patrons.

The plaster-work of the ceilings was elaborately decorative. On the floors, rushes were giving place to carpets and matting ; that meant fewer fleas and diminished the chance of the flea-borne Plague. Good carpets were now made in England, or imported from Turkey and from Persia. But in 1645 the Verneys at Claydon had ' leather carpets for dininge and drawinge rooms,' ' greene wrought velvet furniture ' and ' stooles with nailes guilt ' : most of the company still sat on stools, chairs being reserved for the elder or more honourable. The trestle table was giving place to solid tables with ornamental legs. Many magnificently carved beds and cupboards of the period still survive in their grandeur of polished and time-blackened oak.

Out-of-doors, it was a great age for gardens in England, as indeed it has been ever since. Bacon, after saying that ' God Almighty first planted a garden,' declared that without one ' building and palace are but gross handiworks.' The period of late Elizabeth and the early Stuarts saw the development of the flower garden as distinct from the garden of useful vegetables (to which the potato from America had now been added). Then, too, there was the well-loved orchard with its green walks, and the ' pleached bower ' into which Beatrice stole

Where honeysuckle ripened by the sun
Forbids the sun to enter.

The flower-garden proper was arranged in rectangles and squares, divided by broad walks, set in full view of the house. Box and lavender were trimmed into hedges and ornamental shapes.

Many trees, plants and flowers were introduced into England at this period, among many others the crown imperial, the tulip, the laburnum, the nasturtium, the everlasting, love-in-a-mist, honesty, the tulip tree, the red maple. The love of gardening and of flowers that now became so characteristic of the English, was in part taught them by Huguenot refugees from the low countries, settled in Norwich and in London. The Huguenot weavers of Spitalfields started the first gardening societies in England.

In the reign of Charles I, English books, such as *Paradisus,* praising and describing flowers, taught and popularized the fashion of gardening. (Eleanor Rohde, *Story of the Garden,* 1932.)

Besides the flowers of this period that are still with us, our ancestors had then a passion for herbs, which has not survived to the same extent. Herbs were much used for medicinal and for culinary purposes. Mazes and dials were laid out by plantations of herbs and flowers. These verses of Andrew Marvell, the lesser of Cromwell's two poet secretaries, tell of a side of life that was not destroyed by the wars of Roundhead and Cavalier :

> Here at the fountain's sliding foot,
> Or at some fruit-tree's mossy root,
> Casting the body's vest aside,
> My soul into the boughs does glide ;
> There, like a bird, it sits and sings,
> Then whets and combs its silver wings,
> And, till prepared for longer flight,
> Waves in its plumes the various light.
>
> How well the skilful gardener drew
> Of flowers, and herbs, this dial new ;
> Where, from above, the milder sun
> Does through a fragrant zodiac run,
> And, as it works, the industrious bee
> Computes its time as well as we !
> How could such sweet and wholesome hours
> Be reckoned but with herbs and flowers !

The ideal family life of the period that ended in such tragic political division, has been recorded once for all in the *Memoirs of the Verney Family.* Their household at Claydon, Bucks, represented all that was best in the Puritan and Cavalier way of life, practised in unison by Sir Edmund Verney and by his son Ralph, till the obstinacy of the King and the violence of his enemies, forced even those two men of moderation to take opposite sides in civil war, without less love for one another and without any weakening of their common interest to maintain the family house and estate intact in evil times.

The picture we get of the Verneys at Claydon in the reign of Charles I shows the English country house as a centre not only of estate management but of domestic industry, in which the members of the family, as well as their army of servants and dependants of both sexes, have essential parts to play.

' A great house provisioned itself with little help,' writes the historian of the Verneys.

' The inhabitants brewed and baked, they churned and ground their meal, they bred up, fed and slew their beeves and sheep, and brought up their pigeons and poultry at their own doors. Their horses were shod at home, their planks were sawn, their rough ironwork was forged and mended. Accordingly the mill-house, the slaughter-house, the blacksmith's, carpenter's and painter's shops, the malting and brewhouse, the woodyard full of large and small timber, the sawpit, the out-houses full of all sorts of odds and ends of stone, iron and woodwork and logs cut for burning—the riding house, the laundry, the dairy with a large churn turned by a horse, the stalls and styes for all manner of cattle and pigs, the apple and root chambers, show how complete was the idea of self-supply.'

The dovecots and the stew-ponds full of fish, and the decoy for water fowl were not less important. And game brought down by the hawk or the ' long gun ' was the more valued in winter because otherwise the only meat was that which had been salted at the autumn slaughtering Skin diseases were a frequent result of the salt diet, at Claydon and in all other households high or low. For winter vegetables were scarce ; potatoes and salads were only beginning to come into use.

' The work with the needle and the wheel was a very necessary part of a lady's education, and as some of the poorer relations of the family resided in great houses as " lady helps " (the equivalents of the pages of the other sex) they were useful and welcome in carrying out these important household labours. There are letters from five or six of these ladies, connected with the Verneys, well born, well bred, and as well educated as their neighbours, who seem to have been treated with great consideration.'

Among the employments of the female part of the household at Claydon were spinning at wool and flax, fine and coarse needlework, embroidery, fine cooking, curing, preserving, distillery, preparing medicines from herbs at the prescription of the doctor or by family tradition, and last but not least the making of fruit syrups and home-made wines from currant, cowslip and elder, which played a great part in life before tea and coffee began to come in at the Restoration.

Ten of Lady Verney's children grew up. This large and affectionate family, in which no hand was idle, found time for long correspondence with absent members. In the Verney archives four hundred letters survive from a single year. Frequent journeys were taken by Sir Edmund and his children, on the King's or the Parliament's business, or on family and personal affairs. They were made on horseback at a good pace along the soft roads. In 1639 Sir Edmund rode 260 miles in four days with the King from Berwick to London. Much slower was the walking pace of the family ' coch—a sort of cart without springs, with leathern curtains against the weather, which most un-luxurious luxury was used only by infirm persons or delicate women who could not ride.'

Public conveyances were becoming common in the period of the Commonwealth, but were still expensive and slow. In 1658 ' stage coaches ' set out from the George Inn, Aldersgate, London, to various cities on the following terms :

To Salisbury in two days for 20 shillings.
To Exeter in four days for 40 shillings.
To Plymouth for 50 shillings,
    and to Durham for 55 shillings (no time of arrival guaranteed)
    and every Friday to Wakefield in four days for forty shillings.

The breeding and purchase of horses of every kind and for every purpose was an essential part of the Verneys' way of life at Claydon. In that part of England horses were gradually replacing oxen in cart and plough. Sir Edmund Verney's cart-horses were sent periodically to an estate he had in the fens to ' gather flesh at an easy charge.'

When we compare the life and letters of the Verneys in the reign of Charles I to the life and letters of the Pastons under Henry VI, we are aware of the general resemblance, but we are aware also of higher moral instincts and traditions,

of greater kindliness and less hard outlook on family relationships and on duty to neighbours. Long generations of
peace and order in the countryside, and possibly other
changes as well, had made life more gentle and more just.
Sir Tobie Matthew, a courtier of Charles I who knew
several foreign lands almost as well as he knew his own, and
being a Roman Catholic convert was able to take an outside
and critical view of his countrymen, writes in the preface to
his Letters that the English had a monopoly of ' a certain
thing called Good Nature,' and that ' England is the only
Indies where this bottomless mine of pure gold is to be
found.' ' No man is more remote than an Englishman
from the doggedness of long-lasting and indelible revenge.'
These good qualities were put to an exacting test when
civil war came to every man's gate, a war more ubiquitous
in its scope and area than the Wars of the Roses, but fought
from less selfish and material motives.

Books for Further Reading

Memoirs of the Verney Family in the Civil War (1892) ; Dorothy Osborne's
Letters ; Mrs. Hutchinson's *Memoirs of Colonel Hutchinson* ; Lipson, *Ec. Hist.
Eng.* ; Darby, *Hist. Geog. Eng.*, chap. xi ; Margaret James, *Social Problems and
Policy during the Puritan Revolution*, 1930 ; Godfrey Davies, *The Early Stuarts*
(Oxford Hist. Eng.), chap. xi.

CHAPTER IX

Charles II, 1660-1685. James II, 1685-1688. (The Revolution, 1688-1689.)
William III, 1689-1702.

POLITICALLY, the Restoration of 1660 restored King, Parliament and Law in place of the ' forced power ' of military dictatorship. Ecclesiastically it restored the Bishops and Prayer Book and the Anglican attitude to religion, in place of Puritanism. But socially—and its social aspect concerns us most in this work—the Restoration restored the nobles and the gentry to their hereditary place as the acknowledged leaders of local and national life. The Englishman's proverbial ' love of a lord,' his respectful and admiring interest in ' the squire and his relations,' again had full play. Indeed, as events were to prove, the social importance of the peer and the squire, of the gentleman and his lady, was much more completely ' restored ' than the power of the King. The Englishman was, at bottom, something of a snob but very little of a courtier.

Under the Commonwealth, with its democratic ideals and its military realities, the majority of the hereditary ' upper class,' being Cavaliers, had suffered an eclipse without parallel in our social history. They had not been destroyed as a class, but had been put into cold storage. They had not lost their lands or more than a certain proportion of their wealth by fines. But their place in national and local government and in social importance had for awhile been usurped by successful soldiers, or by politicians who could adapt themselves to the rapid changes of a revolutionary era. Some of these, Algernon Sidney and Ashley Cooper, had been men of good family ; others, like Colonels Pride and Birch, had been such ' plain russet-coated captains ' as Cromwell loved, whom he had raised up with him to rule the land. At the Restoration many of the Roundhead leaders disappeared into obscurity or exile ; but others, like Monk, Ashley Cooper, Colonel Birch and Andrew Marvell retained their status in the Parliamentary or Governmental ranks. Once the Regicides had been disposed of, there was no proscription of former Roundheads, except only of such as obstinately continued to attend ' conventicles,' as the places of Puritan worship were now called.

Throughout the reign of Charles II, religious nonconformists suffered severe though intermittent persecution, under the laws of the ' Clarendon Code.' The victims were members of the middle and lower classes, chiefly residing in the towns. Many of them were wealthy merchants, more were industrious artisans ; and statesmen were soon complaining that religious persecution interfered seriously with trade. Very few of those who suffered belonged to the landowning gentry : among the squires, the Roundhead spirit suffered change into the Whig, which refused to hamper its worldly ambitions by too scrupulous an adherence to the proscribed Puritan religion. A common Whig type was that of the sceptical Shaftesbury or the blasphemous Wharton, although these attitudes were no less fashionable among Cavalier courtiers and Tory leaders of Parliament. There were, however, plenty of Whigs who were good Christians, though never High Churchmen ; the Russells and other Whig families attended the Anglican worship with sincere piety, while they engaged silenced Puritan clergymen as private chaplains and tutors for their children. The distinction between the two Protestant religions was by no means absolute for all men.

After the Restoration, the members of the landowning class who attended conventicles and suffered persecution as Nonconformists were a mere handful. Anglicanism became distinctively the upper-class religion, far more completely than it had been in the days of Elizabeth or of Laud. There were indeed still a certain number of Roman Catholic country gentlemen, especially in Lancashire and Northumberland ; they were shut out from all participation in local and national government by laws which the King was occasionally able to break for their benefit. Otherwise the upper class, the gentlemen of England, were socially united by common conformity to the Anglican worship. Henceforth the services of the parish Church were under the special patronage of the ladies and gentlemen in the

family pew ; the great body of the congregation were their
dependants, the farmers and labourers of the village.
Addison's Sir Roger de Coverley in church affords a pleasant
example of the social side of rural worship as it remained for
many generations to come :

My friend Sir Roger, being a good Church-man, has beautified the
inside of his Church with several texts of his own choosing.   He has
likewise given a handsome pulpit cloth and railed in the communion
table at his own expense.   He has often told me that at his coming to
his estate he found the Parishioners very irregular ; and in order to
make them kneel and join in the responses, he gave every one of them
a hassock and a Common-Prayer book ; and at the same time employed an itinerant singing-master, who goes about the country for
that purpose, to instruct them rightly in the tunes of the Psalms.   As
Sir Roger is landlord to the whole congregation, he keeps them in
very good order, and suffers no body to sleep in it besides himself ;
for if by chance he has been surprised into a short nap at sermon,
upon recovering out of it he stands up and looks about him, and if
he sees anybody else nodding, either wakes them himself or sends
his servants to them.

The dissenting congregations, on the other hand, alike in
times of persecution and toleration, were made up of men
who prided themselves on their independence, and who
liked to feel that the chapel and its minister belonged to
themselves.   Socially at least they were ' at ease in Zion,'
safe from the inquisitorial eye of the squire and his lady.
Until the Wesleyan movement, dissenting congregations
and meetings were almost confined to cities, market towns
and industrial districts, though many villages had isolated
families of Quakers and Baptists.   Some of the Dissenters
were poor artisans like John Bunyan ; others, especially in
London and Bristol, were wealthy merchants who could
have bought up the squires who persecuted them.   And
often such merchants did in fact buy out needy gentlemen,
after accumulating mortgages on their land.   In the next
generation the dissenting merchant's son would be a squire
and a churchman.   Yet another generation, and the ladies
of the family would be talking with contempt of all who
attended meeting-houses or engaged in trade !
Thus the social character of English religious divisions

was stereotyped at the Restoration and continued with little change until the Victorian era.

Though the upper class was now substantially one in the form of its religious observance, it was divided politically into Whigs and Tories. The Tories, who were far the most numerous, sought to extirpate religious Dissent and to make the Anglican Church coextensive with the nation. But the Whig Peers and gentry, an able and wealthy minority, advocated the new doctrine of Toleration, at least for all Protestants. They derived their political power from alliance with the Puritans of the industrial and commercial regions, who were able to control the municipal and Parliamentary elections in many boroughs. The Tories, like the Cavaliers before them, were the section of the society that stood most whole-heartedly in the old ways of rural England. The Whigs, like their Roundhead fathers, were usually those members of the landowning class who were in close touch with commercial men and commercial interests. And therefore Whig rather than Tory policies stood to gain in the long run by the continuous process of economic change, as it moved with gradually accelerating momentum towards an agricultural and industrial revolution which would leave only too little of the ancient ways.

The Restoration world had turned back from that preoccupation with matters ecclesiastical which had characterized Cromwellian England. The popular reaction that overthrew the Puritans had been less religious than secular. *Hudibras* is not a work of Anglican piety. Indeed, the principal reason why the English witnessed the return of the old Church establishment with relief, was because it made less constant and obtrusive demands for professions of religious zeal upon the common occasions of life. The Puritans had made men ' eat religion with their bread,' till the taste of it sickened them.

For a generation after 1660 the Puritans were often bitterly persecuted, but more for political and social reasons than from genuinely religious motives. The object of the ' Clarendon Code ' was to prevent the revival of the Roundhead party, and to avenge the wrongs suffered by Anglicans and Cavaliers. But the spirit of the persecution was not ecclesiastical ; it was not a heresy hunt.   The hard-drinking fox-hunters of the manor-house hated the Presbyterians of the neighbouring Town not because they held the doctrines of Calvin, but because they talked through their noses, quoted scripture instead of swearing honest oaths, and voted Whig instead of Tory.

In 1677 the Writ *De haeretico comburendo* was abolished, and all ' punishment by death in pursuance of any Ecclesiastical Censures ' was abolished by law ; but in fact no heretic had been put to death in England since the Unitarians who had been burnt in the lifetime of Shakespeare. Puritanism in the day of its power had not made for orthodoxy ; Cromwell's England had abounded in strange doctrines and attenuated creeds, and had left to the restored Kings an island of ' a hundred religions.'   Where religions are many and various, irreligion is less likely to be persecuted.   But in Presbyterian Scotland, where sects had little hold and where the spirit of orthodoxy in doctrine was popular with the masses, a lad of eighteen was hanged for denying the authority of the Scriptures as late as the year 1697 ; whereas in England, any time after the Civil War, a reputation for ' atheism,' though it might be socially disadvantageous, no longer endangered a man's life or freedom. By the end of the Century, Unitarian doctrines, for which men were burnt a hundred years before, were not uncommon among English Presbyterian congregations of the highest bourgeois respectability, while many of the leading statesmen, not to mention King Charles himself in his merrier moods, were sceptics in the sense of being scoffers.

It was of graver import that experimental science was spreading fast in England.   Under the Commonwealth there had been a group of remarkable scientists resident at the Universities and in London, whose work came into the limelight of fashion and favour at the Court of the Restoration.   The Royal Society was founded under the patronage of King Charles and of his cousin Prince Rupert, himself a conductor of chemical experiments.

The uses to which science might be turned, in agriculture, industry, navigation, medicine and engineering, appealed to the practical English mind.   Another hundred years were to pass before the Industrial Revolution gathered full force, largely as a result of the application of science to manufacture, but already in the reign of Charles II many subjects of daily importance were being studied in a scientific spirit, and this new spirit already had a great influence on educated thought in England. Robert Boyle, Isaac Newton and the early members of the Royal Society were religious men, who repudiated the sceptical doctrines of Hobbes. But they familiarized the minds of their countrymen with the idea of law in the Universe and with scientific methods of inquiry to discover truth. It was believed that these methods would never lead to any conclusion inconsistent with Biblical history and miraculous religion ; Newton lived and died in that faith. But his law of universal gravitation and his calculus supplied methods of approaching truth that had no relation to theology. The spread of scientific inquiry affected the character of religious belief, though not as yet its content. The age of latitudinarian piety that followed the Revolution of 1688 was being prepared by these intellectual movements of the Restoration.

Early in the reign of Charles II, the first ' History of the Royal Society,' its character and aims, was written by Sprat, some years later Bishop of Rochester, a man highly characteristic of the new age both in the versatility of his mind and the politic flexibility of his opinions. This High Church divine commends the ' learned and inquisitive age ' in which he lives, praises the practical objects of the Fellows of the Royal Society, ' to increase the powers of all mankind and to free them from the bondage of errors,' and claims for these new philosophers the widest range of inquiry—' these two subjects, God and the Soul, being only forborne : in all the rest, they wander at their pleasure.' God was to be praised by studying the plan of His creation, but no further attempt was to be made to fit the findings of science into the scheme of theology, as the schoolmen of old had striven so long and so painfully to do. ' God and the Soul ' were taken for granted—and left aside. It was an orthodox position no doubt, but not essentially religious. God was no longer all in all. In a world governed by such studies, superstition would be exposed, and poetry would yield pride of place to prose ; would even religion be quite the same again ?

Sprat was one of the excellent writers who formed the

lucid prose of the Restoration era, but he was not an original thinker, and his book on the Royal Society (1667) is on that account all the more symptomatic of the mind of the new age.   Like Locke and Newton a few years later, the Bishop concedes to ' the ancient miracles ' of Bible times a passport as privileged phenomena, unusual interferences of God with His creation.   But modern miracles were no longer to be expected in the Protestant, Anglican climate.   ' The course of things,' Sprat declares, ' goes quietly along, in its own true channel of natural causes and effects.'   It is no longer even Shakespeare's world : ' King Oberon and his invisible army of fairies ' are ' false chimeeres ' to this philosopher Bishop.   When the Englishmen of the Revolution epoch laughed at ' Popish miracles,' it was not only because they were Popish but because they were miracles.   Sprat even warns his too credulous countrymen ' not to be hasty in assigning the causes of plagues, or fires or inundations ' to the judgments of God for sin.   Finally, ' the new philosophy ' of the physical sciences is to be the mother of inventions useful to man, enriching and comforting his life. ' While the old philosophy could only bestow on us some barren terms and notions, the new shall impart to us the uses of all the creatures and shall enrich us with all the benefits of fruitfulness and plenty.'

While the episcopal blessing was thus enthusiastically given to the questioning spirit of science, it is not surprising that in the later years of the Century, the reaction of educated minds to charges of witchcraft was very different from what it had been a short time before.   Evidence of these ' odd stories ' was now critically and sometimes contemptuously examined by magistrates.   Popular superstition on this subject was almost as gross as ever, but the gentry were now predisposed to be sceptical.   The accused witches had two advantages ; England was a country where the common Law did not permit the use of torture to extract confession ; and the judges had almost as much control as the juries over the course and outcome of trials.   More generally speaking, it was lucky for the witches that England was still aristocratically governed.   In many rural parts the populace, if it had not been restrained by the gentry, would have continued to drown or burn witches down to the Nineteenth

Century. But in 1736, greatly to the indignation of many simple folk, Parliament repealed the already obsolete law that condemned a witch to die.

We can trace this gradual change of opinion, affecting in the first instance the educated classes, in Sir John Reresby's account of a witch trial that he attended at the York Assizes in 1687 :

A poor old woman had the hard fate to be condemned for a witch. *Some, that were more apt to believe those things than me,* thought the evidence strong against her, the boy that said he was bewitched falling into fits before the bench when he see her. But in all this it was observed that the boy had no distortion, no foaming at the mouth, nor did his fits leave him gradually, but all of a sudden ; *so that the judge thought fit to reprieve her.*

However, it is just to relate this odd story. One of my soldiers, being upon the guard at eleven o'clock at night at Clifford Tower Gate the night the witch was arraigned, hearing a great noise at the Castle, came to the porch, and being there see a scroll of paper creep from under the door, which, *as he imagined by moonshine,* turned first into the shape of a monkey, then a turkey cock, which moved to and fro by him. Where upon he went to the gaol and called the under-gaoler, who came and see the scroll dance up and down and creep under the door, where there was scarce the room of the thickness of half a crown. *This I had from the mouth both of the soldier and gaoler.*

It will be observed that Sir John Reresby and the Judge, the men of education, were more sceptical than the Jury, the soldier and the turnkey.

For their patronage of science, Charles II and his courtiers deserve all praise. Their patronage of the theatre, struggling to revive after its suppression by the foolish bigotry of the Puritans, was also a well-timed service to the nation, but the manner of it was less deserving of unqualified eulogy.

The revived theatres differed in several important respects from those in which Shakespeare had first been played. The whole playhouse was now roofed in, and the stage artificially lighted with candles : there were ' footlights,' a drop curtain and painted scenery. Moreover, the women's parts were no longer, as before the Civil War, taken by well-trained boys, but by women actresses.   Men came to see the actress as much as the play.   Nell Gwynne's personal vigour and charm counted for more perhaps than her professional skill.   It was to a large extent a new theatre and a new dramatic art, with new possibilities and new dangers.

For many years there was one theatre open in London, the Theatre Royal, at Drury Lane, and sometimes one or two more.   But there were no fixed theatres in the provinces and the touring companies were few and bad.   Acting was not, as music then was in the age of Purcell, a national pastime and an art widely practised at home by many small groups of connoisseurs.   The drama was localized in London, and even there it appealed not to the citizens but to the Court and the fashionables of the Town.   It was for their vitiated taste that the drama of the early years of the Restoration catered.

At that time a hard-hearted and cynical frivolity prevailed in Whitehall and Westminster much more than in England as a whole.   The men who haunted Charles II's Court, the first leaders of the Whig and Tory parties in the time of the Popish Plot and the Exclusion Bill, laughed at all forms of virtue as hypocrisy, and believed that every man had his price.

> What makes all doctrines plain and clear ?
> *About two hundred pounds a year.*
> And that which was proved true before
> Prove false again ?   *Two hundred more.*
>
> (*Hudibras.*)

So they thought, being themselves for sale.   Yet two thousand Puritan Ministers had just given up their livings and gone out to endure persecution for conscience' sake (1662), following the example of their enemies the Anglican clergy, who had suffered like things for twenty years past rather than desert the Church in her extremity.   The Puritan and Anglican clergy who refused to save their livelihoods by recantation were nearly ten times as numerous as the Catholic and Protestant clergy who had similarly stood out during the frequent Tudor changes of religion.   Conscience meant more, not less, than of old.   England was sound enough. But her courtiers and politicians were rotten. For the King himself and the younger generation of the aristocracy had been demoralized by the break-up of their education and family life, by exile and confiscation leading to the mean shifts of sudden poverty, by the endurance of injustice done to them in the name of religion, by the constant spectacle of oaths and covenants lightly taken and lightly broken, and all the base underside of revolution and counter-revolution of which they had been the victims.

For these reasons a hard disbelief in virtue of any kind was characteristic of the restored leaders of politics and fashion, and was reflected in the early Restoration drama which depended on their patronage. One of the most successful pieces was Wycherley's *Country Wife* ; the hero, by pretending to be a eunuch, secures admission to privacies which enable him to seduce women ; one is expected to admire his character and proceedings. In no other age, before or after, would such a plot-motive have appealed to any English audience.

However, the theatre had been restored, and much of its work was good. It revived plays by Shakespeare and Ben Jonson. It was adorned by the poetic genius of Dryden's dramas and the musical genius of Purcell's incidental tunes and operatic pieces. And in the following generation Wycherley's brutalities went clean out of fashion. They were succeeded by the new English comedy of Congreve and Farquhar. Those great writers are usually lumped with Wycherley as ' Restoration Dramatists,' but in fact it would be more chronologically correct to call Congreve and Farquhar ' Revolution Dramatists,' for they wrote in the reigns of William and Anne.

So the Wycherley period of the English stage did not last long, but it had done permanent harm, because it had confirmed many pious and decent-minded families, High Church as well as Low, in a hostile attitude to the drama, which had in Shakespeare's time been peculiar to rigid Puritans. Till late in the Nineteenth Century, not a few well-brought-up young people were never allowed to visit the theatre. And if such stringency was the exception rather than the rule, it is at least true to say that the serious part of the nation would never take the theatre seriously.

This misfortune was not a little due to Puritan bigotry and to its outcome in the licentiousness of the early Restoration drama. These unhappy conditions were peculiar to England : the age of Wycherley over here was the age of Molière, Corneille and Racine in France. There the drama, comic as well as tragic, was decent and was serious, and the French have ever since taken their drama seriously, as the Elizabethan English took theirs, regarding it as a civilizing influence and a criticism of life.

The age which produced Newton's *Principia*, Milton's *Paradise Lost*, Dryden's *Absalom and Achitophel*, Purcell's Music and Wren's Churches, and all the varied interests and curiosities of the daily life recorded by Evelyn and Pepys, such an age was one of the greatest for English genius and civilization. It could not have been what it was without the printing press, yet it is remarkable what a small amount of printing served its turn.

In the first place there was a rigid censorship. No book, pamphlet or news-sheet could be legally printed without licence obtained from the authorities. Enemies of the existing establishment in Church or State, could only print their views in secret presses, operated in London garrets by desperate men, who were spied upon by informers in the pay of Roger Lestrange, and savagely punished if caught.

But the censorship that thus stifled debate no longer derived its sanction from the Royal Prerogative, as of old, but from an Act of Parliament. The first Licensing Act, passed in 1663 by the Cavalier Parliament, aimed at preventing the publication of seditious and heretical works— meaning in the first instance Roundhead and Puritan writings. The Act was periodically renewed, except during the period of the Whig Houses of Commons and the years without a Parliament that followed (1679–1685). Revived by the Parliament of James II, the Licensing Act was finally allowed to expire in the more liberal age ushered in by the Revolution. After 1696 an Englishman was permitted to print and publish whatever he chose, without consulting any authority in Church or State ; only he could be called to account for it on a charge of libel or sedition before a jury of his countrymen. Thus Milton's dream of 'liberty of unlicensed printing' was realized in England, a generation after his death.

Under the restrictions of the Censorship while it still existed, men of letters and science had been able to make a freer use of the press than politicians. The ecclesiastical licensers,[1] while refusing their sanction to the specific doctrines of Dissent, were not so obscurantist as to prevent the publication of *Paradise Lost* or *Pilgrim's Progress.* Newton's *Principia* bears the *imprimatur* of Samuel Pepys as President of the Royal Society in 1686.

Yet the aggregate of books and pamphlets published was not large. By the provisions of the Licensing Act the number of master-printers in the Kingdom was reduced to twenty and the number of presses they might each use was rigidly limited. Except for the two University Presses, all the master-printers congregated in London, to the detriment of intellectual life in the country at large. In the following century, when the Licensing Act was no more, printing became widely diffused, to the great benefit of the literary and scientific life of the Provinces. But in Stuart times, London and the two Universities monopolized printing and publishing. When William of Orange occupied Exeter on his famous march from Torbay, the Capital of the West was unable to furnish a single printer or machine to strike off copies of his manifesto.

Except during the few years in Charles II's reign when the Censorship was in abeyance, there were practically no newspapers, for the meagre official *Gazette* could not be so called. News circulated in 'newsletters' written by hand in London and sent down to correspondents in distant towns and villages : the recipients, if they wished, could read or lend them to their neighbours. It was largely by this means that the Whig and Tory parties were formed and held together in the constituencies. And news of all sorts— sporting, literary and general, went round in the same way. The composition and multiplication of these newsletters

[1] By the Licensing Act of 1663 Political treatises were to be licensed by the Secretary of State, Law books by the Lord Chancellor, books of Heraldry by the Earl Marshall or Kings of Arms, and all other publications by the Archbishop of Canterbury and the Bishop of London. These authorities appointed Licensers to read the books.

employed an army of scribes in London, answering to the journalists and the printers of newspapers of later times.

Private libraries were growing more common, varying in size and character from the noble collections of Samuel Pepys and of the Cotton family, to the modest bookshelf in the yeoman's farm. That a fine country house ought to have a fine library was an idea already becoming fashionable, but it was not yet put in practice so generally as in Hanoverian times.

On the other hand, since public libraries were extremely rare outside Oxford and Cambridge, it was difficult for readers of slender means to obtain the use of books. In 1684 a public library in London was established by Tenison, then Rector of St. Martin's in the Fields, afterwards Archbishop of Canterbury ; Evelyn writes in his diary :

Dr. Tenison communicated to me his intention of erecting a library in St. Martin's Parish, for the public use, and desired my assistance, with Sir Christopher Wren, about the placing and structure thereof, a worthy and laudable design. He told me there were thirty or forty young men in orders in his parish, either governors to young gentlemen or chaplains to noblemen,[1] who being reproved by him on occasion for frequenting taverns and coffee-houses, told him they would study or employ their time better, if they had books. This put the pious Doctor on this design ; and indeed a great reproach it is that so great a city as London should not have a public library becoming it.

Tenison built a large house on the ground of St. Martin's churchyard, and used the upper part for the library, the ground floor as a workroom for the poor. (Strype's *Stow's London*, 1720, Ch. VI, p. 68.)

Ten years before, Wren had been engaged by his friend, Isaac Barrow, Master of Trinity, Cambridge, to design the noblest of all College Library buildings ; and the bookcases were adorned by the wood-carving of Grinling Gibbons. If books were still somewhat rare, they were held in all the more honour and were housed like Princes.

A fair proportion of the people, even in remote villages, could read and write. Accounts were made up ; letters of business, gossip and affection were exchanged ; diaries, as

---

[1] Viz., the class of clergymen most likely to rise to Bishoprics and Deaneries in that age of patronage.

we know, were kept both in short and long hand. But though it was an age of reading and writing in the conduct of the ordinary affairs of life, very little printed matter came in the way of the less educated. This gave all the greater importance to the sermon, which dealt as freely with political as with religious doctrines. In the Puritan era gone by,

> The pulpit, drum ecclesiastic
> Was beat with fist instead of a stick.
>
> (*Hudibras*.)

Now the jack-boot was on the other leg ; it was said that the country parsons of the restored Church preached more often about King Charles the Martyr than about Jesus Christ. A fierce political tone was no doubt too common, but much also was taught and preached by the rural clergy that was better than politics. Moreover, there existed, chiefly in London, an influential minority of the Anglican priesthood, whose sermons, broadly human, learned and eloquent— raised the reputation of the Church and its pulpit deservedly high with all men. Such were Tenison, Stillingfleet and Isaac Barrow, and above all Tillotson.

Moreover, the Church of the Restoration and Revolution made great contributions to learning. The ecclesiastico-political controversies of the time, in which all sides appealed to the practice of the past, set a premium on historical research, and helped to produce in England the first great age of mediaeval scholarship. It inspired the researches of clergymen and religious laymen like Sir William Dugdale of the *Monasticon*, Anthony Wood and Hearne of Oxford, Jeremy Collier, Nicholson, Burnet, the first serious historian of the Reformation, Wharton of *Anglia Sacra*, Rymer of the *Foedera* and Wake and Wilkins of the *Concilia*. The publication of mediaeval texts, and the study of Anglo-Saxon and mediaeval antiquities by these men between 1660 and 1730 were astonishing alike in quality and volume. After that, interest in mediaeval history died away under the influence of encyclopaedic ' enlightenment ' in the age of Voltaire, which was in turn succeeded by the sentimental romantic antiquarianism of the epoch of *Ivanhoe*. But when, in the middle and later years of the Nineteenth Century, the two Maitlands and Stubbs and a host of other scholars unearthed the realities of mediaeval life and thought, the work of these moderns was based upon that of the scholars of the later Stuart period, whose exact and monumental studies had been inspired by the desire to defend the Church of England against Rome and Geneva, or by zeal to espouse one side or the other in the Nonjuror and Convocation controversies. (See *English Scholars*, Prof. David Douglas, 1929.)

In classical scholarship, Richard Bentley, Professor of Divinity and Master of Trinity, Cambridge, shone supreme among the English scholars not only of his own day but of all time. The publication of his *Phalaris* in 1699 made a new epoch in Greek studies, as Newton's *Principia* had done in physical science only a dozen years before. The fact that Bentley and his opponents published their lucubrations on *Phalaris* in English, not in Latin, betokened the increasing number of the general public who could take an intelligent interest in a learned controversy. But even Bentley still published the notes of his editions of the classics in Latin, just as Newton published his *Principia*, for scholarship and science still regarded themselves as cosmopolitan first and national afterwards.

Meanwhile the Quaker community was spreading its influence among the people faster than any other of the persecuted sects. Founded by George Fox in the period when the sword of Cromwell guarded the 'liberty of prophesying' against presbyter and priest, the strange religion was able to take root, but the unusual proceedings and manners of the first Friends subjected them to much ill-usage even in that era of sectarian liberty. And when the Restoration brought back the avowed persecution of Dissent, the Quakers suffered most severely of all the sects exposed to the severity of the Clarendon Code. Averse from institutional religion, regardless of sacraments, without priesthood or dogma, the Quakers, if they had come into existence half a century before they did, would have been burnt in batches. But the kind of persecution they had now to undergo, of stripes and imprisonment, enabled them to win proselytes by the display of patience and meekness under suffering.

With the meekness went a strain of mild obstinacy ex-
quisitely calculated to infuriate the self-important bumbledom of that time, as when the Friends refused to remove
their hats before the Court that was to try them. Their
protest against the snobbery and man-worship of the age
was invaluable, but sometimes it took very foolish forms.

The nature of early Quakerism in the lifetime of its
founder (Fox died in 1691) was a popular revivalism,
profuse in its shrill utterance, making converts by thousands
among the common folk. In the reigns of William and
Anne, the Friends had become numerically one of the most
powerful of the English sects. They settled down in the
Eighteenth Century as a highly respectable and rather
exclusive ' connection,' not seeking to proselytize any more,
but possessing their own souls and guiding their own lives by
a light that was indeed partly the ' inner light ' in each man
and woman, but was also a tradition and a set of spiritual
rules of extraordinary potency, handed on from father to
son and mother to daughter in the families of the Friends.

The finer essence of George Fox's queer teaching, common to the excited revivalists who were his first disciples,
and to the ' quiet ' Friends of later times, was surely this—
that Christian qualities matter much more than Christian
dogmas. No Church or sect had ever made that its living
rule before. To maintain the Christian quality in the world
of business and of domestic life, and to maintain it without
pretension or hypocrisy, was the great achievement of these
extraordinary people. England may well be proud of having
produced and perpetuated them. The Puritan pot had boiled
over, with much heat and fury ; when it had cooled and been
poured away, this precious sediment was left at the bottom.

The autobiography of Sir John Reresby, Baronet, of
Thryberg in the West Riding of Yorkshire, supplies a
typical instance of the changing fortunes of a Cavalier
landed family. Sir John's father died in 1646, the year
after Naseby, leaving the estate in debt for £1200, ' not
through ill husbandry but through reason of the war.' He
had been taken prisoner by the Roundheads two years before
his death, ' confined to his own house,' and forced by fines
to sell ' a large wood, all of it great timber, that stood in the

Park.'   His son, Sir John, aged twelve at the time of his succession to the encumbered estate, managed, under the careful conduct of his mother, to pull things round.   In the next twenty years the debts were gradually paid off, and in 1668 Sir John was in a position to begin a series of improvements in his country house.

He rebuilt the exterior of the manor-house with stone in place of rough-cast ; he put ' a new wainscot in several of the rooms ' ; he enlarged the deer park by taking in some arable fields, and ' encompassed it with a stone wall ' ; to replace the timber sold during the troubles, he planted ashes and sycamores, chosen as more suitable to the soil than ' trees of better kinds ' ; he brought the garden up to date, making a ' *jett d'eau* or fountain, in the middle of the parterre, and the grotto in the summerhouse and brought the water in lead pipes,' and he raised the height of the garden wall.   These operations were frugally spread over a number of years.   Finally, just before the Revolution, he was ' at some charge to repair and beautify the Church and the windows and to give a new bell to the steeple.'

So far from being an ' illiterate squire,' Sir John was a fair Latin scholar and had a smattering of Greek ; he talked Italian fluently and French like a Frenchman.   In his youth he had spent some time in Padua University and in Venice, learning music and mathematics.   At home he was an active Justice of the Peace ; his clerk, he tells us, made ' £40 a year out of the place '—more than many clergymen received from their livings.   Sir John sat for the rotten borough of Aldborough (Yorks), where there were only nine electors, privileged owners of ' burgage houses.'   A moderate and cautious Tory, Sir John became a House of Commons man, a courtier, sometimes a paid servant of the Crown.   But he never ceased to be, first and foremost, a country gentleman.

Landowners of this type, with estates of the middling size and with outside connections and sources of profit, could more than hold their own in the Restoration world.   But the small squire who lived on the proceeds of farming his own land but had little or no rents or other property, a man of meagre education and no knowledge of the world outside his own county, was beginning to lose ground in the latter

part of the Seventeenth Century.   The economic situation
was gradually turning against him, for capital was needed
to keep up with the new methods of land improvement.
The fines and losses of the Civil War period might be a
weight round the neck of a small estate for many years after
the Restoration.   And henceforth, more than ever, the
great landowners and the men who had acquired new wealth
by law, politics or commerce, were on the look-out for land,
and ready to buy up the needy small owner with tempting
offers.   In this way the Dukes of Bedford added acre to
acre, and manor to manor, till it seemed as if all Bedfordshire
were theirs.

This process of increasing the great estates by extinguish-
ing the small, culminated in the reign of George III, but it
had already begun in the reign of Charles II.   It accounts
for much of the bitterness of Tory feeling immediately after
the Revolution of 1688 against the moneyed men and the
great Whig Lords.   The small squire was usually a Tory
and he specially detested the burden laid on his vanishing
patrimony by the land tax, raised to pay for the wars of
William and Marlborough, the more so as he believed that
the proceeds of the tax went into the pockets of low-born
army contractors, and of rich Dissenters, Londoners and
Dutchmen who lent money to government.   Though less
fatal to the whole race of landowners than our modern
Income Tax and Death Duties, the Land Tax was a sore
burden to many small estates.

War and taxation certainly hastened the change, but at
bottom the creation of great estates out of small was a
natural economic process, analogous to the absorption of
small businesses by large in the industrial world of our own
day.   If once agriculture came to be regarded as a means of
producing national wealth, and no longer as a means of
maintaining a given state of society, the change was inevitable.   The capital in the hands of the great acquisitive
landowners, and their devotion to the business and profit of
landowning, were necessary conditions of that ' agricultural
revolution ' which in the Eighteenth Century so greatly
increased the productivity of the English soil by wholesale
enclosure and by the general application of new agricultural
methods.

In the reign of Charles II these changes were still in the experimental stage. Agricultural writers were advocating, and a few more enlightened landlords and farmers were practising the improvements which became general in the following century—scientific rotation of crops, proper feeding of stock in winter, roots and clovers, the field cultivation of turnips and potatoes, oil-cake, silos, the storage of water. In the Restoration period all these things were known, but their general adoption was retarded by the open-field system with its half-communal agriculture, and by the want of capital and knowledge among the small squires and yeomen freeholders to whom so much of the land still belonged. And even the big landowners, in the generation immediately following the disturbance of the Civil Wars, had not enough confidence in the future, not enough capital or credit, nor enough personal interest in agriculture to take the lead in land improvement on a large scale, like their descendants in the days of ' Turnip Townshend,' Coke of Norfolk and Arthur Young.

After the Restoration rents were rising, but the landlords put too little of them back into the land and failed to encourage good farmers.

> He that havocs may sit :
> He that improves must flit

was a Berkshire saying of this time. ' Our gentry are grown ignorant in everything of good husbandry,' wrote Pepys. For lack of leadership and capital the age of change was postponed.

So, under merry King Charles, the old rural world still survived, with its wide diffusion of rights in the soil, its comparative economic equality, its open fields and its small productivity. But the movement towards great estates, enclosed fields, and improvement of agricultural methods was already on the way.

For one thing, national policy was already promoting increased production for the domestic and foreign markets. Acts of Parliament restricted the import of cattle from Ireland and of corn from abroad, and offered the English farmer bounties for export. This policy, introduced step by step from Charles II to Anne, was partly meant as a set-off to the heavy incidence of the land tax and was, of course, popular with the small squires and freehold yeomen. Yet, if it helped them at the expense of the home consumer, it helped still more the larger landlords, and the men with capital and enterprise to increase production for the market, the men who were gradually buying up the small estates.[1]

These protective corn laws and bounties did not have their full effect until Hanoverian times, but their adoption under the later Stuarts is significant of the social forces that were moulding our national policy, the more so as export bounties on corn were not a system in general use in other countries. Its singular adoption in England was due to the control of economic policy which Parliament had won from the Crown as a result of the Civil War. The power of the House of Commons over the business affairs of the country was confirmed at the Restoration and further enlarged at the Revolution. And the House of Commons was very much alive to the interests of the landowners, to which class nine-tenths of its members belonged. The voters in the Parliamentary boroughs, most of them small country towns, preferred to be represented by neighbouring gentry rather than by real ' burgesses ' from their own ranks. By this arrangement, so characteristic of the advantages of English snobbery, the interests of the townsfolk received more attention at Westminster and at the same time the political and social power of the House of Commons was increased. If, for example, Aldborough, instead of electing Sir John Reresby, had sent up one of its small shopkeepers to Parliaments, neither King, Lords nor Ministers would have cared what such a man said or thought. Only London and a few other great cities chose their own merchant princes to speak for them on the floor of the national Senate : for what they said carried weight.

But although the House of Commons was becoming, to

---

[1] The actual working of the bounty of five shillings a quarter on wheat exported, may be seen in the following letter from Falmouth in 1675 :

' Much corn is buying up in those parts for the Canaries and Holland, so that the price is raised since harvest three shillings on twenty gallons and is like to be dearer, for the encouragement the merchant has at five shillings per quarter paid them at the custom house very much encourages them to buy, so that the Act, which is good for the farmers, is not beneficial to the town and tradesmen.' (*State Papers, Dom.* 1675, p. 403.)

an ever increasing degree, a House of landlords, whose personal interest was mainly agricultural, it did not follow that trade and industry were neglected. After all, more than four hundred of the five hundred members sat for boroughs ; such a Chamber, consisting mainly of squires whose constituents were townsfolk, was more likely than any other assembly to give due consideration both to the agricultural and to the trading needs of the nation. Moreover, a large proportion of the landlords in both Houses of Parliament, particularly the richer and more powerful among them, were personally interested in industrial or commercial affairs. It is therefore no surprise to find that in this same period Parliament protected cloth manufacture as assiduously as corn growing ; forbade the import of foreign cloth and the export of raw wool, killed the Irish cloth trade for the benefit of the English clothiers, and ordained that everyone who died should be buried in English cloth.[1]

The Navigation Act, which aimed at keeping the trade of the country for English instead of Dutch shipping, had been passed in the Long Parliament in 1651, at a time when State policy was much under the influence of the merchant community of London. The Restoration made no change in this respect. Court and Parliament were at one on the policy of the Navigation Laws, to keep the trade of England and her Colonies in English bottoms, and on the concomitant policy of hostility to our Dutch commercial rivals.

The Princes and Ministers of the Court of Charles II, as well as their critics in Parliament, were in close personal contact with the City magnates who conducted the great adventures of foreign commerce. The highest persons in the land held shares in the joint-stock companies trading in Indian, African and American waters. James, Duke of York, Lord High Admiral and heir to the throne, was Governor of the Royal African Company and shareholder in East Indian stock ; he succeeded Prince Rupert as the Governor of the Hudson's Bay Company and was in turn succeeded by Marlborough.

[1] ' Odious ! in woollen ! 'twould a saint provoke,'
Were the last words that poor Narcissa spoke.
(Pope, *Moral Essays*, I.)

In this way the magnates who controlled English diplomatic, naval and military policy were in the closest possible touch with the mercantile community and personally shared its interests and its outlook.   The wars with Holland in the reign of Charles II, and with France in the reigns of William and Anne were to a large extent mercantile and colonial wars, on the necessity and profit of which Court, Parliament and City were agreed.

The pacifist and ' little England ' feeling of the squires with small rent rolls and rustic outlook played its part in Tory electioneering, but had not much influence on the action of statesmen at Westminster and Whitehall.   A series of wars of commercial and colonial expansion, first against Dutch, then against French, increased the English territories in America and pushed English commerce into the markets of Europe and the world.   These wars were paid for largely by the land tax.   It cannot, therefore, be said that English policy from Charles II to Anne neglected the mercantile or the national interest from a prejudice in favour of the land, or from undue attention paid to the opinions of the majority of the landowners.

Old rural England, on the eve of the wholesale enclosures and the industrial revolution, is often presented to the mind's eye of posterity in one or other of two rival pictures.   On the one hand we are asked to contemplate a land of independent and self-respecting peasants, most of them attached to the soil by small personal rights therein, contented with the country quiet and felicity which have been since destroyed, and celebrating their rural happiness in ale-house songs about ' Harvesthome,' which we have since promoted to the drawing-room ;   and the same land, we are reminded, was also the land of craftsmen in village and market town, not divorced from rural pleasures because they pursued industry, using tools instead of watching machines, and therefore enjoying in their daily work the delight of the individual artist, for which a poor substitute is found in the feverish excitement of our modern amusements, organized *en masse* as a counterpoise to the dullness of mechanical and clerical toil.   On the other hand we are shown the opposing picture :   we are asked to remember the harsh, backbreaking labour of the pre-mechanical ages, continued for thirteen or more hours in the day ; child-labour instead of primary schools ; disease and early death uncontrolled by medical science or hospital provision ; and absence of cleanliness and comforts which we now regard as necessities ; neglectful and unimaginative harshness not only to criminals and debtors but too often to women, children and the poor at large ; and, finally, a population of five and a half millions in England and Wales, with less material comfort than the present population (1939) of more than seven times that number.

Confirmation of both these pictures emerges from a study of the period. But which picture contains the greater and more important body of truth it is hazardous to pronounce, partly because the dispute is about intangible values—we cannot put ourselves back into the minds of our ancestors, and if we could we should still be puzzled ; partly also because, even where statistics would help, statistics are not to be had.

It is true that, about the time of the Revolution, the able publicist Gregory King made a calculation from the hearth tax and other data of the probable numbers in various classes of the community. The figures he gave represent a shrewd guess, but no more. They will indeed serve negatively as a check on the enthusiasm of the *Laudator temporis acti*, by recalling the fact that, even before the great enclosure and the industrial revolution, the number of farmers and yeomen was relatively small and the numbers of the agricultural proletariat large.

The two largest classes by far in King's analysis of the nation are the ' cottagers and paupers ' and the ' labouring people and outservants.' The former represent, we may suppose, those who attempted to be independent of wages and, according to King, made a very poor business of the attempt. Yet such persons, who picked up a living off the common whereon they had squatted, or off the small field they owned behind their hovel, may have been happier than King knew, even if they were poorer than is realized by modern idealizers of the past. King's second large class, the ' labouring people and outservants,' are the wage-earners. But many of them had also some rights on the common, some garden or tiny holding which added to the interest and dignity of life, without entitling the owner to the proud rank of English yeoman. Even the servants of industry had many of them small gardens or plots of land to till in their off hours, especially the woollen weavers in all parts of the island. On the stony heights around Halifax each clothworker had ' a cow or two ' in a field walled off on the steep hillside whereon his cottage stood.

On the other hand, there were very large numbers of employees both in agriculture and industry who had no rights in land and no means of subsistence but their wages.

The wages in agriculture and in industry were supposed to be regulated by schedules issued for each county by the Justices of the Peace, who also occasionally set a limit to the price at which certain goods might be sold. These schedules did not pretend to fix either wages or prices exactly, but only to set a maximum which was not to be surpassed. Variations were therefore permissible inside every county, as well as differences between one shire and the next. Moreover, the maximum announced was very often transgressed in practice.[1]

Judging by negative evidence, we may conclude that concerted strikes and combinations to raise wages were not common ; we hear much more about strikes in the reign of Edward III than in the reign of Charles II.

The Elizabethan Statute of Artificers, that was still partially in force, penalized the leaving of work unfinished, as well as the giving or taking of wages above the maximum fixed by the Justices of the Peace. But the maximum was often exceeded when excess payment was to the interest of both employer and employed. If there was little trade-unionism, there was much individual bargaining about wages.

Even when the low prices are taken into account, some of the wages paid seem low by modern standards. But

---

[1] Wages differed from one estate to another ; in 1701 a Yorkshire squire wrote : ' The wages of a good husbandman in the parts about Barnsley and Wortley I find to be no more than £3 a year, and Sir Godfrey gives his keeper but £3. 14s., and his bailiff £4, so that we are worse served for high wages. About Wortley all the husbandmen are up every morning with their beasts at three o'clock and in our house they lie abed till near seven. But above all Warne's £20 vexes me.' I expect both food and lodging were given, as well as the wages mentioned. That year wheat stood as low as 34s. a quarter and other grain in proportion, and chickens could be bought in the West Riding at twopence apiece.

they were high in comparison with the Europe of that day.
The national characteristic of Englishmen, then as now,
was not thrift but insistence on a high standard of life.
Defoe, writing as an employer, declared that :

> Good husbandry is no English virtue. English labouring people
> eat and drink, especially the latter, three times as much in value as
> any sort of foreigners of the same dimensions in the world.

The staple diet was bread, or rather bread, beer and
usually meat. Vegetables and fruit played a small, and
meat a very large part in the English meal of that date.
Among the middle and upper classes, breakfast was often
a ' morning draft ' of ale with a little bread and butter ; that
sufficed till the noonday dinner, a tremendous meal of
various fish and meats. As to the poorer households,
Gregory King reckoned that half the population ate meat
daily, and that of the other half the greater number ate meat
at least twice a week. The million who ' received alms,'
' eat not flesh above once a week.'

Reliable statistics of the population of England, and of
the classes into which it was divided cannot be obtained
before the first Census of 1801, but the calculations—or
shall we call them guesses ?—that Gregory King made with
the help of the hearth tax and other data at the time of the
Revolution (1688) are well worthy of examination. At
least they represent the map of society as it presented itself
to the thought of a well-informed contemporary. The
reader would do well to study the figures, knowing indeed
that they cannot be exact, but not knowing in what direction
the errors lie.

To interpret this table, several points should be borne in
mind. The ' heads per family ' are the persons living under
one roof : the ' family ' includes the servants in the house as
well as the children. The poor, therefore, are put down as
having much smaller ' families ' than the rich, although the
average number of children still alive and still at home
might be the same in all classes. The ' families and incomes ' given are, of course, guesses at the *average* figure :
in each class, some householders would have larger ' families ' and incomes than the figure set down, while others in
the same class lived on a smaller scale. The ' Freeholders '

Number of Families	Ranks, Degrees, Titles and Qualifications.	Heads per Family	Number of Persons	Yearly Income per Family
160	Temporal lords	40	6,400	£3200
26	Spiritual lords	20	520	1300
800	Baronets	16	12,800	880
600	Knights	13	7,800	650
3,000	Esquires	10	30,000	450
12,000	Gentlemen	8	96,000	280
5,000	Persons in greater offices and places	8	40,000	240
5,000	Persons in lesser offices and places .	6	30,000	120
2,000	Eminent merchants and traders by sea	8	16,000	400
8,000	Lesser merchants and traders by sea	6	48,000	198
10,000	Persons in the law . . .	7	70,000	154
2,000	Eminent clergymen . . .	6	12,000	72
8,000	Lesser clergymen	5	40,000	50
40,000	Freeholders of the better sort . .	7	280,000	91
120,000	Freeholders of the lesser sort . .	5½	660,000	55
150,000	Farmers	5	750,000	42 10s.
15,000	Persons in liberal arts and sciences .	5	75,000	60
50,000	Shopkeepers and tradesmen . .	4½	225,000	45
60,000	Artisans and handicrafts . .	4	240,000	38
5,000	Naval officers	4	20,000	80
4,000	Military officers	4	16,000	60
50,000	Common seamen	3	150,000	20
364,000	Labouring people and out-servants .	3½	1,275,000	15
400,000	Cottagers and paupers . . .	3¼	1,300,000	6 10s.
35,000	Common soldiers . . .	2	70,000	14
	Vagrants, as gipsies, thieves, beggars, etc.		30,000	
	Total		5,500,520	

(Printed in Charles Davenant's Works (1771), Vol. II, p. 184, with further figures.)

K

include, not only owners of their own farms, but also copy-holders and tenants for life. Finally, it must be remembered that 'Labouring people and out-servants,' and 'cottagers and paupers,' the two largest classes in the community, include many who had small rights in land of one kind or another.

According to Gregory King over one million persons, nearly a fifth of the whole nation, were in occasional receipt of alms, mostly in the form of public relief paid by the parish. The poor-rate was a charge of nearly £800,000 a year on the country and rose to a million in the reign of Anne. There was seldom any shame felt in receiving out-door relief, and it was said to be given with a mischievous profusion. Richard Dunning declared that in 1698 the parish dole was often three times as much as a common labourer, having to maintain a wife and three children, could afford to expend upon himself ; and that persons once receiving outdoor relief refuse ever to work, and 'seldom drink other than the strongest ale-house beer, or eat any bread save what is made of the finest wheat flour.' The statement must be received with caution, but such was the nature of the complaint of some ratepayers and employers about the poor-law.

These problems of outdoor relief have a family likeness in all ages. But one peculiarity of the English Poor Law in the Restoration era and the Eighteenth Century was the Act of Settlement, passed by Charles II's Cavalier Parliament. By this Act every Parish in which a man tried to settle could send him back to the parish of which he was native, for fear that if he stayed in his new abode he might at some future date become chargeable on the rates. Nine-tenths of the people of England, all in fact who did not belong to a small class of landowners, were liable to be expelled from any parish save their own, with every circumstance of arrest and ignominy, however good their character and even if they had secured remunerative work. The panic fear of some parish authorities lest newcomers should some day fall on the rates, caused them to exercise this unjust power in quite unnecessary cases. The Act placed a check upon the fluidity of labour and was as much an outrage as the Press-gang itself on the boasted freedom of

Englishmen. Yet it was seldom denounced, until many years later Adam Smith dealt with it in scathing terms. It is hard to ascertain the exact degree to which it operated, and Adam Smith appears to have exaggerated the harm done and the number of cases in which cruel wrong was inflicted. But at best it was a great evil ; it is the reverse side of that creditable effort of Stuart England to provide for the maintenance of the poor through the local public authorities. That effort, on the whole, was not unsuccessful, and largely accounts for the peaceable character of English society.

Nothing marked more clearly the growing power of squirearchy in the House of Commons and in the State than the Game Laws of the Restoration period. By the Forest Laws of Norman and Plantagenet times, the interests of all classes of subjects had been sacrificed in order that the King should have abundance of red deer to hunt ; but now the interests of the yeomen and farmers were sacrificed in order that the squire should have plenty of partridges to shoot. Even more than politics, partridges caused neighbours to look at one another askance : for the yeoman freeholder killed, upon his own little farm, the game that wandered over it from the surrounding estates of game preservers. And so in 1671 the Cavalier Parliament passed a law which prevented all freeholders of under a hundred pounds a year —that is to say the very great majority of the class—from killing game, even on their own land. Thus many poor families were robbed of many good meals that were theirs by right ; and even those few yeomen whose wealth raised them above the reach of this remarkable law, were for that reason regarded with suspicion. The best that even the good-hearted Sir Roger de Coverley can bring himself to say of the ' yeoman of about a hundred pounds a year,' ' who is just within the Game Act,' is that ' he would make a good neighbour if he did not destroy so many partridges '— that is to say upon his own land.

For many generations to come, grave social consequences were to flow from the excessive eagerness of the country gentlemen about the preservation of game. Their anxieties on that score had grown with the adoption of the shot-gun. During the Stuart epoch shooting gradually superseded hawking, with the result that birds were more rapidly destroyed, and the supply no longer seemed inexhaustible. In Charles II's reign it was already not unusual to ' shoot flying.' But it was regarded as a difficult art, the more so as it was sometimes practised from horseback. But the ' perching ' of pheasants by stalking and shooting them as they sat on the boughs, was still customary among gentlemen.

The netting of birds on the ground was a fashionable sport, often carried on over dogs who pointed the game concealed in the grass. It is written that Sir Roger ' in his youthful days had *taken* forty coveys of partridges in a season ' probably by this means. To lure wild duck, by the score and the hundred, into a decoy upon the water's edge was a trade in the fens and a sport on the decoy-pond of the manor-house. Liming by twigs, snaring and trapping birds of all kinds, not only pheasants and wild duck but thrushes and fieldfares, had still a prominent place in manuals of *The Gentleman's Recreation*. But the shot-gun was clearly in the ascendant, and with it the tendency to confine sport more and more to the pursuit of certain birds specifically listed as *game*. In that sacred category a place had recently been granted by Statute to grouse and black-cock ; already the heather and bracken where they lurked were protected from being burnt except at certain times of the year, and the shepherd transgressing the law was liable to be whipped. Addison's Tory squire declared the new Game Law to be the only good law passed since the Revolution.[1]

Fox-hunting, under the later Stuarts, was beginning to assume features recognizably modern. In Tudor times the fox had been dug out of its earth, bagged, and baited like a badger, or had been massacred as vermin by the peasantry. For in those days the stag was still the beast of the chase *par excellence*. But the disorders of the Civil War had broken open deer-parks and destroyed deer to such an extent that at the Restoration the fox was perforce substituted in many districts. As yet there were no county or regional packs supported by public subscription, but private gentlemen

---

[1] The two leading Game Laws are those of 22–23 Charles II, cap. 25, and 4 W. and M. cap. 23.

kept their own packs and invited their nearer neighbours to follow. The idea that gentlemen should hunt ' the stag and the fox with their own hounds and among their own woods,' was gradually yielding to the chase across the country at large, irrespective of its ownership.

In some counties earths were stopped and the endeavour was made with frequent success to run the fox down in the open. Under these conditions runs of ten or even twenty miles were not unknown. But in Lancashire and probably elsewhere ' the hunters ran the fox to earth and then dug him out ; if he refused to go to earth he generally got away. It is possible that there had not yet been developed as tireless a breed of hounds as to-day.' [1]

The chase of the deer, with all the time-honoured ritual of venery, still continued as the acknowledged king of sports, but it was steadily on the decline, as the claims of agriculture for more land reduced the number of forests and set a limit to the size of the deer-park that a gentleman was likely to keep enclosed round his manor-house.

More widely popular than the hunting of deer or fox was the pursuit of the hare, with a ' tunable chiding ' of hounds, the gentlemen on horseback, and the common folk running, headed by the huntsman with his pole. This scene partook of the nature of a popular village sport, led indeed by the gentry but shared with all their neighbours, high and low.

Other popular sports were wrestling, with different rules and traditions in different parts of the country ; various rough kinds of football and ' hurling,' often amounting to a good-natured free-fight between the whole male population of two villages. Single-stick, boxing and sword-fighting, bull and bear baiting, were watched with delight by a race that had not yet learnt to dislike the sight of pain inflicted. Indeed the less sporting events of hanging and whipping were spectacles much relished. But cockfighting was the most popular sport of all, on which all classes staked their money even more than upon horse-racing. But the turf was beginning to take a greater place in the national

---

[1] Thus Thomas Tyldesley writes in his diary—' went early to Sullom a fox hunting to meet brothers Dalton and Frost, found two foxes, but could get neither of them into the earth.' (Notestein *English Folk*, p. 172.) Compare the account of fox-hunting in Bloome's *Gentleman's Recreation*, 1686, II, pp. 137–139.

consciousness owing to the patronage of Newmarket by
Charles II, and the improvement in the breed of riding-
horses by the introduction of Arab and Barb blood.

Under the later Stuart kings, Spas were much frequented
for purposes of fashion and of health.   The waters of Bath
were beginning to attract the great, for the first time since
Roman days, but the fine town of Beau Nash and Jane
Austen had not yet been built.   Buxton and Harrogate
were much attended by northern gentry and their families.
But the Court and the world of London fashion were found
oftenest and in greatest number among the rustic cottages
round the Tunbridge Wells, where in 1685 the courtiers
built a church for their own use, dedicated to King Charles
the Martyr.

As yet the seaside had no votaries : doctors had not yet
discovered the health-giving qualities of its air ; no one
wanted to bathe in the waters of the ocean or to rhapsodize
over its appearance from the shore.   The sea was ' the
Englishman's common,' his way to market, his fishpond,
his battleground, his heritage.   But as yet no one sought
either the seaside or the mountains for the refreshment they
could give to the spirit of man.

During the century of Stuart rule, frequent assessments
of the counties of England were made for fiscal purposes ;
the returns indicate roughly the geographical distribution
of wealth.   The richest county was Middlesex, as it included so much of London ; the poorest was Cumberland.
Surrey, owing to the expansion of London and its market,
rose from the eighteenth place in 1636 to the second in
1693.   Next in order of wealth came Berks and the group
of agricultural counties north of the Thames—Herts, Beds,
Bucks, Oxfordshire and Northants.   Their wealth is remarkable, considering that they possessed no great towns,
industrial districts or coal mines and that their agriculture
was chiefly open-field ; but it was not far from the London
market.   Thus the central counties were on the average the
richest.   Next came the southern, including Kent and
Sussex, with lands of old enclosure and fruit gardens, and
with downland sheep-runs ; next East Anglia, enjoying the
farmer's blessing of a low rainfall, and with Essex abutting

on London ; next in order of wealth came the West, distant from the capital, and suffering from a damper climate. And last of all, the lately turbulent and still impoverished North. The seven poorest counties in England were Cheshire, Derbyshire, Yorkshire, Lancashire, Northumberland, Durham and Cumberland. The poverty of the Northern shires is the more remarkable because they all had coal-mines, and Yorks and Lancs had textiles as well. But the wealth produced by these industries had not yet been applied on a large scale to the improvement of agriculture in these backward northern parts. That was done in the following century, when the wealth of the Tyneside mines was poured out into the soil, to fertilize the moorland farms of the neighbouring counties.

If a line be drawn from Gloucester to Boston, the area of England without Wales is divided about equally into a North-Western half and a South-Eastern half : to-day the majority of the population live North-West of the line, owing to the development of heavy industries, though a return drift towards the South has recently begun. But in Charles II's reign it is probable that only a quarter of the population lived North-West of the line. The land tax returns indicate that the wealth of the North-Western half was only 5:14, while the Excise returns make it 1: 4. (Ogg, *England in the reign of C. II*, p. 51.)

In the course of the Seventeenth Century, changes had taken place in Warwickshire significant of industrial progress and of its reactions on agriculture. In Elizabeth's reign Camden had noted in his *Britannia* that Warwickshire was divided by the Avon into two parts, the Feldon or rich arable district of open field to the South-East of the river, and the Woodland (the Forest of Arden) to the North-West. In the reign of William III, Gibson, afterwards the famous Bishop of London, brought out a new edition of the *Britannia*, adding notes of changes that had taken place since Camden's day : the Forest of Arden had disappeared, and had become a rich arable district :

For the ironworks in the counties round [viz. in Birmingham and the Black Country] destroyed such prodigious quantities of wood that they quickly lay the country a little open, and by degrees made room for the plough. Whereupon the inhabitants, partly by their own industry, and partly by the assistance of marl have turned so much of wood and heath-land into tillage and pasture that they produce corn, cattle, cheese and butter enough not only for their own use but also to furnish other counties.

Meanwhile, on the other side of Avon, the Feldon, once the great arable region supplying Bristol with corn, had been largely laid down to grass, and the population of many villages had been reduced, according to Gibson, to a few shepherds ; the reason for the change to pasture in the Feldon is, he thinks, the superior arable quality of the old forest lands on the other side of Avon recently brought under plough. Here, then, in both parts of Warwickshire, we have a great increase of enclosed fields—to the North-West enclosure of old forest and heath, to South-East hedging of former open fields. All this occurred in the Stuart era, with very little said, for the feeling against enclosure, so vocal in Tudor times, seems to have died away.[1]

In Stuart times, in spite of the rapid growth of iron trades in Birmingham and the Black Country to the west of it, coal or coke fires were not yet applied to iron. Coal, however, was used in many other processes of manufacture ; and it had become the regular domestic fuel in London, and in all regions to which it could easily be carried by water. Under these conditions the Stuart era saw an increase in the coal trade, hardly less astonishing, in the circumstances of that earlier time, than the second great increase in the early Nineteenth Century, the age of ' coal and iron.' [2]

Throughout the Seventeenth Century coal played a great part in developing, not only the national wealth and therewith the well-being of many classes of the community above ground, but also the less pleasant characteristics of the Industrial Revolution in the life of the miners themselves. Their ' capitalist ' employers saw little and cared less about

---

[1] In his ' Additions to Warwickshire ' since Camden's day, Gibson also notes in the 1695 edition of the *Britannia* (pp. 510–512) that in Stratford church ' in the chancel lies William Shakespeare, a native of this place, who has given proof of his genius and great abilities in the 48 plays he has left behind him.' There are only 37 in the present canon ! But the passage at least shows the considerable place Shakespeare already held in his countrymen's estimation.

[2] The following figures given by Mr. Nef in his *Rise of the British Coal Industry*, pp. 19–20, [Routledge], show how rapid was the advance in coal production

their conditions of life and labour. As the pits grew deeper, the miners spent more time far away underground, and were more and more segregated from the rest of humanity ; explosions due to fire-damp became more frequent and more terrible, and women and children were more often employed underground as bearers. In Durham and Northumberland great combinations of thousands of miners and keelmen on the Tyne coal-barges, strove with indifferent success to better their conditions of life. In Scotland the miners were reduced to the condition of ' bondmen ' bound to the service of the mine. In England this could not be done, but the condition of the miners and their families were in many respects worse than that of any other large class of the community.

Mr. Nef, who has collected a great body of facts relating to mining conditions in Stuart and early Hanoverian times, writes :

Coal created a new gulf between classes. The mediaeval peasants and artisans, whatever their disabilities and trials may have been, were not segregated from their neighbours to anything like the same extent as were the coal miners of the seventeenth century in most colliery districts.

Moreover, within the coal-mining industry itself, there was now a complete barrier between the capitalist employer and the manual worker, similar to that which became general in so many other trades in later times. Indeed, under the later

---

between the reigns of Elizabeth and William III, and show also the geographic distribution of the coalfields, much the same as at the present day.

ESTIMATED ANNUAL PRODUCTION IN TONS

	1551–60	*1681–90*	*1781–90*	*1901–10*
Durham and Northumberland	65,000	1,225,000	3,000,000	50,000,000
Scotland	40,000	475,000	1,600,000	37,000,000
Wales	20,000	200,000	800,000	50,000,000
Midlands	65,000	850,000	4,000,000	100,180,000
Cumberland	6,000	100,000	500,000	2,120,000
Kingswood Chase and Somerset	10,000	100,000	140,000	1,100,000
Forest of Dean . . .	3,000	25,000	90,000	1,310,000
Devon and Ireland . .	1,000	7,000	25,000	200,000
	210,000	2,982,000	10,295,000	241,910,000
Approximate increase :		14 *fold*	3 *fold*	23 *fold*

The Midland coal area included mines in Yorks, Lancs, Cheshire, Derbyshire, Shropshire, Staffs, Notts, Warwickshire, Leicestershire and Worcestershire.

K 2

Stuart Kings many new industries which sprang up as a result of the supply of coal for furnaces, tended to be of the same large-scale and capitalistic character.   (Nef, *Rise of the British Coal Industry*, Vol. II, chap. IV.)

But there were many districts which could not obtain coal either by sea or by river.   Some of these regions, owing to the decrease of timber, went short of fuel for the elementary needs of warmth and cooking, and remained in that condition until the improved roads, the canals and finally the railways of later times brought coal to every door.   Thus, in the reign of William III, the adventurous Miss Celia Fiennes,[1] on a riding tour in the South-West, found her supper at Penzance ' boiling on a fire always supplied with a bush of furze, and that to be the only fuel to dress a joint of meat and broth ' ; for the Cornish forests had disappeared, and the French privateers in time of war prevented the delivery of Welsh coal in the south Cornish ports.   In Leicestershire, cowdung, that ought to have enriched the fields, was gathered and dried for fuel.

So too, in 1695, Gibson, in his edition of Camden's *Britannia* comments on the description given by the Elizabethan antiquary of the Oxfordshire hills ' clad with woods '; ' this is so much altered,' writes Gibson, ' by the late civil wars that few places except the Chiltern country can answer that character at present.   For fuel is in those parts so scarce that 'tis commonly sold by weight, not only in Oxford, but other towns in the northern part of the shire.'   Oxford town and gown could, however, warm their parlours and cook their food with coal conveyed by the Thames barges, whereas the ' towns in the northern part of the shire ' found the shortage of wood fuel a more serious matter.

The bread-and-cheese diet to which many English working-class families were increasingly limited in the following century, was largely the result of this lack of kitchen fuel ; and in winter time their poor cottages must have been terribly cold.   In those parts of the country where there was a time-gap between the timber age and the coal age,

---

[1] *The Journeys of Celia Fiennes,* edited by Christopher Morris (1947).   This delightful and important record was composed on tours made partly in the reign of William III, partly in that of Anne.   Miss Fiennes was a lady of means and a dissenter.   She was sister of the Third Viscount Saye and Sele.   She rode through England on tours of pleasure and curiosity.

there was much suffering for the poor and some inconvenience for the rich.

But even before the days of hard roads, coal could at a cost be carried far inland, at a great distance from the mines, wherever the service was well organized. Thus Miss Fiennes describes the barges with ' sea-coal ' from Bristol coming up by river through Bridgwater to a place within three miles of Taunton, ' where the boats unload the coal, the packhorses come and take it in sacks, and so carry it to places all about. The horses carry two bushell at a time, which at the place of disembarkation cost eighteen pence, and when it's brought to Taunton cost two shillings. The roads were full of these carriers going and returning.'

The growth of London, more and more outdistancing all other cities, continued after the Restoration without a check. By the year 1700 the capital contained well over a tenth of the five and a half million inhabitants of England.[1] Bristol and Norwich, the cities next in size, numbered about 30,000 each. And London trade was proportionately great. In 1680 the Custom House administration of the Port of London cost £20,000 a year, of Bristol £2000, of Newcastle, Plymouth and Hull £900 each ; the rest were nowhere. The port of Newcastle lived on the export of coal, three-quarters of it to London ; Hull flourished on the whaling and fishing industries, and on its importance as the chief garrison town of Northern England ; Plymouth, like great Bristol and rising Liverpool, benefited by the growing trade with the transatlantic colonies, and on its own importance as the western base of the Royal Navy.

Whitby, Yarmouth and Harwich had flourishing shipbuilding yards. But many other ports, such as King's Lynn and the smaller harbours of East Anglia, were declining as trade increasingly sought the mouth of the Thames, or shifted to the West to catch the American trade. The

[1] It has been estimated from the registers of baptisms that in 1700 when England and Wales contained rather more than five and a half million inhabitants, the Metropolitan Area contained 674,350. Of these the ' City ' proper contained about 200,000. (Mrs. George, *London Life*, etc., pp. 24-25, 329-330.) On the figures of population for England and Wales see Talbot-Griffith, *Royal Statistical Society Journal*, 1929, Vol. XCII, Pt. II, pp. 256-263.

effect of the Navigation Laws was to foster England's colonial trade across the Atlantic, and diminish her foreign trade with Scandinavia and the Baltic, to the disadvantage of the east coast ports, all save London. And even in the West, smaller ports like Fowey and Bideford suffered from the large size of ships necessitated by the long oceanic voyages. Moreover, London merchants and London capital controlled the trade of other cities.

The vital and recuperative force of London, perpetually fed by the inflow of immigrants and of wealth from outside, was heavily tested by the Plague and the Fire (1665–1666), disasters of the first magnitude, which however seemed scarcely to affect the onward movement of the power, opulence and population of the capital.

The famous ' Plague of London ' was merely the last, and not perhaps the worst, of a series of outbreaks covering three centuries. Between the campaigns of Crecy and Poitiers, the Black Death had first swept over Europe from some unknown source in the Far East, with the ubiquity and violence usual to the incoming of a new disease. The obscurest hamlet had little chance of escape. It is thought probable that a third, and possibly that one half of the fellow-countrymen of Boccaccio, of Froissart and of Chaucer, perished within three years. The Black Death remained in the soil of England, and became known as ' The Plague.' It never again swept the whole country at one time, but it perpetually broke out in different localities, particularly in the towns and ports and the riversides, where the ship-borne, flea-bearing rat multiplied. In London under the Lancastrian and Tudor Kings the plague was for long periods together endemic and nearly continual ; under the Stuarts it came in rare but violent outbursts. The rejoicing in London for the accession of James I had been cut short by an outbreak of the Plague that carried off 30,000 persons; the accession of Charles I was the signal for another, no less destructive. In 1636 a slighter attack occurred. Then followed thirty years of comparative immunity for London, during which other events took place calculated to make men forget in their talk the Plague horrors that their fathers and grandfathers had endured. So when the last outbreak came in 1665, although it did not destroy a much larger proportion of the Londoners than some of its predecessors had done, it struck the imagination more, for it came in an age of greater civilization, comfort and security, when such calamities were less remembered and less expected, and it was followed close, as though at the Divine command, by another catastrophe to which there was no parallel in the most ancient records of London.[1]

The Great Fire (1666) raged for five days and destroyed the whole City proper between the Tower and the Temple ; yet it probably did not unroof half the population of the capital. The ' Liberties ' beyond the walls were only touched, and these contained by far the greater part of the inhabitants. London had been increasing with immense rapidity in the last sixty years. It was just short of half a million. In all other cities of England the townsfolk still lived within breath of the country, under conditions of what we should now call country-town life. In London alone the conditions of great-city life were growing up, in many respects in a peculiarly odious form. The poor were crowded out of the City into the slum districts of the ' Liberties ' beyond—St. Giles's, Cripplegate, Whitechapel, Stepney, Westminster, Lambeth—where they multiplied exceedingly in spite of an enormous death-rate among infants.

The fire and rebuilding made little improvement in the sanitary and moral condition of the slum populations. For the seat and origin of the Plague had always been in the ' Liberties ' outside the City, where the poorest dwelt. Now as these districts were not burnt down they were not rebuilt, and in 1722 Defoe declared that ' they were still in the same condition as they were before.' It is therefore evident that the ' rebuilding of London ' due to the Fire was not the main reason why the Plague disappeared from England after its last great effort.

[1] During the Civil War (1642–1646) the Plague raged in other parts of the island, particularly the South and West ; in some towns, such as Chester, a quarter of the inhabitants died of it. The ' Plague of London ' (1665) was not quite confined to the capital. East Anglia suffered very severely, but the Plague did not extend far west or north. In Langdale, Westmorland, tradition still points to the ruins of an isolated farmhouse where all the inhabitants died of the Plague, owing to the infected clothes of a soldier being sent there ; but the rest of the valley and district remained immune. The soldier's clothes presumably carried the flea that bore the Plague.

The portion of London that was changed by the Fire was the residential and business quarter in the heart of the City itself, the great commercial houses where the merchants with their orderly and well-fed households worked and slept. These abodes of wealth, commerce and hospitality dating from the Middle Ages, with their gardens behind and courtyards within, still presented lath and plaster walls to the narrow and crooked streets ; the gables sometimes protruded so far over the shop fronts that the prentices in their garrets could shake hands over the way. When the Fire came racing before the wind, these old and flimsy structures were tinder to the flame. Only in the few places where the Fire met brick walls was it forced to linger and fight. The merchants took the opportunity to rebuild their houses of brick, and in a more wholesome if less picturesque relation to the street. Sanitation in the City itself was improved by the enforced rebuilding of so many very ancient dwellings.

The fact that the Plague did not again recur in England is due in part to the increase of brick building, and the substitution of carpets and panelling for straw and cloth hangings, since the infected fleas and the rats that carried them were thus deprived of harbourage. But it is probable that the chief cause of the disappearance of the Plague was due to no human agency at all, but to an obscure revolution in the animal world ; about this period the modern brown rat extirpated and replaced the mediaeval black rat, and the brown rat was not a carrier of the plague-flea to nearly the same extent as its predecessor. (Saltmarsh's article in *Cambridge Hist. Journal*, 1941.)

The reconstruction of the City of London was accomplished at a pace that astonished the world.

'The dreadful effects of the fire [wrote Sir John Reresby] were not so strange as the rebuilding of this great city, which by reason of the King's and Parliament's care, and the great wealth and opulency of the city itself, was rebuilded most stately with brick (the greatest part being before nothing but lath and lime) in four or five years' time.'

And London, which had lost a fifth of its population by the Plague made good that loss also without seeming to notice it

at all, so continual was the flow of immigrants from all the
shires of England and half the countries of Europe.

The Mediaeval and Tudor City had disappeared in the
flames ; only the ground plan of its rabbit-warren of streets
and alleys was retained. The layout of the greatest city in
the world continued to be the worst ; and mortal eye has
never yet had a view of Wren's St. Paul's.[1]

Eighty-nine churches, including the old Gothic Cathedral,
had been burnt. If they were doomed to perish, no
happier date could have been chosen for the holocaust since
Christopher Wren, just arrived at the height of his powers,
was beginning to be known in Court and City. His
genius was stamped on the ecclesiastical architecture of
the new London. His churches, which survived general
rebuildings of the streets in which they stand, still (1939)
testify to the spacious classical dignity of the age
and of the man who put them in place of their mediaeval
predecessors.

The rebuilding of St. Paul's was a communal effort
worthy of a great nation. A tax on the coal entering the
port of London was voted by Parliament for the purpose.
The great work went steadily forward year by year, un-
deterred by all the excitements of the Popish Plot, the
Revolution and the Marlborough Wars. It was completed in the height of Queen Anne's glory, a dozen years
before the death of its architect.

The new St. Paul's was built of the white stone of Portland, fetched by sea direct from the quarries of that strange
peninsula. Though the quarries had long been known, it
was only in Stuart times that Portland stone began to be
extensively used. The needs of Wren's colossal work gave
a new life to the ' Isle of Portland ' and its inhabitants.
Vast quarries were opened and roads and piers built.
Great sums were spent on

'salaries to agents and wharfingers and repairing ways, piers and
cranes, with the expenses of several persons sent from London to
view and direct the same, to regulate the working of the quarries
and to adjust matters with the Islanders.' (*Ec. Hist. Rev.*, Nov.
1938.)

[1] This sentence was written before the Blitz !

Henceforth the white Portland Stone plays an important part in architectural history of England, and seems specially associated with the cold majesty of the monumental work of Wren and Gibbs, just as the warm red brick suits the comfortable domesticity of the common dwellings of the same period.

BOOKS FOR FURTHER READING

Besides the books mentioned in the notes to this chapter, see Pepys' and Evelyn's *Diaries,* and Arthur Bryant's *Life of Pepys* ; David Ogg, *England in the Reign of Charles II* (1934), Chaps. II and III ; *The Seventeenth Century Background* (1934), Basil Willey.

CHAPTER X

DEFOE'S ENGLAND [1]

Queen Anne, 1702–1714—George I, 1714–1727—The Marlborough Wars, 1702–1712.—Parliamentary and economic union with Scotland, 1707.

WHEN a survey is demanded of Queen Anne's England and its everyday life, our thoughts turn to Daniel Defoe, riding solitary and observant through the countryside. It was one of his tasks to traverse Britain on such tours of reconnaissance ; after his day's journey, in the inn of some market town, he wrote his report on local opinion to his employer, Robert Harley, a mystery-man like himself, and a lover of exact information secretly given. On Sundays he would attend the Dissenters' Chapel, observant of his fellow-worshippers and inquisitive as to their business affairs. For besides being a trader, he was a Nonconformist, not indeed of the type laden with the proverbial conscience, for Defoe could be all things to all men, but a Puritan in his preference for solid work and homespun to fashionable display. Like Cobbett, who rode and wrote about England a hundred years after him, he was a realist and a man of the people, but he was not, like his successor, half blinded by rage against the powers that be. For the age of Anne was the prelude to a long era of content, and Defoe, more than Swift, was the typical man of his day. Defoe, the trader, hailed the advent of the era of business prosperity as heartily as Cobbett, the disinherited yeoman, bewailed the rural past. He first perfected the art of the reporter ; even his novels, such as *Robinson Crusoe* and *Moll Flanders* are imaginary ' reports ' of daily life, whether on a desert island or in a thieves' den. So then, the account that this man gives of the England of Anne's reign is for the historian a treasure indeed. For Defoe was one of the first who saw

---

[1] Only a few years ago I wrote some chapters on the social life of England under Queen Anne, in my history of her reign, published, like this volume, by Messrs. Longman. As I cannot improve on them now, I have laid them under contribution.

the old world through a pair of sharp modern eyes. His report can be controlled and enlarged by great masses of other evidence, but it occupies the central point of our thought and vision.[1]

Now this picture of England, drawn by Defoe in much wealth of prosaic detail, leaves the impression of a healthy national life, in which town and country, agriculture, industry and commerce were harmonious parts of a single economic system. Much indeed of the administrative machinery of government, particularly of the ' poor decayed borough towns ' which Defoe despised, was antiquarian lumber too religiously preserved. But for many years to come no cry was raised for Reform, because the principle of freedom then peculiar to England enabled individual enterprise to flourish, and new shoots to push through the old jungle. The Bumbledom of that day could not suppress the economic initiative native to the island soil.

The England so ordered was prosperous and in the main contented even in time of war, partly owing to good harvests and cheap food in the first half of Anne's reign. Only during the last three years of a decade of hostilities with France (1702–1712) were there signs of distress and discontent due to war conditions. Otherwise industry, agriculture and commerce all continued to expand ; society moved forward unconsciously towards the Industrial Revolution, which grew in the next hundred years out of the conditions described by Defoe. Overseas trade ; water-carriage on the rivers, particularly of coal ; sheep-farming and the cloth trade ; the national marketing of agricultural produce by wholesale dealers—on these things he lays stress, and it was these things that enabled many landowners to pay the land tax, the mainstay of the Marlborough Wars. They grumbled but they paid, till the war was won, when they sent the Whigs about their business and made peace.

It is true that rural squires over their October ale cursed the moneyed men and traders as economic parasites, war-

---

[1] He published his *Tour through Great Britain* in the reign of George I, but the tours on which he based his observations were largely taken in the early and middle years of Anne. The first edition of the Tour (1724–27) has been edited and republished by Mr. G. D. H. Cole in 1927.

profiteers and Dissenters, would-be intruders into political
life which was the proper sphere of the landed interest alone.
But economically the activities of these undesirables doubled
the rent of many a squire, as indeed he was partly aware.
And the Act of Toleration, though scarcely to be mentioned
without a groan over degenerate times, gave riches as well
as quiet to the land.

In the reigns of Anne and George I the old way of life for
peasant and craftsman was still carried on, but under conditions peculiarly favourable.   The enterprise of trader and
middleman was finding new markets for the products of the
peasant's and craftsman's toil, and had already done much
to relieve their mediaeval poverty without as yet destroying
their rustic simplicity of manners.   Money made in trade
was more and more frequently put into the land by improving landlords, who had won or enlarged their fortunes
as mercantile investors.   This interplay of the activity of
town and country, not yet subversive of the old social order,
gave to Queen Anne's England a fundamental harmony
and strength, below the surface of the fierce distracting
antagonisms of sect and faction.

While religion divided, trade united the nation, and trade
was gaining in relative importance.   The Bible had now a
rival in the Ledger.   The Puritan, sixty years back, had
been Cromwell, sword in hand ; thirty years back, Bunyan,
singing hymns in gaol ; but now the Puritan was to be
found in the tradesman-journalist Defoe.   The Quaker, too,
had ceased to prophesy in public against steeple houses,
and had become a thrifty dealer, studying to be quiet.   For
old sake's sake, Puritans and Quakers were still called
' fanatics ' in common parlance.   But if there were ' fanatics ' at large, one of them surely was Justice Bradgate,
who ' rode a horseback into the Meeting House ' at Lutter-
worth and told the preacher he lied.   Yet that angry zeal
of the High Churchmen was perpetually being tempered
by patriotic and economic considerations that worked
strongly in the minds of the Moderate Tories, led by
Harley, whose secret servant was this same Defoe.   Here
then was an island which, with luck and good leading, might
in wartime display enough unity, wealth and vigour to bring
to his knees the mighty Louis of France, the undisputed

lord of nobles and poor peasants, who had got rid of his
Nonconformists once for all by revoking the Edict of
Nantes.

Already English agriculture had improved so far that
more wheat was grown than in mediaeval times. Wheat
was reckoned at thirty-eight per cent. of the bread of the
whole population ; rye came next, barley and oats a good
third and fourth. Prices were therefore quoted in terms
of wheat and rye.

But wheat formed a much smaller proportion of the actual
corn grown than of the bread baked, because enormous
crops of barley were produced all over the island to make
malt for ale and beer. For example, Cambridgeshire south
of Ely was ' almost wholly a corn country ' and, as Defoe
observed, ' of that corn five parts in six is barley, which is
generally sold at Ware and Royston and other great malting
towns of Hertfordshire.' Except in the cider counties of
the West, ale had been unchallenged in former ages as the
native drink of English men, women and children at every
meal, and it was only beginning to feel the rivalry of strong
spirits on the one hand and of tea and coffee on the other.
It was still the drink of ladies. In 1705 Lady Carnarvon
imputed the fact that Miss Coke was ' extremely fallen
away and her voice weak and inward ' to ' her having had
stale beer all this summer.' Children still drank very
small beer and it was in many cases better for them
than the impure water which was too often the only
alternative.

Not only did barley everywhere provide the staple drink,
but in some districts it provided the staple food. The
small farmers of the Welsh hills supplied themselves with
an excellent barley bread. The peasantry of the northern
counties consumed oats and rye in various forms ; and in
Scotland, oats ' supported the people ' as Dr. Johnson was
still able to assert many years later. In the central districts
of England, rye and barley divided honours with wheat,
and only in the drier climate of the south-east could wheat
be said to preponderate.

But already in the reign of Anne a great interchange of
agricultural products was going on between one district and

another, especially where river traffic was available. Largely for this reason the deepening of rivers and the making of locks was a movement specially characteristic of the period, two generations before the era of the Duke of Bridgewater's artificial canals.[1] The Thames all the way down from Oxford, and its affluents the Wey, the Lea and the Medway, were the scenes of an animated and crowded traffic—food, drink and timber going down to London, and Tyneside coal and overseas products towed up-country in return. Abingdon and Reading were each the emporium of a great agricultural district, of which they dispatched the produce by water to the capital. The coasts of Sussex and Hampshire sent their corn, Cheshire and other western counties sent their cheese, by sea to London, running the gauntlet of the French privateers from Dunkirk. The roads were at many times of year too soft for waggons, but in most weathers the sheep and cattle, the geese and turkeys of the northern and midland shires could be driven to the capital, grazing as they went on the broad grass of the roadside. Even before the Union of 1707, Scotland sent 30,000 head of cattle a year into England : the strange speech of the Welsh drovers was familiar on the roads near London ; only the Irish cattle-trade had been killed by an Act of the reign of Charles II, a sacrifice to the jealousy of English breeders.

England and Wales already formed the most considerable area in Europe for internal free trade, to which Scotland was added half way through the reign of Anne. ' Tis our great felicity in England,' wrote Defoe, ' that we are not yet come to a *gabelle* or tax upon corn, as in Italy, and many other countries.' The shrewd Venetian envoy, Mocenigo, at the end of his residence in our island, reported to his masters in 1706 that freedom from internal *douanes* was one reason why ' industry was further advanced in England

---

[1] The *Statutes* and the *Commons Journals* for Anne's reign, as well as local histories, afford abundant evidence of this. One case may be quoted for all : in 1699 the inhabitants of Wisbech petition the House of Commons to have the River Lark made navigable, as the roads are impracticable, and their district which itself produces only butter, cheese and oats, is supplied with wheat, rye and malt from Suffolk. Among the rivers at this period deepened and supplied with proper locks were the Bristol Avon, the Yorkshire Derwent, the Stour and the Cam ' from Clayhithe Ferry to the Queen's Mill ' in Cambridge.

than in any other part of the world.' London and every provincial city was an open market for provisions, with no toll taken at the gate. Favoured by this freedom, the corn-factors and middlemen of agriculture pervaded the whole island, buying up on speculation the farmers' crops as they grew in the field, or as they lay unthreshed in the barn ; penetrating to the most unlikely places, even to dangerous Highland straths, amid claymores and Jacobites, in search of cattle to be fattened in English parks ; everywhere forwarding the movement towards agricultural progress by opening new markets for the produce of remote estates and hamlets.

Under this regime of enterprise and improvement England was sending corn overseas on a large scale, helped by the bounty on export. In the middle of Anne's reign the employees of the Gloucestershire coal trade rose in revolt against the high price of corn, due to the scale on which the Bristol merchants shipped the local supply abroad. And even north of Trent, homely squires were calculating on sales abroad as an important item in their own and their tenants' fortunes.[1]

Nevertheless, this cheerful picture of agricultural and distributive activity must not delude us into imagining that England was already the land of improved agriculture and reformed traffic that it became by the end of the century. The busy life of the rivers was a measure of the badness of the roads. Corn-lands potentially the best in England—in the midlands, and northern East Anglia—were still for the most part unenclosed. In those regions the vast and hedgeless village field was still being cultivated by mediaeval methods that would have won the approval of a Doomsday commissioner, but were destined to shock the modern intelligence of Arthur Young.

The initiative of improving landlord or farmer was

---

[1] In July 1709 Robert Molesworth writes to his wife from Edlington, near Doncaster : ' If God sends good harvest weather, there will be a very great store of corn in the kingdom, and yet such are the wants abroad that it is likely to bear a very good price for several years to come. This must enrich our farmers.' And next year he writes : ' Corn must certainly rise in price and that very suddenly, for the plague, which is got into the Baltic, will make soon both us and the Dutch to prohibit all trade there and then the Dutch must be furnished with corn from us.'

closely circumscribed on these village fields, wherein the scattered strips of individual owners had perforce to be cultivated on the plan laid down for the whole community. A man could not profitably grow turnips or artificial grasses on his unfenced strips ; for the whole ' field,' as soon as the corn was carried, was opened as pasture to the cattle of the village, which would eat his clover and turnips and he would be without redress. The open field was cultivated on a uniform plan. A small country town like Godmanchester, for example, still employed its bailiffs to summon all the farmers to appear, according to old custom, at the Court Hall, where they ' did agree that none should sow barley in the commonfield before Friday, 21st March ' (1700), ' and that day only headlands.'

More initiative and therefore more progress was possible, though by no means inevitable, on newly enclosed farms which were constantly increasing in number, and in the regions of old enclosure in southern, western and northern England. But the districts where enclosure was commonest were on the average the less productive parts of the island, with the worst climate. It is true that Kentish hop-fields and west country orchards and fruit gardens must be reckoned among the lands of early enclosure, but so must the intakes amid the weather-beaten moorlands of west and north. Most of the best cornlands of the midlands were still unenclosed.

Since many of the sheep and cattle were fed on stubble-fields, heaths and commons, and without the aid of roots or artificial grasses for winter feed, they were pitifully small and thin. Their weight at Smithfield market in 1710 was less than half that of ordinary sheep and cattle in 1795. At the beginning of the century the difficulty of keeping beasts alive in winter was still so great that, when they came off the summer grass, all save the breeding stock were slaughtered and salted, and the survivors were kept on short rations till spring. When the price of salt rose in 1703, the House of Commons was petitioned, on the ground that it was ' a grievance to the poorer sort of people who mostly feed on salted provisions.'

The days of Lord Townshend's turnip-fields and Coke of Norfolk's fat sheep and cattle were still in the future. But already the Wiltshire and Cotswold uplands, that bred sheep for the western wool-clothiers, were a wonder to behold. ' On the pleasant downs ' within a six-mile radius of Dorchester, Defoe was informed that more than half a million sheep were feeding ; and he noted that on Salisbury Plain and the Dorset Downs the land was becoming so much enriched by the folding of sheep with pens in a new place every night, that the chalk lands thus manured, though hitherto fit only for pasture, were rapidly coming under the plough.

Ever since Tudor times, and more particularly since the Restoration, there had flowed from the press an ever broadening stream of books on improved methods of agriculture. The spirit of scientific inquiry emanating from the regions of the Royal Society into the walks of common life, was a constant stimulant but often a sore puzzle to the practical farmer. For the experts and modernizers were so seldom agreed. Jethro Tull, the great improver who introduced the drill and the horse-hoe into his own farming operations in the course of Anne's reign, was quite wrong on many other points, as subsequent experience showed. But men were on the look-out to adopt new methods as soon as their value had been proved, especially where enclosed ground gave liberty for change.

With the idea of agricultural improvement thus in the air, the enclosure of commons and heaths was not only frequently practised as it had been for centuries, but was preached by modern theorists as a duty to the commonwealth. In Tudor times controversialists had been almost all on the side of the commons and the commoners against the enclosures. But when Anne came to the throne the agricultural writers were denouncing the commons as ' seminaries of a lazy, thieving sort of people,' whose sheep were ' poor, tattered and poisoned with rot,' and whose heath-fed cattle were ' starved, todbellied runts, neither fit for the dairy nor the yoke.' Here was another phase of the perennial controversy as to the social value of rights on the common, in which Cobbett a hundred years later was protagonist of the defeated commoners. On the merits of that dispute the historians of our own day are still divided. In Anne's reign there was not yet much enclosure done by

Act of Parliament, but enclosure was going forward under the common law by agreement or otherwise.[1]

The age of Defoe was still a period of prosperity for English freehold yeomen, and it was no ill time for the still rising fortunes of the tenant farmers. The freehold yeomen and their families were reckoned at about one-eighth of the population of the country, and the substantial tenant farmers at a little less ; at the time of the Revolution it had been calculated that the freehold yeoman was on the average a richer man than the tenant farmer. A hundred years later the opposite was probably the case, in so far as the freehold yeoman any longer existed. For in the Georgian era of agricultural improvements, the tenant farmer had the benefit of his landlord's capital poured into his land, while the small freeholder had no financial resources save his own with which to keep abreast of the times. But Anne's reign was perhaps a moment of no very marked economic difference between the two classes.

The difference was political and social. The freeholder had a vote for Parliament and was often in a position to use it as he liked. The tenant farmer had no vote, and if he had, he would have been obliged to cast it as his landlord wished. Even the ideal landlord, Sir Roger de Coverley, was represented by Addison to an approving world as exercising over his tenants an absolute patriarchal sway.

But the independence of the freehold yeoman was deeply cherished and stoutly maintained. In the election correspondence of country gentlemen in the reign of Anne we meet such expressions as ' the freeholders do not stick to say they will show their liberty in voting.' The squire, who had everyone else under his thumb, was all the more anxious to buy out the freehold yeoman for political and

[1] In the summer when Marlborough was marching to Blenheim, a Yorkshire squire was writing to his wife :

' The law in England is (as I know now by experience) that every freeholder can enclose so much of his common as lies upon him (much more a lord of a considerable land), provided he leaves out as much common as is sufficient for those that have rights, and disclaims any further title to put beasts on the rest of the common which he leaves out. This is the instance of Mr. Frettwell, of Hellaby, our neighbour, who carried it even against the Lord Castleton, who is lord of the manor, upon trial. And this is our case between us and Gunsborough.'

game-keeping reasons ; and, as the century went on, many
freeholders, whether yeomen or small gentry, were ready
on fair terms to quit the countryside, in which their old
importance was threatened by the increasing wealth of the
large landlord and his tenant farmers. The process of
buying out the small freeholder to form large compact
estates for the grandees, began after the Restoration and
continued during the next hundred years and more.

But the distinction between the class of freeholders and
the class of tenants was never absolute, because a man often
farmed one piece of land as a tenant and another piece
as its owner.

The squalor of the mediaeval village had long been in
retreat before the homely dignity and comfort of the rural
middle class. In Anne's reign men were everywhere
building or enlarging farmhouses, in stone, brick or half-
timber according to the tradition or material of the district.
The architectural results of rustic prosperity were most
evident in those favoured regions where the cloth-manu-
facture made a great demand for the local wool, as in the
magnificent stone farms of the Cotswolds dating from the
Fifteenth to the Eighteenth Century, or in the dwellings
of the Cumbrian and Westmorland mountaineers whose
fortunes had more recently risen with the improvement of
the local cloth trade.

Besides the fine old farmhouses familiar to the traveller
in the Lake District to-day, there were then many cottages,
since fallen to ruin, wherein the poorer dalesmen brought up
large and sturdy families. The children were kept at their
mother's knee, spinning for the clothiers, until they were
old enough to go up on to the fells to drive the sheep and to
pile those great stone walls up the sides of the precipices,
which are the wonder of our less industrious age. It was
only in the course of the Eighteenth Century that the beauty
of Wordsworth's homeland attained the moment of rightful
balance between nature and man. In previous centuries
the valleys were ' choked, tangled, swampy and featureless ' ;
in our day man is all too successfully regulating the face of
nature with the machine. But in the reign of Anne the
dales were just beginning to take on their brief perfection

of rural loveliness, ordered but not disciplined, in contrast with the mountain magnificence above and around.

Nevertheless visitors were extremely rare in the Lake District, ' the wildest, most barren and frightful ' in England, as it appeared to Defoe and his contemporaries. The few strangers whom business or curiosity caused to ride up the steep stony tracks beyond Windermere and over Hardknot, complained of the bread of the Lake Valleys as ' exceedingly black, coarse and harsh,' and the houses as ' sad little huts ' of unmortared stone, more fit for cattle than for men. But already ' here and there was a house plastered ' and sometimes the ' oat clap bread ' was cunningly baked and delicious. And already the famous Windermere delicacy, ' the fish called charrs came potted to London.' We may conclude from these travellers' impressions that the great improvement in the prosperity of this happy pastoral region (with its well drained valley bottoms, its solid farm buildings and their oak furniture) was by no means complete in the reign of Anne, although it had been in rapid progress since the Restoration thanks to the manufacture of cloth at Kendal.

In the neighbouring county of Northumberland, recently so warlike and barbarous, the travellers along the coast and in the valley of the South Tyne, found ' plenty of good bread and beer ' as well as hens and geese, and famous stocks of claret, no doubt on account of the neighbourhood of Scotland where the gentry imported claret from France in spite of the war. When Anne came to the throne there was still a ' County Keeper ' for Northumberland, who drew a salary of £500 in return for making good out of this sum all cattle stolen and not restored. Although the wild moorlands between Redesdale and the Roman Wall still had a bad name, the County Keeper had the best of his bargain, and ' was able to inform travellers that the moss-trooping trade is very much laid aside, and that a small sum will recompense all the robberies that are yearly committed in the County.' Peace with Scotland, the wealth of the Tyneside mines, and the trade of Newcastle were factors already raising the standard of life along the Border. But the more outlying rural districts of Northumberland, Cumberland and Durham were still very poor, though more thickly inhabited than they afterwards became.   In many a ' township ' that to-day consists of a single prosperous sheep farm, half a dozen cottages of the crofter type cluster-ing round a peel tower then maintained a hardy population of borderers, unused to comfort, and tilling the moorland for a meagre harvest of oats.

Throughout the Stuart period, particularly since the Restoration, fine country houses were rising in place of the castles wherein the gentry of the Border had been forced to live in the turbulent times gone by.   Some of these Stuart mansions, like Chipchase, Capheaton, Wallington and the first Fallodon, already existed in the reign of Anne.   But the work of making the roads, and enclosing and draining the moorland farms of Northumberland, the planting of its beech woods, and the making of its spacious brick-walled gardens, was chiefly the work of the Hanoverian age that followed.   These great changes in the appearance and productivity of a region that had so long been backward and barbarous, were carried out in the course of the Eighteenth Century, favoured by free trade with Scotland after the Union of 1707, and paid for by Tyneside money, made in coal and invested in land.   Political events, such as the Rising of 1715, assisted the economic tendency for industrial and mercantile families to oust old Jacobite and Catholic lords of the soil, as in the case of the Osbaldistones in *Rob Roy*. The newcomers brought with them their industrial wealth and poured it into the estates they had bought, to increase the rent of their farms, the prosperity of their tenants, and the amenity of their new country homes.

In the more southerly districts of England where civiliza-tion was of older date, peace unbroken since the Civil War was multiplying the comforts of life.   Everywhere that perfectly beautiful equilibrium between man and nature, which marked the Eighteenth Century landscape, was in process of being established.   While hedgerow and orchard were gaining on the wild, the multiplication and improve-ment of cottages, farm-buildings and Halls was going on, either in old traditional styles, or in that dignified but simple manner which we know as ' Queen Anne.'   That style, which seems to us to-day native English, in its origin owed something to Dutch influence. Nor was the internal decoration unworthy of the architecture : in 1710 a foreign visitor noted that ' now in England tapestry is no longer in fashion, but all is panelled at great cost.' Spacious panels, five feet high and broad in proportion, were now preferred to the small pattern of earlier Stuart wainscoting. Big sash-windows with large panes of glass replaced gothic and Elizabethan lattices. High well-lighted rooms were the new fashion.

China-ware, brought to Europe by the Dutch and English East India Companies, had become a passion with ladies, and we may conceive the scheme of decoration in many Queen Anne mansions in town and country, as blue and white jars in panelled recesses, and tall grandfather clocks decorated with lacquered work from the East. Grinling Gibbons was still executing his marvels in woodwork. Mahogany was beginning to come in from the American Indies, and with it the lighter and finer furniture that we associate with Eighteenth-Century taste. Already foreign art dealers were amazed by their opportunities over here, and ' fleeced the English rarely, selling for great sums what they imported for a trifle from France and Italy.' Foreign artists declared that the nobility and gentry over whom Anne reigned held secluded in their country Halls as many pictures by renowned Italian masters as were to be found in all the Palaces and museums of Rome itself.

Vanbrugh's Blenheim House, with its magnificent conception and doubtful detail, is by no means characteristic of the architecture of Anne's reign. Usually a purer taste prevailed in the realm of ecclesiastical, academic and public buildings, while in ordinary domestic structure the note of the day was ' simple in elegance.' Wren was still alive and active over his London churches and his Hampton Court, and Gibbs was learning that skill which was soon to produce the Radcliffe Camera at Oxford. Together they taught the succeeding generations to effect ' the fusion of classic grace with vernacular energy.' The rules of proportion which these great men laid down, filtering into the text-books commonly used by local architects and builders, prepared for the Eighteenth Century a long and happy period of common English building in hamlet and country town. It

was only when, in the Nineteenth Century, men attempted
to restore the architecture of ancient Athens or of the Middle
Ages, that the English tradition was lost, and was succeeded
by a hideous anarchy of amateur fancies and exotic modes.

The country gentlemen were of many different grades of
wealth and culture.   At the top of the social hierarchy stood
the Dukes, who would in any other land have been styled
Princes, and whose manner of life outdid in magnificence
the courts of allied monarchs drawing England's pay.   At
the lower end of the scale was the squire reckoned to be
worth two or three hundred a year, farming a part of his
own land, speaking the broadest provincial dialect, but distinguished from the yeomen, among whom he mingled
almost on equal terms, by a small sporting establishment,
by a coat of arms, and by the respect which all paid to him
as a ' gentleman.'   If once in his life he went to London
on business, he was noticeable in the City crowds for his
horse-hair periwig, his jockey belt and his old-fashioned
coat without sleeves.   His library, traditionally at least,
consisted of the Bible, Baker's Chronicle, *Hudibras* and
Foxe's *Martyrs*, and, whether he read these works or not,
his view on Puritans and Papists usually coincided with
those expressed in the last two.

But this type of old-fashioned small squire was beginning
to feel the pressure of the times.   The heavy land tax of
four shillings in the pound to pay for Whig Wars, hit him
hard and added to the zeal of his Toryism.   The style of
living even in rural parts was becoming more expensive as
it became less homely, more elaborate and more influenced
by town example.   And if the small squire found it more
difficult to make two ends meet, it was easier for him to sell
out at a good price, for many large landowners were on the
watch to buy out their neighbours and consolidate their
own great estates.

It may seem remarkable that the land-hunger among the
wealthier members of the community should still have been
so eager, now that so many other forms of investment were
available, depriving land of the quasi-monopoly value which
it had previously enjoyed as the most obvious use for
capital.   Plain merchants who would in Tudor times have

settled land, or rents or tithe on their children, now invested
in the Funds. But for the purposes of social and political
ambition, the attractions of landowning were greater than
ever. Mr. Habakkuk, who has closely investigated
changes in land-ownership in Northamptonshire and Bedfordshire between 1680 and 1740, writes :

People bought land who were peculiarly susceptible to considerations
of social prestige and political power. Among them were a few
large merchants, mainly chairmen of the East India Company, who
went in for politics ; but most of the newcomers were either connected in some way with government or were Judges, who desired
to have that significance in society which only the possession of land
could give. They bought up blocks of land in different parts of the
country, bought out some of the surrounding gentry, bought ad-
vowsons and, in many cases, the manorial rights of Parliamentary
Boroughs. They were not so much investing their money in land
as buying up the perquisites of a social class, the undisturbed control
of the life of a neighbourhood. When they looked over the fields
they wanted to see their own land and nothing but their own land.
The hatred of the small squires and gentry for the great lords, whether
old or new, who were buying them out is the theme of many contemporary plays. (*Ec. Hist. Rev.*, p. 12, Feb. 1940, *English land-
ownership 1680–1740*.)

In picturing to ourselves the country house life of that
time, we think first of the grandees, filling rural palaces with
pictures from Italy, furniture from France, and editions of
Italian, French or Latin authors which they not only collected but read—the men whom young Voltaire during his
visit to England in 1726–1729, contrasted favourably with
the French nobles as patrons of letters and science. There
were philosopher Lords like the Third Earl of Shaftesbury ;
scholar statesmen like Somers and Montagu ; and the
greatest of all antiquarian collectors, Robert Harley, who
when too much engaged as ' the nation's great support '
to hunt books and manuscripts himself, still had his private
agents everywhere on the look-out. The Lords of the
Whig Junto and their followers and foes at Westminster
and St. James's prided themselves on being country gentlemen, whether self-made or to the manner born, each with
his rural seat to which the careworn statesman was ever
anxious, at least in theory, to return.

The London season was over by the first week in June,
when people of fashion dispersed to their country homes or
adjourned to Bath. A longer residence in town would have
ruined many families who had strained a point to bring their
daughters to the London marriage-market, while their
neighbours were fain to be contented with a county capital,
or with the round of such rural visits as ladies could accomplish in the coach in summer, and on the pillion behind their
brothers in the muddy lanes at Christmas.

Lady Mary Wortley Montagu, a brilliant blue-stocking,
in a letter of which the dullest part is a quotation from Tasso,
condemns the squires of a certain southern county as ' in-
sensible to other pleasures ' than the bottle and the chase.
' The poor female part of the family were seldom permitted
a coach, their lords and masters having no occasion for such
a machine, as their mornings are spent among the hounds,
and their nights with as beastly companions—with what
liquor they can get.' Yet in the same letter she regrets and
praises the society of the squires of Northamptonshire. No
less real, if more rare, than boorish Squire Western was the
learned country gentleman, celebrated in Somerville's
sententious lines :

> A rural squire, to crowds and courts unknown
> In his own cell retired, but not alone ;
> For round him view each Greek and Roman sage,
> Polite companions of his riper age.

Nevertheless, the impression left by turning over many
hundreds of letters to the better-to-do gentry of the reign of
Anne, is neither that of country scholar nor of country
bumpkin. We read the actual thoughts of squires, anxious
about their account books, their daughters' marriages and
their sons' debts and professions ; attending to their own
estates, and to the county business on the bench of magistrates, as well as to their hounds and horses ; devoted to
their gardens and their ponds a little more than to their
books ; living, as we should expect, a wholesome and useful
life, half public, half private, wholly leisured, natural and
dignified. Many of the better-to-do gentry, as their letters
and diaries show, were getting several thousands a year
from their estates.

The expenditure required of a country gentleman, rich or poor, was in one respect very small. It was not then considered obligatory that his sons should be sent at great cost to exclusively patrician schools. At the nearest local grammar school, the squire's children sat beside those sons of yeomen and shopkeepers who had been selected for a clerical career ; otherwise the young gentlemen were taught at home by a neighbouring parson, or in wealthier families by the private chaplain. Where a tutor was specially employed, he was often a Huguenot refugee, for the land was full of educated men of this type, welcomed by careful parents for their French, and doubly welcome in Whig families for their sufferings and their principles. Eton, Winchester and Westminster were indeed patronized by many, but not by most, of the aristocracy. And even at Westminster there could be found at the end of Anne's reign ' houses at which boys pay but £20 a year for boarding, and the schooling but five or six guineas.' Harrow, founded under Elizabeth to meet local and plebeian needs, began to rise into the rank of the fashionable schools in the reign of George I.

It followed that, whereas a gentleman of moderate means in our day often thinks himself obliged to spend a sixth part of his income on the schooling of one boy, he could in those days be satisfied to spend a hundredth. Thus squire Molesworth, at a time when he was drawing a rental of just under £2000 paid £20 a year for each of his sons—including board, instruction, clothes and all charges. His heavy parental liabilities only began when the two lads left school, and the younger went into the army. Then indeed ' Dick must be furnished with a hundred pounds or he cannot stir a step. He has both horses, clothes and equipage to buy.' As ' he was not in the list of officers slain in the late glorious battle of Blenheim,' which would have been a sad economy, nor yet ' in any of desperate attacks on Lille,' Dick continued for many years to be an increasing source of expenditure and pride to his Yorkshire home. The elder, Jack, had chosen diplomacy, a no less costly method of serving the State. In 1710 the father writes : ' I verily believe these two sons of ours have spent between them £10,000 within the last seven or eight years ; they and the

L

daughters are all money-bound.   It is well they have a good
father's house to tarry in.'   Five years later Dick's zeal for
his regiment caused him to ' lay out £600 above what was
allowed him, so well he loves the service.'

Smaller squires paid equally little for their sons' schooling,
and then prenticed them to cheaper trades than the army or
diplomatic service.   In the plays of Congreve and Farquhar
the younger son of the manor may still expect to be ' bound
prentice,' perhaps ' to a felt-maker in Shrewsbury ' ; and
Steele declares that ' younger brothers are generally condemned to shops, colleges and inns of court.'   On these
terms the gentry could afford to have large families, and
although a great proportion of their children died young,
they kept England supplied with a constant stream of high-
spirited young men, who led her along the forward path at
home and overseas.   For the younger sons were willing, as
the cadets of the continental nobility were not, to mingle in
the common avocations of mankind and not to stand upon
their gentry.   The fact that the younger son went out to
make his fortune in the army or at the bar, in industry or in
commerce, was one of the general causes favouring the Whigs
and their alliance with those interests, as against the desire of
the High Tories to keep the landed gentry an exclusive as
well as a dominant class.   Dominant it remained for another
century, but only on condition of opening its doors wide to
newcomers, and fostering in a hundred different ways close
alliance with interests other than agriculture, in scenes far
remote from the manor-house and the village church.   The
country gentlemen ruled Eighteenth Century England, but
they ruled it largely in the interest of commerce and empire.

The common schooling of the upper and middle class was
already being criticized for its rigidly classical curriculum.
It was even declared by some that ' a girl which is educated
at home with her mother is wiser at twelve than a boy at
sixteen ' who knows only Latin.   Yet the second classical
language was so ill taught at school and college that the
excellent Latinists of Christ Church had not enough Greek
to be aware that Bentley had proved them dunces over the
Letters of Phalaris.   It was only in the Nineteenth Century
that the typical English scholar was equally at home with
Aristophanes and with Horace.

Even so, Greek scholarship in the England of Bentley
had not fallen as low as in the rest of Europe. In the
Germany of that day not only was classical Greek no longer
studied, but the names and stories of the mythology and
history of Hellas were unknown.[1] But they were familiar
to educated people in England, if not through Greek then
through Latin and English authors. Every man of fashion
in the reign of George I had at least to pretend an acquaintance with Pope's rendering of Homer. Milton was now
rising to a place only a little lower than Shakespeare in the
hierarchy of English literary reputations, and the use that
he made of classical ideas and mythology set an example to
the poets of this later age, though few were scholars of his
calibre. In architecture and its ornaments, the ' Gothic '
had disappeared, and had been replaced by ideas suggested
directly or indirectly by the temples and statues of the
ancient world.

But it would be a mistake to suppose that nothing was
anywhere taught but classics ; there was considerable
variety in the type of school patronized by gentlemen.
Thus Robert Pitt, father of a mighty son, writes in 1704 to
his own scarcely less formidable father, Governor Pitt of
Madras :

My two brothers are at Mr. Meure's Academy, near Soho Square,
esteemed the best in England. They learn Latin, French and
accounts, fencing, dancing and drawing. I think of settling them
in Holland for their better education next summer : and should my
wife's father-in-law, Lt. Gen. Stewart, accompany the Duke of
Marlborough, of placing them under his care to see a campaign.

Among the critics of our educational methods were the
wise Locke and the good-natured Steele, who both urged
that perpetual flogging was not the best method of imparting
knowledge and maintaining discipline. Upper-class education was admitted on all hands to need reform, yet nothing
was done to reform it. Swift, for all his hatred of the Scots,
agreed for once with Burnet that the lairds gave their sons

[1] In 1718 Burckhard declared that the majority of University Students in
Germany did not even know the names of Plato, Aristotle, Homer, Thucydides
or Euripides. Such a statement would have been utterly absurd if made about
England. *The Popular Background of Goethe's Hellenism*, Humphry Trevelyan,
1934, p. 8 and *passim*.

more sound book-learning than the wealthier and idler English.

Yet the Eighteenth Century, in spite of its educational defects, produced a larger proportion of remarkable and original English men from among those who passed through its schools than our highly educated and over-regulated age is able to do. And in spite of cruel flogging by 'those licensed tyrants the schoolmasters,' and cruel bullying by the unlicensed tyranny of ill-disciplined school-fellows, there was also much happiness in boyhood, that still had leisure and still spent it in the free range of the countryside. Nor was severity universal : a young lord, newly arrived at Eton, writes home, ' I think Eaton a very easy scholl. I am shure one cannot offend without they be meare rakes indeed.'

Women's education was sadly to seek. Among the lower classes it was perhaps not much worse than men's, but the daughters of the well-to-do had admittedly less education than their brothers. It was before the days of ' ladies' academies,' and though there were ' boarding schools ' for girls, they were few and indifferent. Most ladies learnt from their mothers to read, write, sew and manage the household. We hear of no fair Grecians, like Lady Jane Grey and Queen Elizabeth in days of old. But a few ladies could read the Italian poets and were therefore held in some awe by their swains. And at least two women could meet Swift on terms of something like intellectual equality. Yet it was he who lamented ' that not one gentleman's daughter in a thousand should be brought to read her own natural tongue, or be judge of the easiest books that are written in it.' The want of education in the sex was discussed as an admitted fact, one side defending it as necessary in order to keep wives in due subjection, while the other side, led by the chief literary men of the day, ascribed the frivolity and the gambling habits of ladies of fashion to an upbringing which debarred them from more serious interests.

Nevertheless, country-house letters of the period show us wives and daughters writing as intelligent advisers of their menfolk. Such correspondents were something better than brainless playthings or household drudges. A whole class of the literature of the day, from the *Spectator* downwards, was written as much for ladies as for their fathers and brothers. And it was observed that the ladies took a part, often too eager, in the Whig and Tory feuds that divided town and country. As to rural pastimes, the prototype of Diana Vernon in *Rob Roy* is to be found in Belinda of Farquhar's play, who tells her friend ' I can gallop all the morning after the hunting horn and all the evening after a fiddle. In short I can do everything with my father but drink and shoot flying.'

In the upper and middle classes, husbands were often found for girls on the principle of frank barter. ' As to Cloky,' writes her father, squire Molesworth, ' we shall not have money enough to dispose of her here,' so she must be sent to Ireland to seek there a husband at a cheaper rate. Another squire, named Guise, who is in search of a wife for himself, writes ' Lady Diana sent a very venerable person to view my estates, and was well satisfied with the report and I think did sincerely desire I might have her daughter.' But the daughter had other views, so Guise found consolation elsewhere :

Being on the Bench at the quarter Session, a Justice of the Peace took me aside and asked me whether I would marry a woman worth twenty-thousand pounds. The lady I had seen but never spoke to, and upon the whole readily accepted his offer.

A Cornet of Horse writes with equal frankness :

Not expecting anything this campaign I had taken thoughts another way, to try my fortune under Venus, and accordingly about a fortnight ago was (by some friends) proposed to a lady of a very good fortune : but how I shall speed (farther than a favourable interview already) I can't tell.

Since almost everyone regarded it as a grave misfortune to remain single, women did not account it a universal grievance that their hands should often be disposed of by others. They were no doubt usually consulted as to their destiny, much or little according to character and circumstance. Swift, in writing ' to a very young lady on her marriage,' speaks of ' the person your father and mother have chosen for your husband,' and almost immediately adds, ' yours was a match of prudence and common good liking, without any mixture of the ridiculous passion ' of romantic love.   And this description would probably have covered a vast proportion of the ' arranged ' marriages of the day.   But since the ' ridiculous passion ' often asserted itself, runaway matches were common enough, as in the case of Lady Mary Wortley Montagu.   And even without that desperate expedient, an ever-increasing proportion of ordinary marriages were the outcome of mutual affection.

Divorce was almost unknown.   It was obtainable only through Church Courts, and then only if followed by a special Act of Parliament ; not more than six divorces were thus legalized during the twelve years of Queen Anne.

Both sexes gambled freely, the fine ladies and gentlemen even more than the country squires.   In London, Bath and Tunbridge Wells the gaming-table was the central point of interest, while in the manor-house it was of less account than the stables and the kennel.   The expenses of gambling and of sport, as well as a noble zeal for building and for laying out gardens and planting avenues, burdened estates with mortgages which proved a heavy clog on agricultural improvement and domestic happiness.   Immense sums of money changed hands over cards and dice.

Drunkenness was the acknowledged national vice of Englishmen of all classes, though women were not accused of it.   A movement for total abstinence was out of the question, in days before tea or coffee could be obtained in every home and when the supply of drinking water was often impure.   But tracts in favour of temperate drinking were freely circulated by religious bodies and anxious patriots, setting forth with attractive detail the various and dreadful fates of drunkards, some killed attempting to ride home at night, others seized by a fit while blaspheming, all gone straight to Hell.   Among the common folk, ale still reigned supreme ; but ale had a new rival worse than itself in the deadly attraction of bad spirits.   The acme of cheap spirit-drinking was not indeed reached till the reign of George II, in the days of Hogarth's ' Gin Lane,' but things were already moving in that direction.

Meanwhile the upper class got drunk sometimes on ale and sometimes on wine.   It is hard to say whether the men of fashion or the rural gentry were the worst soakers.   But perhaps the outdoor exercise taken by the fox-hunting, sporting and farming squire made him better able to absorb his nightly quantum of October, than the gamester and politician of St. James's Square to escape the ill effects of endless Whig toasts in port and Tory toasts in French claret and champagne. Magistrates often appeared on the bench heated with wine ; Courts Martial, by a prudent provision of the Mutiny Act, might only take place before dinner.

Tobacco was still taken in long churchwarden pipes. A 'smoking parlour' was set aside in some country houses. But Beau Nash forbade smoking in the public rooms at Bath, as disrespectful and unpleasant to ladies. Among the common people of the south-western counties, men, women and even children smoked pipes of an evening. When in 1707 the Bill for the Security of the Church of England was passing through Parliament, Dr. Bull, the High Church Bishop of St. David's, being suspicious of the Whig proclivities of some of the Episcopal Bench, kept watch ' sitting in the lobby of the House of Lords, all the while smoking his pipe.' Swift describes how his brother parsons pull his character to pieces at their favourite resort at Truby's coffee house,

> And pausing o'er a pipe, with doubtful nod
> Give hints that poets ne'er believe in God.

The taking of snuff became general in England during the first year of Anne's reign, as a result of the immense quantities thrown on to the London market after the capture of Spanish ships loaded with snuff in the action of Vigo Bay.

The drinking and gambling habits of society, and the fierceness of political faction, led to frequent duels of which many ended ill. The survivor, if he could show there had been fair play, was usually convicted of manslaughter and imprisoned for a short term ; or haply ' pleaded his clergy,' was ' touched with cold iron ' and so set free. It was the privilege of all gentlemen, from a Duke downwards, to wear swords and to murder one another by rule. As soon as men were well drunk of an evening they were apt to quarrel, and as soon as they quarrelled they were apt to draw their swords in the room, and, if manslaughter was not committed on the spot, to adjourn to the garden behind the house, and fight it out that night with hot blood and unsteady hand.   If the company were not wearing swords, the quarrel might be slept upon and forgotten or arranged in the sober morning.   The wearing of swords, though usual in London, as being like the full-bottomed wig a part of full dress, was fortunately not common in the depths of the country, among the uncourtly but good-natured rural squires, whose bark was often worse than their bite.   And even at Bath, Beau Nash employed his despotic power to compel the fashionable world to lay aside their swords when they entered his domain : in this he did as good service to the community as in teaching the country bumpkins to discard their top boots and coarse language at the evening assemblies and dances.   During his long supremacy as Master of the Ceremonies, nearly covering the reigns of Anne and the first two Georges, Nash did perhaps as much as any other person even in the Eighteenth Century to civilize the neglected manners of mankind.   But he encouraged public gambling and took for himself a percentage on the winnings of the bank.

London and the county capitals were the commonest scenes of such duels as Thackeray has immortalized in *Esmond*.   Even more often than Leicester Fields, the open country behind Montagu House, the site of the present British Museum, was selected by duellists as being at that time on the edge of the new London.   It was no unusual thing for the town to be disturbed by such a double event as the following :

Ned Goodyear has killed Beau Feilding as is reported, and made his escape.   The quarrel began at the Play House in Drury Lane.   The same night a captain here did the like friendly office for young Full-wood, so that there will be two Warwickshire beaus the fewer.   The captain is in Newgate.

Ever since the Restoration, foreigners had admired the English bowling greens, ' which are so even, that they bowl upon them as easily as on a great billiard table.   And as this is the usual diversion of gentlemen in the country, they have thick rowling-stones to keep the green smooth.'   In Anne's reign a primitive kind of cricket was just beginning to take its place among village sports alongside of the far more ancient football.   Kent was the county most renowned at the new game, and, ' among the Kentish men, the men of Dartford lay claim to the greatest excellence.'

At cockfighting all classes shrieked their bets round the little amphitheatre. If a foreigner should by chance come into these cockpits, we are told, ' he would certainly conclude the assembly to be all mad, by their continued outcries of Six to Four, Five to One, repeated with great earnestness, every Spectator taking part with his favourite cock, as if it were a party cause.' Horse-racing presented much the same spectacle in a more open arena : the spectators, most of them on horseback, galloped up the course behind the race, yelling with excitement. The meetings were still regional or county gatherings. The only national meeting was at Newmarket. There indeed ' the vast company of horsemen on the plain at a match contains all mankind on equal footing from the Duke to the country peasant. Nobody wears swords, but are clothed suitable to the humour and design of the place for horse sports. Everybody strives to out-jockey (as the phrase is) one another.' Queen Anne, out of the secret service money, gave plates to be run for at Newmarket, and at Datchet near Windsor. Arab and Barb blood was being introduced by Godolphin and other noble patrons of the sport—a change fraught with great future consequence to the character and appearance of horseflesh in England.

When we try to imagine how the generality of our ancestors disported themselves out-of-doors, we must remember that most of them lived widely scattered and in the country. For most men the village was the largest unit of their intercourse. A village cricket match, or hurly-burly at football, or races on the green were very different from the ' organized athletics ' of the modern arena. But most people took their ' exercise ' as a matter of course in doing their work, in tilling the soil, or in walking or riding to and from their daily task. Among the upper and middle class riding was the commonest act of the day.

The most usual sports that lay at many men's door were taking fish, and shooting and snaring birds of all kinds, particularly but not exclusively game. England was alive with game and with many birds now rare or extinct, from the Great Bustard of the Downs and the eagle of Westmorland

L 2

and Wales down to many smaller friends that survived to be recorded by Bewick. Much of the land was strictly preserved and religiously shot by the owners, but great tracts were open to any man who could procure a net or gun or who was clever at setting a springe. In Anne's reign, and indeed for the rest of the century, the fens and uncultivated lands round Cambridge were the common shooting ground of the undergraduates, whence they returned with pheasants, partridges, duck, snipe, bitterns and ruffs, with none to say them nay. And in every part of the lovely island the uncared-for heaths, coppices and marshes, destined ere long to be drained, ploughed up or built over, were still the cover for abundance of wild life of every kind. The Englishman had only to move a few yards from his door to be in contact with nature at its best ; and his love of field-sports led him to wander wide.

Few villagers had seen anything of town life. Most people remained all their lives under the influence of Pan and his magic. The mental food of English children was just such cottage fireside tales of ' the hall-house being haunted, of fairies, spirits and witches,' perhaps only half believed but pleasantly shuddered at. Now that the witch could be pointed out but no longer hanged or ducked, such earth-born legendary lore was no unwholesome fare. For the common people, untouched by the scepticism of the town, the fairies still danced in the woods, though when the wayfarer came round the bush they had always vanished.[1] Books in the village were few. The ordinary farmer and cottager saw no printed matter of any kind except Bible, Prayer Book and

> The ballads pasted on the wall,
> Of Joan of France and English Moll,
> Fair Rosamund, and Robin Hood,
> And the little children in the Wood.

And therefore even at the end of the ' Century of reason ' and of artificial poetry among the governing class, the faculty

[1] The educated upper class had generally ceased to believe in the real existence of fairies. In 1707 the philosopher Lord Shaftesbury, in his *Letter concerning Enthusiasm*, writes to Lord Somers, ' I could put your Lordship in mind of an eminent, learned and truly Christian Prelate you once knew who could have given you a full account of his belief in Fairys,' as if such a belief was unusual and obviously absurd.

of wonder was not dead in the English people. Wordsworth attributed the growth of imagination in his own mind partly to the fairy-tales and ballads of the rustic North that he heard in childhood, in contrast to the rationalism of the Nineteenth Century schoolroom. (*Prelude*, Bk. V, l. 205, *et seq.*) No city-made newspapers or magazines stamped a uniform mentality on the nation. In this isolation from the world at large, each shire, each hamlet had its own traditions, interests and character. Except for some unusual event like the Battle of Blenheim or the trial of Dr. Sacheverell, country folk had little to think or talk about except their own affairs. Their shrewd rustic comment on things that they knew and understood was expressed in the pithy dialect of their own countryside. For gossip and sensation they were satisfied with the daily human drama of their own village, with its poaching affrays and smuggling adventures, its feuds and loves, its ghosts and suicides, its quarrels of miller and innkeeper, of parson and squire.

The still unremedied badness of the roads was due to the want of any adequate administrative machinery for their reconstruction or repair. Every parish through which a road passed was legally bound to maintain it by six days a year of unpaid labour given by the farmers, under no outside supervision ; one of themselves was chosen as surveyor. The unfairness of laying the burden of repair not on the users of the great roads, but on the parishes through which they happened to pass, was equalled by the folly of expecting farmers, who had no interest in the matter, to act gratuitously as skilled makers of highways. The result was that a very inadequate number of hard roads had been made or kept up since the Romans left the island. In the Middle Ages, when there was little commerce, this had mattered less. Under the later Stuarts, when commerce was large and rapidly increasing, it mattered much ; it was beginning to be felt as a national disgrace. The new system of turnpikes to make the users of the road pay for its upkeep was there-fore enforced in a few of the worst sections by Acts of Parliament. When Anne came to the throne the usual machinery of local Justices of the Peace was employed to manage the turnpikes, but towards the end of the reign special bodies of Turnpike Trustees were sometimes established by Statute.   It was not, however, till the House of Hanover had been some time on the throne that anything approaching a general reform was effected by this means. Defoe thus describes a main road in Lancashire :

'We are now in a country where the roads are paved with small pebbles, so that we both walk and ride upon this pavement which is generally about one and a half yards wide.   But the middle road where the carriages are obliged to go is very bad.'

In winter and bad weather wheeled traffic did not attempt to take the road, and riders started early in the morning to get in front of the pack-horse trains which it was difficult to pass on the narrow causeway.

Under such conditions, sea and river traffic, however slow, held a great advantage over road traffic, especially for heavy goods.   Fish could be sent up from Lyme Regis to London by relays of fast trotting horses ; but coal came there by sea. Even so, while it cost but five shillings per chaldron at the Tyneside pit's mouth, it cost thirty shillings in London, and anything up to fifty shillings in the towns of the Upper Thames.   This was partly because sea-borne coal was taxed, both to pay for the rebuilding of St. Paul's and to pay for the French war.   Coal was cheaper in those towns of Yorkshire, Lancashire and the west Midlands to which it could be floated from the pit's mouth on rivers like Calder or Severn. For coal carried on inland rivers was not taxed, like the coal carried by sea, neither was it exposed to the attacks of the Dunkirk privateers, nor harassed by the consequent restrictions of an inadequate convoy system supplied by the Royal Navy between Tyne and Thames.

The ownership of mines and an interest in their working was not deemed beneath the dignity of the greatest noblemen of the land, for in England, unlike most countries of Europe, all minerals except gold and silver have been treated as the property of the owner of the soil.   Among the aristocratic coal owners of that time was Lord Dartmouth, to whom belonged many of the Staffordshire mines near his country house at Sandwell.   He had a rival in a country gentleman named Wilkins, who was said to have ' engrossed the coalworks of Leicestershire to himself.'

It was then usual to leave pillars of coal to support the

roof of the mine, rather than to use timber props. Shafts were sunk to a depth of 400 feet and more, and in Lancashire the science of the engineers had devised in the year 1712 a machine for pumping water out of the mine which has been described as ' the first genuine steam-engine.'   On Tyne-side, wooden rails were used to run the trucks down to the river for loading the keels ; twenty thousand horses were employed in the transport of coal in the environs of New-castle alone.   Since the larger mines were deeper below the surface than in the Middle Ages, explosions due to fire-damp were already frequent, as at Gateshead in 1705, and at Chester-le-Street in 1708, when a hundred miners perished ' besides great damage to many houses and persons for several miles round.   One man was blown quite out of the mouth of the shaft, which is fifty fathom, and found at a prodigious distance from the place.'   Two years later another explosion at Bensham, in the same North Durham district, killed eighty more.   But the amount of surface mining was still considerable ; in the west there were many scores of small workings, each conducted by two or three colliers and sometimes by a single man.

The miners of all kinds and the quarrymen of every county form an important exception to the statement that in old England the method of industry was domestic. Other exceptions there were, but they are harder to specify and define.   Many workshops had premises so large, and contained so many apprentices and paid journeymen, that they may be reckoned as standing half-way between the domestic and the factory system.   The normal basis of industry still was apprenticeship, the only legal doorway to a trade whether for boys or girls.   The apprentice system was often abused by cruel masters and mistresses ; and pauper apprentices were at least as badly treated as children in the worst days of the subsequent factory system. There were no inspectors and no checks on ill usage.   On the other hand, the apprentice was part of his master's ' family,' and the average man does not like to see unhappy faces at his own board and in his own household.   More-over, apprenticeship was invaluable for the discipline and skilled training that it provided during that important ' after-school age ' so much neglected in our own day.   It largely compensated for the deficiency of school education. Apprenticeship was the old English school of craftsmanship and of character.[1]

Before they were old enough to be apprenticed, small children were sometimes set to work in their parents' cottages at an age full as early as the factory children of later times. Especially was spinning for the cloth industry conducted in this fashion : Defoe noticed with approval at Colchester and in the Taunton clothing region, that ' there was not a child in the town or in the villages round it of above five years old, but, if it was not neglected by its parents and untaught, could earn its bread.' Again, in the clothing dales of the West Riding he found ' hardly anything above four years old but its hands were sufficient for its support.' Poor little mites ! But at least, whenever their parents let them go to play, they had fields near at hand, instead of the boundless wilderness of slums.

Spinning was done chiefly in country cottages by women and children, and weaving chiefly in towns and villages by men. Both processes, though conducted under domestic conditions, required capitalist organization and supervision, either by employers, or by middlemen who bought the goods manufactured by the cottager. The methods by which the cloth trade was organized differed in the many different regions of England where it flourished.

The cloth trade was the typical industry of the time. Two-fifths of English exports consisted of cloth woven in England. Many of our domestic laws and many measures of our economic and foreign policy were aimed at the great national object of promoting the manufacture of cloth and pushing its sale at home and abroad. It was felt that here lay our real advantage over Dutch rivals in the carrying trade of the world, for we had this great staple manufacture with which to load our outgoing ships, whereas they had little to export except herrings, and acted mainly as carriers between other nations.

---

[1] Already in Anne's reign there were complaints that apprenticeship was not made as universally obligatory as the laws dictated. In 1702 the Corporation of Kendal petitioned for a new and stricter law, because ' although there are laws against persons setting up any trade without having received seven years' apprenticeship, when such persons come to be prosecuted they meet with such favour that very few have been punished of late.' *H. M. C. Bagot*, R. 10, pt. iv., p. 336.

The desire to keep open the great markets of the world for English cloth was a chief incentive to taking up arms in 1702 against the Franco-Spanish Power, which was at that moment, at the command of Louis XIV, proceeding to close Spain, the Netherlands, South America and the Mediterranean to our goods.   The taking and keeping of Gibraltar in 1704 was symptomatic of more than military and naval ambition : a free entrance to the Mediterranean and Turkish trades was vital to the cloth industry.   Not only were great quantities of our cloth sold in those parts, but our merchants brought back from Spain and Southern Italy oil used here in the manufacture of cloth.   Spanish merino wool was worked up in England and sold back as cloth to Spain herself, whose native industry was in the last stages of decline.   Of late years the fine quality and great quantity of English-grown wool had been yet further increased by means of ' clover and other grass seeds ' to feed the sheep. Our American Colonies were valued largely as markets for our cloth.   In Russia, too, a great demand for it was growing up in the new century.

Only in the Far East was it impossible to sell the heavy English cloth, and this was the most damaging argument which the East India Company had to meet in pleading its cause before Parliament.   But the tea and silk it brought to England sufficed to condone the high economic crimes of failing to sell English cloth and daring to export bullion to buy cloth substitutes.   In vain the merchants of the rival Turkey Company pleaded that ' if silk be brought from India where it is bought cheap with bullion, it will ruin our trade with Turkey, whither we send cloth for their silk.' The demands of fashion and luxury outweighed the arguments of clothiers, Turkey merchants and orthodox economists.   ' Our stately fops admire themselves better in an Indian dressing gown than in one made at Spitalfields.' The ladies, besides, were all drinking ' tay.'   So the Indian Trade was permitted to flourish, and in spite of that the Cloth Trade flourished as well.

Thanks to the East India Company's great ships, not only tea but coffee was now a usual drink at least among the wealthier classes.   From the reign of Charles II to the early

Georges, the London Coffee House was the centre of social
life. It afforded a much needed relaxation of the severe
drinking habits of the time, for alcohol was not to be had on
the premises. A list of some of the Coffee Houses in
Queen Anne's time runs to nearly five hundred names.
Every respectable Londoner had his favourite house, where
his friends or clients could seek him at known hours.

> ' Remember, John,
> ' If any ask, to th' Coffee House I'm gone,'

says the citizen to his apprentice as he leaves the shop.

> Then at Lloyd's Coffee House he never fails
> To read the letters and attend the sales.[1]

The *beau monde* assembled at White's Chocolate House in
St. James's Street, where, as Harley bitterly complained to
Swift, young noblemen were fleeced and corrupted by
fashionable gamblers and profligates. Tories went to the
Cocoa Tree Chocolate House, Whigs to St. James's Coffee
House. Will's, near Covent Garden, was the resort of
poets, critics and their patrons ; Truby's served the clergy,
and the Grecian the world of scholarship ; nor were there
lacking houses for Dissenters, for Quakers, for Papists and
for Jacobites. The ' universal liberty of speech of the
English nation ' uttered amid clouds of tobacco smoke,
with equal vehemence whether against the Government and
the Church, or against their enemies, had long been the
wonder of foreigners ; it was the quintessence of Coffee
House life.

The Coffee House filled the place now occupied by the
Club, but in a more cheap and informal manner, and with a
greater admission of strangers. In days when men stood
much on their rank, it had a levelling influence : at the
Coffee House ' you will see blue ribbons and stars sitting
familiarly with private gentlemen as if they had left their

---

[1] In Ned Ward's *Wealthy Shopkeeper* (1706) his day is thus apportioned : rise
at 5 ; counting-house till 8 ; then breakfast on toast and Cheshire cheese ; in
his shop for two hours then a neighbouring coffee house for news ; shop again,
till dinner at home (over the shop) at 12 on a ' thundering joint ' ; 1 o'clock on
Change ; 3, Lloyd's Coffee House for business ; shop again for an hour ; then
another coffee house (not Lloyd's) for recreation, followed by ' sack shop ' to
drink with acquaintances, till home for a ' light supper ' and so to bed, ' before
Bow Bell rings nine.'

quality and degrees of distance at home.' But that was not all. In days before telegrams and effective journalism, news could be most easily obtained at the Coffee House. The Windsor, at Charing Cross, advertised itself as supplying the ' best chocolate at twelve pence the quart and the translation of the *Harlem Courant* soon after the post is come in.' Not only was news sought for its political, military and general interest, but for the strictly business purposes of commerce, particularly at Lloyd's. Edward Lloyd, whose surname instantly rises to men's lips when they speak of shipping to-day, was, when he walked the earth, nothing more nor less than a Coffee House keeper in Lombard Street in the reign of Queen Anne. To his house merchants came for the latest information and for the personal intercourse and advice necessary for all transactions. Newspapers had then no commercial column and no details of shipping. The spoken word did many things that print does to-day, and for merchants the word was spoken at Lloyd's. Before the end of the Queen's reign, Lloyd had set up a pulpit for auctions and for reading out shipping news.

The feud of High Church against Low Church and Dissent was the chief theme of political and ecclesiastical anger and eloquence. Nevertheless, in another aspect, the reigns of William and Anne were a period of purely religious activity and revival, which left a permanent mark on the life of the country, and sowed the seed of great developments in the future. An age to which we owe the Charity Schools and the Society for Promoting Christian Knowledge was not wholly absorbed in the quarrels of High Church and Low. In some of these better activities, members of the two parties co-operated with each other and with the Dissenters.

The religious revival had its origin in the brief and stormy reign of James II. The Tory pamphleteer, Davenant, in the early years of Anne, thus recalled how those times had stirred men's souls :

The measures King James the Second took to change the religion of the country, roused up fresh zeal in the minds of all sorts of men ; they embraced more straitly what they were in fear to lose. Courtiers

did thrust themselves into the presence to quit their offices, rather
than be brought to do what might prejudice the Church of England.
Nor had the licentious ways of living in fleets and armies shaken our
seamen and soldiers in their principles.   They all stood firm.   The
clergy showed themselves prepared to die with their flocks and
managed the controversial parts of Divinity with primitive courage
and admirable learning.   The Churches were everywhere crowded,
and the prospect of persecution, though peradventure at some distance,
begot devotion.

The symptoms of this moral and religious revival did not
wholly subside with the crisis that gave it birth.   In the first
instance it gave an immense impetus to the work of the
already existing Religious Societies inside the Church of
England.   These Societies were groups of ' serious young
men,' who came together, usually under the influence of
some active clergyman, to strengthen each other in religious
life and practice.   The original idea of John Wesley, many
years later, was merely to form such ' societies ' within the
Church resembling those which that zealous Churchman
his father had helped and defended in the reigns of William
and Anne.   The first object of these groups was to promote
a Christian life in individuals and families, to encourage
church attendance, family prayers and Bible study.   But
more public activities soon grew out of the impulse thus
given.   Of these activities some were carried on in rivalry
to the Dissenters, others with their co-operation.

The Dissenters, who were excluded from both the Universities by law, and from many schools either by law or by
custom, had started all over the country a number of
excellent schools and academies of their own, covering the
whole field of primary, secondary and higher education.
These caused much jealousy, and at the end of Anne's reign
the High Churchmen at last succeeded in passing the
Schism Act to suppress them—an act of persecution repealed under George I.   But the Church also reacted to the
challenge of the Nonconformist schools in a more generous
fashion.   In the reign of Anne, Charity Schools were
founded by hundreds all over England, to educate the
children of the poor in reading, writing, moral discipline,
and the principles of the Church of England.   They were
much needed, for the State did nothing for the education

of the poor, and the ordinary parish had no sort of endowed school, though in many villages ' dames ' and other unofficial persons taught rustics their letters in return for small fees ; here and there an endowed Grammar School gave secondary education to the middle class.

The able men at the head of the Charity School movement introduced the principle of democratic co-operation into the field of educational endowment. They did not depend merely on the support of a few wealthy founders. The policy at headquarters was to excite the local interest of a parish in the setting up of a school. Small shopkeepers and artisans were induced to subscribe and to collect sub-scriptions, and were taught to take a personal interest in the success, and a personal part in the control of the school for which they helped yearly to pay. The principle of ' joint-stock enterprise ' was being applied to many sides of life in that era, among others to the cause of philanthropy and education. By the end of Anne's reign there were 5000 or more boys and girls attending the new Charity Schools in the London area, and some 20,000 in the rest of England. The movement was already being taken up in Presbyterian Scotland by the General Assembly of the Church. Essential parts of the scheme were to clothe the children decently while at school, and to apprentice them to good trades afterwards. In 1708 a 'poor boy ' could be clothed at nine shillings and twopence, and a ' poor girl ' at ten shillings and threepence in one of the London schools.

Another characteristic organization of this period was ' The Society for the Reformation of Manners.' In its open ranks Churchmen and Dissenters co-operated against the licence of the age. Scores of thousands of tracts were issued against drunkenness, swearing, public indecency and Sunday trading. We know not what success attended the *Kind cautions against swearing* distributed among the hackney coachmen of London, and the similar *Kind cautions to watermen* distributed among the West Country bargees ! More effective, perhaps, were the innumerable prosecutions instituted. Magistrates were shamed into enforcing laws which had become obsolete. These activities aroused furious opposition. Some of the High Churchmen, like Sacheverell, clamoured for the ' ancient discipline of the

Church ' to suppress vice, immorality, heresy and schism, instead of this newfangled Society for the Reformation of Manners in which laymen and even Dissenters were allowed to take a part, appealing to lay magistrates instead of to Church Courts.   Some prudent Bishops like Sharp, and Judges like Holt, feared that organized delation would lead to ill-feeling, corruption and blackmail.   Many magistrates positively refused to receive the evidence of the philanthropic informers.   The mob in some places was dangerous, and at least one active member of the Society was murdered outright.

Nevertheless there were tens of thousands of successful prosecutions.   It was said that no one but a person of quality could safely swear in a public place.   There was, indeed, a strong body of opinion that supported these proceedings.   Many quiet citizens had found the magistrates, ever since the Restoration, scandalously lax in restraining drunkards from annoying the sober, in protecting women from insult, and in preserving any show of decency and order.   Nor was Sunday trading really desired by the bulk of the community.   The Mayor of Deal, a courageous and energetic man, undertook single-handed a crusade against the behaviour of the town, carried most of his points and was re-elected Mayor in 1708.   It is indeed probable that many of the prosecutions, especially for swearing and for travelling on Sunday, were vexatious, and the time came under the Georges when the Society was doing quite as much harm as good, and could disappear.   But its activities in the reign of Anne helped to make the streets and taverns less unpleasant for decent people, to reduce drunkenness and to secure Sunday as a day of rest from business and labour.

The more gloomy side of the English Sunday struck a German visitor in 1710 :

In the afternoon to St. James's Park, to see the crowds.   No other diversion is allowed on Sunday, which is nowhere more strictly kept ; not only is all play forbidden, and public-houses closed, but few even of the boats and hackney coaches may ply.   Our hostess would not even allow the strangers to play the *viol di Gamba* or the flute, lest she be punished.

He added, rather sourly, that Sunday observance was the only visible sign that the English were Christians at all.

But the most important and lasting impression of the religious revival was made by the Society for Promoting Christian Knowledge, and its off-shoot, the Society for the Propagation of the Gospel in Foreign Parts. The self-same men were the supporters of both, above all the indefatigable Dr. Thomas Bray. The spirit afterwards characteristic of the movement that abolished the Slave Trade and Slavery, inspired these voluntary societies of evangelists, lay and clerical, High and Low Church, Nonjuror and Nonconformist. The last years of William's reign and the first of Anne's saw them fully at work. The diffusion of Bibles and of other religious literature was their chief object. They were therefore great advocates of the Charity Schools where the poor could be taught to read them ; the two movements went side by side. The Society's publications were welcomed by Marlborough in the army, and by Benbow and Rooke in the fleet. Cheap Bibles and Prayer Books were furnished in the country districts. And a supply of Bibles and other books to America was begun on a large scale, and to the rest of the world on a scale, modest indeed as compared to the gigantic work of the Society in later years, but ever growing with the growing power and wealth of England oversea. These activities betokened an instinctive movement of the English religious world to get away, on one side at least, from the denominational and political feuds in which it was entangled, into a field of broader vision, where zeal might produce something better than hate.

In the reign of Anne, as also long before and long after, religious differences were the motive force behind political passions. It is doubly impossible, therefore, for the English historian to ignore religion, if he would explain other phenomena. But he must not be tempted to forget that there was more in the religious sense of the nation than the feuds out of which, incidentally, our political liberties in large part arose. The religious life of many quiet parishes and humble families moved on its way, little concerned with partisanship of High and Low Church; English religion was, in the main, a free and healthy function of that old-world life, nicely guiding itself between superstition and fanaticism on the one side and material barbarism on the other.

And in spite of bitterness of party warfare, the prevalent frame of mind among educated persons already partook of that calm, broadminded optimism characteristic of the Eighteenth-Century Briton. It has been well said :

Addison's England was fortunate in having behind it not only the Glorious Revolution of 1688, but such a poet as Milton, such a physicist as Newton, and such a philosopher as Locke. All the dearest ambitions of men and of Britons had been realised ; the Constitution had been established and ' freedom ' secured ; Homer and Vergil had been equalled if not outdone, the law which preserves the stars from wrong, had been made manifest, and the true workings of the mind had been revealed. All these things had been done not only by Englishmen but by Christians. The brilliant explanations of Newton and Locke had not only removed the strain of living in a mysterious universe, but confirmed the principles of religion. (Basil Willey, *Seventeenth Century Background*, p. 264.)

Two miles away from the Parliament at Westminster and the Queen's Court at St. James's lay the centre of the greatest City in the world, less amenable to the jurisdiction of Court and Parliament than any other portion of English soil. London was governed by her own freely elected magistrates ; policed, in so far as she was policed at all, by her own constables ; guarded by her own militia ; and rendered formidable to the neighbouring seat of government by the largest and least manageable mob in the island. With only a tenth part of her present population, and much less than a tenth of her present area, London had more than her present relative importance. She surpassed her nearest English rivals, Bristol and Norwich, at least fifteen times in number of inhabitants. Her merchants and her markets controlled the larger business operations of the towns and villages of England, ' sucking the vitals of trade to herself.' It was the peculiar boast of the men of Bristol that they alone kept their trade independent of London, bringing American goods to their own port and disposing of them in the west through their own carriers and agents. Everywhere else the strings of trade were pulled from the capital. ' Norwich buys Exeter serges, Exeter buys Norwich stuffs, all at London.' Every county joined in the great national business of supplying London with food, coal or raw material. In return she sent to every county the finished goods of her own luxury trades, and the distant products of her foreign merchandise. To the port of London belonged practically all the East India trade of the country, most of the European, Mediterranean and African, and much of the American.

The lower strata of the population of the capital, the dockers and unskilled casual labour of a great mart and port, lived under the most filthy conditions of overcrowding, without sanitation, police or doctors, and far beyond the range of philanthropy, education and religion. Such was their state both in the City proper and in the liberties beyond, in the days of Defoe. The death-rate among them was appalling, and was still going up because they were learning to drink spirits instead of ale. The privileged sanctuary of outlaws in 'Alsatia,' so outrageous to the dignity of the neighbouring lawyers at the Temple, had indeed been abolished a few years before Anne came to the throne, but the fraternity of thieves, highwaymen and harlots had only been scattered thence to spread themselves more thickly over the whole metropolitan area. Their secret organizer, the great Jonathan Wild, flourished at this period, ostensibly as a zealous magistrate, really as a receiver of stolen goods on an immense scale. Some of his methods of preserving discipline among his subordinates are ascribed to Peachum in the opening scene of the *Beggar's Opera*, which was written immediately after Wild's belated exposure, trial and execution in 1725. His life's story argues an inefficiency on the part of magistrates and constables that only began to be remedied in the middle of the century, when the famous brothers Fielding set up their office in Bow Street.

Even honest workmen in the ranks of unskilled labour in London were totally without education : Jonathan Brown, a leading personality among the bargemen, confessed to Calamy, the dissenting preacher, that he and his companions ' had never so much as heard who or what Christ was,' though they could easily be set on by their betters to burn Meeting Houses or Popish Chapels according to the political requirements of the hour. It was to combat this state of things that the Charity Schools were being founded by public subscription, and that in 1711 Parliament voted the taxpayers' money to build fifty new churches in the suburbs, to seat several hundred thousand persons unprovided for by the Established Church ; the Dissenters, whom the Parliamentary Committee reckoned at 100,000 in that district, had already provided their own chapels.

But London was above all a city of contrasts. The port and mart where the goods of England and the world were exchanged, required not only the muscular efforts of unskilled labour, but a supervising army of foremen, clerks, shopkeepers and middlemen of every variety. Moreover, London was not only a mart ; she was also the seat of manufactures, of finishing processes and luxury trades, employing the most skilled workmen in the island. Many thousands of Huguenot silk manufacturers had recently settled in Spitalfields, and other skilled trades previously conducted in France were now practised in Long Acre and Soho by refugees who were rapidly becoming Englishmen and were already voting Whig to secure the toleration that they precariously enjoyed for their Calvinist worship. The finest native craftsmanship was also concentrated in London. In the best shops of the City the apprentices were sons of country gentlemen, likely to die richer than their elder brothers, and dressing in full-bottomed wigs when off duty. Greater London was the centre of English literary and intellectual life, and of fashion, law and government. For all these reasons the capital contained, alongside the most brutal ignorance, an immense and varied stock of skill and intellect. London wits were sharpened, not only by the processes of national and world commerce, but by daily contact with the lawyers and politicians of Westminster, and with the noblemen and persons of fashion of St. James's. During the season, the leaders of society lived in private mansions or in boarding-houses west of Temple Bar, and were as much Londoners as the annually returning swallow is English.

Such a city, containing more than a tenth of the population of England and a good half of its trained thinking power, placed beside the seat of government at Westminster in juxtaposition so close as to form a single metropolis, could not fail to exercise a decisive influence on the course of English history in the days when the difficulties of travel still isolated Court and Parliament from the other towns and shires of the land. At no time, indeed, did London seek to govern England as Rome had governed Italy or as Athens sought to govern Greece. She accepted the government of England by the Monarchy or by Parliament, so long as the rulers of the land remained at Westminster outside her gates, leaving her ancient municipal liberties undisturbed, and so long as they conducted the religious and foreign affairs of the country in the main in accordance with principles that were popular in London. The Kings and Queens whom she favoured—Henry VIII, Elizabeth, William III and Anne—left behind them political structures that survived. Those who quarrelled with her built for the day—Mary Tudor, the two Charleses and Jameses, and the Protector—though Oliver and the second Charles each owed his rise to power largely to her support.

The Tower of London, which was to have overawed the citizens, had been built by William the Conqueror on the side of the City away from Westminster. Partly for that reason, it had not overawed them long. In Stuart times it could not, in its isolated position, serve to protect Westminster and Whitehall from the insults of the London mob. In Anne's reign the Tower still served as the great Arsenal whence cannon and gunpowder were shipped to the wars oversea ; it also contained the Mint and its machinery for coining the money of the Realm, presided over by Newton himself as Master. The outer walls enclosed a network of streets inhabited by the officers of these two establishments. On occasion it was still a State prison. But already it had its lighter side, for it served as the Zoo and the Museum of the Capital. Visitors were taken to see the Crown Jewels, and the newly finished Armoury where a line of English Kings sat mounted in battle array. The stock of lions and other wild beasts had been maintained ever since the days when the Tower had been a favourite residence of mediaeval kings ; it was finely replenished by presents to Queen Anne from the monarchs of North African ' Barbary,' with whom the English merchants traded, and with whom the captors of Gibraltar made treaties of alliance against France and Spain.

Between the Tower and Temple Bar stretched the length of the City proper ; its meagre breadth extended north-wards from the river only as far as the bars of Smithfield, Holborn and Whitechapel.[1] But the march of bricks and mortar had burst the municipal bounds, chiefly in a westerly direction, attracted towards the seat of national government at Westminster. At the Strand began the jurisdiction of that City. But the municipal privileges of Westminster were no rival to those of London. Neither London nor the Court nor Parliament had ever wished to have to deal with a Lord Mayor of Westminster. So Westminster was never permitted to enjoy self-government, or to acquire a corporate sense. It was ruled by twelve burgesses ap-pointed for life by the High Steward, and even their powers were being rapidly superseded by those of the Justices of the Peace and of the Vestries of the different parishes. It is true that the parliamentary franchise in Westminster was democratic, and in the days when most boroughs had a narrow franchise, the election of a member of Parliament for Westminster caused unusual political excitement long before the time of Charles Fox, as when General Stanhope stood in 1710 in the Whig interest and was defeated after a fierce contest and a hot canvass. But Westminster's local government was a mere bureaucracy, so far as it was anything better than an anarchy of rival jurisdictions.

On the other hand, the City of London enjoyed complete self-government in an unusually democratic form. At that time very few boroughs in England were so free of the element of oligarchy, unless it were Ipswich and Norwich. In London as many as 12,000 ratepaying householders voted in their respective Wards to elect the 26 Aldermen and 200 Common Councillors. These ratepayers of the Wards were almost identical with the Liverymen of the 89 Gilds and Companies : in their double capacity they controlled by their votes the antique and complicated machinery of London self-government.

The electorate of shopkeepers chose men of their own class to represent them on the Common Council, rather than the great merchant princes known in the world of high

---

[1] These ' bar ' boundaries, were, of course, more extensive than the original City bounded by the wall and gates, e.g. Temple Bar was farther west than Ludgate.

finance and politics. The City magnates were more often chosen as Aldermen. Common pride in the privileges and power of London, and jealous care for her independence, prevented a serious breach between the great men of the Exchange and the shopkeeping democracy. But there was sometimes friction, and in the course of Anne's reign a tendency became apparent for the democratic Common Council to be Tory, and for the Mayor, Aldermen and wealthy City magnates to be Whig.

The jurisdiction of London's elected magistrates was not confined to the area of their own City. Their power stopped short of Westminster, but they clipped it in on every side. They possessed the Shrievalty of Middlesex and the Bailiwick of Southwark. They administered and taxed the port of London. The Lord Mayor was Conservator of the river from Gravesend and Tilbury up to a point just above Staines Bridge—a course of over sixty miles. London levied coal duties in a radius of twelve miles, and enforced her monopoly of markets in a radius of seven.

The City proper was the most densely populated acreage in England. It was not, as in later times, abandoned to ' cats and caretakers ' at nightfall ; the merchant prince and the shopkeeper slept, each with his family, over his place of business—servants and prentices above in the garrets, and porters and messengers packed away anywhere in cellarage and warehouse. Old Jewry and Basinghall Street, in particular, were reputed to contain the homes of some of the richest men in England. But the nobility of the realm had already deserted their ancestral palaces in the crowded City and the Strand, whence gardens were vanishing apace ; the grandees resided, during the season, round Covent Garden, Piccadilly, Bloomsbury or St. James's Square, or in some part of Westminster. And gentlemen from the country, civil servants, members of Parliament and professional men had smaller houses in these same regions, clustering round the mansions of the nobility. Such is the origin of many famous London ' Squares.' [1]

[1] Thus Bloomsbury Square, originally called Southampton Square, was a new fashionable quarter, built after the Restoration. The ' Square ' was the first piece of properly planned development on the Bloomsbury estate of the last Earl

But the rich merchants still inhabited their beloved City for reasons alike of business and sentiment. They had also their country houses and villas among the woods, fields and pleasant villages within a twenty-mile radius of London. In their suburban and riverside retreats—in Hampstead, West Ham, Walthamstow, and below Epsom Downs, and especially along the green shores of the Thames from Chelsea upwards—there was perhaps as much good eating and drinking done by Londoners as in the City itself. The poorer sort walked out for a holiday in the country to favourite spots like Dulwich.

The river was the most crowded of the London highways. Passengers in boats were perpetually threading the heavy commercial traffic, to the accompaniment of volleys of traditional abuse and chaff exchanged between boatmen and bargees. On the north bank, between London Bridge and the Parliament Stairs were at least thirty landing-places, where boats waited by the steps to carry people along or across the river. Statesmen and parsons going over to Lambeth, or prentices and budding barristers on lighter errands to Cupid's Garden hard by, one and all crossed by boat. There were ferries with platforms to take a coach and horses. For until Westminster Bridge was built in 1738, London Bridge was the only road over the river. The street that stood upon it had been rebuilt in a more modern style since the ravages of the Great Fire, but the projection of its ancient piers still hindered and endangered traffic. To ' shoot the bridge ' was still an adventure ; it was said that London Bridge was made for wise men to go over and fools to go under.

The big shipping, therefore, came no higher than the Bridge. Below it, a forest of masts covered the Pool of London, with which no scene in the world save Amsterdam could compare. The fairway was the more crowded because scarcely any of the great docks had then been dug

---

of Southampton, on whose death it passed to his daughter Rachel and her ' dear lord,' the Whig hero executed in 1683. It was one of the earliest of the London squares, and was given that form in order to leave open the view from the front of the great mansion, Southampton (later Bedford) House that occupied its north end. A century passed before Russell Square was similarly developed out of the fields to the north of the great House. *The Russells in Bloomsbury*, Scott Thomson, chaps. II and III.

out, except those at Deptford, and the single dock at Blackwall used for the vessels of the East India Company.

Amid the hayfields on Thames bank stood Chelsea Hospital in solitary grandeur, inhabited by four hundred red-coated pensioners of Sedgemoor, Landen and the Boyne, discussing the weekly news of Marlborough's doings with the professional earnestness of Corporal Trim. A little way off lay the village of Chelsea, where a few persons of fashion had taken the fancy to build themselves retreats, as far removed from the turmoil of London and Westminster as Kensington Palace itself.

Since coal was burnt on almost every London hearth, the air was so infected that a foreign scholar complained ' whenever I examine London books I make my ruffles as black as coal.' On days when the north-east wind carried the smoke cloud, even Chelsea became dangerous to the asthmatic, as the mild philosopher Earl of Shaftesbury had reason to complain. There is no wonder that King William with his weak lungs had lived at Hampton Court when he could, and at Kensington when he must. Anne, on her accession, could safely move the royal residence from country to town, from Kensington to St. James's Palace. But that was all the satisfaction she would give to her loving subjects ; not only was she often at Bath and yet more often at Windsor, but even when she came to town, the doors of St. James's were open only to her Ministers and her female favourites, and to those whom Ministers or favourites introduced by the front stairs or the back. Throughout her reign she was an invalid. What asthma was to William, gout or dropsy was to Anne. To be jolted in a coach to Westminster to open Parliament, or to St. Paul's to give public thanks for some famous victory, was a penance that she could only occasionally consent to endure.

Queen Anne therefore kept Court as little as William. Metaphorically as well as literally, the Whitehall of the Merry Monarch lay in ruins, never to rise again. Except the Banqueting House of tragic memory, the whole Palace had been burnt in 1698, and its roofless walls still cumbered the river bank. Buckingham House was still the residence of a subject. The fashionable world parading in sedan chairs and six-horse coaches in the Mall, or sauntering in the more private garden immediately below the windows of St. James's Palace, had to be content with remembering that they were near the invisible Queen. It was more to the point that in the other direction the Houses of Parliament were but a few minutes' walk away.

'The Court' had been the microcosm and throbbing heart of England ever since the days of Alfred, through Norman and Plantagenet times, through the spacious days of Henry and Elizabeth down to Charles II ; his Court was not only the scene of much pleasure, liberty and scandal, it was also the centre of patronage for politics, fashion, literature, art, learning, invention, company-promoting, and a hundred other activities of the King's eager subjects seeking notoriety or reward. But after the Revolution the glory of the Court grew dim. Neither the political position of the Crown, nor the personal temperament of those who wore it was the same as of old. Stern William, invalid Anne, the German Georges, farmer George, domestic Victoria, none of them desired to keep a Court like Queen Elizabeth's. Henceforth the Court was the residence of secluded Royalty, pointed out from afar, difficult of access save on formal occasions of proverbial dullness. Patronage was sought elsewhere, in the lobbies of Parliament, in the ante-chambers of Ministers, in the country houses of the pleasantest aristocracy in the world,—finally in an appeal to the educated public. This decline of the Court had many consequences, direct and indirect, on English life. It had no analogy in contemporary France, where Versailles still drew men like a magnet, and impoverished the life of chateau and province.

CHAPTER XI

DR. JOHNSON'S ENGLAND [*circa* 1740–1780] [1]

I

Population—Medicine and Philanthropy—Justice—Local administration—Religion—Education—Universities—Wales.

THE first forty years of the Eighteenth Century, the reign of Anne and the rule of Walpole, constitute an age of transition, during which the feuds and ideals of the Stuart era, lately a lava flood scouring the land with devastating heat, were being channelled and congealed into fixed, durable Hanoverian forms. In this way the age of Marlborough and Bolingbroke, of Swift and Defoe, was the meeting point of two epochs. It is only in the years that followed (1740–1780) that we find a generation of men wholly characteristic of the Eighteenth Century ethos, a society with a mental outlook of its own, self-poised, self-judged, and self-approved, freed from the disturbing passions of the past, and not yet troubled with anxieties about a very different future which was soon to be brought upon the scene by the Industrial and the French Revolutions. The gods mercifully gave mankind this little moment of peace between the religious fanaticisms of the past and the fanaticisms of class and race that were speedily to arise and dominate time to come. In England it was an age of aristocracy and liberty ; of the rule of law and the absence of reform ; of individual initiative and institutional decay ; of Latitudinarianism above and Wesleyanism below ; of the growth of humanitarian and philanthropic feeling and endeavour ; of creative vigour in all the trades and arts that serve and adorn the life of man.

It is a ' classical ' age, that is to say an age of unchallenged assumptions, when the philosophers of the street, such as Dr. Johnson, have ample leisure to moralize on the human scene, in the happy belief that the state of society and the

[1] George II, 1727-1760. George III, 1760-1820. Dr. Johnson, *b.* 1709, *d.* 1784. Seven Years' War, 1755-1761. War of American Independence, 1776-1782.

modes of thought to which they are accustomed are not mere passing aspects of an ever-shifting kaleidoscope, but permanent habitations, the final outcome of reason and experience.　Such an age does not aspire to progress though it may in fact be progressing ; it regards itself not as setting out but as having arrived ; it is thankful for what it has, and enjoys life without ' deep questioning which probes to endless dole.'　And therefore the men of this ' classical ' age looked back with a sense of kinship to the far-off Ancient World.　The upper class regarded the Greeks and Romans as honorary Englishmen, their precursors in liberty and culture, and the Roman Senate as the prototype of the British Parliament.　The mediaeval period, with its ' gothic ' aspirations and barbarisms, sank for a while below the horizon of study and sympathy, so that the eye of taste could range back without hindrance across the gulf of time, and contemplate on its further shore the only civilization which could claim to be as classical, as poised, as enlightened and as artistic as the fortunate present.

Compared to the self-complacency of the mid-Eighteenth Century, the proverbial self-complacency of the Victorians is modesty itself, for the Victorians were, within certain limits, ardent and successful reformers, and admired themselves for the improvements they made.　But to the typical men of the period of Blackstone, Gibbon and Burke, England appeared to be the best country possible in an imperfect world, requiring only to be left alone where Providence and the Revolution of 1688 had so fortunately placed her.　Their optimism about England was based on a general pessimism about the human race, not on a belief in perpetual and world-wide ' progress ' such as cheered simple hearts in the Nineteenth Century.

It is true that the men who were least content were those who looked closest at the realities of English life—Hogarth, Fielding, Smollett and the philanthropists ; they indeed exposed particular evils as unsparingly as Dickens himself. But even their strictures kept within the limits of the classical and conservative philosophy of the time.　Nor was the self-complacency of that age altogether unjustified, though it was unfortunate because it sustained an atmosphere inimical to any general movement of reform.   It was a society which, with all its grave faults, was brilliant above and stable below.

In the course of the Eighteenth Century the population of England and Wales rose from about five and a half millions when Queen Anne came to the throne, to nine millions in 1801. This unprecedented increase, the herald of great changes in the life of our island, was not caused by immigration : the entry of cheap Irish labour which now first became an important feature of our social and economic life, was counterbalanced numerically by English emigration overseas.   The advance in population represented a rather larger birth-rate and a very much reduced death-rate.   The survival of many more infants and the prolongation of the average life of adults mark off modern times from the past, and this great change began in the Eighteenth Century. It was due mainly to improved medical service.

In the first decades of the Century the death-rate had risen sharply and passed the birth-rate.   But this dangerous tendency was reversed between 1730 and 1760, and after 1780 the death-rate went down by leaps and bounds.

Both the rise of the death-rate and its subsequent fall have been attributed in part to the growth and decline of the habit of drinking cheap gin instead of beer.   The dire consequences of that change in the habits of the poor have been immortalized in Hogarth's famous delineation of the horrors of ' Gin Lane ' contrasted with prosperous ' Beer Street.'   In the third decade of the Century, the epoch of the *Beggar's Opera*, statesmen and legislators had deliberately encouraged the consumption of gin by throwing open the distilling trade and by placing on spirits far too light a tax.   Distilling, said Defoe, consumed corn and was therefore good for the landed interest, and so thought the Parliament of landlords.   But as the appalling social consequences were gradually brought to their notice by the enlightened philanthropy of the age, a series of hesitating steps were taken to mitigate the evil.   But it was not really checked until 1751, when spirits were highly taxed and their retail by distillers and shopkeepers was stopped (24 G. II, c. 40).

'The Act of 1751,' says the historian of Eighteenth

M

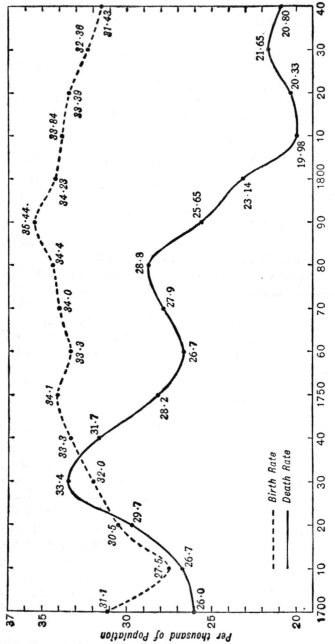

Per thousand of Population

Birth Rate
Death Rate

Diagram from *Population Problems of the Age of Malthus.* G. Talbot Griffith.

Cam. Press, 1926.

Century London, ' really did reduce the excesses of spirit-drinking. It was a turning-point in the social history of London and was so considered when this time was still within living memory.' Even after that blessed date medical men still attributed an eighth of the deaths of London adults to excess in spirit-drinking ; but the worst was over, and after the middle years of the Century tea became a formidable rival to alcohol with all classes, both in the capital and in the country at large.

At the height of the gin era, between 1740 and 1742, the burials in the London region had been twice as many as the baptisms ! The capital had been supplied with inhabitants by the unfailing stream of immigrants from the healthier and more sober countryside. The change for the better after the middle of the Century was very great. In 1750 the London death-rate had been 1 in 20 ; by 1821 it had fallen to 1 in 40. The population of greater London doubled between 1700 and 1820 (674,000 rose to 1,274,000), but the annual number of registered burials was unaltered. In other words, although the target that London exposed to the darts of Death was twice as large in 1820 as it had been a century before, the number of hits he scored showed no increase. (See Mrs. George, *London Life in the Eighteenth Century*, pp. 24–38.)

While the period of cheap gin lasted (1720–1750) it had done much to reduce the population of the capital. In the country at large, its ravages had been severe, but ale had held its own better in the village than in the town. Social historians have indeed sometimes exaggerated the effect of gin-drinking on vital statistics outside the London area. For example, gin cannot account for the rapid increase in the death-rate between 1700 and 1720, for in those years the great consumption of cheap spirits had scarcely begun. And whereas the death-rate in all England, as distinct from the London area, fell rapidly from 1730 to 1750, those were precisely the years when gin-drinking was at its worst.

We must therefore look for other causes, besides the decline of the consumption of spirits, to account for the remarkable fall in the death-rate that marked the middle period of the Century, and still more its last twenty years. The two reasons why death began to take a smaller toll

of English infants, children and adults, were improved conditions of life and improved medical treatment.   The great
advance in agriculture during the Eighteenth Century gave
more abundant food to many, though not to all.   The
advance in locomotion and the changes in industrial method
gave more employment and higher wages and brought
more numerous and more varied articles of purchase within
the cottager's reach.   It is true that the industrial and agricultural revolution had some most unhappy effects on
society and on the amenities of life in village and town.
It did not always make for content, possibly not on the
average for happiness.   But it certainly provided more
food and clothing and other articles per head of the population, though their distribution was scandalously unequal.
And this greater abundance, by lengthening human life,
was one cause why the population continued to rise.

But an even greater check upon the death-rate was the
advance in medicine.   Throughout the Eighteenth Century the medical profession was moving out of the dark ages
of sciolism and traditional superstition into the light of
science.   The Physician, the Surgeon, the Apothecary and
the unlicensed practitioner were all going forward apace in
knowledge and in devoted service, especially to the poor,
who had hitherto been horribly neglected.   Science and
philanthropy were the best part of the spirit of the ' age of
enlightenment ' and this spirit inspired the better medical
training and practice of individuals.

At the beginning of the Century, smallpox had been the
scourge most dreaded, as destructive of beauty and still
more destructive of life.   The woman traveller, Lady Mary
Wortley Montagu, introduced inoculation from Turkey, and
an Inoculation Hospital was set up in London.   Although
the remedy was suspected as unnatural and even impious,
it made some headway and reduced the ravages of the disease.
But smallpox still carried off a thirteenth of each generation until, at the close of the Century, Jenner discovered
vaccination.

Scotland was beginning to make her great intellectual
contribution to life south of the Border.   The union of
brains was following the Union of Parliaments and of commerce.   It was the age of Hume, Smollet, Adam Smith and

Boswell. And in this same period Sir John Pringle, the Hunter brothers and William Smellie came from Scotland to London ; the Hunters, by their teaching, converted British surgery from the trade of the ' barber-surgeon ' into the science of the specialist ; Smellie similarly revolutionized the practice of midwifery ; while Pringle reformed military hygiene, on scientific principles which had also a great influence on the habits and the treatment of the civilian population.

The great improvement in professional skill was supported by the foundation of Hospitals, in which the age of Philanthropy gave sober expression to its feelings, just as the age of Faith had sung its soul in the stones of cloisters and Cathedral aisles. Lying-in hospitals were founded in the principal towns. County hospitals for all sorts of patients were set up. In the capital, between 1720 and 1745, Guy's, Westminster, St. George's, London and Middlesex Hospitals were all founded ; the mediaeval St. Thomas's had been rebuilt in the reign of Anne, and at Bart's teaching and practice were improving apace. In the course of 125 years after 1700, no less than 154 new hospitals and dispensaries were established in Britain. These were not municipal undertakings—municipal life was then at its lowest ebb ; they were the outcome of individual initiative and of co-ordinated voluntary effort and subscription.

At the same time the growing benevolence of the age was moved to cope with the appalling infant mortality among the poor and especially among deserted bastard children. Jonas Hanway, who did much to reduce these evils, had declared that ' few parish children live to be apprenticed.' And thousands of infants did not even live to be parish children, but died abandoned in empty rooms or exposed in streets by mothers to whom they would only mean expense and shame. Captain Coram, with his kind sailor's heart, could not endure the sight of babes lying deserted by the roadside, while respectable citizens passed by with the shrug of the Pharisee. For years Coram agitated the project of a Foundling Hospital ; at length he obtained a charter from George II ; Handel gave an organ ; Hogarth painted a picture ; subscriptions poured in, and in 1745 the Hospital was completed and opened. Many infant lives were saved, and many deserted children were brought up and apprenticed to trades.

A few years after the good Captain had died, a bad moment occurred in the history of the institution he had founded. In 1756 Parliament made a grant to its funds, on condition that all children brought to the Hospital should be admitted. Fifteen thousand were brought, and the not unnatural consequence was that of this unmanageable multitude only 4400 lived to be apprenticed. After that disastrous experiment, the Foundling Hospital again became a private institution with a limited entry—and a reduced death-rate. It long continued to do good work, till in the happier social conditions of the early Twentieth Century it was moved out of town, and the ' Foundling site ' was secured as a playground for all kinds of children, and rechristened ' Coram's Fields.'

Early in the reign of George III, Hanway's persistent efforts were crowned by an Act of Parliament which compelled the parishes of the London area to keep their 'parish infants ' no longer in the workhouses where they died apace, but in country cottages where they lived and throve.[1]

In the same spirit, General Oglethorpe had drawn attention to the scandal of debtors' prisons. In 1729 he induced Parliament to enquire into the horrors of the Fleet and Marshalsea, where the gaolers tortured debtors to death in the endeavour to extract fees from men who in the nature of the case had no money. English prisons remained for the rest of the Century a national disgrace, being still farmed out to wretches of this kind by the local authorities who would not be at the trouble and expense to maintain them by properly paid public officials.[2] But Oglethorpe had at least called

---

[1] Hanway (1712–1786) is also famous for introducing the umbrella into England. For many years he carried one, in spite of the jeers of the populace and the interested anger of sedan chairmen and hackney coachmen, until in the last years of his life his example was generally imitated. But it would be more true to say that he re-introduced the custom, for in 1710, two years before Hanway was born, Swift had written in his *City Shower :*

' The tuck'd up sempstress walks with hasty strides
While streams run down her oil'd umbrella's sides.'

It is therefore probable that Hanway had seen umbrellas in use in London when he was a small boy.

[2] John Howard, in 1773, began his life's work on prisons by a vain attempt to induce the justices of Bedfordshire and the neighbouring Counties to pay regular salaries to the gaolers in lieu of fees extorted from the prisoners.

attention to the state of things and mitigated some of its
very worst abuses. Previous generations had seldom en-
quired what went on inside these houses of woe.

The gallant General also became the founder and first
governor of the new colony of Georgia, whither he transplanted many debtors and impoverished persons. He
well deserved Pope's eulogium—

> One, driven by strong benevolence of soul,
> Shall fly, like Oglethorpe, from pole to pole.

' Strong benevolence of soul ' was characteristic of many
in that age. It dictated the extraordinary domestic arrange-
ments of Oglethorpe's formidable friend Dr. Johnson.
From beginning to end of the Century, the new Puritanism
of the ardently religious, such as Robert Nelson, Lady
Elizabeth Hastings, the Wesleys, Cowper and finally
Wilberforce, strove to practise the charity of the New
Testament in place of the harsher precepts of the Old with
which Cromwell's troopers had marched to battle. It was
no accident that Uncle Toby, the Vicar of Wakefield, Mr.
Allworthy and Parson Adams were leading characters in
English fiction during its first great period. A keener
sensitiveness to the needs and sufferings of others, particularly of the poor, was not only reflected in literature but
was seen in the lives of philanthropists and in the successive
activities of the age—the foundation first of Charity Schools;
then of Hospitals ; and, in the last years of the Century, of
Sunday Schools. It overleapt the boundaries of race and
colour. It melted the hard prudence of statesmen. ' Stormy
pity ' inspired much of the eloquence and some of the errors
of Burke and of Fox on India and on France ; and at length
stirred the great rebellion of the English conscience against
the slave-trade.

Yet while the new humanitarian spirit inspired private
initiative, it had as yet little effect on executive, municipal or
legislative action. Private employers treated their servants
better than the Government treated its soldiers and sailors.
The fleet had to be maintained by the haphazard and iniquitous compulsion of the press-gang, because voluntary recruiting was inadequate owing to the notorious conditions on
board the royal ships. The life of the fisherman and the

merchant sailor was hard enough, but it was better than life on a man-of-war, where the food was foul and scanty, the pay inadequate and irregular, the attention to health nil, and the discipline of iron.   The good Admiral Vernon, who suffered in the reign of George II for being the sailors' outspoken friend, declared that ' our fleets are defrauded by injustice, manned by violence and maintained by cruelty.'

The private of the army was no better treated.   At home he had no barracks, but was billeted in ale-houses on a population that hated the red-coats and treated them accordingly.   They were the more unpopular because they acted as the only efficient police force against rioting and smuggling.   As to discipline, one soldier of George II had received 30,000 lashes in sixteen years—' yet the man is hearty and well and in no ways concerned.'   While such was their lot at home, garrison duty in the West Indies was tantamount to a sentence of death.   These were the men who by sea and land won England her empire and defended her trade and secured her wealth and happiness at home, and such was their reward.

Throughout the Century, Parliament went on adding statute after statute to the ' bloody code ' of English law, enlarging perpetually the long list of offences punishable by death : finally they numbered two hundred.   Not only were horse and sheep stealing and coining capital crimes, but stealing in a shop to the value of five shillings, and stealing anything privily from the person, were it only a handkerchief.   But such was the illogical chaos of the law, that attempted murder was still very lightly punished, though to slit a man's nose was capital.   The effect of increased legal severity in an age that was becoming more humane, was that juries often refused to convict men for minor offences that would lead them to the scaffold.   Moreover it was easy for a criminal, by the help of a clever lawyer, to escape on purely technical grounds from the meshes of an antiquated and over-elaborate procedure.   Out of six thieves brought to trial, five might in one way or another get off, while the unlucky one was hanged.   It would have been more deterrent if they had all six been sure of a term of imprisonment.

To make matters worse, the chances of arrest were small,

for there was no effective police in the island, except the 'runners' of the office which the Fielding brothers, about the middle of the Century, set up in their house in Bow Street.[1] Until the soldiers were actually called out, there was no force capable of dispersing a disorderly crowd. Hence the disgraceful incident of the Gordon Riots (1780), when seventy houses and four gaols were burnt by the London mob. Indeed, the wonder is that our ancestors preserved public order and private property as well as they did. They must have been, on the average, at least as moral and law-abiding a folk as our own generation. For what would be the effect in our great cities to-day of abolishing the police?

Yet, until the Code Napoleon was received on the Continent, it is possible that English justice, bad as it was, may have been the best in the world, as Blackstone boasted. It had at least two advantages over the European codes of the *ancien régime*. It gave the prisoner in political cases a real chance to defend himself against the government, an improvement made by the Treason Law of 1695, and by the general tendency of political and judicial practice since the Revolution. And in no cases, political or other, was torture permitted to extort evidence or confession. But it cannot be said that English justice eschewed torture as a means of punishment, for although breaking on the wheel was unknown in our island, the floggings, particularly in the army and navy, often amounted to torture.

The English were still fond of witnessing the punishment of those whose actions they disapproved. Two passages may be cited from the Diaries of Parson Woodforde, a benevolent soul unusually kind to men and animals :

1777. July 22. Robert Biggen, for stealing potatoes, was this afternoon whipped thro' the streets of Cary [Somerset] by the Hangman at the end of a cart. He was whipped from the George Inn to

---

[1] The novelist Henry Fielding and his remarkable half-brother Sir John, who was blind from birth, were the best magistrates London had in the Century. Actually they were Stipendiary Justices of Westminster. In a ballad of the period, the Highwayman sings :
> I went to London one fine day
> With my sweet love to see the play,
> Where Fielding's gang did me pursue
> And I was ta'en by that cursed crew.

the Angel, from thence back through the street to the Royal Oak in South Cary and so back to the George Inn.   He being an old offender there was a collection of 0.17.6 given to the Hangman to do him justice.   But it was not much for all that—the Hangman was an old Man and a most villainous looking Fellow indeed.   For my Part I would not contribute one Farthing to it.

1781.   April 7.   Gave my servant Will leave to go to Norwich ten miles by road this morning to see the three Highwaymen hung there today.   Will returned about seven o'clock in the evening.   They were all three hung and appeared penitent.

Whether or not English justice was on the whole less bad than the continental practice of the day, the philosophers of Europe and of England now began their famous attack on the existing systems of law and punishment.   This greater sensitiveness to evils which all previous ages had accepted as matters of course, was part of the general humanitarian movement, connected on the continent with Voltaire and the ' philosophers,' and in England connected equally with ' philosophy ' and with religion.   The Italian reformer, Beccaria, in his attack on the penal codes of Europe was followed by Howard's exposure of the still scandalous state of prisons at home and abroad, and by Bentham's analysis of the useless and complicated absurdities of English law, a vested interest dear to the heart of the most conservative of professions.

The excellent idea of the rule of law, as something superior to the will of the rulers, was strong among the Eighteenth Century English.   It had been secured by the events of the Revolution and by the consequent irremovability of Judges, who were no longer jackals of government, but independent umpires between the Crown and the subject.

This high conception of the supremacy of law was popularized by Blackstone's *Commentaries on the Laws of England* (1765), a book widely read by educated people in England and America, for it was a legally-minded age.   The fault was that the law thus idealized was regarded too much as static, as a thing given once for all ; whereas, if law is indeed to be the permanent rule of life to a nation, it must be apt to change with the changing needs and circumstances of society.   In the Eighteenth Century, Parliament showed little legislative activity, except in private acts for enclosure of land, for turnpike roads, or other economic measures. In administrative matters there was a lag in legislation, at a time when great industrial developments were every year changing social conditions, and adding to the needs of a growing population.

Therefore Jeremy Bentham, the father of English law reform, regarded Blackstone as the arch-enemy, who stood in the way of change by teaching people to make a fetish of the laws of England in the form which they actually bore at the moment, a form dictated by the needs not of the present age but of ages long past.[1]

The first blast against Blackstone was blown by young Bentham in his *Fragment on Government* in 1776, that seminal year which saw the publication of Adam Smith's *Wealth of Nations*, the first part of Gibbon's *History*, and the American Declaration of Independence. When the octogenarian Bentham died in 1832, the laws of England had only just begun to be altered from what they had been when he first denounced them in Blackstone's day. Yet his prolonged efforts had not been in vain, for he had converted the rising generation. Onwards from that time our laws were rapidly changed in accordance with the commonsense, utilitarian principles that Bentham had laid down.

Reform was to be the specific work of the Nineteenth Century. The specific work of the earlier Hanoverian epoch was the establishment of the rule of law ; and that law, with all its grave faults, was at least a law of freedom. On that solid foundation all our subsequent reforms were built. If the Eighteenth Century had not established the law of freedom, the Nineteenth Century in England would have proceeded by Revolutionary violence, instead of by Parliamentary modification of the law.

The abuses of the poor-law, of which so much was heard in Eighteenth Century England, were due to want of modern organs of government, and above all to an entire lack of central organization and control. The problem of the

---

[1] Professor Holdsworth thinks that Bentham somewhat exaggerated the conservative optimism of Blackstone, who was not in all ways as blind as his critic made out.

poor and of unemployment was in its essence national—or
at least regional—yet every petty parish dealt with it separately, in a state of hostility to every other.   Rural ignorance
and parochial jealousy were left to cope with the terrible
problem according to their own devices, and the chief
anxiety felt was to drive out of the parish anyone who might
conceivably become a burden on the poor-rate, a policy
which checked the fluidity of labour and severely aggravated unemployment.   But the problem of the poor in
England had this advantage over the problem of police
and prisons, that it was legally obligatory to raise a poor-
rate in every parish to deal with its poor, whereas the
ratepayers regarded it as an unusual hardship if the magistrate raised any rate to pay for roads, prisons, sanitation
or police.

Rural England was governed by the patriarchal sway of
the Justices of the Peace.   It lay with them to decide if a
local rate should be raised for any purpose, and how it
should be spent.   The Justices, nominally appointed by
the Crown, were really appointed by the Lord Lieutenant
influenced by the opinion of the gentry of the shire.   Nominally State officials, the J.P.s really represented local territorial power.   The Privy Council no longer, as in Tudor
and early Stuart days, kept them in awe and guided their
action on national principles.   The Revolution of 1688, in
one of its aspects, had been a revolt of these unpaid local
magistrates against the Central Government which had
overstrained their loyalty in religion and politics.   Owing
to the infatuation of James II, the privileges of Parliament
and the liberties of Englishmen were reasserted at the price
of an excessive lack of central control over local authorities
even in matters that were not political but social.   The
Privy Council by aiming at absolute power in all things, had
lost powers which it had formerly exercised for the general
good.   In the Eighteenth Century the Justices of Peace
might rather have been said to control the Central Government through the grand national Quarter Sessions of Parliament, than to be under any central control themselves.
No local authority had then to consider ' Whitehall.'

The powers and functions of the J.P.s covered all sides of
country life.   They administered justice in Quarter or

Petty Sessions, or in the private house of a single magistrate. They were supposed to keep up the roads and bridges, the prisons and workhouses. They licensed the public houses. They levied a county rate when a rate was levied at all. These and a hundred other aspects of county business lay in their control. Yet they had not any proper staff, or any effective bureaucracy to carry out local administration. For that would have meant a big County rate which men were unwilling to pay ; they preferred inefficient local government provided only it was cheap. Modern English practice is so different in this respect that it is difficult to realize how great has been the change.[1]

In the middle years of the Century, Fielding, Smollett and other observers of the injustices of life, bitterly satirized the irresponsible power of the J.P.s and its frequent misuse in acts of tyranny and favouritism. There was a corrupt type of J.P. known as 'trading justices,' men of a lower order of society who got themselves made magistrates in order to turn their position to financial profit. But generally speaking, the Justices who did most of the work in rural districts were substantial squires, too rich to be corrupt or mean, proud to do hard public work for no pay, anxious to stand well with their neighbours, but often ignorant and prejudiced without meaning to be unjust, and far too much a law unto themselves.

It is a common error to regard the Eighteenth Century in England as irreligious. An ethical code based on Christian doctrine was a rule of life to a much larger proportion of the community than it had been in the late mediaeval and Tudor periods. Indeed, the age of Wesley, Cowper and Dr. Johnson was perhaps as 'religious' as the Seventeenth Century itself, though it had ceased to fight with the sword about rival doctrines of Christianity, and was therefore somewhat more tolerant of still wider differences of opinion.

Locke's argument that Toleration was not merely politically expedient but positively just and right, became

---

[1] The annual cost of poor relief between 1782 and 1793 was two millions a year ; *all other kinds of expenditure met out of local rates did not exceed £200,000 a year !* Halévy, *Hist. of Eng. People*, II, p. 233 (Pelican ed.).

generally accepted as the Eighteenth Century went on.
It is arguable that this does not make that much abused
era any less Christian. Human experience had so long
associated religion with intolerance, that when intolerance
cooled, people thought that religion had decayed. The
deduction may be challenged.

Writing in the reigns of James II and William, even
Locke had maintained that neither Atheist nor Romanist had
an absolute claim on society for toleration, because the one
undermined morality and the other the State. But in
effect both were to benefit by the more liberal and latitudinarian philosophy which his influence helped to impose on
the succeeding age.

Locke's *Reasonableness of Christianity* (the very title
marks a new brand of thought and religion) was the starting-
point of two movements, the Latitudinarianism that became for a while the prevalent tone of the Established
Church, though not of Methodism ; and the English
Deistic movement which all respectable people regarded
askance.

In the first thirty years of the Century the ' Deists,' such
as Toland, Tindal and Collins, were allowed to print their
cautiously expressed views without being prosecuted ; while
they were answered not only by the satire of Swift but by
the arguments of men who outmatched them in intellect—
Bishop Butler, Bishop Berkeley, Bentley and William Law.
Voltaire, the bolder and more formidable disciple of these
English Deists, found no such antagonists in France, but
had more to fear from active persecution by Church and
State. Partly for that reason continental Deism became more
uncompromising and more anti-Christian than English.
Indeed, the most recent historian of Eighteenth Century
thought speaks of ' that peculiarly English phenomenon,
the holy alliance of science and religion, which persisted
(in spite of Hume) till near the close of the Century.' (Basil
Willey, *The Eighteenth Century Background*, p. 136.) David
Hartley, after whom Coleridge named his son, proclaimed
this ' holy alliance.' In the words of Pope's comfortable
epigram :

> Nature and Nature's laws lay hid in night ;
> God said, *Let Newton be !* and all was light !

The harmony of science and religion was nobly symbolized by the erection in 1755 of Roubillac's statue of Newton in the ante-chapel at Trinity College, Cambridge.

It is true that, in the early years of George III's reign, there were Britons of the intellectual calibre of Hume and Gibbon who were avowed sceptics. Yet even Gibbon thought well to veil his real thought in the decent obscurity of the ironical. And as every reader of Boswell's *Johnson* is aware, these great sceptics and their lesser followers were ill spoken of in society, while the batteries opened upon them by orthodox writers were overwhelming in quantity, though no longer in quality. In 1776, a date usually regarded in retrospect as belonging to the period most marked by infidelity and laxity of doctrine, Hume wrote to Gibbon about the reception of the first part of his Roman history, ' the prevalence of superstition in England prognosticates the fall of philosophy and the decay of taste.' Hume was too pessimistic, but he was speaking from real experience.

In any case, the scholarly scepticism of the English Eighteenth Century was addressed only to a highly educated audience. Its optimistic philosophy was the outcome of upper-class conditions of life. When, in the period of the French Revolution, Tom Paine appealed to the multitude on behalf of Deism as the proper creed of democracy, a new age had arrived. In the lifetime of the fastidious and conservative Gibbon, it has been said that infidelity, like hair-powder, could only be worn by the aristocracy. The mass of the nation was either actively or passively Christian, accepting the religion that it was taught. The lowest strata of society had indeed been taught nothing at all, but these also the Charity Schools and the Wesleyan mission were striving to raise out of ignorance to the mental level of understanding Christians.

English Eighteenth Century religion both within the Establishment and among the Dissenting bodies, was of two schools, which we may call for brevity the Latitudinarian and the Methodist. If either is left out of the foreground, the social landscape of that age is wrongly delineated. Each of these two complementary systems had its own function ;

each had the defects of its qualities, which the other made good. The Latitudinarian stood for the spirit of Tolerance, for lack of which Christianity had for centuries past wrought cruel havoc in the world it set out to save ; the Latitudinarian stood also for Reasonableness in the interpretation of religious doctrines, without which they were unlikely to be received by the more scientific modern mind. Methodism, on the other hand, renewed the self-discipline and the active zeal without which religion loses its power and forgets its purpose ; and this new evangelism was allied to an active philanthropy. Both the Latitudinarianism and the Methodism of that era have suffered change with the changing times. But the principles which they respectively rescued and embodied have flourished in new forms and combinations, which preserved religion as a powerful force in English life through many changing generations.

Ever since the Revolution, political circumstances had favoured the Latitudinarians. And after the accession of George I the Whig statesmen, who held the keys of higher Church patronage, felt specially bound to protect the Hanoverian dynasty by encouraging the broader churchmanship of scholar statesmen like Gibson and Wake and even of the questionable Hoadly, and discouraging ' enthusiasm,' which in Walpole's day meant the High Church and Jacobite fanaticism of Atterbury and Sacheverell. As the Century wore on, ' enthusiasm ' of all sorts, including Wesley's, was regarded as bad form by the clergy of the Establishment and by the upper class.

By the time that George III ascended the throne, the Church was fully reconciled to the House of Hanover, and the political motive for Latitudinarianism ceased to operate. But the movement continued, driven forward by its own momentum and by forces deeper than political. Locke and Newton ruled from their graves. The increasingly scientific spirit of the age demanded that ' the reasonableness of Christianity' should be proved and emphasized. The miraculous seemed less actual, and to some less credible. ' Unalterable law ' in the Universe, such as the law of gravitation which preserved the stars from wrong, was now regarded as an attribute of God's glory.

The spacious firmament on high,
With all the blue Ethereal sky,
And spangled Heavens, a shining frame
Their great Original proclaim.
Th' unwearied Sun, from day to day,
Does his Creator's Power display
And publishes to every land
The work of an Almighty hand.

That hymn of Addison's had appeared in the *Spectator* in
1712, but it echoed down the Century, till young Coleridge
and Wordsworth ' took up the wondrous tale.' [1]

It was easy for such a religion to slide into Unitarianism
or Deism.   Indeed, the English Presbyterian body largely
became Unitarian, with the philosopher and scientist
Priestley as its leading man.   In previous centuries religion
had been, first and foremost, dogma.   Now, it was fashionable to preach it as morality, with a little dogma apologetically
attached.   The religion of the Established Church has been
thus described by Canon Charles Smyth :

In the Anglican Church of the Eighteenth Century, the dominant
influence was that of Archbishop Tillotson (1630–1694).   His
legacy was partly good and partly evil.   On the one hand, he established as the idiom of the English pulpit, in an age in which our
churches, like the great churches of the friars in the later Middle
Ages, were designedly ' fitted for auditories,' a plain, practical and
perspicuous prose.   The triumph of the Tillotsonian style marked a
decisive break with the traditional forms of pulpit oratory, deriving
from the mediaeval Church.   Latimer, Andrewes, Donne and
Taylor were all, in their different ways, essentially mediaeval.   It is
possible to see how Tillotson saved Anglican homiletics from
degenerating into a morass of pedantry and affectation.   On the
other hand, the content of his preaching was little more than a
prudential morality, based rather on reason than on revelation, and
appealing deliberately to sober common sense.   The Gospel of Moral
Rectitude rendered to the English character a service which only
bigotry would ignore ; for ' if, as is the case, the Englishman wherever
he is placed, carried with him a sense of duty, this is due to Tillot-
sonianism.' (Baring Gould.)   Yet it falls far short of the Christian

---

[1] *Cf.* Coleridge's *Hymn before Sun-rise, in the Vale of Chamouni.*   For Wordsworth's relation to Locke, etc., see Mr. Basil Willey's *Seventeenth Century Background*, chap. XII, and his later and equally valuable work *The Eighteenth Century
Background.*

gospel : although it still sits enthroned, as our true National Religion, if not in the pulpits of the Church of England, at least in the consciences of English men and English women. (*The Priest as Student*, S.P.C.K., 1939, pp. 263-264.)

In the early years of George III, the parson was rising in the social and cultural scale, living on equal terms with the gentry as never before. But he was not for that any more in touch with the bulk of his parishioners. His sermons, carefully composed, were read from the pulpit as literary exercises, meant to flatter the taste of the elegant young people who sat in the high pew around the slumbering squire, but too abstract and impersonal to move the patient rustic audience in the body of the church. And in the new industrial and mining districts the neglected inhabitants altogether escaped the ministrations of the Establishment, whose antiquated geography was seldom brought up to date by the creation of new parishes. That mission field was left to Wesley.

It was natural that an aristocratic, unreforming, individualistic, ' classical ' age should be served by a Church with the same qualities and defects as the other chartered institutions of the country. There was perfect liberty for the individual parson to act according to his own lights, however eccentric. He might have as many twists in his mind as Laurence Sterne ; he might even, if he were so ill bred, be a ' methodist ' like Cowper's dangerous friend, John Newton, or Berridge of Everton whose preaching threw the people of his own and other men's parishes into the physical agonies of conversion. More often the parson was a ' typical Englishman,' kindly, sensible, mildly pious. It was a Church renowned for scholarship, culture and freedom. But little pressure was exerted either by episcopal authority or by public opinion to compel the clergy to exert themselves more than they wished.[1]

[1] To understand the English Eighteenth Century Church, and the country life of which it was an essential part, read the *Diaries* of the Rev. James Woodforde, beginning with Mr. John Beresford's introduction. The receipt of his tithe and the working of his own glebe farm kept parson Woodforde in touch with agricultural life.

' 1776, Sep. 14. Very busy all day with my barley, did not dine till 5 in the after noon, my harvest men dined here today, gave them some beef and some plumb Pudding and as much liquor as they would drink. This evening finished

A living was regarded, like a seat in Parliament or a
College Fellowship, as ' a piece of patronage ' awarded as a
favour and enjoyed as a privilege. An amusing illustration
of this way of thought is found in the following epitaph,
recorded in Nichols' *Literary Anecdotes* (III, p. 52) :

> Here rests all that was mortal of Mrs Elizabeth Bate,
> Relict of the Reverend Richard Bate,
> A woman of unaffected piety
> And exemplary virtue.
>
> She was honourably descended
> And by means of her Alliance to
> The illustrious family of Stanhope
> She had the merit to obtain
> For her husband and children
> Twelve several employments
> In Church and State.
> She died June 7, 1751, in the 75th year of her age.

It was characteristic of the age that Gibbon in his Autobiography records a passing regret that he ' had not embraced
the lucrative pursuits of the law or of trade, the chances of
civil office or India (sic) adventure, *or even the fat slumbers
of the Church.*' Ecclesiastical history written by Archdeacon Gibbon would have been as scholarly and as volu-
minous, but would perforce have been even more decorous
and subtly ironical than the actual masterpiece of Edward
Gibbon, Esquire.

The social gulf between rich and poor clergy was still
almost as wide as in mediaeval times. But the proportion
of the well-to-do was greater, for they now included not only
prelates and pluralists, but a number of resident parish
clergy of good family and connections, living in the parsonage and attending to its duties. The rise in the value of
tithes and glebe farms, with the improvement of agriculture,
helped this development. In Queen Anne's reign, out
of some 10,000 livings, as many as 5597 had been worth
less than £50 a year ; a hundred years later only 4000 were
below £150. Throughout the Eighteenth Century,
country gentlemen came more and more to regard livings

---

my harvest, and all carried into the Barn—8 acres. Dec. 3. My frolic for my
people to pay tithe to me this day. I gave them a good dinner, surloin of beef
roasted, a leg of mutton boiled and plumb puddings in plenty.'

in their gift as worth the acceptance of their younger sons. The ideal arrangement, well established by the time of Jane Austen, as her readers know, was a good Rectory, with a bow window, built in a pleasant spot a mile from the manor-house, and inhabited by a son or son-in-law of the squire. The family group was kept together in that way, and the religious needs of the village were served by a gentleman, of education and refinement though perhaps of no great zeal—for it was only after the beginning of the Nineteenth Century that the gentleman-parson was likely to be ' serious,' that is to say, evangelical.

But half the livings of England were not so endowed as to support a squire's son. There was still a large class of poor parsons, though not so numerous as in the days of Chaucer, or the days of Charles II when Eachard had written his *Grounds and Occasions of the Contempt of the Clergy*, of which the chief were their poverty and their lowly birth. But even in the reign of George III there were still thousands of impoverished and despised ' black-coats,' occupying livings of fifty to a hundred pounds a year, or drawing salaries of fifty pounds as curates to absentee pluralists. Pluralism was not, however, always an abuse, for often the best arrangement possible was that a single clergyman should serve two neighbouring parishes, neither of which could by itself support a parson.

The Bishops, almost without exception, were either relations of noblemen, or former chaplains to noblemen or tutors to their sons. Some of them, like Joseph Butler, Berkeley and Warburton, were great philosophers or scholars. But none had been raised to the Episcopate for services rendered to the Church, but for services rendered to learning, to lay patrons or to political parties. Church promotion, like many other good things, had been swept into the net of Whig and Tory party patronage, which had succeeded the royal patronage of times gone by. In the Middle Ages the Bishops had been the King's civil servants ; now their secular duties had been cut down to regular attendance at the sessions of Parliament, to vote for the Minister who had appointed them and who might yet promote them—for some Bishoprics were worth ten times as much a year as others.

But the Eighteenth Century prelate, having discharged his Parliamentary duties, had more leisure to devote to his ecclesiastical functions than those mediaeval Bishops could afford who had been whole-time servants of the Crown. Some, though by no means all, of the Hanoverian Bishops laboured arduously in their dioceses, especially on journeys over long, bad roads to confirm the faithful. Between 1768 and 1771 the Archbishop of York laid his hands on the heads of 41,600 candidates for confirmation, and the Bishop of Exeter in 1764–1765 confirmed 41,642 in Cornwall and Devon alone. It is impossible in face of such figures, to say that the Bishops were entirely neglectful of their ecclesiastical duties, or that the religious zeal of the population ran wholly into the Wesleyan mission. There is much evidence that Church life, in many districts at least, was strong and vigorous. Nevertheless, there was elsewhere much laxity and neglect. At any rate, the aristocratic clergy we have described were more often examples of the Latitudinarian merits than of the Methodist virtues.

The way of life which came to be called ' Methodism ' was older than its name and older than the mission of the Wesley brothers. As boys, they had been brought up in its atmosphere in the Epworth rectory of their High Church father. It was a way of life devoted not only to religious observance but to self-discipline and work for others. It was seen to perfection in the lay non-juror Robert Nelson, and it inspired those Churchmen and Dissenters who collaborated with him during the reigns of William and Anne in founding the Society for Promoting Christian Knowledge and the Charity Schools. It was seen to advantage in the strict, beneficent life of the charming Lady Elizabeth Hastings (1682–1739), immortalized by Steele's epigram ' to love her was a liberal education ' ; she devoted her great wealth to charity, in particular to well-devised schemes for the schooling and the University education of poor scholars. ' Methodism ' in one form or another inspired much of the philanthropic work of the century that ended with Wilberforce.

This ' method' of religious life was widely spread among

the trading and professional classes, whether Church or Dissent. It was at once Puritan and Middle Class in character ; it was even stronger among the laity than the clergy ; its devotees were not withdrawn from the business of life but strove to dedicate it to God. ' Conduct, not dogma, stamped the Puritan of the Eighteenth Century. . . He was irresistibly drawn towards the service of man, who through misery or ignorance, or debauchery, deprived God of the glory that was His due. To men of such a mould charity was obligatory.' [1] The citadel of this way of life was the middle-class home, with its family worship, whence it went out to convert the souls, educate the minds and care for the bodies of the neglected poor.

The greatest and most justly famous of the manifestations of ' methodism ' was the revivalist preaching of the Wesleys and Whitefield, which deeply moved a vast mass of human beings hitherto neglected by Church and State. And fortunately John Wesley's genius lay not only in his power as a revivalist preacher but in his gifts as an organizer. By forming his converts into permanent congregations he began a new chapter in the religious, social and educational history of the working class. The coincidence in time of Wesley and the Industrial Revolution had profound effects upon England for generations to come.

The ' steady laicisation of religion ' was the logical outcome of the Protestant atmosphere of the England of that day. The active part taken by the laity, individually and collectively, in religious organization and philanthropic work related thereto had been marked in the days of Robert Nelson under Queen Anne, and was yet more in evidence a hundred years later, particularly among the Wesleyan congregations.

Another important contribution made to modern English religion by the Eighteenth Century was the hymn-book. Isaac Watts (1674–1748), John Wesley's brother Charles and others of less note, produced a body of hymns which, alike in Church and Chapel, gradually displaced the metrical

---

[1] Miss Jones' *The Charity School Movement* (Cambridge Press, 1938), pp. 6–7 and *passim*. That remarkable book and Professor Norman Sykes' chapter in *Johnson's England* (Oxford Press, 1933), and his *Birkbeck Lectures* for 1931–33 and *Life of Gibson* throw new light on Eighteenth Century religion.

version of the psalms in popularity with congregations who loved to make a joyful noise before the Lord.

Among other ways of dedicating life to God and man was the quiet work of the Quakers. They left to Wesley the task of popular revivalism, wherein they themselves had laboured so fervently in the days of their founder. They had now settled down into bourgeois respectability, redeemed by the spirit of love that permeated with its pure influence the exclusive but philanthropic society of Friends. Early in the reign of George II they were already famous for their knack of prospering in honestly conducted business ; the poet Matthew Green, who died in 1737, had written of the Quakers and their unorthodox doctrines :

> They, who have lands, and safe bank stock,
> With faith so founded on a rock,
> May give a rich invention ease
> And construe scripture how they please.

The Friends had ceased to be a scandal to Mr. Worldly Wiseman, and had become an accepted national institution.

The humanitarian spirit of the Eighteenth Century with the care it bestowed on the bodies and minds of the poor and the unfortunate, made a real advance towards better things. But even so it had its faults. The foundation of hospitals and the improvement of medical service and infant welfare were pure gain. But the educational work done, valuable as it was, is more open to retrospective criticism. The Charity Schools, followed by the Sunday School movement that took on such large proportions after 1780, were indeed the first systematic attempt to give any education to the bulk of the working people, as distinct from selected clever boys to whom the old Grammar Schools had given opportunity to rise out of their class. The new Charity Schools and Sunday Schools had the merit of trying to do something for all, but they had the demerit of too great an anxiety to keep the young scholars in their appointed sphere of life and train up a submissive generation. Modern education may in our time have gone too far in an opposite direction, creating an unwanted intellectual proletariat. But the Eighteenth Century fault, carried over into the education of the early years of the Nineteenth, was excessive emphasis on the difference of classes and the need for ' due subordination in the lower orders.'

The historian of the Charity Schools has well written :

The Eighteenth Century was marked by a very real sense of pity and responsibility for the children whose physical and spiritual interests were lamentably neglected, coupled with a determination to reform them by application of what Defoe aptly called ' the great law of subordination.' The political and religious unrest of the Seventeenth Century contributed in no small degree to the desire of the upper and middle classes to establish social discipline among the poor, who in contemporary opinion were peculiarly susceptible to the poison of rebellion and infidelity. . . . But it would be a misreading of the age of benevolence to see in the prominence enjoyed by the principle of subordination a harsh and unsympathetic attitude of the superior to the lower classes. Far from it. The Eighteenth Century was the age of well defined social distinctions, and it used a language in accordance with its social structure.[1]

But in the early Nineteenth Century, the age of Hannah More, too much of the education and charity bestowed on the poor continued to be class-conscious and patronizing, when an equalitarian spirit unknown in the Eighteenth Century was beginning to render such anxious condescension unpalatable and out of touch with the needs and problems of a different age.

> God bless the squire and his relations
> And keep us in our proper stations

was a sentiment that scarcely aroused comment in the days of Sir Roger de Coverley, but this Sunday School attitude became a cause of scoffing and offence after the Industrial Revolution had put an end to the unconscious simplicity of traditional feudalism.

While the Eighteenth Century made a beginning of mass instruction by starting the Charity and Sunday Schools, it lost ground in Secondary Education by permitting many of the old Grammar and endowed schools to decay. It was indeed a general feature of the age that, while private

---

[1] Miss M. G. Jones, *The Charity School Movement*, p. 4. And see Prof. Tawney's review of it in the *Economic History Review* for May 1939.

enterprise and philanthropic zeal opened new paths, chartered institutions grew lazy and corrupt. The resounding defeat of James II's attack on law and chartered rights gave to the hundred years that followed a legal and conservative character that was carried even to excess. To show a charter was to be above criticism. There was no talk of Reform, either of Parliamentary Constituencies, Town Corporations, Universities or Charitable Institutions, until near the end of the Century, and then, alas, ' the unhappy example of France ' made Reform anathema. Just as the co-optive municipal oligarchies spent their corporate revenues on gluttonous feasts and neglected the duties of town government, in the same spirit the headmasters of endowed schools often neglected and in some cases closed their schools and lived on the endowment as if it was their private property.

But the loss thus incurred by Secondary Education was made good by private schools, financed by fees only, which made much progress in the Eighteenth Century. Such schools, including the Dissenters' Academies, supplied at moderate cost a good education, in which living languages and science held a place besides classics. The old endowed schools had no more use than the Universities for such newfangled subjects.

The Dissenting Academies, that contained men of the calibre of Priestley, also to some extent made good the deficiencies of Oxford and Cambridge. The only two Universities in England excluded all who were not churchmen, and gave so bad and so expensive an education to those whom they deigned to admit, that their numbers shrank to miserable proportions, not half what they had been in the days of Laud and Milton.

Indeed, the spirit of chartered monopoly was seen at its worst on the banks of Isis and Cam. The College Don could hold his Fellowship for life, unless he took a Church benefice ; he was not compelled to do any academic work, he was not permitted to marry, and in most Colleges he was forced to take Holy Orders. In their lazy, self-indulgent, celibate clericalism the Dons of the Eighteenth Century resembled the monks of the Fifteenth, and were about as much use. Gibbon, who as a Gentleman

Commoner was admitted to the Fellows' table at Magdalen, Oxford, in 1752, thus describes their habits :

'From the toil of reading or thinking or writing they had absolved their conscience. Their conversation stagnated in a round of college business, Tory politics, personal stories and private scandal ; their dull and deep potations excused the brisk intemperance of youth.'

At both Universities the undergraduates were entirely neglected by the great majority of the Fellows, though here and there a College Tutor zealously performed duties that ought to have been shared by the whole Society. Noblemen's sons and rich Fellow Commoners, who were much in evidence, and for whom large allowance was made in matters of discipline, were often accompanied by private tutors of their own. The Professors of the University seldom performed any of their supposed functions. No lecture was delivered by any Regius Professor of Modern History at Cambridge between 1725 and 1773 ; ' the third and most scandalous ' of the holders of that Chair died in 1768 from a fall while riding home drunk from his Vicarage at Over.

At Oxford, by 1770, no serious examination at all was held for a degree. At Cambridge the Mathematical Tripos offered a real test for the rival merits of the more ambitious candidates for honours. Gibbon indeed declared ' Cambridge appears to have been less deeply infected than her sister with the vices of the Cloyster : her loyalty to the House of Hanover is of a more early date, and the name and philosophy of her immortal Newton were first honoured in his native Academy.'

The movement of internal reform, by which the two Universities put themselves upon the road of self-improvement, only began in the very last years of the Century. It may be dated in Trinity, Cambridge, from the crisis of 1787, when it was decided after a severe struggle which carried the disputants before the judgment seat of the Lord Chancellor, that its Fellowships must be justly awarded according to the results of a careful examination. After that change, the College at length drew ahead of its rival St. John's in numbers and academic pre-eminence, though the College of Wordsworth and Wilberforce continued to produce men of great distinction.

The notorious Jacobitism of Oxford under the first two Georges had been highly significant of the limitation of the power of government, and the immunity secured to the subject by charter and the rule of law. Church patronage was in the hands of the Whig Ministers, who would sooner have made a Mohammedan than a Jacobite Bishop. But the Oxford and Cambridge Colleges were outside their jurisdiction, and the failure of James II's attack on the Universities was a red-light warning which preserved academic liberty in England from interference by future governments. If Oxford Dons, after securing their emoluments by taking Hanoverian oaths, chose to get fuddled on Jacobite toasts, King George's Ministers could do nothing about it. In this manner the essential liberty of the Universities, which had been infringed in various degrees by Tudors, Stuarts and Cromwellians, was established by Eighteenth Century practice. In some respects this immunity was abused, but we may thank God that it was preserved, when we consider the state of slavery into which academic life has fallen in countries which had no such venerable tradition of the rule of law and the liberty of the subject.[1]

Yet in spite of the decadence of the only two Universities that then existed in England, in spite of the decay of the endowed schools specially charged with secondary education, the intellectual life of the country was never more brilliant, and the proportion of men of genius per head of population in the irregularly educated England of George III was immensely greater than in our own day. It would seem that the very highest products of the human mind are the outcome of chance and freedom and variety rather than of uniform organization—of the balance of town and country rather than the dead weight of life in great cities, of literature rather than of journalism, of arts and crafts rather than of the machine. But even if the future can never again produce giants like Burke, Gibbon and Johnson, let alone Milton, Newton and Wren, the number of educated people capable of enjoying an

[1] For the Universities at this period see A. D. Godley's *Oxford in the 18th Century*; C. E. Mallet, *History of the University of Oxford*, vol. III; D. Winstanley, *Unreformed Cambridge*; Gunning's *Reminiscences of Cambridge from the year* 1780. For Oxford in 1774-5 an intimate and delightful picture will be found in Parson Woodforde's *Diaries*.

intellectual life of some kind may yet be greater than in the past.

In the Eighteenth Century the Welsh people recovered, through the instrumentality of religion and education, the consciousness of a spiritual and intellectual life of their own, separate from that of England.   The story is singular as well as important.

The Welsh-Englishman, Henry VIII, intended by his political union of the two countries to make the Welsh a part of the English people on free and equal terms.   To a large extent he succeeded, because there was no English exploitation of the land and its inhabitants as in Ireland, nor did religion divide the two races.   The Welsh gentry in Tudor times adopted the English language, outlook and literature, and ceased to patronize the native Bards.   The peasants, having no other leadership, acquiesced ; but they continued to speak their own tongue, and to sing its songs to the harp.

In Elizabeth's reign the Church, by translating the Bible and Prayer Book into Welsh, began unconsciously to counteract the Anglicizing policy of the State.   That was the seed of much that followed, but it was long ere the full harvest came up.   English Puritanism of the Cromwellian type did not attract the Welsh, who remained Cavalier so far as they took any side at all.   King Charles's regiments of foot who perished at Naseby came for the most part from the hills of Wales.

When the Eighteenth Century opened, the smaller Welsh squires, like their counterparts in England, were being bought out by the larger landlords.   Wales was becoming, legally, a land of great estates ; but in its fundamental social structure it was a land of small peasant farms ; they averaged thirty to a hundred acres each, they were held on short or annual leases, and were devoted to the old-fashioned subsistence agriculture, feeding the families who cultivated them, rather than serving the market.   There were few big farmers, and few middle-class people of any sort.   Under the cloak of the great estate system, Wales was in reality an equalitarian democracy of peasant farmers ; and in South Wales there were miners as well.

Wales was a land of old enclosure, like other Western and

Celtic parts of the island. The open-field system had never existed there, except in those parts of Pembrokeshire where the English had settled ; and there too enclosure was now taking place. The ordinary Welsh farms were fenced with stone walls or sod banks.

The traditional ways of these remote and rustic folk were not in Stuart times disturbed by the impact of any emotional movement—social, national, political or religious. They were devoted to their traditional music of harp and song, and their religion consisted largely in the singing of hymns. But they were too illiterate to be in the full current of the Bible-reading Protestantism of the day. Economically, and intellectually, Wales was shut off from English penetration by the geographic difficulties of approach. As late as 1768 Arthur Young described Welsh mountain roads as ' mere rocky lanes, full of hugeous stones as big as one's horse.'

If, then, the Welsh were to have a religious or educational revival of any sort they must make it for themselves ; and they did. Beginning in the reigns of William and Anne and going on throughout the Eighteenth Century, Welsh philanthropists promoted an educational and religious mission among their countrymen. The Methodist Churches eventually became the most important part of Welsh evangelicalism, but it had started before John Wesley was born.

To teach the peasant to read, and to put the Welsh Bible into his hands were the motives of those who established popular education throughout the length and breadth of Wales. In England, too, no doubt, the Charity and Sunday Schools were founded for religious reasons, but they were associated with the more mundane objects of defending the State Church either against Dissenters or against Jacobites, and of training up the children of the poor to be industrious and amenable members of a carefully graded social economy. In the simpler, equalitarian peasant society of Wales no such problems presented themselves, and ' middle-class ' ideas of utility were unknown ; those who founded the Schools desired only to save the souls of men and women, that is to say, to bring them up as Bible-reading, evangelical Christians. This object was achieved, and at the same time the Welsh people, by becoming literate, had new vistas of intellectual and national culture opened to them, coloured always by religion but spreading out into other spheres.

The historian of the Charity Schools, herself a Welsh woman, has written : [1]

'It would be difficult to exaggerate the importance and effect of the Charity School movement upon the history and character of the Welsh people. The steady concentration upon piety as the aim and end of all instruction changed a gay and simple people, indifferent in religion and lacking in political consciousness, into a people whose dominant interests were religious and political. The Bible had become the Welshman's manual. Its language was his language, its teaching dominated his social and political life. In it, and in the hymns of Williams of Pantycelyn, the emotional and intellectual interests of the peasantry found satisfaction.

The political influence of the Charity School movement was no less important. Modern Welsh nationalism is the child of the literary and linguistic renaissance of the Eighteenth Century, and in this, as in the religious revival, the charity school movement played a part of chief importance. Before the schools began their work, Welsh, once ' the language of princes and poets,' was in danger of destruction. By the end of the Eighteenth Century it was again the medium of poetry and prose, no longer princely, but bearing upon it the marks of its peasant origin and pious inspiration.'

[1] *The Charity School Movement, A Study of Eighteenth Century Puritanism in Action.* M. G. Jones, Fellow of Girton College, 1938, p. 321.

CHAPTER XII

DR. JOHNSON'S ENGLAND

II

The Agricultural and Industrial Revolutions begin—Improved communications—Overseas Trade—The City.

ALTHOUGH ' the Industrial Revolution ' is by far the most important movement in social history since the Saxon conquest, it is as difficult to say when it began as to decide when ' the Middle Ages ' came to an end. Capitalism, coal, transoceanic commerce, factories, machinery, and trade unions had all, as we have seen, had their part in English life long before the Hanoverian epoch. But the last half of the Eighteenth Century is regarded as the time when industrial change, stimulated by scientific invention and a rising population, entered decisively on that headlong career that shows no sign of slackened pace to-day.

With similar qualifications we may ascribe ' the Agricultural Revolution ' to the Eighteenth Century. The immense increase then brought about in the agrarian productiveness of the island was rendered necessary by the rapid growth of its population, which in those days could not have been fed from overseas. This pressing national need was successfully met and exploited, owing to the peculiar social and economic conditions of the time. In the Eighteenth Century the landlords as a class were able and willing to devote their personal attention and their accumulated wealth to the improvement of the land and the methods of cultivation. The capital created by the incipient industrial revolution was much of it conducted by the channel of the great-estate system to fertilize agriculture with money derived from cloth, cotton, coal and commerce. But capital also flowed in the opposite direction, from land into industry : many of the new industrialists who set up factories, mills and businesses in the Eighteenth Century, derived the money they so employed from their own or

171

their fathers' success as cultivators of the land. The County Banks, now growing up in great numbers, assisted this double flow of capital from industry into agriculture and from agriculture into industry.

Indeed, the connection of the agricultural with the industrial revolution was more than a coincidence in time. Each helped on the other. They may indeed be regarded as a single effort by which society was so reconstructed as to be able to feed and employ a population that was rising in numbers with unexampled rapidity, owing to improved medical conditions.[1]

The changes effected in a hundred years may be summarized by contrasting the situation in the reigns of George II and George IV.

When George II (1727–1760) began to reign, manufacture was a function of country life. The ' manufacturers ' —a term then used to describe not the capitalist employers but the hand-workers themselves—inhabited ordinary villages each of which supplied its own clothes, implements, and buildings of the commoner kind, as well as its own bread, meat and beer. Only the ' gentleman's seat,' in the park near at hand, sent to the county capital or to London for its best furniture, its books, china and other amenities in an age of taste and expense, and its more refined wants for the table, though its ordinary food still came off the estate.

Moreover, many rustic villages manufactured not only cheap goods for their own use, but some special line of luxury goods for the market. To take one example out of very many : I possess an Eighteenth Century grandfather clock, still keeping good time, which was made in the small Warwickshire village of Prior's Marston. The woollen cloth, which still constituted the chief item in home and foreign trade, was still manufactured, as regards the main

---

[1] In Eighteenth Century Ireland the population rose even faster, from about one and a half millions to four millions. But social conditions and racial characteristics in that island were not favourable to economic change, and instead of industrial or agricultural revolution, there was chronic starvation and frequent famine among the potato-fed population, culminating in the disaster of 1847.

In a well-known passage of the *Wealth of Nations* (Bk. I, ch. xi), Adam Smith connected the physical strength and beauty of the Irish in London with the potato diet of their own land ! Whether he was right about that or not, potatoes were an easy but dangerous way of feeding a vast population.

processes in the countryside, and the rapidly growing cotton industry was conducted in the cottage. The towns took some part in the manufacture, but were chiefly distributing centres : Bristol and Norwich disposed of cloth made in Cotswold and East Anglian villages ; Leeds and Halifax sold goods woven in the stone farms or cottages each with its field and cow, scattered along the steep sides of the Yorkshire clothing dales.

The towns of early Hanoverian England subsisted, not so much by the goods they themselves manufactured, as by their markets, their shops and their commerce. London indeed was industrial as well as commercial, and already displayed many characteristics of modern ' great city ' life. Birmingham had always been a town of small industries. And the ports had a sea-life of their own, from great Bristol and its growing rival Liverpool, to little Fowey and Aldeburgh, whose best days already lay in the past. But most other towns were appanages of the countryside which each served. They had forgotten the jealous civic patriotism of the walled mediaeval burgh, and had lost the manufacturing monopoly of its gilds. They were markets for farmers, and meeting-places to which the gentry and their families resorted to shop, to dance and to conduct the affairs of the County. Many squires of the middling sort, especially those who lived more than a hundred miles from the capital, not being able to afford a ' London season,' built themselves good houses in or around the county town, whither their families, on matrimonial hopes intent, migrated from their rural homes for a part of every year. Cathedral cities flourished deferentially in the venerable shadow of clerical patronage. But larger county towns such as Newcastle-on-Tyne and Norwich were, in addition, entrepôts of national trade.

The England over which George IV reigned (1820–1830) was already very different. By that time there had grown up, especially in the West Midlands and the North, a new portent—a number of ' manufacturing towns ' and urban districts, given over to factories and machine industry, quite dissociated from the rural life of the country around. The harmonious fabric of old English society suffered a perpendicular cleavage between town and country, as well

N

as expanding the old lateral cleavage between rich and poor. It is true that at that date the harsh distinction between rural and urban life was still confined to certain regions; but during the reign of Victoria it became universal.

A corresponding change in country life itself was already far advanced in the reign of George IV. The manufacture of specialized goods, including many processes of cloth and cotton manufacture, had left the country cottages for the factory regions. The improvement of roads had abolished the need for a self-sufficing village, and dwellers in the country now bought in the town articles which their fathers and mothers had made for themselves. Many a village tailor, carpenter, brewer, miller and harness-maker found his occupation gone. The huswife's spindle seldom now twirled on the cottage floor : the term ' spinster ' was becoming an anachronism. And the modern farmer produced corn and meat primarily for the town market, only secondarily for home consumption.

By 1820 the ' agricultural revolution ' had enclosed the open fields into rectangular hedged fields, where scientific rotation of crops and of pasture could be conducted, and fat stock fed up to a size and weight undreamed of in earlier times. Hundreds of thousands of acres of waste and old woodland had also been enclosed for arable.[1] Even the familiar figure of the highwayman had gone from the macadamized roads, since the heaths and thickets where he lurked had been ploughed up. The orderly new ' plantations ' were guarded by gamekeepers, man-traps and spring guns.

The changes so effected have been called in retrospect ' the agricultural revolution,' because they worked not by expansion of an old economic and social system but by the creation of a new one. Great compact estates cultivated in large farms by leasehold tenants employing landless labourers covered more and more of the acreage of England, at the expense of various forms of petty cultivation and ownership. Small squires, and peasants with diminutive rights in the soil were bought out to make room for the new order. The open fields of the great midland corn area were enclosed

---

[1] If Gregory King's estimate (1696) and the Board of Agriculture return of 1795 are approximately correct, two million acres had been added to the agricultural land of England and Wales in a hundred years.

into the chess-board pattern of fenced fields which has ever since been the hall-mark of the English landscape. And even in the half of England where enclosed fields had always been the rule, analogous social changes were taking place. For everywhere the larger owners were consolidating their estates by purchase ; everywhere squires and farmers were busy with new methods. And everywhere better roads, canals and machines were diverting industry from cottage and village to factory and town, thereby cutting off the peasant family from spinning and other small manufacturing activities by which its meagre budget had been eked out.

Taking into account the great variety of local conditions, it is true to say of England as a whole that enclosure was only one, but possibly the most important, of the many changes that combined to reduce the numbers of the independent peasantry, while increasing the aggregate wealth of the countryside.[1]

These changes were still going forward apace in the era of Trafalgar and Waterloo, but they had set in on a great scale between 1740 and 1789, and the whole process may therefore be considered in this chapter. When completed it had changed the immemorial manner of life in rural England.

In the reigns of the later Stuarts and George I the enclosure of open fields, commons and waste was proceeding rapidly, by agreement between the parties concerned or by purchase ; but enclosure was still a local expedient rather than a national policy. But after the third decade of the Eighteenth Century the work began to be carried on by a

---

[1] In the Lake District, Wordsworth observed that between 1770 and 1820 the number of the freehold ' statesmen ' was halved and the size of their holdings doubled : the little farms were amalgamated, because they proved insufficient to support families when the invention of the ' spinning jenny ' concentrated spinning in factories and so took away profitable work from the peasant's wife and children. Thus the change was not in that district due to enclosure, for the dales had long before been covered by a network of stone walls which the small freeholders themselves had erected round their own fields.

In the Midland shires, on the other hand, enclosure of the open fields was a determining cause of the disappearance of many small peasants with rights in the land. On the other hand, even in Midland and Eastern counties, enclosure did not by any means always reduce the number of owner cultivators of the yeoman type ; see Clapham, I, pp. 103-105, and J. D. Chambers' article in *Ec. Hist. Rev.*, Nov. 1940.

new and more wholesale procedure : private Acts of Parliament were passed which overrode the resistance of individual proprietors to enclosure ; each had to be content with the land or the money compensation awarded to him by Parliamentary Commissioners whose decisions had the force of law. Batches of these revolutionary Acts were hurried through every Parliament of George III (1760–1820), assemblies not otherwise famous for radical legislation. But this was the radicalism of the rich, often at the expense of the poor.

The pace of the enclosure of land grew more rapid every decade from 1740 onwards, and was fastest of all at the turn of the century. By the time Victoria came to the throne the work of enclosing the open cornfields was nearly complete, though the enclosure of commons continued for the first thirty years of her reign. The area seriously affected by the enclosure Acts comprised about half the English Counties, running south from the East Riding of Yorkshire through Lincoln and Norfolk and the Midland Shires to Wilts and Berks. More than half the total acreage of Northamptonshire was enclosed by Act of Parliament, and over forty per cent. of Hunts, Beds, Oxford, and the East Riding ; Leicester and Cambridge Shires were not far behind.

But Kent, Essex, Sussex, the Northern and Western Counties and Wales were little affected by the Enclosure Acts, because so much of their acreage consisted either of fields enclosed many ages ago, or else of moorland pastures so extensive that no one could afford to enclose them until the age of wire fencing. Thus not two per cent. of the area of Northumberland came under the Enclosure Acts, although precisely at this period its landlords were investing great sums of Tyneside capital in agricultural improvement.

For the age of enclosure was also the age of new methods of draining, drilling, sowing, manuring, breeding and feeding cattle, making of roads, rebuilding of farm premises and a hundred other changes, all of them requiring capital. Ever since the Restoration there had been a rapidly increasing movement to accumulate land in large compact estates ; the magnates of the realm, the great political Peers, owned a much larger, and the lesser rustic squires a much smaller acreage of England in 1760 than in 1660.

The landlord class had therefore more capital and more credit to devote to the now fashionable cause of agricultural improvement.

Owners of large compact estates took the lead—men like 'turnip Townshend,' the retired statesman early in George II's reign ; and forty years later ' Coke of Norfolk,' the friend of Fox and enemy of George III. Both Townshend and Coke introduced into Norfolk new crops and new methods—above all, root crops and the marling of light land. Their example put their backward county at the head of English agriculture. Between 1776 and 1816 Coke so improved his land as to raise the rental of his Holkham estates from £2200 to £20,000 a year, and yet make the fortunes of the tenants who paid these higher rents ; he granted them the security of long leases on strict terms as to cultivation. And according to radical Cobbett, they spoke of their landlord as affectionate children speak of their parents. His ' sheepshearings ' at Holkham became famous all over Europe, and were attended by agricultural experts who gathered, sometimes six hundred together, in that remote corner of Norfolk, to see how land should be farmed and sheep fed. Eighty of the visitors at a time could be taken under the roof of their princely host, and the rest were billeted in the neighbouring farms.

Townshend and Coke had imitators among their brother landlords in every shire. And the farmers of the new type, like Robert Bakewell of Leicestershire, breeder of improved sheep and cattle, were themselves active innovators. The net result was a great increase in the amount of corn produced for the national consumption as bread and beer, and an even greater increase in the numbers and size of the animals. For much of the best land in England, hitherto cultivated in vast open cornfields where the cattle strayed among the stubble in search of food, was now enclosed in moderate-sized fields divided by hawthorn hedges, wherein beasts could be pastured on good grass. And at the same time much more of the arable land was used for raising crops such as artificial grass and roots, to feed the cattle and sheep through the winter.

And so, for the first time since mankind took to farming, the wholesale slaughter of stock at the end of autumn ceased.

Salted meat was replaced by fresh beef and mutton. The immediate result was that scurvy and other skin diseases, which had afflicted even the noblest households like the Russells and Verneys in the Seventeenth Century, grew rare even among the poor. The new facilities for feeding animals all the year round encouraged landlords and farmers to purchase pedigree stock and to study scientific breeding. The average weight of cattle and sheep sold at Smithfield doubled between 1710 and 1795.[1]

Nor was this astonishing increase in the production of beef and mutton made at the price of any diminution of arable. On the contrary, the output of wheat and barley was for a long while able to supply bread and beer for a home population that nearly doubled itself in the course of the Century, while the corn bounties kept up English exports ; it was only in the last half of the Century that, as the population rose even more rapidly, the imports of grain from abroad gradually equalled and then passed the quantity exported.

The improvement of land was carried to such a point that wheat was grown where only rye, oats or barley could be grown before. The soil and climate of England is only in a few regions, chiefly in East Anglia, suited to the cultivation of wheat. Yet such was now the artificial improvement of the land by capital supplied by the great estates, that in the course of the Eighteenth Century, Englishmen of all classes became so dainty as to insist on refined wheat bread that had previously been regarded as a luxury of the rich. This new demand began in the town but spread to the country, even to paupers. The abandonment of the coarser wholemeal breadstuffs was bad for the purity of the loaves actually provided by dishonest bakers, bad for the health and bad for the teeth of the English race. But it was a proof of the efficacy of capitalist high-farming.[2]

---

[1] Equally remarkable was the improvement in all kinds of horses in Eighteenth Century England. In the Stuart era the English had gone to Arabia and Barbary for sires to their race-horses and hunters. In the reign of George III all the world came to England for horses, from the race-horse to the hardly less noble cart-horse. The horse was then essential to sport, travel and agriculture, and to all these the English gentlemen of the age were devoted.

[2] *The Englishman's Food*, J. C. Drummond and A. Wilbraham (1939), pp. 157, 195, 222–226 ; *The Bread of our Fathers*, Sir William Ashley, 1928.

The social price paid for economic gain was a decline in the number of independent cultivators and a rise in the number of landless labourers. To a large extent this was a necessary evil, and there would have been less harm in it if the increased dividend of the agricultural world had been fairly distributed. But while the landlord's rent, the parson's tithe, and the profits of farmer and middleman all rose apace, the field-labourer, deprived of his little rights in land and his family's by-employments in industry, received no proper compensation in high wages, and in the Southern Counties too often sank into a position of dependence and pauperism.

The rapid rise in the numbers of the population kept down the market price of labour, at the very time when the labourer was losing his independent sources of livelihood. The wage-earner of George III's reign could therefore make no such bargain for a living wage as his forbears in the reign of Edward III had been able to make, when the Black Death had rendered labour scarce. Moreover, the poor were now unarmed and untrained to war. ' Bows and bills ' no longer rendered the commonalty formidable as in the period of the rising of 1381 : in those days they had not been afraid, in spite of Parliamentary Statutes, to come out again and again, with old archers at their head, on strike for the wages and the rights they claimed.

Nor could the hard case of the peasant any longer win such ready hearing from statesmen and publicists as during the far less extensive enclosures of Tudor times. Enclosure had then been regarded as a public crime ; now it was regarded as a public duty. Without sympathy from the classes that were framing the Enclosure Acts, the peasant was unable to state his own case with effect. If he lost his strip in the open cornfield, or the pasture for his cow upon the common, the few guineas given him in exchange were soon dissipated in the public house. Even if the Parliamentary Commissioner awarded him some distant acre of land in lieu of his common rights, how could he afford to enclose and drain it ? He could only sell it again cheap to the big men, engaged in sharing out the new compact farms that were taking the place of the common and the open field. For they alone could afford to fence and drain at their own charges, as an investment of capital that might some day bring large returns.[1]

In future, to farm the land of England one must either have capital of one's own or have behind one the capital of others. The tenant farmer benefited by his landlord's capital and both had resort to loans from the Bank. The English banking system grew with the enclosure of land, for even the wealthy did much of their fencing and other improvements on borrowed money. Under such a system the poorest class, who had no credit, had little chance of farming with success, and that chance was further diminished by the too frequent disregard of their interests in the new distribution of the village lands. The enclosure of commons, though very desirable from the point of view of national production, meant depriving the poor man of his cow and geese and often of many other small rights of fuel-cutting and so forth, by which he had eked out an independent livelihood. (Ernle, *English Farming*, pp. 305–307.)

It is, indeed, by no means certain that under the new system the rural poor were worse off materially than they had been in the past (Clapham, *Ec. Hist. Mod. Britain*, Bk. I, chap. IV). But they had less economic independence of squire and farmer. In an aristocratic age that did not seem to signify. But when, in the following era, democracy, armed with new strength in the cities, turned a hard, sharp eye on the 'agricultural interest,' it felt an instinctive dislike for an aristocratic preserve. There was no longer in England, as there still was in other European countries, a peasantry to plead for protection. And so, at the end of Victoria's reign, when the pinch of foreign competition came at last, the urban electorate would listen to no proposal to save British agriculture from ruin.

In the Eighteenth Century, many of those who were

---

[1] The great expense and difficulty of enclosing and draining the land of a village is illustrated in detail in the case of Bourn, described in Gunning's *Reminiscences of Cambridge*, II, pp. 244–250. In addition to the fencing, an entirely new system of draining had to accompany enclosure, when the furrows between the old strips (that had acted as drains as well as boundaries) were filled up. This ridge-and-furrow draining had in the long run been bad for the soil and the enclosers spent much money in levelling the surface and putting drains underground. The ridge was sometimes five feet above the furrow !

divorced from the land by the change of system, went off not unwillingly and made good elsewhere. Of the mercantile, industrial and professional families who grew up and flourished in the new and wealthier England, a large proportion were descended from small squires, yeomen and peasants who had migrated to the towns, with the price of their land in their pockets. The biographies of eminent Victorians often begin with the ' yeoman ancestor.' The Colonies too profited by that sturdy type. Many also of the freehold yeomen retained their own farms and rented other farms besides, rising to greater prosperity through the agricultural changes. The Englishman's instinct to ' better himself' gave the impulse to the rapid growth of wealth, power and intelligence in the country, the towns and oversea. It is only in certain directions that the English are ' a conservative nation.' In the industrial and agricultural ' revolutions' they blazed the trail for the whole world. And because they were the first to tread the new ground, they made some terrible mistakes.[1]

The movement from country to town, alike of men and of manufactures, was conditioned by the improvement of roads and of water carriage. Arthur Young, with the interests of the countryside always at heart, rejoiced to note that when a good turnpike road was made, opening out new markets and enabling new ideas to circulate by the come-and-go of more frequent travel, rents in the district soon rose with the improvement of agriculture. On the other hand, he saw and deplored the beginning of that ' rural exodus' which has been going on ever since. And that also he ascribed to the better roads. In his *Farmer's Letters* (ed. 1771, p. 353), he wrote :

To find fault with good roads would have the appearance of paradox and absurdity ; but it is nevertheless a fact that giving the power of expeditious travelling depopulates the Kingdom. Young men and women in the country villages fix their eyes on London as the last

---

[1] On the agricultural revolution of the Eighteenth Century see Mr. Orwin's chap. X of *Johnson's England* (1933) ; Mr. East's chap. XIII of Dr. Darby's *Historical Geography of England* (1936) ; Gilbert Slater's *The English Peasantry and the Enclosures of Common Fields* (1907) ; Hammond's *Village Labourer* (1911) ; Lord Ernle, *English Farming*, chaps. vii–xi. For the early Nineteenth Century see Clapham, vol. I, chap. v.

N 2

stage of their hope. They enter into service in the country for little else but to raise money enough to go to London, which was no such easy matter when a stage coach was four or five days in creeping an hundred miles. The fare and the expenses ran high. *But now !* a country fellow, one hundred miles from London, jumps on a coach box in the morning, and for eight or ten shillings gets to town by night, which makes a material difference ; besides rendering the going up and down so easy, the numbers *who have seen London* are increased tenfold, and of course ten times the boasts are sounded in the ears of country fools to induce them to quit their healthy clean fields for a region of dirt, stink and noise.

Without improving communications neither the industrial nor the agricultural revolution could have taken place. The subjects of Queen Anne had great ships in which they sent heavy goods with ease to America and to India, but inside their own island they were still dispatching sacks of coal and hardware strapped to the sides of pack-horses, because wheeled traffic would have stuck in the mud and broken in the ruts of English roads wherever their route crossed a pocket of clay. This state of things had to be changed before much more could be done in the way of economic progress.

There was no effective highway authority, either local or central. Not the county but the parish was charged, most absurdly, with the upkeep of highroads used for the most part by travellers from a distance. The parish naturally scamped the work or left it undone. As it appeared impossible in the Eighteenth Century to reform or readjust local government, recourse was had to private initiative, in which the improving spirit of that age resided. Turnpike companies were granted Parliamentary powers to erect gates and toll bars, and mulct the actual users of the roads, in return for remaking and maintaining some particular stretch of highway. Between 1700 and 1750 as many as four hundred Road Acts were passed ; between 1751 and 1790 sixteen hundred ! This was the principal machinery by which land communications were steadily improved throughout the Hanoverian epoch. There were many stages in the improvement of roads, and as many in the corresponding improvement of vehicles. In the days of Queen Anne, the ' glass coach ' had been tugged along at a walking pace by a team of six horses. By 1750 the stage-coach, drawn by two or four horses, was lighter and more rapid ; but it still had no springs, had heavy wheels like a waggon, carried six inside but had no seats for passengers outside, though the humble were sometimes allowed to cling to the luggage on the roof. Stoppages and overturns were frequent ; and the red-coated guard with his blunderbuss was much in requisition, for the highwayman, still at the height of his glory, could easily ride down any attempt to escape. In 1775 the Norwich coach was waylaid in Epping Forest by seven highwaymen, of whom the guard shot three dead before he was himself killed at his post.

Private carriages, also, gradually became more light and elegant as the roads improved. To drive a lady in a phaeton built for two, with its high wheels and smart pair of horses, was a fashionable diversion in the last part of the Century. For long journeys a usual practice was to hire post-chaises with postilions, especially on main thoroughfares where a regular change of horses could be obtained at the posting inns. The roads were thronged as they had never been in any past age, for while the number of vehicles increased the number of riders had not yet diminished. The degree of social, commercial and intellectual intercourse in the days of Dr. Johnson, due largely to improved traffic, was a cause and a characteristic of the high civilization of the period.[1]

Indeed, a rage for travel seized on Englishmen of all classes, each according to his means. The wealthiest made the grand tour of France and Italy ; after six months or two years spent partly in inns and partly as guests in the houses of the foreign nobility, they returned to their country homes with a rich spoil of pictures and statues, selected by their good taste or foisted on their ignorance. The walls of English manors were crowded with genuine and spurious Old Masters from oversea, side by side with the home products that Reynolds, Romney and Gainsborough were supplying in such profusion. The English ' milords ' (and all English gentlemen were ' milords ' to the foreign inn-keeper) had almost the monopoly of tourist travel in Europe,

---

[1] In 1774 Parson Woodforde paid £4 8s. for a post-chaise from Oxford to Castle Cary in Somerset, a distance of a hundred miles which he performed in a day. This shows the speed but also the expense of ' post-shaying.'

and their requirements became the standard of posting inns from Calais to Naples. In 1785 Gibbon was told that 40,000 English, counting masters and servants, were touring or resident on the Continent.

At home the improved roads carried visitors so far afield that in 1788, according to Wilberforce, ' the banks of the Thames are scarcely more public than those of Windermere,' though as yet no one but the shepherds went up the neighbouring mountains. Owing to better roads and vehicles, Bath in the days of Beau Nash was so crowded with visitors that it was thought worth while to rebuild its streets in a style befitting the solid splendour and comfort of that age. And at the first census of 1801 this fashionable resort was found to contain 30,000 inhabitants and to stand ninth in the list of English cities in order of population.

But the condition of the roads still varied greatly according to the nature of local soils. As late as 1789 the highways in Herefordshire, after the autumnal rains set in, were impassable to waggons and carts, and for half the year the county families could only visit one another on horseback, the young ladies riding pillion behind their brothers ; towards the end of April the surface was levelled by means of ' ploughs,' each drawn by eight or ten horses. (Gunning's *Reminiscences*, I, p. 100.) In most counties, however, such primitive conditions no longer applied to the main highways but only to the by-roads.

By constant experiment in new engineering methods and new road surfaces, Turnpike Trustees finally reached the perfection of Macadam's roads, along which the Tantivy coaches, with relays of horses at the coaching inns, cantered at anything up to ten miles an hour, in the brief interval of highway glory between Waterloo and the Railways. By 1840 there were 22,000 miles of good turnpike roads in England, with nearly 8000 toll gates and side bars.

As the highways improved, the transport of goods progressed at the same steady pace as the traffic of passengers. The waggon first supplemented and at length superseded the pack-horse. One of the commonest sounds upon the road was the chime of bells announcing the approach of a waggon drawn by four great horses, from whose collars the music was suspended. By an unwritten law of the road, the waggon team had precedence, and all other traffic must draw aside to let it pass.

The improvement of ' inland navigation ' was hardly less important than the improvement of roads in opening the way to industrial change. The first half of the Eighteenth Century had been a period of much activity in deepening the navigable rivers and supplying them with locks ; the second half saw the construction of new artificial waterways. The Duke of Bridgewater is known as ' the father of inland navigation,' but he could be more accurately described as the father of English canals, for there had always been ' inland navigation ' on the natural course of rivers : York, Norwich and many other centres of up-country commerce had always depended on their water traffic. (See the map of English rivers at the end of this volume.) His Grace of Bridgewater, like many other Peers, was a coal owner, and took his duties and opportunities as such very seriously. To link up his Worsley collieries with Manchester by canal, this great nobleman in 1759 allied his Parliamentary influence and his capital to the genius of his half-illiterate engineer Brindley. That famous partnership, so characteristic of the English as contrasted with the continental nobility, set going the movement that in the next fifty years netted all England with waterways. Improved engineering technique pierced tunnels through the Pennines and Cotswolds, and carried aqueducts high across river valleys.

The canal movement began in the rapidly developing industrial region of South Lancashire and the West Midlands, and soon spread over the whole country. In the 'sixties, Brindley, supported by his Duke, carried through the remarkable engineering feat of the Manchester-Liverpool Canal. In the following decade they linked the Mersey to the Trent by the Grand Junction Canal : its effect on those parts of the countryside which it served was thus described by Thomas Pennant in 1782 :

The cottage, instead of being half covered with miserable thatch, is now covered with a substantial covering of tiles or slates, brought from the distant hills of Wales or Cumberland. The fields, which before were barren, are now drained, and by the assistance of manure, conveyed on the canal toll-free, are clothed with a beautiful verdure.

Places which rarely knew the use of coal are plentifully supplied with that essential article upon reasonable terms ; and, what is of still greater public utility, the monopolizers of corn are prevented from exercising their infamous trade ; for, communication being opened between Liverpool, Bristol and Hull, and the line of Canal being through countries abundant in grain, it affords a conveyance of corn unknown in past ages.

The canal system and the turnpike roads did more than stimulate the exchange of goods inside the island ; they hastened the growth of overseas trade. Goods from Europe, America, Asia, and Africa could now be distributed in much greater quantities throughout the length and breadth of England ; and they could be more readily purchased abroad by the increased export of coal and manufactured goods. For the heaviest mineral and textile products of the Black country and the Pennines, and the fragile ware of the Staffordshire Potteries could now be easily carried by water to the ports of London, Liverpool, Bristol or Hull for shipment oversea.

In this way the whole character and scope of British commerce began to assume its modern form of supplying necessaries for all, instead of merely luxuries for the rich. In the Middle Ages, England's overseas trade had been a quest for wine, spices, silks and other fashions for nobles, knights and merchants, little affecting the peasant population. In Stuart times this was still true in the main, although the greater tonnage of ships meant a bigger bulk of imports and exports, and the use of articles of luxury was spreading among the larger and wealthier middle classes of that era. But it was only in the Eighteenth Century that articles of general consumption were brought from oversea to clothe the bodies and quench the thirst of the King's humbler subjects.

To give one example out of many ; in Charles II's reign thousands of well-to-do Londoners frequented the ' coffee-houses,' to enjoy the fashionable new drinks brought over by the East India Company. But early in the reign of George III all classes in town and country were drinking tea in their own homes. In his *Farmer's Letters* for 1767 Arthur Young complained that ' as much superfluous money is expended on tea and sugar as would maintain four millions more subjects on bread.' Tea drinking had become a national habit, a rival to the consumption of spirits and beer ; ' the cups that cheer but not inebriate ' were already as well known and as highly valued in the labourer's cottage as in the poet Cowper's parlour. In 1797 Sir Frederick Eden wrote :

' Any person who will give himself the trouble of stepping into the cottages of Middlesex and Surrey at meal-times, will find that in poor families tea is not only the usual beverage in the morning and evening, but is generally drank in large quantities at dinner.'

The poor sweetened the bitter herb with large quantities of sugar. Sugar from the British West Indian Islands was now on every table, whereas in Shakespeare's day a very limited luxury supply had come from Mediterranean ports.[1]

Until the younger Pitt reduced the high duties, the scale on which smuggling was carried on was prodigious. In 1784 Pitt calculated that thirteen million pounds of tea were consumed in the Kingdom, of which only five and a half millions had paid duty. (Lecky's *England*, ed. 1902, V, p. 296.) Smuggling added to the interest of people's lives almost as much as poaching, and was regarded as equally innocent. Parson Woodforde, a truly good as well as ' respectable ' man, wrote on March 29, 1777 : ' Andrews the smuggler brought me this night about 11 o'clock a bagg of Hyson Tea 6 pound weight. He frightened us a little by whistling under the parlour window just as we were going to bed. I gave him some Geneva and paid him for the tea at 10/6 per pound.' The inhabitants of this inland rectory thought and spoke of ' Andrews the smuggler ' just as one might speak of ' Andrews the grocer ' !

With tea, sugar and tobacco finding their way into all homes (whether through the custom house or the smuggler's cave) and with timber mainly supplied from abroad,[2] we

---

[1] As late as 1700 England consumed only 10,000 tons of sugar, though she had by that time ' sugar colonies ' of her own. But by 1800 she consumed 150,000 tons. That is to say, allowing that the population had doubled, the average use of sugar by each Englishman had risen seven and a half times in the Eighteenth Century. For the tea-habits of the working class, see J. C. Drummond, *The Englishman's Food*, pp. 242–244.

[2] Between 1788 and 1802 Britain imported nearly 200,000 loads of fir timber every year from Northern Europe (Clapham, I, p. 237).

are approaching the historical confines of modern England, a community that subsists as the centre of a great overseas Empire and a greater overseas trade providing articles of common consumption for all classes. And already, when George III came to the throne, some of England's chief home industries, particularly the rapidly expanding cotton manufacture of Lancashire, depended absolutely on raw material brought from distant lands. It was left to the Victorian era to add bread and meat to the list of goods supplied mainly from oversea. That removed the last limit assignable to the expansion of the little island in wealth and population, but gave a dangerous pledge to fortune in time of war.

To return to the mid-Eighteenth Century. The port of London received ships from every quarter of the globe ; but it monopolized the East Indian trade of England. Not only saltpetre, spices and silks continued to pour into the Thames from China and India, but tea, porcelain and woven cotton goods were now being imported from those distant parts in such quantities that they came within the reach of the mass of the population. They created new wants and the popular demand was so great that home-manufacturers took to making cotton goods and china ware.

The American trade was shared by London with Bristol and Liverpool. Liverpool in the Middle Ages had been subsidiary to the port of Chester but, as the estuary of the Dee silted up, the old Roman city gradually lost its sea trade, and the upstart town at the mouth of the Mersey took its place. In the census of 1801 Liverpool showed 78,000 inhabitants, more than any provincial city except its neighbour Manchester-Salford with 84,000.

The branch of American trade specially belonging to Liverpool was the slave-trade, which was closely connected with the cotton manufacture of Lancashire. More than half the slaves carried across the Atlantic made the ' middle passage ' in the holds of English ships, though the horrible commerce was shared by French, Dutch and Portuguese competitors. In 1771 as many as fifty-eight ' slavers ' sailed from London, twenty-three from Bristol and one hundred and seven from Liverpool. They transported 50,000 slaves that year.

One of the first to object to the slave-trade on moral grounds was Dr. Johnson, and another was Horace Walpole, who as early as 1750 wrote to Mann—

' We have been sitting this fortnight on the African Company : we, the British Senate, that temple of liberty, and bulwark of Protestant Christianity, have this fortnight been pondering methods to make more effectual that horrid traffic of selling negroes. It has appeared to us that six-and-forty thousand of these wretches are sold every year to our plantations alone ! It chills one's blood. I would not have to say that I voted in it, for the Continent of America ! '

The Liverpool ' slavers ' carried cargoes of finished Lancashire cotton goods to Africa, exchanged them for negroes, took the slaves across the Atlantic and returned with cargoes of raw cotton, besides tobacco and sugar. The planters of the West Indian Islands and the American mainland bought Lancashire cotton goods to clothe their slaves, and the supply of negro labour from Africa enabled them to provide the raw material of the great Lancashire industry. The guilty trade and the innocent manufacture were mutually assistant in more ways than one.

Cotton goods were also used by all classes in England, and were already a formidable rival to ' good English cloth.' In a pamphlet of 1782 we read : ' As for the ladies, they wear scarcely anything now but cotton, calicoes, muslin, or silks, and think no more of woollen stuffs than we think of an old almanac. We have scarcely any woollens now about our beds but blankets, and they would most likely be thrown aside, could we keep our bodies warm without them.' In the middle of the Century the great increase of the raw material of cotton gave employment to many thousands of men, women and children in their own homes. The cotton worker's cottage was a miniature factory ; the women and children were engaged in picking the cotton, the men in weaving it. This domestic system was a source of independence and livelihood to many families and to many single women who would otherwise have been paupers. But it was not an ideal mode of life. For when the home was a workshop for cotton, it could be neither clean nor comfortable, and the huswife who was in fact a manufacturer could only give odds and ends of her time to cooking and household duties.[1]

As the Century went on, inventions like Arkwright's gradually moved more and more of the work into regular cotton mills. They stood beside running water in the hill country ; until steam replaced water-power, the cotton industry was not concentrated in towns. The Census of 1801 showed that Lancashire had risen in a hundred years from a County of some 160,000 to a County of 695,000 inhabitants, the richest and most populous next after Middlesex. This change was due to the cotton worked in cottage homes or in the mills beside the Pennine streams, to the overseas commerce of Liverpool, and to the trade and various textile manufactures of Manchester.

Cotton was already great, but woollens were still the greatest and by far the most widely diffused national industry, still the favourite of Parliament, protected and encouraged by an elaborate code of laws against the export of raw wool and the import of made cloth. After the invention of Hargreaves' ' spinning jenny ' (1767) and Crompton's ' mule ' (1775) wool spinning gradually moved from the cottage to the factory, from the country to the town, though the process was not complete till the Nineteenth Century. But the more skilled art of weaving was still conducted in farms or cottages containing one or more looms each. The weaving of woollen cloth was still a source of additional wealth to hundreds of agricultural villages all over England. The merchants of the cities— Leeds, Halifax, Norwich and Exeter—collected and disposed of the goods. Only with the coming of steam-power in a later age did the weavers follow the spinners from the cottage to the factory, from the village and small town to the great city. For several generations of gradual change the domestic and the factory systems existed side by side in the textile industries.

The British West Indian islands and the Southern Colonies of the mainland sent to the mother country not only cotton but sugar and tobacco. It was the age of the long churchwarden pipe. Then, rather suddenly, in the early

---

[1] Ivy Pinchbeck, *Women Workers and the Industrial Revolution*, chap. VI.

years of George III smoking went out of fashion among the upper classes. ' *Smoking has gone out*,' said Dr. Johnson in 1773 (Boswell's *Tour to the Hebrides*, Aug. 19). And it remained ' out ' for eighty years. Army officers were still to be seen,

> Like Mars
> A smoking their pipes and cigars,

as a symbol of their dare-devil attitude to life ! But for other gentlemen to take tobacco was regarded as ' low ' or ' fast,' until the Crimean War brought back into fashion smoking and wearing beards, both in imitation of ' our Crimean heroes.'

But the mass of the people were not bound by the vagaries of fashion, and the national consumption of tobacco increased as the reign of George III went on. So did the wearing of cotton and the use of sugar. The West Indian Islands were therefore regarded as the richest jewels of the English Crown. The nearest approach to ' American millionaires ' known in the England of that day were Creoles, British owners of West Indian slave plantations, in which much English capital was invested. The other wealthy class from overseas of whom there was talk and criticism, were the ' nabobs.' The nickname was given to those returned Anglo-Indians who had exploited the new conquests of Clive with an unscrupulous greed, to which the next generation of the English rulers of India put a check. The ' nabobs ' raised the price of Parliamentary seats and made themselves otherwise objectionable to the old-established aristocratic society into which they intruded with their outlandish ways.

The northern colonies of the American mainland took English cloth and other manufactured goods, and sent back timber and pig-iron. Timber, iron and naval stores had also to be sought in Scandinavia and the Baltic, for Eighteenth Century England, having exhausted its natural forests, was short of wood for ship-building, house-building and fuel. Coal largely made good the fuel deficiency for domestic purposes and for many manufactures, but it was only now beginning to be applied on a large scale to the smelting of iron. And so, in spite of England's potential

wealth in iron-ore, much iron was imported from lands
which still had virgin forests to burn.

The manufacturing progress of Eighteenth Century
England, rapid as it was, did little to harm the amenities of
the island in that fortunate era.   London was still the only
' great city,' and Wordsworth in 1802 thought that ' earth
has not anything to show more fair ' than the sight of it
from Westminster Bridge.   For buildings still added to
the beauty of the land, and ships to the beauty of the sea.
The ' coal and iron age ' was yet to come.

Josiah Wedgwood (1730–1795) is a characteristic figure
of this time, when industry, already beginning to move
towards mass production, was not yet divorced from taste
and art.   He is typical of the fine bourgeois life of
Eighteenth Century England.   Middle-class employers,
even while developing their business on a great scale, were
still in close personal touch with their employees, and many
of them took an active part in the best cultural and artistic
life of the period.   ' Captains of industry ' were not
necessarily ' Philistines.'

The importations of the English and Dutch East India
Companies had already inspired Europe to rival Asia in the
beautiful art of porcelain.   Nor was England behind in the
race.   The ' china ' of Chelsea, Bow, Derby and Worcester
vied with the exquisite products of Sèvres and Meissen.
These, indeed, were all luxury articles, above the reach of
ordinary purses.   But Wedgwood, in his Staffordshire
works, catered for all classes with his pottery and jasper
ware, creating a big market both at home and abroad.   He
was equally successful in the ' Useful ' and the ' Ornamental ' Branch of his productions.   He laboured with
equal zeal at finding new types of beauty, some drawn from
the classical models of newly discovered Pompeii, and at
extending and cheapening his business.   He experimented
ceaselessly with new scientific methods, new moulds and
new designs.   He was indefatigable in promoting canals
and turnpikes to reduce his costs of transport and percentage
of breakages, and connect his remote Staffordshire potteries,
built far inland, with his raw material of china clay in Cornwall and with the overseas markets he hoped to exploit.
Between 1760 and 1790 he succeeded in filling not only

England but Europe and America with his goods. During this period pewter went out of general use, and was succeeded by earthenware plates and vessels, so that eating and drinking became more hygienic and more delicate. In the next generation, men no longer spoke of ' common pewter ' but of ' common Wedgwood.' Thus a Radical paper writes satirically of ' lords and ladies ' as the ' china trinkets of the nation, very superior to the common wedgewood pottery of the mass of the people.' (The *Black Dwarf*, Sept. 17, 1817.)

The most potent and characteristic phase of the whole Industrial Revolution, the connection of iron with coal, was only now beginning. From the reign of Queen Anne onwards, successive generations of the Darby family had been evolving by practical business experiment the application of coal-coke to the smelting of iron, in place of wood-charcoal. In 1779 the third of the Abraham Darbys completed the world's first iron bridge, spanning the Severn at ' Ironbridge,' near the family works at Coalbrookdale, Shropshire. The great development of the iron trade that followed, with increasing momentum especially in the early Nineteenth Century, took place chiefly in South Wales, South Yorkshire and Tyneside, regions where coal and iron were found together, either near the sea or with easy access to it by river or canal. But the ' coal and iron age ' cannot be dated earlier than the Napoleonic wars.

' In 1769 Arkwright patented the water frame, and James Watt his steam engine : 1769 therefore was the birth year of mechanical power in cotton and engineering. Both Watt and Arkwright had their atmosphere, the atmosphere of mechanical speculation in the bustling north.' The patents issued in the quarter of a century following 1760 were more numerous than those issued in the previous century and a half. (C. R. Fay, *Great Britain from Adam Smith to the Present Day*, 1928, p. 303.)

The Industrial Revolution was well under way. Of the nine millions to which the population of England and Wales had risen at the end of the Century, about one-third were engaged in agriculture but 78 per cent. still lived in the country.

The constant growth of England's home industry and overseas trade throughout the Eighteenth Century depended on the finding of money for those purposes. And it was not then so readily available as in later times ; government was a strong competitor in borrowing. But the technique of the money market was being perfected in London. After the decline of Holland, the City ' became the centre of the world's finance, where capital was more easily to be had than anywhere else on the globe.'

Joint-stock methods had suffered a set-back with the bursting of the South Sea Bubble in 1720, but they lived down that discredit, and men learnt to be a little wiser in the future. The Joint-Stock Company was indeed admirably suited to the social structure of that aristocratic but commercially minded Century, for the landed magnate could, without becoming that abhorred thing ' a tradesman,' meet on the board the City man and act with him, so that the political influence of the one could be joined to the business brains of the other. But even more than the Joint-Stock Company, the growth of provincial Banks all over the island financed both the industrial and the agricultural revolutions. These Banks were family or one man concerns, therefore not always secure, but on the whole able to supply the needs of expanding business with the necessary funds.

Then, too, there were the Jew and the Quaker, both rising into the front rank in the City and the Banking World of England, each bringing certain qualities of value.

Between the time when the Jews were expelled by Edward I and the time when they were readmitted by Cromwell, the English had learnt to manage their own financial and business affairs. There was therefore no danger of Hebrew domination and of the answering reaction of anti-semitism. By Hanoverian times, England was strong enough to digest a moderate influx of Jews and, as the prosperity of Holland declined, many of them moved from Amsterdam to London and became prominent there in stock-broking. The Jew helped the development of ' the City.' ' He was ubiquitous and enterprising, persistent but not pugnacious ; he ran after customers without regard to his dignity, and made a profit out of articles and transactions which other people rejected or despised. For international finance the Jews had a special bent, overcoming by their tribal bonds the boundaries of nations, and yet as individuals retaining that mental detachment which is so necessary to financial analysis.' [1] During the Seven Years' War, Sampson Gideon was important in the City as a banker ; in the next generation the Goldsmids came to the front ; and in 1805 Nathan Rothschild founded the most famous of all Jewish houses in London, usefully linked with the family's establishments in other European lands. But besides the great City Jews, there was also a low type of Hebrew moneylender now prominent, abhorred not without reason by his victims, the impecunious and unthrifty of all classes.

The Quakers, too, were becoming a power in finance. They took to Banking, like the Gurneys of Norwich, and had much to do with the establishment of the best English tradition therein ; honest, quiet, liberal and peace-loving, they had a steadying effect on the excitable violences and Jingoisms of the financial world.

[1] C. R. Fay, *Great Britain from Adam Smith to the Present Day*, p. 128.

CHAPTER XIII

Dr. Johnson's England

III

Social conditions favourable to art and culture—Love of natural landscape—Country house life—Sport—Food—Drama and music—Newspapers—Printing and publishing—Libraries—Domestic servants.

IF the England of the Eighteenth Century, under aristocratic leadership, was a land of art and elegance, its social and economic structure was assistant thereto. As yet there was no great development of factories, producing goods wholesale, ruining craftsmanship and taste, and rigidly dividing employers from employed. A large proportion of wage-earners were fine handicraftsmen, often as well-educated, as well-to-do and socially as well considered as the small employer and shopkeeper.

Under these happy conditions, the skilled hands produced, for the ordinary market, goods of such beautiful design and execution that they are valued by connoisseurs and collectors to-day : china, glass and other ware, silver plate, books beautifully printed and bound, Chippendale chairs and cabinets, all sorts of articles for ornament and use. Even the commonest type of grandfather clocks that told the time in farmhouse kitchens, were simple and effective in design, the outcome of a tradition followed with individual variations by innumerable small firms.

Architecture was safe in the plain English style now known as ' Georgian.' In those days all buildings erected in town or country, from town halls and rural mansions to farms, cottages and garden tool-houses, were a pleasure to the eye, because the rules of proportion, in setting doors and windows in relation to the whole, were understood by common builders : those simple folk, by observing the rules of proportion laid down for their guidance in Gibbs' handbooks, kept hold of a secret afterwards lost by the pretentious architects of the Victorian era, who deserted the plain English Georgian style to follow a hundred exotic fancies, Greek, mediaeval or what not, and were book-wise in everything concerning their work, except the essential.

In the Eighteenth Century, art was a part of ordinary life and trade. The pictures of Hogarth, Gainsborough, Reynolds, Romney and Zoffany ; the school of miniature portraits that culminated in Cosway ; the engravings of Vertue and Woollett ; the busts and statues of Roubillac ; the furniture and decorations of the Adam brothers—these were not outbreaks of genius in protest against its surroundings, but the natural outcome of the ethos of the age, parts of a process of supply and demand. And the same may be said of the literary world of Gray, Goldsmith, Cowper, Johnson, Boswell and Burke. In its quiet, settled unity of aim and thought it was a classical age, unlike the vexed Victorian, when most of the great men—Carlyle, Ruskin, Matthew Arnold, the Preraphaelites, William Morris, Whistler, Browning and Meredith—were in a state of revolt against the debased ideals of their time, or were fighting berserk each to impose his own strange genius upon the public. Yet the Eighteenth Century, it is true, produced the greatest rebel of all : William Blake was born in 1757.

The spirit bloweth where it listeth : the social historian cannot pretend to explain why art or literature flourished at a particular period or followed a particular course. But he can point out certain general conditions favourable to a high level of taste and production in Dr. Johnson's England.

Wealth and leisure were on the increase, widely diffused among large classes ; civil peace and personal liberty were more secure than in any previous age ; the limited liability of the wars we waged oversea with small professional armies gave very little disturbance to the peaceful avocations of the inhabitants of the fortunate island. Never was an Empire won at smaller cost than was ours in Canada and India. As to Australia, Captain Cook had merely to pick it up out of the sea (1770). Even the disastrous war in which we threw away the affections of the old American Colonies, though it caused a considerable disturbance in trade, otherwise affected but little the even tenor of life in the defeated country, because our hold on the sea, though challenged, was maintained ; even when the French fleet for a while sailed the Channel (1779) it was not starvation but invasion that we had to fear, and the danger soon passed.   And so it was again in the Napoleonic Wars.   The fact that our island grew most of its own food and also commanded the paths of the ocean, was the dual basis

' Of Britain's calm felicity and power,'

which Wordsworth viewed with a just complacency, as he surveyed sea and land together from the summit of Black Comb, in the twentieth year of the War with Revolutionary France.   One year of modern totalitarian war is more dislocating to society and more destructive of the higher branches of civilization in England, than a cycle of warfare in the days of the elder or the younger Pitt.

But wealth and security cannot alone account for a great age of taste and art.   The Victorian age was even more wealthy and even more secure ; yet the houses it built and the things it put into them (except the books) were of no high order.   In the Eighteenth Century, taste had not yet been vitiated by too much machine production.   Both the maker and the purchaser of goods still thought in terms of handicraft.   The artist and the manufacturer were not yet divided poles asunder.   They were both men of a trade supplying a limited public, whose taste was still unspoiled because it had not yet seen much that was really bad.   Life and art were still human, not mechanical, and quality still counted far more than quantity.

Another circumstance favourable to the arts in the Hanoverian epoch was the aristocratic influence which coloured many aspects of life besides politics.   The social aristocracy of that day included not only the great nobles but the squires, the wealthier clergy, and the cultivated middle class who consorted with them on familiar terms, as we read in Boswell's Johnsonian dialogues, and in the life-history of the most princely of professional men, Sir Joshua Reynolds.   That great society, broad-based on adequate numbers, and undisputed in its social privilege, could afford to look for quality in everything.   The higher ranks of this aristocracy set the tone to the bourgeoisie and pro-fessional class, and they in return supplied the nobles with brains and ideas—as, for instance, Burke supplied Lord

Rockingham. The leaders of the Eighteenth Century were not harassed by the perpetual itch to make money and yet more money, to produce more and yet more goods no matter of what sort, as were those mighty children of Mammon who in the Nineteenth Century set the tone to England, America and all the world. The aristocratic atmosphere was more favourable to art and taste than either the bourgeois or the democratic have since proved in England, or the totalitarian in Europe.

Indeed, aristocracy functioned better as a patron of art and letters than even the old-fashioned form of Kingship. Monarchy may sometimes have taste, as in the France of Louis XIV and XV, but it concentrates everything at Court as the one acknowledged centre of light and leading. But the English aristocracy had not one centre but hundreds, scattered all over the country in ' gentlemen's seats ' and provincial towns, each of them a focus of learning and taste that more than made up for the decay of learning at the official Universities and of taste at the Hanoverian Court. George II patronized Handel's music but nothing else. It did not matter, because patronage had passed into thousands of other hands—though not yet into the hands of millions. Oxford University did nothing for Gibbon, and Royalty had nothing to say to him except, ' Hey, what Mr. Gibbon, scribble, scribble, scribble ! ' But the reading public of the day was just of the size and quality to give proper recognition to his greatness the moment his first volume appeared (1776).

Eighteenth Century taste was not perfect. The limits of its sympathy in literature are notorious. Even in art, too much, perhaps, was thought of Reynolds and not enough of Hogarth and Gainsborough. By the foundation of the Royal Academy in 1768 Sir Joshua made the purchase of pictures fashionable among the rising middle class seeking a hall-mark of gentility. No doubt he thereby conferred a material benefit on his brother artists by creating a yet wider demand for their wares. But did that most noble knight unwittingly prepare the way for the vulgarization of art ? And did his Royal Academy serve to stereotype overmuch particular kinds of painting and sculpture ?

The romantic circumstance of the discovery of the buried

cities of Herculaneum and Pompeii excited an immense curiosity, which had better consequences, perhaps, for archaeology than for art. Graeco-Roman statuary of the second order was taken as the standard of judgment, and the next generation of Academy sculptors, Nollekens and Flaxman, insisted that all statues, even of contemporary British statesmen, must be moulded on that fashion, must be draped in the toga of the ancients (like the statue of Fox in Bloomsbury Square) and in other respects must cease to follow the true Renaissance tradition of Roubillac (died 1762). Oddly enough, at the very same time Benjamin West reversed this law of clothes as regards historical *painting* ; in spite of the grave but friendly remonstrances of Sir Joshua himself, West insisted that his picture of the death of Wolfe (exhibited in the Academy of 1771) should show the general and his men in contemporary British uniform and not in ancient armour, as modern heroes in battle were wont to be painted for their greater renown. By his obstinacy in favour of this bold innovation, West won a charter of liberty for the school of historical painting which he founded, and which he made exceedingly popular especially through the medium of engravings.

But in spite of the vagaries of fashion in art and much variety in the powers of its leading practitioners, the tone of the Eighteenth Century was favourable to high quality in the arts and crafts. England was filled full of beautiful things of all kinds, old and new, native and foreign. Houses in town and country were as rich as museums and art galleries, but the books, the engravings, the china, the furniture, the pictures were not flaunted or crowded for exhibition, but were set in their natural places for domestic use in hospitable homes.

Indoors and out it was a lovely land. Man's work still added more than it took away from the beauty of nature. Farm buildings and cottages of local style and material sank into the soft landscape, and harmoniously diversified and adorned it. The fields, enclosed by hedges of bramble and hawthorn set with tall elms, and the new ' plantations ' of oak and beech, were a fair exchange for the bare open fields, the heaths and thickets of an earlier day. Nor indeed had all these disappeared. And near to almost every village was a manor-house park, with clumps of great trees under which the deer still browsed.

In the last decade of the Century arose the great school of landscape painters, chiefly in water-colour—Girtin and the youthful Turner, soon to be followed by many more, including Crome and Cotman of the Norwich school, and Constable himself. They depicted England at her best, at the perfect moment before the outrages on her beauty began. In earlier years the fashionable demand had been for portraits and subject pictures rather than for landscapes, in spite of the power in that line shown by Gainsborough and Richard Wilson. But all through the period there had been growing up a conscious admiration of scenery, of landscape in its broader outlines. It was reflected and stimulated by literature from the first appearance of Thomson's *Seasons* in 1726, onwards through Cowper, till Wordsworth finally transformed and sublimated the theme. But no written word could express the unique glory of our island, which the painters alone could show, the shifting lights and shades of sky, earth and foliage in our water-laden atmosphere. Thus the joy of the English in their land received its expression in letters and in art, at the hands of Wordsworth and the landscape painters, just as the Eighteenth Century closed and the new era began.

As far back as the reign of George II, this novel delight and interest felt in the wilder and larger features of landscape had altered the fashion of laying out the ' grounds ' of a country house. The formal garden, the walks decorated by leaden statuettes in the Dutch style prevalent under William and Anne, and the yew hedges clipped into fantastic shapes, were swept away in order to bring the grass and trees of the park up to the walls of the manor-house ; the fruit and vegetable garden within its high brick walls, now regarded as an essential appendage of a country house, was placed at a little distance, out of sight of the front windows. These changes were conducted under the influence of William Kent and his successor ' Capability Brown,' so called from his habit of saying, when called in to consult on the new laying out of a gentleman's grounds,

' I see great *capability* of improvement here.'

No doubt there was loss as well as gain.   It was sad that hundreds of those charming lead figures were cast away, to be melted down to shoot Americans and French.   But the abolition of Dutch gardens to make room for grass slopes and trees visible from the windows, testified to the growing delight in natural scenery, which soon led English-men to take pleasure even in mountain forms, to flock to the Lake District, and in the following century to the Scottish Highlands and the Alps, hitherto abhorrent to civilized men.

This instinctive craving for the larger features of un-tamed nature was an inevitable reaction on the part of a society growing over-civilized.   In older times forests and thickets were everywhere close at hand, and man was constantly at war with the wilderness ; in those days he sought relief from the struggle in formal gardens.   Now he had conquered.   The countryside, though still beautiful, was tamed down to an affair of hedgerows and ' plantations.' So nature in her shaggy reality must be deliberately sought out further afield, in accordance with Rousseau's mystic doctrines.

The taste for mountains which began in the latter part of the Eighteenth Century, was accompanied by a corre-sponding love for the ' seaside,' hitherto neglected.   It is true that in the first half of the Century the new custom of resort to ' seaside watering-places ' had been medicinal in purpose.   At the doctor's orders people went to inhale the sea air at the village of Brighthelmstone (Brighton), or drink the well-water at Scarborough, and even to dip in the waves.   A picture of Scarborough beach in 1745 shows male visitors swimming ; and at Margate by 1750 ' Beale's bathing machines,' dragged by horses took either sex into the water, which they could enter down a ladder under cover of a hood, and thence if they wished swim out.

But those who went for the medicine of the body, found also a medicine of the soul.   The contemplation of the sea and of coast scenery added an attraction which drew ever larger crowds to the cliffs and sands, primarily for health, but also for a mental pleasure that was a part of health.   It is significant that in the latter part of George III's reign the waves of the sea were, for the first time, being truly and lovingly delineated by Turner. Ships had been well painted before, but not the real waters on which they sailed. Poets had often before described the terrors of the ocean ; now they also described its beauty and exhorted it to roll on !

In the Eighteenth Century, for the first time, the sites of new country houses were chosen for aesthetic, not merely for practical reasons. They were often placed on rising ground to ' command the prospect.' This was rendered possible by the increasing control of the wealthy over artificial supplies of water. Cowper, who disapproved of ' the great magician Brown,' complained that the houses he induced people to build on exposed hill tops were very cold until trees had grown up to protect them, and that his landscape gardening cost so much as to ruin many of his more enthusiastic patrons (*The Task*, Book III). Certainly people tended to ' overbuild ' themselves, and mortgaged their estates in their zeal for ' improvement,' like the last Earl Verney of Claydon.

Fashion has many odd vagaries. A taste for artificial ruins preceded by many years the ' Gothic revival ' in literature, religion and architecture. Before Pugin or Sir Walter Scott were born, and half a century before their influence was felt, ruined mediaeval castles were being erected as part of the ' landscape,' and fanciful ' Gothic ' ornament was fastened on to some houses.[1] But fortunately the mansions which the Eighteenth Century folk built for their own habitation were for the most part sound Georgian, sometimes with touches of the classical, such as porticos and pediments, which could, however, be made to blend not unnaturally with the Georgian style, itself of renaissance origin. The more pretentious were in the Palladian or some other style that the owner had observed on his Italian tour.

In these country houses, great and small, life was lived at its fullest. The zeal for estate management and agricultural improvement took the squire out on his horse at

[1] Even before the building of the Gothic parts of Strawberry Hill begun by Horace Walpole in 1750, Gothic ornament in external and interior decoration of houses, of a very meretricious kind, was not unknown ; it was followed by a taste for ' Chinese ' motifs. But these fancies were exceptional. See Ketton-Cremer *Horace Walpole*, pp. 151–154.

all hours of the day, and the ladies at home were as usefully employed, organizing and providing for their large households, and themselves busy with the needle or in the preserving room. For weeks and months together large parties of visitors were entertained with much eating and drinking, with field sports, with music and literature, with cards and dice which sometimes brought ruin to host or guest. It was usual now for a country house to have a library proportioned to its size, filled with leather-bound volumes stamped with the family arms or crest—the English, Latin and Italian classics, and many large tomes of splendidly illustrated travels, local histories or books of engravings and prints. Twentieth Century civilization has nothing analogous to show to these private libraries.

In many respects it was a free-and-easy society. Charles Fox set the fashion of dressing carelessly. The House of Commons—the central point of the English aristocracy—produced the impression of *déshabillé* on a foreign visitor in 1782 :

'The members have nothing particular in their dress ; they even come into the House in their great coats and with boots and spurs. It is not at all uncommon to see a member lying stretched out on one of the benches, while others are debating. Some crack nuts, others eat oranges. There is no end to their going in and out ; and as often as anyone wishes to go out, he places himself before the Speaker and makes him his bow, as if, like a schoolboy he asked his tutor's permission.' (Moritz, *Travels*, H. Milford, 1924, p. 53.)

Perhaps no set of men and women since the world began enjoyed so many different sides of life, with so much zest, as the English upper class at this period. The literary, the sporting, the fashionable and the political ' sets ' were one and the same. When the most unsuccessful of all great politicians, Charles Fox, said on his deathbed that he had lived ' happy,' he spoke the truth. Oratory at its highest, politics at its keenest, long days of tramping after partridges, village cricket, endless talk as good as ever was talked, and a passion for Greek, Latin, Italian and English poetry and history—all these, and alas also the madness of the gambler, Fox had enjoyed and had shared with innumerable friends who loved him. Nor had he been less happy during the long wet day at Holkham which he spent sitting under a

hedge, regardless of the rain, making friends with a ploughman who explained to him the mystery of the culture of
turnips.

In versatility of action and enjoyment Fox represented
the society in which he was so long the leading figure.   All
the activities of town and country, of public and private
life, were pursued and relished by those liberal-minded,
open-hearted aristocrats, whom their countrymen felt not
the slightest wish to guillotine.   The more fashionable
among them had grave faults.   In spite of the saying ' as
drunk as a lord,' there is indeed ample evidence that excessive drinking was a habit among all classes of Englishmen, low as well as high.   But heavy gambling and connubial infidelity were perhaps most observable in the
highest grade of society at that time, before the evangelical
influence, having dealt first with the common people,
returned to lay a restraining hand on the upper class,
fitting them for the ordeal of the Nineteenth Century, when
their conduct would be canvassed and their privileges
challenged.   Meanwhile the hour was theirs and it was
golden.

This classical age, when Dr. Johnson's Dictionary (1755)
did much to fix the words recognized as good English, saw
also the settlement of spelling by rules now insisted on
among all educated people.   In the age of Marlborough,
even queens and great generals spelt very much as they
liked.   But in 1750 Lord Chesterfield wrote to his son :

' I must tell you that orthography, in the true sense of the word is so
absolutely necessary for a man of letters, or a gentleman, that one
false spelling may fix a ridicule upon him for the rest of his life.
And I know a man of quality who never recovered the ridicule of
having spelled *wholesome* without the w.'

At the same time he advises the young man to read Plato,
Aristotle, Demosthenes and Thucydides, whom none but
adepts know, though many quote Homer.   It is Greek,
adds Chesterfield, that must distinguish a man ; Latin
alone will not.   It is significant that the high-priest of
fashion at that period when fashion meant so much, regarded
classical scholarship of a very real kind as proper to the
character of a gentleman.

o

Older forms of the chase were yielding to the pursuit of the fox. The hunting of deer, the King of sports in all past ages, became a memory, except on Exmoor and in a few other regions. As early as 1728 some Hunts had already come down to the ignominious 'carting' of deer, the beginning of the end. The reason is evident : the destruction of forests, the enclosure of wastes and the encroachments of agriculture caused the continual decrease of the herds of wild deer that used to roam the countryside at large. In the reign of George III, stags browsing under the oaks were an ornament to a gentleman's park, safely enclosed within its pales, but were no longer beasts of the chase. The owner or his gamekeeper would shoot them in season, for the table.

Hare-hunting, beloved of Shakespeare and of Sir Roger de Coverley, went out more slowly. Although fox-hunting was gaining ground throughout the Eighteenth Century, as late as 1835 a sporting magazine enumerated 138 packs of harriers as against 101 packs of fox hounds. The harriers had this advantage, that the countryman on foot could keep within view of the shorter circles of the hunted hare, more easily than he could follow the longer and straighter run of the fox. But although the democratic and pedestrian element formed a smaller part of the field in fox-hunting, 'the hunt,' with its red or blue coats, its hounds and horn, caught the imagination of all classes in the countryside ; spirited fox-hunting songs were shouted as loudly and as joyously on the ale bench as round the dining table of the manor.

In the reign of George III fox-hunting had become in its essential features what it has been ever since, except that very few then joined a Hunt who were not resident in the County. But it had ceased to be an affair of one or two neighbours riding over their own lands. The hounds now ran over a whole district, and great Hunts like the Badminton, the Pytchley and the Quorn carried the science to the point where it has remained ever since. The runs became longer as the Century advanced, and the Enclosure Acts, by cutting up the open fields with hedges in the hunting shires of the Midlands, made a greater call on the qualities of the horse and its rider. But even as early as

1736, Somerville, the squire-poet of *The Chase*, describes jumping as an important part of the game :

> with emulation fired
> They strain to lead the field, top the barred gate,
> O'er the deep ditch exulting bound, and brush
> The thorny-twining hedge.

Shooting in the Eighteenth Century was rapidly taking the place of the hawking, netting and liming of wild-fowl. Its procedure was moving towards present-day practice, but more slowly than that of hunting. 'Driving' the birds had not yet come in. The long, hand-cut stubble still made it easy for sportsmen to get near partridges, walking up to them behind the faithful setter. Pheasants were not driven out of covers high over the heads of the 'guns,' but were flushed out of the hedgerows and coppices by packs of yelping spaniels and shot as they rose. In northern moorlands, grouse were less numerous than to-day, but less wild. Blackgame and duck were very numerous on suitable land, and everywhere troops of hares did much injury to the farmer ; rabbits were not quite such a pest as they are now (1939), because the proportion of grass land to arable was smaller. Ruffs and reeves, bittern, plovers, wheatears, landrails and other wild birds were shot as freely as more regular game.

The muzzle-loading flint-and-steel gun of slow ignition was very different from the modern ejector ; its action being slower, it was necessary to shoot much further in front of the bird, a feat reflecting all the more credit on the performance of Coke of Norfolk, who on more than one occasion killed 80 partridges in less than a hundred shots. Reloading was a matter of time, and, if carelessly done, of danger ; therefore after each shot the sportsman had to halt and the dog was bidden 'down charge' while the 'charging' of the gun took place. In the middle of the Eighteenth Century, gamekeepers, like Black George in *Tom Jones*, were not so generally respectable a class of men as their successors of a later day. They were often 'the worst of poachers, taking one brace for the master, and two for themselves.' But neither the gentry nor their keepers were the only people who took game ; there was never a truce to the poaching war in old England.

In Stuart times cricket had grown up obscurely and locally, in Hampshire and Kent, as a game of the common people. The original method of scoring, by ' notches ' on a stick, argues illiteracy. But in the early Eighteenth Century cricket enlarged both its geographic and its social boundaries. In 1743 it was observed that ' noblemen, gentlemen and clergy ' were ' making butchers, cobblers or tinkers their companions ' in the game. Three years later, when Kent scored 111 notches against All England's 110, Lord John Sackville was a member of the winning team of which the gardener at Knole was captain. Village cricket spread fast through the land. In those days, before it became scientific, cricket was the best game in the world to watch, with its rapid sequence of amusing incidents, each ball a potential crisis ! Squire, farmer, blacksmith and labourer, with their women and children come to see the fun, were at ease together and happy all the summer afternoon. If the French *noblesse* had been capable of playing cricket with their peasants, their chateaux would never have been burnt.

Until the later years of the Century the two wickets each consisted of two stumps, only one foot high, about twenty-four inches apart, with a third stump or bail laid across them. The space between the stumps was known as the ' popping hole,' into which the batsman had to thrust the end of his bat, before the wicket-keeper could ' pop ' the ball into it at the risk of a nasty knock for his fingers. The bowler trundled the ball fast along the ground against the low wicket ; when, as often happened, the ball passed between the stumps without hitting them, the batsman was not out. The bat was curved at the end like a hockey-stick. Towards the end of the Century the game was radically altered by abolishing the ' popping hole,' adding a third stump, and raising the height of the wicket to 22 inches. The straight bat was soon adopted as a result of these changes.

Eighteenth Century Englishmen were much addicted to the pleasures of the table, and our island cooking had already taken on certain characteristic merits and defects. Foreigners were astonished at the vast quantity and excellent quality of the fish and of the red and white meat consumed, but did not appreciate the English policy about vegetables, which only came in as trimmings to meat. English cooks seemed as incapable of turning out a vegetable dish as of producing anything better than ' brown water ' by way of coffee. But, however served, vegetables from the kitchen gardens of rich and poor were now abundant and various : potatoes, cabbages, carrots and turnips, sprouts, cucumbers and salad were eaten with the meat as plentifully as they are to-day. And already sweet dishes and puddings—especially ' plumb pudding ' as Parson Woodforde ominously spelt it—held pride of place on the English table.

Woodforde's flour bill for the year 1790, indicating the very limited amount of bread baked and eaten at the Rectory, was £5.7.6. For the same period his bill for meat was £46.5.0. The English middle-class household of this period was essentially carnivorous and well ' above the bread level ' in its diet. For the same year his bill for malt for his home brewing was £22.18.6. The worthy parson recorded his meals in his diary : a good, ordinary dinner for a fair-sized company (1776) was ' a leg of mutton boiled, a batter pudding, and a couple of ducks.' Another (1777) consisted of ' a couple of rabbits smothered with onions, a neck of mutton boiled, and a goose roasted, with a currant pudding and a plain one, followed by the drinking of tea.' ' A very elegant dinner,' which he enjoyed at Christ Church, Oxford (1774), comes nearer to our conception of those corporate feasts in which the more privileged among our ancestors so much delighted :

' The first course was, part of a large cod, a chine of mutton, some soup, a chicken pye, pudding and roots etc. Second course, pidgeons and asparagus, a fillet of veal with mushrooms and high sauce with it, rosted sweetbreads, hot lobster, apricot tart and in the middle a pyramid of syllabubs and jellies. We had a desert of fruit after dinner, and Madeira, white Port and red to drink as wine. We were all very cheerful and merry.'

In the country parts, riding home on a dark night ' when merry ' was a frequent cause of accidents and death.

The young German, Moritz, who resided in England in 1782 with a meagre purse, fared less well than Parson Woodforde, for he was at the mercy of English landladies, who treated him as too many of them still treat their unlucky guests.

' An English dinner [he wrote] for such lodgers as I am, generally consists of a piece of half-boiled or half-roasted meat ; and a few cabbage leaves boiled in plain water ; on which they pour a sauce made of flour and butter.'

(This fluid, I suspect, was in Voltaire's memory when he said the English had a hundred religions and only one sauce !)

But, adds Moritz :

' The fine wheaten bread which I find here, besides excellent butter and Cheshire cheese, makes up for my scanty dinners.   The slices of bread and butter, which they give you with your tea, are as thin as poppy leaves.   But there is another kind of bread and butter usually eaten with tea, which is toasted by the fire, and is incomparably good.   You take one slice after the other and hold it to the fire on a fork till the butter is melted so that it penetrates a number of slices all at once : this is called *toast*.'

Economic circumstances made the first half of the Eighteenth Century an age of relative plenty for the working class.   Many of them, at least, breakfasted on beer, bread and butter, quantities of cheese, sometimes meat.   At midday many made a plentiful if coarse meat meal.   Smollett, in *Roderick Random* (1748), describes his entry into

a cook's shop, almost suffocated with the steams of boiled beef, and surrounded by a company of hackney coachmen, chairmen, draymen and a few footmen out of place or on board wages, who sat eating shin of beef, tripe, cowheel and sausages at separate boards, covered with cloths which almost turned my stomach.

But the innumerable local varieties of wages and conditions of life make generalizations about working-class diet exceedingly unsafe.   Many lived mainly on bread and cheese, some vegetables, beer and tea.

The theatre had a vigorous popular life in Eighteenth Century England.   In the early years of its resuscitation under Charles II it had been confined to London and to Court patronage.   It now spread far and wide.   Companies were established in the larger provincial towns, and strolling players were always moving round the countryside, acting in barns and town halls before rustic audiences. Parson Woodforde records their periodic appearance in the Court House of Castle Cary, a Somersetshire village of 1200 inhabitants, where from time to time they acted *Hamlet*, the *Beggar's Opera* and other good pieces. Farquhar's *Beaux' Stratagem* remained a favourite long after the untimely death of its author in 1707, but there was a shortage of good new plays, until more than sixty years later Goldsmith and Sheridan again supplied a few first-rate comedies.

On the other hand, as we should expect in the country that so effectually patronized Handel's Oratorios, the musical side of the theatre was excellent. Thomas Arne (1710–1778) set Shakespeare's songs and wrote the incidental music of many plays. And the English light opera (which had a continuous life from the *Beggar's Opera* to Gilbert and Sullivan) flourished exceedingly in the days of Dibdin (1745–1814). As a very young man he wrote the music of *Lionel and Clarissa* ; and he long continued to supply his countrymen with the sentimental, patriotic and nautical songs they loved to sing, such as ' Poor Jack ' and ' Tom Bowling.' To the people of England, music was not then an affair only of listening. They were not ashamed to try their own voices, for they rode and walked and worked out of doors, not always in a hurry and not always in a crowd ; and indoors they had much leisure, and if they wanted music must make it for themselves.

The dramatic genius of Garrick in the middle of the Century, and of Mrs. Siddons after him, made the London theatre famous. The garbled versions of Shakespeare that they acted—*Lear* with a ' happy ending '—arouse our horror. But we must recognize the service done by the actors and the literary critics of that age, who between them persuaded the English that Shakespeare was the greatest glory of our nation. He was read, quoted, known far more generally than to-day, for poetry and great literature had not then to meet any serious competition from printed matter of a more ephemeral kind. The reading world was just the size to give great literature its best chance. Milton was then known and honoured only less than Shakespeare.

The printed newspaper had by the middle of the century quite displaced the written 'news letter.' Early in George III's reign, its price was twopence or threepence owing to the tax, and in size it had grown to the 'folio of four pages' that Cowper expected every evening in his country retreat, and read aloud over the tea-cups to the ladies,

> Fast bound in chains of silence, which the Fair,
> Though eloquent themselves, yet fear to break.

Each of the four folio pages had four columns. After 1771, when the right to publish debates was silently conceded by the two Houses of Parliament, that task became an important function of the newspaper. Since the limited public that bought it was intensely and intelligently political, more than half the news space was in session time given up to these reports. One or more of the four folio pages were devoted to paying advertisements, telling of books, concerts, theatres, dresses and various kinds of people in want of domestic employment. The rest of the paper was occupied by poetry, articles serious and comic, letters to the paper signed with the correspondent's name or pseudonym, snippets of information and gossip theatrical or social, interspersed with *Gazette* announcements and long official reports of foreign affairs. The modern newspaper was in the making. But as yet its circulation was limited : 2000 was regarded as a good circulation ; in 1795 the *Morning Post* fell to 350, while the *Times* rose to 4800. Great fortunes could not yet be made or lost in journalism : the prize was influence, particularly in politics. There were a number of good provincial papers, like the *Northampton Mercury*, the *Gloucester Journal*, the *Norwich Mercury* and the *Newcastle Courant*.

Just as the theatre and the newspaper had, since the reign of Charles II, spread from the capital to the provinces, so had the printing and publishing of books. The lapse of the Censorship and the Licensing Act in the reign of William III had removed the legal restriction on the number of printing presses, with the result that not only were the printing and publishing firms in London greatly increased in number, but provincial presses were set up in many other towns. The business of publishing and bookselling were then conducted by one and the same firm.[1] Between 1726 and 1775 there were about 150 of these firms in England outside London, and about as many in the Capital.

The vigorous literary and scientific life of many provincial towns in Dr. Johnson's day was stimulated by the local newspapers and the local publishing firms, which often attained to a high standard. Before the end of the Century such first-rate work as Bewick's *British Birds* with his famous woodcuts was being printed and published in Newcastle-on-Tyne. Eighteenth Century printing, though less fanciful than the Elizabethan, and less mechanically correct than the Victorian, was superior to both as a beautiful art.

Much publishing, especially of the large and expensive volumes in which that aristocratic century delighted, was done by subscription, for which the author touted among his friends and patrons. The fine private libraries accounted for much of the trade. But Circulating Libraries, of which the first was started in 1740, were to be found both in London and the provinces, particularly in the health resorts. Bath and Southampton had very fine Circulating Libraries. Book clubs among neighbours and private friends were also common.

Poetry, travels, history and novels all had a place in popular reading. The German Moritz, after his residence in England, bore remarkable testimony to our literary civilization at that period (1782) :

'Certain it is, that the English classical authors are read more generally, beyond all comparison, than the German ; which in general are read only by the learned ; or at most by the middle class of people. The English national authors are in all hands, and read by all people, of which the innumerable editions they have gone through are a sufficient proof. My landlady, who is only a taylor's widow, reads her Milton ; and tells me that her late husband first fell in love with her on this very account ; because she read Milton with such proper emphasis. This single instance would prove but little ; but I have conversed with several people of the lower class,

---

[1] The most long-lived of these was Longmans. In 1724 Thomas Longman bought the business. It is still a family concern and was conducted on the old site in Paternoster Row till its destruction by enemy action in 1940. Only the business is of course now confined to publishing only, bookselling having become a separate trade.

O 2

who all knew their national authors, and who all have read many, if not all of them.'

In the course of the Eighteenth Century the accumulation of great consolidated estates by the nobility and wealthier gentry, and the developments of capitalist agriculture, led to the general disappearance of the small squire of £100 to £300 a year, who worked his own land or let a couple of farms. This particular type of man, once so important in the life and government of the countryside, was now much less in evidence. But his place was in some respects taken by an increased number of gentry and professional men living on various kinds of small incomes in the country, but less rooted in the soil than the old rustic squire. There was gain as well as loss in the change. It made for a higher level of culture : Mr. Bennet in *Pride and Prejudice* is an example of the new type, more attached to his library than to the land. Parson Woodforde, the diarist, had only £400 a year, but on that he was able to keep five or six servants indoors and out, to look well after his relations, to travel freely, and to exercise a generous hospitality to rich and poor. His habit of noting in his diary every sixpence he spent or gave, may indicate that he knew he had to be careful and therefore succeeded in living in such good style within a modest income.

The best type of domestic or outdoor employee cost only £10 a year and his keep : many were content with much less. On these conditions, armies of servants, male and female, filled the households of the gentry. Not a few became ' old servants,' privileged and intimate, whom their masters and mistresses never dreamt of turning off ; it was an important and humanizing element in old English life. The floating population of maids, who soon went away to be married, learnt during their term of domestic service many arts of cooking and housekeeping, that afterwards served them well as wives and mothers. Villages and cottages had also their own immemorial traditions in these matters. In those days, when it was not yet possible to buy everything, including tinned meals, in the shop round the corner, the feckless and untrained housewife was more utterly disastrous and therefore less common than in the city life of to-day.

BOOKS FOR FURTHER READING

In the notes and text of this and the previous chapters I have mentioned a number of works of value on special aspects of the subject. I particularly commend the student to the social parts of Lecky's *History of England in the Eighteenth Century* and to a recent work of great value, *Johnson's England,* edited by Professor Turberville for the Oxford Press in 1933, with articles by many different authorities on special aspects of life in that period. This book has now come down to a time in our annals when contemporary memoirs, novels, diaries and biographies and letters like those of Horace Walpole make the study of social history more real and very delightful. A very remarkable short essay on Eighteenth Century England is pp. 72–91 of the first volume of W. P. Ker's *Collected Essays* (1925).

CHAPTER XIV

Scotland at the Beginning and at the End of the
Eighteenth Century

The Union, 1707—Culloden and the Conquest of the Highlands, 1746.

Since the scope of this work is confined to the social history of England, nothing has yet been said about the neighbouring kingdom of Scotland. For more than two centuries after the wars of Edward I and Wallace, English and Scots had few dealings with one another save at the point of the spear. In the reign of Elizabeth they ceased to be active enemies, because they had an interest in common, to defend the island against the powers of the Catholic reaction ; but they adopted radically different forms of ecclesiastical polity, which further differentiated the character of social and intellectual life on the two sides of the Border.

By the accession of James VI of Scotland to the English throne (1603) his two kingdoms were linked by the uneasy bond of a Dual Monarchy. James himself understood Scotland better than England ; but under his son and grandsons the smaller of the two kingdoms was governed in accordance with plans concocted in London by Bishops, courtiers or parliament-men, who knew nothing of Scotland's needs and habits, and only sought to make her serve some English partisan policy of the hour. The Edinburgh Privy Council took its orders from Whitehall. The Scots deeply resented this vassalage to England, whether the absent overlord was named Charles, Oliver or James. They wrapped the plaid of their own prejudices more tightly round them, and were more suspicious than ever of influences emanating from their over-great neighbour.

Under these political conditions, social life in the two countries continued to flow in separate channels. There were also economic and physical obstacles in the way of more international intercourse. Communications were hindered not only by tariffs but by the state of the Great North Road. London was nearly a week's journey from

Orkney Islands

C. Wrath

SUTHERLAND

Moray Firth

Elgin

Culloden
Inverness

I. of Skye

R. Spey

BANFF

ABERDEEN

Aberdeen

R. Dee

Fort
William

Blair Atholl

Highland

Line

(Episcopalians)

FORFAR

Glencoe

R. Tay

Dundee

Perth

CAMPBELLS

Firth of Tay

St. Andrews

FIFE

Inverary

R. Forth

Kirkcaldy

Firth of Forth

LENNOX

Stirling

Carron

Dunbar

ARGYLE

Dumbarton

Edinburgh

HADDINGTON

CAMPBELLS

RENFREW

Glasgow

R. Clyde

LOTHIAN

Berwick

LANARK

R. Tweed

Firth of Clyde

Ayr

AYR

R. Nith

Moffat

Cheviots

(Covenanters)

Annan

R. Esk

R. Tyne

GALLOWAY

Dumfries

Stranraer

Carlisle

SCOTLAND

Scale of Miles

0 10 20 30 40 50

Solway Firth

CUMBERLAND

Emery Walker Ltd. sc.

417

Edinburgh, and the English counties that lay nearest the
Border were the most primitive and the most hostile to the
Scots. In religion, in law, in education, in agricultural
methods, in the mutual relation of classes, Scotland showed
no tendency to approximate to English example, still less
to give any lead to England.

Indeed, so repugnant to one another were the two neighbour nations over which King William uneasily reigned, that
before his death in 1702 it had become clear to the wiser
heads in both his Kingdoms that either there must be a
closer political and commercial union, or else the crowns
would again become separate and war would almost certainly
ensue. For after the Revolution of 1688 the Edinburgh
Parliament assumed a new attitude of independence, that
rendered it impossible for the English any longer to control
the affairs of Scotland through the instrumentality of her
tame Privy Council. The system of Dual Monarchy was
breaking down. The choice before the two countries lay
between a closer union negotiated on equal terms, or the
severance of the existing connection.

The right choice was made, though with deep mis-
givings on the part of the Scots. Under Queen Anne as
first sovereign of the new State of ' Great Britain,' the
Union took place of the Parliaments and commercial
systems of the two nations made one, while their Churches
and laws remained distinct. The Union of 1707 meant,
in effect, that Scotland lost her Parliamentary life (which
had never meant very much to her though it had meant
rather more in recent years), while she gained in return
full partnership in England's markets and colonies. That
privilege opened to her the opportunity of getting rid at
last of her grinding and perennial poverty.

For a generation or more the benefits of the Union
seemed to hang fire. But after the liquidation of the
Jacobite and Highland questions in 1745–1746, Scotland
sprang forward along the path towards happier days. Her
agriculture, which had been to the last degree antiquated
and miserable, could, before the Century closed, give
lessons to the improving landlords of England. Scottish
farmers, gardeners, engineers and doctors came south and
taught the English many things. Englishmen began to

travel in Scotland and to admire both her mountains and her men. Scots took a large share in the commerce and colonization of the British Empire, in the wars of Britain, in the government of India. Released from the prison of poverty where she had languished for ages, Scotland burst into sudden splendour. Her religion lost much of its gloom and fanaticism, while remaining vital and democratic. The genius of her sons gave a lead to the thought of the world : Hume, Adam Smith, Robertson, Dugald Stewart, extended their influence not only over all Britain but into the salons of continental philosophers, while Smollett, Boswell and Burns made their native country famous in letters, and Raeburn in art. Thus the latter part of the Eighteenth Century saw the golden age of Scotland, which was prolonged for a second generation of glory when Sir Walter, with his Lays and romances, imposed the Scottish idea upon all Europe.

To bring out clearly the extent and character of the changes that took place in Scotland during the Hanoverian epoch, I shall in this chapter describe her first as she was at the time of the Union in the reign of Queen Anne,[1] and then as she had become in the middle years of George III.

[1] For this purpose I have availed myself of my account of Scotland in the second volume of my *England under Queen Anne.*

I

King William, 1689–1702—Queen Anne, 1702–1714.

Ever since the days of Burns and Sir Walter Scott the English have delighted in Scottish tradition and story, highland and lowland alike, sometimes to the point of sentimentality. They go to Scotland to admire her scenery, and in their own country and throughout their world-wide Empire they have acknowledged, not without envy, the sterling qualities of her sons. But in the reign of Anne, ignorance was still the fruitful parent of hostility and contempt. Contact between the two peoples was slight, and for the most part unfortunate. Scots still sought their fortunes less often in England than on the Continent of Europe. Jacobite exiles lived in Italy and France. Presbyterian clergy and lawyers went to Dutch universities to finish their education at the fountain-heads of Calvinist theology and Roman law. Scottish overseas merchants dealt with Holland and Scandinavia, but were excluded from the Colonies of England. Englishmen who crossed the Cheviots on business were few, except the Borderers who nursed a traditional hostility to everything Scottish ; the jealous Northumbrians used to warn travellers from the South that Scotland was ' the most barbarous country in the world.' Scottish drovers sold their cattle in the fairs of north England, but otherwise the business done between the two lands was so slight that the London mail bag sometimes brought only one letter to Edinburgh.

Perhaps not more than a dozen people in the year visited Scotland for pleasure. And of these few the weaker sort were speedily driven back across the Border by the badness of accommodation in the slovenly inns, where good French wine and fresh salmon could not alone compensate for the want of other palatable victuals, and for the utter filth of the lodging. And while the English traveller complained of his own treatment, he was no less bitter on the stabling

of his horse in a place 'hardly fit for a hog-house,' where
the poor beast was offered straw to eat in place of hay.
If indeed these tourists had come provided with intro-
ductions and could have enjoyed Scottish hospitality in
gentlemen's houses, as the native gentry did upon their
journeys, they would have fared less ill.

Nor was there in Scotland anything specially to attract
the seeker after the beautiful as it was understood in those
days. No Southerner then admired wild moorland scenery ;
the Scots doubtless loved, in their innermost hearts, the

land of brown heath and shaggy wood,

but they had not yet, through the medium of literature,
expressed that still unconscious passion even to themselves,
still less to their unfriendly neighbours. The Englishman
who rode from Berwick to Edinburgh, despised the Lowland scenery as divided between melancholy wastes and
ill-managed fields of oats. It was unenclosed ; almost
treeless ; devoid, except in the immediate neighbourhood
of Edinburgh, of the fine mansions and parks, well-built
farms and stately parish churches which the traveller had
left behind him in his own country. As to the Highland
mountains, the very few Englishmen who ever penetrated
into their recesses in the way of business or duty pronounced
them 'horrid,' 'frightful' and 'most of all disagreeable
when the heath is in bloom.'

The Scot was either a Jacobite or a Presbyterian, and in
either capacity he alienated four-fifths of English sympathy.
And the English of all religions or none were shocked or
amused at the rigour of the social discipline of the Kirk.
Cromwell's troopers, in their day of power in Scotland, used
to seat themselves in derision on the 'stool of repentance'
in the parish churches ; and in Anne's time that instrument
of moral reformation was as alien to the free spirit of the
English Dissenting sects as it was to the mild authority of
the village parson. Calamy, the leader of the English
Nonconformists, in his tour of fraternization among the
Scottish Presbyterians in 1709, gave offence by calling
some proceedings of their Church Assembly 'the Inquisition revived.' And apart from all questions of politics
and religion, the national and personal pride of the Scot

appeared to the unimaginative Englishman ridiculous when associated with poverty. That a ' gentleman ' should be proud though out-at-elbows seemed absurd to the English merchant in his broadcloth. And the Scot, when at every turn he encountered this vulgar scorn, only became more silent and more dour.

The Scots, indeed, regarded the English with sour aversion, as purse-proud and overbearing neighbours. Popular poetry, tradition, history—strong influences on an imaginative and emotional race—all pointed to England as the ancient enemy. Four centuries of intermittent warfare with the Southerner formed the subject of Scottish legend and ballad. Hardly a place in the Ancient Kingdom but its inhabitants could tell how the English had burnt it. And Flodden, still unavenged, was the lyric theme vibrating in every Scottish heart.

The Edinburgh Parliament, though it had become some-what more important after the Revolution, had never stood for much in the social life and imagination of the people. It held its sessions in the great hall off the High Street, known as the Parliament House ; after the Union it was assigned to the lawyers of the capital, and still remains the most famous room in Scotland. There, under its high, open-timbered roof, Nobles, Barons and Burgesses sat together ; they were reckoned as three separate Estates, but they debated and voted in a single Chamber.

The Barons, or County members, unlike the correspond-ing class in the English House of Commons, were not elected on a popular franchise of forty-shilling freeholders, but were each chosen by a few score gentlemen who happened to be, in the eye of the old Scottish law, tenants-in-chief of the Crown. The Burghs, too, were all of them as ' rotten ' as the rottener part of the English Boroughs. The representative element was therefore weaker in the Scottish than in the English Parliament ; such repre-sentation of the people as there actually was, could only be called ' virtual.' Partly for this reason, partly because the social structure of Scotland was still essentially feudal and aristocratic, the Nobles were the most powerful element in the Chamber. It was chiefly they who led its debates, headed its factions and formulated its acts and policies.

The predominance of the aristocracy was not confined to Parliament. In each district of the countryside the common people were attached by custom, pride, awe and hope of protection to some great House that represented their region in the eyes of Scotland. The lairds, as the Lowland gentry were called, were trained to use the arms with which they commonly rode abroad ; the local nobleman entertained them royally at banquets in his mansion, espoused their quarrels, pushed their interests, and confidently expected them in return to follow his standard, if he raised it for the Government that had given him office, or against the Government that had neglected his claims.

If Whig and Jacobite came to blows, as they nearly did on several occasions under Anne, and as they actually did in 1715, it would be to the banners of Argyle, Atholl, Mar or some other grandee that each region would rally, in the Lowlands only to a less degree than in the Highlands. If all the nobility had been united against the Government, the little Scottish army would not long have availed to hold them down. But like other classes they were divided. And nearly all who engaged in politics were greedy of office, for nearly all were embarrassed by the need of keeping up feudal state on the meagre rentals and payments in kind of a countryside desperately poor ; and they had all been taught to regard office as the natural remedy of a great nobleman's finances. But many, both in the Jacobite and in the Whig camp, were patriots as well as self-seekers, and some were, besides, shrewd and politic statesmen, who knew how to pursue their country's true interest, and whose aristocratic position and upbringing set them above the necessity of courting popularity with the mob. Such were the men who passed the Union.

After the Nobles came the lairds or country gentlemen. Their tall, stone mansions, each with its corbel-stepped gable roof, stood up gaunt and fortresslike in the treeless and hedgeless landscape. Architecture did not flourish as in England. Many of these country houses had grown up by clumsy additions to the war-towers of former days. There was seldom any window on the exposed north side, even when it commanded the best or the only view of the landscape. The day of lawns, avenues and walled gardens was yet to come. The farm buildings, with their homely smells and litter, abutted on the mansion ; the cornfields came up to its walls on one side, and on another was an ill-kept garden of kale, physic-herbs and native flowers.

The interior was equally devoid of luxuries common in the south of the island. The furniture was of the simplest, the floors had no carpets, the walls were usually devoid of paper, panelling, arras or pictures. The bed-chambers had no fire-places, except in the envied ' fire-room.' The drawing-room held a closed bed ready for guests, since it was not always safe for a convivial laird to ride home o'nights, any more than for Tam o' Shanter from his humbler festival. Hospitality took the form of plentiful plain meats served in one course, washed down by Scottish ale and French brandy and claret—and, in the Highlands, by the local whisky. Tea was only known to the Scottish subjects of Queen Anne as an expensive medicine. Thrift was a dire necessity, but hospitality was a national instinct. Neighbours would arrive on horseback on surprise visits of half the day in length ; they were heartily welcome, for the means of passing the time in a country house were fewer than in contemporary England.

Near Edinburgh and other towns golf was a time-honoured institution. And all over Scotland hares, grouse, blackgame and partridges were pursued with dogs, hawks, and snares, and less often with the long gun. But the red deer, once common, were already withdrawing into the Highland glens. The extraordinary abundance of salmon and trout afforded not only good sport, but a cheap food for the people. In some parts the gentry despised salmon as a dish that cloyed, and farm-hands struck if they were fed upon it every day.

The gentry of the Lowlands were divided not unevenly into Presbyterian and Episcopalian, a division scarcely distinguishable from the political division of Whig and Jacobite. Tories there were none, in the English sense of the word, for the Tory was an Episcopalian who had accepted the Revolution Settlement because it left his Church established and privileged, whereas in Scotland the Revolution left the Episcopal Church disestablished, and not even tolerated according to law ; Scottish Episcopalians, therefore, were necessarily Jacobites, looking to a counter-revolution for their relief. This was the essential difference between English and Scottish politics, and it deeply affected social life and relations in the Northern Kingdom.

Family and religious discipline tended to be more strict in Presbyterian than in Episcopalian families. There was usually more pleasure and freedom in a Jacobite household. But deep Presbyterian piety and a strict sense of public duty did not prevent Forbes of Culloden from indulgence in hard drinking, convivial hospitality, profound learning and liberal culture. And when Anne came to the throne, the services of psalmody, preaching and extempore prayer were very much the same in the Episcopal Meeting House as in the Presbyterian Parish Church. The Prayer Book only began to find its way into some of the Meeting Houses in the last half of her reign. The doctrines professed by the rival denominations differed little except on Church government, and not much even on that, seeing that the Episcopalians too had their Presbyteries and Kirk Sessions with inquisition and discipline over morals.

The division therefore was deep only on its political side ; it did not touch the basis of a common Scottish mentality and civilization. Free thought had not yet spread from the land of Shaftesbury and Bolingbroke to the land of Hume. In the reign of William an unfortunate Edinburgh student had been hanged for expressing doubts as to the Trinity and the authority of the Scriptures, in terms that would only have provoked a frowning rebuke in a London coffee house.

Nearly all Scottish families, especially those of the gentry, regularly attended either the Parish Church or the Episcopal Meeting House, where they received much the same spiritual medicine, diluted with different quantities of water. Poverty and religious controversy combined to form a national character, overriding the acute political divisions, and uniting all Scots in a mental and moral antagonism to the wealthier, more libertine civilization on the south of the Cheviots. The popularity of Addison's and Steele's *Spectators* among Edinburgh ladies and gentlemen at the end of Anne's reign was one of the first instances of a real intellectual invasion of North by South Britain. As a consequence of the Union such influences began to multiply.

The intellectual unity of the nation and the good understanding of its component classes were all the greater because Scottish lairds in those days sent their own bairns to the village school. The idea of sending a Scottish gentleman's son to an English public school was rendered unthinkable alike by thrift and by patriotism. Education in the village school strengthened the young laird's love of his native land and landscape, and inclined him when he came to man's estate to sympathy with his tenants who had once been his schoolfellows. The broad Scots tongue, of which the highest were not ashamed, the traditions and ballads of the countryside, were the common heritage of all. That was why, two generations later, in the days of Burns and Scott, the poetry and traditions of Scotland went forth to conquer the imagination of men bred in less fortunate countries, where rich and poor had no culture in common. Scotland was at once more feudal and more equalitarian than England. An amazing freedom of speech, between classes that were yet perfectly distinct in a strict social hierarchy, characterized the relation of men who had sat on the same bench at school, and whose fathers had ridden shoulder to shoulder to fray and foray.

But in the age of Anne no literary or intellectual palms were won by Scotland in the world's arena. Her poverty was still too bitter and her religion was still too narrow. But the seeds of greatness were there ; that very poverty and that very religion were forming the national mind and character. Already Swift, who hated the Scots as Presbyterians, confessed that their youth were better educated than the English ; while Defoe wrote, though with some exaggeration :

You find very few gentry either ignorant or unlearned. Nay, you cannot ordinarily find a servant in Scotland but he can read or write.

When Forbes of Culloden, in 1705, went to finish his legal education at Leyden University, he was led to contrast the grave and studious habits of his own countrymen abroad with the 'riot and debauchery' of the young English spendthrifts making the grand tour, 'who repaid the for-bearance and politeness of the inhabitants with contempt and ignorance.'

Scottish school education would, however, by modern standards, be judged miserably inadequate. At the Refor-mation the Nobles had stolen the Church endowments, which had been earmarked for education by the 'devout imagination' of John Knox. Since then, the Church had continued to strive for the cause of educating the people, but with all too little support from the gentry and the cheeseparing 'heritors' who controlled the money spent on the schools. The excellent laws of 1633 and 1696 had ordained that a well-appointed school should be set up in every parish and maintained by local rates. But the reality was very different. In Anne's reign many parishes had no school at all, and where a school was to be found it was too often a dark, draughty, dirty hovel, and the master or mistress usually lived on starvation wages. In Fife, at the end of the Queen's reign, only two men out of three could sign their names, and one woman out of twelve, while in Galloway few of the people could read.

On the other hand, though there were not enough schools, in those that there were Latin was very often taught ; and it was usually well taught in the Burgh schools maintained by the towns. The village and the Burgh schools were not merely primary schools ; some of the older and better scholars were being prepared for the University by masters who were themselves College men. Many, indeed, of the half-starved dominies, though they could not afford to buy books, had the root of the matter in them ; and though they taught only a part of the population, that part was the pick of the Scottish democracy, lads taught to make sacrifices to obtain education, who used the slender equipment of learning available to them as no other nation in Europe could do, and so in the end raised themselves and their country to higher ranges of civilized life.

The Universities of Scotland were in a dull condition at sunrise of that century which was to set in the golden glow of Principal Robertson, Adam Smith and the Edinburgh philosophers. An age of violent civic commotion is seldom favourable to academic institutions controlled by the State.

The Episcopal regime of Charles II had excluded half the Scottish men of learning from academic life, and the Revolution extruded most of the other half, replacing them by men who had learnt more fanaticism than scholarship in moorside conventicles subject to attack by dragoons.

The students were of all classes, sons of nobles, lairds, ministers, farmers and mechanics. The most part were seeking to be beneficed clergymen, but there were far too many candidates. The number of small bursaries and the Scottish peasant's zeal for knowledge overcrowded the sacred profession in days when there were few other openings for an educated man. The lot of the ' stickit minister,' the laird's tutor and the underpaid schoolmaster was hard. But those who were able to obtain charge of a parish were not so ill off by the modest standards of that day. Calamy, the English Nonconformist leader, wrote after his visit to the Presbyterians of North Britain in 1709 :

> As for the settled ministers of the Church of Scotland, though they are not so plentifully or profusely provided for as many of the Established Church in England, yet are there none but what have a competency, whereupon to live easily and conveniently and above contempt.

The Scottish lad, in his hard struggle to reach this harbour, supported life at the University from the sack of oatmeal leaning against the wall of the garret where he lodged in the town. On holidays fixed for the purpose, the rustic student tramped home with the empty sack, and returned with it refilled from the harvest of his father's ' infield.'

The peasants on a Scottish estate lived on terms of traditionally familiar intercourse with the laird, who on his daily ride across his lands had to listen to the sharp tongues of an outspoken race. None the less they were living under him in a position of servitude at once feudal and economic. This kind of relationship was remarked on by English travellers as something new in their experience. Private jurisdictions over tenants, civil in some cases, civil and criminal in others, were common all over Scotland, though such feudal courts had long ago ceased in England. Statesmen in London held that the Protestant Succession was in imminent danger from these *superiorities*, which removed the Scottish vassal from the protection of the royal courts and subjected his person and property to Jacobite overlords.

The peasantry held their farms on annually terminable leases which left them at the mercy of the laird or his factor, and fatally discouraged any attempt on their part at improving the land they tilled. And the laird on his side seldom put capital into the improvement of his tenants' farms. Had he wished so to do, he lacked the means. A rent-roll of £500 sterling was considered great wealth in Scotland, £50 was common, and many ' bonnet lairds ' supported their families on £20 of rent and the produce of their own ' infield.' These figures could be multiplied by ten to represent the wealth of the corresponding grades of the English squirarchy. Moreover, Scottish rents were paid more than half in kind : sheep, poultry, oatmeal, barley and peat were brought to the door of the manor house by the tenantry—not in carts, for they had none, but balanced on the backs of half-starved horses. Another source of supply for the laird's household was the cloud of pigeons from his dovecot, which preyed on the surrounding fields, transforming a large proportion of the tenants' meagre crops into flesh for the landlord's table. For the rest, the Scottish farmer, like the villein of mediaeval England, had to manure, sow and reap the ' infield ' of the laird, often on days between two spells of bad weather, when he might otherwise have saved his own precarious harvest and secured his family against starvation during the coming year.

Under these conditions it is no wonder that in Queen Anne's reign nine-tenths of the fields of Scotland were unenclosed by wall or hedge. The cattle had to be tethered or watched all day and shut up all night. Only in the Lothians the wealthier landlords had begun the process of enclosing by stone walls. Quick-set hedges were hardly anywhere to be seen, and the want of them was not regretted, for it was believed that they harboured birds which would eat the corn. A similar suspicion attached to trees. Saplings were not only eaten off by the cattle but deliberately broken by the peasants, in spite of proclaimed penalties. But there were few trees for them to injure except close round the manor-house and the kirk. The ancient forests where, according to the instructions of Robert Bruce's 'testament,' the population used to shelter in time of English invasion, had now almost everywhere disappeared. And the modern movement for plantations, to keep the wind off the land and supply the market with timber, was only in its infancy. The general aspect of Scotland was then more treeless than ever before or since. Here and there, particularly in Clydeside, could be seen woods of some size and pretension ; and, in the distant and un-visited North, old forests still rustled their branches to the Highland winds. Even in the Lowlands the denes and steep banks of the burns sheltered in their dank recesses the sparse remains of the blanket of birch, alder and dwarf oak that had once been spread over the land.

The houses of the peasantry were in keeping with the starved aspect of the landscape and the want of any proper system of agricultural improvement. Rightly to imagine the home of a Scots farmer in Queen Anne's reign, we must forget the fine stone farms of a later date, and think of something more like the cabins of Western Ireland. It consisted almost always of one storey and often of one room. The style and material of building and the degree of poverty varied in different regions, but walls of turf or of unmortared stone, stopped with grass or straw, were very common ; chimneys and glass windows were rare ; the floor was the bare ground ; in many places the cattle lived at one end of the room, the people at the other, with no partition between. The family often sat on stones or heaps of turf round the fire of peat, whence the smoke made partial escape through a hole in the thatch overhead. Since they worked on an ill-drained soil, only half reclaimed from marsh and rushes, and came back to a damp home in wet clothes for which they too seldom had any change, it followed that rheumatism and ague plagued and shortened their lives.

Men and women wore clothes made up in the immediate neighbourhood by local weavers and tailors ; often spun and dyed in the wearer's own cottage. Children always and grown-ups often went bare-foot. The men wore the broad, flat, round, blue bonnets of wool, the distinctive headgear of Scotland in the eyes of the world. The laird and the minister alone sported a felt hat ; but they too wore home-spun clothes made up by a country tailor. To the surprise of Dissenters from South Britain, the minister wore no black or clerical garments, either in or out of church, but made his rounds and preached his sermon in lay neck-cloth, and in coloured coat and waist-coat of homely wool.

In Scotland yet, as in the England of pre-Saxon times, much of the land that was potentially the best for agri-culture was still uncultivated marsh cumbering the valley bottoms, while the peasants painfully drove their teams on the barren hillsides above. The enormous ploughs of primitive design were all of wood except the share and coulter, and were usually made by the farmers themselves ; they were dragged along the slope by eight or ten small and meagre oxen, urged on by the blows and shrill cries of half a dozen excited farmers. The cortège, with the united efforts of beasts and men, scratched half-an-acre a day.

A group of farmers usually tilled their lands together, and shared the profits on the ' run-rig ' system, each farmer claiming the produce of a ' rig ' or ' ridge '—a different ' rig ' being assigned to him each harvest. A single farm, paying £50 sterling rent or its equivalent in kind, might have half a dozen or more tenants, among whom the land was every year re-divided by lot. This system, and the precarious annual leases granted by the laird rendered agricultural improvement impossible. The quarrels inside the group of co-operating farmers—some of them of that dour type that bred Cameronians and Kirk seceders—too often held up the common cultivation for weeks at a time. Farmers had to wait every morning till the lazier or more sulky of their neighbours arrived to join in the clumsy operations of the field.

The farm was further divided into an ' infield ' and an ' outfield.' On the ' infield,' near the houses of the clachan, was lavished all the manure that could be locally collected, including sometimes the thatch covering the turf on the goodman's cottage roof. But the ' outfield,' perhaps three-quarters of the total acreage, was left unmanured, used as rough feed for cattle for eight or ten years on end, and then cropped for a year or two before relapsing into moorish pasture. This system was very inefficient compared to the three-field system usual in English open-field cultivation, but something like it was found in parts of West England, Wales, Cornwall and the East Riding.

Scottish crops consisted of oats for the staple food ; and barley to make scones, or the Scots ale which was still the wholesome national drink of the Lowlander before the ill-omened invasion of whisky from the Highlands. Kale, pease and beans were grown for the cottage kitchen. But turnips and artificial grasses for cattle were unknown, and potatoes were grown only by a few gardeners to season the laird's dish of meat, not by farmers as part of the people's food.

The tyranny of these primitive customs of cultivation, approved by the people themselves, kept them always near the verge of famine. Their grain, but little multiplied by such methods of agriculture, went in the three shares celebrated in the old saying :

' Ane to gnaw, and ane to saw, and ane to pay the laird witha'.'

The lairds were bound fast by their own poverty, unable to help themselves or their tenants. Yet it was the lairds who, in the century now dawning, learnt so to make use of the commercial conditions introduced by the Union as to revolutionize the system of agriculture and create a new prosperity for all classes.

The last half-dozen years of William's reign had been the ' dear years ' of Scottish memory, six consecutive seasons of disastrous weather when the harvests would not ripen. The country had not the means to buy food from abroad, so the people had laid themselves down and died. Many parishes had been reduced to a half or a third of their inhabitants. This sombre experience, from which the nation was slowly emerging during the years when the Treaty of Union was under debate, coloured the North Briton's outlook, deepened his superstitions and darkened his political passions, especially in relation to the hated English who had watched the kindly Scots die of hunger, and had moved no finger save to make their lot worse by opposition to the Darien scheme. Fortunately a cycle of fat years under

Queen Anne followed the lean years under King William. Then in 1709, after the Union was safely passed, the failure of the harvest again produced famine—unpeopling farms and hamlets and filling the villages with beggars. Until the methods of agriculture had been completely changed, such might always be the result of a single season of bad weather.

In these circumstances, the principal source of agricultural wealth, as distinct from mere subsistence, was sheep and cattle. The sheep's wool supported the home cloth manufacture, and both sheep and cattle were sold into England in great numbers. Stock-breeding flourished most in Galloway, but even Galloway had hardly recovered from the depredations on her livestock made by the Highlanders and other emissaries of a paternal government in the ' killing times ' of the persecution under Charles II. It was reckoned that in 1705 Scotland sold 30,000 cattle into England ; the usual price was something between one and two pounds sterling a head. This marketing of ' black cattle ' was one of the most important of a Scottish laird's few sources of wealth. The sheep and cattle were small, even as compared to the small English beasts of that period. Their pasture was for the most part unimproved moorland. The cattle were shut up all night for want of fences. Of the remnant that had not been sold south to the English pastures, many had to be slaughtered at Martinmas on the approach of winter, for there was little hay and no root-crop on which to feed them. During the next six months salted meat supplied the tables of the gentry ; but meat seldom graced the peasant's board at any time of year. On the return of the tardy Scottish spring, the poor beasts, mere skeletons after their winter-long imprisonment in the dark on rations of straw or boiled chaff, were led back from the byre to the pasture, a pitiful procession, half supported, half carried by the farmers. This annual ceremony was only too well named the ' Lifting.'

The standard of life in Scotland was very low in almost every material respect, but hardships had not crushed the spirit of the people, not even after the ' dear years ' of William. To avoid the receipt of alms was a passion with

common folk more decidedly than in wealthier England.
The poor law system was totally different in the two
countries. In England the poor had been, ever since
Elizabeth's reign, a charge on the community ; they were
maintained by compulsory parish rates that amounted at
the end of Anne's reign to a million pounds a year, then
regarded as a heavy national burden. In Scotland there
was no compulsory rate, and poor-relief was an obligation
not on the State but on the Church. Endowments of the
poor were made by private persons, announced in the kirk,
and sometimes commemorated on boards hung upon its
walls. In the kirk also stood the poor's box, which the
thrifty Scots constantly replenished with most of the bad
copper of the neighbourhood, besides a useful minority of
good coins. The deacon was a lay officer of the Church,
found in many parishes, though not in all ; it was the
deacon's business to distribute these alms among the
necessitous, who were for the most part creditably unwilling
to receive it. The duty of keeping their relations independent of such relief was keenly felt and nobly undertaken
by persons themselves desperately poor.

Licences to beg from door to door in a given area were
also issued by the Kirk Session to privileged ' gaberlunzies,'
or ' blue gowns.' Many of them, like Edie Ochiltree,
acted as welcome carriers of news to lonely farms, re-
positories of regional lore and legend—popular, respectable
figures with a place of their own in rural society.

But unhappily there was a much larger number of unlicensed and less desirable vagabonds. The ' sorners ' of
Queen Anne's Scotland answered to the ' sturdy beggars '
of Tudor England. The ' dear years ' under William had
swelled this army of broken and masterless men, though
there is no support to Fletcher of Saltoun's wild guess that
they numbered 200,000, which would have made them
between a fifth and sixth of the whole population. But the
' sorners ' were numerous enough to terrorize a countryside
of lonely farms and clachans of two or three houses apiece ;
a company of ' ill men ' could rob in the face of day, taking
the last crust from the cottage, the cow from the byre, and
sometimes wresting the child from its unhappy parents.
The number and power of the ' sorners ' was the penalty

paid by Scotland for the want of a regular poor-law like the English. And in neither country was there any attempt at a proper police. Fletcher of Saltoun, the grim republican patriot who lent a flavour of his own to the Scottish politics of the age, proposed as a remedy that the ' sorners ' should be put into compulsory servitude ; his idea was only the extension of existing practice in Scotland. Coal-mines and salt-mines were worked very largely by ' bondsmen,' veritable serfs, who could be caught and punished for running away. Even in modern establishments based on free contract, like the New Mills cloth factory in Haddingtonshire, there was a ' prison att the manufactory,' and hands who ran away or broke their contracts could be dealt with by summary methods. But the conditions of the employees of the New Mills was not bad by the standard of those days, whereas the hereditary bondsmen in the mines were treated by their masters as chattels, and were spoken of by the rest of the population with a kind of pitying terror, as ' the brown yins ' or ' the blackfolk.' [1]

If Scotland at the time of the Union lagged behind England in agricultural methods, her industry and commerce were in no better way. Almost all her articles of export were food or raw materials—cattle and salmon for England, coal and salmon for Holland, salt and lead for Norway, herrings for the Iberian Peninsula. The Scots themselves wore cloth woven by village websters for local consumption ; but only a very little linen or woollen cloth was sold abroad. The Haddington New Mills were famous, but they were not flourishing. There were, besides, other woollen factories, as at Musselburgh and Aberdeen, all clamouring to the Scots Parliament to support them with money and monopolies, and being only in part satisfied. The wool-growing landlords, on their side, compelled the legislature to allow them to export raw wool to Sweden and Holland, to the detriment of the market for

---

[1] This iniquitous system of serfage was abolished at the end of the Eighteenth Century. Till then the Scottish miner, together with his wife and children who carried up the coal he cut, were transferable with the pit on any change of proprietorship. They could not leave their employment during life.

Scottish cloth in those countries, and of course clean contrary to the established policy of England. The herring trade was a chief source of the nation's wealth, but even so the Dutch fishermen took many more herrings off the Scottish coast than did the Scots themselves. A great part of the business of the Edinburgh Parliament consisted of regulations to encourage and direct the meagre manufacturing and trading efforts of the country.

Though Scottish officers and regiments were winning honour for the land of their birth—the Scots Greys were as famous in the armies of Marlborough as in those of Wellington—the war with France meant little to the Scots at home. It was England's war, not theirs. Four years before the Union, the Edinburgh Parliament passed a Wine Act, to legalize the most popular part of trade with the enemy. The English were scandalized at this bold defiance of propriety in war-time, when they themselves were content with illegal smuggling to the French ports. But they dared do nothing, for if one of their cruisers had seized a Scots ship freighted with brandy, claret and Jacobite agents, they might have woken up one morning to find themselves at war with Scotland.

Since the Restoration, Glasgow had been reckoned as the second city in the kingdom, and the first for trade and manufacture. Probably on account of the famine and distress in William's reign, the population had recently declined : when the Union of 1707 was passed, it numbered only 12,500 souls out of a total of a million or more for all Scotland. The Glasgow merchants owned between them fifteen trading ships, with an aggregate tonnage of 1182 tons, and even these small vessels had to unload more than a dozen miles below the town, as the Clyde was still unnavigable to anything larger than a boat. Since no Scottish firm was permitted to trade with an English dependency, their commerce was confined to Europe, until the Union Treaty opened the tobacco trade with the English colonies to Bailie Nicol Jarvie and his fellow-citizens. In Anne's reign Glasgow was still a pretty little country town, with colonnades at the cross roads in the centre, where the merchants met to transact their modest affairs. It was, moreover, one of the four University towns of Scotland : ' there are only forty scholars that lodge in the College,' an English traveller noted in the year of Blenheim, ' but there are two or three hundred that belong to it, and all wear red gowns, as do likewise those at Aberdeen and St. Andrews.'

The fourth university town was Edinburgh herself—the headquarters of Scotland's law and law courts, the meeting place of the Parliament of the three Estates, and of that other Parliament which proved more enduring—the General Assembly of the Church. There, too, was Holyrood Palace, the empty nest whence Scotland's Kings had flown. At the other end of the mile-long Canongate and High Street—' the stateliest street in the world,' as a traveller of the period called it—rose the Castle on its rock, where the absent Queen Anne was represented by the red coats of her small Scottish army. The idle soldiers looked down upon the reek and roofs of Edinburgh, in perpetual wonder as to what might be brewing in the turbulent town below, and what riot, religious, political or economic, it would be their next duty to quell.

Although the antique City Guard of Edinburgh, with their Lochaber axes, were the laughing-stock of Scotland, yet housebreaking and robbery were almost unknown in the chief city of the kingdom, where men left their house doors unlocked all night. The fact speaks well for the honesty of the Scots, and is a credit to the hard religious system under which they were bred. It ruled the town effectually, preventing, in Scotland's very capital and centre of fashion, all theatrical shows and all dances ; and on the Sabbath all ' idle gazing from windows,' all loitering and all walking fast in the streets. No wonder Dr. Pitcairn wrote his witty rhymes lampooning the clergy, and no wonder ' Hell-fire Clubs ' and ' Sulphur Clubs ' met surreptitiously to flout the Church in ways more questionable than the drama and the dance.

But not even the Church attempted on week-days to stop horse-racing on Leith sands, golf, cock-fighting or heavy drinking. On six evenings of the week the taverns were filled with men of all classes at their ale and claret, till the ten o'clock drum, beaten at the order of the magistrates, warned every man that he must be off home. Then

P

were the High Street and Canongate filled with parties of every description, hurrying unsteadily along, High Court Judges striving to walk straight as became their dignity, rough Highland porters swearing in Gaelic as they forced a passage for their sedan-chairs, while far overhead the windows opened, five, six, or ten storeys in the air, and the close stools of Edinburgh discharged the collected filth of the last twenty-four hours into the street. It was good manners for those above to cry ' Gardy-loo ' (*gardez l'eau*) before throwing. The returning roysterer cried back ' Haud yer han',' and ran with humped shoulders, lucky if his vast and expensive full-bottomed wig was not put out of action by a cataract of filth. The ordure thus sent down lay in the broad High Street and in the deep, well-like closes and wynds around it making the night air horrible, until early in the morning it was perfunctorily cleared away by the City Guard. Only on Sabbath morn it might not be touched, but lay there all day long, filling Scotland's capital with the savour of a mistaken piety.

This famous sanitary system of Edinburgh aroused much comment among English travellers and made the Scots ' traduced and taxed of other nations,' as being, in Defoe's words, ' unwilling to live sweet and clean.' But it is only fair to quote his defence of them in the matter :

Were any other people to live under the same unhappiness, I mean as well of a rocky and mountainous situation, thronged buildings from seven to ten or twelve story high, a scarcity of water, and that little they have difficult to be had, and to the uppermost lodgings far to fetch, we should have a London or Bristol as dirty as Edinburgh ; for though many cities have more people in them, yet I believe that in no city in the world so many people live in so little room.

Edinburgh indeed was an extreme example of the French type of town, kept within its ancient limits for reasons of safety and defence, and therefore forced to find room for growth by pushing its tenement flats high in air—in contrast to the ground plan of the easy-going peaceful towns of England, that sprawled out in suburbs ever expanding, to give each family its own house and if possible its own garden. French influence and the disturbed condition of Scotland in the past had confined the capital within its walls and pushed its growth up aloft. It was not, indeed, so long since it had been a matter of great peril for a gentleman to pass the night in a house without the walls, like Darnley in Kirk o' Fields.   And so the Scottish grandees had no fine Edinburgh mansions like those of the English nobles in Bloomsbury and the Strand, but were fain, during the session of Parliament, to live each in a flat over the High Street.

In such a town, where every flat was accounted as a separate ' house,' and no houses were numbered, it may well be imagined that it was difficult for letters to reach their destination, or for strangers to find their way.   Indeed, without the services of the self-disciplined regiment of keen-eyed, quick-witted, dependable ' caddies,' business could scarcely have been carried on in the mazy wynds and stairways of old Edinburgh.

Scottish literature was centred in the capital, but it gave no sign as yet of the great awakening that lay before it in the latter half of the new century.   The material was there in the heart and mental habits of the nation, but the Promethean fire had not yet descended.   The mind of the people throve on the ballads sung, the stories told, the doctrines debated round the peat-fire in the peasant's cottage.   Printed books, other than the Bible, consisted chiefly of theology or political pamphlets.

There was no native journalism.   The two papers, issued three times a week at Edinburgh, were the old-established *Gazette* and its rival the *Courant*, started in 1705 ; both existed by special permission of the Privy Council ; they were tame organs of officialdom, in form mere imitations of the London papers, full of continental and English news but telling the Scots nothing about their own affairs.   With the disappearance of the Scottish Privy Council soon after the Union, the Edinburgh press acquired a certain freedom, and in the last years of Anne's reign began to have a life of its own, with a somewhat larger variety of newspapers.

The Scottish peasant, cramped in feudal bonds and mediaeval poverty, had one method of escape from his material lot—religion.   Other intellectual food was not offered him.   Bible on knee, in harsh, delightful argument with his minister or his cronies, he inhabited a realm of thought and imagination, deep, narrow, intense, for good and for evil utterly unlike the merry-go-round of disconnected information and ideas in which the popular mind of our own day gyrates.   Never consulted by his betters about politics, and without representation in the Estates of Parliament, he took all the keener interest in the proceedings of the assemblies where his influence was felt, the hierarchy of Church courts—the Kirk Session of the Parish, the Presbytery of a dozen parishes, the Provincial Synod, and the national General Assembly annually held at Edinburgh.   In all of these the laity were represented, as they were not in the purely clerical convocations of York and Canterbury.   It has often been said that the Church Assembly was Scotland's Parliament more truly than the three Estates.   And in the absence of any representative local government, the Kirk Session, where the lay elders kept the minister in awe, was the nearest approach to a parish council.

The parish church, with its roof of turf or thatch, was a small and tumble-down building ; it had no mediaeval splendours or amenities, and would in England have been deemed more fitted for a barn.   In the country churches there were seldom pews, except for the elders and a few privileged families.   Most men and women stood during the service, or else sat on ' creepies,' stools such as that with which Jennie Geddes had marked her disapproval of the Prayer Book service.   Yet the hard, ill-furnished room was crowded every Sabbath for two services of three hours each by a congregation of whom many had come on foot long miles across the moor.   So small was the space inside the church that an overflow of the pious was often crowded out into the churchyard, where the Bible was read to them by a lad put up upon a tombstone.

The most solemn and impressive of popular religious rites were the Communions, held out of doors at long tables, gatherings under the eye of summer heaven that reminded everyone present of more dangerous meetings held on the moorside in the ' killing times.'   Eight or ten parishes combined to hold a communion each in turn, from June to August, and many persons attended them one after the other, thinking nothing of walking forty miles over the hills to get there. The older Presbyterian clergy in Queen Anne's reign were men whose education had been interrupted and whose spirits had been disturbed and embittered by persecution. One who knew them in their later years described them as—

weak, half-educated men, their lives irreproachable, and their manners austere and rustic. Their prejudices coincided perfectly with their congregations who in respect of their sound fundamentals made great allowances for their foibles and weaknesses.

'Presbyterian eloquence' was a byword with English hearers for its uncouth treatment of religious mysteries, its familiar apostrophes of the Almighty, its denunciation of such harmless acts as wearing smart clothes in church or taking in the London *Spectator*. But it was an Englishman who wrote :

Were the ministerial office in England discharged as it is in Scotland, in that laborious and self-denying manner, and under such small encouragements, thousands of the clergy I daresay would wish to have been brought up mechanics rather than parsons. Here are no drones, no idle parsons, no pampered priests, no dignities or preferments to excite ambition.

Indeed, the ambition of a peasant's son, such as most of the ministers were in origin, was honourably satisfied with the leadership of a parish and the confidence of its people. Meanwhile there was growing up a younger generation, better educated in less troublous times, with more sense of proportion in thought and refinement in language, who were soon, as ' Moderates,' to be openly at odds with the older men whom Claverhouse had dragooned into bigotry.

The Kirk Session of self-important lay elders, acting conjointly with the minister, interfered in ordinary life to an excessive degree. Week in, week out, the Kirk Session and the superior court of the Presbytery were trying cases of alleged swearing, slander, quarrelling, breach of Sabbath, witchcraft and sexual offences. Some of these enquiries and judgments were properly conducted and useful, being such as were dealt with by ordinary magistrates in England. Others were intolerably vexatious, as when a woman was arraigned for carrying a pail on a Fast Day, and a crowder

for fiddling at a christening feast. The adulterer or forni-
cator of either sex was exposed on the stool of repentance in
church, to the merriment of the junior half of the congregation, to the grave reprobation of the more respectable, and
to the unblushing denunciations of the minister, renewed
sometimes for six, ten or twenty Sabbaths on end. There
was often a long row of penitents, and the ' gowns ' in
which they were clad were in such constant use that they
had frequently to be renewed. To avoid this intolerable
humiliation, poor girls often resorted to concealment of
pregnancy and sometimes to child murder. The Privy
Council was constantly dealing with the question of re-
mitting or enforcing the extreme penalty in such cases.

These activities of the Kirk Session and Presbytery had
much support in public opinion or they could not have so
long survived the disuse of similar Church jurisdiction in
England. But they aroused deep resentment in many, not
least among the upper classes. It is true that commutation
of penance for fines was often allowed in the case of the
gentry. But even with these mitigations, the jurisdiction
over conduct claimed by low-born elders and clergymen
was an offence to the proud families of lairds and nobles ;
it was an underlying cause of Episcopal religion and Jacobite
politics in many who had otherwise no quarrel with the
services and doctrines of the Presbyterian Church. Anti-
clericalism strengthened the Jacobites in Scotland, as it
strengthened the Whigs in England. Yet it must be
remembered that the stool of repentance and the jurisdiction
of Kirk Sessions had gone on even in the Episcopal days
of Charles II, and had not yet ceased in those numerous
parishes still ruled by Episcopalian ministers.

On the whole, the Episcopalian or Jacobite party depended on upper-class support more than the Presbyterian or Whig. The more rigorous the discipleship of
Knox, the more democratic were doctrine and practice
likely to be. The clash came in the appointment of ministers, which the true-blue Presbyterian claimed for the
people of the parish, both on grounds of religious doctrine
as to the call of pastors, and because the private patrons
who claimed to appoint were often very doubtful in their
Presbyterianism.

Episcopalian pamphleteers twitted the Presbyterians with their want of policy in ' constant taking part with the mob in all the disputes that happen betwixt them and the Nobility and Gentry in the choice of ministers, as if you relied upon them for the security of your establishment. . . The Nobility and Gentry in Scotland have the commons so much under, that it argues no small stupidity in you to have blundered in so plain a case.' Even English Nonconformist visitors to Scotland were astonished and alarmed at the boldness of the Church in its dealings with ' the Great.' Whatever its other faults, the Church of John Knox raised the downtrodden people of Scotland to look its feudal masters in the face.

The position of the Episcopalians at the beginning of the Eighteenth Century was most anomalous. Their services, doctrines, organization and discipline—except for the presence of Bishops who in fact exercised small authority—differed little save in emphasis from those of the Presbyterian Establishment. Yet the greatest bitterness prevailed between the two communions, because the difference of the Churches answered to the political difference of Whig and Jacobite, behind which lay two generations of feuds and wrongs inflicted and remembered on both sides.

The Episcopalians of Scotland were at once better and worse off than the Nonconformists of England. On the one hand there was not, until 1712, any Act of Toleration to legalize their services. On the other hand, more than a sixth of the parish churches were still occupied by their ministers. In Aberdeenshire, in the Highlands and along their eastern border, Presbyterian clergymen who showed themselves were liable to be attacked by mobs as savage as those who had ' rabbled ' the Episcopal ' curates ' of the South-West. When in 1704 the Presbyterian minister was to be inducted at Dingwall, he was stoned, beaten and driven away by a mob of men and women crying ' King Willie is dead and our King is alive.'

The popular feeling that thus found expression in the North-East arose less from religious differences than from political feuds, regional hatred of the Whiggamores of the South-West, and personal loyalty to old and tried pastors. In 1707 there were still 165 out of some 900 parishes in

Scotland where the minister adhered to the Episcopal Church.   But the great majority of the Episcopalian clergy had been deprived at the Revolution.   In Anne's reign they were living miserably enough, the more fortunate as chaplains in some great house, too many on alms collected from their co-religionists in Scotland, or from English churchmen who regarded them as martyrs in a common cause.

I have explained in an earlier chapter how the belief in witchcraft had already so far declined in the upper strata of English society that the persecution of witches in accordance with the law and with the dictates of popular superstition was ceasing to be permitted, in a country that was then ruled according to the ideas of its educated class.   In Scotland the same phenomena were repeated, a generation or two later.   At the beginning of the Eighteenth Century, part of the upper class was already dubious as to the frequency of diabolic agency, but popular and clerical fanaticism was still very strong.   Several supposed witches were put to death in Queen Anne's Scotland, and several more were banished forth of the realm.   In the reign of George I capital punishment was inflicted on witches for the last time in this island, in the recesses of far Sutherlandshire. In 1736 the law punishing witchcraft with death was repealed for Great Britain by the Westminster Parliament. After yet another generation had passed, witches and ' the muckle black de'il ' were a subject of jest rather than of dread to Burns and his farmer friends, although Presbyterians of the stricter way continued to regard disbelief in witchcraft as ' atheism ' and flying in the face of God's word.

The Presbyterian Church was not the fount and origin of popular superstitions.   It fostered some kinds and discouraged others.   But all had their roots far back in Popish, in pagan, in primeval instincts and customs still strong in a land of mountains, moors and yet unconquered nature, amid a population which even in the Lowlands was largely Celtic in origin and which lived under conditions in many respects little changed since the remote past.   Still, when the goodman came splashing home across the ford at

midnight, he heard the water kelpie roaring in the spate.
Fairies still lurked in the thorn trees of the dene, known
visitants to be propitiated by rites lest they should slay the
cattle in the byre or take the child from the cradle.   North
of Tay, men lit Beltan fires and danced round them, on
traditional heights, upon the first of May.   Crops and
cattle were defended by a number and variety of local
formulas of propitiation, some dating back to the earliest
times of agricultural and pastoral man,

> When holy were the haunted forest boughs,
> Holy the air, the water and the fire.

Magic wells were visited, and trees and bushes were decked
with rags of tartan and offerings of the fearful and grateful.
In parts of the Highlands such rites were the main religion
of the people ; in the Lowlands they were a subordinate but
still a real part of life and belief among a nation of Christian
kirk-goers.

In the absence of proper doctors for the countryside,
popular medicine was traditional, and it was sometimes hard
to distinguish it from a popular form of witchcraft.   There
were wise men and women who helped human happiness,
as well as warlocks and witches who hampered it.   The
Church encouraged the people to destroy the latter, but
could not prevent them from seeking the aid of the former.
The minister was not all-powerful.   How could he be,
since he forbade harmless pleasures ?   Lads and lassies,
'danced promisky' to fiddle or pipes at every festal
meeting, in spite of the Church's ban ; and neither old nor
young could be held back from rites older than Presbyter
or Pope.   There were a hundred different charms and
customs to avert ill-luck, suited to every event in life—
birth, marriage, death, the churning of milk, the setting
forth on a journey, the sowing of a field.

Miracle was looked upon as an everyday occurrence, far
more than in unimaginative, sceptical England.   Ghosts,
omens, apparitions were of the ordinary pattern of Scottish
life ; tales of living corpses taking part in the common
affairs of men were told with circumstance and believed ;
like the Greek of Homer's time, the Scot who met a stranger
on the moor might well be uncertain whether he was what

P 2

he seemed to be, or was ' no that canny.' The ' muckle black de'il ' was often seen waiting in the shadow at evening outside the cottage door, or slipping away over the north side of the kirkyard wall. The men who had been hunted on the moors by the dragoons, like Wodrow their historiographer, were always agape for the wonderful, moving in an element of divine and diabolic manifestations of power. Ministers encouraged such beliefs in their congregations. Shepherd lads, out alone for long hours upon the hills, had strange and sometimes beautiful fancies : Wodrow tells us in 1704 of one who declared that ' when herding in such a lee, there was a bonny man came to him, and bade him pray much and learn to read ; and he supposed it was Christ.' Next year he tells us of another lad who was once drowning in a well, but ' a bonny young man pulled him out by the hand. There was nobody near by at the time, so they concluded it was no doubt ane angel.' This is an older Scotland, not the Scotland of David Hume, Adam Smith or the Edinburgh Reviewers, not even the Scotland of Burns and Walter Scott, though it supplied them with matter for their argument.

If even in the Lowlands primitive and natural conditions bred primitive belief and natural fancies, it was even more so in the Highlands, the very home of the fairies and spirits of the mountain, of the formless monster that brooded unseen in the deep water beneath the boat, of second-sight, of omens and prophecy with which the little life of man was girt round. Beyond the Highland line, seldom passed by the Lowlander, and never without those qualms which beset Bailie Nicol Jarvie on his famous expedition, lay the grim, unmapped, roadless mountains, the abode of the Celtic tribes, speaking another language ; wearing another dress ; living under a system of law and society a thousand years older than that of Southern Scotland ; obedient neither to Kirk nor Queen, but to their own chiefs, clans, customs and superstitions. Till General Wade's work a generation later, there was no driving road through the Highlands. Nature reigned, gloomy, splendid, unchallenged—as yet unadmired—and man squatted in corners of her domain.

Far less accurate knowledge was available in London or even in Edinburgh about the state of the Highlands than can now be bought across the counter of a bookshop concerning the remotest parts of Africa. There was no tolerable book on the Highlands until Mr. Burt's letters of the following generation. A few pages at the beginning of Morer's account of Scotland told the English of Queen Anne's time almost all they cared to know about the unreclaimed northern end of the strange island they inhabited :

The Highlanders are not without considerable quantities of corn, yet have not enough to satisfie their numbers, and therefore yearly come down with their cattle, of which they have great plenty, and so traffick with the Low Landers for such proportions of oats and barly as their families or necessities call for. . . . Once or tweice a year great numbers of 'em get together and make a descent into the Low-Lands, where they plunder the inhabitants and so return back and disperse themselves. And this they are apt to do in the profoundest peace, it being natural to 'em to delight in rapine.

Defoe, writing to Harley from Edinburgh in November 1706, gives his Englishman's impression of the Highlanders :

' They are formidable fellows and I only wish Her Majesty had 25,000 of them in Spain, as a nation equally proud and barbarous like themselves. They are all gentlemen, will take affront from no man, and insolent to the last degree. But certainly the absurdity is ridiculous to see a man in his mountain habit, armed with a broadsword, target, pistol, at his girdle a dagger, and staff, walking down the High Street as upright and haughty as if he were a lord, and withal driving a cow ! '

What manner of life did the tribesman lead, unobserved at home, when he was not trading with the Lowlander or driving off his cattle ? It is a pathetic fallacy to suppose that the tribal land was the people's, and that they lived on it in rustic felicity, until the chiefs, in a sudden access of wickedness, took it from them after the ' forty-five.' In fact, the crofter of Queen Anne's reign was fain to hire a patch of ground from the ' tacksman ' or leaseholder of the chief, who sublet it on rack-rent terms that were usually most oppressive. The soil on the mountain-side was thin and stony, denuded by torrents, unimproved by manure ;

the agricultural implements and methods were more primitive than even in Southern Scotland ; the crofts were the merest hovels.   It could not be otherwise, for the scanty population was yet too large for the glens to support.   As the clansmen multiplied, the little farms were divided and subdivided with disastrous results.   It might easily have been prophesied that if ever the Highlands were brought into connection with the outer world by roads, or by military and political conquest, a great emigration would result as soon as the clansman had grasped the idea that change was possible in their mode of life.   In Anne's reign there was only a trickle of emigration into the Lowlands for the rougher types of service, and to the Continent to join the ' Irish ' regiments in French pay, which owed much to the Scottish Highlanders in their ranks.

The Chief had the power of life and death, and exercised it to the full, keeping his clan in awe, that was always strengthened by traditional loyalty and often by affection. But it depended on the uncertain personal factor whether a Chief was a tyrant or a father, or something between the two.   Just as Louis XIV taxed his peasants to keep up his army, so the Chief moved about with a train of armed relations and attendants, whom he supported in idleness at the expense of the rest of the clan ; but any more economical and peaceful habit of life would not have been appreciated by a race in whom personal and tribal pride was the dominant passion.

Many of the Highland Chiefs, besides the great Argyle, were also noblemen with a place in Edinburgh politics, and with something of the culture of France or of England.   But always the civilized Chief and his uncivilized followers had much in common—the pride of clan, the love of the harp and of the pipes, the stories and songs in which old feuds and fancies were still being woven by tribal poets into a living Gaelic literature.   If in the shadow of the glen and beside the hill-girt arms of the sea there was more of poverty and savagery than in other parts of the island, there was also more of poetry and wild imagination.

This state of things aroused the zeal of the Church Assembly and of the Society for Promoting Christian Knowledge ; from 1704 onwards many thousands of pounds were raised to initiate libraries, schools and Presbyterian missions in the Highlands, where religion was divided between Presbyterian, Roman Catholic, Episcopalian and primitive Pagan, in proportions which it would be difficult to determine. Some success was achieved at once, but in some places the mission was suppressed by violence at the orders of the Chief, and in others it lapsed in the course of years. It was after the ' forty-five,' when tribalism had been effectively put down by military and political invasion from the south, that the Presbyterian missionary had his chance, and the real evangelization of the Highlands took place.

Such, in some sort, was Scotland, when the circumstances of the passing hour brought to a final issue the ever-recurring problem of the closer Union of the whole island. In that design stark King Edward had failed, and Cromwell's arm had laxed its hold in death ; where force had been tried in vain, Queen Anne was to succeed by means more befitting her womanhood. The freely negotiated Treaty between the two countries, that united their Parliamentary and commercial systems, came into force in 1707 and opened the way to the movements that made modern Scotland.

BOOKS FOR FURTHER READING

H. G. Graham, *Social Life of Scotland in the Eighteenth Century.* A number of other books on the subject are cited in the second volume of my *England under Queen Anne (Ramillies and the Union with Scotland).*

II

SCOTLAND AT THE END OF THE EIGHTEENTH CENTURY

George III, 1760–1820

'PROGRESS,' as we of the Twentieth Century are better aware than our Victorian ancestors, is not always change from bad to good or from good to better, and the sum total of ' progress ' associated with the Industrial Revolution has not been wholly for the good of man. But the ' progress ' of Scotland in the second half of the Eighteenth Century was not only very rapid but very much in the right direction. No doubt it bore in itself the seed of future evil, but Scotland in 1800 was a better place than Scotland in 1700. The lifting of the pressure of dire poverty from the bulk of the population, and of penury from the higher classes, set the Scottish spirit free for its greatest achievements.

Release from the conditions of misery described in the first part of this chapter came mainly through a revolution in agricultural methods. It was analogous to the contemporary movement in rural England, but it marked an even greater change, for Scottish agriculture had been far worse than English when the Century opened. Improvement was begun by the action of certain Scottish landlords, who introduced English ploughmen and farmers to teach their tenants new ideas from South Britain ; and it culminated triumphantly during the Napoleonic Wars when stewards and ploughmen from the Lothians were taken to England to teach methods that had by that time been evolved in Scotland. Between 1760 and 1820 English agriculture had been progressing much faster than ever before or since ; yet during those very years Scottish agriculture caught it up and passed it.

As in England, the first movers in the change were individual landlords with a little capital, enterprise and outside knowledge. Their success set an example which was generally followed. The first thing to be done was to break up the ' run-rig ' system of common tillage (p. 431

above) ; it was conducted on methods more primitive than those of the English ' open fields ' ; it prevented individual initiative and gave neither security of tenure nor motive for exertion to the community of petty farmers, crushed under an obsolete feudalism. Unlike the old English copyholders, the Scottish tenants had no legal rights in the land, and they had short leases or none. But this system, bad as it was, had one advantage, that it could be easily terminated. There was nothing to prevent landlords bent on improvement from abolishing the ' run-rigs ' and re-dividing the land in compact farms, which they let to individual farmers at long leases of nineteen years or more. By this great reform the tenant obtained for the first time a motive to exert the long dormant energy and enterprise of the Scottish race.

There was indeed an obvious danger, as in the analogous case of the English enclosures, that some of the old tenants would be turned off the land altogether, as victims of reform. For instance, where a ' run-rig ' farm previously let to a community of a dozen tenants was enclosed and re-divided among half that number, what became of the rest ? A few went to the now prosperous towns or to the Colonies opened by the Union to Scottish emigration. But generally speaking, the number of people employed in Scottish agriculture increased rather than diminished, owing to the constant enlargement of the area of cultivated land. And the new acres won from the waste were often the best, being situated in the fertile valley bottom which only required artificial draining to be more valuable than the fields of older cultivation on the self-draining hillside above.

Both the old lands and the new were now enclosed with stone walls or hedges ; the high ' rigs ' were levelled ; the fields were drained, limed, manured ; one or two good horses took the place of the long train of starveling oxen at the plough ; men could now afford leather harness instead of horses' hair or rushes, iron ploughs instead of wooden, carts instead of sledges. Potatoes grown in the fields and vegetables in the garden varied the food of the population, while roots and other crops fed the cattle through the winter. Plantations of trees broke the wind and served the timber-requirements of the estate ; and, on a larger scale, new forests covered the hillsides in many parts of Scotland.[1]

After the Turnpike Act of 1751, the roads were so generally improved as to increase the marketing opportunities of farmers and industrialists alike. Agricultural prosperity supplied capital to be put back into the land. And Banks, established in County towns early in the reign of George III, helped both lairds and farmers to finance the changes they were together carrying out. The industrial and commercial growth of Clydeside created a market for agriculture and supplied capital for further improvement of the land. Estates were bought and developed by ' tobacco-lords ' of the Glasgow shipping world, and by adventurous Scots returned from British India where they had amassed fortunes. In short, there was simultaneous growth in all kinds of economic and social life, none at the expense of any other : for in that fortunate era industry and commerce were not the enemies but the allies of agriculture.

In this way the periodic famines, which had taken toll of the lives and energies of the Scottish people, lost their worst terrors. And, in ordinary years, real wages, farm profits and rents were all much higher than in former times. Potatoes, vegetables, cheese and occasionally meat were added to the porridge and milk, which was still the staple diet of the poor though the bowl was fuller than of old ; in Scotland as in England the smuggler helped to bring tea and tobacco into the homes even of the poorest. Scandalous as Scottish housing remained, there was great though not universal improvement even there ; in some regions solid stone farms, and cottages with one or even two rooms, with chimneys, glass windows, beds, furniture and outside privies, replaced the hovels which the peasantry used to share with their cattle. The sturdy Scots of the time of Burns (1759–1796) looked a different race from their grandfathers, whom want of food, clothing and warmth had too often rendered haggard, slovenly and lethargic to the view.

---

[1] Dr. Johnson, who travelled in Scotland in 1773, continued to joke about its lack of trees. In fact some great plantations had already been made, but the trees were still saplings when he was there. Thirty years later the aspect of many parts of the country had been greatly changed in this respect.

Moreover the Scots were now free men.   The last evils
of moribund feudalism, which survived in Scotland for
centuries after they had ceased in England, were abolished
in 1748 by the Act which put an end to ' hereditable jurisdictions.'   In Lowlands and Highlands alike, the baron or
chief who had his private court to try his vassals and tenants,
had been able, at will or whim, to imprison the disobedient
in fetid dungeons, without appeal lying to the King's
tribunals.   These powers, it was believed, helped Jacobite
lairds and chiefs to ' call out their men ' in 1745.   They
were accordingly abolished three years later, and there were
plenty of good reasons why they should go, apart from the
political motive that hastened their end.

In the Highlands, much disappeared besides the hereditable jurisdictions.   In the years following the suppression
of the ' forty-five,' the whole manner of life and society,
which had prevailed in the mountains of Scotland with
little change since prehistoric times, was swept away at a
blow.   The tribal system, the kilted warrior with broadsword and target, the patriarchal rule of the chief, vanished
for ever.   The Highlands became, for the first time in their
history, one with the rest of Scotland, so far as law, land-
tenure, education and religion could make Highlander and
Lowlander one.   The construction of the first roads
through the Highlands effected by General Wade in the
generation before 1745, had already carried Lowland
influence into the hills, and prepared the way for the great
change ; it must have come ere long, but would have come
more gradually, if the Jacobite invasion had not provoked
the long-suffering South to put an end once for all to the
thousand-year-old nuisance of the raiding tribes.
A population that had always lived for and by war was
at last effectively disarmed ; but its fighting instincts were
canalized into the Highland regiments of the Crown, that
did good service abroad for the Empire now common to
Englishmen and Scots, to Gael and Saxon.   The Chiefs
were turned into landlords, like the lairds in the South.
Henceforth justice and administration were royal and
national, not personal and tribal any more.   The
acceptance of these immense changes in the structure of

society indicated that the time for them was ripe. For some years after the Rebellion there was a period of tyranny and repression, the period described in Stevenson's *Kidnapped*, when the personal devotion of the clansmen to their banished chiefs was touchingly demonstrated. But there was no popular movement to restore an outworn state of society, and when the ex-Jacobite chiefs were permitted to return from abroad and their estates were restored to them under the new system of tenure, the conflict of loyalties came to an end. The tribal tartan, which had been proscribed, was again allowed to be worn, for the proud sentiments attaching to it were no longer disruptive of society and law.

Meanwhile Presbyterian missionaries and schoolmasters had been at work in the Highlands, and had from the first shown more tact and more sympathy with the Gael than the emissaries of the civil power. The imagination and intellect of the mountaineers, hitherto illiterate and poetical, had new channels opened to it by the work of the schools. Reading and writing were brought into the Highlands mainly by the Scottish Society for Propagating Christian Knowledge, which began its mission in that wild region in the reign of Anne, but was only able to succeed there on a large scale when the country was opened by the breaking of the clans after Culloden. The unity of Scottish society was achieved on the religious and educational side before the century ended, though the Highlands remained bilingual. In the glens where the Roman Catholic religion prevailed, its hold was unshaken ; but the old paganism disappeared.

Closely connected with this educational movement was the great change in the economic side of Highland life. Under the tribal system, the population had been much larger than the barren mountains could maintain. The ambition of each Chieftain had been to increase not the amount of his rents but the number of his armed followers ; while the tribesmen, accustomed to dire poverty and periodic famine, had neither the knowledge nor the opportunity to emigrate into the lands where Gaelic was an unknown tongue. But the new times were more favourable to emigration. The Chief, when transmuted into a peaceful landlord, wanted money more than men. And his sorely oppressed tenants became aware, by means of the new roads and schools, of a wealthier world outside the mountains and beyond the sea. The age of Highland emigration set in, very largely to Canada, while at home sheep-runs often replaced the little holdings of the crofters. In the 'seventies there were great emigrations from the Highlands and the Islands, and again in 1786–1788 as a result of the terrible famines of 1782–1783. Under the old system such famines had often taken place, but had not been followed by emigration, because the tribesmen had not known how or whither to emigrate.

Now, in some districts, the landlords themselves stimulated emigration by evictions. But elsewhere they strove to keep people at home by the introduction of the potato, and sometimes by their opposition to the schools of the S.P.C.K. For the missionary-schoolmasters were the real promoters of emigration. They even accused the gentry of trying ' to keep the people at home in ignorance and subjection.' The Highlander could only hope for a higher standard of living if he went oversea, or at least outside the mountain region. And as a preparation for departure, he must learn English, as he could now do at the missionary schools.

The English tongue and the Gaelic Bible suggested two ways of escape from conditions which were fast becoming intolerable. Far from undermining the characteristic independence of the Highlanders, the Charity Schools provided them with the only means of translating it into effective action. To men of vigour and courage the English language offered a new world across the seas ; to those who remained behind, the schools made possible independent access to the consolations of the Bible.[1]

The Union of the political and commercial systems of England and Scotland had alone rendered possible the social revolution in the Highlands, the colonization of the British Empire by Scots, the development of Glasgow's transatlantic trade and the consequent industrialization of Clydeside. These changes, like the agricultural revolution, were mainly an affair of the last half of the Century, but during that period they were very rapid.

[1] Miss M. G. Jones, *The Charity School Movement of the* 18th *Century,* chap. **VI.**

At the time of the Union of 1707 Glasgow was a market
and University town with a population of 12,500, an out-
post of Southern civilization against the Highland tribes,
the capital of the Covenanting West ; its inhabitants were
rigid and censorious in their Presbyterian zeal, simple in
manners, frugal in expense, and strictly sober ; its leading
citizens, such as Bailie Nicol Jarvie, lived among their
fellow-citizens in modest quarters in the heart of the town.
By 1800 great changes had taken place : Glasgow numbered 80,000 inhabitants, sharply divided by differences in
wealth and manner of life, and no class among them was
any longer famous either for church going or for abstention
from drink.   Well-to-do suburbs and new slum tenements
had spread over the surrounding land.   There were shops
to suit every taste, with wares from England, Europe and
America ;   there were sedan chairs, concerts, balls, cards
and dice, punch, wine and English literature for the rich,
and Highland whisky for the poor.   The University had
won European fame through Professor Adam Smith.

These social changes had taken place, because the
American and West Indian trade, chiefly in tobacco and
raw cotton, had by 1800 transformed not only Glasgow but
all Clydeside into a commercial and industrial district as
up to date as any in England ;   it had already given the
world James Watt, one of the lords of the new ascendant,
the inventor of the modern condensing engine.   Western
Scotland was already beginning to suffer from the advent of Irish labourers, who made the Glasgow slums even
worse than bad housing would in any case have rendered
them.

In the last twenty years of the Century, cotton mills were
rising in villages of Lanark, Renfrew and Ayr, with social
consequences described in Galt's *Annals of the Parish*, that
little story book, first published in 1821, which still remains
the most intimate and human picture of Scotland during her
period of change in the reign of George III.

The opening of the Scottish-American trade by the Union
had naturally had less influence on the fortunes of towns
upon the East Coast.   Indeed, the old-established commerce
of Leith and Dundee with the Baltic and German ports lost
rather than gained by the British mercantilist policy of

the Navigation Acts, which aimed at enlarging colonial trade with America at the expense of commerce with Europe.

On the other hand it was in the East that the first Scottish ironworks were erected. At Carron, between Stirling and Edinburgh, iron-ore, coal and water-power were found together ; coal-coke was now applied to the smelting of iron. The Carron Company, founded in 1760, prospered ; one of its early articles of production was the short naval gun known therefore as the ' carronade.' Such was the beginning of the Scottish iron industry that took on such great proportions in the following century.

But the only town of the Scottish East Coast that made striking advance in the Eighteenth Century was Edinburgh. No longer a political capital, it was still the legal, fashionable and intellectual capital of the country ; and law, fashion and intellect were all rapidly on the upgrade in the wealthier and more active-minded Scotland of the new era. Moreover, the now famous agriculture of the Lothians had advanced even faster than the agriculture of the West. The South-Eastern Scotland of Walter Scott's youth was a land of rural wealth and mental energy centred on Edinburgh. The Scottish capital was famous throughout Europe for its ' philosophers'—Hume, Robertson and Dugald Stewart ; its lawyers and academicians were men of remarkable personality and intellectual power. Joined with these professional classes, the nobles and gentry of the region, busy with the improvement of the land and the planting of forests, combined to form a splendid society, worthy of the immortality given to it by its own artist, Raeburn.

It is indeed true that, during this golden age of Scotland, her political life was dead. To use Cockburn's words, she ' had no free political institutions whatever ' : the absence of ' political institutions ' was indeed a feature of the whole period from the Union to the Reform Bill, under Whig and Tory rule alike, but as long as Jacobitism had been active, there was a diseased kind of political life—a constant sedition. After 1746 that too had gone, till the Radical movement arose in 1790, to be at once suppressed by a harsh government persecution. Under the rule of Pitt's friend Dundas, Scotland was ' a lodge at a great man's gate,' as the Reformers bitterly said. But politics are not every-thing. The social, imaginative and intellectual life of the land of Burns and Scott was vigorous in inverse proportion to the political atrophy ; it sprang from native sources, and though closer connection with England had given it an impulse, it paid back to England more than it borrowed. Adam Smith devised policies for the statesmen of Great Britain. And for several years at the beginning of the Nineteenth Century, while the *Lay of the Last Minstrel* and *Marmion* were initiating the ' romantic' period of letters in our island, the very unromantic *Edinburgh Review* en-joyed almost a monopoly of literary and philosophic criticism in England. The rival *Quarterly* was soon set up against it, largely by the efforts of Scotchmen. For some years Edinburgh was hardly less important than London in the British world of letters.

Physically, too, Edinburgh had grown out of her hard old shell. The insanitary warren of deep wynds and lofty tenement flats off High Street, where the greatest men in Scotland and their families had formerly consented to be cabined in darkness and dirt, were deserted for the spacious and dignified houses, built after 1780 in the region of new squares beyond Princes Street. The bridging of the Nor' Loch in 1767 had opened out for development this new Edinburgh. Instead of paying £15 a year for an ill-lighted flat seven storeys off the ground, persons of position could now afford to pay £100 a year for a comfortable town house. Similarly in the countryside, the tall, grim, gothic towers rising from the naked fields, that had served for the country seats of the gentry, were, at least in many cases, replaced by Georgian or classical mansions, cheerful, well lighted and sheltered by trees. But architecture never attained in Scotland to the importance which it had for centuries had in England. In spite of much improvement, particularly the fine stone farms of the Lothians, housing north of the Tweed remained on the average below the level of South Britain. Even in the Lowlands there were still many one-roomed cottages, still in some cases shared by the cow ; and the high slum tenements of Glasgow and Edinburgh were worse than ever because they had now been abandoned by the well-to-do. Nevertheless there had during the

Century been great progress in housing, though less than in food, clothes and education.[1]

The rapid changes in Scottish mind and manners during the Eighteenth Century did not come into any serious collision with the influence of the Church, such as marked contemporary movements of opinion in France. For the clergy and religious laity of Scotland moved with the times towards a more tolerant and a more reasonable outlook. Presbyterian bigotry, which had been so crude in the years immediately following the Revolution of 1688, began to soften as a generation of younger clergy and elders, who knew not Claverhouse, gradually took the place of the fierce old prophets of the moss-hags. The enjoyment of toleration, better education, English influence, and the indefinable ' spirit of the age ' broadened their vision as the years went by. Witch hunting died out. The latitudinarian movement prevailing in the contemporary Church of England had a close analogy in the views of the Moderates, who became the most influential section of the Scottish clergy. The sage leadership of the historian Robertson (1721–1793) guided the Church Assembly into the ways of peace.

It is possible that some of the Moderates went too far in the sweet reasonableness of their moderation, and the more zealous of their ever critical hearers had perhaps some reason in their complaints against sermons that were ' a cauld clatter of morality,' lacking in orthodox doctrine and apostolic zeal. In due course the pendulum swung back, and in the early Nineteenth Century the Evangelical revival, connected with men like Dr. Chalmers (1780–1847), breathed fresh power into Scottish religion. But the religion of Chalmers was no longer a narrow and persecuting creed : the ' Moderates ' had done their work.

The Eighteenth Century also saw great changes in the fortunes and in the spirit of the Episcopalian minority. At the time of the Union of 1707 the Episcopalians were a formidable body, practically identical with the Jacobites, and prepared to fight for a Restoration of their Church and

[1] An interesting comparison of Scottish and English housing of the working classes about 1820, with its local variations, will be found in Professor Clapham's Economic History of Modern England, I, pp. 21–41.

of their King ; they did not, however, use the Prayer Book, and their religion was only a milder form of that of the Presbyterian Establishment.   But as the Century went on they drew nearer to the rest of the nation in politics and further from it in religion.   After the death of Jacobitism they became loyal subjects of George III, while their adoption of a Prayer Book closely resembling the English divided them off from their fellow Scots as a religious community with an ethos of its own.   Their numbers dwindled. In Anne's reign they had been the Church of the People in many parts of Eastern Scotland, and had as such been permitted at the Revolution to continue in occupation of parish churches and manses in spite of the law.   But as that generation of incumbents died off, they were replaced by Presbyterian ministers.

On the other hand, the position of the Episcopalians was improved in one important respect.   They had not, at the Revolution, been granted an Act of Toleration like the English Dissenters.   Their position was in every respect anomalous, depending not on law but on local opinion and force.   At length in 1712 the Tories of the Westminster Parliament passed a Toleration Act for Scotland—a first-fruit of the Union eminently right and proper, but regarded with deep suspicion by the Presbyterians as the herald of further attacks on the established order.

Indeed, there followed in a few weeks another and more questionable interference of the British Parliament in the affairs of the Scottish Church.   In 1712 Patronage was restored—that is, the right of individual proprietors to appoint to livings.   To an Englishman accustomed to the system in the Anglican Church this may seem a small matter, but Scottish religious and social history was profoundly affected for 150 years to come by the restoration of Patronage.

The democratic element in the appointment of ministers to parishes was regarded by orthodox Presbyterians as an essential point of religion ; and apart from all theory, there was a practical danger in presentation by patrons many of whom were latitudinarians, Episcopalians or Jacobites. For these reasons Patronage had been abolished by a law of the Scottish Parliament at the Revolution : by the Act of 1690 the Protestant heritors and elders should ' name and

propose ' a minister to the whole congregation, which if
dissatisfied might appeal to the Presbytery, whose decision
should be final.   But now, in 1712, the ' prelatic ' Parliament of Westminster altered this law, in defiance of the
spirit of the Union Treaty.   The right of presentation was
restored to the old patrons, unless they were Roman
Catholics.

Although the new law was deeply resented, its consequences were not remarkable for the first generation after
its passage.   But the ultimate outcome was momentous
indeed.   Patronage was the root cause of a long series of
secessions of Presbyterian bodies from an Established
Church bound by this State-made law.   For good or for
evil, Scotland, hitherto inimical to Sects such as flourished
in England, saw the rise of a number of Nonconformist
Churches, competing with the Establishment, though
differing from it in doctrine and ritual hardly at all.

The restoration of Patronage had also the effect of helping
the rise of the Moderate Party in the Church.   In the
Eighteenth Century the rights of the patrons were often
exerted to place moderate-minded ministers in parishes of
zealots, who objected to their intrusion, yet benefited by
their mild ministrations.   Readers of Galt's *Annals of the
Parish* will not forget that in the first year of George III's
reign the excellent Mr. Balwhidder was thus intruded, ' for
I was put in by a patron, and people knew nothing what-
soever of me, and their hearts were stirred into strife on the
occasion.'   Some critics of the bigotry of the older Calvinism have said in their haste that the Scots were ' a priest-
ridden people.'   It would be truer to say that theirs was
' a people-ridden clergy.'   The zealots in the congregation
kept a close eye on their minister's orthodoxy.   In the
Eighteenth Century many of the placed clergy did all they
could to liberalize Scottish religion, often at the price of
unpopularity with their lay parishioners.

In the Nineteenth Century the long-drawn-out consequences of the Patronage Act of 1712 culminated in the
secession of the Free Church under Chalmers, a protest on
behalf of evangelical liberty which is one of the great facts
of the modern history of Scotland (1843).   At length, in
1875, the measure so lightly passed in Anne's reign was

reversed, with the consequence that a path was opened for the ultimate reunion of the divided parts of the Church of Scotland, which took place in our own day, after the State had still further declared the unfettered freedom of the Church over the entire field of matters spiritual by the Act of 1921.

In the course of the Eighteenth Century the inhabitants of Scotland rose in numbers from about a million to 1,652,000. This represents a natural increase, as the emigration of the Highlanders can be set against the immigration of the Irish. The rise in population, unprecedented in any previous century of Scottish history, was due, like the contemporary rise in the numbers of Englishmen, to the rapid fall of the death-rate. It was the outcome of improved conditions of life, and of better doctoring, a science in which Scots in the reign of George III were already able to instruct the English.

Rapid as was the rise of Scotland's population in the Eighteenth Century, it had not been as rapid as the increase of her wealth. The Excise revenue in 1707 was £30,000 ; in 1797 it was close on one million three hundred thousand. The day of small things was over.

But Scotland had still a bad hour to pass through. The Napoleonic Wars witnessed a great rise in prices of food, accompanied by much general distress. Again there were ' dear years ' in 1799 and 1800, when ' oatmeal was as high as ten shillings a stone,' and Thomas Carlyle's father noticed the labourers ' retire each separately to a brook, and there drink instead of dining—without complaint, anxious only to hide it.' But they no longer died of starvation by scores and hundreds, depopulating whole clachans, as in the ' dear years ' of King William a century before.[1]

[1] The last half of Carlyle's sketch of his father James Carlyle in the *Reminiscences*, contains many vivid particulars of Scottish peasant life in the last half of the Eighteenth Century. At Langholm, James Carlyle ' once saw a heap of smuggled tobacco publicly burnt. Dragoons were ranged round it with drawn swords ; some old women stretched through their old withered arms to snatch a little of it, and the dragoons did not hinder them.' The working women of those western parts, including Thomas Carlyle's mother, smoked tobacco in short clay pipes.

CHAPTER XV

I

Change in Town and Country—Factories—Working-class conditions—Coloni-
zation—Education—Luddites—Trade Unions.
(The Wars with France, 1793–1815. Waterloo, 1815. Peterloo, 1819.
The Reform Bill, 1831–1832.)

BETWEEN the classical world of the Eighteenth Century with
its self-confidence and self-content, and the restless England
of Peterloo and the rick-burnings, of Byron and Cobbett,
were interposed twenty years of war with Revolutionary
and Napoleonic France (1793–1815).

Coming at a critical moment in our social development,
the long war was a grave misfortune. With its violent
disturbances of economic life, and its mood of 'anti-
Jacobin' reaction against all proposals for reform and all
sympathy with the claims and sufferings of the poor—the
war formed the worst possible environment for the industrial
and social changes then in rapid progress. The modern
English slum town grew up to meet the momentary needs
of the new type of employer and jerry builder, unchecked
and unguided by public control of any sort. A rampant
individualism, inspired by no idea beyond quick money
returns, set up the cheap and nasty model of modern
industrial life and its surroundings. Town-planning,
sanitation and amenity were things undreamt of by the
vulgarian makers of the new world, while the aristocratic
ruling class enjoyed its own pleasant life apart, and thought
that town building, sanitation and factory conditions were
no concern of government. Great cities would in any case
have been bad enough, as the slums of Eighteenth Century
London had already shown, but the circumstances of the
Napoleonic period in England were peculiarly unfavourable
to the better development of the grim factory towns of the
North, and to the relations of the new type of employer to

the new type of employee.   Man had acquired formidable tools for refashioning his life before he had given the least thought to the question of what sort of life it would be well for him to fashion.

Since municipal lethargy and corruption had long lost all touch with the civic traditions and public spirit of mediaeval corporate life, the sudden growth of the new factory quarters did not disturb the slumbers of the town oligarchies, who were so well accustomed to neglect their old duties that they were incapable of rising to a new call. And when, as usually happened, the development took place outside the area of any corporate town, the gentlemen magistrates of the County made no pretence to control housing activities.

When Waterloo was fought, rural England was still in its unspoilt beauty, and most English towns were either handsome or picturesque. The factory regions were a small part of the whole, but unluckily they were the model for the future. A new type of urban community was permitted to grow up which it was fatally easy to imitate on an ever increasing scale, until in another hundred years the great majority of Englishmen were dwellers in mean streets. When, as the Nineteenth Century advanced, local government was gradually made to attend to its duties, by being subjected to democratic local election and to central control from Whitehall, then indeed large provision was made for health, convenience and education. But even after these belated reforms in the utilitarian sphere, ugliness remains a quality of the modern city, rendered acceptable by custom to a public that can imagine only what it has seen.

The course of the Napoleonic wars, with blockade and counter-blockade, made business a gamble. There was every incitement to manufacturing enterprise, except security. England's control of the sea, and her new power of machine production, not yet imitated in other lands, gave her a monopoly of many markets in America, Africa and the Far East. But the European markets were alternately opened and closed to British goods according to the vagaries of diplomacy and war. One year an allied State would have its armies clothed and shod by British workmen : next year it might be under the heel of France, a part of Napoleon's 'continental system.' The unnecessary war with the United States (1812–1815) was another element of disturbance to trade. The sufferings of the English working class were increased by these violent fluctuations of demand and employment ; and unemployment was worst of all during the post-war slump after Waterloo.

The war had also the effect of shutting out the supply of European corn, which had at last become necessary to steady food prices in our thickly populated island. Wheat rose from 43 shillings a quarter in 1792, the year before the war broke out, to 126 shillings in 1812, the year Napoleon went to Moscow. The poor, both in town and country, suffered terribly from the price of bread, though it put money into the pockets of tenant farmers, freehold yeomen, and receivers of tithe and rent. During the twenty years of war, the extent and character of land cultivation was adapted to these high prices, so that when corn fell at the return of peace many farmers were ruined and rents could not be paid. In these circumstances the protective Corn Law of 1815 was passed, with the aim of restoring agricultural prosperity at the expense of the consumer. It encountered the most violent opposition from the town population of all classes irrespective of party. The landlord members of Parliament complained that, as they went down to the House to vote for the Bill, they had been savagely mauled by a mob set on ' by the inflammatory speeches of Baring the banker, and the false statements of the Lord Mayor of London.' (Sir R. Heron's *Notes*, ed. 1851, p. 50.) For a generation to come, until the Repeal of the Corn Laws in 1846, the question of agricultural protection divided England, and gave a political focus to the differentiation between urban and rural life which the Industrial Revolution was making more marked every year, as the inhabitants of the town lost all touch with the farming, and the inhabitants of the village with manufacture.

The observant eyes of Defoe, as he rode through Queen Anne's England, had been pleased by the harmony of the economic and social fabric. It was shattered now, giving place to a chaos of rival interests, town against country, rich against poor. A hundred years after Defoe, another horseman, William Cobbett, on his ' rural rides ' noted the new symptoms ; the wrongs of the disinherited poor inspired his headlong, single-handed crusade against the phalanx of their oppressors. The poor, perhaps, had in reality always been as poor and as ill used ; but their evil plight became more obvious to themselves and to others, now that they were segregated and massed together. In the past, poverty had been an individual misfortune ; now it was a group grievance.   It was a challenge to the humanitarian spirit which the Eighteenth Century had engendered.   That spirit had been obscured for awhile by England's angry fright at the French Revolution, but in the new Century it could no longer regard the victims of economic circumstance with the hard indifferent eye of earlier ages.   So Cobbett's blustering words had weight.

The poor suffered by the war.   But at no period had the landed gentry been wealthier or happier, or more engrossed in the life of their pleasant country houses.   The war was in the newspapers, but it scarcely entered the lives of the enjoying classes.   No young lady of Miss Austen's acquaintance, waiting eagerly for the appearance of Scott's or Byron's next volume of verse, seems ever to have asked what Mr. Thorpe or Mr. Tom Bertram were going to do to serve their country in time of danger.   For in those happy days the navy was a perfect shield to the safety and to the amenities of island life.   While Napoleon was ramping over Europe, the extravagance and eccentricity of our dandies reached their highest point in the days of Beau Brummell, and English poetry and landscape-painting enjoyed their great age.   Wordsworth, whose mind had, in time of peace, been aroused and disturbed by the French Revolution, so completely recovered his equanimity during the long war that he was able to produce a body of philo-sophic poetry expressive of

> ' central peace subsisting at the heart
> Of endless agitation,'

a mood which it is more difficult to catch and keep under the conditions of modern totalitarian warfare.

During half the years of the struggle with France,

England sent no expeditionary force to Europe, and even the seven campaigns of the Peninsular War cost less than 40,000 British dead : the blood tax was a light one for all classes. Mr. Pitt's income tax was more vexatious, but rent and tithe had risen with the price of corn, so that landowners did well upon the balance. The ' gentlemen of England ' beat Napoleon, the professional, and they deservedly won praise and prestige for a victory which, not being abused, gave us the priceless boon of a hundred years' immunity from another ' great war.' But the gentlemen had fought and conquered the upstart on very easy terms for themselves, and so in the years that followed the restoration of peace they were, somewhat ungratefully perhaps, denounced by the rising generation of reformers as having been war profiteers.

> See these inglorious Cincinnati swarm,
> Farmers of war, dictators of the farm ;
> *Their* ploughshare was the sword in hireling hands,
> *Their* fields manured by gore of other lands ;
> Safe in their barns, these Sabine tillers sent
> Their brethren out to battle. Why ? for rent !
> Year after year they voted cent for cent,
> Blood, sweat, and tear-wrung millions—why ? for rent !
> They roar'd, they dined, they drank, they swore they meant
> To die for England,—why then live ? for rent !
>   (Byron, *The Age of Bronze*, 1823.)

If the war proved a source of increased wealth to the landlords and of prolonged calamity to the wage-earner, it was a gamble to ' the middling orders of society ' : it made this merchant a profiteer, like old Osborne in *Vanity Fair*, and that other, like poor Mr. Sedley, a bankrupt. As a whole, ' the nation of shopkeepers' longed for peace, to bring security, to open the European markets once for all and to reduce taxation. But they had no thought of surrender to Bonaparte. Many of the wealthier—the bankers, the old-established merchants and moneyed men, and their families—shared the Tory politics of the ' quality,' to whose society they were admitted, with whom they married, and from whom they bought seats in Parliament and commissions in the army. But many a manufacturer of the new type, himself or his father sprung from the yeoman or from the working class, more often than not a Dissenter, his thoughts engrossed by the factory he had built beside some Pennine stream, had no love for the aristocracy, and dumbly resented the war as something from the glory and interest of which he was excluded. Such men were making the new wealth of England, but they had no part in her government either central or local, and they were jealous of the haughty class that kept them out. They felt too little sympathy with the real victims of the war, their own employees—as little indeed as the landlords and farmers felt with the ill-fed workers of the field whose labour filled their pockets so full. It was a hard world of sharply divided interests, with small sense of national brotherhood, save occasionally in face of the foreign foe.

For all that, we must not exaggerate the actual amount of discontent, particularly in the first part of the war. The democratic movement, inspired by the original French Revolution and the writings of Tom Paine, was suppressed in the ''nineties,' quite as much by public opinion as by government action : working-class mobs in Birmingham and in Manchester sacked the chapels and houses of the Dissenting reformers, and the Durham miners burnt Tom Paine in effigy. In the bulk of the working class, discontent only grew slowly as a result of very real suffering, and for a long time it was sectional and regional, not national. Even during the period of anti-Jacobin repression, when it was ' safer to be a felon than a reformer,' the majority of Englishmen were still proud of themselves as being a free people. In the year of Trafalgar, a distinguished American scientist, visiting the London theatres, notes that

Enthusiastic applauses were bestowed by the Galleries this evening on this sentiment, that if a poor man had an honest heart there lived not one in England who had either the presumption or the power to oppress him. In this incident may be seen the active jealousy of liberty which exists even in the lowest orders of England.[1]

It is to be feared that the ' sentiment ' was unduly optimistic, but the fact that it could be applauded by the ' gallery ' is not without pleasant significance.

[1] B. Silliman's *Travels in England in 1805,* New York 1810, I, p. 252.

Bread and cheese became, in many southern counties, the staple diet of the labourer, washed down with beer or tea. They seldom saw meat, though many grew potatoes in the cottage garden. The danger of sheer starvation with which the rural poor were faced in many districts owing to war prices and low wages, was averted by a remedy that brought much evil in its train. In May 1795 the magistrates of Berkshire were summoned to meet at Speenhamland, a northern suburb of Newbury, for the expressed purpose of fixing and enforcing a minimum wage for the county in relation to the price of bread. It would have been a difficult policy to carry out against the resistance of recalcitrant farmers, during a period of violent price fluctuations ; but in principle it was the true remedy. If it had been adopted for Berkshire and for all England, it might have diverted our modern social history into happier channels. It was the right course, and it was appointed by ancient custom and existing law. Unfortunately, the J.P.s who had come to Speenhamland for this good purpose, were there persuaded not to enforce the raising of wages but to supplement wages out of the parish rates. They drew up and published a scale by which every ' poor and industrious person ' should receive from the parish a certain sum per week in addition to his wages, so much for himself and so much for other members of his family, when the loaf cost a shilling. As the loaf rose, the dole was to rise with it. This convenient scale, vulgarly known as the ' Speenhamland Act,' was adopted by the magistrates in one county after another, till the evil system was established in perhaps half rural England, particularly in the Counties of recent enclosures. The Northern Counties were among those outside the system, for in the North the near neighbourhood of factories and mines tended to keep up rural wages by competition.

This payment of rates in aid of wages relieved the large employing farmer from the necessity of giving a living wage to his workpeople, and most unjustly forced the small independent parishioner to help the big man, while at the same time it compelled the labourer to become a pauper even when he was in full work ! The moral effect was devastating on all concerned. The large farmers were confirmed

Q

in their selfish refusal to raise wages, the independent classes staggered under the burden of the poor-rate, while idleness and crime increased among the pauperized labourers. An American observer wrote with too much truth in 1830 :

'The term pauper as used in England and more particularly in agricultural districts, embraces that numerous class of society who depend for subsistence solely upon the labour of their hands.' [1]

It is not, however, true, as was thought at the time, that rates in aid of wages were an important cause of the rapid rise of population which Malthus was teaching his contemporaries to dread so much. In the Nineteenth as in the Eighteenth Century, the rise of population was due not to an increase in births but to a decrease in deaths. Not the foolish magistrates of Speenhamland but the good doctors of Great Britain were responsible for the fact that between 1801–1831, the inhabitants of England, Wales and Scotland rose from eleven to sixteen and a half millions.

The price of corn during the war, while it starved and pauperized the labourer, not only benefited the landlord and large tenant farmer, but for a time checked the decline of the freehold yeoman and the copyhold peasant. But after Waterloo, with the crash in corn prices, the reduction in the ranks of the small cultivators was resumed. It was upon them that the Speenhamland system weighed hardest financially, for in many Southern Counties, particularly in Wiltshire, the numerous farmers who employed no paid labour themselves were forced to pay heavy poor-rates in order to eke out the wages paid by the large employing farmers, their rivals who were destined to supersede them. And the small cultivator still suffered by the continued enclosure of the open fields and commons, and by the progressive decline of cottage industries.

Yet we must not exaggerate the pace and extent of change. The Census of 1831 shows that out of just under a million

---

[1] Between 1792 and 1831 poor-law expenditure in the County of Dorset increased 214 per cent., expenses for prosecutions for crime 2135 per cent., whilst the population had only increased 40 per cent. (*Victoria County History, Dorset*, II, 259). In 1813 more than seven millions were raised in all England for poor-rate, while local taxation for all other purposes only amounted to one and a half millions.

families engaged in agriculture, nearly 145,000 were those of owners or farmers who hired no labour, as against 686,000 families of field labourers for hire. That is to say, on the eve of the Reform Bill, the agricultural proletariate proper were only two and a half times as numerous as the independent cultivators of the soil. And there was still a 'small peasantry' left, almost as numerous in fact as the farmers who paid wages to employees. But much the greater part of the acreage cultivated was now in the hands of the large farmers, and the open fields and commons had for the most part gone.

Once the war and its reactions were well over, it appears from statistical calculation of real wages that the agricultural labourer was no worse off in 1824 than he had been thirty years before, taking the average of the country as a whole.[1] In some regions he was decidedly better off. But his standard of life had declined in those parts of the rural South which lay farthest from the wage-competition of factories and mines, particularly where the poor-rates were being employed to keep wages down, and where the labourer depended on the farmer who employed him for the clay-built hovel in which he lived. He was often forced to take part of his wages in bad corn and worse beer. In those counties rick-burning and rioting gave expression to the sense of hopeless misery. In earlier and simpler days the labourer had more often been lodged in the farm and ate at the board of the farmer. This had meant, of course, that he was just as dependent on his employer as when in later times he was provided with a tied cottage. But it had meant also a closer and often therefore a kinder personal contact, and less segregation of classes. Cobbett speaks of the old-fashioned labourer sharing his employer's meal on equal terms, except that the farmer might reserve for himself a stronger brew of beer.

In the winter of 1830, a few months before the introduction of the Great Reform Bill, the starving field labourers of the Counties south of Thames marched about in a riotous manner demanding a wage of half-a-crown a day. The revenge taken by the Judges was terrible : three of the rioters were unjustly hanged and four hundred and twenty

[1] See Clapham, *Ec. Hist. of Modern England*, I, pp. 125-131.

were torn from their families and transported to Australia, as convicts. Such panic cruelty showed how wide a gap of social misunderstanding divided the upper class from the poor, even when the anti-Jacobin spirit had been exorcised from the political sphere and ' Reform ' had become the watchword of the King's ministers. (Hammond, *Village Labourer*, chaps. XI and XII.)

It would, however, be a great mistake to regard the unhappy condition of the labourers in the Counties south of Thames as characteristic of all rural England. In the North, and indeed in all regions where factory life and mines were expanding, the wages even of agricultural labourers were higher, the poor-rate lower, and the number of people in receipt of poor relief less. The average standard of life was almost certainly higher than in the previous century, if all regions and all classes are taken into account. Not only Cobbett but everyone else, complained that farmers were ' aping their betters,' abandoning old homely ways, eating off Wedgwood instead of pewter, educating their girls and dashing about in gigs or riding to hounds. Whether this was good or bad depends on the point of view, but in any case it was a ' rise in the standard of life.' [1]

And among humbler rural classes there was much happiness and some prosperity, varying with place, year

---

[1] The change in the farmer's life was complained of in the Waterloo period, and thirty years later the complaint was still being made as these verses, written in 1843, show :

Old Style.

Man, to the plough ;
Wife, to the cow ;
Girl, to the yarn ;
Boy, to the barn,
And your rent will be netted.

New Style.

Man, Tally Ho ;
Miss, piano ;
Wife, silk and satin ;
Boy, Greek and Latin,
And you'll all be Gazetted.

Lord Ernle (*English Farming*, p. 347) is scornful of these charges, not as wholly untrue, but as inadequate to account for agricultural distress ; he observes that this explanation of farmers' difficulties is ' as old as the hills,' and that in 1573 Tusser had alluded to farmers who neglected their business in order to go hawking.

and circumstance. The life of the village children, let loose to play in the hedges, heaths and thickets, was wholesome and sweet, as Bewick, Wordsworth and Cobbett recorded from their own boyhoods' experience in the previous generation, and Howitt in the new century. William Howitt, George Borrow and other writers who shared the life of the common people in lane, field and cottage in the 'twenties and 'thirties, leave an impression of much widely diffused health and happiness as well as much hardship.[1] Village sports and traditions, and the daily contact with nature—and nightly contact too in the surreptitious taking of hares and rabbits in their hedgerow runs by ' old Hobden's ' ancestors—how are these things to be assessed in computing the ' condition of the rural poor ' ? And how is the great variety of life in different counties and regions, on different estates and farms to be reduced to the compass of a single generalization ?

As far back as 1771 Arthur Young had deplored the fact that, with better facilities of travel, the drift of country lads and lasses to London was on the increase. But now other towns were also drawing away their thousands from all parts of rural England. The movement was most marked in the North, the region of mines and factories and cotton mills. Indeed, the Census figures for 1801 to 1831 show that some outlying parishes in the North were already diminishing in population every decade. This was not yet true of the average English village ; but although a rural parish in the first thirty years of the Century might show no drop in the number of its resident inhabitants, it was none the less sending many of its young people to the Colonies or United States, or to the centres of industry and commerce at home.

The continual rise in the population made it indeed impossible to provide work for everyone in the English village. Agriculture had absorbed all the hands it required. And many traditional kinds of rural occupation were disappearing. Great national industries, like cloth, were

---

[1] Howitt's delightful *Rural Life in England* and *Boy's Country Book* cover experiences from 1802 to 1838 ; Borrow's *Lavengro* records experiences from 1810 to 1825.

migrating back out of the country districts to which they had moved in the later Middle Ages and Tudor times. The village was becoming more purely agricultural ; it was ceasing to manufacture goods for the general market, and, moreover, was manufacturing fewer goods for itself.

With the improvement of roads and communications, first the lady of the manor, then the farmer's wife and lastly the cottager learnt to buy in the town many articles that used to be made in the village or on the estate. And a 'village shop' was now often set up, stocked with goods from the cities or from oversea. The self-sufficing, self-clothing village became more and more a thing of the past. One by one the craftsmen disappeared—the harness maker, the maker of agricultural implements, the tailor, the miller, the furniture maker, the weaver, sometimes even the carpenter and builder—till, at the end of Victoria's reign, the village blacksmith was in some places the only crafts-man left, eking out a declining business in horseshoes by mending the punctured bicycle tyres of tourists ! The reduction in the number of small industries and handi-crafts made rural life duller and less self-sufficient in its mentality and native interests, a backwater of the national life instead of its main stream. The vitality of the village slowly declined, as the city in a hundred ways sucked away its blood and brains. This century-long process had already begun between Waterloo and the Reform Bill.

But the English village during the first half of the Nine-teenth Century was still able to provide an excellent type of colonist to new lands beyond the ocean. The men were accustomed to privation and to long hours of out-of-door work, and were ready to turn their hands to tree-felling, agriculture and rough handicraft. The women were ready to bear and rear large families.

All the circumstances of post-war England helped the great movement of colonization. The over-population that terrified the contemporaries of Malthus, the economic and social troubles, the resentment felt by the freer spirits against the rule of squire and farmer, were all factors that went to build up the Second British Empire, filling Canada, Australia and New Zealand with men and women of British speech and tradition. 'In Canada,' wrote one immigrant, ' we can have our liberty, and need not be afraid of speaking of our rights.' ' We have no gamekeepers and more privileges,' wrote another. The Scots, too, High-lander and Lowlander alike, had discovered the Canadian trail. The forests fell, the log huts rose and the rich wilderness began its yield of crops and men. In Australia in the early decades of the Nineteenth Century, capitalist ' squatters ' introduced cattle and sheep farming on a large scale, and opened out an attractive field of enterprise for adventurous spirits. The settlement of New Zealand came a little later, chiefly between 1837 and 1850, being some-what more regularly organized by the zeal of Gibbon Wakefield and by the pious efforts of Anglican and of Scottish Presbyterian committees. The Briton of the Hanoverian and early Victorian era was a villager, or was only at one remove from the villager : he was not wholly a product of the city, incapable of going back to the land, or of plying more trades than one. He was still able to adapt himself to the hardships of pioneer life, and to its variety of requirements and opportunities. And so the British Commonwealth of Nations was founded just in time.

But while many English villagers were crossing the ocean, many others were drifting into the industrial districts at home. During the Napoleonic Wars this movement within the island had been specially marked. The age of ' coal and iron ' had come in earnest. A new order of life was beginning, and the circumstances under which it began led to a new kind of unrest.

Immigrants to the mining and industrial districts were leaving an old rural world essentially conservative in its social structure and moral atmosphere, and were dumped down in neglected heaps that soon fermented as neglected heaps will do, becoming highly combustible matter. Very often their food, clothing and wages were less bad than they had been in the farms and country cottages they had left. And they had more independence than the agricultural labourer whose wages were eked out by poor relief. But migration to the factories had meant loss as well as gain. The beauty of field and wood and hedge, the immemorial customs of rural life—the village green and its games, the harvest-home, the tithe feast, the May Day rites, the field sports—had supplied a humane background and an age-long tradition to temper poverty. They were not reproduced in mine or factory, or in the rows of mass-produced brick dwellings erected to house the hands. The old rural cottages whence they came had indeed often been worse places to live in materially—picturesque but ruinous and insalubrious. Yet it was not impossible to have some feeling for a rickety window embowered in honeysuckle, or a leaking roof that harboured moss and doves ! Words-worth's ' Poor Susan,' the exile in the great city, remembered the country cottage where she was born,

' The one only dwelling on earth that she loves.'

Such affection could not be transferred to town slums. It cannot even to-day be felt for the model workman's flat.

The worst slums in the new urban areas were those inhabited by the immigrant Irish. They came from rural slums far worse than those of the worst English village, and brought with them proportionately bad habits. England's treatment of the Irish peasant was perpetually being avenged over here. But the worst period for sanitary conditions in the industrial regions was the middle of the Nineteenth Century rather than the beginning, because so many of the new houses had then had time to become slums, since no one repaired or drained them as the years went by.

The factory hands, like the miners, were brought together as a mass of employees face to face with an employer, who lived apart from them in a house of his own in a separate social atmosphere ; whereas under the old rural system they had been scattered about—one, two or at most half a dozen hands to each farm—in close and therefore often in kindly personal relation with their employer the farmer, at whose board the unmarried hands took their meals, cooked by the farmer's wife.

The mass of unregarded humanity in the factories and mines were as yet without any social services or amuse-ments of a modern kind to compensate for the lost amenities and traditions of country life. They were wholly uncared for by Church or State ; no Lady Bountiful visited them with blankets and advice ; no one but the Nonconformist minister was their friend ; they had no luxury but drink, no one to talk to but one another, hardly any subject but their grievances.   Naturally they were tinder to the flame of agitation.   They had no interest or hope in life but Evangelical religion or Radical politics.   Sometimes the two went together, for many Nonconformist preachers themselves imbibed and imparted Radical doctrines.   But the political conservatism with which the Wesleyan move-ment had started was not yet exhausted, and acted as a restraining element.   In the opinion of Elie Halévy, the great French historian who wrote for us the history of the English Nineteenth Century, the power of Evangelical religion was the chief influence that prevented our country from starting along the path of revolutionary violence during this period of economic chaos and social neglect :

' Men of letters disliked the Evangelicals for their narrow Puritanism, men of science for their intellectual feebleness.   Nevertheless during the Nineteenth Century, Evangelical religion was the moral cement of English society.   It was the influence of the Evangelicals which invested the British aristocracy with an almost Stoic dignity, restrained the plutocrats who had newly risen from the masses from vulgar ostentation and debauchery, and placed over the proletariat a select body of workmen enamoured of virtue and capable of self-restraint. Evangelicalism was thus the conservative force which restored in England the balance momentarily destroyed by the explosion of the revolutionary forces.'   (Halévy, *Hist. of English People*, transl. by E. I. Watkin, III, p. 166.)

But there is another reason, besides the restraints and consolations of a powerful popular religion, to account for the moderate character and the limited success of the Radical movement in the generation after Waterloo.   It is true that it swept over the factory districts, but the factory districts were still a relatively small part of England.   In 1819 factory conditions were not widely spread outside the Lancashire cotton area, and the Radical movement was therefore capable of being temporarily suppressed by the Peterloo massacre and the Six Acts.   The future lay with the factory system, but for the present the great majority of the English working class were still employed under the old conditions of life, whether in agriculture, in industry,

Q 2

in domestic service, or in seafaring. Peterloo was an important event, because that unhappy charge of the Yeomanry, sabre in hand, among the cotton operatives of Manchester disgusted the rising generation of Englishmen with anti-Jacobin Toryism. But the victims of Peterloo, though they were a class typical of South Lancashire, were not typical of the England of that day.

Mr. Pickwick's world, the world of the fast stage coaches and of the First Reform Bill, was a transition world, combining the old with the new economic society, and the old still predominated. The agricultural labourers and the industrialists in small workshops still for a while outnumbered the miners and factory hands. And then there were the great army of men and women in household service. In the third decade of the century the female domestic servants alone were ' fifty per cent. more numerous than all the men and women, boys and girls, in the cotton industry put together.' (Clapham, I, p. 73.) The conditions of work and wages for domestic servants have been little examined by economic or social historians, and would indeed be very difficult to assess, for they varied greatly from house to house according to the occupation and character of the employer. Mr. Samuel Weller, as we all know, was a peculiarly favoured specimen of his class, with ' little to do and plenty to get.' He and his Mary (' Housemaid to Mr. Nupkins ') were not Radicals by outlook or tradition, though they probably cheered for the Reform Bill.

Another large class, equally far removed from factory or domestic employment, was the mobile army of unskilled labour known as ' navvies ' engaged in gangs that moved from place to place, digging canals,[1] making roads and in the next generation constructing embankments and tunnels for railways. In the North, the Irish were found in their ranks in great numbers ; but in the South they consisted almost entirely of the surplus labour of English villages, which in those parts had fewer outlets to factories and mines. Some highly-paid engineers were officers in the army of navvies, and were specially numerous and highly rewarded when it came to railway construction and the piercing of tunnels. But as a whole the ' navvies ' were among the

---

[1] Hence the term ' navvies,' for ' inland navigators.'

least skilled, the most ignorant and the least well paid of the new industrial classes. They were the nomads of the new world, and their muscular strength laid its foundations.

At the opposite end of the ranks of labour were the skilled engineers and mechanics. The men who made and mended the machines were the *élite* of the Industrial Revolution and its true body-guard. They were better paid than their fellow-workmen, they were on the average more intelligent, and they took the lead in educational movements. They were respected by their employers, who had to consult them and to bow to their technical knowledge. They were in the forefront of progress and invention, and rejoiced in the sense of leading the new age. Such workmen were the Stephensons of Tyneside ; there was nothing ' middle class ' about the origins of the man who invented the locomotive, after having taught himself to read at the age of seventeen.

It is indeed easier to reconstruct the early history of the coal-miners and textile hands, than that of the mechanics and engineers, because the latter were scattered up and down the country. But any picture of the earliest and worst stage of the Industrial Revolution is too black if it omits the life of the mechanics. The motto of the coming age was ' self-help,' a doctrine that left behind many of the weaker and less fortunate ; but there were from the first other classes beside employers and middlemen who reaped a share of its benefits, and who grew to a larger manhood under the moral and intellectual stimulus of the individualist doctrine.

Adult Education received its first impetus from the Industrial Revolution in the desire of mechanics for general scientific knowledge, and the willingness of the more intelligent part of the middle class to help to supply their demand. It was a movement partly professional and utilitarian, partly intellectual and ideal. Disinterested scientific curiosity was strong among the better class of workmen in the North. From 1823 onwards Mechanics' Institutes, begun in Scotland by Dr. Birkbeck, spread through industrial England. The flame was fanned by the bellows of Henry Brougham's organizing and advertising genius, in the period of his greatest public service, when he stood for the real ' Opposition ' in Parliament and country, pointing to the future and its needs. Self-satisfied classical scholars like Peacock might laugh at the ' learned friend ' and his ' steam-intellect society,' but the new world could not live wholly on classical scholarship carefully locked away from common use in the close ecclesiastical corporations of the Oxford and Cambridge of that day. Nor, in an age that needed first and foremost to be converted to see the need for education, was there so much harm in this ' semi-Solomon, half knowing everything,' but irrepressible in zeal as a propagandist and not afraid of making a fool of himself before the learned if he could help the ignorant to learn.

The success of these Mechanics' Institutes, with an annual subscription of a guinea, showed that whatever was happening to other classes of workers, prosperity was coming to the engineers and mechanics from the Industrial Revolution which had called them into being. Francis Place, the Radical tailor, had seen the first efforts of the working classes at self-education crushed in the anti-Jacobin panic a generation before ; but in 1824 he described his pleasure at seeing ' from 800 to 900 clean respectable-looking mechanics paying most marked attention ' to a lecture on chemistry. That year the *Mechanics' Magazine* sold 16,000 copies ; and 1500 workmen subscribed a guinea apiece to the London Institute. Encyclopaedic knowledge was now circulated in cheap books and periodicals by enterprising publishers, and was absorbed by eager students in garret and workshop.

While adult education and self-education were on the move before a strong new breeze, the foundation of London University (1827) was inspired by the same spirit. Nonconformists and secularists, excluded from Oxford and Cambridge, had drawn together to found an undenominational teaching centre in the Capital, on the basis of keeping theology out of the curriculum, and having no religious tests for teachers or taught. The tendency of the embryo university was towards modern studies, including science. The strict classical curriculum was identified in men's minds with the close educational establishments of the Church and State party. ' Utility ' appealed more to the unprivileged city population. The founding of

London University was therefore an educational event of the first importance, but at the time its real significance was lost in sectarian and partisan recrimination, and not a little good-humoured satire of Brougham and his ' cockney college.'

Primary education both lost and gained by the religious and denominational squabbles, characteristic of an age when Dissenters had become numerically formidable, but Churchmen were still unwilling to abate a jot of their privileges. On the one hand, public money could not be obtained for educating the people, because the Church claimed that it must be spent under the aegis of the State religion, and the Dissenters would not agree to the use of public funds on such terms.   On the other hand, the hostile denominations vied with each other in collecting money voluntarily for the erection of Day Schools and Sunday Schools.   Readers of Miss Brontë's *Shirley* will remember the scene (chap. XVII) of the rival school feasts, when the column of Church schoolchildren, ' priestled and women officered,' its band playing *Rule Britannia*, marches at quick step down the narrow lane and scatters the column of Dissenting schoolchildren and their pastors, who raise a feeble hymn and then turn tail.   In that comedy we have the secret of much in old English politics, religion and education.

' The British and Foreign School Society,' under Dissenting and Whig Patronage, worked on the basis of undenominational Bible-teaching, while the Churchmen countered by the foundation of the ' National Society for the Education of the Poor according to the Principles of the Church of England.'   The ' National ' or Church schools became the most usual mode of popular education in the English village.

Though much was lacking in the organized education of that age as compared to our own, very many people of all classes at the time of Waterloo knew the Bible with a real familiarity which raised their imaginations above the level of that insipid vulgarity of mind which the modern multiplicity of printed matter tends rather to increase than diminish.

With the growth of new industrial conditions, involving the disappearance of apprenticeship and of the personal relation of the journeyman with his employer, Trade Union action was essential to protect the interest of the employee, especially as the State refused any longer to carry out its old Tudor policy of fixing wages. But during the anti-Jacobin period (1792–1822) all combinations of workmen, whether for political or for purely economic purposes, were regarded as ' seditious.' The only wonder is that this attitude on the part of the State as bottle-holder to the employer did not lead to more violence and bloodshed. It did lead to the ' Luddite ' trouble.

In the middle of the Napoleonic wars, unemployment, low wages and starvation were periodic among the industrialists of Nottinghamshire, Yorkshire, and Lancashire, partly owing to the first effects of new machinery. In 1811–1812 the ' Luddites ' began to break the frames on a systematic plan of action. Although there was a tendency to violence among some Irish in the Luddite ranks, there was no likelihood of a serious rebellion, and the fear of one was simply due to the absence of any effective police in the island. For that reason alone, resort had to be made to the soldiers to repress the mobs and protect the machines. The non-existence of a civilian police aggravated the symptoms of political and social disturbance, and was a direct cause of the Peterloo tragedy. Peel's initiation of the famous blue-coated corps, with its top hats and truncheons, in the year 1829 was the beginning of a better state of things. Formed in the first instance for the London area, ' the new police ' saved the Capital, during the Reform Bill agitation two years later, from suffering at the hands of Radical mobs as Bristol and some other towns suffered, and as London itself had suffered from the Gordon riots fifty years before. As Peel's police were gradually established throughout the whole country, riot and the fear of riot ceased to have their former importance in English life.

But there was another aspect of the movement of 1812 besides machine-breaking. The Luddites demanded, by the legal method of petition to Parliament, that existing laws, some as old as the reign of Elizabeth, should be put into force for the State regulation of wages and hours fairly as between employer and employed.[1] This was a perfectly

---

[1] In fact, since the middle of the Seventeenth Century, the fixing of wages by magistrates, when it was resorted to at all, had been the fixing of a maximum wage only and therefore of no use to employees.

just demand, the more so as these ancient statutes were being partially enforced to prevent combinations of workmen to protect their own interests : indeed, the position had recently been strengthened against working-class Unions by Pitt's Combination Act of 1800. The laws were supposed to apply against combinations both of masters and men, but in fact the masters were allowed to combine as freely as they wished, while their employees were prosecuted for strike action. Finally, in 1813 Parliament repealed the Elizabethan statutes which gave magistrates power to enforce a minimum wage.

To leave the workman unprotected by the State as to wages, hours and factory conditions, while denying him the right to protect himself by combination was frankly unjust. It was not *laissez-faire*, but liberty for the masters and repression for the men. The high pundits of the *laissez-faire* doctrine, such as Ricardo, were on the side of the employees in this matter, demanding the legalization of Trade Unions.

After 1822 the anti-Jacobin tide at last began to ebb. With Peel at the Home Office, repression ceased to be the sole method of government, and in 1824–1825 the House of Commons, in the spirit of a new and better age, was induced by the skilful lobbying of Joseph Hume and Francis Place to repeal Pitt's Combination Act and make Trade Unions legal. Henceforth the various forms of working-class association and corporate action grew up rapidly as a normal and recognised part of the social structure, instead of becoming revolutionary as they must needs have done if the Combination Act had remained in force.

It must not be supposed that the strife of classes was ever an absolute thing in England, or that all masters were harsh to their workpeople or indifferent to their hardships. An enlightened minority of employers had supported the legalizing of Trade Unions. And during the Napoleonic wars the enterprising manufacturer, Sir Robert Peel the elder, father of a greater son, had begun to agitate for State control of the conditions of children in factories, especially for the protection of the pauper apprentices, in whom a horrible slave traffic was carried on by the public authorities. No doubt the good Sir Robert, who himself employed 15,000 hands, was in part anxious to restrain the unfair competition of his more unscrupulous rivals.   But the Factory Acts of the period before the Reform Bill were not only very limited in scope, but remained dead letters for want of any machinery to enforce them.

Unfortunately, in the earlier years of the Century, State control in the interest of the working classes was not an idea congenial to the rulers of Britain.   They turned a deaf ear to Robert Owen when he pointed out to them that his own New Lanark Mills were a model ready to hand, to teach the world how the new industrial system could be made the instrument of standardized improvement in sanitation, welfare, hours, wages and education, raising the conditions of working-class life to an average level that could never have been attained under the domestic system.   Let the State, said Owen, enforce similar arrangements in all factories.   But the world, though sufficiently interested to visit and admire the New Lanark Mills refused to imitate them.   Men were still unable to comprehend the modern doctrine which Owen first clearly grasped and taught, that environment makes character and that environment is under human control.   The great opportunity that his vision had perceived was missed, until in the slow evolution of a Century the State has come round to his doctrine of the control of Factories and the conditions of life for all employed therein, which he had vainly preached to the Cabinet of Liverpool and Castlereagh.   At the end of the Nineteenth Century, partly by successive Factory Acts, partly by Trade Union action, factory life had proved a means of raising standards, while the ' sweated ' domestic trades, like dressmaking which could not be brought under factory control, were still for awhile longer the scene of the worst oppressions, especially of women.

To form a true picture of the processes of social change going on in the post-war period, we must avoid the mistake of supposing that the working classes as a whole were financially worse off than before the Industrial Revolution, although their grievances being of a new kind were more resented, and their complaints were more vocal than in the past. Professor Clapham, the greatest authority on the economic history of the period, roundly condemns

' the legend that everything was getting worse for the working man, down to some unspecified date between the drafting of the People's Charter and the Great Exhibition. The fact, that after the price fall of 1820-1 the purchasing power of wages in general—not, of course, of everyone's wages—was definitely greater than it had been just before the revolutionary and Napoleonic wars fits so ill with the tradition that it is very seldom mentioned, the work of statisticians on wages and prices being constantly ignored by social historians.' (Preface to the *Economic History of Modern Britain.*)

This is true and important ; but the purchasing power of wages is not the whole of human happiness, and for not a few the amenities and values of life were less than those enjoyed by their rural forefathers.

CHAPTER XVI

Cobbett's England [1793–1832]

II

Women and the new world—The fund-holders—Religion—Shipping—Navy and Army—Sporting events—Game Laws—Humanity.

THE growth of the factory system and of capitalist agriculture involved a number of changes in the employment of women, which altered conditions of family life, and therefore in the long run affected the relation of the sexes.[1]

From the earliest ages of mankind, women and children had conducted certain industries in the home, and the variety and complication of cottage manufactures had increased in Stuart and early Hanoverian England. Their sudden decay, owing to the invention of new machines, was of profound consequence to the life of the poor. The first result, in the closing years of the Eighteenth Century, was much unemployment and misery for single women, and the breaking up of many small rural households whose budget had always been balanced by the earnings of the wife and children.

The move to the factories could not be effected at once, and in many cases was not effected at all. During the Napoleonic wars women, deprived of their old means of livelihood by the decay of cottage industries, went into field work beside their men folk. The big capitalist farmers began to employ gangs of women in hoeing and weeding. Such employment had always been occasional among country women, and they had always turned out at haytime and harvest. But the big farmers in the age of Speenhamland employed females all the year round, because the newly enclosed lands required much weeding and preparation ; because there was less charge on the poor-rate if the wife earned wages as well as the husband ; and because if women

---

[1] Many facts relative to this subject will be found in Dr. Ivy Pinchbeck's *Women Workers and the Industrial Revolution*, 1930.

were drawing pay it helped to keep down the wages of the men. It was a vicious circle: the fact that the husband's wages were not at that time enough to support the whole family forced the wife and daughters into this competition with the men for farm service. It was only as the field labourer's wages gradually rose in the second half of the Nineteenth Century, and as agricultural machinery enabled farmers to dispense with many kinds of hand work, that female employment in agriculture again became as restricted as it had been in earlier times.

Under the old system of life, many village women took an active part in tilling the family patch of ground, looking after the pig or cow, marketing the goods or helping to conduct some small local business : in the England of the past, as in the France of to-day, the wife was often her husband's partner and fellow-worker. But the growth of high farming and big business tended to drive women out of these activities, turning some of them into ' ladies ' of no occupation, others into field-labourers or factory hands, others into workmen's wives entirely devoted to the care of the home.

As in most changes in human affairs, there was gain as well as loss. The working-class home often became more comfortable, quiet and sanitary by ceasing to be a miniature factory : for example, the removal of the picking and cleaning of cotton from the cottage to the mill made many huswifes happier and many homes more pleasant.

Moreover, the women who went to work in the factories, though they lost some of the best things in life, gained independence. The money they earned was their own. The factory hand acquired an economic position personal to herself, which in the course of time other women came to envy. This envy, based on the aspiration to independence, was not confined to girls of the working class. It came to be felt also in higher circles. By the middle of the Nineteenth Century, members of the leisured class like the Brontë sisters and Florence Nightingale were beginning to feel that the independent factory hand, earning her own bread, was setting an example that might be of value to the ' lady.'

For the early Victorian ' lady ' and her mother of the Regency period, too often had nothing in the world to do but to be paid for and approved by man, and to realize the type of female perfection which the breadwinner of the family expected to find in his wife and daughters.[1] No doubt the ever increasing numbers of leisured women usefully enlarged the reading public and the patronage of art and literature. Indeed, leisured women, like Jane Austen, Maria Edgeworth and Hannah More, had time and education enough to become authors and artists themselves. That was good. But many of the young ladies who doted on Scott's and Byron's romances, and strove to look like their heroines, were suffering from too much leisure. Fashions in art and literature, as they pass, affect the habits of life and sometimes even the appearance of the more sophisticated classes. Scott's pseudo-mediaeval ideals of the ' lady ' worshipped by the enamoured hero, and Byron's sultanic vision of woman as odalisque, helped to inspire the artificial uselessness of the would-be fashionable sisterhood.

As the upper and middle classes grew richer, and as the rural gentry fell more under the influence of town life, it became a point of social pride that the young ladies should be taught by a governess in the schoolroom, and thence pass to the drawing-room, and do at all times as little domestic work as possible. The ladies in Miss Austen's novels, representing the smaller gentry and upper bourgeoisie, have little to do but to read poetry, retail local gossip and await the attentions of the gentlemen. To be sure it was different in the great political families : in Lansdowne or Holland House a lady's life was by no means so limited or so dull.

Moreover, ' ladies ' were not encouraged to exercise their bodies except in dancing. Very few women at this period hunted ; that became more usual in the strenuous Victorian days, as we see in *Punch's* pictures and in Trollope's novels. The lady of this earlier period was expected to keep herself in cotton wool. When Elizabeth Bennet walked three miles in muddy weather and arrived at Netherfield ' with weary ankles, dirty stockings and a face glowing with warmth and exercise,' Mrs. Hurst and Miss Bingley ' held

---

[1] Before the Married Women's Property Acts of the late Victorian period, a woman's property became her husband's at marriage. The law was in curious contrast to the words of the marriage service, when the man was made to say ' with all my worldly goods I thee endow.' It was really the other way round.

her in contempt for it.' Even in the hardy North, Words-worth in 1801 wrote a poem, as its title tells us, to console and encourage ' A Young Lady, who had been reproached for taking long walks in the country ' ! It was all very absurd, for in less artificial classes of society, women were walking long distances to and from their work ; there were Welsh women who annually walked the whole way to London and back in pursuit of seasonal employment in the fruit and vegetable gardens round the Capital.

The upper-class woman was being devitalized and cut off from life and its interests, as a result of the increasing wealth of her men folk and the more artificial conditions of modern life. In the old self-supplying manor-house, with its innumerable jobs to be done within and without doors, the ladies of good family, like the Pastons and Verneys, had had their allotted tasks. But now it became the hall-mark of a ' lady ' to be idle.

There were, of course, even among the well-to-do, many women who lived active and useful lives, some of the old domestic type ; others, like Hannah More's, of a modern, philanthropic and intellectual variety. But there lay a real danger for the new century in the false ideal of the ' sheltered ' lady. And in a snobbish society like England, where those below were always seeking to imitate those just above them, the false ideal spread downwards among the smaller bourgeoisie now multiplying in the new suburbs of the towns.

Even in the countryside the wives of wealthy farmers were accused of setting up as ' ladies,' too fine to work. In old days the farmer's wife had always been (as she usually is to-day) a very busy woman, with all the cares of the house and some of the cares of the farm on her shoulders. In dairy farms she was herself the foreman labourer, getting the milkmaids up before sunrise and often working on at butter or cheese making until a late hour at night. Dairy farming, especially in the regions of the West that supplied the London market with cheese and butter, was the most arduous and the most profitable of the occupations of women. On other farms the wife was more occupied with housework. She had to cook and care not only for her own family but for the labourers who fed at her husband's board and lodged under his roof.   She was a hard-working woman with little leisure.

But in the early Nineteenth Century these domestic conditions had changed on the large enclosed farms of the new order.   The hands employed were more numerous, but for that very reason they no longer boarded or fed with their employer.   The farmhouse, as Cobbett complained, was becoming 'too neat for a dirty-shoed carter to be allowed to come into.'   The big farmers engaged a better type of domestic servant to relieve their wives of drudgery and to give a gentlemanlike appearance to the parlour, even if the kitchen was still usually preferred for family life on ordinary occasions.   The farmer's daughters, it was said, ' instead of being taught their duty and the business of a dairy at home, receive their education at a Boarding School, are taught to dance, to speak French and to play upon the harpsichord.'

But this was only true to its full extent in the case of the wealthier farmers, some of whom were indeed gradually becoming gentlemen.   The farming class included a number of different social grades and standards.   The farmers in the North did not ape the gentleman like some farmers of the Speenhamland regions.   The northern ' hind ' was more independent than the pauperized labourer of the South, and the social demarcation between him and his employer was less marked ; this was specially true of the moorland shepherds.   And all over England there were still thousands of farms where the women of the family took a share in all kinds of work, and many where the farm hand still fed with those who employed him.

An account of women's life at this period ought to include a reference to the great army of prostitutes.   It had existed in all ages, and its ranks had grown with the increase of wealth and population in the country.   Except for ' rescue work ' which the pious were now actively taking in hand, the evil was left untouched.   It infested the towns without the least public control ; ' the harlot's cry from street to street ' made public resorts hideous at nightfall. The growing ' respectability ' of the well-to-do classes in the new era diminished the numbers and position of the more fortunate 'kept mistresses,' who had played a considerable part in Eighteenth Century society. But for that very reason the demand was increased for the common prostitute who could be visited in secret. The harshness of the world's ethical code, which many parents endorsed, too often drove a girl once seduced to prostitution. And the economic condition of single women forced many of them to adopt a trade they abhorred. The decay of cottage manufacture starved orphan girls till they bowed the head for bread. Low wages in unregulated sweated industries made temptation strong. On the whole, the more regular pay and the general conditions of life in factories tended towards a higher standard of morals, although the critics of the factory system long denied it. As the new Century went on and factory pay and conditions steadily improved, the self-respect of the women employed was put on a sounder economic basis.

The new age was bringing into being a large leisured class which had no direct relation either to the land, to the professions, to industry or to trade. In the years following the Napoleonic Wars there was much talk of the 'fund-holders,' who enjoyed incomes secured on the national credit.

Ever since the reign of William III, the constant increase in the funded National Debt with each new war, was always expected to prove fatal to the country as the figures soared up decade after decade. But in fact the Debt never outran the increasing financial power of Britain, and the interest paid on it was nearly all spent within her four shores. At the beginning of George III's reign the 'fund-holders' had been reckoned at 17,000 persons, and about one-seventh of the total debt was at that time held abroad, largely by Dutch investors. But after Waterloo only a twenty-fifth part of Britain's now colossal debt was held by foreigners. In 1829 official statistics showed that the fund-holders numbered 275,839 persons, of whom more than 250,000 were small investors each receiving an annual interest of £200 or less.[1]

This meant a wide diffusion of safe and easily realizable

[1] Halévy, *Hist. of Eng. People* (Pelican ed.) II, pp. 204–212.

wealth among a very great number of families. They were thrifty folk ; in 1803 it had been calculated that a fifth of the interest paid by the State to its creditors was reinvested in the public funds. It is probable that most of the fund-holders were earning additional incomes in one way or another, but some were living inactive, respectable lives on their small, carefully treasured investments, particularly un-married women, like the innocent ladies whom Mrs. Gaskell described in *Cranford*.

When Cobbett abused the ' fund-holders ' as blood-suckers eating the taxes of the people, and demanded the repudiation of the National Debt, he hardly realized what an enormous number of inoffensive, humble folk he pro-posed to ruin, over and above the ' stock-jobbers ' who were perhaps fair game. Them he hated above all, partly because they helped to swell the ' wen ' of greater London. The inexorable ' march of bricks and mortar,' burying for ever the green farmlands of Middlesex, was creating residential areas for the business men of the capital and for the stock-jobbers and fund-holders. With his heart in the old yeoman past of his country, Cobbett could not abide the sight of this new featureless swamp of houses, and this new artificial society with no roots in the soil. Yet of such towns and such people the England of the future would largely consist.

Brighton, famous for the patronage of George IV and for the Pavilion he had built there, was already an adjunct of London. ' Mark the process,' growled Cobbett ; ' the town of Brighton, in Sussex, fifty miles from the wen, is on the seaside, and is thought by the stock-jobbers to afford a salubrious air. It is so situated that a coach which leaves it not very early in the morning, reaches London by noon. . . . Great parcels of stock-jobbers stay at Brighton, with the women and children. They skip backwards and forwards on the coaches and actually carry on stock-jobbing in Change Alley though they reside at Brighton.' (*Rural Rides*, May 5, 1823.)

During the first thirty years of the Century many changes in habits of life and thought were due to the steady infiltra-tion of evangelical religion into all classes of society, finally not excepting the highest ; it was a movement that spread from below upwards.   An active individualist Protestant-ism, closely connected with humanitarian activity, strictness of personal conduct and avowed profession of piety had, as we have seen, been an important element in Eighteenth Century England, but had then exerted little influence on the latitudinarian Established Church or on the free lives of the enjoying classes.   But when those classes saw their privileges and possessions threatened by Jacobin doctrines from across the Channel, a sharp revulsion from French ' atheism and deism ' prepared a favourable soil for greater ' seriousness ' among the gentry.   Indifferentism and latitudinarianism in religion now seemed seditious and un-patriotic, and a concurrent change in manners took place, from licence or gaiety to hypocrisy or to virtue.   Family prayers spread from the merchant's household to the dining-room of the country house.   ' Sunday observance ' was revived.   ' It was a wonder to the lower orders,' wrote the *Annual Register* in 1798, ' throughout all parts of England, to see the avenues to the churches filled with carriages.   This novel appearance prompted the simple country people to enquire what was the matter.'

If this change to religious seriousness had been nothing more than a symptom of the anti-Jacobin panic, it would have passed away with the passing of the danger.   But it survived the return of peace in 1815, and came to terms with the liberal reaction that followed.   The Victorian gentleman and his family were more religious in their habits and sober in their tone of thought than their predecessors in the light-hearted days of Horace Walpole and Charles Fox.   The English of all classes formed in the Nineteenth Century a strongly Protestant nation ; most of them were religious, and most of them (including the Utilitarians and Agnostics) were ' serious,' with that strong preoccupation about morality which is the merit and danger of the Puritan character.   In their double anxiety to obey a given ethical code and to ' get on ' in profitable business, the typical men of the new age overlooked some of the other possi-bilities of life.   An individualist commercialism and an equally individualist type of religion combined to produce a breed of self-reliant and reliable men, good citizens in

many respects—but ' Philistines ' in the phrase popularized
by their most famous critic in a later generation.   Neither
machine industry nor evangelical religion had any use for
art or beauty, which were despised as effeminate by the
makers of the great factory towns of the North.

In the lower ranks of society, horror of French Republican
atheism helped the Wesleyan movement to spread more
widely than ever after the death of its great founder in
1791.   Not only did the new Methodist Churches increase
their membership to hundreds of thousands, but the
methodist spirit was infused into older Nonconformist sects
like the Baptists.   On the eve of the French Revolution,
the latitudinarian and radical spirit of Priestley and the
Unitarians had to some extent penetrated other dissenting
sects that were nominally orthodox.   But that liberalizing
influence was destroyed by the reaction with which the
Century closed, and its place was taken by a strong, narrow
evangelicalism.   The various Nonconformist sects, thus
reinspired to a fresh proselytizing activity, undertook the
mission of Christianity in the new industrial districts, a
task for which the Established Church at that time had
neither the organization nor the zeal.

While the war lasted, the influence of the new type of
Nonconformity was anti-French and on the whole conservative ; the governing classes therefore regarded its
increasing influence and numbers with less alarm than
might otherwise have been felt.   Common antipathy to
Roman Catholics and to their reviving claim to civil equality,
formed yet another link between the Tory upper class of
the day and the Dissenting Sects under the new evangelical
influence—to the chagrin of the aristocratic Whigs, in
whom alone the broader Eighteenth Century attitude survived.   But as soon as the war was over and anti-Jacobin
fears had receded, the unreformed and highly privileged
Church Establishment was left face to face with a number
of powerful Nonconformist sects, all inspired by a new
evangelical vigour, and no longer grateful for a bare toleration, like their feebler predecessors of a hundred years before.

The bridge between Establishment and Dissent, as also
between anti-Jacobin and Liberal, was found in the small
but influential Evangelical party which had now effected a

lodgment inside the Church. Its ethos was not clerical like that of the Oxford Movement in the following generation. The most energetic among the Church clergy were indeed the Evangelicals, but they cared less about the Church as an institution than about the saving of souls, and they made no high claims on behalf of their own priesthood. Except Charles Simeon and Isaac Milner of Cambridge, the leading ' Saints ' (as the Evangelicals were popularly called) were laymen—Wilberforce himself, the Buxtons and the Clapham ' Sect.' The strongest type of English gentleman in the new era was often evangelical. The army knew them with respect and India with fear and gratitude. Through families like the Stephens, their influence on Downing Street and on the permanent Civil Service and on Colonial administration was constantly increasing during the first forty years of the Century.

Humanitarian activity was the characteristic form in which their religious piety expressed itself. In the cause of the slaves they were ready to co-operate not only with their fellow Evangelicals, the Wesleyan and other Dissenters, but with free-thinkers and Utilitarians. Wilberforce confessed with chagrin that the ' high-and-dry ' conservative party then prevalent among the Church clergy obstructed the anti-Slavery cause or were at best indifferent, while Nonconformists and godless reformers proved his staunchest allies. And the old free-thinker Bentham on his side exclaimed : ' If to be an anti-slavist is to be a Saint, saintship for me.' The same combination of forces, Church Evangelical, Dissenter and free-thinking Radical—worked for the education of the poor in the British and Foreign School Society, and in the following generation for Shaftesbury's Factory legislation.

This cross-cut, traversing established party and denominational lines, indicated that the public mind was becoming more active and independent. Many were now thinking and acting for themselves, on subjects chosen by themselves, and were no longer content merely to make a crowd at the hustings for the benefit of the Whig or Tory aristocracy. This new power of organized public opinion carried the abolition of the Slave Trade in 1807, in the teeth of powerful vested interests, in the middle of the anti-Jacobin reaction. The movement was not allowed to drop after that first triumph, but was carried on to effect the further object of freeing all the slaves in the British Empire ; Fowell Buxton in the 'twenties took on the leadership of this cause, which triumphed in 1833, the year Wilberforce died.

Thus was Wilberforce rewarded for his complete honesty of purpose. He had never shrunk from the pursuit of his great humanitarian object even when after the French Revolution it had become for a while extremely unpopular in the world of politics and fashion ; he had always been ready to work with persons of any party, class or religion who would support the cause. He was an enthusiast who was always wise. He was an agitator who always retained his powerful gift of social charm, the outcome of his sweet disposition. He is the classic example of the use of the cross-bench politician in our two-party public life. He could not have done what he did if he had desired office. With his talents and position he would probably have been Pitt's successor as Prime Minister if he had preferred party to mankind. His sacrifice of one kind of fame and power gave him another and a nobler title to remembrance.

The hold of Wilberforce and the anti-slavery movement on the solid middle class in town and country was a thing entirely beautiful—English of the best, and something new in the world. For a whole generation, the anti-slavery champion was returned at every election for the great popular constituency of Yorkshire. He could, if he himself had consented, have sat for it during the rest of his life. In those days, all the freeholders had to come up to the Cathedral city to vote. ' Boats are proceeding up the river (from Hull) heavily laden with voters,' says a letter in 1807, ' and hundreds are proceeding on foot.' ' Another large body, chiefly of the middle class, from Wensley Dale, was met on their road by one of the Committee. " For what parties, gentlemen, do you come ? " " Wilberforce, to a man," was their leader's reply.' When on Sunday the vast floor of York Minster was packed with the freeholders of the three ridings, ' I was exactly reminded,' writes Wilberforce, ' of the great Jewish Passover in the Temple, in the reign of Josiah.'

Wilberforce and the anti-slavery men had introduced into English life and politics new methods of agitating and educating public opinion. The dissemination of facts and arguments; the answers to the mis-statements of the adversary on the pleasures of the ' Middle-passage ' and the happiness of negro life in the plantations; the tracts; the subscriptions; the public meetings—all these methods of propaganda were systematized by methods familiar enough to-day but strange and new in that age. The quiet force of the Quakers was brought out of its long hibernation and launched into public life, taking the party politicians in flank. The methods of Wilberforce were afterwards imitated by the myriad leagues and societies—political, religious, philanthropic and cultural—which have ever since been the arteries of English life. Public discussion and public agitation of every kind of question became the habit of the English people, very largely in imitation of Wilberforce's successful campaign. Voluntary association for every conceivable sort of purpose or cause became an integral part of English social life in the Nineteenth Century, filling up many of the gaps left by the limited scope of State action.

The British mercantile marine, which together with the Royal Navy thwarted the ambition of Bonaparte, was incomparably the greatest in the world. In the reign of George IV (1820–1830) its tonnage, close on two and a half millions, was still moved by wind and sail, though in 1821 steamers undertook the passenger service between Dover and Calais, reducing the passage to three or four hours in favourable weather. By sea as well as land the age of steam was drawing near, though still in the future. But already engineering progress had transformed the approaches and harbours of the island. Between 1800 and 1830 Trinity House established lighthouses and floating lights round the coasts of England; docks were built in every considerable port town; the dock system of London was rapidly brought into being, though the ' Pool ' was still thronged with tall masts in the river as far up as the bridge. Pleasure piers, like those of Margate and Brighton, were also being built to attract the crowds of visitors to seaside resorts.

The Thames estuary still held unchallenged supremacy as the centre of Britain's trade and the World's. On the eve of the Reform Bill a quarter of the country's tonnage was owned and registered in London, including the great East Indiamen built for voyages of more than six months round the Cape to the India and China seas ; Newcastle came next with 202,000 tons, chiefly coal ships, many of them to supply London ; Liverpool came third with 162,000 tons, chiefly for the American trade ; Sunderland and Whitehaven were fourth and fifth, dealing in coal along the East and West coasts respectively ; Hull had 72,000 ; no other English port had over 50,000 tons. Clydeside had 84,000. (Clapham, *Ec. Hist. Modern Britain,* I, pp. 3–8.)

The relation of the Royal Navy to the merchant marine and to the rest of the seagoing population—including fishermen, whalers and smugglers, was of the first importance in time of war. The link between the two was the chaotic and atrocious system of the press-gang. Some form of compulsion was required to man the fighting ships when they were put into commission, for conditions of life in the King's service were too bad to attract the required numbers of volunteers. But the method by which compulsion was applied was the worst possible. A proper register of seamen from whom conscripts might be taken in a just and orderly manner had been proposed by officials of the Admiralty during the wars against Louis XIV, but nothing had been done. The incompetence characteristic of State action and organization throughout the Eighteenth Century held good in this matter, even during the heroic age of the Navy. Still in the days of Nelson the press-gang was the terror of life along the coasts and in the harbours of England. Bands armed with cutlasses were led by the King's officers to crimp mariners and landsmen from ships in harbour or at sea, from ale-houses and streets, or even at the church-door whence bridegroom and congregation were sometimes carried off. Widespread injustice and misery were caused; families were ruined or broken up ; and often very unsuitable recruits were obtained.[1]

---

[1] Mrs. Gaskell's *Sylvia's Lovers* gives a picture of Whitby about the year 1800, which throws much light on the ways of the press-gang, and on the English whalers of the Greenland and Arctic seas.

Once on board the King's ship, the pressed man had too much reason to bemoan his fate. The food provided by swindling contractors was often disgusting, and the pay doled out by a penurious government was always insufficient. Improvement in these respects only followed as a consequence of the dangerous mutinies of Spithead and the Nore in 1797. Thereafter the sailor's lot was gradually improved, on lines that had been advocated for generations past by the best naval officers in their struggles with the authorities at home. Nelson's own relations to his men were a pattern of kindness. But it must stand on record that the common sailors who saved Britain at St. Vincent, Camperdown and the Nile, were many of them mutineers in the intervals of their magnificent service. The contrast between their grievances and their indiscipline on the one hand, and their splendid spirit in action and on the blockade service, may seem unaccountable. The explanation lay in this : the men before the mast knew that, for all the ill treatment they received, the nation regarded them as its bulwark and glory ; that at the sight of one of Nelson's men with his tarry pig-tail, the landsman's eye kindled with affection and pride. The country that used them so ill, looked to them confidently to protect her, and they knew it.

The naval officers, from among whom Nelson drew his ' band of brothers,' were more uniformly satisfactory than of old, though still occasionally quarrelsome and self-willed. In Stuart times the service had suffered from constant strife between the rough ' tarpaulin ' captains of humble origin who knew the sea, and the fashionable landsmen sent from Court to share the command of the fleet. Those days had long gone by. The naval officers were now the sons of gentlemen of modest means (Nelson was a poor parson's son), sent to sea as boys, and combining what was best in the ' tarpaulin's ' experience and training with the manner and thought of an educated man. Fanny's brother William, in *Mansfield Park*, and Captain Wentworth in *Persuasion* stand for all that was most attractive in the type. But there were all sorts of characters and idiosyncrasies among officers and men in the fleets of Nelson and Collingwood, which have been described by one of themselves in Captain Marryat's immortal *Peter Simple* and *Mr. Midshipman Easy*.

In the last few years of the struggle with Napoleon, the army became for a short time even more popular with the nation than the navy.   The very completeness of victory at Trafalgar placed our ' storm-beaten ships ' in the background of the war of which they remained the invisible support.   It was now Wellington's victories that filled the minds of men.   From 1812 to 1815, when the laurel-wreathed coaches cantered through village and market town bearing the news of Salamanca, Vittoria or Waterloo, the army became popular as it had never been before and never was again until the German Wars of the Twentieth Century, and then it was the nation itself in arms.

But Wellington's army was not the nation in arms, as was the conscript French army against which it fought.   It consisted of aristocrats commanding privates taken from the lowest ranks of society, ' the scum of the earth ' as Wellington declared them to be, though he added (as is often forgotten) ' it is really wonderful we should have made them the fine fellows they are.'   (Stanhope's *Conversations with the Duke of Wellington*, ed. 1889, pp. 14, 18.)   The principal causes of enlistment were drink, unemployment, and personal trouble with a woman or with the laws of the land.   The harsh discipline of the lash, considered necessary to keep such rough customers in order, served to prevent the more self-respecting members of society from joining the army as privates.   In the earlier years of the Peninsular War the British soldiers plundered in spite of all Wellington's efforts, though never as badly as the French whom Napoleon encouraged to live on the lands they conquered. But by the time our troops entered France in 1814, their discipline was excellent, and their self-respect and just pride as the best troops in Europe and the favourites of the folks at home was a credit to the odd social system on which the British army was based.

The military officers came from more aristocratic circles than the naval men.   They were, many of them, like Wellington himself, cadets of the great families who led fashion and politics at home ; others, like George Osborne, in *Vanity Fair*, were of the wealthy bourgeoisie who could afford to buy their commissions and to mingle with the scions of the nobility. Between such officers and the men they led, the social gulf was immense and often resulted in gross neglect of the private soldier by officers too fashionable and sometimes too drunken to attend to their duty. The inefficiency and corruption of the army when the war began in 1793 was tested and exposed by the first campaigns in the Low Countries. A few years before, Cobbett, who had enlisted in the ranks and been promoted to sergeant-major, discovered that the Quarter-master of his regiment ' who had the issuing of the men's provision to them kept about a fourth part of it to himself,' and when Cobbett gallantly attempted to expose the scandal, he found that such proceedings were very generally connived at throughout the army ; he fled to America to escape the vengeance of the authorities who would suffer no such prying into their methods and their perquisites.

As the long war went on, Sir Ralph Abercromby, Sir John Moore and Wellington gradually reformed this state of things ; the British officer recovered his sense of duty and the army its discipline. But alike in the ill-managed and the well-managed regiments, the personal care and control of the privates was left to the sergeants, the ' non-commissioned officers,' who were indeed ' the backbone of the army.' The regiment was a society made up of grades answering to the social demarcations of the English village whence men and officers had come. It has been observed that when the ensign fresh from Eton was handed over to the respectful care and tuition of the colour-sergeant, the relation of the two closely resembled that to which the younger man had been accustomed at home, when the old gamekeeper took him out afield to teach him the management of his fowling-piece and the arts of approaching game.

There was no very strong professional feeling among the army officers of our most unmilitary nation. From the Duke downwards they hastened to get into mufti when off duty, though even the Duke was angry when some dandies in the Guards put up umbrellas to keep off the rain on the battlefield, as if it had been outside a club in St. James's Street ! Only a few of the officers looked to the army as their real means of livelihood ; as such, indeed, it could not be very profitable, considering the price that had to be paid

R

for commissions at each step in the service. It was a way of seeing life ; of enjoying in Spain a sport even more exciting and arduous than big-game shooting ; of making entry into the best society ; of serving one's country in a manner suitable to one's youth. The Peninsular War produced a number of good English officers, and fostered a number of great regimental traditions, but it did not make an English military caste or an army organization of permanent value. When peace returned, most of the officers were willing enough to go home to the duties and pleasures of country-house life, to rural parsonages, or to the world of fashion and politics in town. England's army was not, like the army of France, of Spain and of Prussia, a military power rival to the civil power ; it was a part-time occupation of some members of the governing aristocracy.[1]

During the long war two changes took place, indicating that at last the nation had accepted the standing army as a necessary national institution. At last barracks were built to house the troops, and the haphazard billeting of the soldiers on public houses came to an end, to the great relief both of the civilian population and of the soldiers themselves. At the same time the county militia ceased to be regarded as a line of defence, and was used as a source whence to supply the regular army with a reserve of trained recruits. The old idea that the defence of the island could be entrusted to the ' constitutional ' militia of the shire, and that the ' standing army ' was a dangerous temporary expedient, had been out of date for more than a hundred years, and now altogether passed away.

After Waterloo, a small standing army was maintained, but its popularity came to an end with the war. Though no longer regarded as a menace to the Constitution, it was regarded as an unnecessary expense by the economic anti-militarism of the new age. Moreover, the reformers now rising to influence disliked it as an aristocratic preserve. Such indeed it was ; but the reformers, instead of proposing to reform it and democratize it, preferred to starve it and cut it down. Meanwhile the respectable working classes

---

[1] George Borrow's father, so well described in the opening chapters of *Lavengro*, was a fine example of the rarer type of officer who was not a man of fashion and to whom the army life was all in all.

continued to regard enlistment in the army as a sign of failure in life, if not of positive disgrace. Nineteenth Century England, having the good fortune to be safe from attack for several generations, conceived that so long as her navy was efficient her army could safely be neglected. And since it continued to be an aristocratic institution, it became increasingly unpopular with the rising democracy both of the middle and the working class. It was regarded as a proof of British freedom that, unlike the other inhabitants of Europe, no man over here could be required to learn to defend his country in arms. This new and strange definition of liberty was

'The imposthume of much wealth and peace.'

It became so ingrained during the hundred years of security that it proved very difficult to shake it off when danger returned in the Twentieth Century more formidably than ever before.

News of Wellington's campaigns in Spain were not awaited with greater national eagerness than reports on the prospects of famous horse-races and prize-fights. With the improvement of roads and communications, 'sporting events' ceased to be of purely local interest and became matters of intense concern to high and low in all parts of the country. Horse-racing indeed had flourished under royal patronage ever since Stuart times, but scientific pugilism had grown out of rude and vulgar beginnings in the reign of George II into the chief national interest in the Regency period. Just as the good-natured democracy of present-day England is well represented in the vast crowds of all classes, mingled together on terms of perfect equality, to watch a Test Match or a Cup Tie, so the more variegated social structure and rougher manners of that earlier time were best seen in the 'patronage' of 'the ring.'

When the date and place of a prize-fight had been announced, hordes set out, driving, riding and walking to the spot from all parts of the island. Sometimes twenty thousand spectators assembled. In one aspect these vast outdoor assemblies were festivals of the common people. But the priests of the national cult were fashionable members of the aristocracy, who presided over the ceremonies and held the rough and often violent multitude in awe. It was these men of fashion and rank who hired and backed the gladiators. Among those sturdy ' bruisers,' whose business it was to give and take ' punishment,' not a few ruffians could be found, but the real champions, men like Broughton, ' the father of British pugilism ' in the reign of George II, and in the later times Belcher, Tom Cribb and Tom Spring were fine fellows and honourable men. Their lordly patrons were proud to be seen driving them to the ring-side in coach or gig. So too at race-meetings, the horses were owned by the men of fashion. Without aristocratic patronage sporting events would have lost half their zest and picturesqueness, and would very soon have degenerated into orgies of brutality and fraud, for the lower type of sporting men who surrounded the ring included too many like Thurtell, the murderer.

Indeed, with so much money wagered by the public, it was an uphill struggle for noble patrons to keep either the turf or the ring even comparatively honest. Without the moral jurisdiction of the fashionable Jockey Club, horse-racing would have become too disreputable to survive. That fate actually befell the prize-ring in the early days of Victoria, because ' cross ' fighting and the sale of victories had become too common. The decline of prize-fighting was further hastened by the growing humanitarianism and religiosity of an age which forbade the setting on of animals to fight one another, and could scarcely do less for men. The recent revival of prize-fighting tempered with gloves, is more democratic, and largely American and cosmopolitan. It has not the peculiar tone of the English prize-ring in the days when handsome George was Regent and leader of fashion.[1]

---

[1] The prize-ring in its ' most high and palmy state ' was thus described by that soul of chivalry and honour, Lord Althorp, speaking in his old age to a friend : ' He said his conviction of the advantages of boxing was so strong that he had been seriously considering whether it was not a duty he owed to the public to go and attend every prize-fight which took place. In his opinion, cases of stabbing arose from the manly habit of boxing having been discouraged. He gave us an account of prize-fights he had attended, how he had seen Mendoza knocked down for the first five or six rounds by Humphreys and seeming almost beat, till the Jews got their money on ; when a hint being given him, he began in earnest and soon turned the tables. He described a fight between Gully and the

When such was the most popular English sport, it can well be imagined that ordinary Englishmen were often at fisticuffs when they quarrelled, as readers of *Lavengro* and the *Pickwick Papers* are well aware. Indeed, young Dickens in 1836 could scarcely have drawn so popular a character as he meant Sam Weller to be, without endowing him with special gifts in knocking down his man.

As the century went on, when growing humanitarianism, evangelicalism and respectability helped to put down ' the ring,' they did the greater service of putting down the duel. The duel in the Eighteenth Century had been fought at push of rapier ; in the early Nineteenth Century it was fought with pistols—like poor Rawdon Crawley's ' same which I shot Captain Marker.' As the spirit of the age became less aristocratic and more bourgeois, less military and more completely civilian and more ' seriously ' religious and, let us say at once, more sensible, duelling gradually dropped out. But the change had only begun by the time of the Reform Bill. Statesmen still quarrelled and fought with political opponents or rivals. In 1829, Wellington, then Prime Minister, being an old-fashioned fellow, thought it necessary to call out Lord Winchilsea and have a shot at him. Pitt, too, had exchanged shots with Tierney, and Canning with Castlereagh ; but in Victoria's reign Prime Ministers and other gentlemen were restrained, by a changed code of public morals, from vindicating their honour by a method so absurd.

These early years of the Century saw the culmination of a delightful popular art, the ' coloured print.' It ruled the mind and imagination of the age, as photography and the film rule ours. The shop windows were filled with ' coloured cartoons,' fiercely political and libellously personal, glowing with the genius of Gillray or the no less vigorous social comedy of Rowlandson. Other favourite themes, illustrated in a more conventionally heroic style, were the battles of the Peninsula, and incidents in the wars

---

Chicken. How he rode down to Brickhill—how he was loitering about the inn door, when a barouche-and-four drove up with Lord Byron and a party, and Jackson the trainer—how they all dined together, and how pleasant it had been. Then the fight next day ; the men stripping, the intense excitement, the sparring ; then the first round, the attitude of the men—it was really worthy of Homer.'

of all Europe, as far as the Russian snows strewn with frozen Frenchmen, or sea-pieces of our ships engaging the enemy. In quieter colours, Ackermann's beautiful prints showed the homely dignity of Oxford and Cambridge Colleges.

But above all, the coloured prints represented the outdoor world of sport, from big-game shooting in India and Africa to the field-sports and the life of the road at home. It is through these sporting prints still treasured and often reproduced, that our generation best knows the spirit of that bygone epoch. Through them we are still familiar with the bustle of the galleried inn-yard when the coaches were starting, the young swell seated in the expensive place of honour beside the mail-coachman on the box, the heavy middle-aged men of business well wrapped up on the seats behind, the red-coated guard in rear of all ; then the scene on the open road, the post-chaises, gigs and dog-carts racing each other and the coach, over Macadam's hard, smooth surface ; the adventure when the travellers are held up by flood or snow. Then the shooters in their top hats approaching the partridges that their dogs have pointed in the stubble ; the spaniels flushing the cock pheasants out of the brushwood ; the hardy sportsman wading through ice and snow after geese, wild duck and swan. Last, but not least, the hounds in full cry, and the career of the red-coated hunt, to whom the countryside, recently enclosed and drained, presents with its new hedges and channelled watercourses the cheerful aspect of innumerable ' jumps.'

There was no luxury about the field-sports of those days. Hard exercise and spartan habits were the condition of all pursuit of game. This devotion took the leaders of the English world out of doors, and helped to inspire the class that then set the mode in everything from poetry to pugilism, with an intimate love and knowledge of woodland, hedge-row and moor, and a strong preference for country over town life which is too seldom found in the leaders of fashion in any age or land.

Indirectly, therefore, the passion for shooting game did much for what was best in our civilization. But it was un-fortunately connected with the poaching war and all manner of unneighbourliness. The legislation affecting ' game ' was exclusive and selfish, not only towards the poor but towards everyone except an aristocratic few. It was illegal for anyone to buy or sell game—with the result that prices obtainable by professional poachers were much increased ; and it was illegal for anyone who was not a squire or a squire's eldest son to kill game even at the invitation of the owner. This inconvenient law could indeed be evaded by a process known as ' deputation.' And it was abolished by the Whig legislators of 1831, in spite of the opposition of the Duke of Wellington, who was convinced that these extraordinary restrictions were the only means of keeping game in the countryside, just as he thought that the rotten boroughs were the only way of keeping gentlemen in politics. In both cases the event proved that he was too pessimistic.

By a new law of 1816, the starving cottager who went out to take a hare or rabbit for the family pot could be transported for seven years if caught with his nets upon him at night. Less sympathy need be felt for the bands of armed ruffians from the towns who invaded the preserves and fought pitched battles, twenty a side, with shot-guns at close range, against the gentlemen and gamekeepers who came out against them. The poaching war had become a very ugly business.

One of its worst features was the protection of pheasant preserves by hiding mantraps and spring-guns in the brush-wood, thereby maiming and killing innocent wanderers, quite as often as the poachers for whom the engines of death were intended. The English judges pronounced the infamous practice to be legal, until Parliament put it under the ban of the law by an Act of 1827. The humanitarian spirit was beginning to be too strong even for the zealots of game preservation, against whom it then proceeded to win a long series of victories in the matter of the game laws. As those laws became milder and were more justly executed, the preservation of game became less difficult as well as less scandalous.

Indeed, as the Nineteenth Century advanced and as the anti-Jacobin spirit receded, humanitarianism invaded one province of life after another, softening the rude and often brutal temper of the past, and fostering instead a cheerful benevolence of heart sometimes running to sentimentality.

The destined prophet of this new phase of popular feeling in its strength and its weakness, was Charles Dickens, who grew to sensitive manhood in the hard school of London streets in the 'twenties. During that decade the 'bloody code' of death penalties for innumerable offences was being repealed, under pressure from juries who often refused to convict a man for theft if he was to be hanged for it. The age of Eldon was passing, the age of Bentham and Brougham was coming in. The movement for the abolition of negro slavery aroused passionate popular enthusiasm sometimes excessive in its sentiment for the 'dusky brother.'

These changes of feeling were a striking improvement upon all past ages. As the Nineteenth Century grew older, humanity pervaded more and more all the dealings of life, particularly the treatment of children. The advance in humanity, far more than the boasted advance in machinery, was the thing of which the Nineteenth Century had best reason to be proud ; for in the wrong hands machinery may destroy humanity.

CHAPTER XVII

Between the Two Reform Bills [1832–1867]

The interval between the Great Reform Bill of 1832 and
the end of the Nineteenth Century may, if we like, be called
the Victorian Age, but it was characterized by such constant
and rapid change in economic circumstance, social custom
and intellectual atmosphere, that we must not think of these
seventy years as having a fixed likeness one to another, merely
because more than sixty of them were presided over by ' the
Queen ' (1837–1901). If any real unity is to be ascribed
to the Victorian era in England, it must be found in two
governing conditions : first, there was no great war and no
fear of catastrophe from without ; and secondly, the whole
period was marked by interest in religious questions and
was deeply influenced by seriousness of thought and self-
discipline of character, an outcome of the Puritan ethos.
This ' seriousness ' affected even the ' agnostics ' who, in the
last part of the period, challenged not the ethics but the
dogmas of Christianity, with increasing success on account
of Darwinism and the discoveries of science. Moreover,
the High Church movement, originated by Evangelicals
who had seen a new light, inherited this strain of Puritanism.
Mr. Gladstone, an Anglo-Catholic of that breed, appealed
to the heart of his Nonconformist followers, because both
orator and audience regarded life (including politics and
foreign policy) as a branch of personal religion.

Throughout the last seventy years of the Nineteenth
Century the State was rapidly undertaking new social
functions, rendered necessary by new industrial conditions
in an overcrowded island ; but the real strength and felicity
of the Victorian age lay less in that circumstance, important
as it was, than in the self-discipline and self-reliance of the
individual Englishman, derived indeed from many sources,
but to a large extent sprung from Puritan traditions to which
the Wesleyan and Evangelical movements had given
another lease of life. ' Self-help ' was a favourite motto

with leading and characteristic men in all classes. In the Twentieth Century, on the other hand, self-discipline and self-reliance are somewhat less in evidence, and a quasi-religious demand for social salvation through State action has taken the place of older and more personal creeds. Science has undermined the old forms of religious belief, but even now the strength and the weakness of England cannot be understood without some knowledge of her religious history. In the twenty years between the two German wars (1919–1939) the moral idea, though less in-fluential on personal conduct, was still expected, by the emancipated descendants of the Victorian religionists, to dictate our foreign policies and our disarmament, with all too little regard to actualities in other European nations who had never been Puritan, and had never regarded morals as having anything to do with policy.

During the period of the Napoleonic Wars and the first decade of peace that followed, the Evangelical clergy had become an integral part of the Church Establishment, to which they brought a vitality and enthusiasm that was still lacking in its other sections. The life's work of Charles Simeon (1759–1836), Fellow of King's and Minister of Holy Trinity Church, Cambridge, had done much to recon-cile the proselytizing fervour of Evangelicalism to the discipline of the Church. Had it not been for Simeon, the evangelical clergy would have continued to drift into Dissent, as the easier method of conducting a peripatetic mission after the manner of Wesley, athwart the bounds of the parish system and in defiance of Church order. If this movement had continued in the new Century the Church of England might perhaps have fallen when the tempest of ' Reform ' blew high in the 'thirties. But the Simeonite clergy, though friendly to Dissenters, effectively defended the Church whose mission to souls they did so much to revive.[1]

Except for the Evangelicals, the Church under the Regency remained very much as it had been in the early years of George III ; only its latitudinarian liberalism had hardened into anti-Jacobin orthodoxy, unaccompanied by

---

[1] *Simeon and Church Order*, Canon Charles Smyth's Birkbeck Lectures, Cam. Press, 1940.

any spiritual awakening except what was supplied by the Simeonite leaven. Still, as in the Eighteenth Century, the clergy of the Establishment were sharply divided into rich and poor. The Bishops, the Cathedral clergy and wealthier parish priests were part of the ' enjoying ' class ; they had obtained preferment not as a reward of work done for the Church, but through aristocratic connection or family favour. The parishes were often perfunctorily served or were left to the ministration of underpaid curates and threadbare incumbents of poor livings, who were not in the circle visited by the manor-house or acknowledged by Lady Catherine de Bourgh. All this had been highly congenial to the Eighteenth Century, when a ' place ' in Church or State was regarded not as a solemn public trust but as a coveted prize. But in the new Age of Reform, opinion began to demand that a man should do the work for which he was paid. Every institution, from the ' rotten borough ' to the Church benefice, was subjected to the rude Benthamite enquiry : ' What is the use of it ? '

Moreover, the clergy of the Establishment were unpopular because they adhered, more faithfully than any other class or profession, to the High Tory party in the day of its decline and downfall. The formidable hosts of Nonconformists and of free-thinking Radicals, though loving each other little, united to attack ecclesiastical privilege. Young intellectuals, like John Sterling at Cambridge in 1826, described the parson in every village as ' a black dragoon,' kept there to do battle for the powers of tyranny and obscurantism.

Another and perhaps more just description of the well-connected parson as village autocrat at this period may be quoted from Dean Church. (*The Oxford Movement*, pp. 4, 10.)

When communication was so difficult and infrequent, he filled a place in the country life of England, that no one else could fill. He was often the patriarch of his parish, its ruler, its doctor, its lawyer, its magistrate, as well as its teacher, before whom vice trembled and rebellion dared not show itself. The idea of the priest was not quite forgotten ; but there was much—much even of good and useful—to obscure it.

Dean Church also recalls the type of ' country gentlemen in orders, who rode to hounds, and shot and danced and farmed, and often did worse things,' and the ' pluralists who built fortunes and endowed families out of the Church.'

Under these general conditions, it is not wonderful that the Radical Press, in lampoons, articles and gross caricatures of plump, red-faced eaters of tithe, attacked the Anglican clergy more fiercely than they had been attacked since the days of the Long Parliament.   Their unpopularity came to a head in 1831, when the Spiritual Peers in the House of Lords voted by twenty-one to two against the Reform Bill. That winter, the Reform mobs took a special delight in stoning the coaches and burning the palaces of Bishops.

Trembling churchmen and their exultant enemies both assumed that the first work of the reformed Parliament of 1833 would be to remedy the admitted grievances of the Dissenters and that before very long the Church would be disestablished and disendowed.   'No human means are likely to avert the threatened overthrow of the Establishment,' wrote the Tory Southey.   ' The Church as it now is, no human power can save,' wrote Dr. Arnold of Rugby, the Liberal-Conservative.   But a Century has since gone by, and the Establishment, though shorn of its Irish and Welsh excrescences, maintains its endowments and its connection with the State, scarcely any longer challenged. Even the removal of the most obvious grievances of the Dissenters, instead of being carried at a rush in the first decade after the Reform Bill, was spread over fifty years.

The threatened ecclesiastical revolution was side-tracked, and the chief causes of the unpopularity of the Church were done away by friendly hands.   Parliament reformed the unequal distribution of clerical wealth, and there was a rapid revival of religious activity among the clergy themselves, which evoked a rally of the laity to defend the Church and to participate in its parochial work.

The Parliamentary measures necessary for Church reform were carried out by the co-operation of the Conservative leader Peel with the Whig statesmen.   The men of the new Oxford Movement protested against the interference of the State with ecclesiastical revenues, but no other machinery existed to effect these necessary changes, and the wiser members of the Episcopal Bench, like Blomfield, co-operated with Whig and Tory statesmen in the work of the Ecclesiastical Commission and the Acts of Parliament which were passed on its advice between 1836 and 1840.

These Acts removed the worst abuses in the distribution of endowments, and partially at least bridged the gap between rich and poor clergy—though not completely, as readers of Trollope's novels will remember. Plurality was restricted by law, members of chapters being forbidden to hold more than one benefice or to belong to more than one chapter. The Cathedral clergy were reduced in numbers and in wealth. By such measures one hundred and thirty thousand pounds a year were saved and were applied to raise the stipends of the poorer parsons and curates. The diocesan boundaries were altered, and the Bishoprics of Manchester and Ripon were created to cope with the new industrial population of the North. The great inequalities in episcopal revenues were remedied, and scandalously large incomes cut down.

As a consequence of these reforms the Church was no longer assailed as a part of 'old Corruption.' Radical cartoons ceased to represent Bishops, deans and prebendaries as fat, worldly, rapacious men, living on the sweat of the poor.

At the same time the Church, under the inspiration of the spirit of the age, began to supplement by her own action the mediaeval geography of the parish system. New parishes were created, and churches were built in industrial districts, till then abandoned to the activity of the Nonconformists, or to no religion at all. Bishop Blomfield raised a great fund for building churches in outer London. For there was no longer any question of obtaining new churches out of public funds. Tory Parliaments had voted taxes to build churches in Anne's reign, and again after Waterloo. But after 1832 no government dared propose to mulct the taxpayer for such a purpose.

It was difficult to preserve the fabric even of the existing churches by forcing parishioners to pay the Church Rate, which continued for another generation to be a subject of fierce local controversy wherever the Dissenters were strong, especially in the industrial districts of the North. At

Rochdale in 1840, when a poll was being taken to decide whether or not a Church Rate should be levied, passion ran so high that troops were drafted into the town to keep order with fixed bayonets.

For all further development and new undertakings, the Church had therefore to rely on raising money by voluntary subscription, as the Free Churches had always done. And the maintenance of the Anglican Schools, at that time the principal part of the primary education of the country, depended almost entirely on voluntary contribution.

The Whig government also relieved the Church of the worst unpopularity of the tithe system, which from time immemorial had caused heart-burning not only to Dissenters but to the whole agricultural community. The harvest song—

> ' We've cheated the parson, we'll cheat him again,
> For why should the Vicar have one in ten ? '

expressed a sentiment as old as Anglo-Saxon England. The tithe was levied from the tenant farmer, very often in kind : the tenth sucking-pig went to the parson's table ; the tenth sheaf was carried off to his tithe barn. Long before the Reformation it had been a cause of friction and bitterness. Chaucer had praised the good parson who did not ' cursen for his tithes,' that is, excommunicate the recalcitrant tithe-payer.

The Tithe Commutation Act of 1836 laid this ancient grievance to rest. It stopped payment in kind. Tithes were commuted for a rent-charge on land. In 1891 it was made payable by the landowner, no longer by the tenant farmer except perhaps indirectly through his rent. The squires, who were socially and politically allied to the parsons, did not object to paying tithe as strongly as their tenants. The Commutation Acts gave peace to the country-side. It was only in our own day, when after 1918 so many cultivating farmers bought their own land and having become landowners found themselves directly chargeable with tithe, that a fresh agitation arose leading to fresh concessions at the expense of the Church.

Another grievance was remedied by the Marriage Act of 1836. By Lord Hardwicke's Marriage Act of 1753, no one could be legally married except by a Church of England parson, an intolerable insult to the religious feelings of Protestant Dissenters and still more of Roman Catholics. The Act of 1836 permitted religious ceremonies in Catholic or Protestant dissenting places of worship, that should be legally binding if notified to the Registrar.   For the Act established civil officers called Registrars of Births, Deaths and Marriages—in itself a notable reform consonant with the new era of statistics and exact information.   Religious marriage in the Church of England was left as before, on condition that the parson sent to the Civil Registrar a duplicate of the entry of marriage made in the Vestry.   This typical English compromise between the modern secular State and the old religious world is still the law of the land.

These various reforms saved the Church from the serious attack upon her that had been predicted alike by friend and foe.   Nevertheless, political and social divisions remained very largely religious.   The leading Conservatives in each town and village were usually the keenest churchmen ; while their most active opponents, Whig and Liberal, were Dissenters or Anti-clericals.   The lower-middle and working classes attended the same chapels and took part in the same religious activities.   Politics in the Nineteenth Century were as much a matter of denomination as of class. The religious cleavage running through society was maintained all the more because the Whigs after 1832 failed to remedy the Dissenters' grievances about Church Rates, Burials and admission to Oxford and Cambridge.   For a long time to come England was less ' class-conscious ' than ' church-and-chapel conscious.'

In the more old-fashioned parts of England—let us say in ' Barsetshire '—the clergy were still under the patronage and influence of the upper class.   But in other parts of England many now served parishes where there were few or none of the higher orders of society, owing to the geographic segregation of classes which the Industrial Revolution was bringing about.   The ' slum parson ' came into being, a man with a different set of ideas and functions from those of the clerical autocrat of the old English village.

The internal vigour of Church life in the middle decades of the Nineteenth Century was derived from a variety of sources. The average parson of no particular school of thought was aware that he must bestir himself in a critical age. The specifically evangelical influence was much more widely diffused and fashionable in Church circles than in the early years of the century : the ' low Churchmen,' as the Evangelicals were now called, were strong enough to enforce, both by law and custom, more ' Sabbath observance ' than in the previous easy-going age. And at the same time, the Anglo-Catholic ideal, emanating from the Oxford of the 'thirties and 'forties, gradually spread its thoughts and practices throughout the land. In each of these aspects, the ecclesiastical picture of the Church of the 'fifties and ' sixties is well known to readers of Trollope's ' Barsetshire ' novels. In shires less remote, there was also the ' broad church ' school of Frederick Denison Maurice and Charles Kingsley, called ' Christian socialist ' because of its interest in working-class life and education, derived in part from the exhortations of Thomas Carlyle, himself no churchman. The Broad Church school was never strong in numbers, but its ways of thought came to have influence on many more orthodox clergymen, though at first both its ' heresies ' and its ' socialism ' had been regarded with grave reprobation. Thus the Church of England, not without many invigorating controversies and vain attempts to expel either ritualism or heresy, became the multiform body to which we are now so well accustomed, liberally receptive of many different ways of life and thought.

After Newman's conversion to Rome in 1845, the Oxford Movement, which he had done so much to originate, divided itself into two separate currents. One, guided by Pusey and Keble, continued to promote the Anglo-Catholic cause in the established Church.[1] The other, led by Newman and later by Manning, stimulated the revival of the long depressed Roman Catholic mission in England.

---

[1] ' Anglo-Catholicism ' was a novelty in the early Nineteenth Century, but it was not new in the longer range of Anglican History. The Laudian clergy perhaps, and the Nonjurors certainly, might have been called ' Anglo-Catholics ' : the Oxford Tractarians resembled the Nonjurors, *minus* their Jacobitism. Two Irish Churchmen, Bishop Jebb and Alexander Knox, had also adumbrated Anglo-Catholic principles a generation before the Oxford movement gave them a national importance. The ritualistic side of Anglo-Catholic services only developed as the Century went on : it was not a marked feature of the original Oxford Movement.

Having been accorded the status of civic equality by the Catholic Emancipation Act of 1829, and being perpetually recruited by Irish immigration into England, the Roman community went on increasing in numbers and influence. But in 1850 it was still obnoxious to a strongly Protestant nation, as was shown by the misdirected popular outburst against the so-called ' Papal aggression,' when the Pope set up territorial Bishops in England.

Meanwhile the Nonconformist strength went on increasing, as the middle and working classes of the new industrial order continued to grow in numbers, wealth, political power and social esteem.   In the 'sixties, when Matthew Arnold held up an unflattering mirror to the bloated face of English society, it was above all the Nonconformist ' Philistines ' whom his Oxford soul abhorred ; he saw in them the representative men of their generation, proud of their old English liberties and their new gotten wealth, but with too little other idea of the social and intellectual needs of a community deficient in ' sweetness and light.'   But many of these wealthier industrialists of the new order joined the more fashionable Established Church, and passed into the ranks of the upper class by self-assertion or by marriage.   ' Society was getting mixed.'

Another poet, Robert Browning, not of Oxford, perceived better what strength and comfort was added by Puritan religion to the lives of the poor and the hardworking orders of society.   And, indeed, to judge from Matthew Arnold's sonnet *East London*, he too sometimes understood.[1]

The enormously increased wealth and manufacturing power of England in the first half of Victoria's reign—the

' Mammon-quakings dire as earth's '—

and their twin progeny, a new middle class without tradition and a raw industrial proletariat, needed a corresponding development of education to fructify and enlighten them. Unfortunately no government before Gladstone's in 1870 dared to evoke the battle of rival denominations which was

---

[1] William Law Mathieson, *English Church Reform 1815-40* ; Dean Church, *The Oxford Movement; Pretractarian Oxford* by W. Tuckwell ; Matthew Arnold, *Culture and Anarchy*.

certain to ensue from any proposal for State Education, when Church and Dissent would assuredly fly at one another's throats over the question of religious teaching. In 1841 Sir James Graham wrote to Brougham : ' Religion, the keystone of education, is in this country the bar to its progress.' All that the timid State ventured to do,

> ' Between the pass and fell incensed points
> Of mighty opposites,'

was to make a grant of twenty thousand pounds a year towards the school buildings of the various voluntary societies. This was begun in 1833 and the meagre allowance was annually renewed. To distribute this pittance, an Educational Committee of the Privy Council was set up, with a permanent Secretary and a system of inspection of the State-aided schools. Such was the humble origin of the present Ministry of Education. The insistence on government inspection as a condition of a government grant was a principle destined ere long to dominate many spheres of life. The Factory inspectors, set up by the Factory Act of 1833, bred School Inspectors ; Mine Inspectors shortly followed. Government inspection was on the march ; the time would come when it would affect half the activities of the land.

Meanwhile, twenty thousand pounds a year was not much for the richest State in the world to spend on education. The Prussian State was educating the whole Prussian people. The paternal rulers of Germany in the early Nineteenth Century educated their subjects, but gave them little political freedom and no share in government. The English State gave the common people great political freedom and some share in government, but left them to be educated by private religious charity. Only after the working classes of the towns had been enfranchised by the Reform Act of 1867, did the politicians at last say : ' We must educate our masters.'

While such was the inadequate provision for the primary education of the masses, secondary education of the well-to-do underwent a remarkable development in the growth of the ' Public School system.'

At the beginning of the Century there were three kinds

of secondary schools : the fashionable 'Public Schools' (really private) like Eton, Winchester and Harrow, still few in number, with a purely classical curriculum and shockingly ill disciplined ; secondly, the private Academies, where the unfashionable Dissenting middle class received a more scientific and modern education under better discipline ; and finally the old endowed Grammar Schools, many of which had decayed through the negligence and corruption characteristic of public institutions in the Eighteenth Century.

With the growth of the power and wealth of England and the need for every kind of leadership at home and overseas that the new Century demanded, a great increase of secondary education was essential. And it was to some extent supplied, but in an unexpected way that had important social consequences. It might have been supposed that the age of Reform and the approach of democracy would lead to the improvement and multiplication of endowed Grammar Schools by State action ; in that case a common education would have been shared by the clever children of very various classes, as had been done in the Grammar Schools of Tudor and Stuart times with such excellent results. But in the Victorian era the Grammar Schools remained less important, in spite of some striking exceptions as at Manchester. At the same time the Dissenting Academies, so useful in the previous century, petered out. The new fashion was all for the 'Public School,' modelled on the old ideals of Eton, Westminster, Winchester and Harrow, of which Rugby became the great exemplar.

This development was partly due to chance, in the advent of a single man. The great educational reformer of the 'thirties was Dr. Thomas Arnold, Head Master of Rugby. His emphasis on religion and the chapel services, his monitorial system and his largely successful attempt to suppress bullying, drinking, profligacy and the worst indiscipline of the old ' bear-garden ' type of Public School, set an example that proved infectious. The old establishments were reformed and others were started in eager competition. ' Organized games,' which Arnold himself had by no means over-emphasized, grew up automatically, dominating and further popularizing Public School life, and spreading in due course to Oxford and Cambridge.[1]

The ' middling orders of society ' found in the reformed Public School the door of entrance for their sons into the ' governing class.' The old landed gentry, the professional men and the new industrialists were educated together, forming an enlarged and modernized aristocracy, sufficiently numerous to meet the various needs of government and of leadership in Victoria's England and Victoria's Empire.

In many respects the Public Schools were a success and filled the part required. But the subjects which they taught were too much confined to the Classics to meet all the requirements of the new age, though they formed the basis for a high development of literary culture at Oxford and Cambridge, and in Tennyson's England at large. In the microcosm of ' public school ' life, wherein the boys were left to form and govern their own society, character gained more than originality, and intellect was less encouraged than sturdy schoolboy faithfulness to comrades. Twenty and more years after Dr. Arnold's death, his critical son Matthew called the English governing class ' barbarians ' : the Public Schools had tended to preserve both the virtues and the limitations of ' earth's primitive, vigorous sons.'

The upper, the upper-middle and the professional classes were welded together in the Public Schools, and by the same process were further divided from the rest of the nation brought up under a different educational system. The tendency to social segregation, enhanced by the geographic division of the various class ' quarters ' in the

---

[1] How much reason careful and pious parents had to dread the influence on their sons of the Public School before the period of ' Arnold ' reforms and the growth of organized games, can be read in Cowper's *Tirocinium* (1785) **:**

> ' Would you your son should be a sot or dunce,
> Lascivious, headstrong, or all these at once ;
> Train him in public with a mob of boys,
> Childish in mischief only and in noise,
> Else of a mannish growth, and five in ten
> In infidelity and lewdness men.
> There shall he learn, ere sixteen winters old
> That authors are most useful pawned or sold **;**
> That pedantry is all that schools impart
> But taverns teach the knowledge of the heart.'

The whole poem is worth the attention of the student of social history.

lay-out of great modern cities, was thus further accentuated by education. Moreover, the expenses of a Public School, so much higher than those of the Grammar School and Day School, became a terrible self-imposed burden on middle-class and professional families. Indeed, at the end of the Century it became a principal cause of the lamentable decrease in the number of children in some of the best sections of the community.

Much of the success and much of the failure of modern England can be attributed to the Public Schools. They were one of the great institutions unconsciously developed by English instinct and character, and even less than Parliaments could they be successfully imitated oversea.

In the middle years of the Century the secondary education of girls was very ill provided for. They were sacrificed to pay for the expensive education of their brothers. In that and in other matters concerning women, the great emancipation and improvement was postponed till the last thirty years of Victoria's reign—the real period of the ' emancipation of women ' in England.

Yet in spite of Matthew Arnold's pert and challenging phraseology about upper-class ' barbarians ' and middle-class ' Philistines,' he himself was a prophet and poet of the age he abused, and in spite of his scorn for our system of secondary education as ' the worst in the world,' the fact remains that the higher culture of Nineteenth Century England was varied, solid and widespread over a large proportion of the community. The world is not likely to see again so fine and broad a culture for many centuries to come.

Already in the middle years of the Nineteenth Century, industrial change was creating the mass-vulgarity which was destined ere long to swamp that high standard of literary culture with the advent of the new journalism, the decay of the countryside, and the mechanization of life. Scientific education, when at last it came, inevitably displaced humanism. But in the mid-Nineteenth Century, education was still humanistic not scientific, and though this had some serious practical disadvantages, it made for the time being a great literary civilization, based on scholarship, with an even wider following of intelligent readers than in the Eighteenth Century, and with a much more varied and catholic scope in style and matter than in the days when Boileau and Pope were the standards of taste. In literature and thought as well as in society and politics it was an age of transition from aristocracy to democracy, from authority to mass-judgment ; and for literature and thought such conditions were propitious, so long as they lasted.

Serious historical works were addressed to a very wide public and hit their mark, by no means in the case of Macaulay alone. The atmosphere of free religious controversy, of moral reflection, of anxious and reverent doubts on orthodox creeds and the search for a substitute, gave body and interest to imaginative writers like Carlyle, Ruskin and the author of *In Memoriam*, and made Wordsworth in his old age more popular than Byron in his grave. At the same time the critical analysis of actual society, perceived to be very faulty and believed to be remediable, helped to inspire and to popularize Dickens, Thackeray, Mrs. Gaskell and Trollope. And the rights of personality, even in the case of women, were represented in the writings of the Brontë sisters no less than in the life's work of Florence Nightingale. John Stuart Mill on *Liberty* (1859) and on the *Subjection of Women* (1869) attacked the bondage of convention and proclaimed the rights of individual men and women to free life and thought, in a manner that may be taken as a turning-point between the early and the later Victorian age.

The aspect of science which is nearest akin to humanism, the close and loving interpretation of nature, was another source that inspired the literature of the time and another cause of its wide appeal. In the later Eighteenth Century, the way had been prepared by White of Selborne, Bewick and other naturalists both professional and amateur, who taught their countrymen to observe and reverence the world of nature, in which it was man's privilege to dwell. At the turn of the Century this widespread habit found further expression in the landscapes of Girtin, Turner and Constable, and in the poetry of Wordsworth and Keats. In the following generation, in the 'thirties, 'forties and 'fifties, de Wint, David Cox, Edward Lear and many others were added to the list of landscape painters of real talent, who could not even in water-colour paint fast enough to satisfy the public demand. And in poetry the long reign of Tennyson covered most of the Victorian era. His strongest appeal lay in the strength, beauty and accuracy of his pictures of nature.

Indeed, Tennyson, when at his best, was able to clothe the accurate observation of natural objects with ' the light that never was on sea or land.' That commended him to the Victorians, who were susceptible both to the magic of words and the loveliness of nature. The more precise pictures that Tennyson's poetry evoked displaced the vaguer nature-scenes of Thomson's *Seasons*, which until his advent had retained the affections of the middle-class reading public. Early in Victoria's reign the ladies of *Cranford* were told about Tennyson : ' This young man comes and tells me that ash buds are black ; and I look and they *are* black.'

Very similar was the source of Ruskin's influence over the same reading public, which sprang up suddenly in the 'forties and continued for many years. In *Modern Painters*, written to advocate the claims of English landscape painting, particularly that of Turner, and later to defend the Pre-Raphaelites, he analysed in prose at once lucid and magnificent the beauty of form in clouds, mountains and vegetation—the work of God spread wide for the delight of man. He may have erred in testing the value of pictures overmuch by their approximation to truth in these respects, but he gave new eyes to his countrymen in their journeys to the Alps and to Italy, and in their walks in their own familiar woods and fields.

Europe, then a world of comparative peace and variegated beauty, not yet mechanized and not yet closed by war and national hatred, was the great playground of the English, who flocked abroad in thousands to spend their newly gotten wealth in exploring the mountains and flower-meadows of Switzerland, the architecture, the galleries, and the landscapes of the Netherlands, Italy and France. The English traveller of this period took abroad a full mind equipped by some knowledge of history, literature and natural science to observe and appreciate the glory of the world of nature and of man.

At the same time the new railway system of Britain opened out the Highlands of Scotland to pedestrians and tourists with a zeal for mountain air and scenery. The wealthier and more fashionable had their deer-forest or their grouse-moor where they entertained their guests every autumn. The moorland expeditions of the Queen and Prince Albert from Balmoral, and the deer that the Prince shot and Landseer painted, popularized Highland scenery with all classes of the English, who were now able to see the landscape of Scott's romances for themselves.

Thus, in the middle years of the Century, Victoria's subjects developed eyes for many kinds of natural beauty and historical interest. They enjoyed a great literary civilization, both in reading the classics of the past and producing classics of their own age. But these grandfathers and great-grandfathers of ours, though they compassed sea and land to admire Roman aqueducts and Gothic Cathedrals, themselves produced deplorable buildings, and filled them with appropriate furniture and knick-knacks. In these respects the decay of taste between the period of the Regency and the period of the Prince Consort was astonishing. The most refined and educated classes were as bad as any : the monstrosities of architecture erected by order of the Dons of Oxford and Cambridge Colleges in the days of William Butterfield and Alfred Waterhouse give daily pain to posterity.

An unfortunate habit of the time was the demolition of beautiful old manor-houses of manageable size, to make room for ugly rural palaces where the rich men of Britain's most prosperous era entertained their troops of guests from London. Their descendants, with better taste in architecture and with less money in the Bank, have reason to regret the burdens thus bequeathed them.

It is not altogether easy to account for this architectural blind spot in the Victorian vision. But Ruskin, as chief priest, was in part responsible, in that he condemned, on fantastic religious grounds, the whole Renaissance tradition, of which real English architecture was essentially a part. His influence filtered down through society till it reached people who never read a line of his books, and jerry-builders believed that if they ' stuck on a bit of Gothic ornament,' all was well. The real secret of architecture, proportion, was lost. At bottom the Industrial Revolution was to blame : the mechanization of building and other trades, and the decline of craftsmanship were no doubt the deep underlying causes. Local customs in architecture, based on the use of local materials, were destroyed by the railways, which supplied standardized cheap bricks and slates, to take the place of local stone, stone-tiles, thatch and thin brick, which previous generations of countrymen had known how to use aright by inherited skill and regional tradition. But now building everywhere became a process of cheap mass-production of houses by modern methods. New furniture, machine-made, was as bad. The fat up-holstered arm-chairs might be more comfortable, the new houses might be more convenient, but beauty spread her wings and flew away.

In the 'forties, 'fifties and 'sixties painting was still a great trade, supplying a great demand. For the photo-grapher had not yet sufficiently developed his science to take the place of the painter's art in the production of family portraits, copies of famous pictures and representa-tions of ancient buildings and favourite landscapes. At Rome, and in every artistic capital of Europe, resided an army of artists, good and bad, painting landscapes and copying ' old masters ' to sell to the touring English, who carried back these mementoes of their travels. And the Royal Academy was in its heyday, commercially speaking, supplying the rising manufacturers with portraits, land-scapes and historical pieces—to cover the large walls of their comfortable, new, pretentious homes. It was partly because this trade was so extensive that Ruskin became so important. He exercised over art the kind of dictatorship which the *Edinburgh* and *Quarterly* reviews had formerly exercised over literature. The complaint of the demoded R.A. was thus parodied :

> I paints and paints,
> Hears no complaints,
>   And sells before I'm dry ;
> Till savage Ruskin
> Sticks his tusk in
>   And nobody will buy.

The same dangers from the same combination of religious and social forces, which in the years immediately preceding the Reform Bill had threatened the clergy of the Establishment, threatened also the old Municipal Corporations with which the Church interest was allied.[1] But unlike the Church, the old Corporations were as incapable of recovery or self-reform as the Parliamentary Rotten Boroughs with which their fate was closely associated. Three years after the death of the ' Rotten Boroughs,' the rotten Town governments were abolished by the Municipal Reform Act of 1835.

That important measure meant much to the social life of cities, by the immediate transference of power to new classes ; and it meant more than was then foreseen, as the basis on which was to arise, during the next hundred years, the great structure of municipal social service for the benefit of all classes of the community, particularly of the poor. No one in 1835 foresaw the day when the ' new municipalities ' would not only light and pave the streets, but control the building of houses, and the sanitation and health of the borough ; convey the workmen to and from their work ; provide public libraries ; carry on great municipal trades and industries ; and finally educate the people.

The immediate change that excited contemporaries was the transference of municipal authority, such as it then was, to Dissenters and shopkeepers, in place of the co-optive oligarchies of Tory lawyers, Churchmen and noblemen's agents who had enjoyed a close monopoly of the old corporations. There was not much ' sweetness and light ' in the new style of city governor, but they had a certain rough vigour, and were disposed to welcome ' improvements, ' while the fact that they were periodically chosen by a real democracy, kept them up to the mark in those matters in which the electors themselves felt any interest. The limitation of the Parliamentary franchise to ' ten pound householders ' in the Reform Bill of 1832 was not imitated in the more radical Municipal Reform Bill, which gave the local franchise to all ratepayers. The working class had

---

[1] Light on this alliance is thrown in the article entitled *A Leicester Election of 1826* in the *Royal Historical Society Transactions* for 1940. See also Halévy's *Hist. of Eng. People* (Ernest Benn, Watkin's transla. 1927), III, pp. 217–220.

a say at least in local elections in the new Boroughs. The town administration thus passed into entirely new hands; moreover, the judicial bench of magistrates in large urban areas was filled up by the Whig governments, acting on behalf of the Crown, with Dissenters and middle-class citizens of the newly dominant types. There were to be no more ' Peterloo magistrates ' in the cities of England.

The Reform Bill of 1832 and its sequel in the Municipal Reform Bill of 1835, taken together, emphasized and increased the differentiation between the social life of town and country which economic forces were every day making more complete. Victoria's England consisted of two strongly contrasted social systems, the aristocratic England of the rural districts and the democratic England of the great cities. The counties and the market towns were still ruled and judged by country gentlemen to whom all classes bowed. But the cities were governed by a totally different type of person, in accordance with a very different scale of social values which, whether middle or working class, were essentially democratic.

Owing to economic causes and the progress of locomotion, the new society of the town was perpetually encroaching on the old society of the country till, in the Twentieth Century, urban thought, ideas and government conquered the countryside itself. But that was a long process and the Nineteenth Century was an age of transition. Agriculture was not at once ruined by the Repeal of the Corn Laws in 1846, nor was aristocratic government of the villages and market towns overthrown by that measure. Until the American prairies were able to empty their grain and cattle into the English market a generation later, English agriculture flourished, sustaining the social system with which it was associated.

But agriculture was not capable of indefinite expansion ; by the middle of the Century it had reached its highest development and the acreage of land could not be increased. On the other hand, the Industrial and Commercial Revolution was only then gathering its full strength, and the increase of town wealth and population went on decade after decade. The Census of 1851 showed that already half the population of the island was urban, ' a situation that had probably not existed before, in a great country, at any time in the world's history.' (Clapham, I, p. 536.) And since there was no visible limit to this process, it was ominous of a queer future. John Bull was ceasing to be a countryman and a farmer ; when once he was wholly urbanized or suburbanized, would he any longer be John Bull, except in the cartoons of *Punch* ?

The new urban conditions, under which so large a pro-portion of the English people were already living in 1851, began at length to attract attention and demand a remedy. The old life of the open countryside, blown through by the airs of heaven, needed, or was thought to need, less control of housing and sanitation : bad as rural cottages were, the death-rate was lower in the country than in the town. But owing to the increased proportion of town dwellers, the rapid fall of the death-rate that had so happily distinguished the period between 1780 and 1810 was positively checked between 1810 and 1850. Taking the island as a whole, the death-rate did not again rise as high as in the early part of the Eighteenth Century, but it ceased to decline any further, in spite of the constant advance in medical service and science. (See p. 342.) The chief reason was the growth of the area covered by industrial slums, and their progressive deterioration as years went by.
    In the matter of guardianship of public health, the rule of shopkeepers, builders and publicans, elected by the rate-payers under the Municipal Reform Act of 1835, was no real improvement on the lethargy of the Tory oligarchs who had been displaced amid such general rejoicings. Still throughout the 'forties nothing was done to control the slum-landlords and jerry-builders who, according to the prevalent *laissez-faire* philosophy, were engaged from motives of self-interest in forwarding the general happiness. These pioneers of ' progress ' saved space by crowding families into single rooms or thrusting them underground into cellars, and saved money by the use of cheap and insufficient building material, and by providing no drains— or, worse still, by providing drains that oozed into the water-supply. In London, Lord Shaftesbury discovered a room with a family in each of its four corners, and a room with

a cesspool immediately below its boarded floor. We may even regard it as fortunate that cholera ensued, first in the year of the Reform Bill and then in 1848, because the sensational character of this novel visitation scared society into the tardy beginnings of sanitary self-defence. A full-page cartoon in the most popular journal of the time represents Mr. Punch as Hamlet in meditation over a City sewer—' Why may not imagination trace the remains of an Alderman till we find them poisoning his Ward ? '

The first Public Health Act dates from 1848. It resulted from the cholera and from the efforts of Edwin Chadwick, who as Secretary to the Poor Law Commissioners had come to realize the facts.

' The prisons [he wrote] were formerly distinguished for their filth and bad ventilation ; but the descriptions given by Howard of the worst prisons he visited in England (which he states were among the worst he had seen in Europe) were exceeded in every wynd in Edinburgh and Glasgow inspected by Dr. Arnott and myself. More filth, worse physical suffering and moral disorder than Howard describes are to be found amongst the cellar populations of the working people of Liverpool, Manchester or Leeds and in large portions of the Metropolis.'

But the Public Health Act of 1848 of which the main principle was permission rather than compulsion to act, was not properly carried out by the municipalities for another twenty years. It was only in the 'seventies that the establishment of the Local Government Board to enforce the law, and the rise of Joseph Chamberlain, the social-reforming Mayor of Birmingham, ushered in a new age. Then at last the fact that the Municipalities were elected bodies produced real public benefits on a large scale, while the State increasingly insisted on a compulsory standard. Not till the 'seventies did the death-rate decisively fall as a result of building and sanitary reform, and not till the end of the Century was sanitation in English cities at all what it should have been.

But even in the middle years of the Century slight improvement had been made. Lord Shaftesbury had, by voluntary subscriptions, established some model lodging houses, and their immunity from cholera induced Parliament to pass an Act for the inspection of common lodging

houses in 1851 ; at the same time the window tax, that old
enemy of health and light, was at last repealed.   In that
year, when the Great Exhibition spread its hospitable glass
roof high over the elms of Hyde Park, and all the world
came to admire England's wealth, progress and enlightenment, an ' exhibition ' might profitably have been made of
the way in which our poor were housed, to teach the admiring foreign visitor some of the dangers that beset the
path of the vaunted new era.   Foreign slums were indeed
many of them as bad or worse, but a much smaller proportion of the populations of Continental States had been
removed from the wholesome influence of the countryside.

If we ask why those who sympathized with the victims of
a lopsided ' Political Economy ' called it the ' dismal
science,' we get some answer in the following unctuous
passage from the *Economist* newspaper, written in May 1848
in opposition to Chadwick's Public Health Act :

' Suffering and evil are nature's admonitions ; they cannot be got
rid of ; and the impatient attempts of benevolence to banish them
from the world by legislation, before benevolence has learnt their
object and their end, have always been more productive of evil than
good.'

Doctrine of one kind or another has been the cause of half
the woes of mankind, but fortunately the English of this
period were not entirely doctrinaires, and passed the Ten
Hours Bill and the Public Health Act in despite of the
prevalent *laissez-faire* theories of the age.[1]

Meanwhile, if public health still lagged behind, public
order had been well secured.   Sir Robert Peel's great
institution of the civilian police with their truncheons, blue
coats and top hats (later exchanged for helmets) had only
applied to the Metropolitan area in 1829.   But a people
fond of liberty, property and personal safety liked the good-
natured and effective ' Bobbies ' of London and demanded
their establishment elsewhere.   By 1856 every county and
borough had to employ a police force, half local, half
national in its administration, discipline and finance.   The
days of the inefficient Watchman of the Dogberry and

---

[1] Clapham, I, pp. 536-547 ; Fay, C. R., *Great Britain from Adam Smith to
the present day*, pp. 362-365 ; *Ec. Hist. Rev.*, Ap. 1935, pp. 71-78 ; Griffith,
Population problems of the age of Malthus, pp. 39-42.

Verges type were gone by for ever ; person and property were well guarded at last without any sacrifice of freedom, and mobs and meetings could be dealt with, punctually and quietly, without calling on armed force as at Peterloo.

The period between the two first Reform Bills (1832–1867) was the ' age of coal and iron ' now working at full blast, or in other words it was ' the Railway Age.'

The railways were England's gift to the world. They originated from experiments in the best method of moving coal from the pit-head in the vast quantities required for smelting and manufacture as well as for domestic use. In the 'twenties there had been much controversy as to the rival merits of drawing coal along wooden or iron rails by horses, or by stationary engines, or by George Stephenson's ' locomotive.' The triumph of the latter opened out unexpected vistas not only for the carriage of all classes of goods but as a new method of passenger traffic. Not only the canals but the stage-coaches were doomed ; Mr. Weller senior's occupation was gone. Short local lines laid down in the coal districts were developed in the 'thirties and 'forties into a national system for the whole island, as a result of two distinct periods of railway investment and speculation, in 1836–1837 and in 1844–1848.

Many of the railroad promoters and investors who led the way in the 'thirties were Dissenters, and more particularly Quakers of the Midlands and the North—Peases, Croppers, Sturges. The original *Bradshaw's Railway Time Table* was issued in 1839 by a Friend wishful to help mankind ; until the Twentieth Century the outside cover of ' Bradshaw ' still bore the Quaker's designation of the month—' First Month ' instead of January, and so forth.

But in the 'forties, under the less scrupulous leadership of George Hudson, the ' Railway King,' the general public plunged headlong into the speculation of the ' railway mania,' and lost much money in bogus or unsuccessful companies. Thackeray's Diary of *Jeames de la Pluche, Esq.*, humorously chronicles the excitement of the boom and the crash. But when all was over, though the more foolish part of the public had been gulled, a large residuum of successful new lines survived. Hudson was not a mere swindler ; he had scored his mark across the face of England. In 1843 there had been about 2000 miles of railway in Great Britain ; in 1848 there were 5000.[1]

Henceforth the normal way of transporting heavy goods and the normal way of long-distance travelling was by rail. The canals, after half a century of prosperity and public service, were most of them ruined, and were many of them bought up by local railway companies that had in fact been started with the object of cutting them out. At the same time the main roads ceased to be the chief arteries of the life-blood of the nation. The posting inns and postilions disappeared, and with them went the public mail-coach, and the heavy family coach in which the aristocratic households had moved about. In the Capital, the convenient 'landau,' the light ' Victoria,' the smart ' hansom cab ' (called by Disraeli ' the gondola of London '), the homely four-wheeler and the democratic omnibus held the streets. In the country at large it was the age of the gig, the wagonette, the pony-cart and the dog-cart. Horse-traffic, both for travellers and for goods, became ancillary to the railway and flourished on that basis. There were not railways everywhere and in any case it was necessary to ' get to the station.' Byroads continued to increase in number, quality and use. But long journeys by road went out, and the great highways were relatively deserted, until the coming of the motor car.[2]

The growth of the electric telegraph was almost contemporaneous with the change in locomotion, and originated as an adjunct of the new railway system. By 1848 over 1800 miles of railways, a third of the whole mileage in use, were already equipped with telegraph wires. The Electric Telegraph Company, formed in 1846, had seventeen offices in London by 1854, of which eight were at the railway

---

[1] Sir Roger Scatcherd, in Trollope's *Dr. Thorne*, represents a ' self-made man ' of this rough vigorous period of railway and engineering development carried out by English initiative at home and abroad. For the autobiography of a real engineer of the period, of a more respectable type than the imaginary Scatcherd, see *John Brunton's Book*, Cam. Press, 1939.

[2] Seymour's well-known illustration of the row with the cabman in Chap. II of *Pickwick* shows the aboriginal form of the ' hansom cab ' in the 'thirties, with the driving-seat not above but at the side of the high roof. From the 'forties onwards changes in locomotion, dress, games and social customs can be followed in the pictures of *Punch*.

termini. As early as 1847 arrangements for the candidature of the Prince Consort for the Chancellorship of the University were in part conducted by telegram, even by such old-fashioned people as the dons of Cambridge.

The same decades that saw the rapid growth of the railway system and the electric telegraph, saw the triumph of the penny post, established by the unselfish and tireless efforts of Rowland Hill, supported by the popular demand, against the indifference of statesmen and the angry obstruction of the unreformed civil service. Prior to this great change, the poor who moved in search of work either inside the island or by emigration overseas, could seldom exchange news with the parents and friends they had left behind, owing to the heavy charge made for the receipt of letters. Rowland Hill's plan for a postal delivery prepaid by a cheap adhesive stamp, enabled the poor, for the first time in the history of man, to communicate with the loved ones from whom they were separated. And since the business world found cheap postage a boon, and since it proved a great financial success after it had been forced upon the obdurate Post Office, the new method was soon imitated in every civilized country in the world. In this great reform the State had necessarily to be made the instrument, but the thought and the leadership had come from an individual, backed by public opinion.

The rapid growth of railways in the island during the 'forties was followed by the substitution of steam for sail, and of iron for wood in the British mercantile marine. As late as 1847 our steamships were few and small, with a total tonnage of 116,000 out of the three million tons of the whole merchant service. But in the 'fifties and 'sixties the great ocean-going ships were increasingly propelled by steam, and built first of iron and then of steel. The change coincided with the enormous development of English iron and steel output, and the increased use of steam and metal in every sort of manufacturing process and product. In 1848 Britain already produced about half the pig-iron of the world : in the next thirty years her output was trebled. The West of Scotland, hitherto behindhand, was soon producing a quarter of Britain's pig-iron. Staffordshire, Wales and the North-Eastern England of Tyneside and

s

Middlesbrough were also the regions of the great iron-masters, who by due attention to scientific discovery carried on their supremacy into the age of steel.[1]

The wealth accruing from these developments in the mid-Victorian era greatly relieved the pressure of the social problem by raising the real wages of a large proportion of the working class, while Trade Union action and the Co-operative movement helped to distribute the enormous national dividend a little more evenly.

The national dividend was indeed enormous. The Californian and Australian gold discoveries ushered in a great period of expanding trade of which England, by her lead over other countries both in commerce and industry, was able to reap the principal benefit in the middle years of the Century. In 1870 the volume of the external trade of the United Kingdom exceeded that of France, Germany and Italy together and was between three and four times that of the United States.

While these great industrial and commercial developments were going forward at revolutionary speed, British agriculture continued along a steady path of progress, helped by abundance of capital and the increasing application of machinery to farm work. The Repeal of the Corn Laws in 1846 steadied prices, but gave no check to agricultural prosperity for another generation to come, because America was not yet ready to flood England with her farm products. In 1851 it was reckoned that only one quarter of the Englishman's bread came from oversea.

Corn Law Repeal was a political triumph for Manchester and for the urban population ; and it certainly helped industry. But it effected no immediate economic or social revolution. The cities belonged to democracy, but the countryside was still in the hands of the landlord class, and of their deputies and allies the tenant farmers, whose affairs were much more flourishing in the 'sixties than they had been a generation before. Country-house life, with its

---

[1] Clapham (II, 515) points out that in Petermann's census map of the location of industries in 1851, neither Middlesbrough nor Barrow, neither Cardiff nor Newport are marked as the seat of iron industry. Their rise as such was very rapid after that date.

hunting and shooting, and its political and literary 'house-parties' was more prosperous, easy and delightful than ever, though its moral standards were more ' respectable ' than in the days of Eighteenth Century aristocratic licence.   In the rural parts there was still no elective local government. Administrative and judicial authority still rested with the gentlemen Justices of the Peace, chosen from among the landowners.   The immemorial rule of the squire magistrate still prevailed, though subject, through the newspapers and the spirit of the age, to a more wholesome and effective criticism than in the early Hanoverian times.

With locomotion constantly diminishing the distance between the village and the city, with the spread of science and machinery even in the processes of agriculture, in a small island with a dense urban population that had now lost all tradition of country life, it was only a question of time before urban ways of thought and action would penetrate and absorb the old rural world, obliterating its distinctive features and local variations.   But the time was not yet.   In the 'sixties two things were still lacking before the change could be complete—the economic ruin of British agriculture, and a town-made system of universal education.

When Victoria came to the throne the ' great estate ' system was already an accomplished fact.   Ever since the days of the last Stuart Kings, more and more land had been passing from small squires and cultivating owners into the possession of the big landlords, into whose circle the men of the new town-made wealth were constantly intruding themselves by marriage, by the purchase of large continuous estates, and by the building of new ' country houses.'   The small squires had gone, their manor-houses converted into tenant farms ;   the freehold yeomen were fewer than of old ;   large and middle-sized estates were the general rule.

But if estates were large, it did not follow that farms had proportionately increased in size.   On the average they were bigger than before.   But moderate-sized farms worked by a single family without hired labour were still very common.   And indeed such farms are very numerous even to-day, especially in the pastoral counties of the North, the more so as machinery has reduced the number of hands required.[1]

So far was land from falling out of cultivation during the two decades following the Repeal of the Corn Laws in 1846, that more and more acres were enclosed and cultivated.   There was a constant increase of the island population, that had still to be fed mainly by home produce. The gold discoveries of the 'fifties raised prices.   In the 'sixties, while wars raged in Europe and in America, England was at peace.   Great progress was still being made in live-stock breeding.   Improved draining and manuring ; the gradual introduction of machine ploughing, reaping and threshing into one county and village after another ; the work of the Royal Agricultural Society ; the capital invested and the pride taken by the great landlords in the improvement of their estates—all these things brought more fields under the plough in Lord Palmerston's England.   When Matthew Arnold revisited in the 'sixties the Oxford hillsides where he had strayed with his friend Arthur Clough twenty years before, it was not yet ' bungaloid growth ' that the poet had to bemoan, but the more innocent spread of cultivation !

> I know these slopes ; who knows them if not I ?—
>> But many a dingle on the loved hillside,
>>> With thorns once studded, old, white-blossomed trees,
>> Where thick the cowslips grew, and far descried
>>> High towered the spikes of purple orchises,
>>>> Hath since our day put by
>> The coronals of that forgotten time ;
>>> *Down each green bank hath gone the ploughboy's team,*
>>>> And only in the hidden brookside gleam
>> Primroses, orphans of the flowery prime.

[1] In 1851, omitting holdings under 5 acres, the size of farms in England and Wales was thus scheduled :

Size—acres	No. of farms	Acreage of group
1. 5–49	90,100	2,122,800
2. 50–90	44,600	3,206,500
3. 100–299	64,200	11,015,800
4. 300–499	11,600	4,360,900
5. 500–999	4,300	2,841,000
6. 1000 and upwards	771	1,112,300

Clapham, *Ec. Hist. of Modern Britain*, II, p. 264.

At Victoria's accession, the enclosure of the ' open fields ' and therewith the end of the ' strip ' system of agriculture, was already an accomplished fact, except for a few scattered survivals. But the enclosure of commons was not yet complete and still went on apace, stimulated by the General Enclosure Act of 1845.

The movement for the enclosure of common land—for so many centuries past a source of disputes and grievances, as well as a means of greatly increasing the productivity of the island—was halted at last in the decade between 1865 and 1875. It was characteristic of the altered balance of society that enclosure of commons was ultimately stopped by the protest not of the rural peasantry, but of the urban population, who objected to exclusion from its holiday playgrounds and rural breathing spaces. The Commons Preservation Society effectively opposed the destruction of the remaining commons, in the interest, nominally and legally, of the vanishing ' commoner ' of the village, but really of the general public in quest of ' air and exercise.' The great battle of Berkhamsted Common (1866) and the saving of Epping Forest ushered in a new age. Enclosure had done its work in England, and was to do no more. (*Clapham*, I, 450 note, 454 ; II, 258–9.)

The prosperous agriculture of the eighteen-sixties still showed a great variety of method, from the fully mechanized farming of scientific Scots in the Lothians, to fields in Sussex where oxen still dragged the plough. Those lands that had been enclosed during the last two hundred years from open field, sheep-run and fen into large rectangular fields, were most easily subject to modern scientific and mechanical cultivation, as for instance in Cambridgeshire. Lands of the West and South-East, where enclosure had existed from time immemorial, were still cut up by old hedges into small and irregular fields that impeded agricultural efficiency. But in almost every shire there was much diversity of method, due either to variety of soils or difference in the economic and social past.

The condition of the agricultural labourer, particularly in the South, was often very wretched in the 'thirties and ' hungry 'forties,' when even the farmer who employed

him was suffering from the bad times.   And on the ' labouring poor,' in field and factory, fell the heavy weight of the
New Poor Law of 1834, when outdoor relief was abolished
(not indeed quite universally) and the ' workhouse test '
was imposed on applicants for public alms.   Such was the
remorseless utilitarian logic of the Poor Law Commissioners,
to whom the Act gave power.   It was a harsh remedy for
a terrible disease :   the Speenhamland policy of granting
the poor-rate in aid of wages had pauperised even the
employed workman and kept wages down ; moreover, it
was now ruining the ratepayers. (See p. 469.)   An
operation was necessary to save society, but the knife was
applied without anaesthetics.   The need to make life in
the workhouse less attractive than employment in field
and factory was the principle on which the Commissioners
worked, and as they could not in that era raise the attractive-
ness of employment by enforcing a minimum wage, they
felt obliged to lower the standard of happiness of the workhouse.   Moreover, in their preoccupation with the problem
of the adult workman, the Commissions overlooked the
justice and expediency of treating old people, children and
invalids with the tenderness that was in every sense their
due.

Dickens's *Oliver Twist* was an attack on workhouse
management, to which the greater sensibility of the Victorian
public responded.   The working class in town and country
regarded the New Poor Law as an odious tyranny, as indeed
it often was.   But it had created a central machine which,
by displacing the old local autonomy, was used as years
went by to remedy the grievances of the poor and to make
a national system of which the country had less reason to
be ashamed.   The national and centralized character which
the first Commissioners had stamped on the Poor Law
made it easier to carry out the many improvements suggested
later on by a philanthropy that gradually became more
humane as it became more experienced and more scientific.
Imperfect and harsh as was the Poor Law in 1834, it had
been intellectually honest within its limits, and contained
the seeds of its own reform.

For the system erected for the new Poor Law was based
not on *laissez-faire* but on its opposite.   It was pure

Benthamism, a combination of the elective with the bureaucratic principle, as advocated in Bentham's ' Constitutional Code.' The three government Commissioners (bureaucrats representing the Central government) are to lay down the rules for poor law administration and to see they are enforced. But the actual people to administer these rules are local elective bodies—the boards of guardians. Every ' union ' of parishes is to be administered by a ' board of guardians of the poor,' to be elected by all the ratepayers. Both the centralized bureaucrats at the top, and the democratically elected Boards of guardians in the localities, are the Benthamite substitute for the old methods of government by country gentlemen acting as unpaid Justices of the Peace.

But the new Poor Law of 1834 was a very unfortunate beginning for reformed methods of governing the countryside. Its harshness, especially in the separation of families,[1] gave the rural poor a distaste for Benthamite improvement, and reconciled them to the old paternal government of the Justices of Peace in all other matters, which went on for another fifty years. The New Poor Law might have served as a model for other changes in local government, but it was too unpopular.

Why did the Whig and Tory squires acquiesce in this encroachment on their right to rule the countryside, in this one matter of poor law administration ? It was only in the case of the Poor Law that they allowed State bureaucracy and electoral democracy to invade the rural parts. The reason is clear. The country gentlemen had a direct interest in the change. Under the old system of rates in aid of wages, the poor-rate which they paid was growing

[1] In 1838 the popular writer William Howitt in his *Rural Life of England* (II, p. 131), after describing the simple pleasures of country life for the cottager, adds : ' I often thank God that the poor have their objects of admiration and attraction ; their domestic affections and their family ties, out of which spring a thousand simple and substantial pleasures ; that in this country at least the hand of arbitrary power dare seldom enter this enchanted circle, and tear asunder husband from wife, parent from children, brother from sister, as it does in the lands of slavery. Yet our New Poor Laws have aimed a deadly blow at this blessed security. And, till the sound feeling of the nation shall have again disarmed them of this fearful authority, every poor man's family is liable, on the occurrence of some chance stroke of destitution, to have to their misfortune, bitter enough in itself, added the tenfold aggravation of being torn asunder and immured in the separate wards of a Poverty Prison.'

heavier every year, and pessimists prophesied that it would finally absorb the entire rent of the kingdom. The Whig Ministers had presented the Bill as 'a measure of agricultural relief,' and Peel and Wellington accepted it as such. At Wellington's orders, the Lords resisted the temptation to throw out this very unpopular measure.

With the increasing prosperity of industry and agriculture in the 'fifties and 'sixties, the lot of the wage-earner in town and country was greatly relieved. Shortly after 1870 agricultural wages had reached a point that they were never again to touch for many years. All along, in bad times and good, the wages of the field worker in the North were higher than in the South owing to the neighbourhood of coal-mines and higher paid industries. Agricultural Wages in the West Riding of Yorkshire had been fourteen shillings a week when they were seven shillings in Wilts and Suffolk. (Clapham, I, pp. 466–467 ; II, p. 286, table.)

The labourer, driven off the enclosed common and open field, had sometimes found compensation in allotments and potato-patches provided for him by philanthropic squires, parsons and farmers. The potato was of great service to the field labourer in the Nineteenth Century. But the allotment movement went slowly, and was no more than an occasional palliative.

In the 'fifties and 'sixties, while agriculture still flourished, good brick cottages, with slate roofs and two or even three bedrooms apiece, were being built by landlords as 'estate cottages,' particularly on large estates like those of the Duke of Bedford. The bad cottages were the old ones, of which there were plenty, built of mud, lath and plaster, and roofed with ill-repaired thatch, with only two rooms to the whole cottage. 'The worst were generally the small freeholds, inhabited by the person who owned them.' The farmhouses were not only larger but on the average more habitable than the cottages. The best had usually been erected recently by the landlord. Where a good farmhouse was two centuries old, it was nearly always a former manor-house, once belonging to some family of small squires. (Clapham II, p. 505–512.)

The English landlord, if not a philanthropist, was not a mere ' business man ' dealing with land for profit. The rent of the new ' estate cottages ' seldom covered the expense of their building and maintenance. There were of course bad landlords, and as a rule the squire had insufficient sympathy with the labourers' desire for a better standard of life, as was shown during the attempt of Joseph Arch to secure them higher wages, by forming agricultural unions (1872–1873). But the English rural landlord did much for the countryside and its inhabitants, whereas the rural landlord of Ireland, like the town landlord of England was a mere exploiter of other people's labour. The ill odour into which the town landlord most justly fell, made the radical and socialist of the town regard all ' landlords ' with too indiscriminate reprobation, and helped to increase his misunderstanding of rural questions.

Thus, when British agriculture reached its peak of prosperity about 1870, prior to the sudden catastrophe of the next decade, it was based on an aristocratic social system, the ' dual ownership ' of landlord and farmer, which had done marvels in the way of production, but gave too little of the increased dividend of rural life to the field labourer. It is true that he received higher wages than agricultural labourers on the Continent, but by English standards they were not high. It is true that he was materially better off than most of the self-employed peasantry of Europe. It is true also that there were in England many small-sized farms run on a family basis. But there was no longer an independent peasantry as numerous in proportion to the other inhabitants of the country as had once existed in England and still exists in continental countries. The consequence was that when after 1875 Free Trade completed its work by destroying the prosperity of British agriculture, the town-bred electorate was indifferent to the decay of rural life—because it was associated with an aristocratic system. Too many Englishmen looked on almost with satisfaction at the progress of the national disaster, as being a free and natural economic change.

The passing of the Reform Bill of 1832 was at once followed in the industrial North by a fierce agitation of the factory hands against the hard condition of their lives, particularly in the matter of hours. In Yorkshire it was to some extent a Radical and Tory coalition. At Westminster members of all parties took part in it, and in 1833 the Whig government gave it legislative form. The principal leaders in the country, Oastler, Sadler and Shaftesbury, were Tories ; they were also all three Evangelicals. Evangelical humanity was a strong motive in providing the educated leaders, while the popular drive behind the movement came from the factory population itself, who were mostly Radicals. But the Tory country gentlemen were not hostile to the movement, for they were jealous of the parvenus of the master-manufacturer class. The squires were incensed at the attacks made by these upstarts upon the gentlemen of England for grinding the faces of the poor with their corn-laws ; they replied by denouncing the evils of factory employment, though their fathers had scouted all such Luddite complaints as ' Jacobinical.' The split in the ranks of the well-to-do gave the wage-earner a hole through which to thrust up his head, and make his case heard. And behind these class recriminations lay the genuine humanitarianism of the age, focused by the Evangelicals, but not confined to any religious sect or political party.

The sentiment of humanity was now a great force in politics. In 1833 it abolished slavery in the Empire at a cost of twenty million pounds cheerfully paid by the British taxpayer. That same year it stopped the abuse of children's labour in the textile factories at home.

The promoters of Factory legislation found that the appeal to humanity was most easily made about the children.

' It is true [writes Mons. Halévy] that the operatives were seeking a restriction of working hours for themselves—not for the children who were very often the victims of their brutality rather than of the employer's tyranny. But the number of children employed in the factories was so great in proportion to the adults that it was out of the question to restrict the working hours of children without restricting at the same time the hours of the adults. It was for the children that Oastler sought to awaken the pity of the English middle class, but his aim was the legal protection of the adult worker.' (Halévy's *Hist. Eng. People*, trans. by Watkin, III, p. 111.)

Lord Althorp's Factory Act of 1833 set legal limits to the working hours of children and young personsr espectively, and its provisions were enforced by the appointment of factory inspectors, with power of entry into the factories. Their appointment had been suggested by some of the better disposed among the employers themselves. For it was not merely bad employers but bad parents living on their children's labours, who required watching. Moreover, the better employers wanted the government to prevent the worse employers from undercutting them by defying this Act as they had defied the earlier laws.

Out of this children's charter of 1833 grew the Ten Hours Bill. This second crisis of Factory legislation came to a head in 1844–1847, contemporaneously with the repeal of the Corn Laws, and was heated with the fires of that great dispute. The Ten Hours Bill limited the daily work of women and youths in textile factories, and thereby compelled the stoppage of all work after ten hours, as the grown men could not carry on the processes alone. This measure had for years been the aspiration of the employees and the storm-centre of a fierce controversy. In Parliament it produced curious cross-voting. Among the Liberals—Melbourne, Cobden and Bright were against it: Russell, Palmerston and Macaulay were for it. And the Conservatives were no less divided, Peel being strongly against the Bill, while a majority of the Protectionist squires voted in its favour. But the man who finally carried the Bill through the House of Commons was Fielden, ' the largest cotton spinner in England ; and the man who told with him in the lobby had passed from the position of worker to that of employer in the same industry.' (Hammond, *Lord Shaftesbury*, p. 121 and *passim*.)

What the Reform Bill of 1832 was to all later extensions of the Franchise, the Factory Acts of 1833 and 1847 are to the far-spreading code of statutory regulation which now governs the conditions and hours of almost all branches of industry. The factory system which at its first coming bade fair to destroy the health and happiness of the race, has been gradually converted into an instrument to level up the average material conditions under which labour is carried on. It is far easier to inspect factories than it would ever have been to inspect the old system of domestic work. Robert Owen's vision of decent conditions of life for factory hands, which he had first embodied in his own New Lanark Mills, was destined in the course of a hundred years to be made the standard for the greater part of the industrial world. And the decisive first steps were taken in 1833 and 1847, during the period which it is usual to condemn as obsessed by the doctrine of *laissez-faire*. It is difficult to obsess people with a doctrine if once either their hearts or their pockets are touched. A former generation, in anti-Jacobin days, being in a mood to grind the faces of the poor, had chosen out those parts of *laissez-faire* which suited their purpose and neglected the rest. Now the process was being reversed : the self-same House of Commons that repealed the Corn Laws in the name of *laissez-faire* passed the Ten Hours Bill in flat defiance of that doctrine. At no period was *laissez-faire* in force in all directions at once. Benthamism was in many respects its exact opposite, calling for the creation of organs of government to control and harmonize the rival interests of society.

In the years following the Ten Hours Bill of 1847, the principle of factory regulation was extended by a series of Acts to other manufactures besides textiles. And the revelation of the appalling conditions of female and child labour in the coal-mines, an evil several centuries old, had led to Lord Shaftesbury's Mines Act of 1842, by which the underground employment of women and of children under ten was forbidden. By an Act of 1850 adult males were also protected by a Mines Inspectorate, and step by step the provision of safety in the Mines became the care of the State.

The gross ill-usage of little boys as sweeps, by masters who found it cheaper to drive them through the soot-choked chimneys than to use a long brush, had been exposed to the public indignation, but in vain. In 1875 Shaftesbury wrote in his diary : ' One hundred and two years have elapsed since the good Jonas Hanway brought the brutal iniquity before the public, yet in many parts of England and Ireland it still prevails with the full knowledge and consent of thousands of all classes.' That year Shaftesbury obtained the passing of an Act that at last cured the evil. The previous Acts of 1840 and 1864 had been rendered dead letters by the callous connivance of private householders, local authorities and magistrates. (Hammond, *Lord Shaftesbury*, chap. XV.)

The passing of the abortive chimney-sweeper's Act of 1864 had been in large measure due to the publication in the previous years of Charles Kingsley's *Water Babies*, describing the relations of little Tom to his master Grimes. Dickens had already done much to interest the public in the sufferings and feelings of children ; *Water Babies* did that and it did something more, it created a fairy world of fantasy and fun which grown-ups and children could share together. The sympathetic interest in the games, fancies and thoughts of children was one of the best features of an age that thought much of family life, and reared numerous offspring. In the middle years of the Century, Grimm's and Andersen's fairy tales came over from the Continent and conquered England. Boys' and girls' story books were multiplied apace. Children's books of which the pleasure was intended to be shared with grown-ups was a characteristic invention of the time. In the previous century *Gulliver* and *Robinson Crusoe* had been written for men and women, though children and boys delighted in them and in the *Arabian Nights*. But in 1855 Thackeray published the *Rose and the Ring, a Fireside Pantomime for great and small children*, and ten years later *Alice*, written for the little daughter of the Dean of Christ Church, was published by 'Lewis Carroll.' These masterpieces of a peculiar type of literature have since been imitated by a host of writers, including Stevenson, Barrie and Andrew Lang.

This enlarged sympathy with children was one of the chief contributions made by the Victorian English to real civilization. But such feelings were not universal, as the long delay over the chimney-sweep scandal testified. Neglect and ill-usage of children died hard. The streets of the slums were still the only playground for the majority of city children, few of whom had schools to go to until 1870, and none of whom had Play Centres till the turn of the Century. The Society for the Prevention of Cruelty to Children was not founded till 1884 ; since that year it has dealt effectively with more than five million cases. The

Nineteenth Century saw the gradual disuse of cruel flogging of boys, which educational reformers had deplored in vain for ages past. In many directions life was being humanized, as some set-off against its increasing ugliness and sordidness in the growth of great cities under their pall of soot and fog.

Disraeli's famous saying that England was divided into two nations, the rich and the poor, had in it an uncomfortable amount of truth. But like all epigrams it was only half true. Certainly the Industrial Revolution had in the Victorian era increased the disparity of wealth between the very rich and the very poor, and had segregated classes geographically by substituting great cities divided into various social quarters, in place of the life of villages and market towns with some features and interests common to all. But industrial change had also increased the number of middle classes of varying levels of wealth and comfort ; and it had raised the standard of life of the better-to-do working classes, such as engineers, far above that of the unskilled labourer and slum-dweller. There were many more ' nations ' than two ; if only two were to be reckoned, it would have taxed the wit of Disraeli himself to say where the line was to be drawn.

The improvement of the lot of the wage-earners in the 'fifties and 'sixties, was partly due to the prosperity of trade in those fortunate years when England was the workshop of the world ; partly to the social legislation of Parliament ; and partly to Trade Union action to raise wages, and stop truck payments and other abuses. Trade Unionism was particularly strong among the working-class aristocracy, the engineers and the men of other skilled trades.

To this period also belongs the growth of the Co-operative movement, which has done so much to stop the exploitation of the consumer by the retail dealer, and to train the working classes in self-government and business management. It originated from the enterprise of two dozen Chartist and Owenite workmen of Rochdale, who in 1844 opened in Toad (T'owd) Lane the store of the Rochdale Pioneers. It was a humble affair, and many larger attempts at co-operation had failed. But these men chanced to have hit on the right plan for realizing Owen's dream. Their rules were—the sale of goods at market prices, followed by division of surplus profit among members in proportion to their purchases. This secured democratic interest in the management of the business, while eliminating profit at the expense of the consumer. It was on these lines that the Co-operative movement reached such enormous development before the century closed.

The practical success of the movement was helped in the 'fifties by the zeal with which its idealist aspect was preached both by the Secularists led by Holyoake, the pupil of Owen, and by the Christian Socialists whom Frederick Denison Maurice had inspired, especially Tom Hughes, the author of *Tom Brown's Schooldays*. The attempts of the shopkeepers to establish a boycott of the movement only increased its strength. In the 'seventies the Co-operative Societies added production on a considerable scale to their original activities.

The Co-operative movement was of more than financial importance. It gave many working people a sense that they also had 'a stake in the country.' It taught them business habits and mutual self-help, and drew them together in societies that encouraged the desire for education and self-improvement. 'It is,' writes one of its historians, 'in its intellectual and moral influence upon its members, even more than the financial savings that it effects and encourages, that the Co-operative movement has wrought a beneficent revolution among tens of thousands of working-class families, and has contributed so largely to the social transformation of Great Britain.'

The expedients by which the new Britain was striving to remedy the evils attendant on the Industrial Revolution— Co-operation, Factory Laws, Trade Unionism, Free Trade —were all, like the Industrial Revolution itself, British in conception and origin.

The second quarter of the Nineteenth Century was the period in the settlement of Canada, Australia and New Zealand, which decided that those lands should be peopled mainly from Britain and should become parts of a free British Commonwealth of Nations.

The overpeopling of Great Britain deplored by Malthus, and the sorry plight of the English peasantry at home, caused in these years the great rural exodus to the Colonies on which the modern Empire was rebuilt. The tide of emigration also ran strongly to the United States, and might have run there almost to the exclusion of British territories but for the organized effort of emigration societies, and the occasional assistance of Government, inspired by the propaganda of Gibbon Wakefield. He preached to his countrymen that emigration was the true relief of their economic miseries, and that the colonies need not in all cases be mere ports of call or places of trade, but might become new British nations. To him is largely due the systematized and aided emigration that founded modern Canada, Australia and New Zealand.

The condition of England's happiness in the Nineteenth Century, and the cause of that peculiar belief in ' progress ' as a law of history which cheered the Victorian mind, was the fact that we were not engaged in any great war for a hundred years after Waterloo. The Crimean War (1854– 1856) was no exception. It was merely a foolish expedition to the Black Sea, made for no sufficient reason, because the English people were bored by peace, in spite of the flood of pacifist talk in which they had been indulged three years before at the time of the Great Exhibition in Hyde Park. The bourgeois democracy, played upon by its favourite newspapers, was worked up to crusading ardour on behalf of Turkish rule over the Balkan Christians, which in the following generation the same forces, when led by Gladstone, precisely reversed. We fought the Crimean War on a principle of limited liability and broke it off when the desire for foreign adventure had been satisfied. It is a fact in our social history that foreign policy was becoming less of a mystery of statesmen and more of an interest of the people at large. Whether statesmen or people have been most foolish it is perhaps difficult to say.

But the Crimean War had one serious and beneficent consequence, the institution of nursing as a profession for trained women of a better type than Mrs. Gamp. The astonishing personal success of Florence Nightingale lay in the forcing of her modern methods of hospital management on the Crimean Army authorities, who in all else were so antiquated : they would not even make a railway for the few miles from Balaclava port to the siege lines before Sebastopol, till compelled by public opinion at home, stirred up by the press and its first ' War Correspondents.'

The idea of nursing as a serious profession, thus advertized by the sensations of the Crimean War, spread fast in civil life and soon made a new era in public health and medical practice. Moreover, the idea of training women to professions, due to Florence Nightingale's initiative, invaded other spheres of life besides nursing. The ideals of the age of Scott and Byron had demanded that a lady should prove her ladyhood by the beauty of idleness and by touching dependence upon her male protectors. But in the last half of Victoria's reign a very different idea began to gain ground, namely that upper and middle class women, more particularly the unmarried, should be trained to support themselves and to be of some use to the world.

The Crimean War had also its effects in lesser matters. In imitation of our heroes in the trenches before Sebastopol, smoking became fashionable again after being banished from polite circles for eighty years. For the same reason beards returned after an absence from well-bred society of two centuries. The typical mid-Victorian of all classes was a man with a beard and a pipe.

It was the era of ' muscular Christianity,' strenuousness and cold baths. Organized games, particularly cricket and football, were spreading fast in schools, Universities and in ordinary life. Walking and the new diversion of mountain climbing were characteristic of an energetic and athletic generation ; even ladies were now allowed to walk. The days of lawn tennis had not yet come, and could scarcely have come so long as the hampering crinoline was in fashion. But ladies and gentlemen contended in the milder tournaments of the croquet lawn, where sometimes a member of the fair sex, in preparing her stroke, would gently move the ball into a more favourable position under the ample cover of the crinoline !

One thing that the Crimean War did not produce was Army Reform. It was indeed recognized that though the veteran soldiers had fought well, maintaining the regimental traditions inherited from the Peninsula, they had been ill supplied with recruits, ill led, ill fed and ill organized as an army.   But the army recovered its prestige next year in the Indian Mutiny, when the Victorian virtues of self-help and individual initiative showed at their best.   And in any case the reformers of that age were not interested in the army.   They regarded it as a hopelessly aristocratic institution, not really needed by a civilized State.   They were concerned not to gain security by improving it, but to save money by cutting it down.

Only in 1859 there was a panic over the supposed ill intentions of Napoleon III, though his real desire was to live on friendly terms with England.   So the islanders had one of their periodic frights that punctuated their perpetual unpreparedness, and the result on this occasion was the starting of the Volunteer movement, the drilling of business men and their employees in off hours, consonant with the civilian and individualist spirit of the time.   But the reform of the regular army remained unattempted, until the Franco-Prussian war of 1870 made the English public vaguely aware that something was going on among those unaccountable foreigners.   And on this occasion panic fortunately produced the Cardwell reforms, which included the abolition of the purchase of officers' commissions, and the short-service system of enlistment, creating at last an army reserve.

CHAPTER XVIII

The Second Half of the Victorian Era [1865-1901]

One of the difficulties of an attempt to write the social as distinct from the political history of a nation is the absence of determining events and positive dates by which the course of things can be charted. The social customs of men and women and their economic circumstances, particularly in modern times, are always in movement, but they never change completely or all at once. The old overlaps the new so much that it is often a question whether to ascribe some tendency in thought or practice to one generation or the next.

But on the whole the most marked changes of tendency in Victorian England may be ascribed to the later 'sixties and the 'seventies. The old landmarks are still there, but they are no longer so prominent. The territorial aristocracy still rules the rural parts, and still leads society in London and in its country-house gatherings ; the individualist business man still flourishes, with the honest, limited virtues of bourgeois self-help. But these classes no longer fill so much of the scene as in the days of Palmerston and Peel ; and the ideas or lack of ideas for which they stand are challenged now by others beside ' low Radicals.' In all ranks of life free debate of social customs and religious beliefs is taking the place of the settled creeds of the early Victorian era. John Stuart Mill in his *Liberty* (1859) preached the doctrine of revolt against the tame acceptance of conventional opinions, and a dozen years later, such an attitude has become very general. It is a liberal, out-spoken age, whose most representative men are neither the aristocrats nor the shopkeepers, but men of University education, or of trained professional intelligence, readers of Mill, Darwin, Huxley and Matthew Arnold, George Eliot and Browning—the gentlemanly bearded intellectuals whose family life Du Maurier delighted to delineate in the pages of *Punch*.

Democracy, bureaucracy, collectivism are all advancing like a silent tide making in by a hundred creeks and inlets. A short list of some of the changes which marked off the 'seventies from the previous generation, may at least be suggestive. The impact of Darwinism on the Bible religion of the English was being widely, though not yet universally, felt ; in 1871 Oxford and Cambridge were thrown open to all irrespective of religious belief ; science and history were rapidly taking their place beside classics and mathematics in the academic world ; in 1870 competitive examination was made the normal method of entry to the Civil Service, in order to enlist the ablest young men from the Universities in the new bureaucracy ; the working men of the towns had received the Parliamentary franchise by the Reform Bill of 1867 ; and three years later Forster's Act provided primary education for all ; by the legislation of 1871–1875 the Trade Unions received a new Charter of rights corresponding to their growing power ; in business administration, limited liability companies were taking the place of the old family firms ; the professional and social emancipation of women went forward on the lines advocated in Mill's *Subjection of Women* (1869) ; women's colleges were founded at Oxford and Cambridge and women's secondary schools were much improved ; the Married Women's Property Act released the wife, if she had money of her own, from economic bondage to her husband : the ' equality of the sexes ' began to be advocated in theory, and found its way increasingly into the practice of all classes. The demand for the political enfranchisement of women was the outcome of a very considerable degree of social enfranchisement already accomplished.

But the greatest single event of the 'seventies, fraught with immeasurable consequences for the future, was the sudden collapse of English agriculture.

From 1875 onwards the catastrophe set in. A series of bad seasons aggravated its initial stages, but the cause was the development of the American prairies as grain lands within reach of the English market. The new agricultural machinery enabled the farmers of the Middle-West to skim the cream off virgin soils of unlimited expanse ; the new railway system carried the produce to the ports ; the new steamers bore it across the Atlantic. English agriculture was more scientific and more highly capitalized than American, but under these conditions the odds were too great. Mass production of crops by a simpler and cheaper process undercut the elaborate and expensive methods of farming which had been built up on well-managed English estates during the previous two hundred years. The overthrow of the British landed aristocracy by the far-distant democracy of American farmers was one outcome of this change of economic circumstance. An even more important consequence has been the general divorce of Englishmen from life in contact with nature, which in all previous ages had helped to form the mind and the imagination of the island race.

The other States of Europe, which still had peasantry and valued them as a stabilizing element in the social fabric, warded off the influx of Amercian food by tariffs. But in England no such policy was adopted or even seriously considered. The belief in Free Trade as the secret of our vast prosperity, the unwillingness to interfere with the world-commerce on which our power and wealth seemed to stand secure, the predominance of the towns over the country in numbers and still more in intellectual and political leadership, the memories of the ' hungry 'forties ' when the Corn Laws had made bread dear for the poor—all these circumstances prevented any effort to save the rural way of life. Least of all did the late Victorians see any need to grow food in the island to provide for the necessities of future wars. After two generations of the safety won at Waterloo, real national danger seemed to have passed away for ever, like a dream of

> ' Old unhappy far-off things
> And battles long ago.'

In 1846 Disraeli had prophesied the ruin of agriculture as an inevitable result of Free Trade in corn. For thirty years he had been wrong. Now he was suddenly right— and now he was Prime Minister. Yet he did nothing about it, and allowed the ' curse of Cobden ' to blight the English cornfields. Immersed in oriental policies, the old man made no attempt to oppose the spirit of the age at home, to which in fact he had become a convert.

Statesmen regarded the fate of agriculture with all the more indifference because it involved no acute problem of unemployment. The farm labourer did not remain on the land when his occupation there was gone, as unemployed miners hang round a closed mine. When ' Hodge ' lost his job, or when his wages fell, he slipped away to the towns and found work there. Or else he migrated overseas, for the Colonies and the United States were still receiving the overplus of our still rapidly rising population. As a class, the English agricultural labourer was well accustomed to the idea of leaving the land. He could not love the fields that he tilled as a hireling for others, as passionately as the Irish peasant loved the plot of earth from which he wrung the food of his family and which he regarded as by right his own. The English rustic moreover, knew more about the town and the opportunities and the wages it offered. He had the desire characteristic of our people to ' better himself,' and so he raised no outcry when this involved exile from the scenes of his boyhood.

Meanwhile the landlords and farmers, who had neither the wish nor the power to divorce themselves from the soil, suffered and complained in vain, for their day as the political rulers of England had gone by. Both the Liberal and the Conservative intelligentsia of the 'seventies and 'eighties were saturated with the Free Trade Doctrine : they believed that if one industry, agriculture for instance, went under in free competition, other industries would gain proportionately and would take its place—and so all would be well. But all was not well. For political economy does not cover the whole field of human welfare. The men of theory failed to perceive that agriculture is not merely one industry among many, but is a way of life, unique and irreplaceable in its human and spiritual values.

In the first decade of the decline that began in 1875, the acreage of wheat in England fell by nearly a million acres. Already in 1881 there were some hundred thousand fewer farm-labourers than ten years before, and that was only the beginning of the exodus. Whole regions of cornland in the

West, Midlands and North were laid down in grass, but without any corresponding rise in the number of livestock, though there was a considerable substitution of cattle for sheep. The introduction of frozen meat from Australia, New Zealand and South America was a new feature of the ' eighties and 'nineties. From 1891–1899 a second wave of agricultural depression followed, as severe as that of 1875–1884. By the end of the Century the corn area in England and Wales had shrunk from over eight million acres in 1871 to under six million. Permanent pasture had greatly increased, but the fall in cattle and sheep prices kept pace with the fall in the price of corn. And the agricultural labourers, in spite of the fact that they had been given the franchise in 1884, continued to flock into the towns or to pass oversea.

The historian of English farming thus epitomizes the last decades of Victoria's reign :

' The legislature was powerless to provide any substantial help. Food was, so to speak, the currency in which foreign nations paid for English manufactured goods, and its cheapness was an undoubted blessing to the wage-earning community. Thrown on their own resources, agriculturalists fought the unequal contest with courage and tenacity. But as time went on, the stress told more and more heavily. Manufacturing populations seemed to seek food-markets everywhere except at home. Enterprise gradually weakened ; landlords lost their ability to help, farmers their recuperative power. Prolonged depression checked costly improvements. Drainage was practically discontinued. Both owners and occupiers were engaged in the task of making both ends meet on vanishing incomes. Land deteriorated in condition ; less labour was employed ; less stock was kept ; bills for cake and fertilizers were reduced. The counties which suffered most were the corn-growing districts, in which high farming had won its most signal triumphs.' (Ernle, *English Farming*, p. 379.)

The damage indeed was the greater because English agriculture was a highly capitalized system for producing the staple products—corn, particularly wheat so costly to grow in most parts of England, and the best sheep and cattle in the world. Other uses of land had been unduly neglected. There was a fixed acreage of hops, chiefly in Kent. But potatoes occupied only two per cent. of the cultivated area.

Not enough had been done either with fruit or vegetables. Market gardening had never been systematically organized. Neither the small cultivators nor the State were playing their proper part. It was only after the war of 1914–1918 that the State undertook the large-scale forestry which it is specially fitted to conduct. The landlords, who had planted diligently in the Eighteenth and early Nineteenth Centuries, lost interest in forestry as a trade, when government no longer required great oaks to build our battleships, and when timber of all other sorts poured in from Scandinavia and North America at prices that discouraged the home-grower. The vast demand for pit-props and for builder's wood was supplied from oversea.

England in 1880 could boast of finer trees than any other country, if judged by aesthetic, not by commercial standards. The forests had all gone, save a patch or two like the New Forest and the Forest of Dean. Yet seen from the air, the landscape would not have appeared ill wooded. The trees were hedgerow timber scattered over the countryside, or park trees preserved for their beauty, or coverts planted for game. Estate agents were not interested in timber values and neglected to remove ivy, to thin out, and to cut and sell at the right time. The conifer was creeping in for the purpose of the new plantations, and so was the rhododendron, approved by the taste of that age. Both were exotic in most parts of the island, but both were well fitted to lodge the ' kept cock pheasant, master of many a shire,' whom the youthful Kipling disliked as the symbol of an England going to fat, in a dream of wealth and peace that might some day have a rude awakening.

The fate of agriculture was only one example of the near-sightedness characteristic of English State policy. The later Victorians laid no far plans for the future. They were content to meet those demands and to solve those problems of which the pressure was already felt. But within those limits they were more active reformers than their self-satisfied fathers of the Palmerstonian era : they brought up to date the civil service, local government, education, Universities—and even to a limited extent the army. For the English had already lost some of the complacency and cocksureness of the 'fifties and 'sixties. In those lucky days gone by, England had manufactured for a world that was still a generation behind her in industrial machinery ; there had been no military power more formidable or more hostile than the France of Napoleon III ; in 1848, the year of Continental Revolution and Reaction, Macaulay's country-men had rejoiced to think that in wealth, in liberty and in order our country was ahead of every other, ' the envy of less happier lands.' The Franco-Prussian war of 1870 was the first shock. And during the three following decades America and Germany rose as manufacturing powers rival to our own. The immensely greater natural resources of America, the scientific and technical education provided by far-sighted governments in Germany, told more and more every year. To meet this new situation, our island liberty, Free Trade and individualist self-help might not alone be enough. Some sense of this led to improved technical education over here. It led, also, to greater interest in our own ' lands beyond the sea,' the Imperialist movement of the 'nineties ; and it induced a more friendly and respectful attitude to America than our political classes had shown during her Civil War at the end of the Palmerstonian epoch. The democratic England of the new era was better able to understand both the United States and ' the Colonies,' as Canada and Australasia were still called.

The new situation led also to an anxious interest in modern Germany, which our countrymen until 1870 had been content to ignore. In that fateful year two books, Matthew Arnold's *Friendship's Garland* and George Mere-dith's *Harry Richmond* warned England that national education and national discipline in the Teutonic heart of Europe was creating a new kind of power that had a jealous eye on our easily won, carelessly guarded, ill-distributed wealth. At the same time Ruskin nobly spent the popularity and influence which he had won as interpreter of art and nature, in a new role as social prophet, denouncing the ill employment of our boasted wealth in destroying beauty, and its ill distribution so corrupting alike to the superfluously rich and the miserably poor.

There was no strong movement of socialism among the working class till the last years of the Century, but discontent with the spirit of *laissez-faire* had been growing long before. John Stuart Mill died in 1873, bequeathing a testament of neo-liberal philosophy that strongly influenced the thought and practice of the age that followed. Mill's doctrine was semi-socialistic. He urged the better distribution of wealth by direct taxation, particularly taxes on inheritance ; the bettering of conditions of life by social legislation enforced by an effective bureaucracy, national and local ; a complete system of manhood and womanhood suffrage not only for Parliament but for the bodies entrusted with local government. In Mill's thought, democracy and bureaucracy were to work together, and it is largely on these lines that the social fabric of modern England has in fact been constructed, even after Mill himself and his philosophy had passed out of fashion.

But in spite of the decay of England's agriculture, in spite of the diminution of her industrial lead over all other nations, in spite of the increasing sense that all was not well with her social system and the conditions of life in her city populations, nevertheless the last thirty years of Victoria's reign were on the whole years of great prosperity and increasing wealth in which most sections of the community shared. The Queen's Jubilees of 1887 and 1897 were celebrated by all classes with real pride and thankfulness, due in part to a sense of delivery from the conditions endured at the beginning of her reign, for the ' hungry 'forties' were still remembered. Manners were gentler, streets were safer, life was more humane, sanitation was improving fast, working-class housing, though still bad, was less bad than ever before. Conditions of labour had been improved, real wages had risen, hours had shortened. But unemployment, sickness and old age, not yet regularly provided for by the State, still had terrors for the workman.

The Free Trade finance of Peel and Gladstone had lifted the weight of taxation from the poor by reducing indirect taxation to a minimum. Yet the income tax in the 'eighties varied from a bare twopence in the pound to a mere sixpence halfpenny. It is now ten shillings (1941), to say nothing of the surtax.

Free Trade, besides relieving the burdens of the poor,

also claimed credit for the enormous increase of our shipping
and overseas trade. Even our coastal trade had been
thrown open to the ships of all nations, but the foreigner
had, in open competition, only secured one half of one
per cent. of it. And in the 'eighties this coastal trade,
which included so large a proportion of home-consumed
coal, was greater in cargo tonnage than the whole of our
vast overseas commerce. Yet the oceans of the world
were the highways of England. In 1885 a third of the
world's sea-going ships were on the British register, including four-fifths of the world's steamships. Masts and
sails were on the decline, but the fast ocean-going ' clippers '
were British, and in 1885 our tonnage under sail was still
as large as it had been in 1850, while our steam tonnage
was four millions greater.

The tonnage of the port of London was still sixty per
cent. greater than that of the Mersey, though Liverpool,
dealing in Lancashire's cotton, exported more British goods
than the Capital. The great Thames and Mersey docks
were both completed in the 'eighties. The railway system
had greatly increased the volume of overseas trade, but had
further reduced the number of ports, a process begun in
the Eighteenth Century. Whitby, Lancaster, Ayr and
many other small harbours had now gone the way of Fowey,
Chester and the Cinque Ports. But in the last half of the
Nineteenth Century, thanks to the railways, Barrow had
sprung to greatness out of nothing, and Grimsby out of
' almost nothing.' Southampton had revived, after a long
eclipse, for it was now the headquarters of the P. and O.
line to the East. Cardiff had increased its population
thirteen-fold, and had just passed Newcastle as the world's
greatest coal exporter, though Tyneside, in the great days
of Armstrong's Elswick, was itself mightily on the increase.
Such was the work of reconstruction of industry and commerce done by the railways. But ' railways had not made
Tyneside ; it was Tyneside that made them.' (Clapham,
II, 519–529.)

Under such conditions of ' free trade ' prosperity, many
articles that were luxuries in 1837 were common comforts
in 1897. Food, clothing, bedding, furniture were far

more abundant than in any previous age. Gas and oil-
lighting were giving way to electricity. Holidays by the
seaside had become a regular part of life to the lower
middle class and even to large sections of the working class,
particularly in the North. Already in 1876 Blackpool had
grown to the size and status of a Borough, as the scene of
the annual holiday of the Lancashire artisan, and he supported Llandudno and the Isle of Man as well. Distant
Cornwall was already the holiday resort of the well-to-do
at Easter and of the masses in August. In the summer, the
lodging-houses in Keswick and Windermere and the farms
of the Lake District were thronged with family parties.

Even before the age of railways, Londoners had swarmed
on the pier at Brighton and darkened the sands of Margate
with their multitude. Now the whole coast of England
and Wales was opened out to ' trippers ' and ' lodgers,' by
steam locomotion and by the increased earnings and savings
of all ranks. In remote creeks and fishing hamlets, where
families from town came to lodge, children and their
parents bathed and dug and searched the tidal treasuries of
the rocks ; here was at least some mitigation of the divorce
of the city-dweller from country life.

But if seasonal holidays away from home were now
common, the ' week-end out of town ' was only beginning.
It was already a custom among owners of big country
houses and their guests, but the ' week-end cottage ' for
the middle-class family was scarcely yet known. Family
church-going and business tradition still kept folk in town
for seven days of the week.

Women were becoming more athletic and better walkers
as their skirts became somewhat shorter and less redundant ;
after the disappearance of the crinoline and the long sweep-
ing dress, the active movements of lawn-tennis took the
place of croquet in the 'eighties as the game for the
encounter of ladies and gentlemen. In the 'nineties
the bicycle became fashionable, as soon as the two low
wheels succeeded the dangerous ' high bicycle ' ; this
further emancipated women, by sending them out to scour
the countryside alone, or in company with the other sex.
The common use of the motor-car and motor bicycle was
still in the future when Victoria died.

While the town-dwellers were learning to explore the by-ways of their own land on foot or on bicycle, others swarmed over France, Switzerland and Italy in greater numbers than ever ; they were the chief patrons of the best hotels of Western Europe, of the Mediterranean and of Egypt. And Thomas Cook's ' tours ' gave a taste of the delights of continental travel to multitudes of the thrifty and the humble. In the 'sixties and 'seventies, the period of Leslie Stephen, Whymper and Professor Tyndall, the English, with the help of the splendid race of Swiss guides whom they employed, developed mountain craft on rock and snow, and conquered the great summits of the Alps. In the last decade of the Century rock-climbing in Wales and the Lake District became a skilled pastime at home.

John Buchan in his Memoirs has thus described the London society of his youth, on the eve of the South African War of 1899 :

London at the turn of the Century had not yet lost her Georgian air. Her ruling society was aristocratic till Queen Victoria's death and preserved the modes and rites of aristocracy. Her great houses had not disappeared or become blocks of flats. In the summer she was a true city of pleasure, every window box gay with flowers, her streets full of splendid equipages, the Park a show ground for fine horses and handsome men and women. The ritual went far down, for frockcoats and top-hats were the common wear not only for the West End, but about the Law Courts and in the City. On Sunday afternoons we dutifully paid a round of calls. Conversation was not the casual thing it has now become, but was something of an art, in which competence conferred prestige. Also Clubs were still in their hey-dey, their waiting lists were lengthy, membership of the right ones was a stage in a career. . . Looking back, that time seems to me unbelievably secure and self-satisfied. The world was friendly and well-bred as I remember it, without the vulgarity and the worship of wealth which appeared with the new century. (*Memory Hold-The-Door*, pp. 92–94.)

Yet already ' society was getting mixed,' and men of mere wealth, like Sir Gorgius Midas in Du Maurier's *Punch* pictures, had been prominent in London drawing-rooms for twenty years before the Queen died—the more prominent perhaps for being still somewhat exceptional.

'Society,' in the older and stricter sense of the term, had
still in Palmerston's day been a limited world, its entry
closely guarded by certain Whig and Tory Peeresses.   But
in the 'eighties 'society' had a vaguer meaning, perhaps
covering the whole of the upper and professional classes,
perhaps including all the well-dressed men and women,
who crossed and recrossed each other in Hyde Park parades,
or made conversation during the innumerable courses of a
London dinner-party.   Yet, as John Buchan truly records,
these people maintained, at least in the Capital, a certain
aristocratic flavour and convention until the end of the
Century.   They were different from the well-to-do
bourgeois of the provinces, who still in Yorkshire and
Lancashire preferred 'high teas' to dress dinners.

In the 'seventies and 'eighties, large families were still
customary in the professional and business world, as well
as in the working class, and the population rose apace
since so many of the children born were now kept alive.
The death-rate dropped with the improvement of town
sanitation and the constant progress of medical knowledge
and practice.   In 1886 the excess of births over deaths in
England was 13·3, as against Germany's 10·8 and the
French 1·4.

After 1870, the parents of working-class families had
the relief of a universal system of primary education, but
even so it was a hard struggle, and except in school-time
the children of the poor still roamed the streets uncared for.
In middle-class homes, it was the era of the rocking-horse
and Noah's ark : the full nursery and schoolroom were
lively, noisy societies, where childish impressions and
characters were formed, till Tomkins major, minor and
minimus successively went off to the boarding-school, and
could no longer be the joy or the plague of their sisters
except during the holidays.   Governesses, nurses, butlers,
housemaids and cooks were still plentiful and their demands
for wages and nights out were still moderate.   Many of
them became attached and valued members of the household ; others came and went, dimly recollected.   Their
services were arduous and essential, for the tall, narrow
town-houses of the middle class were not fitted up with
labour-saving appliances ; armies of maids staggered up

the stairs with hot water for the nursery tubs, and coals for
every room, that helped to thicken London's fog.

Only in the 'nineties did it become evident that a reduction was beginning in the size of families, in the first
instance in those of the professional and middle class,
charged with heavy ' public-school' fees, and among the
better-to-do artisans struggling to keep up a high standard
of life. In 1877 a prosecution of Bradlaugh and Mrs.
Besant for publishing a neo-Malthusian pamphlet had
given methods of birth-control their first national advertise-
ment. But the slum population, of whom these reformers
were chiefly thinking, were the slowest to adopt the advice.
The families best able to rear children as they should be
reared, were, unfortunately, those that became most addicted
to 'race suicide ' in the coming century.

The 'seventies and 'eighties had been a period not only
of large families but of puritanism in ethical and sexual
ideas, qualified by the too frequent weakness of human
nature in practice. Queen Victoria had put the example of
her court on the side of the stricter code. The genuine
honesty of most British merchants as men of business had
been one of the causes of our great commercial prosperity.
The popular heroes of the period—and they were true
heroes—were religious men first and foremost : Living-
stone the African explorer and missionary ; General
Gordon the soldier-philanthropist ; Lord Shaftesbury and
Mr. Gladstone ; to these four, so different from one
another and from everyone else, life was the service of God.

But the older and more definite religious beliefs that
meant so much to these men were being successfully
attacked by the ' Agnostics ' of the same period. Yet
even the ' Agnostics ' were Puritan in feeling and outlook.
Matthew Arnold, the prophet of ' culture,' spoke of ' conduct ' as ' three parts of life,' though his idea of ' conduct '
was neither narrow nor purely negative. The fame and
authority enjoyed by George Eliot's novels were largely
due to the fact that they were taken by many as ' restating
the moral law and process of soul-making, in terms acceptable to the rationalist agnostic conscience.' Carlyle's
prophetic utterance in *Sartor* supplied a vague but emphatic

creed to many, including Darwin's militant champion Huxley, who defied the clergy at the famous meeting of the British Association in Oxford in the spirit of Luther at Worms. Leslie Stephen's and John Morley's passionate refusal to compromise with dogmas they had come to disbelieve, breathed the unyielding spirit of Seventeenth Century Puritanism. Leslie Stephen had once been a clergyman, and so had J. R. Green, the popular liberal historian. In literature and thought it was a period of quasi-religious movement away from religion.

In its many-sided curiosity and competence, its self-confidence and alertness, this Late Mid-Victorian culture is Greek. In its blend of intellectual adventure and moral conservatism, it is really Athenian. I doubt if any lines of Tennyson were more often quoted by contemporaries than these :

> Let knowledge grow from more to more,
> But more of reverence in us dwell ;
> That mind and soul, according well,
> May make one music as before,
> But vaster.

No words could express more perfectly the Victorian ideal of expansion about a central stability. But would anyone guarantee that they are not a translation from Sophocles ? (*Daylight and Champaign,* p. 264, G. M. Young.)

The Puritan attitude to life and conduct was inculcated not only by the Bible religion of the mass of the Victorians, but by the Anglo-Catholic religion that had grown out of the Oxford Movement of the 'thirties, and was now spreading wide, with such men as Gladstone and Salisbury among its lay representatives. But Anglo-Catholicism was strongest among the parish clergy, to many of whom it gave a new professional pride and motive, to take the place of the fast vanishing social ascendancy that had once belonged to the ' clergy of the Establishment ' as such. The Anglo-Catholic influence made easier some concessions to ordinary human nature, including a less strict observance of the ' Sabbath ' than Evangelicals could approve. The gradual modification of the ' English Sunday ' has had effects both good and bad. In this transition period, between the overgreat strictness of the past and the entire laxity of the present day, there was much good in the practice of many families who still insisted on 'Sunday reading' of serious though not necessarily religious books. For one day in the week, novels and magazines were laid aside, and great classical literature like the Bible, Pilgrim's Progress and Paradise Lost, besides more secular poetry and history had a chance of perusal which they no longer enjoy.

Not only a modified Sunday observance, but Bible reading and family prayers were common until near the end of the Century. Canon Smyth has written in his study of the effect of Charles Simeon's influence on English life :

Evangelicalism was the religion of the Home ; and in this revival of Family worship it won the most signal and the most gracious of its triumphs. It may well be that this revival was virtually restricted to the upper and middle classes of society, especially the latter : but within these limits it was so widely spread that in 1889 the Provost of King's (Cambridge) in a circular letter addressed to the undergraduates of that College on the subject of voluntary attendance at morning Chapel, could write : 'You, most of you, come from homes where family prayers are the custom.' . . . Today that pious custom is virtually extinct : not only because the Victorian piety is virtually extinct, but also because the Victorian family is virtually extinct.' (*Simeon and Church Order*, Charles Smyth, 1940, pp. 19–20.)

English religion had been an imposing fabric in the middle of the Nineteenth Century, but there had been a weakness in its foundations which the movement of scientific discovery was certain to undermine : the belief in the verbal inspiration of the Bible was common to the Nonconformists, to the Church Evangelicals and, to a scarcely less degree, to High Churchmen like Bishop Samuel Wilberforce and Mr. Gladstone. Charles Darwin was as unlike Voltaire as any human being could well be ; he had no wish to be an iconoclast ; he did not regard the Church as 'the infamous' ; and in the end she reverently buried him in Westminster Abbey. But his scientific researches led him to conclusions incompatible with the narrative of the early chapters of Genesis which were as much a part of 'the English Bible' as the New Testament itself. More

T

generally speaking, the whole idea of evolution and of
' man descended from a monkey ' was totally incompatible
with existing religious ideas of creation and of man's
central place in the Universe.

Naturally the religious world took up arms to defend
positions of dateless antiquity and prestige.   Naturally the
younger generation of scientific men rushed to defend
their revered chief, and to establish their claim to come to
any conclusion to which their researches led, regardless of
the cosmogony and chronology of Genesis, and regardless
of the ancient traditions of the Church.   The strife raged
throughout the 'sixties, 'seventies and 'eighties.   It came
to involve the whole belief in the miraculous, extending
into the borders of the New Testament itself.   The
' intellectuals ' became more and more anti-clerical, anti-
religious and materialistic under the stress of the conflict.

During this period of change and strife, causing much
personal and family unhappiness and many searchings of
heart, the world of educated men and women was rent by
a real controversy, which even the English love of compromise could not deny to exist.[1]   In the Twentieth
Century that storm has rolled away ; that battle is ended
and its dead are buried.   Faith and Denial are both in a
different position.   The materialism of the scientist of the
'seventies is felt to be as unsatisfactory as the literal truth
of all parts of the Bible is felt to be untenable.   Both sides
wistfully acknowledge that the whole truth about the
Universe cannot be discovered in the laboratory or divined
by the Church.   But where it can be found is a more
difficult matter to determine.

The shaking of dogmatic assurance within the pale of
the Anglican and Protestant Churches in the latter years of
the Nineteenth Century helped the propaganda of the
Roman Church, whose undeviating claim to full and
certain knowledge appealed to persons who could not
bear to be left in doubt.   The Irish immigration below,

---

[1] People unduly depreciate Tennyson's intellectual acumen, as shown in the
poems he wrote in the formative period of his youth before he took to hymning
King Arthur's knights.   His *In Memoriam*, written in the 'forties, and published
in 1850, nine years before the appearance of Darwin's *Origin of Species*, anticipated
the poignancy of the struggle between Faith and Science that convulsed the
following era.

the flow of converts from the fashionable and intellectual classes above, and the high Roman Catholic birth-rate gave to the Roman Communion a very much more important place in English life at the end of Victoria's reign than that which it had enjoyed at the beginning.

In the last half of the Nineteenth Century, Archaeology and History were in rapid progress, and their discoveries strengthened the hands of science in the strife against orthodox beliefs. Lecky's wise *History of Rationalism* (1865) and the over-confident materialism of Buckle's *History of Civilization* (1857) were part of the strong current that carried men away from ancient faiths. An academic ' liberal ' party, of great intellectual distinction and very much in earnest, fought the battle to free Oxford and Cambridge from the bondage of Church monopoly, and won it by the Test Act of 1871. The younger Universities of London and Manchester had long enjoyed such freedom as their birthright.[1]

The two older Universities became so far assimilated to the new that before the end of the Queen's reign Oxford and Cambridge were much more lay than clerical in the personnel of their ' dons,' who were, moreover, now allowed to marry while continuing to hold Fellowships. Academic study now embraced physical science and mediaeval and modern history as strongly as the older humanism and mathematics. In the last decades of the Century, Cambridge was represented to the world by great men of science like Clerk Maxwell, Rayleigh and young J. J. Thomson, while Archdeacon Cunningham was founding Economic History, and the more brilliant genius of Maitland was revealing the common thoughts of mediaeval men through the harsh medium of their law. Even more rapid had been the change at Oxford, which had been dominated, in the early years of the reign by Newman and his antagonists, disputing over the miracles of Saints and the authority of the Fathers. Very different, thirty years later, was the atmosphere of the University, of which the practical and

---

[1] Most of the Provincial Universities were founded later still, in the first years of the Twentieth Century. The want of a proper system of popular secondary education prior to Balfour's Bill of 1902 was the fundamental reason why the new Universities developed so slowly.

liberal character was represented to the world by Jowett as Master of Balliol, while the scholarship of Stubbs and Gardiner revealed the growth of the English Constitution, and T. H. Green opened out a new scheme of ethical philosophy.

The last half of Victoria's reign was indeed the period when Oxford and Cambridge were most in the public eye. Their reform, particularly the abolition of religious tests for academic posts (1871) was one of the chief political questions of the day. The liberal-minded and highly educated governing class of the 'seventies were more nearly affiliated to the Universities than to the declining aristocracy or the rising plutocracy. Gladstone abolished patronage in all public offices and made competitive examination the normal entrance to the Civil Service. To select men for practical careers on the report of examiners had seemed an absurd proposal to Palmerston and the aristocratic politicians of the previous era. It was a compliment paid to the reputation of the Oxford and Cambridge system of examination for degrees, and it had the effect of making closer than ever the connection of University men with public life. Trained intellect was henceforth to be a young man's best passport, instead of social patronage or fashionable friends. The evils of the Examination system, especially in its effect on school education, were not yet realized, nor were they yet as great as they have since become.

But perhaps the most characteristic achievement of the last years of the reign was the *Dictionary of National Biography*. It was not the undertaking either of a University or of the State. It was initiated and largely financed by a private individual, George Smith the publisher, whose personal friendship with many authors prompted him to this great undertaking. The Dictionary is a monument of the business ability, the enlightened public spirit and the widespread literary and historical scholarship of the Victorian age at its final culmination. It is the best record of a nation's past that any civilization has produced.

It has already been pointed out that the agnosticism of the English revolt against early Victorian religion had no connection with hedonism in theory or in conduct. Only in the 'nineties, the *fin de siècle* as the time was called, a change in the direction of levity, if not of laxity, was observed, due no doubt in part to the gradual crumbling of definite religious beliefs with which a strict and slightly ascetic moral code had been associated. When religion had been transformed, from the ' public and documented system of beliefs, practices and aspirations ' that it had been when the Queen came to the throne, into a ' provision for personal needs,' it could no longer influence the conduct of those who felt no such need for themselves. The movement away from family prayers and church-going, the movement towards ' week-ends out of town,' towards the race-course and other pleasures, some innocent and some less innocent, was led by the Prince of Wales (afterwards Edward VII) himself, reacting against an unsympathetic mother and an unwise education. This last decade of the Century is the era of the *Yellow Book* and ' art for art's sake.' But its greatest writers, Meredith, Hardy, William Morris, Stevenson and Housman, though all opposed to orthodox religion, were each in his own way as deeply ' serious ' as the earlier Victorians.

The conflict between science and religion among the educated classes was crudely but effectively reproduced in Charles Bradlaugh's militant atheism, preached on public platforms to mass meetings of working men ; while the last great evangelical revival, the Salvation Army, founded by ' General ' Booth, brought the enthusiasm of ' conversion,' after Wesley's original fashion, to the army of the homeless and unfed, to the drunkard, the criminal and the harlot. It was significant of the coming era that the Salvation Army was more sensational in its methods than the older Nonconformist bodies. To bring street bands and coloured uniforms into the service of Protestant religion was something new. It was no less significant that the Salvation Army regarded social work and care for the material conditions of the poor and outcast as being an essential part of the Christian mission to the souls of men and women. It was largely for this reason that its power has become a permanent feature in modern English life. It does not depend on revivalism alone.

Another movement, analogous to the Salvation Army in its combination of religious and social motive, was Total Abstinence, or ' Teetotalism.' Drunkenness and excessive expenditure on drink constituted one of the major evils of city life, one of the chief causes of crime and the ruin in families, especially since spirits had largely taken the place of beer. Our great caricaturists had held up the mirror to this unpleasant aspect of English nature, from the days of Hogarth's *Gin Lane* to George Cruikshank's prints of *The Bottle* and *The Drunkard's Children* (1847–1848), which were circulated by tens of thousands. In the years that followed, an organized and largely successful attack was made on the drinking habits of all classes by the ' Blue Ribbon Army ' : takers of the total abstinence pledge wore the blue ribbon on their breasts, to pledge them in the face of the world to keep their promise. In the 'seventies the Temperance party, specially strong among the Noncon-formists [1] became a force in Liberal politics ; but there was an element of fanaticism in their legislative proposals to suppress the drink traffic, that long postponed more practical measures. The movement provoked the better led activities of the drink interest ; the brewing companies were backed by a great army of shareholders, and in the last decades of the Century they captured the Conservative Party, with whom after 1886 the government of the country principally lay.

Not only ' Teetotalism ' but the proper and moderate use of wine and beer were encouraged by the increasing amenity and diminishing monotony of life, by rival amuse-ments and occupations such as reading, music, playing and watching organized games, bicycling and sight-seeing, country and seaside holidays, above all by more active and educated minds and more comfortable homes. All these things helped to counteract the dullard's itch for the bottle in the cupboard, and diminished the attraction of the lights of the ' gin palace ' glaring out its promise of warmth and welcome on to the wet inhospitable street. Moreover, the

[1] But all religious bodies promoted the Temperance movement. In 1909 the Church of England Temperance Society contained 639,233 members. Of these 114,444 were pledged to ' total abstinence,' and as many as 486,888 were ' juvenile members.' For it was a regular policy of Temperance Societies to enlist children before they acquired the taste for drink.

brewing companies were gradually frightened or shamed into a more enlightened policy in the management of the public houses they controlled, making them more decent, more ready to sell other things besides drink, less anxious to send their customers away tipsy. And Balfour's Licensing Act of 1904 at length found a practical method of reducing the excessive number of houses of sale.

In the Twentieth Century, drink has found fresh enemies in the cinema at the street corner, and the wireless at home ; and the increase of skilled and mechanical employments, particularly the driving of motor-cars, has put a premium on sobriety. Gambling perhaps now does more harm than drink. But when Queen Victoria died, drinking was still a great evil from the top to the bottom of society, more widely prevalent than in our day, but decidedly less than when she came to the throne.

In the Victorian era photography made its effective impact on the world. Already in 1871 it was acclaimed by an observer as ' the greatest boon that has been conferred on the poorer classes in later years.'

' Any one who knows what the worth of family affection is among the lower classes, and who has seen the array of little portraits stuck over a labourer's fireplace, still gathering into one the " Home " that life is always parting—the boy that has " gone to Canada," the " girl out at service," the little one with the golden hair that sleeps under the daisies, the old grandfather in the country—will perhaps feel with me that in counteracting the tendencies, social and industrial, which every day are sapping the healthier family affections, the sixpenny photograph is doing more for the poor than all the philanthropists in the world.' (*Macmillan's Magazine*, Sept. 1871.)

By the cheapest and most accurate form of portraiture possible, photography had indeed brought to all classes a prolongation of poignant and of delightful memories of the dead, of the absent, of past years, incidents and associations.

Its effect on art was of more doubtful benefit. Many thousands of painters had formerly lived on the demand for portraits of persons, for accurate delineations of events, scenes and buildings and for copies of famous pictures. Photography henceforth supplied all these. By reducing the importance of picture-painting as a trade, and surpassing it in realistic representation of detail, it drove the painter to take refuge more and more in theory, and in a series of intellectualized experiments in Art for Art's sake.

If the English language at the end of Victoria's reign be compared to its predecessor in the last years of Elizabeth, it will be seen that it is the same language : a modern Englishman can easily understand the Bible of 1611, and he can even understand the more idiomatic dialogues of Shakespeare much more easily at any rate than he can understand Chaucer. For the three centuries between Elizabeth and Victoria had been a period of transactions by writing, governed by a literate upper class who defended the language against fundamental changes in grammar or in the structure of existing words. But in another sense the language had changed—from a vehicle of poetry and emotion to a vehicle of science and journalism. An Elizabethan reading a Victorian newspaper article or listening to the conversation of modern educated people, would be bewildered by long words unfamiliar to him, which have been formed, usually from the Latin, not for the purposes of poetry like ' the multitudinous seas incarnadine,' but for the prosaic purposes of science and journalism, and for the discussion of social and political problems : *opportunist, minimize, international, centrifugal, commercialism, decentralize, organization,* and the yet more technical terms of physical science—a useful but unlovely jargon.[1]

In the last half of the Nineteenth Century ' capital ' and ' labour ' were enlarging and perfecting their rival organizations on modern lines. Many an old family firm was replaced by a Limited Liability Company with a bureaucracy of salaried managers. The change met the technological requirements of the new age by engaging a large professional element, and prevented the decline in efficiency that so commonly marred the fortunes of family firms in

[1] Mr. Pearsall Smith, in his *The English Language* (Home University Library, p. 124) says : ' Science is in many ways the natural enemy of language. Language, either literary or colloquial, demands a rich store of living and vivid words—words which are " thought pictures," and appeal to the senses and also embody our feelings about the objects they describe. But science cares nothing about emotion or vivid presentation ; her ideal is a kind of algebraic notation, to be used simply as an instrument of analysis ; and for this she rightly prefers dry and abstract terms, taken from some dead language, and deprived of all life and personality.'

the second and third generation after the energetic founder. It was, moreover, a step away from individual initiative, towards collectivism and municipal and State-managed business. The Railway Companies, though still private concerns managed for the benefit of shareholders, were very unlike old family businesses. They existed by reason of Acts of Parliament, that conferred on them powers and privileges in return for State control. At the same time the great municipalities went into business to supply lighting, trams and other services to the ratepayers.

The growth of the Limited Liability Company and municipal trading had important consequences. Such large, impersonal manipulation of capital and industry greatly increased the numbers and importance of shareholders as a class, an element in the national life representing irresponsible wealth detached from the land and the duties of the landowner ; and almost equally detached from the responsible management of business. All through the Nineteenth Century, America, Africa, India, Australasia and parts of Europe, were being developed largely by British capital, and British shareholders were thus being enriched by the world's movement towards industrialization. Towns like Bournemouth and Eastbourne sprang up to house large 'comfortable' classes who had retired on their incomes, and who had no relation to the rest of the community except that of drawing dividends and occasionally attending a shareholders' meeting to bully the management. On the other hand, 'shareholding' meant leisure and freedom which was used by many of the later Victorians for the highest purposes of a great civilization.

The 'shareholder' as such had no knowledge of the lives, thoughts or needs of the workmen employed by the Company in which he held shares, and his influence on the relations of capital and labour was not good. The paid manager acting for the company was in more direct relation with the men and their demands, but even he had seldom that familiar personal knowledge of the workmen which the employer had often had under the more patriarchal system of the old family business now passing away. Indeed, the mere size of operations and the numbers of workmen involved rendered such personal relations

T 2

impossible. Fortunately, however, the increasing power and organization of the Trade Unions, at least in all the skilled trades, enabled the workmen to meet on more equal terms the managers of the companies who employed them. The harsh discipline of the strike and lock-out taught the two parties to respect each other's strength and understand the value of fair negotiation.

Under these conditions the increasing national dividend was rather less unevenly distributed between classes. But the distinction between capital and labour, the personal segregation of employer from employed in their ordinary lives still went on increasing. The mere fact that philanthropic ' settlements ' were formed in working-class districts in order to show the well-meaning bourgeois how the poor lived, was significant of much. Marxian doctrines, therefore, as to the inevitability of the ' class struggle ' were rife at the end of the Century ; and the more opportunist collectivism preached by the Fabian Society was still more influential.

But these doctrines were too theoretic to affect the English working man very much. It was no theory, but the practical need to defend Trade Union rights against judge-made law that brought Labour into politics to form a party of its own. For the English law courts developed a most unfortunate habit of discovering that liberties which Parliament intended by its Acts to grant to Trade Unions, had not in fact been granted by those Acts at all. By the legislation of 1825, Trade Unions and combinations to raise wages had been legalized—at least so Parliament and everyone else had supposed for forty years. But in 1867, in the Boilermakers' case, the Judges headed by the Lord Chief Justice decided that Unions, being ' in restraint of trade,' were illegal associations. Fortunately, by the Reform Bill of the same year the working classes were granted the Parliamentary franchise and were therefore able to remedy their grievances by constitutional pressure on politicians. Consequently Gladstone's Act of 1871 restored to Unions the right to exist on very favourable terms, and Disraeli's Act of 1875 legalized ' peaceful picketing.'

After that, the Judges left the Trade Unions alone **for**

another generation, during which the movement spread from the skilled to the unskilled trades, particularly in the great strike of the London dockers led by John Burns in 1889. By the end of the Century, Trade Unionism was in most trades and in most regions of England a very powerful weapon of defence for workmen's wages, on the whole wisely used. Then, in 1901, the Judges struck again with their Taff Vale decision, when the work of former Parliaments was again undone, and strike action by Unions was again pronounced illegal. This decision provoked the effective formation of a separate Labour Party in Parliament at the opening of the new Century, and the Act of 1906 which secured to the Trade Unions highly privileged immunity from legal action. But these events belong to another chapter of social history, beyond the date and outside the atmosphere of Victorian England.

The close of the reign and the end of the Century saw the so-called ' feudal ' society of the countryside still in being, but under changing conditions indicative of the advance of democracy even in rural England, and the penetration of village life by forces and ideas from the cities. In the following generation, with the coming of motor transport, the intrusion of urban life upon the rural parts became a flood, turning all England into a suburb. But when Victoria died (1901) the process had not gone so far ; country roads and lanes were still country roads and lanes, with all their sleepy charm come down from countless centuries, which the invading bicyclist could enjoy without destroying. The ' country houses,' great and small, still flourished, with their shooting parties and their week-end guests from town ; and the estate system was still the method by which English agriculture was organized.

But the country houses and the country estates were less than ever supported by agricultural rents, which American imports had lowered and brought into arrear. The pleasures of the country house and the business of the estate system were now financed by money which the owner drew from industry or other investments, or from his income as ground landlord of more distant urban areas. He was still a country gentleman, but he paid for himself by being other things as well. For British agriculture as an economic proposition had collapsed.

Under these circumstances, the estate system, ' feudal ' as it might be, was fairly popular in the countryside, because it brought money from the industrial world to support decadent agriculture, and because the squire and his family brought into village life educated interests and friendly leadership.

But even before the coming of the motor-car with the advent of the new century, the old village life was being transformed into something half suburban by newspapers, ideas, visitors and new residents from the cities. The contrast between the democratic city and the ' feudal ' countryside, which had characterized Trollope's England in the middle of Victoria's reign, was less marked in the last decades of the Century. As the result of the Education Act of 1870 the agricultural labourer of the next generation and his women folk could all read and write. Unfortunately, this power was not directed to foster in them an intelligent and loving interest in country life. The new education was devised and inspected by city folk, intent on producing not peasants but clerks. Before Victoria died, the *Daily Mail* was being read on the village ale bench and under the thatch of the cottage. The distinctive rural mentality was suffering urbanization, and local traditions were yielding to nation-wide commonplace.

In the realm of politics also, town and country were becoming assimilated. In 1884 the agricultural working man received the Parliamentary vote, which had been denied to him in 1867 when his brother of the town was enfranchised. Protected by the ballot, the agricultural labourer could vote as he wished, regardless of farmer and landlord. Proof of this was given in the General Election of 1885, the first held under the new Franchise Bill. On that occasion the boroughs voted Conservative, but the counties unexpectedly voted Liberal, in defiance of squire and farmer. The control over English country life which the squire had exercised for so many centuries was in fact drawing to an end, as far as Parliamentary elections were concerned. It followed inevitably that the local government of the counties must also be put on an elective basis.

In 1888 therefore the Local Government Act established elected County Councils as the administrative organs of country life, in place of the patriarchal rule of the Justices of the Peace. The Justices of the Peace were preserved in their judicial capacity as magistrates. But their administrative functions were handed over to the elected County Councils, strengthened a few years later by the creation of elective Urban and Rural District Councils. Thus, more than fifty years after the Municipal Reform Act of 1835 had set up democratic local government in the boroughs, the same principle was applied to the rural districts. It was an irony of fate that the farm hand was given the Parliamentary and local franchise only after the destruction of English agricultural life had set in, with American competition and the fall of food prices. The agricultural labourers, if they stayed in the countryside, could now take part in its government, but in fact they were trooping off to the towns.

The Municipal Reform Act of 1835 had affected only a limited number of towns, but the scheme of urban self-government was made general throughout England by the Local Government Act of 1888.

The legislators of 1835 had shirked the problem of the Capital : greater London, that is to say, all London outside the old City boundaries, had been left without unity of administration. Fifty years later, a bewildering chaos of overlapping authorities still carried on the affairs of the five million inhabitants of the Capital in haphazard fashion. The Local Government Act of 1888 applied a remedy long overdue. It established the London County Council, which has since governed London, all except the area of the ancient City, reserved as an historical monument under the Lord Mayor and Aldermen. Foreigners come to see the Lord Mayor, but the head of London's government is the Chairman of the London County Council.

The newborn London County Council sprang at once into vigorous life, and in the first twenty years of its existence carried out many new schemes of social welfare. And the London School Board during the same period made many leading experiments in education, till the Education Act of

1902 merged its activities in those of the London County Council. This forward move in local government by London, hitherto so backward, was conducted by the Progressive party that got the majority on the Council at one election after another. It called itself the *Progressive* party—so as not to be completely identified with either the Liberal or the Labour party ; but it had close affinities to both. It existed for municipal purposes only, and therefore people who voted Conservative at Parliamentary elections could vote Progressive at the County Council Election. The average London voter in the 'nineties was conservative and imperialist in national politics, but wanted democratic social improvement for himself and his City. It was in this atmosphere of a municipally progressive London that the Fabian Society flourished ; the intellectual leadership of the Fabian publicists, the Sidney Webbs and Graham Wallas, had much to do with the Progressive government of London. But the popular leader was John Burns, who represented the coming alliance of Labour and Liberal. John Burns of Battersea was the first great apostle of a London patriotism, as distinct from pride in the ' City,' now shrunk within its ancient boundaries, a dignified memory of the past.

The towns, therefore, in the last decades of Victoria's reign were undergoing rapid improvement in sanitation, lighting, locomotion, public libraries and baths, and to some extent in housing. The example set in these matters by the Birmingham municipality under Joseph Chamberlain in the 'seventies, and by the London County Council twenty years later, was widely followed elsewhere. And the Central Government supported the efforts of the local authorities to better the life of the citizen by grants from taxes in aid of the local rates, conditional on favourable reports by Government Inspectors.

This movement of municipal reform supported by the State prevented an utter social catastrophe. The death-rate, so high in the early Victorian city, rapidly declined, town life was made increasingly tolerable on its purely material side, and primary education became universal. Nevertheless, it was in many respects a dreary heritage to pass on to the Twentieth Century. The modern city, in the unplanned swamp of its increase, lacks form and feature ; it is a deadening cage for the human spirit. Urban and suburban life in modern England made no appeal through the eye to the imagination, as had the old village life of our island, or the city life of ancient and mediaeval Europe. Civic pride and civic rivalry among the industrial towns of the north was almost entirely materialistic and not at all aesthetic. The pall of smoke and smuts in itself was enough to discourage any effort after beauty or joy in the visible aspect of life.

The new cities were too big to have individual unity or character, or even to be seen by the eye as Athens, Rome, Perugia, Nuremberg, Tudor London and a thousand other older cities had been seen and loved. And to make matters worse there had been practically no town planning of the Victorian cities. The State had permitted the landlord and the speculative builder to lay out modern England as best suited their own private gain, too often without a thought given to amenity or to the public welfare. In vast areas of London and other cities there were no open spaces within reach of the children, whose only playground outside the school yard was the hard and ugly street. To millions the divorce from nature was absolute, and so too was the divorce from all dignity and beauty and significance in the wilderness of mean streets in which they were bred, whether in the well-to-do suburb or the slum. The new education and the new journalism were both the outcome of these surroundings and partook of their nature. The race bred under such conditions might retain many sturdy qualities of character, might even with better food and clothing improve in physique, might develop sharp wits and a brave, cheery, humorous attitude to life, but its imaginative powers must necessarily decline, and the stage is set for the gradual standardization of human personality.

The later Victorians, though incapable of coping with their own distress, were beginning to be aware of it. Ruskin had inspired the rising generations of writers and thinkers with disgust at the industrial civilization that had filled their fathers with such pride. Looking back through history, they thought they saw a fairer world than modern

Lancashire ; as early as 1868 William Morris, in the Prologue to *The Earthly Paradise,* had written :

> Forget six counties overhung with smoke,
> Forget the snorting steam and piston stroke,
> Forget the spreading of the hideous town ;
> Think rather of the pack-horse on the down,
> And dream of London, small, and white and clean,
> The clear Thames bordered by its gardens green . . .

But there was no going back, except in imagination.

The year 1870 was a turning-point in educational and therefore in social history. Education was not only a national requirement on the necessity for which politicians were agreed ; it was also the chief battleground of religious denominations. The main reason why English Education lagged behind in the mid-Victorian period was that no government, Whig or Tory, could conceive a means of setting up a national system at the public expense that would not have given the bitterest offence either to the Dissenters or to the Established Church. Until Gladstone's gallant venture in 1870, every government had shrunk from embarking on that sea of trouble. A network of Voluntary Schools paid for by private subscription had been spread over the country owing to religious and sectarian zeal ; but the same zeal had frightened off both political parties from tackling the Education question as a national affair.

The great majority of the Voluntary Schools by which the primary education of the people was supplied, were conducted on Church principles : they were known as National Schools, because founded by the (Anglican) National Society. They had been aided by a very small grant since 1833. Gladstone's Bill of 1870 was the work of W. E. Forster, an ardent churchman though of Quaker origin. Forster's Bill doubled the State Grant to the existing Church Schools and to the Roman Catholic Schools, so as to enable them to become a permanent part of the new system, while it introduced publicly controlled schools to fill up the large gaps in the educational map of the country. These new Schools, called Board Schools, were to be paid for out of the Local Rates, and they were to be governed by popularly elected School Boards. In most of the old Voluntary Schools, that is, in all National Schools, Church teaching was to be continued. But in the new Board Schools the Act prohibited the use, in the religious teaching, of catechism or formulary distinctive of any denomination.

The grievance of the Dissenters was that the State thus perpetuated the Church Schools of the villages, and in each village there was only one school available to which all children had to go. In the towns there were Board and Voluntary Schools side by side. It was unfortunate that the Church Schools were found most of all in the villages where there was no alternative school. That is so very largely to this day (1941), but it is less resented now than in 1870, partly because the hostile feeling between Church and Dissent has very much subsided, and partly because by Balfour's Act of 1902 the Church Schools have been brought under a considerable measure of control by County Councils as the public Educational Authorities.

By the religious compromise of 1870 England was enabled to obtain, better late than never, a system of universal primary education without which she must soon have fallen into the rear among modern nations. Between 1870 and 1890 the average school attendance rose from one and a quarter million to four and a half millions, while the money spent on each child was doubled.

But the State did little as yet for Secondary Education ;[1] nor was there a sufficient ladder of school scholarships to the Universities for the ablest children in Primary Schools. The new School Boards were charged with Primary Education only. In 1900 the Law Courts decided, in the famous Cockerton judgment, that the ratepayers' money could not be spent on any form of Secondary or Higher Education, under the terms of the Act of 1870.

Another defect in that measure was the smallness of the School Board areas. Each School Board being the affair of a single town or village could have no wide educational outlook. And their parochial character made the feud of Church and Dissent more personal and intense.

---

[1] 'In 1899 the amount of public money spent per head on Secondary Education was only three farthings in England, as compared with one shilling and a penny three farthings in Switzerland.' Bernard Allen's *Sir Robert Morant*, p. 141.

These defects in the Act of 1870 were remedied by Balfour's Education Act of 1902, inspired by the great public servant, Sir Robert Morant. This measure abolished School Boards and gave the power to provide for Education, both Primary and Secondary, to the elected County Councils, and to certain large Borough Councils. Such is our system to-day. The Councils do their educational work through their Education Committees. The improvement due to the larger area and broader views of these County Education Committees has been of great benefit to Primary Education, and of still greater benefit to Secondary Education ; and an effective ladder to the Universities was created by Balfour's Bill.

Without the Education Acts of 1870 and of 1902 England could not have competed in the coming era of machinery and organization, and her people would have sunk into the barbarism of an uneducated city population, a far worse form of society than the uneducated rural population of old times, where the mind and character of ploughmen and craftsmen were formed by the influences of nature, the agricultural life and the old system of apprenticeship.

Our modern system of popular Education was indeed indispensable and has conferred great benefits on the country, but it has been a disappointment in some important respects. Being a town-made system it has failed to meet rural needs, of which the Board of Education failed to recognize the distinctive character. It has speeded up rather than diminished the rural exodus. More generally speaking, it has produced a vast population able to read but unable to distinguish what is worth reading, an easy prey to sensations and cheap appeals. Consequently both literature and journalism have been to a large extent debased since 1870, because they now cater for millions of half-educated and quarter-educated people, whose forbears, not being able to read at all, were not the patrons of newspapers or of books. The small highly educated class no longer sets the standard to the extent that it used to do, and tends to adopt the standards of the majority. Whether in the twentieth or twenty-first centuries the lower forms of literature and journalism will completely devour the higher has yet to be seen. If they do not, it will be due to improved Secondary and Higher Education forming a sufficiently large class to perpetuate a demand for things really worth reading.

The subject-matter of this book has been confined to the social history of England, and has not included the vast and varied expanse of lands beyond the ocean associated in the British Commonwealth of Nations and Dependencies. But social life in little England would have been a very different thing if it had not been the centre of a great maritime trade and, moreover, of an Empire. We had long prided ourselves on being a seafaring people ; that was part of the island habit. But consciousness of the Empire of which we had become the centre, lagged far behind the reality. In the middle of the Nineteenth Century popular patriotic songs still celebrated ' the right little, tight little island.' And that island was not yet generally thought of as the heart of ' an Empire on which the sun never set.' That aspect of our position was first fully appreciated at the two Jubilees of Queen Victoria (1887, 1897) when the pageant of distant and diverse lands, all come to pay homage to the little lady in grey, was first fully displayed, with startling effect, in London streets.

Yet, for generations past, the ways of thought and habits of life in English towns and villages had been strongly influenced by overseas connections. In the Eighteenth Century tea and tobacco had become as much the national food as beef and beer. And ever since the Seventeenth Century the adventurous and the discontented had been going across the ocean, first to the American colonies, then to the United States, to Canada, to Australia, to South Africa. It is true that until the Nineteenth Century the emigrant usually parted for ever from the folk he left behind and, however he fared, little more was heard of him. But in Victoria's reign, when the tide of emigration was still running stronger than ever, the postage stamp kept the cottage at home in touch with the son who had ' gone to the Colonies,' and often he would return on a visit with money in his pocket, and tales of new lands of equality and self-help and maybe an affectionate contempt for slow old ways at home. In this very human manner the middle and lower classes knew quite as much about the Empire as their ' betters,' and rather more than their ' betters ' about the United States, as was shown at the time of the Civil War of 1861–1865. But the professional and upper classes also went out to careers all over the world, to govern, and trade, and shoot big game, in Africa and India. And all ranks of the army knew India, so far as it could be seen from the lines.

In this manner, a vast and varied overseas experience was for ever pouring back into every town and every hamlet in Victoria's England. Since Tudor times the influence of the sea had been strong even in upland villages, no one of which is more than seventy miles from a tidal estuary. And to the old maritime influence was now added in equally full measure the Colonial. Our island people were, in some respects, the least insular of all mankind. To Europeans we appeared insular, because we were not continental. But our experiences and opportunities were greater than those of the folk of other lands.

Victorian prosperity and Victorian civilization, alike in their grosser and their higher aspects, were due to a century's immunity from great wars and from any serious national danger. Safe behind the shield of the navy, Englishmen thought of all the problems of life in terms of peace and security which were in fact the outcome of temporary and local circumstances, and not part of nature's universal order. No great country except English-speaking America has ever been so utterly civilian in thought and practice as Victorian England. Service in the army was regarded by the middle and working classes as disgraceful—except in time of war.

' It's Tommy this and Tommy that, and chuck him out the brute ;
But it's ' thank you Mr. Atkins,' when the guns begin to shoot.'

It was a vulgar attitude, especially as it went with occasional fits of Jingoism like those which preceded the Crimean and Boer Wars, and nearly caused several others. But for a hundred years after Trafalgar and Waterloo it led to no fatal results. For we held the surface of the sea, and the surface was then all the sea for human action. On the whole our supremacy in the oceans and along the shores of the world was used in the Nineteenth Century on the side of peace, goodwill and freedom. If it were to be destroyed, mankind would breathe a harsher air.

The carefree Victorians knew little about the spirit and inner workings of the militarized continent, off which this green and happy isle was anchored. They knew more about Australia, America, Africa in a human and business way. Europe was the Englishman's playground, with its Alps, its picture galleries, its ancient cities. We were islanders with an overseas Empire, not continentals. We were sailors not soldiers. We thought of European politics not in terms of power or of our own national security, but according as we liked or disliked the governments of Turkey or Russia, Napoleon III or the Italian *risorgimento*. Sometimes these sympathies led us right, sometimes wrong. But in any case there could be no consistent national policy with armaments adapted to it. To the Englishman, foreign affairs were a branch of Liberal and Conservative politics, tinged with emotion, a matter of taste, not a question of existence.

In the Victorian era this attitude could be indulged without disaster. But when the reign and the Century came to an end, a tremendous revolution in all human affairs was imminent. The internal combustion engine had been invented, and its space-annihilating consequences were about to be disclosed. The motor-car and motor-lorry, the submarine, the tank, the aeroplane were about to plunge the world into a new era, widely different from the past in peace and in war. And England would be the country most concerned of all, because she would lose half the benefit of her insular position. The surface of the sea could no longer be held by ships alone ; and whether it was held or not, the aeroplane could violate the thousand-year-old sanctities of the peaceful island. In such new conditions our happy-go-lucky attitude towards power on the Continent, and our wholly civilian way of life, our refusal to arm ourselves adequately to new needs, if continued too long, might become a terrible danger.

And even in peacetime the new age of motor traction on

the roads made a more rapid social and economic revolution in the first forty years of the Twentieth Century than railways and machinery had made before.   In the age of the railway, supplemented by horse traffic and bicycles, the pace of changes, the disappearance of local and provincial differences though rapid, was limited.   But under the new conditions England bade fair to become one huge unplanned suburb.   Motor traction created the urgent need for the State to control the development of the whole island, but unhappily the matter was left to chance and the building exploiter.   Political society could not at once adjust its habits of thought to new conditions coming on with unexampled speed.

But there are good points in this latest age.   The progress actually made in the first forty years of the new Century, particularly in education [1] and in social services, has perhaps been as much as can be expected of limited human wisdom. The material conditions of the working class in 1939 were much better than in the year Queen Victoria died.

What will now happen to England in peace and in war the historian is no better able to guess than anyone else. And the tremendous changes that have already taken place in the first forty years of the new Century will no doubt, a short time hence, look different from what they now appear, and will fall into a new historical perspective. The best place, therefore, to bring to an end a social history of England is the death of Queen Victoria and the end of the railway age.

---

[1] The battle of Waterloo was won, not on the playing fields of Eton, but on the village greens of England.   The men who fought in the ranks on June 18, 1815, were little educated but they had the qualities of countrybred men.   To-day we are urban and educated.   The flyers of the R.A.F. are not and could not be the product of rural simplicity.   If we win this war, it will have been won in the primary and secondary schools (1941).

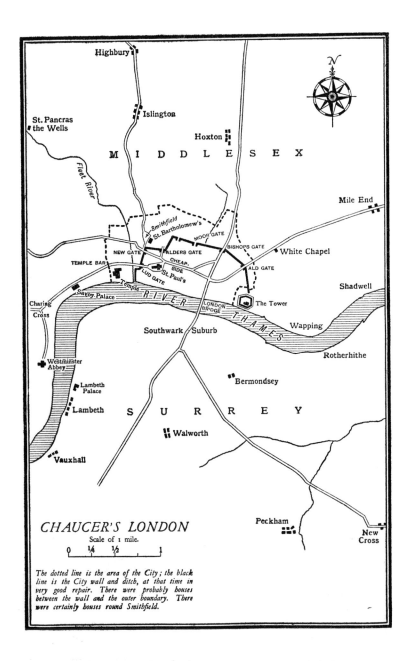

Highbury

St. Pancras the Wells

Islington

Hoxton

M I D D L E S E X

Fleet River

Mile End

Smithfield
St.Bartholomew's

MOOR GATE

BISHOPS GATE

White Chapel

NEW GATE

ALDERS GATE

TEMPLE BAR

CHEAP.
SIDE

LUD GATE

St. Paul's

ALD GATE

Shadwell

Temple

R I V E R

Savoy Palace

Charing
Cross

LONDON
BRIDGE

The Tower

T H A M E S

Wapping

Southwark Suburb

Rotherhithe

Westminster
Abbey

Lambeth
Palace

Bermondsey

Lambeth

S   U   R   R   E   Y

Vauxhall

Walworth

CHAUCER'S LONDON

Scale of 1 mile.

0   ¼   ½   1

Peckham

New
Cross

*The dotted line is the area of the City ; the black
line is the City wall and ditch, at that time in
very good repair. There were probably houses
between the wall and the outer boundary. There
were certainly houses round Smithfield.*

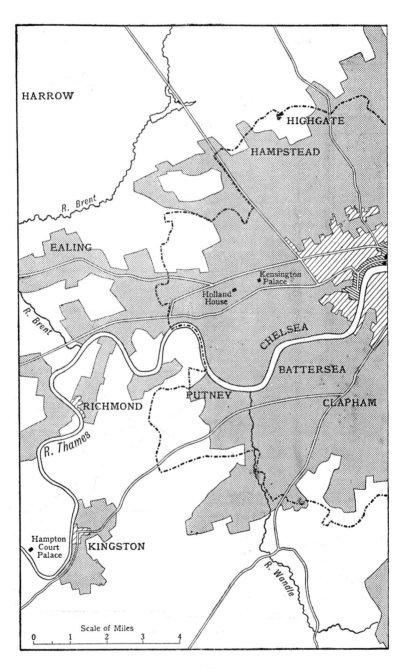

HARROW

HIGHGATE

HAMPSTEAD

R. Brent

EALING

Kensington
Palace

Holland
House

CHELSEA

BATTERSEA

R. Brent

PUTNEY

CLAPHAM

RICHMOND

R. Thames

Hampton
Court
Palace

KINGSTON

R. Wandle

Scale of Miles

0   1   2   3   4

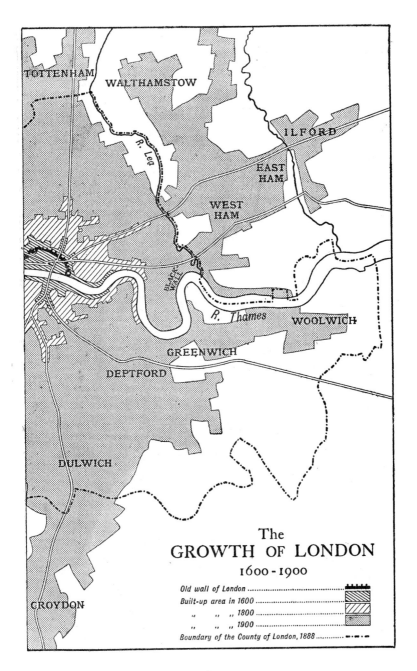

The
GROWTH OF LONDON
1600 - 1900

Old wall of London ....
Built-up area in 1600 ....
    ,,   ,,   ,,   1800 ....
    ,,   ,,   ,,   1900 ....
Boundary of the County of London, 1888 ....

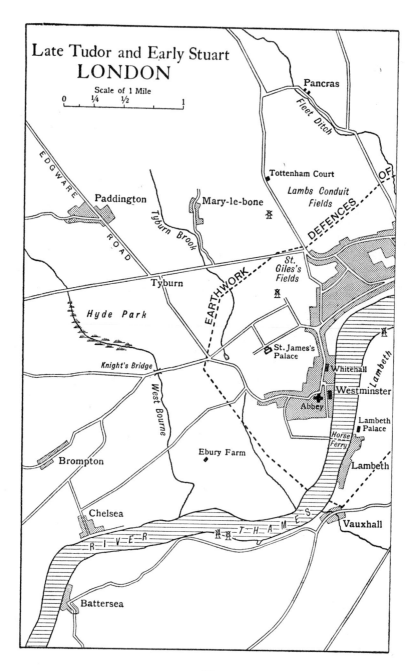

Late Tudor and Early Stuart
LONDON

Scale of 1 Mile
0   ¼   ½   1

Pancras

Fleet Ditch

EDGWARE

Tottenham Court

OF

Paddington

ROAD

Mary-le-bone

Lambs Conduit
Fields

DEFENCES

Tyburn Brook

St.
Giles's
Fields

Tyburn

EARTHWORK

Hyde Park

Lambeth

Knight's Bridge

St. James's
Palace

West Bourne

Whitehall

Westminster

Abbey

Lambeth
Palace

Horse
Ferry

Brompton

Ebury Farm

Lambeth

Chelsea

R - I - V - E - R

T - H - A - M - E - S

Vauxhall

Battersea

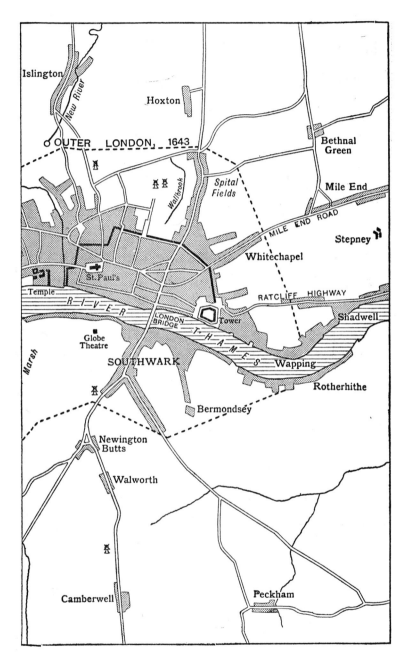

Islington

Hoxton

New River

Bethnal Green

OUTER LONDON, 1643

Spital Fields

Mile End

Wallbrook

MILE END ROAD

Whitechapel

Stepney

St. Paul's

Temple

RATCLIFF HIGHWAY

R I V E R

Shadwell

LONDON BRIDGE

Tower

Globe Theatre

T H A M E S

Wapping

Marsh

SOUTHWARK

Rotherhithe

Bermondsey

Newington Butts

Walworth

Camberwell

Peckham

591

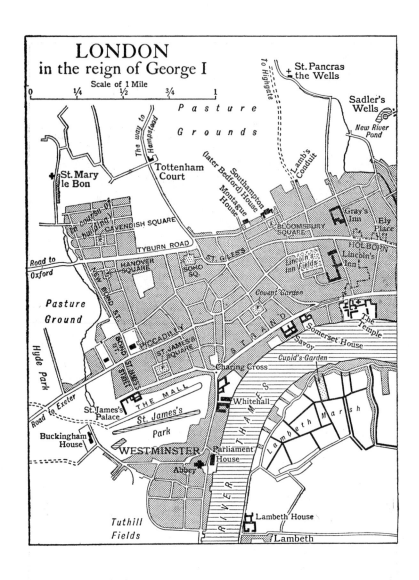

LONDON
in the reign of George I

Scale of 1 Mile

0   ¼   ½   ¾   1

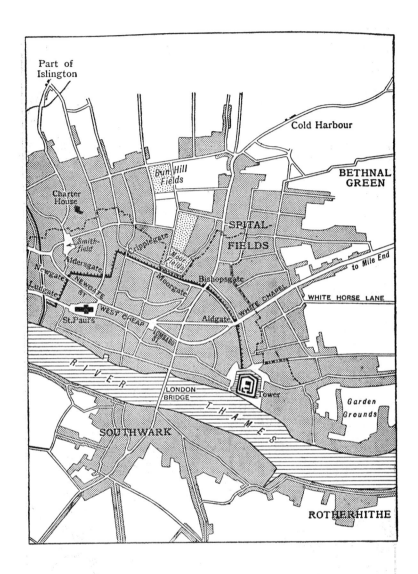

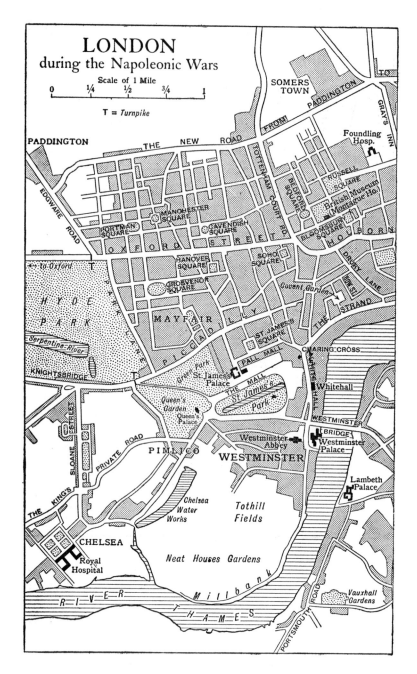

LONDON
during the Napoleonic Wars

Scale of 1 Mile

0   ¼   ½   ¾   1

T = *Turnpike*

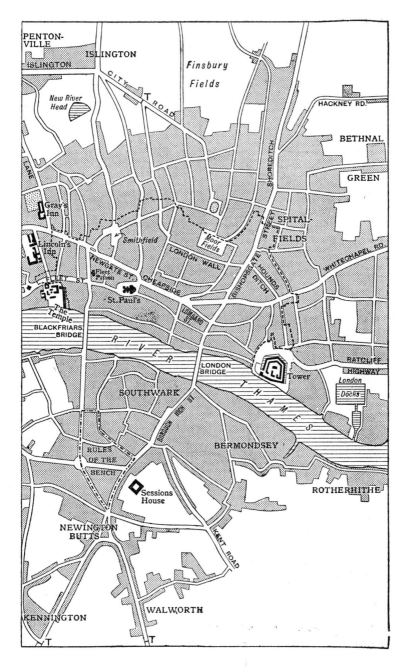

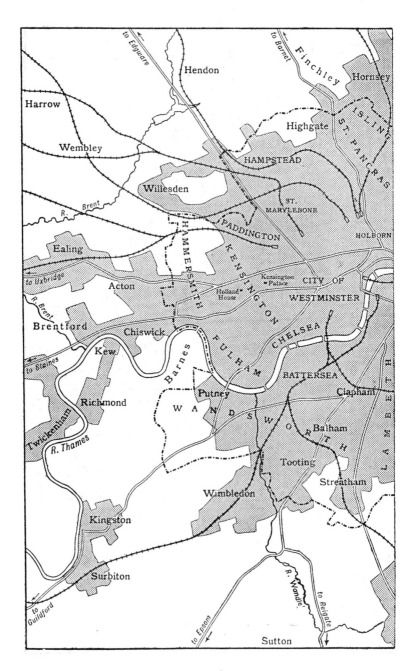

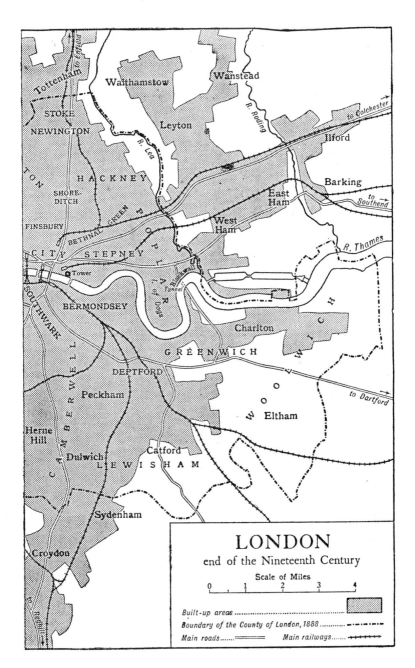

LONDON
end of the Nineteenth Century

Scale of Miles

| 0 | 1 | 2 | 3 | 4 |

Built-up areas ....

Boundary of the County of London, 1888 .... — · — · —

Main roads ...... ═══   Main railways .... ┼┼┼┼┼

INDEX

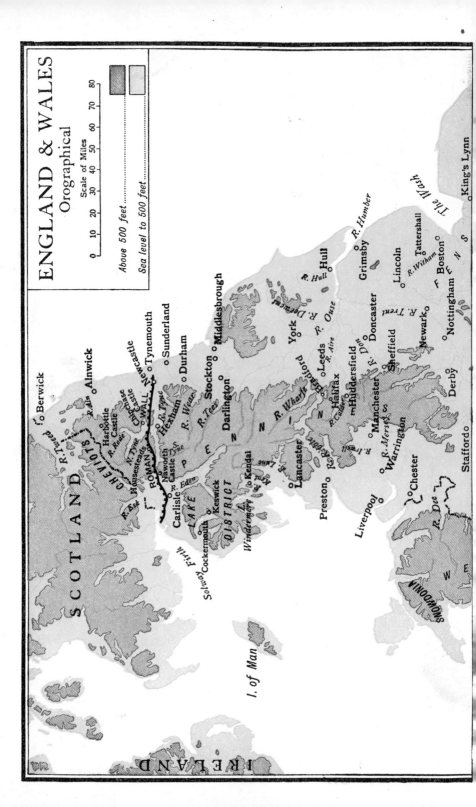

ENGLAND & WALES
Orographical

Scale of Miles
0   10   20   30   40   50   60   70   80

Above 500 feet ....
Sea level to 500 feet ....

SCOTLAND

IRELAND

I. of Man

Berwick
R. Tweed
Alnwick
R. Aln
CHEVIOTS
Harbottle
R. Rede
R. Esk
Housesteads
ROMAN
N. Tyne
Naworth Castle
Carlisle
R. Eden
LAKE
DISTRICT
Cockermouth
Solway Firth
Keswick
Windermere
Kendal
WALL
Chollerford
Corbridge
Hexham
R. Tyne
R. Tyne
S. Tyne
Newcastle
Tynemouth
Sunderland
Durham
R. Wear
R. Tees
Stockton
Middlesbrough
Darlington
Lancaster
Preston
R. Lune
Kent
P E N N I N E
R. Ribble
Liverpool
Chester
R. Dee
Stafford
Derby
Warrington
R. Mersey
Manchester
R. Irwell
Huddersfield
Halifax
R. Calder
Bradford
R. Aire
Leeds
R. Wharfe
York
R. Ouse
Sheffield
R. Don
Doncaster
Newark
Nottingham
R. Trent
R. Derwent
Hull
R. Hull
Grimsby
R. Humber
Lincoln
R. Witham
Tattershall
Boston
The Wash
King's Lynn
SNOWDON
W